THE OXFORD BIBLE COMMENTARY

THE OXFORD BIBLE COMMENTARY

THE
PENTATEUCH

EDITED BY
JOHN MUDDIMAN
AND
JOHN BARTON

ASSOCIATE EDITOR
Rex Mason, *Emeritus Fellow of Regent's Park College, Oxford*

OXFORD
UNIVERSITY PRESS

OXFORD

UNIVERSITY PRESS

Great Clarendon Street, Oxford OX2 6DP

Oxford University Press is a department of the University of Oxford.
It furthers the University's objective of excellence in research, scholarship,
and education by publishing worldwide in

Oxford New York

Auckland Cape Town Dar es Salaam Hong Kong Karachi
Kuala Lumpur Madrid Melbourne Mexico City Nairobi
New Delhi Shanghai Taipei Toronto

With offices in

Argentina Austria Brazil Chile Czech Republic France Greece
Guatemala Hungary Italy Japan Poland Portugal Singapore
South Korea Switzerland Thailand Turkey Ukraine Vietnam

Published in the United States
by Oxford University Press Inc., New York

First published in this updated selection 2010

First published in this updated selection 2010

British Library Cataloguing in Publication Data

Data available

Library of Congress Cataloging in Publication Data

Data available

Typeset by SPI Publisher Services, Pondicherry, India
Printed in Great Britain
on acid-free paper by
Clays Ltd., St Ives plc

ISBN 978–0–19–958024–8

1 3 5 7 9 10 8 6 4 2

LIST OF CONTENTS

LIST OF CONTRIBUTORS

John Barton, *Oriel and Laing Professor of the Interpretation of Holy Scripture, University of Oxford*

Christoph Bultmann, *Professor of Biblical Studies, Universität Erfurt, Germany*

G. I. Davies, *Professor of Old Testament Studies, Fellow, Fitzwilliam College*

Terence E. Fretheim, *Elva B. Lovell Professor of Old Testament, Luther Seminary, St Paul, Minnesota*

Lester L. Grabbe, *Professor in Theology, University of Hull*

Walter J. Houston, *Mansfield College, University of Oxford*

R. N. Whybray†, *formerly Professor of Hebrew and Old Testament Studies at the University of Hull*

ABBREVIATIONS

AB	Anchor Bible
ABD	D. N. Freedman (ed.), *Anchor Bible Dictionary* (6 vols.; New York: Doubleday, 1992)
AfO	*Archiv für Orientforschung*
AnBib	Analecta biblica
ANET	James B. Pritchard (ed.). *Ancient Near Eastern Texts Relating to the Old Testament* (Princeton: Princeton University Press, 3rd. edn. 1969)
AOAT	Alter Orient und Altes Testament
ASOR	American Schools of Oriental Research
ATD	Das Alte Testament Deutsch
B	4th-cent. MS of part of NT, in the Vatican Library
BA	*Biblical Archaeologist*
BAR	*Biblical Archaeologist Reader*
BBB	Bonner biblische Beiträge
BBET	Beiträge zur biblischen Exegese und Theologie
BCE	Before Common Era
BETL	Bibliotheca ephemeridum theologicarum lovaniensium
BEvT	Beiträge zur evangelischen Theologie
BKAT	Biblischer Kommentar: Altes Testament
BWANT	Beiträge zur Wissenschaft vom Alten und Neuen Testament
BZAW	Beihefte zur ZAW
CBQ	*Catholic Biblical Quarterly*
CChr.SL	Corpus Christianorum Series Latina
CE	Common Era
ConBOT	Coniectanea biblica, Old Testament
CTA	A. Herdner, *Corpus des tablettes en cunéiforme alphabétiques*
D	Deuteronomist source in the Pentateuch
DJD	Discoveries in the Judaean Desert
E	Elohist source in the Pentateuch
EI	*Eretz Israel*
ErFor	Eträge der Forschung
ET	English Translation
ETR	*Études théologiques et religieuses*

FAT	Forschungen zum Alten Testament
FRLANT	Forschungen zur Religion und Literatur des Alten und Neuen Testaments
H	Holiness Code
HAT	Handbuch zum Alten Testament
HB	Hebrew Bible
Heb.	Hebrew
HSM	Harvard Semitic Monographs
HUCA	*Hebrew Union College Annual*
ICC	International Critical Commentary
IDB	G. A. Buttrick (ed.), *Interpreter's Dictionary of the Bible* (Nashville: Abingdon Press, 1976)
IDBSup	Supplementary volume to *IDB*
J	Yahwist source in the Pentateuch
JBL	*Journal of Biblical Literature*
JCS	*Journal of Cuneiform Studies*
JJS	*Journal of Jewish Studies*
JNES	*Journal of Near Eastern Studies*
JQR	*Jewish Quarterly Review*
JSJ	*Journal for the Study of Judaism in the Persian, Hellenistic and Roman Period*
JSOT	*Journal for the Study of the Old Testament*
JSOTSup	Journal for the Study of the Old Testament—Supplement Series
JTS	*Journal of Theological Studies*
LXX	Septuagint
m.	*Mishnah*
MS	Monograph Series; manuscript
Mt.	Mount
MT	Masoretic Text
NCB	New Century Bible
NICOT	New International Commentary on the Old Testament
NJPS	New Jewish Publication Society Translation
OBL	Orientalia et biblica lovaniensis
OBO	Orbis biblicus et orientalis
OTL	Old Testament Library
OTS	*Oudtestamentische Studiën*
P	Priestly Work source in the Pentateuch
par.	parallel(s)
pl.	plural

RB	*Revue biblique*
SAA	State Articles of Assyria
SBAB	Stuttgarter biblischer Aufsatzbände
SBL	Society of Biblical Literature
SBLDS	SBL Dissertation Series
SBLMS	SBL Monograph Series
SBT	Studies in Biblical Theology
SCM	Student Christian Movement
SHAW	Sitzungsberichte der Heidelberger Akademie der Wissenschaften
SJLA	Studies in Judaism in Late Antiquity
SOTS	Society for Old Testament Study
SOTSMS	Society for Old Testament Study Monograph Series
SPCK	Society for Promoting Christian Knowledge
SUNT	Studien zur Umwelt des Neuen Testaments
TDOT	*Theological Dictionary of the Old Testament* (G. J. Botterweck, H. Ringgren, and H.-J. Fabry, Theologisches Wörterbuch zum Alten Testament tr. J. T. Willis, Grand Rapids: Eerdmans 1974–)
tr(s).	translation(s), translated (by)
TWAT	G. J. Botterweck and H. Ringgren (eds.), *Theologisches Wörterbuch zum Alten Testament* (Stuttgart: Kohlhammer, 1970–)
TZ	*Theologische Zeitschrift*
v.	versus
VT	*Vetus Testamentum*
VTSup	Vetus Testamentum, Supplements
WBC	Word Biblical Commentary
WMANT	Wissenschaftliche Monographien zum Alten und Neuen Testament
YNER	Yale Near Eastern Researches
ZAR	*Zeitschrift für Altorientalische und Biblische Rechtsgeschichte*
ZAW	*Zeitschrift für die alttestamentliche Wissenschaft*
ZDPV	*Zeitschrift des deutschen Palästina-Vereins*
ZTK	*Zeitschrift für Theologie und Kirche*

CLASSICAL

Philo	Philo Judaeus
Spec. leg.	*De specialibus legibus*

1. General Introduction

A. Studying the Bible. 1. People's reasons for studying the Bible—and therefore for using a biblical commentary—are many and various. The great majority of Bible readers have a religious motivation. They believe that the Bible contains the 'words of life', and that to study it is a means of deepening their understanding of the ways of God. They turn to the Bible to inform them about how God desires human beings to live, and about what God has done for the human race. They expect to be both challenged and helped by what they read, and to gain clearer guidance for living as religious believers. Such people will use a commentary to help them understand the small print of what has been disclosed about the nature and purposes of God. The editors' hope is that those who turn to the Bible for such religious reasons will find that the biblical text is here explained in ways that make it easier to understand its content and meaning. We envisage that the Commentary will be used by pastors preparing sermons, by groups of people reading the Bible together in study or discussion groups, and by anyone who seeks a clearer perspective on a text that they hold in reverence as religiously inspiring. Jews, Catholics, Protestants, and Orthodox Christians have different expectations of the Bible, but we hope that all will find the Commentary useful in elucidating the text.

2. A somewhat smaller group of readers studies the Bible as a monument to important movements of religious thought in the past, whether or not they themselves have any personal commitment to the religious systems it represents. One of the most striking developments of recent decades has been the growth of interest in the Bible by those who have no religious commitment to it, but for whom it is a highly significant document from the ancient world. Students who take university or college courses in theology or religious or biblical studies will often wish to understand the origins and meaning of the biblical text so as to gain a clearer insight into the beginnings of two major world religions, Judaism and Christianity, and into the classic texts that these religions regard as central to their life. We hope that such people will find here the kinds of information they need in order to understand this complex and many-faceted work. The one-volume format makes it possible to obtain an overview of the whole Bible before going on to use more advanced individual commentaries on particular biblical books.

3. Finally, there are many Bible readers who are committed neither to a religious quest of their own nor to the study of religion, but who are drawn by the literary quality of much of the Bible to want to know more about it. For them it is a major classic of Western—indeed, of world—literature, whose influence on other literature, ancient and modern, requires that it should be taken seriously and studied in depth. A generation ago 'the Bible as literature' was regarded by many students of the Bible, especially those with a religious commitment to it, as a somewhat dilettante interest, insufficiently alert to the Bible's spiritual challenge. Nowadays, however, a great deal of serious scholarly work is being done on literary aspects of the Bible, and many commentaries are written with the needs of a literary, rather than a religious, readership in mind. We think that those who approach the Bible in such a way will find much in this Commentary to stimulate their interest further.

B. Biblical Criticism. 1. The individual authors of commentaries have been free to treat the biblical books as they see fit, and there has been no imposition of a common editorial perspective. They are, however, united by an approach that we have called 'chastened historical criticism'. This is what is traditionally known as a *critical* commentary, but the authors are aware of recent challenges to what is generally called biblical criticism and have sought (to a greater or lesser extent) to take account of these in their work. Some explanation of these terms is necessary if the reader is to understand what this book seeks to offer.

2. Biblical criticism, sometimes known as historical criticism of the Bible or as the historical-critical method, is the attempt to understand the Bible by setting it in the context of its time of writing, and by asking how it came into existence and what were the purposes of its authors. The term 'historical' is not used because such criticism is necessarily interested in reconstructing history, though sometimes it may be, but because biblical books are being studied as anchored in their own time, not as freely floating texts which we can read as though they were contemporary with us. It starts with the acknowledgement that the Bible is an ancient text. However much the questions with which it deals may be of perennial interest to human beings (and perhaps no one would study it so seriously if they were not), they arose within a particular historical (and geographical) setting. Biblical criticism uses all available means of access to information about the text and its context, in order to discover what it may have meant when it or its component parts were written.

3. One precondition for a critical understanding of any text is a knowledge of the language in which it is written, and accordingly of what individual words and expressions were capable of meaning at the time of the text's composition. The critical reader is always on guard against the danger of anachronism, of reading later meanings of words into their use in an earlier period. Frequently, therefore, commentators draw attention to problems in understanding particular words and phrases, and cite evidence for how such words are used elsewhere in contemporary texts. A second prerequisite is that the text itself shall be an accurate version of what the author actually wrote. In the case of any ancient text this is an extremely difficult thing to ensure, because of the vagaries of the transmission of manuscripts down the centuries. Copying by hand always introduces errors into texts, even though biblical texts were often copied with special care because of their perceived sacred status. In all the individual commentaries here there are discussions of how accurately the original text is available to us, and what contribution is made to our knowledge of this by various manuscripts or ancient translations. The art of textual criticism seeks to explain the evolution of texts, to understand how they become corrupted (through miscopying), and how their original form can be rediscovered.

4. In reading any piece of text, ancient or modern, one needs to be aware of the possibility that it may not be a unity. Some documents in our own day come into existence through the work of several different authors, which someone else then edits into a reasonably unified whole: such is the case, for example, with documents produced by committees. In the ancient world it was not uncommon for books to be produced by joining together, and sometimes even interweaving, several already existing shorter texts, which are then referred to as the 'sources' of the resulting single document. In the

case of some books in the Bible it is suspected by scholars that such a process of production has resulted in the texts as we now have them. Such hypotheses have been particularly prevalent in the case of the Pentateuch (Genesis–Deuteronomy) and of the Synoptic Gospels (Matthew, Mark, and Luke). The attempt to discover the underlying sources is nowadays usually called 'source criticism', though older books sometimes call it 'literary criticism' (from German *Literarkritik*, but confusing in that 'literary criticism' usually means something else in modern English), or 'higher criticism'—by contrast with 'lower', that is, textual criticism. It is important to see that biblical critics are not committed to believing that this or that biblical book is in fact the result of the interweaving of sources (R. N. Whybray's commentary on Genesis in this volume argues against such a hypothesis), but only to being open to the possibility.

5. A further hypothesis that has had a long and fruitful history in the study of both Testaments is that our present written texts may rest on materials that were originally transmitted orally. Before the biblical books were written, the stories or other units of which they are composed may have had an independent life, circulating orally and being handed on from parent to child, or in circles where stories were told and retold, such as a 'camp-fire' or a liturgical context. The attempt to isolate and study such underlying oral units is known as form criticism, and it has been much practised in the case of the gospels, the stories in the Pentateuch and in the early historical books of the Old Testament, and the prophetic books. Again, by no means all critics think that these books do in fact rest on oral tradition, but all regard the question whether or not they do so as important because it is relevant to understanding their original context.

6. Where texts are composite, that is, the result of weaving together earlier written or oral sources, it makes sense to investigate the techniques and intentions of those who carried out the weaving. We should now call such people 'editors', but in biblical studies the technical term 'redactor' tends to be preferred, and this branch of biblical criticism is thus known as 'redaction criticism'. Once we know what were a biblical redactor's raw materials—which source and form criticism may be able to disclose to us—we can go on to ask about the aims the redactor must have had. Thus we can enquire into the intentions (and hence the thought or the 'theology') of Matthew or Luke, or of the editor of the book of Isaiah. Redaction criticism has been a particular interest in modern German-speaking biblical study, but it is also still widely practised in the English-speaking world. It is always open to the critic to argue that a given book is not composite in any case and therefore never had a redactor, only an author. Most scholars probably think this is true of some of the shorter tales of the Old Testament, such as Jonah or Ruth, or of many of Paul's epistles. Here too what makes study critical is not a commitment to a particular outcome, but a willingness to engage in the investigation. It is always possible that there is simply not enough evidence to resolve the matter, as R. Coggins argues in the case of Isaiah. This conclusion does not make such a commentary 'non-critical', but is arrived at by carefully sifting the various critical hypotheses that have been presented by previous scholars. An uncritical commentary would be one that was unaware of such issues, or unwilling to engage with them.

7. Form and redaction criticism inevitably lead to questions about the social setting of the underlying units that make up biblical books and of the redactors who put them into their finished form. In recent years historical criticism has expanded to include a considerable interest in the contribution the social sciences can make to understanding the Bible's provenance. The backgrounds of the gospels and of Paul's letters have been studied with a view to discovering more about the social context of early Christianity: see, for example, the commentary here on 1 Thessalonians by Philip Esler. In the study of the Old Testament also much attention has been directed to questions of social context, and this interest can be seen especially in D. L. Smith-Christopher's commentary on Ezra–Nehemiah.

C. Post-Critical Movements. 1. In the last few decades biblical studies has developed in many and varied directions, and has thrown up a number of movements that regard themselves as 'post-critical'. Some take critical study of the Bible as a given, but then seek to move on to ask further questions not part of the traditional historical-critical enterprise. Others are frankly hostile to historical criticism, regarding it as misguided or as outdated. Though the general tone of this commentary continues to be critical, most of its contributors believe that these newer movements have raised important issues,

and have contributed materially to the work of biblical study. Hence our adoption of a critical stance is 'chastened' by an awareness that new questions are in the air, and that biblical criticism itself is now subject to critical questioning.

2. One important style of newer approaches to the Bible challenges the assumption that critical work should (or can) proceed from a position of neutrality. Those who write from feminist and liberationist perspectives often argue that the older critical style of study presented itself as studiedly uncommitted to any particular programme: it was simply concerned, so its practitioners held, to understand the biblical text in its original setting. In fact (so it is now argued) there was often a deeply conservative agenda at work in biblical criticism. By distancing the text as the product of an ancient culture, critics managed to evade its challenges to themselves, and they signally failed to see how subversive of established attitudes much of the Bible really was. What is needed, it is said, is a more engaged style of biblical study in which the agenda is set by the need for human liberation from oppressive political forces, whether these constrain the poor or some other particular group such as women. The text must be read not only in its reconstructed 'original' context but also as relevant to modern concerns: only then will justice be done to the fact that it exercises an existential claim upon its readers, and it will cease to be seen as the preserve of the scholar in his (sic) study.

3. Such a critique of traditional biblical criticism calls attention to some of the unspoken assumptions with which scholars have sometimes worked, and can have the effect of deconstructing conventional commentaries by uncovering their unconscious bias. Many of the commentators in this volume are aware of such dangers in biblical criticism, and seek to redress the balance by asking about the contribution of the books on which they comment to contemporary concerns. They are also more willing than critics have often been to 'criticize' the text in the ordinary sense of that word, that is, to question its assumptions and commitments. This can be seen, for example, in J. Galambush's commentary on Ezekiel, where misogynist tendencies are identified in the text.

4. A second recent development has been an interest in literary aspects of the biblical texts. Where much biblical criticism has been concerned with underlying strata and their combination to make the finished books we now have, some students of the Bible have come to think

that such 'excavative' work (to use a phrase of Robert Alter's) is at best only preparatory to a reading of the texts as finished wholes, at worst a distraction from a proper appreciation of them as great literature just as they stand. The narrative books in particular (the Pentateuch and 'historical' books of the Old Testament, the gospels and Acts in the New) have come to be interpreted by means of a 'narrative criticism', akin to much close reading of modern novels and other narrative texts, which is alert to complex literary structure and to such elements as plot, characterization, and closure. It is argued that at the very least readers of the Bible ought to be aware of such issues as well as those of the genesis and formation of the text, and many would contend, indeed, that they are actually of considerably *more* importance for a fruitful appropriation of biblical texts than is the classic agenda of critical study. Many of the commentaries in this volume (such as those on Matthew and Philippians) show an awareness of such aesthetic issues in reading the Bible, and claim that the books they study are literary texts to be read alongside other great works of world literature. This interest in things literary is related to the growing interest in the Bible by people who do not go to it for religious illumination so much as for its character as classic literature, and it is a trend that seems likely to continue.

5. Thirdly, there is now a large body of work in biblical studies arguing that traditional biblical criticism paid insufficient attention not only to literary but also to theological features of the text. Here the interest in establishing the text's original context and meaning is felt to be essentially an antiquarian interest, which gives a position of privilege to 'what the text meant' over 'what the text means'. One important representative of this point of view is the 'canonical approach', sometimes also known as 'canonical criticism', in which biblical interpreters ask not about the origins of biblical books but about their integration into Scripture taken as a finished whole. This is part of an attempt to reclaim the Bible for religious believers, on the hypothesis that traditional historical criticism has alienated it from them and located it in the study rather than in the pulpit or in the devotional context of individual Bible-reading. While this volume assumes the continuing validity of historical-critical study, many contributors are alive to this issue, and are anxious not to make imperialistic claims for historical criticism. Such criticism began, after

all, in a conviction that the Bible was open to investigation by everyone, and was not the preserve of ecclesiastical authorities: it appealed to evidence in the text rather than to external sources of validation. It is important that this insight is not lost by starting to treat the Bible as the possession of a different set of authorities, namely historical-critical scholars! Canonical approaches emphasize that religious believers are entitled to put their own questions to the text, and this must be correct, though it would be a disaster if such a conviction were to result in the outlawing of historical-critical method in its turn. Contributors to this volume, however, are certainly not interested only in the genesis of the biblical books but are also concerned to delineate their overall religious content, and to show how one book relates to others within the canon of Scripture.

6. Thus the historical-critical approach may be chastened by an awareness that its sphere of operations, though vital, is not exhaustive, and that other questions too may reasonably be on the agenda of students of the Bible. In particular, a concern for the finished form of biblical books, however that came into existence, unites both literary and canonical approaches. Few scholars nowadays believe that they have finished their work when they have given an account of how a given book came into being: the total effect (literary and theological) made by the final form is also an important question. The contributors to this volume seek to engage with it.

D. The Biblical Canon. 1. Among the various religious groups that recognize the Bible as authoritative there are some differences of opinion about precisely which books it should contain. In the case of the New Testament all Christians share a common list, though in the centuries of the Christian era a few other books were sometimes included (notably The Shepherd of Hermas, which appears in some major New Testament manuscripts), and some of those now in the canon were at times regarded as of doubtful status (e.g. Hebrews, Revelation, 2 and 3 John, 2 Peter, and Jude). The extent of the Old Testament varies much more seriously. Protestants and Jews alike accept only the books now extant in Hebrew as fully authoritative, but Catholics and Orthodox Christians recognize a longer canon: on this, see the Introduction to the Old Testament. The Ethiopic and Coptic churches accept also *Enoch* and *Jubilees*, as well as having minor variations in the other books of the Old Testament.

2. In this Commentary we have included all the books that appear in the NRSV—that is, all the books recognized as canonical in any of the Western churches (both Catholic and Protestant) and in the Greek and Russian Orthodox churches and those in communion with them. We have not included the books found only in the Ethiopic or Coptic canons, though some extracts appear in the article Essay with Commentary on Post-Biblical Jewish Literature.

3. It is important to see that it is only at the periphery that the biblical canon is blurred. There is a great core of central books whose status has never been seriously in doubt: the Pentateuch and Prophets in the Old Testament, the gospels and major Pauline epistles in the New. Few of the deutero-canonical books of the Old Testament have ever been of major importance to Christians—a possible exception is the Wisdom of Solomon, so well respected that it was occasionally regarded by early Christians as a New Testament book. There is nowadays comparatively little discussion among different kinds of Christian about the correct extent of the biblical canon (which at the Reformation was a major area of disagreement), and our intention has been to cover most of the books regarded as canonical in major churches without expressing any opinion about whether or not they should have canonical status.

E. How to Use this Commentary. 1. A commentary is an aid towards informed reading of a text, and not a substitute for it. The contributors to this volume have written on the assumption that the Bible is open before the reader all the while, whether in hard copy or electronic form. The NRSV is the normal or 'default' version. When other versions or the commentator's own renderings are preferred this is indicated; often this is because some nuance in the original has been lost in the NRSV (no translation can do full justice to all the possible meanings of a text in another language) or because some ambiguity (and these abound in the text of the Bible) has been resolved in a way that differs from the judgement of the commentator.

2. The NRSV is the latest in a long line of translations that go back to the version authorized by King James I of England in 1611. It is increasingly recognized as the most suitable for the purposes of serious study, because it is based on the best available critical editions of the original texts, because it has no particular

confessional allegiance, and because it holds the balance between accuracy and intelligibility, avoiding paraphrase on the one hand and literalism on the other. But comparison between different English translations, particularly for the reader who does not know Hebrew or Greek, is often instructive and serves as a reminder that any translation is itself already an interpretation.

3. *The Oxford Annotated Bible*, based on the NRSV, is particularly useful for those who wish to gain a quick overview of the larger context before consulting this Commentary on a particular passage of special interest. It is useful in another way too: its introductions and notes represent a moderate consensus in contemporary biblical scholarship with which the often more innovative views of the contributors to this Commentary may be measured.

4. When a commentator wishes to draw attention to a passage or parallel in the Bible, the standard NRSV abbreviations apply. But when the reference is to a fuller discussion to be found in the Commentary itself, small capitals are used. Thus (cf. Gen 1:1) signifies the biblical text, while GEN 1:1 refers to the commentary on it. In the same way GEN A etc. refers to the introductory paragraphs of the article on Genesis. The conventions for transliteration of the biblical languages into the English alphabet are the same as those used by *The Oxford Companion to the Bible* (ed. B. M. Metzger and M. Coogan, Oxford: Oxford University Press, 1994).

5. The traditional kind of verse-by-verse commentary has in recent times come under attack as a 'disintegrating' approach that diverts the attention of the reader from the natural flow of the text. The paragraph or longer section, so it is argued, is the real unit of thought, not the verse. However, certain commentators commenting on certain texts would still defend the traditional approach, since they claim that readers chiefly need to be provided with background information necessary to the proper historical interpretation of the text, rather than a more discursive exposition which they could work out for themselves. Examples of both the older and newer methods are to be found in the commentaries below. But even when a particular commentator offers observations on individual verses, we would recommend readers to read the whole paragraph or section and not just the comment on the verse that interests them, so as to gain a more rounded picture. And to encourage this we have not peppered the page with indications of new verses in capitals (V.1) or bold type (**v.1**), but mark the start of a new comment less obtrusively in lower case (v.1).

6. The one-volume Bible commentary, as this genre developed through the twentieth century, aimed to put into the hands of readers everything they needed for the study of the biblical text. Alongside commentaries on the individual books, it often included a host of general articles ranging from 'Biblical Weights and Measures' to 'The Doctrine of the Person of Christ'. In effect, it tried to be a Commentary, Bible Dictionary, Introduction (in the technical sense, i.e. an analysis of evidence for date, authorship, sources, etc.) and Biblical Theology all rolled into one. But it is no longer possible, given the sheer bulk and variety of modern scholarship, even to attempt this multipurpose approach: nor indeed is it desirable since it distracts attention from the proper task of a commentary which is the elucidation of the text itself. Readers who need more background information on a particular issue are recommended to consult *The Oxford Companion to the Bible* or the six volumes of *The Anchor Bible Dictionary* (ed. D. N. Freedman, New York: Doubleday, 1992), though older bible dictionaries may be used instead: the basic factual information they contain remains largely reliable and relatively stable over time.

7. Each article concludes with a bibliography of works cited. But in addition at the end of the volume there is an aggregated bibliography that points the reader towards the most important specialist works in English on the separate books of the Bible, and also major reference works, introductions, theologies, and so forth.

8. The contributors to *The Oxford Bible Commentary*—and this will probably apply to its users as well—belong to different faith traditions or none. They have brought to their task a variety of methods and perspectives, and this lends richness and depth to the work as a whole. But it also creates problems in coming to an agreed common terminology. As we have noted already, the definition of what is to be included in the Bible, the extent of the canon, is disputed. Further, should we refer to the Old and New Testaments, or to the scriptures of Israel and of early Christianity; to the Apocrypha or the deutero-canonical literature? How should dates be indicated, with BC and AD in the traditional manner or with BCE and CE in reference to the *Common Era*? The usages we

have actually adopted should be understood as simple conventions, without prejudice to the serious issues that underlie these differences. A particular problem of a similar kind was whether or not to offer some assistance with a welter of texts, dating from the late biblical period up to 200 CE, which, while not biblical on any definition, are nevertheless relevant to the serious study of the Bible: these are the Dead Sea scrolls, the Old Testament pseudepigrapha, and the apocryphal New Testament. The compromise solution we have reached is to offer not exactly commentary, but two more summarizing articles on this literature (chs. 55 and 82) which, however, still focus on the texts themselves in a way consistent with the commentary format. Some readers may wish to distinguish sharply between the status of this material and that in the Bible; others will see it as merging into the latter.

9. In addition to the overall introductions to the three main subdivisions of the commentary, there are other articles that attempt to approach certain texts not individually but as sets. The Pentateuch or Five Books of Moses functions not only doctrinally but also in terms of its literary history as one five-part work. Similarly, the letters of Paul were once a distinct corpus of writings before they were expanded and added to the growing canon of the New Testament. The four gospels may properly be studied separately, but, both as historical and theological documents, may also be read profitably 'in synopsis'. No attempt has been made by the editors to make these additional articles that group certain texts together entirely consistent with the individual commentaries on them, for the differences are entirely legitimate. The index of subjects at the end of the volume relates only to this introductory material and not to the commentaries themselves. To locate discussions of biblical characters, places, ideas etc. the reader is recommended to consult a concordance first and then to look up the commentary on the passages where the key words occur.

The Bible is a vast treasury of prose and poetry, of history and folklore, of spirituality and ethics; it has inspired great art and architecture, literature and music down the centuries. It invites the reader into its own ancient and mysterious world, and yet at the same time can often surprise us by its contemporary relevance. It deserves and repays all the efforts of critical and attentive reading which the *Oxford Bible Commentary* is designed to assist.

2. Introduction to the Old Testament

JOHN BARTON

A. The Old Testament Canon. 1. 'The Old Testament' is the term traditionally used by Christians and others to refer to the Holy Scriptures of Judaism, which the Church inherited as part of its Jewish origins and eventually came to see as a portion of its own composite Bible, whose other main section is the New Testament. The early Church recognized as Old Testament Scripture both those books which now form the Hebrew Scriptures accepted as authoritative by Jews, and a number of other books, some of them originally written in Hebrew but now (with a few exceptions) found only in Greek and other, later, translations. Since the Reformation, the Hebrew Scriptures alone are recognized as part of the Bible by Protestants, but Catholic and Orthodox Christians continue to acknowledge also these 'Greek' books—sometimes called the 'deuterocanonical' books—which are referred to as 'The Apocrypha' in Protestantism. In this commentary all the books recognized by any Christian church have been included, just as they are in the NRSV, but (again as in the NRSV) we have followed the Protestant and Jewish custom of separating the Apocrypha from the Hebrew Scriptures.

2. The official list of books accepted as part of Scripture is known as the 'canon', and there are thus at least two different canons of the OT: the Hebrew Scriptures (for which Jews do not use the title 'Old Testament'), and the OT of the early church, which contained all the Hebrew Scriptures together with the deuterocanonical/apocryphal books. This second canon has in turn been received in a slightly different form in the Catholic and Orthodox churches, so that there are a few books in the Orthodox canon which do not appear in the Catholic Bible (e.g. 3 Maccabees, Ps 151) and one book (2 Esdras) which is often found in Catholic Bibles but is not extant in Greek and therefore not canonical in the Orthodox churches. The Protestant Apocrypha has traditionally included the deuterocanonical books of the Catholic rather than of the Orthodox church. For a comparison of the Hebrew and Greek canons, see the chart at 1.

3. How did this situation arise? There are many theories about the origins of the various canons, but one which is widely accepted is as follows. By the beginning of the Common Era, most if not all of the books now in the HB were already regarded as sacred Scripture by most Jews. Many, however, especially in Greek-speaking areas such as Egypt, also had a high regard for other books, including what are now the deuterocanonical or apocryphal books, along with others which are no longer in any Bible. The early Christian church, which was predominantly Greek-speaking, tended to accept this wider canon of books. In due course, mainstream Judaism decided to canonize only the books extant in Hebrew, but the Christian churches continued to operate with a wider canon. Certain Church Fathers, notably Melito of Sardis (died c.190 CE) and Jerome (c.345–420) proposed that the church should exclude the deuterocanonical books, but this proposal was not accepted. It was only at the Reformation in the sixteenth century that Jerome's suggestion was reconsidered, and Protestants opted for the shorter, Jewish canon of the Hebrew Scriptures as their OT. The Catholic Church continued to use the longer canon, and the Orthodox churches were unaffected by the Reformation in any case. Some Protestants, notably Lutherans and Anglicans, treated what they now called the Apocrypha as having a sub-scriptural status, but Calvinists and other Protestants rejected it entirely. (See Sundberg 1964; 1968; Anderson 1970; Barton 1986; 1997a; 1997b; Beckwith 1985; Davies 1998.)

4. Since we have included a separate Introduction to the Apocrypha in this Commentary, little more will be said about these deuterocanonical books here. But it is important to grasp that the term 'Old Testament' does not identify a corpus of books so simply as does the corresponding 'New Testament', since different Christians include different books within it. 'Hebrew Bible' or 'Hebrew Scriptures' is unambiguous and is nowadays often preferred to 'Old Testament', but it cannot be used to refer to the longer OT of the ancient church.

B. Collecting the Hebrew Scriptures. 1. If the Hebrew Scriptures were complete by the beginning of the Common Era, that does not mean that the collection was new at that time. Many of the OT books were recognized as authoritative long before the first century BCE. The Pentateuch, or five books of Moses (Genesis, Exodus, Leviticus, Numbers, and Deuteronomy), probably existed in something like its present form by the fourth century BCE, and the historical and prophetic books (Joshua, Judges, Samuel, Kings, Isaiah, Jeremiah, Ezekiel, and the twelve Minor—i.e. shorter—prophets) may well have been compiled no later than the third century BCE. The Jewish arrangement of the Hebrew Scriptures recognizes these two collections, which it calls respectively 'the Torah' and 'the Prophets', as having a certain special prestige above that of 'the Writings', which is the Hebrew title for the third collection in the canon, consisting of other miscellaneous works (Psalms, Proverbs, Job, Daniel, Chronicles, Ezra, Nehemiah, and the five scrolls read at festivals, Esther, Ruth, Song of Songs, Lamentations, and Ecclesiastes). This may well be because the Writings were formed rather later, perhaps not until the first century BCE—indeed, some of the books contained in them, notably Daniel, are themselves much later than most of the books in the Torah and Prophets, and so did not exist to be collected until that later time.

2. In the Greek Bible, followed by the traditional, pre-Reformation Christian canon, this division into three collections is not followed, but a roughly thematic arrangement is preferred, with all the 'historical' books at the beginning, the 'wisdom' or teaching books such as Proverbs in the middle, and the prophetic books (including Daniel) at the end. This produces what looks like a more rational arrangement, but it may obscure the process of canonization to which the Hebrew arrangement is a more effective witness. This commentary follows the traditional Protestant arrangement, which adopts the order of books in the Greek Bible but extracts the deuterocanonical books and groups them into the separate Apocrypha. The different arrangements can be seen in the chart at 1.

3. The collection of scriptural texts was probably undertaken by learned scribes, the forerunners of the people described as 'scribes' in the NT. But it should not be thought of as a conscious process of selection. On the whole the HB probably contains most of what had survived of the writings of ancient Israel, together with more recent books which had commended themselves widely. Growth, rather than selection, was the operative factor. Specific Jewish communities, such as that which produced the Dead Sea scrolls, may have worked with a larger corpus of texts, but there too the texts we now know as biblical had pride of place. There is no evidence of disputes about the contents of the Bible until some time into the Common Era: in earlier times, it seems, old books were

venerated and not questioned. Even where one book was clearly incompatible with another, as is the case with Kings and Chronicles, both were allowed to stand unreconciled within the one canon.

C. Writing the Hebrew Scriptures. 1. People often think of the books of the Bible as each having an author. This was normal in ancient times, too: Jews and Christians thought that the 'books of Moses' were written by Moses, the 'books of Samuel' by Samuel, the Psalms by David, the Proverbs by Solomon, and each of the prophetic books by the prophet whose name the book bears. This raises obvious historical problems—for example, Moses and Samuel then have to be seen as having recorded the details of their own deaths! But modern study has made it clear that many of the books of the OT are the product not of a single author but of several generations of writers, each reworking the text produced by his predecessors. Furthermore, some material in the biblical books may not have originated in written form at all, but may derive from oral tradition. In their finished form most of the books are the product of redactors—editors who (more or less successfully) smoothed out the texts that had reached them to make the books as we now have them.

2. Modern scholarship recognizes important collections of material in the OT that are not coterminous with the books in their present form. In the Pentateuch, for example, it is widely believed that earlier sources can be distinguished. These sources ran in parallel throughout what are now the five books, in particular an early (pre-exilic) strand called 'J' which is to be found throughout Genesis–Numbers, and 'P', a product of priestly writers after the Exile, which is now interwoven with J to form the present form of these books (see INTROD. PENT.). Scholarship has also pointed to the existence of originally longer works which have been broken up to make the books as they now stand. An example is the so-called Deuteronomistic History, supposed by many to have been compiled during the Exile and to have comprised what are now the books of Deuteronomy, Joshua, Judges, Samuel, and Kings, with points of division falling elsewhere than at the present limits of the books. The Psalter has clear evidence of the existence of earlier, shorter collections, such as the Psalms of Asaph and the Psalms of the sons of Korah, which were partly broken up to make the book of Psalms as we now have it. The book of Isaiah seems likely to have consisted originally of at least three lengthy blocks of material, chs. 1–39, 40–55, and 56–66, which have been brought together under the name of the great prophet.

3. Underlying these longer works there were legends, tales, prophetic oracles, wise sayings, and other traditions which may once have existed without any larger context, and circulated orally in particular areas of Israel. The stories of the patriarchs in Genesis, for instance, may go back to individual hero-tales which originally had only a local importance, but which later writers have incorporated into cycles of stories purporting to give information about the ancestors of the whole Israelite people. Individual proverbs may have originated in the life of this or that Israelite village, only much later collected together to form the book of Proverbs. Prophets taught small groups of disciples about matters of immediate concern, but later their words were grouped together by theme and applied to the history of the whole nation and its future.

4. Thus the process which gave us the OT is almost infinitely complicated. Recently, however, literary critics have begun to argue that alongside much anonymous, reworked material, there are also books and sections of books which do betray the presence of genuinely creative writers: the popular idea of biblical 'authors', that is, is not always wide of the mark. The story of David's court in 2 Samuel and 1 Kings, for example, is now widely regarded as the work of a literary genius, and similar claims have been made for other narrative parts of the OT, including segments of the Pentateuch. This Commentary tries to maintain a balance between continuing to hold that most OT books came about as the result of a process stretching over several generations, and a willingness to recognize literary artistry and skilful writing where it can be found. The general trend in OT study at present is towards a greater interest in the present form of the text and away from an exclusive concentration on the raw materials from which it may have been assembled. This present form is often more coherent than an older generation of critics was willing to accept, even though evidence of reworked older material often remains apparent. (See Rendtorff 1985; Smend 1981.)

D. Language. 1. The original language of the OT is predominantly Hebrew, though there are a few sections in Aramaic (Ezra 4:8–6:18, 7:12–26; Dan 2:4–7:28). Aramaic and Hebrew are related, but not mutually comprehensible, languages belonging to the Semitic family, which also includes Arabic, Ethiopic, and the ancient language Akkadian. Aramaic was more important historically, since it was the lingua franca of the Assyrian, Babylonian, and Persian empires, whereas Hebrew is simply the language of Palestine, closely related to the tongues of Israel's neighbours, Moab, Edom, and Ammon.

2. Hebrew and Aramaic, like some other Semitic languages, were originally written without vowels. In any language written with an alphabet more information is provided in the writing-system than is actually needed to make sense of most words: for example, if we wrote 'Th Hbrw lngg' no-one would have any difficulty in understanding this as 'the Hebrew language', especially if they were helped by the context. So long as Hebrew was a living language, this caused few problems. Although some words might be ambiguous, the context would usually determine which was meant. Modern Hebrew is usually written without vowels, too, and this seldom causes difficulties for readers. Once biblical Hebrew became a 'learned' language and passed out of daily use, however, systems of vowel points—dots and dashes above and below the consonant letters—were devised to help the reader, and the system now used in printed Bibles is the work of the Masoretes (see E.2). The unpointed text continues in use today in the scrolls of the Torah read in synagogue worship.

3. Most scholars think that two phases in the development of Hebrew can be found in the pages of the OT: a classical Hebrew which prevailed until some time after the Exile, and a later Hebrew, first attested in Ezekiel and P, which develops through Ecclesiastes and Chronicles in the direction of later Mishnaic Hebrew—the learned language of Jews from about the first century CE onwards, by which time Aramaic had become the everyday tongue. However, this is disputed, and anyone who acquires classical Hebrew can read any biblical book without difficulty. As in many languages, there are wide differences between the Hebrew of prose narrative and that used in verse, where there is often a special vocabulary and many grammatical variations. In some cases these may be due to the use of dialect forms, though this is not certain. Some scholars believe that the oldest parts of the OT, such as the Song of Deborah in Judg 5, preserve an archaic form of the language. (See Saenz-Badillos 1993.)

E. The Text. 1. Until the discovery of the Dead Sea scrolls, which include at least portions of every biblical book except Esther, scholars were dependent on Hebrew MSS no earlier than the ninth century CE. The three most important are the Cairo Codex (of the Prophets only), written in 896 CE; the Aleppo Codex (c.930 CE), unfortunately damaged by fire in 1947; and the Leningrad Codex, dated 1009 CE. The latter is a complete text of the whole HB, and has become the standard text which modern printed Bibles take as their basis.

2. In general terms the Dead Sea discoveries have confirmed the accuracy with which the Leningrad Codex has transmitted the Hebrew text. Although there are innumerable differences in detail, the Dead Sea MSS, though one thousand years older, do not show major deviations from the text as we know it. The HB was transmitted from the beginning of the Common Era by schools of scribes, the most important of whom are the Masoretes, who worked from 500 to 1000 CE; and their claims to have transmitted the Hebrew text with great faithfulness is on the whole confirmed by the evidence from the Dead Sea. One of their tasks was to record the traditional pronunciation of biblical Hebrew, by then a dead language, by adding pointing, that is, signs indicating vowels, to the basic Hebrew text (see D. 2). The Masoretes set themselves the task, almost impossible to imagine in an age before computers, of recording every detail of the text: they compiled lists of unusual spellings, the frequency with which particular words or combinations of words occurred, and even obvious errors in the text. Their work can be seen in the margins and at the top and bottom of the text in a printed HB, in the form of many tiny comments, written in unpointed Aramaic. Their object was not to improve or emend the text they had received, but to preserve it accurately in every detail, and they succeeded to an astonishing extent. The student of the Bible can have confidence that the text translated by modern versions such as the NRSV rests on a faithful tradition going back to NT times.

3. This of course is not to say that that the text was preserved with equal faithfulness between NT times and the times of the original authors. The work of the Masoretes, together with the evidence of the Dead Sea scrolls, ensures that we can feel confident of knowing in general terms what text of Isaiah was current in the time of Jesus. That does not mean that we can know what version of Isaiah was current in

the days of the prophet Isaiah himself. Here we are dependent on conjecture, and the reconstruction of the *original* text, in the literal sense of 'original', is beyond our powers. What we can say is that the HB we possess today is the HB we possess today is the HB that was known to Jews and Christians in the first centuries of our era, carefully preserved even where it does not make sense (which is occasionally the case)! (See Weingreen 1982; Würthwein 1979; Talmon 1970.)

F. Ancient Translations of the Old Testament. 1. By the end of the Second Temple period (4th–2nd cents. BCE) there were substantial communities of Jews who no longer had Hebrew as their first language, certainly outside the land of Palestine and perhaps even inside it. For many, Aramaic had become the everyday tongue, and all around the Mediterranean Greek became the lingua franca in the aftermath of the conquests of Alexander the Great (d. 323 BCE). Aramaic paraphrases of the HB began to be compiled, for use in the liturgy, where readings in Hebrew would be followed by an Aramaic translation, or Targum. Initially Targums were apparently improvised, and there was a dislike of writing them down for fear they might come to seem like Holy Scripture themselves. But later they were collected in writing, and a number have survived to this day.

2. Various Greek versions of the Bible were also made. A legend says that the initiator of Greek translations was Ptolemy Philadelphus of Egypt (285–247 BCE), who ordered that a translation of the Torah should be made so that he could know under what laws his Jewish subjects lived. According to the legend, seventy-two scholars worked on the project for seventy-two days: hence their work came to be known as the Septuagint (meaning 'seventy', traditionally abbreviated LXX). The truth is probably more prosaic, but the third century remains the period when Greek translations of the Torah began to be made, followed by versions of other books too. Later translators set about correcting the LXX versions, among them Aquila, Symmachus, and Theodotion (see Salvesen 1991). About six different translators can be detected in the LXX itself. The version is in general faithful to the Hebrew, and far less of a paraphrase than the Aramaic Targums. Quite often the LXX seems to be a translation of a different Hebrew original from the one that has come down to us, and in some books, notably Jeremiah, it is obvious that the translators were dealing with a quite different (in this case, shorter) version of the book. Any quest for an 'original' text of Jeremiah underlying the MT therefore has to treat the evidence of the LXX very seriously.

3. In the early church Greek was at first the commonest language, and the LXX has come down to us largely because it was preserved in Christian hands. Its divergent ordering of the books, as well as its inclusion of more books than the Hebrew Scriptures, came to be regarded as distinctively Christian features, even though in origin it is plainly a Jewish work. Once Latin displaced Greek as the language of the Western church the need was felt for a further translation into Latin, and various Old Latin MSS have survived, alongside the evidence of biblical quotations in Christian writers who used Latin. The Old Latin versions are translations from the Greek and thus stand at two removes from the Hebrew text. In the fifth century CE Jerome made a complete Latin version of the whole Bible from the original languages. This translation, which came to be known as the Vulgate, became the official Bible of the Western church until the Reformation, and continues to enjoy a high prestige in the Catholic church. Naturally both the Greek and Latin Bibles, like the Hebrew, have come down to us in a range of different MSS, and the quest for 'the original LXX' is no easier than that for the original HB. (See Roberts 1951.)

G. Contents of the Old Testament. 1. The OT contains a huge variety of material, much wider than the contents of the NT, embracing every aspect of the social and political life of ancient Israel and post-exilic Judaism. The variety can be suggested by looking briefly at some of the genres of literature to be found there.

2. Narrative. More than half the OT consists of narrative, that is, the consecutive description of events set in the past. It is hard to distinguish between what we might call history, legend, saga, myth, folktale, or fiction. There are passages in the books of Kings which seem to be excerpts from official documents and thus approach close to something we might recognize as history. At the other end of the spectrum there are at least three stories—Jonah, Ruth, and Esther—which from our perspective are probably fiction, since they rest on no historically true data at all. Then there are a lot of stories that seem to lie between these two extremes: the stories about the creation, the first human beings, and the ancestors of the Israel-

ites in Genesis, the early history of Israel from Exodus through into the books of Samuel, tales about early prophets such as Elijah and Elisha, an account of the court of David which is almost novelistic, and the retellings of older stories in the books of Chronicles, as well as a very small amount of first-person narration in Ezra and Nehemiah. But the OT itself shows no awareness of any differences or gradations within this range of material, but records it all in the same steady and neutral style as if it were all much on a level. Sometimes God or an angel makes regular appearances in the narrative, as in Genesis and Judges, sometimes events are recorded without overt reference to divine causation, as in 2 Samuel; but the OT itself does not draw attention to the difference, and we cannot assume that the writers saw any distinction between 'sacred' and 'secular' history. (See Barr 1980.)

3. Law. Within the narrative framework of the Pentateuch we find several collections of laws, such as the so-called Book of the Covenant (Ex 21–4), the Holiness Code (Lev 17–26), and the Deuteronomic legislation (Deut 12–26). In fact the whole of Leviticus and large parts of Exodus and Numbers contain legal material, and from the perspective of the redactors of the Pentateuch the giving of the law is the main purpose of Israel's sojourn at Sinai. At the heart of the law lie the Ten Commandments (Ex 20, Deut 5), and the rest of the legislation is presented as a detailed exposition of the principles the Commandments enshrine.

4. From a historical point of view the laws in the Pentateuch have much in common with the laws of other nations in the ancient Near East, such as the famous Code of Hammurabi. But they also differ from them in striking ways—e.g. in a higher valuation of human life, much more interest in regulations concerning worship, and a greater tendency to lay down general principles. As presented in the Pentateuch, however, the laws are understood as the foundation of the highly distinctive relationship of Israel with its god, YHWH. They are the terms of the solemn agreement, or 'covenant', made between YHWH and the people through the mediation of Moses. The idea of a legislative framework which regulates the relation between a god and his people was unusual in the ancient world. It led in post-biblical times to the idea of Torah, a complete ethical code covering all aspects of life as lived before God, which would become the foundation-stone of later Judaism. This tendency can already be discerned in Deuteronomy, where the laws are not just to be enacted and observed jurisprudentially but are also to be a subject for constant meditation and delight. (See Noth 1966.)

5. Hymns and Psalms. The Psalms have sometimes been described as the hymnbook of the temple, though since they are hard to date there is no agreement as to whether they are best seen as the hymnbook of Solomon's Temple or of the Second Temple, built after the Exile. We do not know which psalms were intended for public liturgical and which for private prayer—indeed, that distinction may be a false one in ancient Israel. There have been many theories about the use of the Psalms in worship, but all are highly speculative. What can be said is that Israel clearly had a tradition of writing sophisticated religious poems, and that this continued over a long period: Ps 29, for example, seems to be modelled on a Canaanite psalm and must therefore have originated in early pre-exilic times, while Ps 119 reflects a piety based on meditation on the Torah, and is generally dated in the late post-exilic period. Psalms can also be found outside the Psalter itself, for example in Ex 15, 1 Sam 2, and Jon 2. (See Gillingham 1994.)

6. Wisdom. There are at least three kinds of wisdom literature in the OT. The book of Proverbs preserves many sayings and aphorisms which draw moral and practical conclusions from aspects of daily life. These may in some cases have originated in the life of the Israelite village, in others in the royal court, but all have been gathered together to form the great collection of sayings that runs from Prov 10 to 30. A second kind of wisdom is more speculative in character, concerned with theological and cosmological questions, as seen e.g. in Prov 8:22–36. Frequently in such passages Wisdom is itself personified as a kind of goddess, and the writer speculates on the involvement of this being in the creation of the world and on its/her relationship to YHWH. Thirdly, we find what is sometimes called mantic wisdom, which draws on ancient Near-Eastern traditions about the interpretation of dreams and portents to gain insight into the future, and this is manifested by Joseph in Genesis, and in the book of Daniel. Two books, Job and Ecclesiastes, seem to reflect on deficiencies within the traditions of wisdom, and argue for a generally sceptical and non-committal attitude towards the mysteries of life. They are part of a general tendency towards greater pessimism about human capabilities of reason and

understanding, characteristic of post-exilic Jewish thought. (See Crenshaw 1981.)

7. Prophecy. 'Prophecy', like 'wisdom', is something of a catch-all term covering a wide diversity of material. Its basic form is the oracle: a (usually) short, pithy saying in which the prophet either denounces some current evil, or predicts what YHWH will do in the immediate future as a response to human conduct. One of the difficulties of studying the prophetic books is that these oracles are often arranged in an order which reflects the interests of the editors, rather than registering the chronological sequence of what the prophet himself said. The matter is complicated further by the insertion of many non-authentic oracles, representing perhaps what later writers thought the prophet might or would have said in later historical situations, had he still been alive and able to do so. It is probably in the prophetic books that the concept of authorship breaks down most completely. Many prophetic books also contain brief narratives and biographical details about the prophet whose name they bear. Sometimes these are indistinguishable in style and approach from narratives in the 'historical' books—e.g. Jeremiah contains many stories about the prophet that would not be out of place in Kings, and perhaps comes from the same school of writers.

8. Sometimes the prophets relate visions and their divine interpretations, and towards the end of the OT period this became the normal way of conveying divine revelation, in the form usually called 'apocalyptic'. Daniel is the only book in the HB generally called apocalyptic, but later portions of the prophetic books show developments in this direction and are sometimes referred to as proto-apocalyptic. Prime candidates for this description are Isa 24–7, Joel, and Zech 9–14. (See Blenkinsopp 1984.)

H. Themes of the Old Testament. 1. Despite its variety, the OT is a document from a religious tradition that retained, over time, certain characteristic features. These can be introduced here only in the most sketchy outline, but it may be helpful to the reader to be aware of four interlocking themes.

2. Creation and Monotheism. YHWH is consistently presented throughout the OT as the God who created the world, and as the only God with whom Israel is to be concerned. Older strands of thought do not yet treat him as the only God there is (strict monotheism), a development generally thought to have taken place around the time of the Exile. But it is never envisaged that any other god is a proper object of worship for Israelites. There are occasional survivals of a polytheistic system—e.g. in Ps 82—but no extended text in the OT speaks of the actions of gods other than YHWH as real or other than purported. The OT presents much of the life of the pre-exilic period as one of warfare between YHWH and the gods of Canaan for Israel's allegiance. We know that as a matter of historical fact many people were far from being monotheistic in their religious practice in this period. But all our texts imply or affirm that for Israel there can in the end be only YHWH.

3. Alongside the majestic account of creation in Gen 1, where God creates by mere diktat, the OT is familiar with older creation stories in which creation was accomplished when the chief god killed a dragon and made the world out of its body (see Ps 74, Job 3)—a pattern of thought widespread in the ancient Near East. However, this theme seems to be used in a literary way, rather than reflecting a genuine belief of the authors—much as English poets in the past might conventionally invoke the Muses though they did not believe these beings actually existed. Jews and Christians alike have seen the Hebrew Scriptures as important, among other reasons, because they affirm the oneness of God and his absolute power over the creation, and in this they have correctly captured a theme which is of central importance in the Bible itself. It finds its most eloquent expression in the oracles of Deutero-Isaiah, as the author of Isa 40–55 is known: see especially Isa 40:12–26. (See Theissen 1984; Whybray 1983.)

4. Covenant and Redemption. It is a central point in many OT texts that the creator God YHWH is also in some sense Israel's special god, who at some point in history entered into a relationship with his people that had something of the nature of a contract. Classically this contract or covenant was entered into at Sinai, and Moses was its mediator. As we saw above, the laws in the Pentateuch are presented as the terms of the contract between YHWH and his people. Acting in accordance with his special commitment to Israel, YHWH is thought to have guided their history, in particular bringing them out of Egypt and giving them the promised land as a perpetual possession. Later prophets hoped for a restoration to this land after the Jews had lost political control of it to a succession of great powers: Assyria, Babylonia, and Persia.

5. In the prophetic version of the covenant theory, the contractual nature of the arrangement

is stressed in such a way as to imply the possibility of the destruction of Israel if the nation is disobedient. It is not too much to say that the main preoccupation of most of the prophets was with how YHWH would 'manage' this strict interpretation of the covenant, punishing his people and yet somehow preserving the special relationship with them which the covenant implied. In other strands of OT thought, however, the emphasis falls more heavily on YHWH's commitment to his people and the idea of a bargain is less apparent. Thus the covenant with Abraham, and that with David and his descendants, tend to be presented as almost unconditional. Either the obedience required from the human partner is seen as minimal, or else disobedience (though it will be punished) does not have the power to lead to a complete breakdown in the relationship with YHWH. After the Exile the covenant between YHWH and Israel was often seen as unbreakable on the national scale, but individuals had a duty to remain *within* the covenant community by faithful adherence to Torah.

6. The God who makes a covenant with Israel is a God of redemption as well as of creation. He saves his people from Egypt, and then constantly intervenes in their history to deliver them from their enemies, even though he can also use these enemies as agents of his just punishment. In every national crisis Israel can call on YHWH for help, and though his mercy must not be presumed on, he is a reliable source of support in the long term. (See Nicholson 1986; Spriggs 1974.)

7. Ethics. In some OT traditions, such as that of the law, ethical obligation is tightly bound up with Israel's contractual obligations to YHWH, whereas in others (notably wisdom) there is more appeal to universally applicable standards of justice and uprightness. Everywhere in the OT, however, it is taken as given that God makes moral demands on both Israel and all human beings. These demands characteristically include two aspects which to modern, non-Jewish readers do not seem to belong naturally together: a strong commitment to social justice, and a deep concern for ritual purity. Ritual and ethical punctiliousness are seen as points on a single spectrum, so that some texts can speak of gross moral outrages such as murder as polluting the sanctuary of YHWH just as do ritual infringements (see Ezek 18). Pagan writers in the ancient world often drew attention to the high moral standards of Jews, while simultaneously being puzzled that they were so concerned about matters of diet and ritual purity. At the same time there are prophetic books, such as Amos and Hosea, which seem to distinguish the two types of ethical concern, and which argue that YHWH requires social justice more than ritual purity, and perhaps that he does not care about ritual purity at all: this latter possibility is also envisaged in some wisdom texts.

8. The OT's moral code is remarkably consistent throughout the period covered by the literature. It stresses justice, both in the sense of fairness to everyone, rich and poor alike, and in the sense of intervention on behalf of those who cannot help themselves. It forbids murder, theft, bribery and corruption, deceitful trading standards (e.g. false weights and measures), and many sexual misdemeanours, including adultery, incest, bestiality, and homosexual acts. It insists on the duty of those in power to administer justice equitably, and forbids exploitation of the poor and helpless, especially widows and orphans. All moral obligation is traced back to an origin in God, either by way of 'positive' law—YHWH's explicit commands—or else through the way the divine character is expressed in the orders of nature. Some moral obligations at least are assumed to be known outside Israel (as was of course the case), and especially in the wisdom literature appeal is made to the consensus of right-minded people and not only to the declared will of YHWH. (See Wright 1983; Barton 1998; Otto 1994.)

9. Theodicy. In a polytheistic system it is easy to explain the disasters that overtake human societies: they result from disagreements among the gods, in which human beings get caught in the crossfire, or from the malevolence of particular gods towards humankind. This kind of explanation is not available in a monotheistic culture, and consequently the kind of problem which philosophers deal with under the title 'theodicy'— how to show that God is just in the face of the sufferings of the world—bulk large in the writings of the OT.

10. On the corporate level, the Exile seems to have been the crisis that first focused the minds of Israel's thinkers on the problem of how to make sense of apparently unjust sufferings. Lamentations is an extended expression of grief at the rough treatment that YHWH has apparently handed out to the people he had chosen himself; Jeremiah also reflects on the problem. Ezekiel tries to show

that God is utterly just, and that those who complain of his injustice are in fact themselves to blame for what has befallen them. Second Isaiah combines a conviction that God has been just to punish Israel with an assurance that destruction is not his last word, and that he will remain true to his ancient promises to Abraham, Isaac, and Jacob. Through reflection on the disaster that has befallen Israel all these thinkers come to an affirmation of the superior justice of God—greater, not less, than that of any human power.

11. At the level of the individual the problems of theodicy are discussed in Job and, to some extent, in Ecclesiastes. Here explanations in terms of human guilt are for the most part rejected, since we are told at the outset that Job is a righteous man, who manifestly does not deserve to suffer as he does. The book concludes that God cannot be held to account, and that his ways are imponderable, though perhaps also that there are forms of fellowship with him in which understanding why one suffers is not a first priority. For Ecclesiastes, the world manifests no moral order such that the righteous can expect to be rewarded and the wicked punished, but 'time and chance happen to all'.

12. Convictions about the justice of God are crucial to the way the story of Israel is told in the historical books: Kings and Chronicles in particular are concerned to show that God is always just in his dealings with his people. Kings sees this as manifested in the fact that sin is always avenged, even if it takes many generations for God's justice to be implemented; while Chronicles believes instead in immediate retribution. The Psalms, too, contain many reflections on the respective fate of righteous and wicked, and contain some profound insights on this theme—see especially Ps 37, 49, and 73. There are, in fact, few books in the OT where the theme of theodicy is absent. (See Crenshaw 1983.)

I. Arrangement of Books in Hebrew and Greek Bibles

The Hebrew Bible	The Greek Bible
Torah:	*Historical Books:*
Genesis	Genesis
Exodus	Exodus
Leviticus	Leviticus
Numbers	Numbers
Deuteronomy	Deuteronomy

The Hebrew Bible	The Greek Bible
Prophets:	
Joshua	Joshua
Judges	Judges
Samuel	Ruth
Kings	1 Samuel
Isaiah	2 Samuel
Jeremiah	1 Kings
Ezekiel	2 Kings
The Twelve:	1 Chronicles
Hosea	2 Chronicles
Joel	1 Esdras
Amos	Ezra
Obadiah	Nehemiah
Jonah	Esther (*with additions*)
Micah	*Judith*
Nahum	*Tobit*
Habakkuk	*1 Maccabees*
Zephaniah	*2 Maccabees*
Haggai	*3 Maccabees*
Zechariah	*4 Maccabees*
Malachi	
Writings:	*Didactic Books*:
Psalms	Psalms
Job	Proverbs
Proverbs	Ecclesiastes
Ruth	Song of Songs
Song of Songs	Job
Ecclesiastes	*Wisdom of Solomon*
Lamentations	*Ecclesiasticus*
Esther	
Daniel	
Ezra-Nehemiah	*Prophetic Books*:
Chronicles	Twelve Minor Prophets:
	Hosea
	Amos
	Micah
	Joel
	Obadiah
	Jonah
	Nahum
	Habakkuk
	Zephaniah
	Haggai
	Zechariah
	Malachi
	Isaiah
	Jeremiah
	Baruch 1–5
	Lamentations
	Letter of Jeremiah (= *Baruch 6*)
	Ezekiel
	Susanna (= *Daniel 13*)

The Hebrew Bible	The Greek Bible
	Daniel 1–12 (with additions
	Song of Azariah and *Song of*
	the Three Jews)
	Bel and the Dragon (= *Daniel 14*)

Notes: Books additional to the HB are in italics.

Books are given the names familiar to English readers: Samuel and Kings are in Greek the 'Four Books of Kingdoms', and Ezra-Nehemiah is '2 Esdras'.

REFERENCES

Anderson, G. W. (1970), 'Canonical and Non-canonical', *Cambridge History of the Bible* (Cambridge: Cambridge University Press), i. 113–59.

Barr, J. (1980), *The Scope and Authority of the Bible*, Explorations in Theology, 7 (London: SCM).

Barton, J. (1986), *Oracles of God: Perceptions of Ancient Prophecy in Israel after the Exile* (London: Darton, Longman & Todd).

—— (1991), *What is the Bible?* (London: SPCK).

—— (1997a), *Making the Christian Bible* (London: Darton, Longman & Todd).

—— (1997b), *The Spirit and the Letter: Studies in the Biblical Canon* (London: SPCK).

—— (1998), *Ethics and the Old Testament* (London: SCM).

Beckwith, R. T. (1985), *The Old Testament Canon of the New Testament Church and its Background in Early Judaism* (London: SPCK).

Blenkinsopp, J. (1984), *A History of Prophecy in Israel from the Settlement in the Land to the Hellenistic Period* (London: SPCK).

Crenshaw, J. L. (1981), *Old Testament Wisdom: An Introduction* (Atlanta: John Knox).

—— (1983) (ed.), *Theodicy in the Old Testament* (Philadelphia: Fortress).

Davies, P. R. (1998), *Scribes and Schools: The Canonization of the Hebrew Scriptures* (Louisville, Ky.: Westminster/John Knox).

Gillingham, S. E. (1994), *The Poems and Psalms of the Hebrew Bible* (Oxford: Oxford University Press).

Nicholson, E. W. (1986), *God and his People: Covenant and Theology in the Old Testament* (Oxford: Clarendon).

Noth, M. (1966), 'The Laws in the Pentateuch: Their Assumptions and Meaning', in his *The Laws in the Pentateuch and Other Essays* (Edinburgh: T. & T. Clark), 1–107.

Otto, E. (1994), *Theologische Ethik des Alten Testaments* (Stuttgart: Kohlhammer).

Rendtorff, R. (1985), *The Old Testament: An Introduction* (London: SCM).

Roberts, B. J. (1951), *The Old Testament Text and Versions: The Hebrew Text in Transmission and the History of the Ancient Versions* (Cardiff: University of Wales Press).

Saenz-Badillos, A. (1993), *A History of the Hebrew Language* (Cambridge: Cambridge University Press).

Salvesen, A. (1991), *Symmachus in the Pentateuch* (Manchester: University of Manchester Press).

Smend, R. (1981), *Die Entstehung des Alten Testaments* (Stuttgart: Kohlhammer).

Spriggs, D. S. (1974), *Two Old Testament Theologies* (London: SCM).

Sundberg, A. C. (1964), *The Old Testament of the Early Church* (Cambridge, Mass.: Yale University Press).

—— (1968), 'The "Old Testament": A Christian Canon', *CBO* 30: 143–55.

Talmon, S. (1970), 'The Old Testament Text', *Cambridge History of the Bible* (Cambridge: Cambridge University Press), i. 159–98.

Theissen, G. (1984), *Biblical Faith: An Evolutionary Perspective* (London: SCM).

Weingreen, J. (1982), *Introduction to the Critical Study of the Text of the Hebrew Bible* (Oxford: Oxford University Press).

Whybray, R. N. (1983), *The Second Isaiah*, Old Testament Guides (Sheffield: Academic Press).

Wright, C. J. H. (1983), *Living as the People of God* (Leicester: Intervarsity Press).

Würthwein, E. (1979), *The Text of the Old Testament: An Introduction to the Biblia Hebraica* (Grand Rapids: Eerdmans).

3. Introduction to the Pentateuch

G. I. DAVIES

A. What is the Pentateuch? 1. The name 'Pentateuch' means literally 'the work comprising five scrolls', from Greek *pente* and *teukhos*, which can mean 'scroll'. It has been used since at least early Christian times for the first five books of the OT, Genesis to Deuteronomy. The Jewish name for these books was usually and still is 'the law': Hebrew *tôrâ*, Greek *nomos* or *nomothesia* (the latter is literally 'legislation'), and it is this name which appears in the NT: e.g. Lk 24:11, 'What is written in the *law*, the prophets and the psalms', where we meet the threefold subdivision of the Hebrew canon that continues to be used, with the substitution of 'writings' for 'psalms' as the third section. Cf. also the Greek Prologue to Sirach (*c.*132 BCE).

2. But there is a much deeper way of asking, and answering, the question, 'What is the Pentateuch?', one which goes beyond merely defining its external limits to enquire into its nature. In other words, what sort of a thing is this section of the Bible? This question can only really be answered after a full examination of the text, and one justification for the kind of detailed critical analysis which has been popular in modern OT scholarship is that it enables us to give a well-judged (if complicated!) answer to that question. It is a question of considerable theological importance, as can be seen from an introductory look at a few answers that have been given to it, some of which will be examined more fully later on.

2.1. Four of the five books in the Pentateuch deal with the time of Moses, and one recent suggestion has been that we should think of the Pentateuch as *a biography of Moses* with an introduction, that is, Genesis. This attempts to answer the question in terms of the literary genre of the Pentateuch.

2.2. Its main weakness, however, is that it puts Moses as an individual too much in the centre of the picture, important as he undoubtedly is as the leader of his people Israel. We might do better to call the Pentateuch the *story of Israel in the time of Moses*, with an introduction (Genesis) which sets it in the light of universal creation and history.

2.3. To many, however, this would not be theological enough to do justice to the strongly religious element that pervades the story from beginning to end. Gerhard von Rad suggested that the Pentateuch (or to be more precise, the Hexateuch, that is the Pentateuch plus the sixth book of the Bible, Joshua—see below) was an amplified creed, more specifically *an amplified historical creed*, as will be seen in more detail later. The implication is then that the Pentateuch is a product and an expression of faith—it is preceded as it were by an implicit 'I believe in God who ...', it is a confessional document, as one might put it. Of course the adjective 'historical' before 'creed' raises some problems, for example whether the story which the Pentateuch as a whole tells is real history, a question whose answer has important theological implications which critics of von Rad were quick to point out. But there are also problems of a simpler kind which relate specifically to its accuracy as a description of Genesis 1–11. Von Rad was, for much of his scholarly career, fascinated by the historical focus of so much of Israel's faith, and he tended to overlook or play down its teaching about God the Creator. This may well have been due to an understandable wish on his part not to allow a foothold in the OT for crude Nazi ideas about racial supremacy grounded in the order of creation which were current at the time he wrote his earliest works on the Hexateuch. It is, nevertheless, necessary to emphasize that the beginning of Genesis is not about history in the ordinary sense of that word, or indeed in any sense, and the idea that the Pentateuch is a 'historical' creed is in danger of losing sight of the important theological statements about creation in those chapters.

2.4. A different way of representing the theological character of the Pentateuch is of course the traditional Jewish expression: *the law*. This is as characteristic of Judaism as von Rad's emphasis on faith is characteristic of his Lutheranism. If it seems at first sight to focus too much on the second half of the Pentateuch, where the laws are concentrated, and to give insufficient attention to the 'story' character of the earlier books, it is worth saying that this problem has not escaped the notice of Jewish commentators, and a very early one, Philo of Alexandria, in the first century CE, had what he thought was a perfectly satisfactory answer to it. It is that while written law is indeed mainly found in the later books of the Pentateuch, the personalities who appear in Genesis, for example, constitute a kind of 'living law', since through their example, and in some less obvious ways, it was God's intention to regulate human behaviour, just as he does later by the written law. Another way of making the description 'law' more widely applicable involves going back to the Hebrew term *tôrâ*. Although commonly translated 'law', its original meaning is something like 'instruction', and it could be used of other kinds of instruction as well as law in the strict sense. For example, the word *tôrâ* is found in Proverbs, where the context shows that the reference is to the kind of teaching contained there, not to the law as such. If we use *tôrâ* as a description for the Pentateuch in this more general sense of 'teaching' or 'instruction', it can easily embrace the non-legal parts of these books as well as the legal ones. On the other hand, while *tôrâ* understood in this wider way does preserve an important truth about the Pentateuch (especially if it is thought of as 'The Teaching', with a capital T), it is in danger of being too vague a description to identify its distinctive character within the OT.

2.5. Another theological definition, which has the merit of combining the advantages of the last two, is to call the Pentateuch a *covenant book*, a document which presents the terms of God's relationship to his people, in the form of his promises to them and the laws which he requires them to obey. The support of the apostle Paul can probably be claimed for this description, for when he speaks of 'the old covenant' in 2 Cor 3:14 it is very likely that he means specifically the Pentateuch. He is clearly thinking of a written document, because he refers to the 'reading' of the old covenant, and the substitution of the expression 'whenever Moses is read' in the following verse points firmly to the Pentateuch (for 'Moses' as shorthand for 'the books of Moses' see Lk 24:27). A somewhat earlier Jewish reference to the Pentateuch as 'the book of the covenant' occurs in 1 Macc 1:57. Despite the antiquity and authority of this description, it scarcely does justice to the narrative element in the Pentateuch, especially in Genesis.

2.6. A description which combines the literary and the theological aspects has been proposed by David Clines: he regards the Pentateuch as *the story of the partial fulfilment of the promise to the patriarchs*. This has the great advantage of highlighting the important theological theme of promise in Genesis, and of showing how Genesis is linked to the later books theologically, and not just by the continuation of the story. But of course it says nothing about Gen 1–11, and one may wonder whether it takes enough account of the vast amount of legislative material in Leviticus and Deuteronomy especially.

2.7. One might legitimately wonder whether there can be any brief answer to the question which is not open to some objection or another! If nothing else these quite different descriptions, and the comments on them, should have shown that the Pentateuch is a many-sided piece of literature and one which has features which appeal to a variety of religious and other points of view. The final description that I will mention is that the Pentateuch is an incomplete work, a *torso*, because the story which it tells only reaches its climax in the book of Joshua, with the Israelites' entry into the land of Canaan. For von Rad, as we saw, the real literary unit is the 'Hexateuch', 'the six books', and he had many predecessors who also took this view. It was especially popular among the source-critics of the late nineteenth and early twentieth centuries, who believed (as some still do) that the sources out of which the Pentateuch was composed were also used by the editor or editors who composed Joshua. It is less popular today, because Joshua is generally treated as part of the long historical work which extends to the end of 2 Kings, the Deuteronomistic History. In fact since Deuteronomy formed the introduction to that work and, even when taken alone, its connection with the first four books of the Bible can seem very weak, some scholars therefore speak of 'the Tetrateuch', that is the four books from Genesis to Numbers, as the primary literary unit at the beginning of the Bible. From this point of view the Pentateuch would be not so much a torso as a hybrid, the combination of one literary work with the first section of another. If nothing else this view serves to underline the differences in character, concerns, and origin of Deuteronomy, as compared with the earlier books. Yet those differences should not be exaggerated, and it can be argued that Deuteronomy belongs as much with the Tetrateuch as with the books that follow it, and when we come to look at the theology of the Pentateuch in more detail that will become clearer.

B. The Documentary Hypothesis. 1. To make further progress with our question, 'What is the Pentateuch?', we need to dig deeper and consider more closely how it came to exist and what kinds of material it is made up of. A useful way into such study is to review, critically where necessary, the main directions which Pentateuchal scholarship has taken over the past century and a half (see also Clements 1997: ch. 2).

2. The year 1862 was auspicious for the development of Pentateuchal study in England and Germany. It was in that year that Julius Wellhausen went, at the age of 18, as a new student to the German university of Göttingen to study theology. That same year a young British student, T. K. Cheyne, was also in Göttingen, and he was to play an important part in bringing Wellhausen's later ideas to prominence in Britain—he became a professor at Oxford. The year 1862 was also when a series of books by John Colenso, a Cambridge mathematician,

began to be published, and so brought critical OT scholarship very much into the public eye in Britain only shortly after the publication of Charles Darwin's *Origins of Species* and the collection called *Essays and Reviews*. And yet by 1862 the critical study of the Pentateuch was already some 150 years old.

3. There is no need to amplify this statement here—the details are in most Introductions to the OT—except to say that particularly since about 1800 strenuous efforts had been made, chiefly in Germany, to discover the process by which the Pentateuch had reached its present form, and that at the beginning of the 1860s the leading scholars held to what was known as the Supplementary Hypothesis (*Ergänzungshypothese*). According to this, the original core of the Pentateuch was a document known as the Book of Origins (*Das Buch der Ursprünge*), which was put together by a priest or Levite in about the time of King Solomon. A distinguishing mark of this book was that in Genesis and the beginning of Exodus (up to ch. 6) it avoided using the name YHWH for God, and employed other words, especially *'ĕlōhîm*, which means 'God', instead. This core, it was held, was expanded in the eighth century BCE, the time of the first great classical prophets, by the addition of stories and other matter in which the name YHWH was freely used from the very beginning. Later still, in the time of Jeremiah (7th cent.), the work was further supplemented by the addition of the major part of Deuteronomy and shorter sections with a similar spirit elsewhere, and so the Pentateuch reached its present form, before the Babylonian Exile. Wellhausen's teacher at Göttingen, Heinrich Ewald, had played an important part in the development of this theory and still held to it in its essential points in 1862, though not with the rigidity of some of its other adherents.

4. But changes were in the air. An important challenge to this theory had already been made by the publication in 1853 of a book by Hermann Hupfeld. Its main theses were: (1) that the so-called 'original core' contained some passages which were of later origin than the rest and represented a first stage of expansion of the core; and (2) that both these later passages and the passages which the Supplementary Hypothesis itself had distinguished from the core were not fragments picked up from all over the place but had been parts of large preexisting narrative compositions which the compilers of the Pentateuch had drawn on as sources.

5. Hupfeld thus did two things. He refined the analysis of the Pentateuch into its component parts, which were now seen to be not three but four in number, and he replaced the idea of the expansion of an original core with a truly documentary theory of Pentateuchal origins. His four originally independent source-documents correspond closely in extent to those of later theories, three parallel narrative sources and the law-code of Deuteronomy (with some other passages related to it). His oldest narrative corresponds closely to what is now called the Priestly Work (P), the remainder of the Book of Origins is the later Elohist (E), and the source which uses the name YHWH is the Yahwist (J). Hupfeld did not depart from the dominant view at the time about the relative ages of the materials in these sources, and his position can be represented in terms of the modern symbols for them as P-E-J-D (for a fuller account of the sources as later understood see sections c.7 and G).

Hupfeld's new ideas did not succeed in displacing the dominant Supplementary Hypothesis, at any rate not immediately. But some time before 1860 Ewald had recognized the existence of a second Elohist and the character of J and E as continuous sources—which places him very close to Hupfeld. A. Knobel, though less well-known, had reached similar conclusions independently of Hupfeld about the same time, and over a larger range of texts. His work is ignored in most modern accounts of the history of Pentateuchal criticism (though not by Wellhausen) and deserves greater recognition. These scholars brought the *analysis* of the Pentateuch to a state which received only relatively minor modification at the hands of those such as Wellhausen, whose work was to become the classical account of Pentateuchal origins and indeed remained so until very recently. Hupfeld's contribution at least was fully recognized: Wellhausen, for example, wrote in his own work on the composition of the Hexateuch: 'I make Hupfeld in every respect my starting-point.' Where he and subsequent scholarship departed from Hupfeld was in the chronological *order* in which the sources were to be placed.

6. Two changes were in fact made. One, the placing of the YHWH-source—what we now call J—before the second Elo-him-source—what we now call E—did not make a fundamental difference to the time at which either source was thought to have been written, and we shall not spend long on it. Once Hupfeld had made the separation between E and P it was really inevitable, as it was the supposed antiquity of the P texts which had led to the idea

that the Book of Origins was the earliest source. When E was detached from this, it could easily be seen that in certain respects it had a more sophisticated approach to religion than the rather primitive J, and so it was natural to date it a little later.

7. The second change in order was much more decisive, in fact it was quite revolutionary. According to both the Supplementary Hypothesis and Hupfeld's theory, the oldest part of the Pentateuch was a Book of Origins that began with the account of creation in Gen 1 and included most of the priestly laws in Exodus, Leviticus, and Numbers. Doubts about the antiquity of these texts had already been expressed in the 1830s, but detailed critical arguments only began to appear in the early 1860s. One can see this in the work of the Dutch scholar Abraham Kuenen (1828–91), whose *Introduction to the OT* began to be published in 1861. Kuenen, who accepted Hupfeld's division of the Book of Origins into earlier and later layers, also held that the priestly laws in the supposedly earlier layer were not in fact all ancient but had developed over a long period of time, some of them being later in date than Deuteronomy. An even more radical conclusion had been reached by a German schoolteacher, Karl Heinrich Graf, who on 7 October 1862 wrote to his former OT professor, one Eduard Reuss, 'I am completely convinced of the fact that the whole middle part of the Pentateuch [apparently Exodus 25 to the end of Numbers] is post-exilic in origin,' i.e. it all belongs to the final, not the first, stage of the growth of the Pentateuch, after the writing of Deuteronomy. Wellhausen himself, looking back on his early student days, also in the early 1860s, wrote that he had been puzzled at the lack of reference to the allegedly very old priestly laws in the early historical books such as Samuel and Kings and in the prophets, though he had no idea at the time why this was. It was not until 1865 that these very new ideas came out into the open, when Graf published his views in book form. But while he maintained that all the legal parts of the Book of Origins were post-exilic in origin, he still held to the traditional early date for its narratives. In response to the appearance of Graf's book Kuenen now argued that the Book of Origins could not be divided up in this way, because the narratives were intimately related to the laws; so, if (as Graf had so powerfully demonstrated) the laws were late in origin, the narratives associated with them in the 'earlier' part of the Book of Origins must be late too. Graf's letter to

Kuenen accepting the validity of this point sur-vives—it is dated 12 Nov. 1866—and subse-quently Graf put this change of mind into print in an article in which he responded to various criticisms of his book, though the article only came out in 1869 after Graf's death. In this way the order (as represented by the modern symbols) P-E-J-D of Hupfeld was transformed into the J-E-D-P that became standard.

8. It is clear that Abraham Kuenen played a very important part in the development of this revised theory, although it (like Knobel's contri-bution) is often overlooked. What is interesting is that Kuenen gave a great deal of the credit for the contribution which he himself was able to make to John Colenso's series of volumes en-titled *The Pentateuch and The Book of Joshua Critic-ally Examined*. These books were one reason why an attempt was made to depose Colenso from the see of Natal, which he held, an attempt which was only the beginning of a long wrangle in the Anglican Church in South Africa. Much of what Colenso wrote merely echoed what was already being done in Germany, but in the first volume of the study he presented what seemed to him to be a devastating attack on the genu-ineness of the narratives of the Book of Origins and particularly the large numbers which they give for the participants in the Exodus (e.g. Ex 12:37), the very thing which had seemed to others a guarantee of the accuracy and antiquity of the source; on the contrary, argued Colenso, it was quite impossible that the numbers could represent real historical facts: they must be fic-tional. This argument so impressed Kuenen that he found no difficulty at all in regarding those narratives, as well as the priestly laws which Graf had examined, as a late and artificial composition.

9. It is evident from all this that the classical documentary theory of Pentateuchal origins owes little or nothing, as far as its origin is concerned, to Wellhausen: this was mainly the work of Hupfeld, Graf, and Kuenen, themselves of course building on much earlier work. To call it 'the Wellhausen theory', as is often done, is a misnomer, though a revealing one. What the new theory still needed, and what Wellhausen was to provide, was a presentation of it which would convince the many scholars who still held either to the Supplementary Hypothesis or to Hupfeld's version of the documentary theory. The work in which Wellhausen did this so successfully was originally called *History of Israel. Volume I* (*Geschichte Israels I*)—when no further volumes appeared this was changed to

Prolegomena to the History of Israel (*Prolegomena zur Geschichte Israels*)—and it was published in 1878. It is still worth reading and its thorough atten-tion to detail, its treatment of evidence from all parts of the OT, and the force and vigour of its arguments still make a strong impression on the reader.

10. Two criticisms are often made of it. The first is that it embodies a Hegelian view of history which has been imposed upon the data of the OT (so e.g. W. F. Albright and R. K. Harrison). This is not justified as a criticism of Wellhausen's method of working, whatever similarities may be traced between some of his conclusions and those of Hegel-inspired his-tory-writing. It is a complicated issue but essen-tially it seems that what Wellhausen did was to approach the Pentateuch as a secular ancient historian would approach his primary sources in an effort to discover their character and closeness to the events described: his presup-positions and methods are those of a historian rather than those of a philosopher, and not significantly different from those with which more recent historians have worked. Where he does refer to Hegel once it seems to be an implied criticism. The other criticism is that Wellhausen presented his theory in isolation from knowledge of the ancient Near East, which makes it of no more than antiquarian interest: so Harrison again and especially K. A. Kitchen. Wellhausen did not of course have the benefit of knowing many of the archaeological discoveries of subsequent years, and what he did know he did not regard as of primary im-portance for interpreting the OT (unlike Gun-kel: see below). But the main structure of his source-critical arguments has seemed to most subsequent scholars to be unaffected by these discoveries, rightly in my opinion. Where they have departed from them it has been because they sensed weaknesses in his treatment of the OT evidence, and not because of fresh evidence from the ancient Near East.

11. This brief historical introduction to the origins of the so-called Graf–Wellhausen theory about the sources of the Pentateuch should have removed some misconceptions about it, and in particular it has shown that far from being the product of one man's mind it was arrived at through a process of research and discussion which lasted over several decades and involved a number of different scholars in several countries. But it also begins to open up a topic of quite central importance at the present time when some very searching questions are once again being asked about the validity of what, for brevity, we may continue to call Wellhausen's theory.

C. The Logic of Source-Criticism. It is in fact possible to distinguish, logically at least and to some extent chronologically as well, four stages in the argument which led to the formulation of Wellhausen's account of the origins of the Pentateuch, and if we define them appropriately we shall find that they are quite generally applicable to all attempts to analyse the Pentateuch into its constituent parts, and indeed to all attempts at discovering what sources were used in biblical and other writings.

I. The first step was the acceptance that an enquiry into the sources of the Pentateuch was permissible at all, i.e. that it was *not ruled out by the tradition* which regarded Moses as the author of the whole Pentateuch. This tradition goes back to the NT and contemporary writings, though it is probably not implied by anything in the OT text itself. Clearly if this tradition is not open to question, there is little room for Pentateuchal criticism of any kind: one could only enquire into the sources that Moses may have used for the writing of Genesis, which is exactly what one early work of criticism, published in 1753, purported to uncover (Jean Astruc's *Conjectures sur les mémoires originaux dont il paroit que Moyse s'est servi pour composer le livre de la Genèse*). The reasons for questioning the tradition of Mosaic authorship of the Pentateuch are broadly of two kinds: (1) the relatively late date of the first appearance of this tradition (not at any rate before the Babylonian exile); (2) various data in the Pentateuch itself which seem to be inconsistent with it: an obvious one is the account of Moses' death (Deut 34).

2. The second step was the *analysis* of the text, the demonstration of its lack of unity in detail. In the eighteenth century, well before the formulation of the Wellhausen theory, theories had been developed to account for what seemed to be signs of composite authorship, or the use of sources. Some passages, such as the Flood Story, appeared to arise from the combination of two originally separate accounts of the same event. In other cases it seemed unlikely or even impossible that two separate passages could have belonged to the same continuous account, the two creation stories for example. In the history of Pentateuchal criticism the distinction between this, analytical, stage of the enterprise and the next stage, synthesis or the attribution of passages or parts of passages to a particular source or layer, has not always been carefully observed. Indeed a clear distinction is perhaps not to be found before the handbook of Wolfgang Richter (*Exegese als Literaturwissenschaft*, 1971). But the two operations can and should be regarded as separate. To put it in a quite general formula: if ABCD represents a section of the Pentateuch, the assertion that A is of separate origin from B and that C is of separate origin from D is one thing; but the question of whether A belongs to the same source as C or D or neither, for example, is another question, and different answers to it will produce different theories about the larger sources of the Pentateuch.

So on what basis is it argued that the Pentateuch is of composite origin? Four main kinds of *criteria* have commonly been used:

1. repeated accounts of the same action or story.
2. the occurrence of statements (or commands) that are incompatible or inconsistent with each other.
3. vocabulary and style—the use of different words for the same thing, including e.g. different names for God; and variations of style.
4. the appearance of different viewpoints on matters of religion in particular, but also on other matters.

Two observations on these criteria should be made at this stage: their use will be clarified by an example later on.

1. The argument for disunity is strongest when several of these criteria occur together—so for example in the analysis of Gen 1–3.
2. In recent years it has been generally realized that criteria 3 and 4 are of far less value for analysis, at least when they occur alone, than 1 and 2. Variations in relation to 3 and 4 may perfectly well occur within a single account (so Noth 1972 and Westermann 1984). In fact it is much more at the next, constructive, stage that such factors enter in, by suggesting which of the various fragments into which the Pentateuch has been analysed have a common origin, i.e. belong to the same source or layer.

3. The third step is the development of hypotheses about *the major constituent parts* of the Pentateuch and their interrelation. Various *models* are possible, of which the idea that a number of independent source-documents

have been combined is only the best-known because it is the pattern exemplified by the classical Documentary Hypothesis of Graf, Kuenen, and Wellhausen. Other 'models' are possible, however, and indeed have been tried, such as that the Pentateuch is simply a conglomeration of small units put together by an editor (the Fragmentary Hypothesis) or that an original core was amplified by the addition of fresh material, either material that had previously existed independently as small units or new material that was composed for the first time for the purpose of modifying the existing core (a Supplementary Hypothesis such as that which was dominant in the middle of the 19th cent.). It is also possible, and in fact common today, to have a combined theory which exhibits features of all three models.

With all of these models (except the Fragmentary theory) there is the problem of *attribution*, deciding what material belongs to the same source or stage of supplementation. Sometimes this can be determined by what we may call narrative continuity: i.e. an episode in the story presupposes that an earlier part of the story has been told in a particular way. For example, Gen 9:6, 'Whoever sheds the blood of a human, by a human shall that person's blood be shed; for in his own image God made humankind,' clearly presupposes the account of the creation of human beings in Gen 1:26–7 (note the reference to 'in his own image'), rather than that in Gen 2:7, and so they presumably belong to the same source or layer. Fortunately the character of the Pentateuch is such that this kind of argument can quite often be used. Where it cannot, one must have recourse to such factors as agreement over criteria such as 3 and 4 at c.2 above to argue that sections of the Pentateuch have a common source.

4. The fourth step is that of arranging the sources (or supplements) in *chronological order* and dating them. It is in this area that Graf, Kuenen, and Wellhausen made a real innovation. In relation to c. 1, 2, and 3 they did little more than refine the results of their predecessors, especially Hupfeld: but on this point they made a radical change from him, in arguing that the Book of Origins/First Elohist (P) was the latest, not the earliest of the four sources, and in dating it to the post-exilic period. How are such conclusions reached, in general terms? Along two main lines, which must still be taken into consideration in any discussion of the matter:

4.1. The *relative age* of the sources can be considered in various ways: Does one source or layer take for granted the prior existence of another one? Is one source obviously more primitive in its way of presenting events, or its legal requirements, than another? Numerous examples of both these kinds of arguments can be found in Wellhausen's *Prolegomena* (1885). They can be cogent, but it must be pointed out that the argument from primitiveness to antiquity and from sophistication to lateness is a dangerous one, because it too quickly assumes that the religion of Israel developed in a single line with no setbacks or decline throughout its history or divergent patterns of religion coexisting at the same time. In practice the classical theory has relied much more heavily on arguments of a second kind.

4.2. The actual or *absolute dates* of the sources can be fixed by reference to evidence outside the Pentateuch. Such arguments can themselves be subdivided according to whether reference is being made to fixed points in the events of Israel's political and religious history (such as the Babylonian exile) as we know them from the historical books of the OT, or to doctrines (such as the demand for the centralization of worship in Jerusalem) whose first formulation we can date by reference to these same historical books and the writings of the prophets, for example. Even here it is fair to say that the strength of the arguments used varies, and where a link can be established with something like the Exile, it can still be difficult to deduce a very precise date for the source in question. But for all that, it has seemed possible to define in broad terms the time when the various source-documents were put into their definitive form. I emphasize that last phrase because when scholars assign a date to a source they are not saying that this is when it was suddenly created out of nothing. They recognize that much of the material in the sources is older than the sources themselves, it comes from earlier tradition. What they are looking for when they date a source is the latest element within it, because that will show when it reached its definitive form.

D. An Example of a Source-Critical Argument: The Analysis of the Flood Story (Gen 6–9) into its sources. 1. Now we shall move back from theory to practice, and look at some of the detailed claims made by the classical theory associated with Wellhausen and the arguments that were used to support them. Historically,

Pentateuchal source-criticism seems to have begun with the observation that Genesis opens with not one but two different *accounts of creation* (so already H. B. Witter in 1711): 1:1–2:3 (or 2:4*a*) and 2:4 (or 2:4*b*)–25). The second repeats a number of events already described in the first, but not in exactly the same order, and with some notable differences in presentation. The difference that was to be put to most productive use in subsequent scholarship was, of course, the difference over the divine names: the fact that whereas the first account refers to God only by the word 'God' (*'ĕlōhîm*); the second used the compound phrase 'the Lord God' = YHWH *'ĕlōhîm*, combining with the word 'God' the proper name by which Israel knew her God, YHWH.

2. According to the word used to refer to God, the second account of creation was referred to as 'Yahwistic' and given the symbol J. J was used (after the German form, *jahwistisch*) because the abbreviations were worked out in Germany and the 'y' sound is represented by 'j' in German. The first account could be and was for a time called Elohistic (E), although this description of it was given up after Hupfeld's discovery that there were two major source-documents which avoided the name YHWH in Genesis. This source is known today as the Priestly Code, or Priestly Work (abbreviated as P), because of the prominent place given to priesthood and ritual in its later parts, particularly in the books from Exodus to Numbers. *The early history of mankind*, prior to the Flood, is also described twice, once in the form of a series of stories (chs. 3–4, 6:1–4), and once in the form of a genealogy (ch. 5). The first of these connects directly with ch. 3, while the second has various similarities to ch. 1, so they were attributed to J and P respectively.

3. In *the Flood story* (6:5–9:17) things are not so tidy. Does it belong to J or P? Uses of the name YHWH do occur, but only in restricted parts of the story (6:5–8; 7:1–5, 16; 8:20–2): elsewhere the word 'God' (*'ĕlōhîm*) is employed. Thus the story is hardly typical of P, which avoids YHWH, but yet it is not typical of J either, which uses YHWH much more consistently. What is one to make of this situation? Should one attribute the Flood story to a third source occupying an intermediate position with regard to the divine names between P and J? Or has either J or P changed its practice at this point?

4. Careful attention to the details of the story suggests that neither of these solutions is correct. We may note that there are a surprising number of repetitions or overlaps of details in it. Thus (1) vv. 5–7 describe how YHWH saw the evil which men did on the earth and declared that he would therefore destroy the human race. When, after three verses referring specifically to Noah, we come to vv. 11–13 we find another reference, this time to God seeing the corruption of 'all flesh' and saying that he will therefore destroy it. (2) The paragraph then continues with instructions to Noah about how the ark is to be built (vv. 14–16), how Noah and his family are to enter it (vv. 17–18) and how he is to take a pair of every kind of living creature with him (vv. 19–21). And this, we are told, is exactly what Noah did, 'he did all that God commanded him' (v. 22). It therefore comes as something of a surprise when, in 7:1–4, we find YHWH telling Noah again to enter the ark with his family and the animals, and it again being said (v. 5) that Noah did as he was told. (3) By the time we get to the actual entry into the ark we are more prepared for repetitions, and we are not disappointed: 7:7–9 make explicit that Noah, his family, and the animals entered the ark, apparently with plenty of time to spare, as it was another 7 days before the flood started (v. 10). Then the rain began (vv. 11–12), and then we are told again that Noah, his family, and the animals all went into the ark, cutting it a bit fine this time we may suppose! It is a strange way to tell a story, and there are further curiosities to follow which we must forgo because of shortage of space, as we must do also with some details of the explanation which seems to be required to do justice to them.

5. But let us consider again the first two cases of repetition, in a slightly different way. We have in the paragraph 6:11–22 a speech of God to Noah with introduction and conclusion, a passage which makes perfectly coherent sense. But before it are two verses which parallel vv. 11–13, and after it are five verses which parallel vv. 17–22. And the striking thing is that whereas 6:11–22 use the word God (vv. 11, 12, 13, 22), the parallel passages placed before and after it use YHWH (6:5, 6, 7; 7:1, 5). That is, we seem to have here two versions of a part of the Flood story, one of them, like the creation account in Gen 2, using the name YHWH, the other, like the creation account in Gen 1, avoiding it and using *'ĕlōhîm* instead. But instead of being placed one after the other, as with the creation accounts, the two versions of the Flood story have been interwoven, with sections from one alternating with sections of the other. This interpretation of the situation is strengthened by two additional factors:

1. tensions or contradictions within the story which seem likely to be due to the combination of two different versions of it; e.g. the number of pairs of animals taken into the ark (one pair according to 6:19–20; seven pairs of clean animals, i.e. those that could be eaten, and of birds, but only one pair of the unclean animals according to 7:2–3).
2. the fact that when the whole story is analysed, one is left with two substantially complete accounts of the Flood, one showing affinities (including the name YHWH) with the second creation account and the other showing affinities with the first.

One or two details remain unclear but the majority of scholars are agreed on something very like the following analysis: (a) 6:5–8; 7:1–5, 7–10, 12, 16b–17, 22–3; 8:2b–3a, 6–12, 13b, 20–2 (= J); (b) 6:9–22; 7:6, 11, 13–16a, 18–21, 24; 8:1–2a, 3b–5, 13a, 14–19; 9:1–17 (= P). A more detailed presentation of the argument can be found in the commentaries on Genesis by S. R. Driver (1904: 85–6) and J. Skinner (1910: 147–50); cf. Habel (1971: 14–15).

6. This brief but important example will give an idea of how the analysis of the Pentateuch proceeds in the classical documentary hypothesis. It is work of this kind which lies behind the lists of passages belonging to J, E, D, and P in the standard introductions to the OT. There are, it should be said, some passages where scholars have not been unanimous about the recognition of the sources, and here caution is necessary. The following sketch will give a general idea of what has been thought to belong to each of the four sources:

Genesis: Chs. 1–11 are formed from J (2:4b–4:26; 6:1–4; part of the Flood Story (see above); 9:18–27; parts of 10; 11:1–9) and P (1:1–2:4a; most of 5; the rest of the Flood Story; 9:28–9; the rest of 10; most of 11:10–32); most of chs. 12–50 come from J (including 12–13; 18; most of 19 and 24), E (including most of 20–2 and 40–2), and P (17; 23; 28:1–9; 35:9–13; and most of the genealogies).

Exodus: Chs. 1–24 are again made up of extracts from J, E, and P. The only passages of any length which are clearly from E are 1:15–21 and 3:9–15. P is the source of 6:2–7:13; 12:1–20, 40–51, and various shorter passages. Traditionally the Decalogue (20:1–17) and the Book of the Covenant (20:22–23:33) were ascribed to E, but it is now widely doubted if they appeared in any of the main sources. Chs. 32–4 are usually thought to have been based on J and E (32 E; 34 J; 33 parts

from both), but they may be all J except for some late editorial additions. Chs. 25–31 and 35–40 are all from P.

Leviticus: The whole book, together with Num 1:1–10:28, is from P, though it is clear that already existing collections of laws have been incorporated in Lev 1–7 and Lev 17–26 (the latter section being known as the Holiness Code = H).

Numbers: The rest of the book, from 10:29, is again a mixture of J, E, and P. E is most clearly present in the story of Balaam (ch. 23 and some verses in 22). P provided the sections of chs. 16–18 that deal with the revolt of Korah and the vindication of the Aaronite priesthood, most of 25:6–36:13, and some other passages; again older documents (including the wilderness itinerary in ch. 33) have been worked in.

Deuteronomy: from the D source, with the exception of a few passages, mostly at the end. But an original core in 4:45–29:1 from pre-exilic times can be distinguished from a framework placed around it in the Babylonian Exile (so esp. chs. 4 and 29–30).

7. Fuller details can be found, (1) in commentaries, among which special mention should be made of the 'Polychrome Bible', published from 1893 onwards, in which the sections drawn from the various sources were marked in different colours, a custom which has been widely followed by theological students in their own copies of the Bible as an *aide-mémoire* (The proper title of the series was The Sacred Books of the OT, gen. ed. P. Haupt. A less colourful way of achieving the same end is by using different typefaces, as in von Rad's commentary on Genesis and Noth's on Exodus in the Old Testament Library series, where the P sections are printed in italics and the rest in ordinary type); and (2) in a synopsis of the Pentateuch, like those which are produced to show the relationships between the Synoptic Gospels, though they are hard to come by in English (but see Carpenter and Harford-Battersby (1900), ii; Campbell and O'Brien (1993) gives the texts of the sources separately, but not in parallel columns).

E. A Second Example: The Dating of the Priestly Source (P). 1. The second example of source criticism to be given here concerns the dating of the sources (step c.4), and in particular *the claim that P is the latest* of the four. Wellhausen used two kinds of argument to establish this view. First he noted the almost unbroken silence of the older historical books, Samuel and Kings, with regard to the distinctive institutions of the cult prescribed by P (the tabernacle, detailed laws about sacrifice, the Day of Atonement, the limitation of full priesthood to the descendants of Aaron, and the development of tithing as a means of support for the priests). In view of the fact that these books have plenty to say about ritual, this must imply that these institutions were not yet known in the pre-exilic period. It follows that P could not yet have been written. The specific reference to 'the older historical books' is deliberate, so as to exclude the books of Chronicles. The force of this argument could only be felt when a true appreciation of the late date and largely fictional character of Chronicles had been gained, and the dating of P is closely connected with the study of Chronicles. Graf's epoch-making essay of 1865 on the Pentateuch was published along with a study of the books of Chronicles, while Wellhausen devoted more than 50 pages of the *Prolegomena* to them. Chronicles does relate the existence of institutions characteristic of P in the pre-exilic period, and it was only when it had been shown that these elements of the Chronicler's account were fictional that a clear view of the nature of pre-exilic religion could be obtained, and so the necessity of a late date for P established.

2. The second kind of argument was based on the relationship of the laws and narratives of P to the laws in Deuteronomy and the final chapters of Ezekiel. The origin of Deuteronomy in the eighth or seventh century BCE was generally regarded in the mid-nineteenth century as having been established beyond doubt by the critical arguments of W. M. L. de Wette and others, and Ezekiel was of course a prophet of the early sixth century. In a number of ways it was argued that the Priestly texts must be later than those in Deuteronomy and Ezekiel. This is not just a simple evolutionary argument, saying that the practices referred to by P must by their very character lie at the end of a long process of development. The argument is rather that in some cases Deuteronomy and Ezekiel make no reference to features of P which one might have expected them to mention if it were indeed a document of pre-exilic origin; while elsewhere what Deuteronomy and Ezekiel prescribe would make no sense if P already existed.

3. As an example we will look at Wellhausen's argument in the case of admission to the priesthood (1885: 121–51). The crucial points in the argument are set out in the first few pages of the chapter (pp. 121–7), but Wellhausen believed that they received some confirmation from the more thorough account of the history of the

priesthood which follows. He begins by summarizing the regulations about priesthood in the P sections of Exodus–Numbers. He points out that there are two important distinctions made in them: the first between the Levites and the twelve secular tribes, which is vividly reflected in the arrangement of the camp in Num 2; and the second between the Levites and the sons, or descendants, of Aaron, which receives, to quote Wellhausen, 'incomparably greater emphasis'. He continues: 'Aaron and his sons alone are priests, qualified for sacrificing and burning incense; the Levites are *hieroduli* [temple servants], bestowed on the Aaronidae for the discharge of the inferior services.' The unique privilege of the descendants of Aaron is underlined in the story of the Korahite rebellion in Num 16–18. The setting apart of the two priestly groups is the result of two separate acts of a quite different character. First Aaron is chosen by YHWH to be a priest (Ex 28:1–5), and then later the Levites are given their role, by being offered at YHWH's bidding by the people as a substitute for their firstborn who, according to the law, belonged to YHWH (Num 3:40–4:49; cf. also ch. 18).

4. This picture of the demarcation of the Aaronide and Levite groups is located by P at Mount Sinai in the time of Moses—but how ancient is it really? Wellhausen believed that the answer was to be found in Ezek 44:6–16, a passage from the early years of the Babylonian exile (40:1 refers to the year 573), which both refers to pre-exilic practices on admission to the priesthood and prescribes what practices shall be followed in this matter in the future. According to this account, in the pre-exilic temple in Jerusalem ('my sanctuary') the menial tasks had been performed by foreigners (44:8), a practice of which Ezekiel very strongly disapproved. And in the future, he says, these tasks are to be performed by Levites (vv. 9–14). Not however in accordance with a role assigned to them by the people in ancient times—of this explanation (the one given by P) Ezekiel says not a word—but as a punishment for their sins in the pre-exilic period. 'They shall bear their punishment', it says in vv. 10 and 12 (cf. v. 13*b*). This only makes sense as a degradation from a previously higher position, which was no doubt that of full priesthood, which the Levites had enjoyed previously to this (cf. v. 13*a*). That Levites were full priests in pre-exilic times is implied also by Deuteronomy (cf. ch. 18). To what is their punishment due? It is because they 'went astray from me after their idols when Israel went astray' (v. 10—cf. v. 12). This evidently refers to service at the high places or *bāmôt* outside Jerusalem: because those who had been priests at the Jerusalem temple, 'my sanctuary' (vv. 15–16), are explicitly excluded from blame and are to retain an exclusive right to full priesthood in the future: they are called 'the sons of Zadok' after Zadok the priest under David and Solomon. The antithesis between the Jerusalem temple, the one place of legitimate worship, and all other shrines had of course been at the heart of the reform programme of King Josiah (640–609) half a century earlier which, as described in 2 Kings 23, was inspired by the somewhat earlier prescriptions of Deuteronomy (cf. esp. Deut 12:1–14). Ezek 44 is fully at one with Josiah and the Deuteronomists on this point though he differs from Deuteronomy on the extent of the priesthood for the future. He agrees with P that most Levites are to have an inferior role, but he gives a completely different reason for it and he has a different view about what they were originally meant to do.

5. The relationship between what Ezekiel says and the regulations of P is most forcibly expressed in two quotations, one from Wellhausen himself and the other from Kuenen. First Wellhausen:

What he [Ezekiel] regards as the original right of the Levites, the performance of priestly services, is treated in the latter document [P] as an unfounded and highly wicked pretension which once in the olden times brought destruction upon Korah and his company [Wellhausen is referring to the (P) story of the rebellion of Korah in Num 16–17]; what he [Ezekiel] considers to be a subsequent withdrawal of their right, as a degradation in consequence of a fault, the other [P] holds to have been their hereditary and natural destination. The distinction between priest and Levite which Ezekiel introduces and justifies as an innovation, according to the Priestly Code has always existed; what in the former appears as a beginning, in the latter has been in force ever since Moses—an original datum, not a thing that has become or been made. That the prophet [Ezekiel] should know nothing about a priestly law with whose tendencies he is in thorough sympathy admits of only one explanation—that it did not then exist. (1885: 124)

The quotation from Kuenen uses an analogy which is particularly comprehensible in Britain: 'If by reason of their birth it was already impossible for the Levites to become priests [as P lays down], then it would be more than strange to deprive them of the priesthood on account of their faults—much as if one were to threaten the commons with the punishment of being disqualified from sitting or voting in the House of Lords' (ibid.). This was written before the introduction of life peerages! One may put the essential argument as follows: if P had been in existence in 573, Ezekiel surely would have developed his argument in a different way.

6. For these reasons, then, Wellhausen concluded that the regulations about the priesthood, which are absolutely central to P, could not have originated before Ezekiel, but only afterwards. Arguments of similar kinds were brought forward to justify a late date for other aspects of the ritual system prescribed by P. But how much later than Ezekiel was P to be dated? Quite a lot later, according to Wellhausen (ibid. 404–10). He took as his point of departure the statement in Ezra 7:14 that when Ezra came from Babylon to Jerusalem in 458 BCE he had the law of God in his hand. This Wellhausen understood to be a new law book, which consisted of the completed Pentateuch, incorporating not only the older sources J, E, and D but the Priestly Code, which had quite recently been compiled. He seems to have believed that the completed Pentateuch (and the new Priestly Code) must owe its authority to some act of authorization, and only Ezra's mission seemed to be available to meet this requirement. According to Wellhausen, Neh 8–10 describes Ezra's publication and the people's acceptance of the new (or rather partly new) law code, and these events are dated not earlier than 444 BCE (compare Neh 1:1 with 8:2). This, Wellhausen held, gave the approximate date when the Priestly Code was written up and combined with the older Pentateuchal sources. A different kind of argument which lends some support to this position was used by Kuenen: early post-exilic literature, such as the books of the prophets Haggai and Zechariah, shows no awareness of the P legislation. The book of Malachi, probably from the early fifth century BCE, is especially significant, as it says quite a lot about priests, but calls them Levites, not sons of Aaron. By contrast the Chronicler, writing some time after 400 BCE is clearly familiar with P's regulations. So a date within the fifth century becomes likely on this argument too.

7. In the last quarter of the nineteenth century a majority of scholars gradually came to accept the conclusions of the Newer Documentary Hypothesis, as the viewpoint propounded by Graf, Kuenen, and Wellhausen came to be known. In essence they held that the Pentateuch had been composed from four documents or sources, whose dates and places of origin were as follows:

J   9th cent., Judah
E   8th cent., northern kingdom of Israel
D   7th cent., Judah
P   5th cent., Babylon

8. There have, however, from the beginning been those who repudiated this position vociferously. In Britain and the United States today the best-known opponents of the theory are among conservative evangelical Christians. In an earlier generation scholars such as J. Orr and A. H. Finn, later E. J. Young and G. C. Aalders, and most recently K. A. Kitchen and R. K. Harrison, sought to minimize the force of such arguments as those which we have been considering. But opposition came from other quarters too. In the Roman Catholic church the theory became a matter of controversy in the first decade of the twentieth century and the Pontifical Biblical Commission decreed in 1906 that the Mosaic authorship of the Pentateuch was not a subject that was open to discussion. This ban lasted until the 1940s. Some Jewish scholars too have been resolutely opposed to the documentary theory, e.g. U. Cassuto and M. H. Segal of Jerusalem, but others have disagreed only at one particular point, the rejection of the idea that P is the latest of the documents (see below). Among Protestant Christian scholars there has been a further group consisting mainly of Scandinavian scholars, who, for a distinctive reason, have rejected many of the conclusions of the documentary theory. The leader of this group was I. Engnell of Uppsala, who wrote mainly in Swedish. Engnell proposed to replace the dominant theories by the use of what he called 'the traditio-historical method', which as far as the Pentateuch was concerned meant that its origin lay not in the combination of written sources for the most part but in developments that took place while the stories etc. were being transmitted orally, by word of mouth, a process which, according to Engnell, only ended at the time of the Babylonian exile or even later. The enthusiasm which Engnell's approach generated seems now to have waned, and it belongs for the most part to the history of Pentateuchal study rather than to its present concerns.

9. There have also been several modifications proposed to the classical theory. Some scholars have taken up a suspicion already expressed by Wellhausen himself that the

J material in Gen 1–11 is not an original unity, and have gone on to argue that the whole of J is the result of the combination of two originally separate sources or the enlargement of the original J by additions. This is only a minority view, but it has obtained wide publicity through its presentation in two *Introductions* that were at one time popular, those of Otto Eissfeldt and Georg Fohrer. Eissfeldt called the extra source L ('Lay Source', because of the absence of cultic material) and Fohrer called it N ('Nomadic Source', because it seemed opposed to settled life), but both attribute much the same passages to it: e.g. in Gen 1–11 Fohrer ascribed a few verses in chs 2–3 to N, as well as 4:17–24 and 11:1–9, all it is said expressing the frustration of man's attempts to develop. Similar subdivisions have been proposed of the other sources, with more justification in the cases of D and P, but hardly so in the case of E.

10. In fact it has been repeatedly suspected that E is not a true source at all, that is that the passages attributed to it do not belong to a single continuous account of Israel's early history (partial rejection of step c.3 in the systematic presentation). Two German scholars, P. Volz and W. Rudolph, pressed the case for this view between the First and Second World Wars, and Noth was influenced by it to some extent, although he never gave up a belief in E altogether. The problem was that what were supposed to be the remnants of E seemed to show neither the completeness nor the theological unity that appears in J. However, important defences of the existence of E as an independent source have been put forward (Bruegge-mann and Wolff 1975: 67–82; Jenks 1977).

11. A further kind of modification, or rather extension, of the theory has been the claim that the Pentateuchal sources extend into the following books of the OT, the historical books. This is quite widely held for Joshua, but it was also maintained by some scholars for Judges, Samuel, and even parts of Kings (so Eissfeldt, C. A. Simpson). There are certainly some signs of duplicate or parallel narratives in these books, especially in 1 Samuel, but few scholars today accept this explanation of them.

12. Despite all these modifications and even rejections of the theory, the great majority of OT scholars were prepared, after the early years of debate, to accept it substantially as it left Wellhausen's hands. This was true, in recent times, of the major figures in Britain (e.g. Rowley, G. W. Anderson), Germany (von Rad, Noth,

Weiser) and America (Albright, Bright). For close on a century the view that the Pentateuch was composed from the four documents J, E, D, and P, which originated in that order, belonged to what used to be called the assured results of Old Testament criticism. This was an unfortunate phrase, and it would have been better to speak of the dominant or most satisfactory theory: neither a proven fact nor mere speculation, but a plausible account of the phenomena of the text. It needs to be emphasized that Mosaic authorship is also a theory: all that we *know* is that the Pentateuch existed by about the fourth century BCE. And Mosaic authorship is a theory which seems to account less well for the phenomena than critical theories; so at least the majority of scholars have believed. And since this theory seemed a solid foundation to them, their fresh thinking about the Pentateuch was until recently generally not about source criticism but proceeded along two rather different lines of enquiry: (1) the study of the traditions, both narrative and law, in the *preliterary stage* of their history, before they were incorporated into the Pentateuchal source-documents; (2) the definition of the particular *theological content* of the different source-documents.

F. The Preliterary Origins of the Pentateuch. 1.
By 1900 the source-critical theory was in need of a corrective of a much more fundamental kind than any of those mentioned so far, for both historical and literary reasons. On the one hand there had opened up a significant gap between the dates attributed to even the earliest sources of the Pentateuch (9th–8th cents. BCE) and the period which they purported to describe, which ended about 1200 BCE or even earlier. How much, if any, real historical information had survived this passage of time? Was it necessary to conclude, as Wellhausen (1885: 318–19) tended to imply, that the sources could inform us only about conditions in the time when they were written? On the other hand, the investigations of the source-critics had isolated the Pentateuch from the life of the people of ancient Israel, and left the text as a product of writers and redactors who were to some extent created in the image of the scholars who studied them—an intellectual *élite* far removed from ordinary people. Was it really from such circles that the Pentateuch had ultimately originated? These are in fact very topical issues for biblical scholarship at the present time, when interest has reverted to the discussion of sources and especially the work of redactors or editors. Although there

are some more positive aspects of the situation now, this preoccupation with the later, literary stages of composition poses exactly the same threat today to a historical and living appreciation of the Pentateuch as it did around 1900. Then the way forward was marked out by Hermann Gunkel, who was in fact much more of a pioneering, original thinker than Wellhausen. His correctives are as much needed today as they ever were.

2. In 1901 Gunkel (1862–1932) published a commentary on the book of Genesis, with a long introduction which was separately published and also translated into English under the title *The Legends of Genesis*. The change of perspective can very quickly and easily be seen if we compare the contents of this introduction with the introductions to other commentaries on Genesis which appeared in the years immediately before 1901, such as that of H. Holzinger of 1898. (In English Driver (1904) still shows the pre-Gunkel approach.) Holzinger's introduction of some 18 pages included the following subsections: Content of the Hexateuch and of Genesis; Tradition about the Author; History of Criticism [i.e. source criticism]; the source J; the source E; the source P; the Combination of the Sources. This clearly reflects, almost exclusively, the preoccupations of the source critics. Although Holzinger was aware that the material in J and E was ultimately derived from popular oral tradition, as indeed Well-hausen had been before him, he was not apparently interested in, or perhaps capable of, exploring the character of this 'popular oral tradition'.

3. The contrast with Gunkel's introduction could hardly be greater. Its first subsection has a polemical title which sums up the whole thesis: 'Genesis is a collection of legends (German *Sagen*)'—the English translation waters this down to 'The Significance and Scope of the Legends'. Then follow sections on 'The Varieties of the Legends'; 'The Artistic Form of the Legends'; 'History of the Transmission of the Legends in Oral Tradition'. These four sections, all of them dealing with the stages of tradition prior to the written sources, comprise about 80 pages, that is over three-quarters of a much enlarged introduction. Only after this does Gunkel bring in two more traditional-sounding sections: one on 'Yahwist, Elohist, the Older Collections' (but note how what were 'sources' are now 'collections', reflecting the change of perspective); the other on 'The Priestly Code and Final Redaction'. An English commentary which shows the influence of Gunkel's work was J. Skinner's International Critical Commentary, published in 1910: sections 2–5 of the introduction are taken over almost directly from Gunkel.

4. There were in fact two basic changes of approach with Gunkel: (1) *chronologically*, he dug deeper, there is the concentration on the pre-literary form of the tradition, instead of the written sources of Genesis themselves, as we have seen; and changes in the tradition at the earlier stage are regarded as a possible and indeed necessary subject for study; (2) but there is also, *analytically*, a transfer of attention away from long connected narratives to individual sections or episodes, each of which turns out to comprise a more or less self-contained story, which Gunkel believed had once existed independently of the larger narrative context. These two new departures are interconnected, but it may be said with good reason that the first of them led to *tradition criticism*, as particularly practised later by von Rad and Noth, while the second gave rise to *form criticism*, which is where Gunkel himself made his main contribution. In fact both of these methods were designed by Gunkel to reach a higher goal, a more adequate account of the history of Hebrew literature, and his work is most accurately described as literary history: he could see that source criticism alone would never do justice to the art of the Hebrew writers.

5. The general principles of Gunkel's form-critical work on Genesis are the same as those used by him elsewhere, for example on the Psalms. Briefly we may distinguish: (1) determination of the literary genre; (2) classification of the material; and (3) the reconstruction of its social setting (*Sitz im Leben*).

6. Gunkel begins by making the general point that history-writing as we know it, and as it is represented in the later historical books of the OT, is not 'an innate endowment of the human mind'. 'Only at a certain stage of civilization has objectivity so grown and the interest in transmitting national experiences to posterity so increased that the writing of history becomes possible. Such history has for its subjects great public events, the deeds of popular leaders and kings, and especially wars.' Apart from such political organization, the past is remembered and cherished in the form of popular tradition, for which Gunkel used the genre-description *Sage* (pl. *Sagen*); 'legend' is a better English equivalent for this than saga, and perhaps 'tale' is best of all. The preservation of some historical memories in *Sage* is not ruled out—Gunkel

speaks of 'the senseless confusion of legend with lying' in discussion of this issue—but at the same time strong emphasis is laid on the creativity of the story-tellers and it is significant that Gunkel followed up his remark that 'Legends are not lies' with 'on the contrary they are a particular form of poetry': this is perhaps a pointer to the kind of truth which he believed them to contain, it is more the truth of poetry, i.e. general truths about the (or a) human situation, than the truth of history. His argument that the stories in Genesis are to be classed as *Sagen* is quite a simple one. The basic difference, he says, between history-writing as a literary genre and *Sage* is that history-writing is a written composition, whereas *Sage*, as its derivation from the German word 'to say' shows, is a genre of oral tradition. The stories in Genesis, at least most of them, bear the marks of having been originally composed orally—he gives more detail later, but here mentions especially the existence of variant versions of essentially the same story (e.g. the patriarch who passed his wife off as his sister (Gen 12; 20; 26))—and therefore they are *Sagen*. In addition, the general lack of interest in political events, the long period between the events reported and their being put in written form, and the inclusion of numerous details that are, from a modern point of view, fantastic (such as Lot's wife turning into a pillar of salt: Gen 19:26), serve to confirm the general description as *Sagen*. This description of the stories as *Sagen* has important consequences for Gunkel's understanding of them which he illustrates by reference to the sacrifice of Isaac in Gen 22: 'The important matter [sc. for the narrator] is not to establish certain historical facts, but to impart to the hearer the heart-rending grief of the father who is commanded to sacrifice his child with his own hand, and then his boundless gratitude and joy when God's mercy releases him from this grievous trial.' The positive implications of using such language about the Genesis stories were to be developed further by Karl Barth (*Church Dogmatics*, iii. 1) as well as by Gerhard von Rad (in the introduction to his commentary on Genesis).

7. Gunkel went on to subdivide the *Sagen* of Genesis into various types, first of all making a sharp distinction between those of Gen 1–11, which tell of the ancestors of the human race as a whole, and Gen 12–50, which tell of the ancestors of particular peoples, especially Israel. Nowadays it seems appropriate to use the terms 'myth' and 'legend' to distinguish these two types of story, but they were not often so used by Gunkel. Gen 12–50 was further subdivided into *Sagen* of different types: the two main ones being tribal legends and aetiological legends. The former (1) can be either (a) historical, if they represent events in the history of tribes, such as the treaty between Abraham or Isaac and Abimelech king of Gerar (21:22–34; 26) or the migrations of the various patriarchs from one place to another; or (b) ethnographic if they represent tribal relations, as in the stories of Jacob and Esau. Aetiological legends (2) are those whose purpose is to explain the origin of some aspect of contemporary experience, and they subdivide into (a) ethnological legends, which explain why different peoples live where they do, e.g. Gen 19; (b) etymological legends, which explain the meaning of names, e.g. Beersheba in Gen 21:31; (c) cultic legends, which explain why a place is holy, or a particular ritual act carried out (32:32); (d) geological legends, explaining features of the landscape (19:26). These categories are not mutually exclusive, a particular legend may exhibit the characteristics of two or more of them, e.g. Gen 22. This is the analysis worked out by Gunkel for the first edition of his commentary in 1901: an important consequence of it was that, while the aetiological legends were of little or no use for the historian, the tribal legends could (if read correctly) provide information about the history of the various tribes. In the course of his preoccupation with Genesis over the next few years Gunkel changed his mind over certain topics, and in particular he gave up the 'tribal' interpretation of groups (1)(a) and (1)(b) above and supposed instead that they too were based on folklore motifs and had no historical kernel at all.

8. Gunkel's account of the social setting of such stories is given in a chapter in which he attempts to formulate their literary character more clearly. 'The common situation which we have to suppose is this: In the leisure of a winter evening the family sits about the hearth; the grown people, but more especially the children, listen intently to the beautiful old stories of the dawn of the world, which they have heard so often yet never tire of hearing repeated.' It is to be noted, because of the contrast with von Rad and Noth, that it is a domestic scene that Gunkel reconstructed, not one of a cultic festival. He lived before the time when all (or nearly all) the OT was thought to be related to the setting of worship. In the remaining chapters he reconstructed the processes by which the originally separate stories were collected together, so as eventually to form the source-documents J and E—this is really tradition-history—and, as we have seen, went on to deal with the sources themselves and their combination together by the editors of the Pentateuch. Gunkel's views about the origins of Genesis have been enormously influential and have shaped subsequent research just as much as the documentary source-theory. They are not however satisfactory in every respect, as we shall see.

9. Form-critical study of the Pentateuch was extended to the stories involving Moses by Hugo Gressmann in 1913 and to the Pentateuchal laws by Albrecht Alt in 1934 (Alt 1966: 87–132: see further below), and many others followed them. But at the same time the study of the preliterary history of the Pentateuch began to be carried forward in a different way, which considered not isolated individual stories or laws but the overall structure of the Pentateuch, with its sequence of creation, patriarchs, Exodus, revelation at Sinai, wilderness wandering and conquest of Transjordan. Was this order of events, which already appeared in the J source, simply derived from the historical sequence of events; or was it to be explained as the result of some process or processes of development in the tradition which had oversimplified an originally more complicated story? We come with this to the traditio-historical work of von Rad and Noth (see on this especially Nicholson 1973).

10. Von Rad's very influential views on this subject are set out in a long essay published in 1938 and entitled 'The Form-Critical Problem of the Hexateuch' (von Rad 1966: 1–78). The reference to form criticism in the title is at first surprising but is justified by the use, at the beginning of the essay, of the basic principles of that discipline, the difference being that von Rad suggested applying them to the Hexateuch as a whole (like others before and since he believed that the book of Joshua was intimately linked with the Pentateuch) instead of only to the short episodes or pericopae from which it was made up. So he asks first about the literary genre of the Hexateuch in its final form, and answers that it is essentially a statement of faith, a creed: not just popular tradition, or history, but a historical creed. Then he proposed the question of other and especially earlier examples of this genre, the historical creed, in Israel, and coupled with it the question of its social setting or *Sitz im Leben*. He found the answers to these questions given above all in the prayer prescribed in Deut 26:5–9 to be said at the presentation of the first fruits of the harvest, in which the following 'confession of faith' bears a striking resemblance to the outline of the narrative of the Hexateuch:

A wandering Aramaean was my ancestor; he went down into Egypt and lived there as an alien, few in number; and there he became a great nation, mighty and populous. When the Egyptians treated us harshly and afflicted us, by imposing hard labour on us, we cried to the Lord, the God of our ancestors; the Lord heard our voice and saw our affliction, our toil and our oppression. The Lord brought us out of Egypt with a mighty hand and an outstretched arm, with a terrifying display of power, and with signs and wonders; and he brought us into this place and gave us this land, a land flowing with milk and honey.

11. This 'short historical creed', as it has come to be called, was taken by von Rad to be a very ancient formula embedded in the Deuteronomic law book and one which had originally been composed for just the purpose which Deuteronomy gives it, namely to accompany a ritual action in the cult. This passage represented, according to von Rad, the first stage in the history of the genre 'historical creed', at the end of which stood the composition of the Hexateuch in its final form, and it indicated an originally cultic setting for the genre. This implied for von Rad that the origin of the Hexateuch too was bound up with the history of the Israelite cult, a subject which had already before 1938 come to interest OT scholars considerably, particularly through the work of Sigmund Mowinckel on the Psalms, and von Rad was in fact only developing suggestions made previously by other scholars about particular sections of the Hexateuch (Mowinckel on the Sinai peri-cope (1927), Alt on a covenant-festival as a setting for apodictic law (1934), and Pedersen on the link between Exodus and Passover (1934)).

12. At this point we move out of the strictly form-critical sphere into that of tradition criticism or tradition history. Von Rad noticed that the creed in Deut 26:5–9 does not mention the meeting with God at Mount Sinai among the events which it enumerates, and that the same is true of various other 'credal' passages in the OT, especially Deut 6:20–4 and Josh 24:2–13. On the other hand, the final form of the Hexateuch does give considerable space to events at Mount Sinai, and thus represents a departure from the original form of the creed. Even within the Hexateuchal narrative itself, von Rad believed, there were signs that the Sinai narrative had been artificially fitted into an original sequence, running from the Exodus to the Conquest, in which it did not appear. This sequence on the one hand and the Sinai narrative on the other at one time therefore existed quite independently of one another. As we have seen, von Rad had come to the conclusion from his study of the genre 'creed' that the origins of the Hexateuch were bound up with the history of the cult, and he proceeded in the next stage of his essay to develop this view by a detailed argument that these two blocks of tradition had been the theme-material of two different festivals celebrated in the period of the Judges at two different sanctuaries. The patriarchs–Exodus–Conquest sequence (which von Rad usually refers to as the 'settlement-tradition' from its concluding item, the possession of the promised land) belonged to the festival of Weeks or First-Fruits, celebrated at the sanctuary of Gilgal near Jericho, while the Sinai narrative belonged to a festival of the Renewal of the Covenant, referred to in the OT as Tabernacles or Booths, which took place at Shechem in the central highlands of Israel.

13. If that is so, the question arises as to when and by whom the two blocks of tradition were combined together. Von Rad's answer is that it was the author of the J source in the Hexateuch, whom he dates to the tenth century BCE, for in it, as traditionally reconstructed, the canonical sequence already appears. It is also to the Yahwist that the prefacing of Gen 1(2)–11, the primeval history, to the pattern dictated by the creed is attributed, so that this writer takes on immense stature as the originator of the canonical form of the narrative, and indeed in other ways too, which von Rad also spelt out at the end of his essay.

14. Noth's work on the Pentateuch (he did not believe that Joshua was so closely connected) is to be found above all in his book published in 1948 and later translated into English under the title *A History of Pentateuchal Traditions* (1972). It sets out to be a comprehensive and systematic treatise, which builds on von Rad's work, but also introduces fresh ideas and draws in elements of Gunkel's work on particular passages. Beginning from the conclusions of source criticism, Noth observed that the canonical pattern of narrative from the patriarchs to the settlement appeared not only in J but also in E, and since it seemed unlikely to him that E simply imitated J (since sometimes one seems more primitive and sometimes the other), he proposed that both were drawing on a common source in which the canonical pattern already appeared. He seems to have been unsure whether to postulate a written source or just common oral tradition, but he proposed the symbol G (for *Grundlage*, 'foundation') to represent it. This is already an important departure from von Rad's view, since it implied that J inherited the canonical pattern from earlier tradition and was not himself the first to combine the Sinai narrative with the others, as von Rad had thought.

15. But in general Noth regarded von Rad's account of the preliterary history of the tradition as sound. He accepted the idea that the Sinai narrative had once been separate from the rest, and the early Israelite cult as the locus of preservation and transmission of the traditions. Von Rad was only at fault in that he did not take the process of analysis far enough for Noth. In Noth's view there were not just two originally separate blocks of tradition but five, which he generally refers to as 'themes'. These were the promise to the patriarchs, the deliverance from Egypt (Exodus), the leading through the wilderness, the revelation at Sinai, and the settlement in the land of Canaan.

16. To understand what Noth has to say about the origin of these themes it is necessary to remind ourselves of his views about the earliest history of Israel. For him there can be no question of a history of Israel before the settlement in Canaan, because prior to the settlement various groups of semi-nomads existed quite separately and they only became 'Israel' when they combined together in a sacred tribal league or 'amphictyony' on the soil of Canaan. Whatever came before was not, could not be, the history or story of the 'children of Israel', but could only be the history or story of parts of what later became Israel. The arrangement of Noth's own book on the history of Israel is the logical consequence of this view: its first main chapter deals with the arrival in Canaan of those groups which were eventually to become Israel, and only in the third chapter are the traditions about the Exodus, the patriarchs, and Mount Sinai dealt with, under the heading 'The Traditions of the Sacral Confederation of the Twelve Tribes'. In Noth's picture these traditions could only have originated as the traditions of one of the constituent parts of Israel in each case: that is, the implication of the Pentateuchal texts themselves that they are talking about the origin of 'all Israel' is historically false. Further there is no reason to think that the same

constituent part of Israel was involved in the events of all the five themes, and it is quite possible that each theme derived originally from a different group, so that there was no original historical continuity at all between them.

17. Apart from these general considerations about the history of the tradition, Noth continued with the examination of the individual stories that had been begun by Gunkel and Gressmann, emphasizing their typical and legendary features. He seems to have held that the tradition began with five raw statements of faith corresponding to the five themes, of the form 'YHWH brought us out of the land of Egypt', to which only the slightest historical recollections were attached. These statements of faith then became the inspiration for a process of amplification by the creativity of story-tellers or bards, who developed the various episodes with which we are familiar.

18. One result of Noth's theory was his reluctance to regard any element of the tradition which represented continuity between the different themes as an early component of the story. The most celebrated example of this is his treatment of Moses, who of course appears throughout the central section of the Pentateuch, in the Exodus, wilderness, and Sinai themes. In all of this, Noth argued, Moses is dispensable and therefore a secondary element. He originally belonged in fact to the story of the settlement in Canaan, because his grave was located in land claimed by the Israelite tribes (cf. Deut 34:1–6 with Josh 13:15–23), and those elements of the stories about him that are not likely to have been invented (his foreign wife, criticism of his leadership) therefore originally belong here.

19. While the views of von Rad and Noth have been very influential, they have also come in for criticism from many scholars. Among the counter-arguments the following may be mentioned:

1. von Rad's reliance on Deut 26:5–9 may have too readily assumed that it is an ancient piece of traditional liturgy: its style is strongly Deuteronomic, and perhaps it was composed by the authors of Deuteronomy in the eighth or seventh century BCE.
2. whether that is so or not, von Rad's reconstruction of the history of the genre 'creed' too readily assumes that shorter forms are earlier than longer ones, a common misconception of form critics; or to put it another

way, that development invariably proceeds by supplementation and never by selection or subtraction. It is not necessarily the case that the 'canonical pattern' of the creed with Sinai included is later than the shorter form.

3. Even if Noth's historical views about the settlement are true, they do not in fact rule out the possibility that all the themes represent experiences of the *same* group of 'ancestors of Israel', so that there might be an element of historical continuity between them.

4. Noth too quickly disposed of Moses, who is very firmly linked with the Exodus, Sinai, and wilderness traditions and scarcely as 'dispensable' as Noth believed. But if he is allowed to remain in them, this is an indication of an original historical continuity between Exodus, Sinai, wilderness, and settlement.

20. In addition to these objections, which are widely current, it should be observed that many of Noth's arguments are only possible if it is assumed that the tradition possessed the degree of creativity ascribed to it by Gunkel and Gressmann: and it is not at all certain that it did, particularly as far as the tradition about the Exodus and subsequent events is concerned. In fact, a number of questions have been raised in recent years about the validity of some of Gunkel's inferences. Two questions in particular need to be asked: (1) Is Gunkel's overall description of the stories as 'legend' (*Sage*) adequate? (2) Was his growing conviction that Genesis lacked any historical basis justified? These are clearly related questions, for the historical reliability of the stories is bound to be affected by the type of stories that we suppose them to be.

21. The description 'legend' was arrived at by Gunkel by a deceptively simple process of reasoning: the stories originated before the Israelites organized themselves politically into a state, therefore they are oral compositions, therefore they are legends (*Sagen*), and their purpose is to convey experiences of human existence which are not to be equated with particular historical events. The attraction of this line of reasoning is that at its end there is something that certainly needs to be said if we are to do justice to the literary art of the Genesis narratives. But it is not a cast-iron argument, and cogent objections can be raised to it at virtually every point. To take only one point, is it really true that oral literature knows only the genre of *Sagen* as defined by Gunkel? Comparisons over a wider range than he undertook

have suggested that oral literature is a much more varied phenomenon, with several different functions. Detailed studies of the text of Genesis itself also suggested weaknesses in Gunkel's description. He seems to have lost sight of the essential difference in character between the myths of Gen 1–11, which are pure imagination as far as the events they describe are concerned, and the stories of the patriarchs, where imagination is constrained by a particular historical situation.

The most comprehensive attempt to develop a new form criticism of the patriarchal stories has been made by C. Westermann, in the introduction to the second volume of his commentary on Genesis. Westermann's main assertion about the patriarchal narratives is that they are above all *family narratives*, not only in the sense that they are about family life but also because they are told and handed on by people who are the descendants (or think they are the descendants) of the chief characters in the story. In his commentary he makes a comparison between them and Galsworthy's 'family novels', *The Forsyte Saga*. Plato in the *Hippias Major* said that people in his day liked hearing stories of the foundation of cities; other classical parallels can be found in stories of the founding of colonies and in Virgil's *Aeneid*. According to Westermann, it is also possible to show that the aetiological stories and motifs, which are where creativity is at its greatest, belong to a comparatively late stage of the process of growth of the patriarchal stories. In the rest of the tradition, there is no reason why memories of quite ancient situations should not have been preserved, indeed this is to be expected. This is not to say that we can read Genesis as if it were a series of biographies: for the sequence of stories is less to be relied on than some of the stories themselves, and in addition there are some individual stories which owe a lot to later narrators with a particular theological point to make.

22. In looking at Westermann's fresh description of the patriarchal stories we thus encounter some pointers to a somewhat more positive historical evaluation of them than Gunkel allowed. To these archaeological evidence lends some support, though this must not be exaggerated. The claim that such evidence can prove the substantial reliability of the stories has rightly been criticized by T. L. Thompson and J. Van Seters. There are no direct references to Abraham, Isaac, or anyone else in Genesis in contemporary Near-Eastern texts. But in a variety of ways certain details of the stories (though not others) can be shown to fit in with our knowledge from external sources of how life was lived in the second millennium BCE. That is, the stories of the patriarchs did transmit to ancient Israel and do transmit to us some authentic information about conditions of life, both external and internal, social and spiritual, in the time before the Exodus. Creative development there may indeed be, but it is not creation in this case out of nothing: it is an enlarging and deepening of the story of a family, or families, who came to be regarded as the ancestors of all Israel and the recipients of a divine promise whose fulfilment was believed to have been worked out in the life of Israel as a historical people.

23. Despite the various criticisms we have looked at, it needs to be remembered that, even if the answers have weaknesses, the questions posed by von Rad, Noth, and Gunkel about the preliterary stage of the tradition are still with us and are ultimately unavoidable. I have already mentioned Wester-mann's more fruitful treatment of the patriarchal stories from this point of view. There is nothing quite comparable yet for the Exodus and subsequent episodes—T. L. Thompson's work suffers from the same defect as Gunkel's—but B. S. Childs's commentary contains some useful material and G. W. Coats recently brought out an excellent study, based on a series of articles written over a period of some twenty years, which, in direct contrast to Noth's position, takes Moses as its central theme (Coats 1988).

G. The Theology of the Pentateuchal Sources. 1. General considerations.
Twentieth-century scholars have been occupied by another development in Pentateuchal study, going beyond the analysis into sources: that is, the theology—or rather theologies, for they differ considerably—of the sources. In fact the realization of the differences is one of the main benefits of source-analysis. One may draw an analogy with what has happened in NT study of the Gospels—there too a source-critical phase and a form-critical phase have been followed by a phase that focuses on the theologies of the different evangelists. The theological study of the sources of the Pentateuch seems to date from von Rad's 'Hexateuch' essay (1938), in which he identified the author of the J source as a creative theological writer. The modifications which von Rad thought J had made to the tradition (combination of Sinai and settlement; addition of primeval history) were clearly an

advance in theology and not just innovations on the literary level. It is now widely recognized that the interpretation of a particular Pentateuchal passage must take account of its setting within the context of the source-document to which it belongs and ask, 'How is the inclusion of this passage related to the author's overall purpose and plan?' Von Rad again is a good illustration of this at many places in his Genesis commentary, though he concentrates mainly on the J source. Further studies of this kind can be found in Brueggemann and Wolff (1975). Before looking briefly at each source in turn I want to make some general, and rather polemical, points about our method and aim.

2. First, the method must be addressed: how are we to determine the theology of a document which is essentially in narrative form? There are various possibilities:

2.1. The best-known studies of this topic have tended to concentrate either on *specific passages* that make clearly theological statements or on *expressions* which recur in a number of passages. For example, Gen 12:1–3 has been regarded as almost the motto of the J writer (so by von Rad, Wolff, and others), with special emphasis being laid on Abraham as the means of blessing for all the peoples of the earth. Other passages have also been thought to shed particular light on the theology of this writer: thus, in Gen 1–11; 6:5; 8:21, and later on 18:22b–33. Again, Wolff's brilliant study of the theology of E is largely concerned with the recurring expressions 'the fear of God' (20:11, etc.) and God 'testing' or 'proving' someone (Gen 22:1; Ex 20:20). In the case of Deuteronomy the key terms 'covenant' and 'law' have often been picked out, or the demand for the centralization of the cult (Deut 12:1–14). Finally, in his essay on the theology of P, Brueggemann sees the declaration of blessing in Gen 1:28 as 'the central message in the faith of the priestly circle', which is recapitulated in later passages such as Gen 9:7; 17:20; 28:1–4; 35:11; Ex 1:7. There is no doubt that this is a natural and useful approach to take, but if it is used alone as it sometimes is, it is in danger of producing an account of the theology of the sources that is both one-sided and oversimplified. For that reason it is very important to look also at two other aspects of the texts.

2.2. One of these is the *range of contents* of a particular source, that is, particularly, where it begins and ends. Again the study of the Gospels is an illuminating comparison, for they all begin and end at different points, at least if it is kept in mind that Luke's Gospel is only the first part of a 2-volume work. The different beginnings were already noticed by Irenaeus in the second century CE. The Pentateuchal sources also all begin at different points, but unfortunately the question of their endings is not so simple, and it is much argued whether J, E, and P did or did not go on to describe the conquest of Canaan under Joshua, while Deuteronomy can be said to 'end' at two very different places. Still, the different beginnings are clear enough, and they have important implications for the theology of the sources.

2.3. Also important is what I would call the *form* of presentation and the *arrangement* of the contents of the source, and in fact von Rad makes these factors fundamental for his exploration of the theology of the Yahwist. What I have in mind is first the general shape of the source—is it essentially a narrative or a collection of speeches? And what kind of narrative or speeches?—and then the more detailed structure of the contents.

3. Secondly, the aim must be decided: what is it that we are trying to do? I would see this as being to state the religious assertions that are made by *the document as a whole,* or at least in so far as it has been preserved. I say this over against the approach which seeks out only what is distinctive or what is new in a particular source. This has sometimes been the way of putting the question—it is in these terms that von Rad puts it in relation to the Yahwist—but (1) we then presuppose that we can make a clear distinction between the contribution of an author himself and what he inherited from his predecessors. This may sometimes be possible but frankly we are often not in a position to do that with any certainty when dealing with the Pentateuchal sources, and that is an important part of the reason why scholars have found it difficult sometimes to agree in this area. (2) In any case the theology of an author is shaped and expressed as much by what he reproduces from earlier tradition as by the fresh insights (if any) which he brings to it himself.

4. One further point: the authors produced their work in particular *historical situations* and addressed themselves to those situations. It must therefore be part of our aim to discover what those situations were, i.e. to date the work, and to relate what it says to the events of its time. But since most of the evidence for dating comes from the theological themes that are prominent in the sources, this part of our task can only be approached after we have reached

an understanding of its theology by the methods described above.

5. Two important features are common to all four sources of the Pentateuch: (1) they all alike seek to define the character of the relationship between YHWH and Israel; (2) they do this by reference to certain ancient events, among which the sequence patriarchs–Exodus–Sinai–occupation of the land is present in all of them. Nevertheless in their handling of these common features they differ considerably.

6. The Theology of J. J, in overall shape, is clearly a narrative. But what kind of narrative? Some of the important events described would clearly justify von Rad's term, used of the Hexateuch as a whole, 'creed', but others, such as the stories of Abraham's or Jacob's exploits, do not fit this description very well. One might say then that there is a credal framework filled out with what might be called illustrative material. An alternative approach is to begin at the other end with the genre-description 'epic', and then qualify this by a term such as 'religious' or 'theological'. Somewhere at the convergence of these two approaches an accurate description is to be found. The narrative shape of J has led to the view that his theology, like that of other OT writers, is a theology of history, i.e. a witness to and interpretation of the acts of God in history. The question does of course arise as to how far the 'history' in J's account is real history, especially in Gen 1–11, and the recently coined term 'narrative theology' is more widely applicable. Either way, the difference between J's theology and a timeless, philosophical theology needs to be noted.

7. J begins with creation: but it is worth amplifying this to 'the creation of human beings', because in Gen 2:4–5 the references to the creation of the natural world are in a subordinate clause, and not part of the actual story, which begins only in v. 7: 'Then the Lord God formed man . . . '. J's story is thus human history from its beginning to—wherever J ended! That we do not know for sure, but the occupation of the land of Canaan by Israel seems the most likely ending, whether, as some still think, that ending is preserved in the book of Joshua or not.

8. The contents of J can be subdivided into two parts: Gen 2–11, 'The Early History of Mankind in General'; and Gen 12 onwards, 'The Early History of Israel and their Ancestors'. An account of J's theology must address both parts of the document and, which is very important, the fact that they have been brought together.

In Gen 2–11 we have a number of stories about the earliest ages of human history, which now have an interesting parallel in the Babylonian *Epic of Atrahasis*, which covers a similar span of early history. They do not pretend to present a complete history of these times, but only certain episodes with a particular importance for later generations. These episodes are presented either as the cause of a present state of affairs (human mortality, the need to work for a living, the existence of many languages, for example) or as paradigms of situations that may occur at any time (the rivalry of brothers, the attempt to break through the limits imposed on man by God), or as both. Westermann points out how the family is often in view. Of course in all cases the context is theological, and the sequence of sin–punishment–mercy appears several times, both as the cause of the present state of the world and as typical of God's government of the world at all times.

9. J's presentation of the early history of Israel is shot through with the idea of election, that Israel is YHWH's own people, which he brought into being, protected, and settled in her land, to fulfil the promises which he had made to her distant ancestors Abraham, Isaac, and Jacob. That history too illustrates the themes of sin–punishment–grace (especially in the wilderness), but more especially that of YHWH as a powerful deliverer and provider of his people's needs: corresponding to this, faith in God is the primary virtue (Gen 15:6, cf. Ex 4:30–1; 14:13, 31). There are some passages, chiefly poetic, in this section which seem to relate to events of J's own time and are the basis for attempts to date him to the tenth century BCE: according to them Israel is destined to be a great nation, who will rule her neighbours and have a king from the tribe of Judah (Gen 24:60; 27:27–9; 49:8–12; Num 24:15–19). Interestingly none of these passages is exactly in the form of a divine promise and perhaps this means that J did not regard political power as of the very essence of Israel's relationship to YHWH.

10. What is the significance of the combination of the two parts together? There has of late been a tendency to focus on the gloomy side of Gen 1–11, which ends, as von Rad points out, with the story of the scattering of the nations. Unlike earlier acts of judgement, this one is not mitigated by any word of grace and mercy. The word of mercy to the nations comes, according to this view, in a quite new form, in 12:1–3, where YHWH promises his blessing of Abraham's descendants, i.e. of Israel, and that 'in you [or: your seed] all the families of the earth shall be blessed' (12:3—cf. 26:4; 28:14), i.e. that Abraham/Israel is destined to mediate YHWH's blessing to other nations. J's theology is thus universalistic: it looks beyond Israel to God's work in the wider world. There is however a snag with this interpretation (see the note on this verse), and that is that the crucial words in Gen 12:3 could be translated in a different way: 'by you all the families of the earth shall bless themselves', that is, Abraham would be the standard to which all others would want to rise, without it being implied that this was in fact YHWH's intention for them (cf. Ps 72:17; and for the idea Zech 8:13). Then J is only speaking directly about YHWH's purpose for Israel. However that may be, we must certainly not make the mistake of thinking that Gen 1–11 serves in its present context only to indicate what the world needs to be saved from. In other respects, as we saw, it specifies the unchanging conditions under which human life has to be lived, as much in Israel as anywhere else, and shows YHWH's dominion as creator over the whole world. This is also a kind of universal theology and ethics, but it differs from the salvation-history kind that has been found in 12:3 etc. and is not dependent upon it. Other signs of a universal interest are the Table of Nations (ch. 10) and the use of Mesopotamian materials in the Flood story, as well as the Tower of Babel story in ch. 11, which seems implicitly to challenge the pretensions of the great world-empires of the ancient Near East, and especially those of Babylon. The approach is reminiscent of the wisdom literature in a number of ways. In this respect Gen 2–11 is not the antithesis to the kerygma of 12:1–3, law to gospel as it were, but displays God's wider work in creation and providence as the basis for his work in his own people's history.

11. *The Theology of E.* The E source survives to a much smaller extent than J. In *shape* or general character E seems to have been very similar to J, and what was said earlier about this in relation to J applies broadly to E. On the other hand the *range* covered seems to be less, for there is no evidence that E had any account of creation or the early history of the human race as a whole: it began its account with the patriarchs, specifically with Abraham. Most of Gen 20–2 is attributed to E, and it has commonly been thought that part of Gen 15, which describes the making of a covenant between God and Abraham, is also from E and indeed its beginning. It is certainly an appropriate place to begin the story of Israel's origins.

12. From Abraham on the contents of E apparently corresponded closely to those of J, with even greater uncertainty about whether it originally included an account of the occupation of Canaan or not. This means that the theological affirmations of E about the actions and character of YHWH are to a large extent the same as J's, and to save repetition it is possible to note just some important differences:

12.1. The most obvious difference is the lack of the universal perspective (in whatever sense) provided in J by the primeval history (Gen 1–11) and perhaps by Gen 12:3. For E God's purposes are in the main limited to his people Israel. Individual foreigners are, however, shown to have recognized the authority of Israel's God (cf. Abimelech in Gen 20 and Jethro in Ex 18). This is reminiscent of the widow of Zarephath in 1 Kings 17 and Naaman in 2 Kings 5, in prophetic stories from the northern kingdom, which is often seen as the environment in which E was composed.

12.2. It is apparently the view of E that the special name for God, YHWH, was not known to the patriarchs, but was first revealed to Moses (Ex 3:14–15: the same view is also held by P (Ex 6:2–3)). This has two effects: it links the beginning of Israel's religion particularly strongly with the Exodus and the mountain of God in the wilderness, and it makes a distinction between patriarchal religion and Israelite religion which, while not absolute, remains important. The character of God as conveyed in his name is given a rare, though elusive, exposition by E in 3:14: 'I am who I am', or 'I will be what I will be' (see the commentary).

12.3. On the subject of political power, E also includes passages which speak of Israel's great destiny (cf. Gen 46:1–4; Num 23:18–24), but it is noticeable that they do not give any special place to Judah, but rather celebrate the supremacy of the northern tribes Ephraim and Manasseh (cf. Deut 33:13–17; also Gen 48:15–16). This is one reason for thinking that E originated in the northern kingdom (cf. Jenks 1977).

13. Each of these three features in which E differs from J is probably due to E's having retained the attitudes and presentation of the story which were current in earlier times, while J represents a new approach in each. Two other differences are more likely to be due to E's own contribution.

13.1. H. W. Wolff (1975) has noted the concern of E for 'the fear of God', as an all-embracing religious attitude (in addition to Gen 20:11 cf. 22:12; 42:18: Ex 1:17, 21; 18:21; 20:20).

13.2. E's narratives reflect a greater preoccupation than the corresponding passages in J with ethical standards of behaviour as the condition of God's blessing of his people. This is particularly clear if one compares the parallel stories in Gen 12:10–20J and 20:1–18E, where the latter passage includes Abimelech's protestation of his innocence and the implication that Abraham's behaviour is reprehensible. It would be even clearer if it were certain that the Decalogue and the Book of the Covenant were included in E, as used to be thought, but this has been questioned in recent years, perhaps rightly.

14. The Theology of Deuteronomy (D). Deuteronomy/D stands in great contrast to J and E in both its *shape* and its *range*, not to speak of its structure, whether one considers its original nucleus (4:44–29:1) or its amplified form. As regards its shape it consists not of narrative, but of a series of *speeches*, which can most adequately be described as preaching: they speak directly to the people in the second person and urge them to do certain things for reasons that are also stated. Events of the early history are generally referred to in passing and are not the main subject of what is being said. This leads on to the range of the contents: in the nucleus there is no attempt at a connected description of early history as found in J and E, but rather the portrayal of a single event in great detail, namely Moses' parting speeches to the Israelites as they are encamped on the banks of the river Jordan. The structure is consequently also quite different and has been a topic of major interest to scholars, who have related it to the liturgy of a festival for the renewal of the covenant (von Rad) or to the pattern of ancient Near-Eastern treaties (Weinfeld), or indeed to both. The amplified form (i.e. chs. 1–34 as a whole), on the other hand, is most probably the first section of a long *historical work* with a quite different range from J and E, extending through the books of Joshua, Judges, Samuel, and Kings, commonly referred to as the Deuteronomistic History. So in neither form is D at all similar externally to J and E.

15. There is more common ground with the other sources, not surprisingly, when we come to look at its actual teaching, though here too there are new features. In the speeches of Deuteronomy the themes of the promise to the patriarchs, YHWH's deliverance and protection of his people, and his gift to them of the land of Canaan as a land full of every good thing, repeatedly appear. Thus far there is a real continuity with the older sources. The creation story, however, is ignored (though cf. 4:32), and the book is dominated by the theme of the covenant based on God's laws and obedience to them. This central concern is reflected in the title of the original core of Deuteronomy (4:45): 'These are the decrees and the statutes and ordinances, that Moses spoke to the Israelites...' (cf. Moses' opening words: 'Hear, O Israel, the statutes and the ordinances that I am addressing to you today' (5:1)). The picture of Moses himself is changed: instead of being the inspired leader of his people in all kinds of circumstances, he has become above all what we might call a 'prophetic legislator'. The laws too in chs 12–26 go far beyond the most that can be ascribed to J and E and allude to many aspects of life, both private and national—in the latter sphere it is notable that they make provision for the offices of priest, judge, prophet, and king, and imply that public worship is to be concentrated at a single sanctuary, which is referred to as 'the place that the LORD your God will choose as a dwelling for his name' (e.g. 12:11). National prosperity, indeed survival in the land which YHWH has given, now depends upon observance of these commands (cf. ch. 28). It is not the connection of sin and punishment which is new in Deuteronomy but the explicit definition, in the form of a code of laws, of what counts as sin in the sight of YHWH and the dire threats ('curses') held out in the case of disobedience.

16. The amplified form of D incorporates one additional theme of great significance to the community in exile, which is evidence of its origin in the sixth century BCE: this is the call to return to YHWH (cf. 4:27–31; 30:1–6). If sinful Israel, now under the judgment of YHWH, will once more be obedient to YHWH's law, then he will bring them back to Canaan and will even transform them inwardly so that they do not fail again (30:6), a thought that is closely related to Jeremiah's teaching of a new covenant and Ezekiel's of a new heart.

17. The Theology of P. As regards its *shape*, P stands somewhere between J and E on the one hand and D on the other. It does have a narrative structure, with its story extending from creation (this time explicitly including the natural world) to at least the eve of the Israelites' entry into Canaan. But in Genesis one can scarcely speak of a real story, as hardly any episodes are described in detail and the P material is mostly genealogies and chronological

notes. And throughout this source long *speeches* (as in D) are very much in evidence, but this time in the form of divine revelations (or rather promises and commands) communicated to such figures as Noah, Abraham, and Moses. Not infrequently it is clear that a narrative episode is only there to reinforce what has been said in one of the divine speeches. So despite some superficial resemblance to J and E we are clearly in a quite different world. It is difficult to specify the genre of P as a whole. An anthropologist once suggested that because of his interest in myth, kinship, and ritual P could rank as the world's first social anthropologist! But anthropologists are only observers, while for P (which was probably produced by priests for priests) these things clearly have existential importance. Perhaps a report of a Liturgical Commission is a closer modern analogy!

18. While the theology of P is without doubt very largely a theology of ritual (especially priesthood and sacrifice), it does have a broader base. God/YHWH is the creator of the whole world (Gen 1), which he declared to be good and on which he bestowed his blessing. Humanity as such, male and female, is made 'in his image', a difficult phrase which should probably be translated 'as his image', implying that they are God's representatives on earth, to whom dominion over the earth is therefore naturally given (1:26). Gen 9:1–17, which incorporates the covenant with Noah and all living creatures (v. 10), amplifies this definition of the place of mankind in the world. Alongside these universal statements P also reaffirms the tradition of the election of Israel in her ancestor Abraham (Gen 17) and tells in his own way the story of the Exodus, the meeting with God at Mount Sinai, and the wilderness wanderings.

19. But already in Genesis P's interest in ritual can be seen: God himself, by his own example, inaugurates the sabbath (2:2–3); the instructions to Noah include the ban on eating meat with the blood, a basic element of Jewish food laws (9:4); and Abraham receives and obeys the command to be circumcised (17:9–14, 22–7). It is interesting that the three rituals given such great antiquity by P are all private, domestic rituals, which did not need a temple and could therefore be practised in the diaspora, in exile. There is some sign that P thought of four great epochs of revelation, beginning at creation (where God is called Elohim), Noah (again Elohim), Abraham (El Shaddai), and Moses (YHWH), and it used to be customary to speak of P as the Book of the Four Covenants, leading to the use (for example in Wellhausen's early work) of the symbol Q (for *quattuor*, Latin for 'four'). But in only two of the cases (Noah and Abraham) does P actually speak of the making of a 'covenant' (*běrît*), and other common features, such as the presence of a 'sign', are also hard to trace all through the series.

20. Be that as it may, the weight of P's emphasis certainly falls on the making, according to a detailed, divinely revealed plan, of the tabernacle, or desert shrine, at Mount Sinai (Ex 25–31; 35–40). This, or rather the altar outside it, was of course a place of sacrifice, and P has a lot to say, both practical and theological, about the ritual of sacrifice and the priests who were needed to carry it out. But this was not all. The name 'tabernacle' (*miškān*) means 'dwelling-place' (sc. for the divine glory) and it was also known as the 'tent of meeting' (i.e. for meeting with God). That is, what made the tabernacle a holy place, and an appropriate place to offer sacrifice, was that YHWH was in a special sense there, in the midst of his people. And that was its purpose. According to Ex 25:8 YHWH said to Moses: 'And have them [the Israelites] make me a sanctuary, that I may dwell among them.' And after the work was finished (40:34), 'Then the cloud covered the tent of meeting, and the glory of the LORD filled the tabernacle.' P's account of the relationship of YHWH to Israel, therefore, while it does not bypass other categories, is above all a theology of the divine presence in the midst of the people, which necessitates the construction of a sanctuary. For P God's presence is inconceivable without a sanctuary and its associated personnel and rituals. The people need also to know about what is holy and profane, what is clean and unclean, and it is a major part of the priests' task to instruct them in such matters: they are 'to distinguish between the holy and the common, and between the unclean and the clean' (Lev 10:10). This emphasis on the necessity of a sanctuary makes the most natural time for the composition of P the period between the destruction of the First Temple in 587/6 BCE and the completion of the Second Temple in 516, and not later, as Wellhausen and Kuenen thought.

H. Law. 1. What is law? The most familiar, and most general Hebrew word for 'law', *tôrâ*, is not necessarily the best place to begin an answer to this question. The very fact that it has the wider meaning 'instruction, teaching' led to its use for the teaching given by parents (Prov 1:8; 4:2), by the wise (Prov 13:14), or by prophets

(Isa 1:10; 8:16, 20), as well as for what is commonly meant by law. This is an important insight, but it does not help with the definition of law as distinct from these other kinds of instruction. For that a more general (though possibly anachronistic) account is needed, which would recognize that what holds together the different types of law (constitutional, civil, criminal, cultic) is their prescriptive character, the regulation of specific kinds of recurrent (interpersonal) behaviour between members of a community, their enactment (and modification) by a recognized authority, political or ecclesiastical, and the existence of sanctions or penalties and procedures for their determination.

2. Most biblical law is found in the Pentateuch (some cultic law is included in 1 Chr 23–7). The *main collections of laws* in the Pentateuch are (1) the Decalogue or Ten Commandments (Ex 20:1–17; Deut 5:6–21); (2) the Book of the Covenant (Ex 20:22–23:23: for the title cf. 24:7); (3) the cultic commandments in Ex 34:10–27; (4) the Priestly laws about sacrifice, priesthood, and related matters, including land tenure (Ex 25–31 *passim*; Lev 1–7; 11–16; 27; Num 5–6; 8:1–10:10; 15; 18–19; 27:1–11; 28–30; 33:50–34:15; 35–6), among which (5) the Holiness Code (Lev 17–26) forms a distinct section; and (6) the law of Deuteronomy 4:1–30:20). All these collections are presented as having been revealed by God to Moses (and sometimes Aaron) for proclamation to the people at Mount Sinai/Horeb (or, in certain cases, most notably (6), elsewhere). There are, however, numerous instances where the same topic is dealt with more than once, often in different and even contradictory ways (cf. e.g. Ex 21:7 with Deut 15:17). From this, and from comparison with other biblical texts, scholars have concluded that the legal collections derive from very diverse times and situations, and that most probably none goes back to Moses himself. There is also reason to think that several of the collections at least have been revised since their original promulgation. In several cases the collections have an introductory or concluding exhortation or both, and much of the legal collection in Deuteronomy is interleaved with exhortations and 'motive clauses' (cf. G. von Rad's description 'preached law': on biblical law in general see further Patrick (1986) and art. 'Law' in *ABD*).

3. Within these collections it is possible to distinguish different styles or *types of law*. In an essay first published in 1934, A. Alt initiated a new phase in the study of biblical law. He began from the important axiom that 'The making of law is basically not a literary process at all, but part of the life of a community' (Alt 1966: 86). Using the form-critical method, mainly on the Book of the Covenant (as being the oldest collection), he distinguished two major types of law. One, which he called 'casuistic', was conditional and (originally) expressed in the third person: 'If a man...then...'. This type was represented by most of Ex 21:2–22:17, and was similar to the form of law found among other ancient Near-Eastern peoples (see below). Alt concluded that such laws provided the norms for the village courts 'at the gate' in early Israel and that they had probably been taken over from the Canaanite inhabitants of the land. By contrast there was another type of law which Alt called 'apodictic'. Some examples of it express the same kind of case-law in a different way (e.g. Ex 21:13–14, 23–5; 21:12, 15–17; 22:19–20): most of these laws require the death penalty, and they are formulated in a simpler, more direct style than the laws referred to above. But generally laws of this type contain no explicit penalty at all: they are in many cases direct commands or prohibitions, like the Decalogue (cf. also Ex 22:18, 21–2, 28; 23:1–3, 6–9; and the 'table of affinity' in Lev 18:7–18), but they also appear as curses (Deut 27:15–26). Alt argued that these laws were of a distinctive Israelite form and origin, and that they originated not in the local courts but in a religious context, specifically in a festival for the renewal of the covenant celebrated at Shechem in the Judges period (cf. Deut 27; 31:10–13; Josh 24). Indeed the major impulse for such a formulation of law might well go back into the pre-settlement period, when the worship of YHWH began.

4. The key difference between apodictic and casuistic law as defined by Alt is that the former prescribes before the event what ought or ought not to be done, while the latter declares to a situation after the event what the appropriate penalty is. Thus the former belongs to a context of teaching or instruction, while the latter belongs to a judicial context. This distinction can be extended to cover the laws about worship to which Alt gave very little attention. Some of these lay down in the apodictic style what forms worship is or is not to take (e.g. the largely parallel series in Ex 23:10–19 and 34:11–26, and the later Priestly ordinances of Ex 25–31 and Lev 23); others provide, in the casuistic style, guidance for the remedy for particular circumstances that may arise (e.g. Lev 4–5, 12–15). In the context of worship and ritual the apodictic laws may well have been intended

for occasions of public instruction or modelled on them, but the casuistic cultic laws were presumably not administered by judges, but by the priests at the temples.

5. Some of Alt's conclusions, especially about apodictic law, have been rejected by more recent scholars. The 'festival for the renewal of the covenant' is no longer widely accepted as an ancient feature of the religion of Israel. It can be questioned whether all the subtypes of apodictic law have the same origin. Even Alt's more general claims that the apodictic laws are distinctively Israelite and come from a liturgical context have been challenged on the basis of parallels in non-Israelite, non-legal texts. Direct commands and prohibitions have been found in Egyptian wisdom literature, in Hittite and Assyrian treaties, and even occasionally in Mesopotamian law-codes. There is a growing consensus that much if not all apodictic law originated in a family or clan setting and that it originally had nothing to do with the cult or the covenant (Gerstenberger 1965, summarized in Stamm and Andrew 1967; Otto 1994). It is striking that the cases where such a view is most difficult to accept are those where laws about worship are involved: the opening of the Decalogue and the cultic commandments in Ex 34 (cf. 23:10–19). It may be that initially it was only laws such as these which formed part of a cultic ceremony. On the other hand, if that much is accepted, one ought not perhaps to rule out the possibility that other commandments dealing with everyday life also had a place in such a ceremony. The fact that commands and prohibitions are found in a school or family or treaty context elsewhere does not mean that they may not have had a cultic context in Israel. Those who deny this have to see the literary formulation of the law-codes as commandments of God as a relatively late innovation. The alternative view is, with Alt, to see the literary formulation of all law as continuing what had been the basis for some law since its beginning.

6. Since the archaeological discoveries of the late nineteenth century it has become clear that Pentateuchal law has an important relationship with other *ancient Near-Eastern law* (cf. Boecker (1980) and, for specific parallels, *IDBSup* 533). Whether that relationship is one of dependence or just similarity is not the main issue here. Several collections of laws are now known from ancient Mesopotamia. The best known is the Code of Hammurabi of Babylon, from the eighteenth century BCE. The most fully preserved copy was taken in antiquity from Babylon to Susa in Elam, where it was found during excavations in 1901–2. It is now in the Louvre. Other copies of parts of the text are also known. The Code consisted of 282 laws and a prologue and epilogue (see *ANET* 164–80 for ET). The laws deal with such matters as the administration of justice, state and temple property, service to the king, private property, borrowing, family relationships, bodily injury, and agriculture. Earlier and later legal collections from Mesopotamia are also known: the Code of Ur-Nammu (21st cent.), the Code of Lipit-Ishtar (19th cent.), the Code of Eshnunna (18th cent.), the Middle Assyrian Laws (13th cent.), and the Neo-Babylonian Laws (?7th cent.). Another important collection is the Hittite Laws (14th cent.: the surviving parts of all these collections are translated in *ANET* 160–3, 180–8, 523–5). These collections are all apparently state law and they are predominantly in the 'casuistic' form, with a penalty or remedy specified for each particular set of circumstances. At present no comparable documents are known from ancient Egypt or Canaan.

7. The *history of law* in the OT, in the sense of the study of how and why the prescriptions about particular matters arose and developed through the OT period, is not straightforward. It requires that the relative ages of the different legal collections be determined and that, where appropriate, the inner growth of each individual collection be examined. Wellhausen's conclusions about the ages of the major Pentateuchal sources J, E, D, and P were largely based on such a history of law, specifically of the laws about worship. The source-critical approach held that the cultic laws in Ex 34 belonged to the J source and the Decalogue and the Book of the Covenant to E. Both sources were dated to the early monarchy period and it was thought that the legal collections might be earlier still. Deuteronomy came from the seventh century and P (including the Holiness Code) from the fifth century. In the latter two cases a specific link could be made with official ratifications of law, by Josiah (2 Kgs 22–3) and Ezra (Neh 8–10), which gave the biblical laws a similar official status to that enjoyed by the Mesopotamian legal collections. It was not so clear what gave authority to the earlier legal collections, especially the Book of the Covenant. M. Noth made the important observation that both the content of these collections and the linking of their promulgation with Moses asserted their validity for 'all Israel',

which he took to be based on the memory of the 'amphictyony' (sacred tribal league) of the Judges period. But the existence of such a union of the tribes is widely doubted today. Recently Albertz has suggested that the Book of the Covenant was in its original form the basis for reforms introduced by Hezekiah *c*.700 BCE, thus giving it too a royal stamp of approval. But there is little solid evidence for such an association with Hezekiah. Recent scholarship, much influenced by redaction criticism, has tended to doubt whether J or E originally contained any of the legal collections.

8. The *distinctiveness of biblical law* can be seen in its form, its ethics, and its theology. Attention has already been drawn to the hortatory element which is frequently present in the OT legal collections, and a specific feature of this is the numerous 'motive clauses', which ground the laws in the divine will, a historical event, or a promise of future well-being (Sonsino 1980). Close comparisons between the contents of biblical and non-biblical laws have shown that, despite many similarities, there are differences here too. The laws apply equally to all free-born Israelites, whereas in Mesopotamia the penalty imposed may vary according to the social status of the other party. Biblical law goes further in its provision for the disadvantaged in society, including the 'resident alien' (*gēr*) as well as widows and orphans. More generally, a higher value tends to be set on human life as opposed to property, as can be seen in the respective laws about the 'goring ox' (Ex 21:28–32) and theft (Ex 22:1–4). Finally, the mingling of laws on sacred and secular matters, found in the Decalogue, the Book of the Covenant, Deuteronomy, and the Holiness Code, reflects a sense of the unity of life and especially of the claim made by the religion of Israel on the secular as well as the sacred. This latter point is closely associated with the theological, and specifically covenantal, context in which all the laws now stand, as well as the motive clauses already mentioned. The historical fiction whereby the lawgiving of Moses occurs at the behest of YHWH in the period between the creative event of the Exodus from Egypt and the entry into the land of Canaan promised to Israel anchors the law in the fundamental structure of OT faith. This is explicitly brought out in such passages as Ex 20:1 and Deut 6:20–5. Particularly in the later collections, Deuteronomy and the Holiness Code, the observance of the law is presented as a communal responsibility and failure to keep it as the cause of a national catastrophe, ultimately exile from the land. In several places this theology is specifically summed up by a reference to the establishment of a covenant between YHWH and his people (Ex 24:7–8; 34:10, 27; Lev 26:42, 44, 45; Deut 5:2–3, 29:1).

I. Recent Questioning of the Classical Documentary Theory. 1. The work on oral tradition and theological interpretation that we reviewed earlier was based on the assumption that the classical (Wellhausen) theory of Pentateuchal origins is correct. It would need at least considerable revision if that theory proved to be wrong, though no doubt some of the insights would survive. When a theory has come to support such a superstructure of further speculation, it is clearly important that its own foundations should be examined from time to time and possible alternatives to it should be considered. Perhaps this is one reason why recent years have seen a return of interest to the source-critical questions which the classical theory sought to answer. At the present time the study of the Pentateuch is a matter of discussion and controversy such as it has scarcely been since the time of Wellhausen and Kuenen. A variety of fresh approaches is being tried, and discarded ones revived, to seek a well-founded way forward in this most basic of all Pentateuchal studies. Much of what will be described in the following sections is still very much a matter for discussion.

2. The fresh approaches have taken two main forms:

2.1. New attempts to formulate the principles according to which study of the Pentateuch and other parts of the Bible must proceed, i.e. a concern with methodology; which has arisen partly from the need to define more closely the relationship between source criticism and other methods such as tradition criticism and form criticism, and also partly from the impact on biblical studies of 'structural analysis' and other modern literary methods for the exegesis of texts (see esp. Barton 1984).

2.2. The development of particular alternative theories about the origins of the Pentateuch, involving a partial or total abandonment of the classical theory.

We have, then, two lines of research, reflection on method and the formation of new theories, which have sometimes reinforced one another but sometimes proceeded quite separately. For some evaluation of them in print see the *Introductions* of Soggin and Childs, and Whybray (1987). It is possible to distinguish six 'new directions in research' in this area.

3. An earlier date for P. First we have the view that P is not the latest of the four sources, from the exilic or post-exilic period, but is earlier in origin than D or at least contemporary with it. This view has recently been argued for at some length (Haran 1979). But it in fact originated with the Israeli scholar Y. Kaufmann as long ago as 1930 and it has been accepted widely among Israeli scholars, though hardly at all elsewhere. In the form that Haran presents it, this view holds that the composition of P is to be dated to the reign of Hezekiah, c.700 BCE, and that P was in fact the stimulus for Hezekiah's reforms of national religion reported in 2 Kings 18:3–5. As with Wellhausen, we find that the dating of P by Haran is based on the place which P's regulations seem to occupy in the history of Israel's religion, and Haran argues that, contrary to what Graf and Wellhausen had said, all the P regulations make sense, and some of them only make sense, if P was composed before the exile.

4. A 'sounding' can be made by considering what Haran says about the issue considered earlier in connection with Wellhausen's dating of P, namely admission to the priesthood. In order to show that P's regulations reflect pre-exilic conditions, Haran draws attention to the list of Levitical cities in Josh 21, in which the descendants of Aaron appear as a distinct group, and are assigned cities in the tribal areas of Judah and the related Benjamin and Simeon, that is the southernmost tribes, while the other Levites are given cities in the other tribal areas. A number of scholars have argued, on grounds of historical geography, that this list is pre-exilic in origin, which would, if taken seriously, imply that the Aaronides were a recognizable group before the exile, and that they already then had an exclusive right to full priesthood (cf. v. 19) and not only afterwards. Nevertheless, while the list may have a pre-exilic basis, its present context is in a historical work of the exilic period (the Deuteronomistic History), so that it is not clear evidence of pre-exilic practices. Haran also claims support from references to Aaron in the older Pentateuchal sources J and E; but they do not present Aaron and his descendants as having the sole right to the priesthood, as P does. Nor is there any greater force in the passages cited to show the existence of Levites in subservient positions before the exile, as prescribed by P: 2 Kings 11:18 and 1 Sam 2:31–3. In the former case there are subordinate cultic

officials but there is no indication that they are Levites, while in the latter case it is not actually said whether Eli's descendants were to be given any role at all, even an inferior one, in the future temple service.

5. An argument against Wellhausen's view which is perhaps more telling arises from statistics. P appears to envisage a large number of Levites compared with priests (cf. the tithe-law), whereas the lists in Ezra and Nehemiah suggest that there were actually relatively few Levites in post-exilic times. This makes it difficult to believe that P originated in the time to which these lists refer. Even the force of this argument, however, is reduced if P is dated to the years of exile itself in the sixth century, as this would leave time for conditions to have changed before Ezra and Nehemiah, and more Levites than had at first been anticipated may have been able to lay claim to full priestly status by finding a genealogical link with Aaron, thus reducing the number of ordinary Levites. The nub of Wellhausen's argument was Ezek 44, and Haran does attempt a different interpretation of this which would leave room for an older distinction within the priesthood. But it does not convince.

6. In general, many of Haran's arguments seem to turn out on examination to be less conclusive than they at first appear. Moreover, it is surely revealing that Haran has after all to concede that 'it was only in the days of Ezra ... that P's presence became perceptible in historical reality and began to exercise its influence on the formation of Judaism' (1979: p. v). To attribute a document nearly three centuries of existence before it became perceptible is rather unsatisfactory when set against the very explicit arguments of Wellhausen.

7. Other Israeli scholars have used different arguments to support similar views. Weinfeld has argued that D presupposes P at various points so that P must be earlier: but these turn out either to be in passages which are for other reasons not thought to be an original part of D, or else to concern regulations which there is every reason to think existed on their own before their inclusion in P, so that D may have known them without knowing P as a whole. Again, Hurvitz has examined the language of P and shown that the vocabulary includes many words characteristic of pre-exilic rather than post-exilic Hebrew. This need not mean that P is pre-exilic: it could be due to the use of traditional vocabulary in priestly circles—a not unheard of phenomenon—and in fact there

are several cases where P's vocabulary seems closest to Ezekiel, an argument again perhaps for a sixth-century date. Further, Hurvitz's study of vocabulary must be viewed in the light of R. Polzin's work on syntax, which shows that in this respect P's language differs from that of pre-exilic writings and represents a transitional stage in the development to Late Biblical Hebrew, as represented by the books of Chronicles—just what would be expected from a sixth-century work.

8. It has not been established that this earlier dating of P should be adopted. Discussion of it has, however, been useful for two reasons: (1) it has emphasized that the P document did not emerge out of thin air, but in some passages is a compilation of older traditions, particularly laws; (2) it has brought to light one or two reasons for preferring a sixth-century date for the composition of P to the fifth-century one advocated by earlier critics.

9. Renewed emphasis on the final form of the text. A second feature of recent Pentateuchal scholarship has been the tendency of certain scholars to direct attention to what they sometimes refer to as 'the final form of the text', that is the form in which the Pentateuch actually appears in the OT, as distinct from the sources and traditions which lie behind, or beneath the surface of, the biblical text itself. Those who have advocated this approach are agreed that the style of scholarship which has been dominant in academic circles for a century and more has been too preoccupied with questions of origin and sources, and has neglected the interpretation of the text in the form that became standard for synagogue and church for twenty centuries. In their view it is not so much a revision of particular theories that is needed but a completely new approach to the study of the Pentateuch. Indeed it is not only the Pentateuch that needs a new approach, but the whole OT (and perhaps the NT as well). Within this group of scholars it is possible, and perhaps useful, to distinguish two different kinds of concern for the final form of the text.

10. On the one hand there are those who emphasize the need to treat the Pentateuch as a work of literature in its own right, which means seeking to understand its present form, purpose, and meaning, just as one would with, say, a play by Shakespeare or a novel by D. H. Lawrence. A good example of this literary approach is David Clines's *The Theme of the Pentateuch* (1978): he is quite explicit (cf. ch. 2) about his debt to the general study of literature.

Another kind of literary approach is represented by structuralist studies of parts of the Pentateuch which appear from time to time, and sometimes claim to be the sole representatives of a general literary approach to the biblical text, an impression that is far from being a true one. A good indication of the rich possibilities of such a literary approach to the Pentateuch can be gained from Robert Alter's *The Art of Biblical Narrative* (1981), which has been very well received.

11. To be distinguished from this literary approach there are those, above all Brevard Childs, who have urged afresh the need for exegesis to read the OT as the Scripture of synagogue and church, and who speak of a 'canonical approach' to the OT. Here too the exegete is thought of as having much to learn from an unfamiliar direction, and in view of the emphasis on the term 'Scripture' it is not surprising to find that it is the history of biblical interpretation, among both Jews and Christians, that is meant: the great (and not so great) commentaries and other works which grappled with the meaning of Scripture long before the modern historical approach was thought of. One can see Childs's high respect for the commentaries of the past in his own on Exodus, in which one section of the treatment of each passage is reserved for a consideration of them (see also Childs 1979: chs. 3, 5).

12. Clearly both varieties of this development have a real attraction, which is due partly to the fact that they recognize important dimensions of the texts which are commonly overlooked in other OT scholarship, and partly to the fact that what they say seems so much simpler and more familiar than talk of sources and stages of tradition does. At the same time it is important to recognize their limitations, which mean that they cannot and should not take the place of traditional historical scholarship. Clines and Childs are both clear that their methods leave room for historical study of the origins of the Pentateuch, but they do not stress this point sufficiently. One can see the limitations as well as the advantages of their methods if one remembers the descriptions of the Pentateuch which lie at their foundation: on the one hand, a unified work of literature, on the other, Scripture. It is only questions arising out of these descriptions which the methods proposed are capable of answering: that is the questions of students of literature and of preachers and systematic theologians. For the answering of historical questions they are of little or no use:

such questions are ones that can and should be asked, and they will be answered by the use of other, more appropriate methods. I think it is also necessary to go a stage further and ask whether Childs's canonical approach is really adequate, by itself, even for the answering of theological questions about the Pentateuch. Does it not involve turning one's back on matters of enormous theological importace, such as the original message of the Pentateuchal sources taken one by one, and the relation of this to the historical situation which they addressed? For Childs the only historical situation which seems ultimately to matter is that addressed by the text in its canonical form, sometime in the post-exilic or even intertestamental period, and the only theological viewpoint which ultimately matters is that of the final redactor of the text. Is not a theological exegesis based on such principles going to be impoverished compared with what historically based exegesis has to offer?

13. This is also an appropriate place for a brief comment on R. N. Whybray's recent book, *The Making of the Pentateuch* (1987). It contains a review of recent (and not so recent) work on the Pentateuch, and as such it has many useful things to say. The conclusion is, however, rather different from that which will be proposed here: Whybray supports the more far-reaching criticisms of the Documentary Theory, and he takes the view that the final author of the Pentateuch, sometime in the post-exilic period, employed such a 'high degree of imagination and [such] great freedom in the treatment of sources' that source criticism of the traditional kind is not possible and one must limit oneself to the study of the final form of the text, but on critical rather than literary or canonical grounds. This view has found very little support among critical scholars, whose continued discussion of the composition of the Pentateuch from earlier material shows that they do not consider that the situation is as desperate as Whybray proposes. In particular it is remarkable that Whybray does not even seem to recognize the possibility of distinguishing Deuteronomy and the Priestly material from the remainder.

14. Redaction criticism. Back in the world of traditional biblical criticism, it is necessary to consider the growing emphasis on redaction criticism. This can be defined as the study of the way in which *editorial processes* have shaped the Pentateuch. In early biblical criticism the redactor was chiefly thought of as a scribe who combined together older sources into a composite narrative, without contributing much if anything out of his own head by way of interpretation or additional material. He was what has sometimes been called a scissors-and-paste man. He was thought to have taken extracts from existing documents and joined them together, often in a rather careless way. The symbol R^{JE}, for example, was used to denote the redactor who combined the J source with the E source of the Pentateuch. Over the years the emphasis has changed, and when scholars speak of a redactor today they are thinking more often of a figure who may only have had in front of him a single document or account, and amplified it by the addition of words or sentences which would alter its overall meaning to present more clearly the teachings which he himself believed to be most important for his day. This development can be seen with particular clarity in recent study of the prophetic and historical books of the OT, but it has also considerably modified the way in which some scholars have seen the composition of the Pentateuch as taking place. It of course brings attention firmly back to the written stage of the tradition and sometimes there is an explicit polemic against the oral tradition approach. Some scholars in Germany have applied this approach to the detection of layers within the sources recognized by earlier scholarship (e.g. E. Zenger; P. Weimar). But, perhaps because of the importance of Deuteronomic/Deuteronomistic editing in other parts of the OT, this approach often asserts that redactional work by the same 'school' of writers can be traced in the Pentateuch, or rather the Tetrateuch. This is particularly true of L. Perlitt's book, *Bundestheologie im Alten Testament*, 'Covenant Theology in the OT', which made a big impression through the acceptance of some of its theses by influential scholars (cf. Nicholson 1973). For our purposes what is most important is that Perlitt reckons with an extensive Deuteronomic reworking of the chapters in Exodus which deal with events at Mount Sinai. According to Perlitt, all passages in these chapters which imply the making of a covenant between YHWH and Israel at Sinai belong to this redactional level, which he calls Deuteronomic, because he believes that covenant theology is peculiarly the creation of the authors of Deuteronomy, and was imposed by them and their disciples on the other parts of the OT. Much of Perlitt's detailed work on the Sinai narrative is directed at showing that verses normally attributed to J or E do not belong to

them, but are part of this later redactional layer, the result of which is to argue that covenant was not an original component of the Sinai tradition. There is something of a vicious circle in this argument. The references to a covenant in Exodus are said to be due to a late Deuteronomic redactor—because the covenant idea is no older than Deuteronomy—but this can only be sustained by assuming that the verses in Exodus are due to a Deuteronomic redactor. Little attention seems to be given to the possibility that the covenantal texts in Exodus are the seeds from which the Deuteronomic theology grew. There is also a failure to notice important differences between the way that the Sinai covenant is presented in Exodus and the Deuteronomic literature (cf. the critique of Perlitt in Nicholson 1986: ch. 8).

15. However redactional explanations have been brought forward for other sections of the Pentateuch as well. Auld has argued that the passages at the end of Numbers which speak about plans for the conquest of Canaan and its division among the tribes are dependent on passages in Joshua which describe these episodes, and did not form part of any of the main Pentateuchal sources (Auld 1980). It has also been suggested that many of the notes of movement from place to place in Exodus and Numbers, which form a framework to the wilderness narrative as we now have it, were added in an 'itinerary-redaction', which made use of a full account of the wilderness journey preserved in Num 33:1–49. On a more theological level it has been argued that the promises to the patriarchs in Genesis were greatly multiplied and enlarged by redactors working at a time when one of the themes of these promises, the possession of the land of Canaan, was threatened in the late monarchy or even the exilic period by the appearance of the great imperial powers of Assyria and Babylon. Nicholson, again, has argued that the Decalogue in Ex 20 did not originally appear there but was inserted by a redactor who took it more or less as it stood from its other occurrence in Deut 5. Each of the theories has of course to be judged on its merits.

16. It is appropriate to refer briefly here to C. Westermann's massive commentary on Genesis. Westermann does not accept that there is any trace of an E source in Genesis. The passages usually said to have been derived from E, such as most of chs. 20–2, he takes to be stories that had circulated separately before being added to the J narrative, which was already in a connected form. They are, in effect, supplements to J, and with Westermann here we are right back in the world of the supplementary theory of Pentateuchal origins. It is for that reason that he is included here, even though the additional matter is too extensive and too self-contained for the process of its inclusion really to be referred to as a redaction. In coming to this view, Westermann is taking up the approach advocated by W. Rudolph many years ago, and also followed by S. Mowinckel. It is not clear that he has made that approach any the more likely, but it remains an option that must be carefully examined. Wolff's essay on the theology of E, of course, noted some important recurring features in the E material which suggest that it did come from a connected narrative or source.

17. With redactional explanations covering so much of the Pentateuch, it is not a big step to suggest that comprehensive redactional activity has sought to remould the whole Pentateuch into a new form. This is the direction in which William Johnstone has moved. He argues that the Pentateuch is the result of a Priestly revision of an original Deuteronomic version of the story, which was based on Deuteronomy (he does not say on what else), so that a close parallel exists with the composition of the historical books, where the 'priestly' Chronicles is seen by most scholars as a revision of the Deuteronomic historical books of Samuel and Kings (Johnstone 1998). This leads straight into a wider questioning about the nature of P.

18. P as a supplement, not a source. Questions have been raised not only about the date, but about the nature of the Priestly Source. F. M. Cross and others have argued that P is not a separate source which once existed independently of J etc., perhaps as a rival version of the story of Israel's origins, but a series of supplements overlaid on the older narrative. According to this view, P was thus reworking the older narrative by expanding it with material of a new, generally cultcentred character, so as to shift the balance of the story in this direction. Like the elimination of E as a separate source, this is in fact an old view revived which can be traced back to P. Volz in the years between the two World Wars. It is also the view that was held by the Scandinavian scholar Ivan Engnell, whose views on oral tradition were mentioned briefly earlier. The important difference it makes is that the purpose of the P writer must now be investigated on the assumption that he reproduced the older traditions, e.g. about legislation at Sinai, as well as incorporating material

reflecting his own special interests. It is, for example, then no longer possible to say, as some have done, that P knows nothing of a covenant at Sinai but only the founding of a pattern of ritual. P incorporated the older covenant-making story and had no need to add one of his own. One of the attractions of this view, and indeed of the other 'supplementary' theories, is that it appears to spare us the allegedly unreal picture of redactors sitting at their desks with scissors and paste, selecting half a verse from here and half a verse from there in the four sources to make the completed Pentateuch. There are also some passages, especially in the patriarchal stories, where the P material is so meagre that it seems at first sight unlikely that it ever existed alone, and unjustified to claim that it represents extracts from a fuller, now lost, parallel account of the events, and it might better be explained as amplification of an existing narrative.

19. And yet there are a number of passages which seem to defy explanation in these terms, and to require a hypothesis of the traditional kind, which allows for the existence of an independent P source (see especially Emerton 1988; Davies 1996). These are passages where it is possible by analysis to identify both a relatively complete P version of the story and a relatively complete version from one of the older sources. The Flood story is a prime example, but there are others. A redactor would not compose duplicates such as we observed in the Flood story: whether it seems 'natural' or 'likely' to us or not, the only explanation which makes sense of the situation there is that he had two complete narratives of the Flood and combined them. Another point arises from the P passage Ex 6:2–3, according to which God did not make himself known to the patriarchs by the name YHWH but only as El Shaddai/God Almighty. This corresponds well to the beginnings of speeches in P such as Gen 17:1 and 35:11, but it conflicts directly with passages where the patriarchs show familiarity with the name YHWH, which are quite frequent in J (12:8 etc.). It is hardly conceivable that P would have left such passages unamended if he had included them in his overall presentation. This implies that there is a continuing need to reckon with the independent existence of P prior to its combination with the other sources. But it also seems that there has been some minor editing of the completed Pentateuch by a Priestly writer at a very late stage which has introduced the vocabulary of P into older material (e.g. Ex 16:1, 17:1, the

phrase 'the congregation of the people of Israel'), and this could help to explain the isolated 'P' verses in the patriarchal stories that were mentioned.

20. A late date for J. A further recent development concerns the dating of J. The first scholar to mention here is H. H. Schmid who argued in his book *Der sogenannte Jahwist* (1976) ('The So-Called Yahwist') that the composition of the whole of J took place after the rise of classical prophecy and is contemporary with the rise of the Deuteronomic movement. In his own words: 'The historical work designated in research by the word "Yahwist", with its comprehensive theological redaction and interpretation of the Pentateuchal material cannot derive from the time of Solomon, but already presupposes pre-exilic prophecy and belongs close to the deuteronomic-deuteronomistic shaping of the tradition and literary activity.' He declines to give an absolute date but this view would put the composition of J in the 7th or 6th century BCE. How, briefly, does Schmid arrive at this conclusion? By two main kinds of argument: (1) he points to features in the J narrative which, according to him, are prophetic in character and are not found in literature before the classical prophets in the eighth century and later. For example, the 'call of Moses' in Ex 3 resembles the call-narratives found in the books of the prophets Isaiah, Jeremiah, and Ezekiel, but finds no earlier analogues. (2) He points to traditions in J which are noticeably absent from pre-exilic literature outside the Pentateuch: the meeting with God at Mount Sinai, Moses (with one exception), the patriarchs (with one or two exceptions), the unity of all Israel in her early history. The 'silence' of the other texts is strange if J (and E) had existed since the early monarchy, but is readily explicable if J did not originate until the late pre-exilic period.

21. The consequences of such a view for the history of Israelite religion are considerable. It implies that there was no connected written account of the early history of Israel until the seventh century BCE, and also conversely that the seventh and sixth century BCE made an even greater contribution to the shaping of OT tradition than has been recognized in the past, even more than Perlitt thinks. If one asks, 'What then was the nature of Israelite religion before this?', Schmid's books on wisdom and the cult provide an answer: YHWH was seen above all as the creator of an order in the world, which wisdom sought to understand and the cult sought to maintain, very much like the gods of Israel's neighbours. Israel's specific faith in a God of history was the result of insights of the prophets and the Deuteronomic school. But is Schmid's late date for J correct? It is clearly as valid or invalid as the arguments on which it stands. They need careful examination. Let us look at the two main types:

21.1. The similarity between the call of Moses and, say, the call of Isaiah is undeniable, but it should not be exaggerated. Moses in J is not called to be a prophet in the later sense, but to lead his people out of Egypt, in a manner similar to that by which Gideon in Judg 6 and Saul in 1 Sam 9 were called, older narratives without doubt. In so far as there are real prophetic motifs, these can be attributed either to the old Moses-tradition itself or to the influence of the early prophetic movement, which we know to have been active already in the tenth or ninth century. There is no need to come any later.

21.2. The 'silence' about certain Pentateuchal themes in other pre-exilic literature is remarkable but it really proves too much, for if taken with full seriousness it would imply not just that J was a late composition but that these themes were only invented in the late pre-exilic period, an extremely radical position which Schmid clearly does not wish to take up. And yet if he is ready to conceive that the prophetic and other texts might have failed to mention a tradition which nevertheless existed in oral form, surely it is not appreciably more difficult to conceive of their failing to mention what was written down, in J? Moreover, the silence is not, as Schmid has to recognize, total, at least in some of the cases. The prophet Hosea, for example, clearly refers to a number of events in Israel's early history.

Many of Schmid's arguments are open to criticism along one of these lines, and he has given no compelling reason why J should not have originated in the early monarchy or why it should be dated to the late monarchy or the exilic period. J is after all notably lacking in references to the great powers or the possibility of exile (contrast Deuteronomy).

22. Another scholar who dates the Yahwist very late, in the exilic period, is John Van Seters. In his first book-length study on the subject, *Abraham in History and Tradition* (1975), he did not date all of J so late. In fact he suggested that the Pentateuch had 'grown' through a series of expansions of an original core, and that core consisted of part of the J source. To this was added first E, then D, then the rest of J (the larger part of it in fact) and finally P. Even then, however, he was saying that the J material as a whole only came into being in the exile, shortly before P. In Van Seters' more recent work it is on this stage of composition that he has concentrated. Already in *Abraham* Van Seters was developing a series of arguments for a late date for the Yahwist: they include historical anachronisms, the use of formulae from prophecy and the royal cult, and particularly the prominence given to Abraham as the source of Israel's election. This, he argued, corresponds closely to the view of Deutero-Isaiah (see Isa 41:8 and 51:2), but it is a theme which is not yet emphasized in the late pre-exilic writings of Deuteronomy, Jeremiah, and Ezekiel. It does, of course, reappear in P, which is also exilic.

23. In his more recent books Van Seters has widened the textual base of his studies by looking at the rest of the Pentateuch, at least its non-Priestly sections. An important new stage in his work was *In Search of History* (1983). This actually has very little to say about the Pentateuch—it is mostly about the Deuteronomistic History. But in it Van Seters draws numerous comparisons between Old Testament history-writing and comparable literature from other cultures, and he particularly emphasizes the similarity with ancient Greek historians such as Herodotus, who lived in the fifth century BCE. From these comparisons Van Seters argued for a greater appreciation that the Deuteronomistic History was a literary work whose author was ready to write creatively where his sources did not provide what he needed, and in fact was the beginning, as far as Israel was concerned, of such historical literature. These findings have worked their way into his more recent work on the Pentateuch and strengthened his opinion that in J we are dealing with a highly literate, but also quite late, author. Actual Greek parallels to passages in the Pentateuch have also come to play a more important part in his work, though Near-Eastern ones are still cited.

24. A good example of this work is Van Seters' study of Gen 1–11 (1993; see also *The Life of Moses* (1994)). He notes some parallels of form and substance between the Yahwist's primeval history and Hesiod's *Catalogue of Women*, which is thought to have been written about 550 BCE. He sees this as representative of a 'Western genealogies tradition', which influenced the J author in Genesis about the same time. Some of the parallels are probably not very significant: it is difficult to see, for example, how similarities of form are likely to have been

transmitted independently of content; and different communities could easily have brought their traditions together independently in similar ways. The most impressive parallel concerns Gen 6:1–4: the *Catalogue* is very largely about such divine–human liaisons which produced the 'heroes' or demi-gods of primeval times, and one passage suggests that a natural disaster may have been sent by Zeus to get rid of them (cf. the Flood). Van Seters sees several of the 'origins of civilisation' stories in Gen 2–11 as linked to 6:1–4 and modelled on the 'Western tradition'. In most cases it is possible to say that similar stories may have originated independently. But in the case of Gen 6:1–4 Van Seters may be right: this story is very much the odd one out among the stories in Gen 1–11 and perhaps it does have a distant origin. However, it may not be necessary to look as far as Greece for this: the Ugaritic myths include at least one description of a god having sexual intercourse with human women (Shachar and Shalim, *CTA* 23). A different kind of argument is used by Van Seters to place the composition of Gen 2–3 (J) in the exilic period. He sees these chapters as the end of a development which begins with a Babylonian myth about the creation of a king, dated to the seventh or sixth century: this, he argues, was the basis for Ezekiel's oracle against Tyre, which speaks of a mythical king who was once in the Garden of Eden but was expelled from it (Ezek 28), and Gen 2–3 in turn was a transformation of this oracle to describe the creation and fall of mankind generally. Hence Gen 2–3, and therefore J, would be later than Ezekiel. It remains possible, however, that the relationship between these three texts is a different one: Ezekiel may have combined motifs from a myth about the origins of kingship and Gen 2–3 or something like it. In that case Gen 2–3, and J, would be, as generally thought, earlier than Ezekiel.

25. The new tradition-criticism. But—and this brings us to the final issue that has been raised in the recent debate—was there a J at all? This is the question that has been asked—and answered in the negative—in a book published in 1977 (cf. Rendtorff 1990). In certain respects Rendtorff's arguments and conclusions are similar to those of the redaction critics and of Schmid, and in subsequent discussion they have been able to find quite a lot of common ground with him. For example, Rendtorff also believes that P never existed as a separate document, but should rather be described as a redactional layer or rather a series of redactional layers belonging to a late stage of the Pentateuch's composition. But Rendtorff has arrived at his views by a quite different route and maintains some theses which go far beyond the views of the other scholars.

26. The key to Rendtorff's approach is the high value which he places on tradition criticism. The origins of this method, which seeks to trace the history of the Pentateuchal traditions from their beginning to the stage of the completed Pentateuch, can be found in Gunkel's introduction to his Genesis commentary and it was taken further by von Rad and Noth in their famous works. Now all these scholars regarded tradition criticism as a method which was complementary to and needing to be combined with source criticism, the JEDP analysis or something like it. And in this, according to Rendtorff, they made a serious error: to quote some words of his from an earlier paper, 'It must be said that adherence to the Documentary Hypothesis is an anachronism from the point of view of tradition-criticism.' That is, the two methods are not complementary, they are incompatible with each other. We may note, in passing, that this had been said before, by Ivan Engnell, the Scandinavian scholar, and his closest followers. In Rendtorff's polarization of source and tradition criticism the theses of Engnell have received, in part, a new lease of life.

27. Why does Rendtorff polarize the two methods? Because according to him, they represent the use of diametrically opposed starting-points in the analysis of the text. Source criticism begins from 'the final form of the text' and examines the question of its unity, and seeks to explain its apparent diversity in terms of the combination of parallel 'sources' (such as J, E, and P). Tradition criticism, on the other hand, starts from the smallest originally independent unit, say an individual episode in the story or a law, and seeks to explain how it was combined with other similar units to make a series to make a yet larger whole, and how editorial processes or redaction shaped the units until they reached their present form. So it is not a matter of doing source criticism first and then tradition criticism: you have to choose your starting-point and follow through the analysis until you reach the other end. As it stands this is not a very strong point: tradition criticism too has to start with the present text. The contrast of approaches could be put better by saying that traditional source criticism has been ready to believe that a sequence of narratives

was a unity unless it was proved otherwise; whereas Rendtorff wants to say that prior to the present text narratives were not united unless that can be positively proved. This is not specifically a traditio-critical view: it is noticeable above all in fact in some of the newer revisions of source criticism, specifically in those emanating from the pupils of W. Richter.

28. Quite apart from this methodological point, Rendtorff is in little doubt that source criticism is a bankrupt business. In a chapter of his book entitled 'Criticism of Pentateuchal Criticism' he exposes at length the disagreements of source critics both about individual passages and about the number and nature of the sources they find. There is no consensus, he repeatedly affirms; there is no 'classical documentary theory', but several competing theories, none of which has been able to drive the others from the field. In particular the status of the J document, which according to von Rad gave the Pentateuch its canonical shape, is very doubtful. Is it one document or two (cf. its subdivision by Eissfeldt and Fohrer)? And more generally, what evidence is there of its unity? Here Rendtorff points to the method of elimination which lies so often behind the identification of J passages. First the easily recognizable P sections are eliminated from the existing Pentateuch, to reveal the older sources; then likewise the book of Deuteronomy (D) is removed; then E, marked by its use of Elohim in Genesis; and then what is left is called J. But how do we know that what is left is a unity? To give an analogy: how do we know that the Pentateuch is not like a basket containing many kinds of fruit, from which the apples, bananas, and oranges are removed, to leave—just pears? No, surely a mixture of these with peaches, grapes, strawberries, and so on.

29. It is not of potential disunity in a source-critical sense (i.e. two parallel Yahwist (J) strands, as with Eissfeldt and Fohrer) that Rendtorff is primarily thinking, but rather in a traditio-historical sense: what reason have we for thinking that the residue was a single continuous narrative describing everything from creation to the conquest of the land, rather than a series of smaller-scale stories, one about the patriarchs, one about the Exodus, etc.? In fact Rendtorff believes that it is possible to show that the J material is in this sense definitely not a unity. This he endeavours to do by an examination of the various sections of the Pentateuchal narrative taken one by one: the sections bear a notable resemblance to Noth's themes—patriarchs, Exodus, Sinai, wilderness, and settlement. The primeval history seems to be passed over, but the same approach could be applied to it. Rendtorff's point is that the theological perspective of the editing is not consistent throughout but varies from one section to the next. Comprehensive theological evaluations of the whole history are surprisingly rare, and tend to be concentrated in what look like late passages. In his book Rendtorff did not spell his argument out in full detail for all the sections, but he indicated his method of applying tradition criticism in a very detailed study of the patriarchal narratives. He begins with the observation (which is not new) that the theological texts of the patriarchal stories are chiefly concentrated in the 'promises': passages, that is, where YHWH makes a promise or several promises to Abraham, Isaac, or Jacob. The interrelation of the contents of these promise-passages to one another is extremely complex, and Rendtorff attributes it to a succession of stages of editing of the patriarchal traditions. At any rate it is clear that the promises are the major theological theme of the patriarchal narratives. Now von Rad had seen this and attributed the main body of the promises to the Yahwist, who he supposed inserted them to impress on the Pentateuchal material his theological understanding of Israel's early history: it was a history worked out under the shadow of YHWH's promise. But against this Rendtorff is able to show that this theme virtually vanishes at the end of Genesis, and is missing from JE passages such as Ex 3, which mention the land to which YHWH now says he will lead the Israelites without any hint that this had been promised long ago to their forefathers, time and time again! The conclusion he draws is that the development of the promise theme in Genesis is not the work of a J author who composed or compiled a document extending the whole length of the Pentateuch, but rather the theological enrichment of a story which did not extend beyond the limits of the patriarchal period itself. Only at the time of the Priestly redaction and a further stage of editing related to the Deuter-onomic school is there any sign of the various sections of the Pentateuch being co-ordinated together into a continuous narrative. Prior to this there existed only shorter compositions which circulated separately and were edited separately— Rendtorff seems not to have any suggestion to offer about the social context in which this took place or the purpose that such compositions

might have served, but clearly there are in some cases at least possibilities of an association with cultic festivals.

30. It is not clear whether Rendtorff's particular proposals will be able to withstand detailed criticism. The denial of a unity in J will have to contend not only with von Rad but with the more wide-ranging studies of G. Hölscher and H. Schulte. There are in fact various ways in which scholars might respond to the dilemmas with which Rendtorff has faced us, apart from accepting in full his own reading of the situation. But he has, whatever we may decide, exposed some tensions at the heart of modern critical method which need to be resolved. I do not myself think that tradition criticism is a very secure base from which to attack the literary-critical enterprise. It is a bit like trying to move a piano while standing on a tea-trolley!

31. Since it was first put forward in 1977 this view has been rather neglected. Rendtorff himself quite quickly lost interest in it: he was persuaded by Childs's arguments that attention ought to be focused on the final canonical form of the text—a dramatic change for him—and he became particularly interested in the coherence of the book of Isaiah as a whole. His *Introduction to the Old Testament* (ET 1985) reflects this change of perspective, though it also shows that he retains some interest in older traditions and redaction criticism. A student of Rendtorff's, Erhard Blum, has continued some of his ideas in two large books on the Pentateuch (1984, 1990), but it is noticeable that he too increasingly concentrates not on the earliest stages of the tradition, when the stories of the primeval history, the patriarchs, the Exodus, etc. may have been told separately from one another, but on the stages at which they were already combined together: he investigates what he calls the Deuteronomistic Composition (KD)—which does not include the J portions of Gen 1–11—and the Priestly Composition (KP), which successively amplified the traditions from their particular points of view (cf. John-stone 1990).

J. Review and Assessment. 1. In reviewing these recent developments it should be noted that by different routes quite a lot of scholars are coming to support more or less the same alternative to the older source-critical view. The developments outlined in the last four sections are increasingly merging into what is in effect the same understanding of the origin of the Pentateuch. This holds that:

1. The first major comprehensive Pentateuchal narrative was composed either late in pre-exilic times or in the Babylonian exile (7th or 6th cent. BCE), rather than in the early monarchy. Some prefer to speak of a 'late Yahwist' (Schmid, Van Seters), some of a Deuteronomistic narrative (Johnstone, Blum), but they are largely talking about the same thing and using the same arguments.

2. The Priestly Work never existed as a separate source, but involved the insertion into the older narrative of the specifically Priestly narratives and laws, so as to produce a work very like our present Pentateuch.

In each case the model or overall approach is a 'supplementary' one, that is, the old idea of redactors interweaving extracts from distinct sources, a verse from here and a verse from there, is abandoned and we go right back to the approach that was followed in the first half of the nineteenth century and think of a core which in successive stages was amplified until the present Pentateuch was produced: the major difference being—and it is a very significant one—that then what we call P was (part of) the original core, while now it represents the final stage of the process. An important theological consequence of the new approach is the increased prominence which it gives to the sections of the Pentateuch which contain or are associated with law, namely the Deuteronomistic and Priestly passages. It should be noted that theses 1 and 2 are in fact logically independent. It is possible to accept one of them and not the other, and some scholars have done and still do this, following the Wellhausen approach or something like it on the other issue. Thus Cross accepts 2 but not 1; and Schmid and Blenkinsopp hold 1 but not 2.

2. The supporters of the new views are not having things all their own way. Some difficulties with them have already been mentioned, and some further criticisms of thesis 1 have been made by E. W. Nicholson in a recent paper (see also Nicholson 1998). This thesis also fails, in its strongest form, to do justice to the evidence of Deuteronomy itself. The very setting of Deuteronomy on the eve of the conquest of the promised land presupposes a tradition about Israel's origins; likewise there are many passing allusions to features of that tradition in the text of Deuteronomy which would only have made sense if the hearers of the Deuteronomic preaching had been familiar with a quite detailed account of the Exodus and so on.

As for thesis 2, we have seen that some passages, such as the Flood story, are very difficult for it to accommodate.

3. So what are we to think? Which view will prevail? As far as 1 is concerned, I think we are at a stage when all the emphasis is on late elements of the Pentateuch, and some scholars write as though that is all there is. The arguments for lateness are of varying strength. For myself I am more convinced that the Decalogue is a late addition to the Sinai narrative in Exodus than that the idea of a covenant is a latecomer in Exodus, for example. But more important, I think we shall before long find more work being done again on what we may call for now the 'pre-Deuteronomic Pentateuchal narratives and laws'—their contents, their theology, and their origins. Then the Deuteronomic or late J layer (which may turn out to be 'thinner' than currently thought!) will be seen as more clearly that, rather than seeming to comprise the whole of the non-P part of the Pentateuch. On 2 an interesting mediating position has been put forward by R. E. Friedman (1981). He thinks that at a first stage there were independent P versions of certain parts of the Pentateuch, such as the Flood story; but the major composition of P as a whole took place at a second stage in very much the way Cross proposed, i.e. by supplementation of the older narrative. Where P texts from the first stage had to be worked into the older narrative, they were sometimes interwoven with the older version, as in the case of the Flood story. Blum, working in detail on certain passages, ends up with a partly similar view to this. Maybe it will be necessary to hold some such view to accommodate all the evidence—the case for supplementation has been argued to be particularly strong in relation to the Table of Nations and the plague-story by Van Seters—or maybe it will be better, in view of the coherence of so much of the P material, to retain the idea of an original, once-separate source, and explain the most intractable counter-indications by a further, still later layer of redaction.

4. But there are problems within the literary-critical method itself, arising from the fact that we now feel compelled to treat each unit separately for analysis. While it is quite clear that the Pentateuch is not a literary unity and that analysis can separate out parallel strands at numerous points, it is not so obvious that a rigorous approach to the assembly of the 'bits' leads automatically to the division of the Pentateuch into four or five major sources, such as traditional source criticism proposes. In other

words the model for synthesis (step c.3) need not be a wholly documentary one. About the coherence and original independence of the bulk at least of the P material, it seems to me, there is little doubt, and equally about the separate character and development of Deuteronomy. However it is more difficult to be sure how the residue of the books Genesis–Numbers is to be thought of and Rendtorff's thesis of shorter works may well have a part to play, and equally processes of redaction which did not extend the whole length of the Pentateuch, but concerned only a particular range of the narrative.

5. We may conclude by returning, very briefly, to the question with which we began, 'What is the Pentateuch?', in the light of the modern study of the text which we have just reviewed. Whichever of the approaches that have recently been advocated prevails, or even if things eventually stay very much as they were, we must build into our view of the Pentateuch the fact that it is the product of a long process of tradition. In other words we must recognize that its teaching, while organized into some sort of unity by the various redactors, derives from various periods in the history of Israel within which certain individuals or schools have contributed an especially creative shaping and rethinking of the traditions which they inherited. In varying degrees these individuals or schools deserve the name 'theologians'. To some extent the difficulty of finding a fully satisfactory description for the Pentateuch as a whole is due to the differing emphases of these writers. In a real sense, then, the Pentateuch bears witness to the whole history and life of Israel, and not just to the period which it purports to describe. As a comprehensive description I would suggest the following, which I think can apply to all stages of the composition of the Pentateuch:

'The charter of YHWH's people Israel, which lays down the founding principles of their life in creation, history and law, under the guidance of his word of promise and command.'

REFERENCES

Alt, A. (1966), 'The Origins of Israelite Law', in *Essays on Old Testament History and Religion*, ET (Oxford: Blackwell), 87–132; 1st edn. 1934.

Alter, R. (1981), *The Art of Biblical Narrative* (London: George Allen & Unwin).

Auld, A. G. (1980), *Joshua, Moses and the Land* (Edinburgh: T. & T. Clark).

Barton, J. (1984), *Reading the Old Testament* (London: Darton, Longman & Todd).

Boecker, H.-J. (1980), *Law and the Administration of Justice in the OT and the Ancient Near East*, ET (London: SPCK).

Brueggemann, W., and Wolff, H. W. (1975), *The Vitality of OT Traditions* (Atlanta: John Knox).

Campbell, A. F., and O'Brien, M. A. (1993), *Sources of the Pentateuch: Texts, Introductions, Annotations* (Minneapolis: Fortress).

Carpenter, J. E., and Harford-Battersby, G. (1900), *The Hexateuch According to the Revised Version* (2 vols. (London: Longmans, Green and Co.); vol. ii is a synopsis).

Childs, B. S. (1979), *Introduction to the OT as Scripture* (London: SCM).

Clements, R. E. (1997), *A Century of Old Testament Study* (Guildford: Butterworth).

Clines, D. J. A. (1978), *The Theme of the Pentateuch* (Sheffield: JSOT).

Coats, G. W. (1988), *Moses: Heroic Man, Man of God* (Sheffield: JSOT).

Davies, G. I. (1996), 'The Composition of the Book of Exodus: Reflections on the Theses of E. Blum', in M. Fox *et al.* (eds.), *Texts, Temples and Tradition: A Tribute to Menahem Haran* (Winona Lake, Ind.: Eisenbrauns), 71–85.

Driver, S. R. (1904), *The Book of Genesis*, Westminster Commentaries (London: Methuen).

Emerton, J. A. (1988), 'The Priestly Writer in Genesis', *JTS* NS 39: 381–400.

Friedman, R. E. (1981), *The Exile and Biblical Narrative* (Chico, Calif.: Scholars Press).

Gerstenberger, E. (1965), *Wesen und Herkunft des 'apodiktischen Rechts'*, WMANT 20 (Neukirchen-Vluyn: Neukirchener Verlag).

Habel, N. C. (1971), *Literary Criticism of the OT* (Philadelphia: Fortress).

Haran, M. (1979), *Temples and Temple-Service in Ancient Israel* (Oxford: Oxford University Press).

Jenks, A. W. (1977), *The Elohist and North Israelite Traditions* (Chico, Calif.: Scholars Press).

Johnstone, W. (1998), *Chronicles and Exodus: An Analogy and its Application* (Sheffield: JSOT).

Nicholson, E. W (1973), *Exodus and Sinai in History and Tradition* (Oxford: Blackwell).

——(1986), *God and his People* (Oxford: Oxford University Press).

——(1998), *The Pentateuch in the Twentieth Century: The Legacy of Julius Wellhausen* (Oxford: Clarendon Press).

Noth, M. (1972), *A History of Pentateuchal Traditions*, ET (Englewood Cliffs, NJ: Prentice-Hall), from Germ. orig., *Überlieferungsgeschichte des Pentateuch* (1948).

Otto, E. (1994), *Theologische Ethik des Alten Testament* (Stuttgart: Kohlhammer).

Patrick, D. (1986), *Old Testament Law* (London: SCM).

Rad, G. von (1966), 'The Form-Critical Problem of the Hexateuch' (1938), in his *The Problem of the Hexateuch and Other Essays* (Edinburgh: Oliver & Boyd), 1–78.

Rendtorff, R. (1990), *The Problem of the Process of Transmission in the Pentateuch*, ET (Sheffield: JSOT), from German original, *Das überlieferungsgeschichtliche Problem des Pentateuch*, BZAW 147 (1977).

Skinner, J. (1910), *A Critical and Exegetical Commentary on Genesis*, International Critical Commentary (Edinburgh: T. & T. Clark).

Soggin, J. A. (1989), *Introduction to the Old Testament*, 3rd edn. (London: SCM).

Sonsino, R. (1980), *Motive Clauses in Biblical Law*, SBLDS 45 (Chico, Calif.: Scholars Press).

Stamm, J. J., and Andrew, M. E. (1967), *The Ten Commandments in Recent Research*, SBT 2/2 (London: SCM).

Van Seters, J. (1992), *Prologue to History* (Louisville, Ky.: Westminster/John Knox).

——(1994), *The Life of Moses: The Yahwist as Historian in Exodus–Numbers* (Louisville, Ky.: Westminster/John Knox).

Wellhausen, J. (1885), *Prolegomena to the History of Israel*, ET (Edinburgh: A. & C. Black); from German original, *Geschichte Israels I* (1878).

Westermann, C. (1984), 'The Formation and Theological Meaning of the Primeval Story', in *Genesis 1–11: A Commentary* (Minneapolis: Augsburg), 567–606; German original *Genesis 1–11* (Neukirchen-Vluyn: Neukirchener Verlag, 1974–6).

Wolff, H. W. (1975), 'The Elohistic Fragments in the Pentateuch', in Brueggemann and Wolff (1975), 67–82.

Whybray, R. N. (1987), *The Making of the Pentateuch* (Sheffield: JSOT).

4. Genesis

R. N. WHYBRAY

INTRODUCTION

A. Genesis and the Pentateuch. Genesis forms part of a series of 'historical' books that begin with the creation of the world and end with the destruction of the tiny kingdom of Judah in the sixth century BCE (the final chs. of 2 Kings). The events narrated are all arranged in a single chronological sequence into which the non-narrative material, mainly poems and laws, has been fitted. But this great history was not originally conceived as a single work. It is generally agreed that it consists of two complexes, but the point at which the first ends and the second begins has long been a disputed question. According to ancient tradition the first complex comprises the first five books, ending with Deuteronomy. This is known to the Jews by the name of Torah (or 'the law'), and is the first and most sacred part of the canon of the Hebrew Scriptures. Modern scholars know it as the Pentateuch, a Greek word meaning '(of) five books'. However, its integrity was challenged in the nineteenth century CE, when many scholars held that it is incomplete without Joshua: it is only in Josh that God's promise, made in Genesis, of possession of the land of Canaan is fulfilled (hence the term Hexateuch, *six* books). This hypothesis has few supporters today. In 1948 Martin Noth (ET 1972) also rejected the traditional view but in a contrary sense: the first *four* books constituted a complete work (the Tetrateuch). Deuteronomy, though later joined with these to form the Pentateuch, belonged to a second and distinct work, the Deuteronomistic History, comprising Deuteronomy, Joshua, Judges, Samuel, and Kings. Noth's theory has been widely accepted. It may perhaps seem that these questions are irrelevant to a study of Genesis; but this is not so. Genesis, although it has its own distinctive character—it is the only book in the Pentateuch that is not dominated by the figure of Moses—is intimately linked with the books that follow, and can only be fully understood as part of a more extended history. It is essentially a book of promise, a preface to all that follows in the history of Israel, having specific links to many events narrated in those books. It establishes the identity of the nation of Israel and of its God. In particular, it is a necessary prelude to the great events associated with the Exodus from Egypt, which is the foundation of Jewish history and faith. At the same time it presents the reader with the God who is creator of the world but also a God who cares for his human creatures and reveals his nature especially in his protection and guidance of those whom he chose to be his special people.

B. Literary Genre. It is important for an understanding of Genesis (and of the Pentateuch as a wₙₒle) to see it as a literary work and to attempt to define its literary genre. This involves an appreciation of the nature of ancient, pre-scientific, historiography, of which the most notable examples are to be found in the work of certain early Greek historians of the sixth century BCE. The aim of these historians was to write accounts of the origins, genealogical descent, and history of the notable families of their own day, tracing them back to a remote, heroic age: see Van Seters (1983: 8–54; 1992: 24–38). In their accounts of past ages they did not distinguish between myth, legend, and what we now call 'historical facts'. It was not their primary purpose to establish the exact truth of the events that they described, but rather to raise in their readers a consciousness of their own identity and a feeling that they were citizens of a great and noble city or race. These historians made full use of extant traditions about the past, but they were also *creators* of tradition: where extant traditions were lacking or scanty, they did not hesitate to fill them out with details, and even entire stories, supplied from their own imaginations. This kind of imaginative writing has analogies with that of the Israelite historians; but the purposes of the latter were somewhat different. They were certainly concerned to create—or, perhaps, to restore—a sense of national identity in their readers; but their intention was far from triumphalist: the principal human characters were not heroes in the fullest sense. For them it is always God who has the principal role; the human characters are represented as foolish and frequently sinful creatures who time and time again frustrate God's good intentions towards them.

C. Types of Material. The character and intention of Genesis as a completed book cannot be deduced from the wide miscellany of materials which constitute its sources. Gunkel (1901) (see Gunkel 1964 for ET of the Introduction to his commentary) identified many of the sources and demonstrated their nature. Particularly in chs. 12–36 he identified many *Sagen*—that is, brief, originally independent, folk-tales—which had been strung together only at a relatively late stage, eventually taking shape as accounts of the lives of Abraham, Isaac, and Jacob. The somewhat different characters of chs. 1–11, which narrate cosmic and universal events (often classified as 'myths'—an ambiguous term) and of the story of Joseph in chs. 37–50, a single, homogeneous narrative not formed by the combination of *Sagen*, has

long been recognized. All this material has been pieced together and provided with a continuous narrative thread and a chronological sequence by a skilful editor and compiler, who by his selection and arrangement of material and his own original contributions converted it into an expression of his own view of history and theology. With regard to the *Sagen* used by this compiler, Gunkel held that much of this material had previously been transmitted in oral form over many generations and so may be seen as preserving, even though in garbled form, genuine reminiscences of the persons and events described, but this has recently been questioned: see Whybray (1987: 133–219).

D. Composition. About the process or processes by which the diverse material was combined to form a single literary work there is at present no consensus of opinion. The Documentary Hypothesis (see INTROD.PENT B), which was the dominant theory for about a century, envisaged an interweaving of comprehensive 'horizontal' written sources (in Genesis, J, E, and P); but this view has met strong opposition during the last twenty years; and none of the alternative theories that have been proposed has yet found general acceptance. One thorough investigation of the composition of the patriarchal stories (Blum 1984), which envisages a gradual process of composition in which the traditions about each of the patriarchs were gradually and independently built up before their combination into larger complexes, has considerable plausibility; on the other hand, the notion of a fragment hypothesis according to which there was no lengthy process of growth but a single act of composition in which a mass of material was collated by a single author, as in the case of the early Greek historians cited above, has undergone something of a revival: see Whybray (1987: 221–42). In this commentary the Documentary Hypothesis is referred to only occasionally. Obvious differences of point of view implied in the material employed have been noted; but no attempt has been made to define or to date these. References to the 'author', 'editor' etc., are to those responsible for the final shaping of the book.

E. The Date of Genesis. Nothing in the book directly indicates the time when it reached its final shape. However, many passages reflect episodes and situations of post-patriarchal times: the tradition of a nation comprising twelve tribes (49:16, 28); the Exodus from

Egypt (15:13–14); the future possession of Canaan and the areas occupied by the various tribes (15:17–20; 17:8; 28:4); the predominance of the tribe of Judah (49:10) and of the Joseph tribes (especially Ephraim (48:17–20)); and the Davidic monarchy (49:10). There are also anachronisms such as the references to the 'land of the Philistines' (21:32, 34), whose arrival in Canaan was roughly contemporary with that of the Israelites, and to the Chaldeans (11:28, 31; 15:7), a people of southern Mesopotamia whose names do not appear in historical records before the time of the neo-Assyrian empire (from the 8th cent. BCE) and who were otherwise unknown to the OT before the sixth century BCE. Other features of the book—for example the constantly reiterated theme of the promise of possession of the land of Canaan—are perhaps best understood as particularly relevant to a time when the nation had been dispossessed from the land—that is, either the Babylonian exile during the sixth century BCE or the ensuing period when the Jewish community living in and around Jerusalem were once more, like the patriarchs of Genesis, aliens in the land, needing encouragement to hope that God would enable them to throw off the yoke of Persian domination and would restore to them the fullness of his blessing as the rightful owners of the land which he had promised long ago to them.

F. Themes. I. The primeval history (Gen 1–11) heralds some of the main themes of the book. It defines Israel's place in the world of nations and links the human figures of the remote past with Abraham and his descendants by a series of genealogies. It also functions as a universal history of beginnings. It afforded the author the opportunity to state his belief that there is only one, supreme God and that he created the world with all its inhabitants. It is concerned with the nature of this God and with the nature of his human creatures. This universal history taught the Israelite readers a moral lesson as well as a theology: human beings are both foolish and prone to sinful rebellion against God, arrogant and ambitious, seeking to achieve divine status for themselves and capable of murderous intentions towards one another. It warned about the consequences of such behaviour: God, who at the beginning had approved his created world as good, determined to obliterate the human race when it became corrupted; but he mercifully refrained from carrying out this intention: he punished, but did not destroy. So the first

man and woman were banished from the garden but allowed to live outside it; the first murderer also was banished, but his life was preserved; the human race, despite its total corruption, was given a second chance in the persons of Noah and his family; the builders of the Tower of Babel were scattered and divided, but survived and peopled the world. The picture of humanity painted in these chapters is dark but realistic; however, it is lightened by the corresponding theme of divine forbearance which, in the context of the book as a whole, foreshadows a more hopeful destiny for a human race that will be blessed in Abraham.

2. The two main themes of chs. 12–36 are God's choice of Abraham and his descendants out of the entire human race and the promises that he made to them. The particularity of this choice is striking: it is seen not only in the initial selection of Abraham but also in a series of subsequent choices: not Ishmael but Isaac, not Esau but Jacob are chosen. (The theme is pursued further in the succeeding Joseph story: Joseph, Jacob's eleventh son, is chosen to be the saviour of his family, and even in the next generation Ephraim is preferred before Manasseh.) The promises in their fullest form comprise divine blessing, guidance and protection, wealth and political power, and the possession of the land of Canaan as a permanent home. But there is also an important counter-theme: that of the perils into which the recipients of the promises (and their wives) constantly fall, sometimes through their own fault and sometimes at God's instigation (Gen 22). It is this counter-theme that gives liveliness and excitement to the narratives; indeed, without it there would be no story to tell. The failure of the promise of the land to materialize within the timespan of the book gives these narratives a forward-looking character: the possession of the land is clearly the goal to which they aspire. There are, of course, a number of subsidiary themes, corresponding to the variety of the material. There is throughout a strong emphasis on the inscrutability of God's purposes.

3. The story of Joseph (chs. 37–50) continues that of the previous section, but has its own independent character and its own themes. Except at the very end of the book the divine promises are not specifically mentioned in these chapters, though the theme of the endangered heirs continues to be prominent: at different times both Joseph and his family are placed in peril. The Egyptian setting is a major feature of the Joseph story and is described in some detail, partly to give it a plausible local colour but mainly in order to enhance the impression of Joseph's eminent position in Egypt. Joseph's character is portrayed with consummate skill. This final part of the book leaves the readers with hopes of a splendid future. The final verses specifically foretell the Exodus from Egypt which will lead at last to the possession of the promised land.

COMMENTARY

A History of Origins (chs. 1–11)

These chapters may be regarded as a prologue to Genesis, and indeed to the whole Pentateuch. Beginning as they do with the activity of God even before the universe came into existence (Gen 1:1–2), they clearly cannot be based on any record of what actually occurred; and the fact that in them a number of persons are reported as having lived preternaturally long lives is sufficient to show that the world depicted here is different even from that of the later chapters of the book. These stories do not constitute a connected sequence; they have been linked together only in a very artificial way by a series of genealogies (Gen 4:17–22; 5:1–32; 10:1–32; 11:10–32). They are universal stories, depicting not human beings as we know them but giants or heroes in something like the fairytale sense of those words. What is being conveyed is how the authors or collectors of the stories imagined that it might all have begun. However, as we shall see, these stories were intended to convey a much more profound meaning than that.

Many peoples have at an early stage of their development possessed a fund of stories about the origin of the world and the earliest history of the human race; and many of the stories in Gen 1–11 have a family likeness to origin-stories current in the Near-Eastern milieu to which ancient Israel belonged (cf. ANET 3–155). These Israelite versions, however, are unique in that they are monotheistic: all the divine actions that they depict are attributed to a single deity, and there is no mention of other gods. The term 'myth' is often applied to them; but since there is no agreement about the meaning of that term it is probably best avoided.

It is possible that the final author or compiler of these chapters has left an indication of their structure by his use of the word tôlĕdôt, especially in the phrase 'These are the tôlĕdôt of . . .' (2:4; 6:9; 10:1; 11:10, 27; cf. also 5:1). However, this phrase, which also occurs at intervals in the

later chapters of the book, can hardly be adequate as a structural marker since it is used with different meanings, e.g. genealogy or list of descendants (6:9; 10:1) and story or history (2:4; 37:1). One way of viewing the purpose and structure of chs. 1–11 is to see them as presenting a picture of the growing power of sin in the world, together with a parallel picture of a 'hidden growth of grace' (von Rad 1966a: 64–5). This view has some plausibility as regards chs. 3–9. If this is so, however, the story of the Tower of Babel (11:1–9) surely stands outside the pattern. There, as also in ch. 3, it appears to be God's concern for his own status rather than his grace that is to the fore. It may be best to regard this story as an appendix to chs. 1–9, or as a negative foil to the story of Abraham that begins at the end of ch. 11.

Why does the Pentateuch preface its history of Israel's ancestors with these universal stories? It is of interest to note that the origin-stories of other nations (see Van Seters 1983) show a similar pattern: many of them also begin with mythical tales and then proceed gradually to the more historical. The aim of such works, apart from a wish to satisfy the readers' natural curiosity about 'how it all began', was to create or strengthen their sense of national or ethnic identity, especially at critical times when for specific reasons this was threatened. In order to foster such a sense it was thought necessary to account for the nation's place in the world; and, since the human race was thought to have had a single origin, to explain how the various peoples had come into existence. In Gen 1–11 these aims come to the fore in ch. 10, which was clearly intended to be a 'map' of all the peoples of the world, and in 11:1–9, which accounts for their failure to remain united. At this point the history of Israel's ancestors could begin.

But beyond these motives Gen 1–11 was designed to reflect certain distinctive Israelite (Yahwistic) articles of faith. Not the least of these was monotheism. Despite the inclusion of the phrases 'Let us make man in our own image' (1:26) and 'like one of us' (3:22), on which see below, this monotheistic stance is quite striking and sometimes even polemical—that is, anti-polytheistic—especially in ch. 1. The conflict-tradition of Mesopotamia, according to which the creator-god had had to fight and kill a hostile monster before he could create the world, although traces of it are to be found elsewhere in the OT (e.g. Ps 74:13–14; Isa 51:9), is entirely absent here: the 'great sea monsters' (tannînîm, 1:21) are simply listed together with

God's other creatures. Similarly the sun, moon, and other heavenly bodies, which in the Near-Eastern religious systems are powerful deities coexisting with the creator-god, are here a part of God's creation and are entirely subservient to him, being assigned by him their proper functions (1:14–18). Equally distinctive of Israelite religion is the setting aside by God of the seventh day, the day on which he rested from his work of creation, to be observed as a day of rest—presumably by the whole created world—in the institution of the Sabbath (2:1–3).

Some scholars have interpreted these chapters as reflecting the experiences of the Babylonian exile or the early post-exilic period. Thus the themes of punishment for sin, especially banishment from God's presence and/or dispersal or destruction (3:23–4; 4:12, 16; 6–8; 11:4, 9), have been taken as symbolic of Israel's richly deserved banishment from the land of Canaan, while the signs of divine grace and forgiveness, especially God's acceptance of Noah's sacrifice and the covenant which he made with him (8:20–9:17) would suggest to the exilic or post-exilic reader that God had even now not cast off his people but was a God of infinite patience and forgiveness who would rescue Israel from its folly and its guilt as he had done for humanity in ancient times.

Some of these stories also betray an interest in aetiology: that is, in seeking the origin of various phenomena of universal human experience which appear to defy rational explanation. These aetiologies are of many kinds. One of the most important ones concerns the reason for human mortality, a common theme in both Near-Eastern and classical literature that sometimes took the form of narratives in which human beings attempted to wrest immortality from the gods but failed; this is alluded to in Gen 3:22—which appears to imply that mortality is inherent in mankind's status as creature— and in the mysterious incident of 6:1–3. The nature of the relationship between man and woman is discussed in 2:18, which explains why both sexes are necessary to a complete humanity, and in 2:23–4, which explains the attraction between the sexes and the forming of permanent relationships between them as due to God's providence. In ch. 3, however, the less ideal realities of the relationship are attributed to disobedience to God's command, in which both partners are implicated.

There is also an aetiology of work here. Work in itself is not regarded as a punishment: rather, it is a natural (male) activity (2:15); but—it is implied—it is an agreeable one. The cursing of the ground and the consequent harshness of agricultural labour (3:17–19) are the result of disobedience. The final line of 3:19 ('You are dust, and to dust you shall return'), possibly a common saying, does not imply that human mortality is the result of disobedience.

Another matter that evidently called for explanation was the wearing of clothing. The feeling of shame at appearing naked before others (cf. 9:20–7) and the universal custom of wearing clothes are explained as a consequence of the eating of the forbidden fruit (3:7–12, 21): previously (2:25), nakeness had not been shameful. Other aetiologies in these chapters include the reason for the human dislike of snakes and for the ability of snakes to move without legs (3:14–15), the reason for the rainbow (9:12–17), and the origin of the sabbath.

It is generally agreed that the stories in Gen 1–11 are not a pure invention of the final compiler: however much he may have adapted them for his own purpose, he was using material current in his own time. On the nature and date of this material, however, there is at present no agreement. Arguments have recently been advanced which suggest that, at least in their present form, these chapters cannot be older than the sixth century BCE. For example, the Chaldeans, referred to in 11:28, a verse assigned by the followers of the Documentary Hypothesis to the oldest source J, did not become significant on the international scene until about that time, while the garden of Eden is nowhere mentioned in OT texts before the time of the exilic Isaiah (Deutero-Isaiah, Isa 51:3) and Ezekiel (Ezek 28:13; 36:35). Similarly Abraham (Abram 11:26–30) appears to have been unknown in the pre-exilic period: he is never mentioned by the pre-exilic prophets, and his name occurs only in two OT passages which may be pre-exilic but are probably not (1 Kings 18:36; Ps 47:9). This fact is, of course, significant also for the dating of the story of Abraham in chs. 12–25. Finally it is remarkable that there is no extant ancient Near-Eastern text that in any way covers the same ground as Gen 1–11, and no evidence that any other people compiled a comparable narrative before the Graeco-Roman period.

(1:1–2:4a) The Creation of the World This creation story is only one of many current in the ancient Near East; there are, for example, several extant Egyptian ones in which the creation of the world is attributed to different gods, and the creator-god is not necessarily the principal god. This multiplicity is due to the existence of different local traditions. In the OT also, where there is only one God, we find several quite distinct creation traditions. In addition to Gen 1 there is a different account in Gen 2, and another version is reflected especially in Ps 74:13–14 and Isa 51:9, in which the creation of the world appears to have followed a conflict in which YHWH defeated and killed a sea monster or monsters. Other somewhat different versions are found in Prov 8:22–31, in parts of the book of Job, and elsewhere.

The creation story in Gen 1:1–2:4 has long been thought to have particular affinities with the Babylonian *Enuma Elish* (*ANET* 60–72); but a glance at the latter shows that the relationship is at most a very remote one. Apart from the fact that the Genesis story is monotheistic, the most crucial difference between the two accounts is that *Enuma Elish* belongs to the category of the conflict tradition, which is entirely absent from Gen 1. In the former, the god Marduk first summons the other deities and, after killing the sea monster Tiamat, creates heaven and earth by splitting Tiamat's body into two. (The commonly repeated notion that the word 'the deep'—*tĕhôm*, in 1:2—is a pale reminiscence of Tiamat cannot be sustained.) There is no trace of a conflict here: God is alone, and he is supreme.

This account contains no explicit statement about God's *purpose* in creating the world; but this purpose is clearly implied in the great emphasis that is placed on the position of mankind in God's plan: the creation of mankind, the last of God's creative acts, is evidently the climax of the whole account, and receives the greatest attention (1:26–30). The creatures created on the previous days—light, day and night, dry land, heavenly bodies, plants and animals—are all by implication provided for mankind's use and convenience; human beings are given the plants for food, and power over the animals. Above all they are created in God's image and likeness (1:26–7). Whatever may be the precise meaning of that phrase—this question has been endlessly debated (see below)—it sets human beings apart from all the other creatures and puts them in a unique relationship with God himself.

A further clue to God's intention when he created the world is to be found in the successive statements made at the conclusion of each act of creation, that 'God saw that it was good' (1:4, 10, 12, 18, 21, 25), culminating in the final comprehensive statement that he 'saw everything that he had made, and, indeed, it was

very good' (1:31). This is the craftsman's assessment of his own work; and it says something about his intention as well as about his artistry. A competently crafted artefact implies a good intention. The word 'good' (*tôb*) here, however, refers more directly to the *usefulness* of the world—presumably primarily its usefulness to mankind. It does not necessarily have an ethical connotation: it is not mankind that is said to be 'good', but God's work as craftsman. The author was well aware of the subsequent catastrophic introduction of evil into the world.

In its cosmology—that is, its understanding of the structure and different parts of the universe—this account of the creation conforms to that generally current in the ancient Near East. (In some OT passages this cosmology is described in more detail.) The pre-existent watery waste (1:1–2) was divided into two by the creation of a solid dome or vault (the sky, 1:6–8), so that there was water both above and below it. The lower mass of water was then confined to a limited area, the sea, revealing the dry land, which God called 'the earth' (1:9–10). (According to Gen 7:11 the sky had 'windows' which when opened allowed the rain to fall.) The heavenly bodies, sun, moon, and stars, moved across the vault of the sky, giving light and following a prescribed programme (1:14–18).

A characteristic feature of this account of creation is its precise and meticulous style. It frequently repeats the same phraseology, listing the various acts of creation with the dryness of a catalogue, and possesses nothing of the imaginative or dramatic skill characteristic of chs. 2–3. Yet, as has long been recognized, there remain a number of variations or inconsistencies of detail, which suggests that two or more accounts have been combined. In particular, the creative acts are introduced in different ways. While in some cases God creates simply by speaking ('And God said ... '), in others we are told that he performed certain actions: he made, separated, named, blessed, placed. A second anomalous feature is that although the entire work of creation was carried out in six days (presumably to conform to the concept of six days of creation concluding with a Sabbath rest on the seventh day), there are in fact eight creative acts: on the third day and again on the sixth (1:9–13, 24–31), *two* acts of creation are performed. It is not possible, however, to reconstruct the earlier accounts whose existence is thus implied.

The sentence with which ch. 1 begins (1:1–2) has been translated in several ways (see NRSV marg.). The older English versions have 'In the beginning God created...'. Some other features of these verses call for comment. The use of the word 'God' (*ʾĕlōhîm*) rather than YHWH (2:4*b*–3:24 mainly uses 'the LORD God'—*YHWH* (*ʾĕlōhîm*) is found elsewhere in Genesis and has been taken to indicate the use of different sources. The word rendered by 'created' (*bārāʾ*) is a rare and probably late term confined almost entirely in the OT to Gen 1–6, where it occurs 9 times, and Isa 40–66; it is used exclusively of the creative activity of God. Elsewhere in the OT that activity is denoted by words meaning 'to form' or 'to make', which are also used of human activity.

1:2 refers to the situation before God's creative action began. There is no question here of a *creatio ex nihilo*, a 'creation out of nothing'. The earth (*hāʾ ʾāreṣ*) already existed, but it was a 'formless void' (*tōhû wābōhû*)—not a kind of non-existence but something empty and formless, without light and covered by the water of the deep (*tĕhôm*). There are echoes here of the Near-Eastern cosmologies. The word *rûaḥ*, rendered by 'wind' in NRSV, can also mean 'spirit' (see NRSV marg.). Whichever is the correct interpretation, NRSV's 'swept' is a participle, denoting a continuous action; it should perhaps be rendered 'was hovering'.

In 1:3 as in some later verses God creates by means of a command. His words are presumably addressed to the 'formless void' of 1:2. The creation of light before that of the sun and moon (1:14–18) has led to the suggestion that this feature of the account is derived from an earlier, somewhat different tradition. God's separation of light from darkness and his naming them (1:4–5), like his other acts of separating and naming (1:6, 8, 10, 14, 18), are the acts of a sovereign who determines the destinies of his subordinates.

In 1:11, 12, 21, 24, 25 the phrase 'of every kind' might be better rendered by '(each) according to its species'. The reference to signs and seasons and days and years in the description of the heavenly bodies in 1:14 suggests the establishment of the calendar with particular reference to the determination of the dates of the sacred festivals. When the account moves on to the creation of the animal kingdom, first the water animals and birds (1:20–3) and then the land animals (1:24–5), these are distinguished from all that had been previously created as being 'living creatures' (*nepeš [ha] ḥayyâ*, 1:20, 21, 24, 30)—clearly a higher status than that of the plants. They receive God's blessing (1:22, 28).

Unlike the plants which are to serve as food for both human beings and animals (1:29, 30) it is significantly not said of them that they may be killed and eaten. This is a vegetarian regime.

The meaning of the statement that mankind was created in God's image (*ṣelem*) and likeness (*dĕmût*) (1:26, 27) has always been a matter of discussion, as also has been the use of the plural form ('Let *us* make', 'in *our* image', 1:26, although in 1:27 the singular form 'in *his* image' is used). The most probable explanation of the second point is that the plural is used to denote the court of heavenly beings who exist to do God's bidding. The terms 'image' and 'likeness' are probably not to be differentiated: the double phrase is simply for emphasis. It clearly defines human beings as resembling God in a way that is not the case with the animals (cf. 1:28 and Ps 8:3–8). The nature of this resemblance is not apparent, however, and hypotheses abound. Since God is often represented elsewhere in the OT as having bodily organs—hands, feet, eyes, etc.—and the word *ṣelem* is elsewhere used of images of gods, it has been supposed that the passage refers to a resemblance to God's external form. It is more probable, however, that some less material resemblance is intended: that human beings, in distinction from the animals, possess the unique capacity to communicate meaningfully with God, or—particularly with reference to the animals—are God's representatives or vicegerents on earth.

The ordinance that mankind is to rule over the animal kingdom (1:26, 28), like the statement that the sun and moon are to rule over the day and the night (1:16), determines mankind's function in the world. It does not imply exploitation, for food or for any other purpose; rather, it is a consequence of the gift to mankind of the image of God. Mankind is, as it were, a manager or supervisor of the world of living creatures. The blessing, accompanied by the command to 'be fruitful and multiply' (1:28) is, as with the animals (1:22), a guarantee that life is to continue.

God's rest (*šābat*, 2:2) on the seventh day implies the sabbath (*šabbāt*—the word itself does not occur here—which is thereby 'hallowed' or made holy (2:3; cf. Ex 20:8). The same reason for the observance of the sabbath is given in the Decalogue (Ex 20:11).

(2:4*b*–3:24) This narrative, which could stand by itself as an independent story, has taken up themes and motifs quite different from those employed in 1:1–2:4*a*. It was once generally believed to be older and more primitive in its theology than the preceding chapter (J as contrasted with P); but more recently this view has been challenged. Blenkinsopp (1992: 63, 65), for example, suggests that it may have been 'generated by reflection on the creation account in Genesis 1' and may be seen as 'standing in a wisdom tradition which indulged in "philosophizing by means of myth" '. Undoubtedly some of the motifs employed are considerably older than the author's own time; but the telling of tales for edifying or didactic purposes is more a characteristic of a late stage of civilization than an early one. There is evidence, too, that some elements of the vocabulary employed here are late rather than early.

This is a story about two people, a man and a woman, and what happened to them. Although in the context they are necessarily pictured as the *first* man and woman, they are symbols as well as ancestors of the human race: behind his statements that 'This is what happened' the author is saying 'This is how human beings behave, and these are the consequences that follow.' The eating of the fruit is not a single event of the remote past, but something that is repeated again and again in human history. The traditional view that it was the first sin that caused all later generations to be born in 'original sin' is not borne out by this story, although it has the aetiological purpose of explaining the present conditions of human existence. It teaches that God's intention for human beings is wholly good, but that they can be led astray by subtle temptations; and that, while disobedience to God, which is self-assertion, may bring greater self-knowledge, it leads to disaster: the intimate relationship with God is broken. Life then becomes harsh and unpleasant; however, God does not entirely abandon his creatures but makes special provisions for their preservation. An Israel that had suffered devastation and exile from its land could hardly fail to get the message.

It is hardly correct to call ch. 2 a second and alternative creation story. The reference to the creation of the world only occupies 2:4b–6, and is expressed in a subordinate clause: 'In the day when...'. It is introduced in order to provide a setting for the main story. It belongs to a different tradition from that of ch. 1 with its Mesopotamian perspective—that of Palestine, where *rain* (2:5) is vitally important for the existence of plant and animal life. But other motifs may have Mesopotamian or other origins. In 2:7 the author chose to depict the creation of the first

(male) human in terms of formation from the soil (perhaps rather, clay). This is a tradition also found among modern preliterate peoples (Westermann 1984: 204). In Egyptian mythology the god Khnum fashioned living creatures on a potter's wheel (*ANET* 368, 431, 441), while in the Babylonian tradition the wild man Enkidu was fashioned from clay (*ANET* 74).

Eden (2:8—the word means 'delight') as the garden of God occurs again in Ezek 28:13; 31:9; Joel 2:3, and Eden by itself in a few passages in Ezekiel and in Isaiah (51:3), always as a place of ideal fertility and beauty. (It also occurs in Gen 4:16 as a place-name.) In Ezek 28:13–16 there is an allusion to a myth of an expulsion from the garden, but this differs markedly from Gen 2–3.

The two named trees in the garden—the tree of the knowledge of good and evil (2:9, 17, and also, it must be presumed, the 'tree that is in the middle of the garden', 3:3; cf. 3:11, 12) and the tree of life (2:9; 3:22) constitute a puzzle in that the latter does not appear in the main story but only in the two verses mentioned above. The problem is usually, and probably rightly, solved by supposing that the author combined two variant traditions in order to introduce the theme of life and death, and was not concerned with consistency of detail. Both trees have connections with wisdom themes. In the book of Proverbs knowledge is a synonymous with wisdom; and in Prov 3:18 it is stated that wisdom is 'a tree of life to those who lay hold of her'. This might lead one to suppose that the two trees are the same, but it is clear from 2:9 and 3:22 that this is not so. So knowledge and (eternal) life are *not* synonymous in this story.

2:15 resumes the main narrative after what appears to be a digression. The identity of the first two of the four rivers of 2:10–14 is not known. 2:16–17 contain the first instance of a divine prohibition, on which the plot of ch. 3 depends. The naming of the animals by the man in 2:19–20 establishes their distinct characteristics and confirms the man's rule over them. The creation of woman from the man's rib is a detail that no doubt derives from an older tradition. In 2:23 the word 'woman' (ʾiššâ) is stated—erroneously—to be derived from 'man' (ʾîš). 2:24a is an aetiology explaining the origin of the relation between the sexes; it appears, however, to run counter to actual practice. 2:25b probably expresses a view that was generally held about primitive man. It also points ahead to 3:8–11: shame is one of the consequences of sin.

The serpent (3:1) is neither a supernatural enemy threatening God's creation from outside nor some kind of inner voice within the woman urging her to disobedience. It is specifically stated that it was one of God's creatures, but that it was craftier (ʿārûm) than all the others. (There is a play on words here: ʿārôm (2:25) means 'naked'.) ʿārûm is an ambiguous word: it can also denote 'wisdom' in a positive sense. But here it is the wrong kind of wisdom possessed by the serpent that initiates mankind's fall into disaster. Snakes played a significant part in the mythologies and religious practices of the ancient Near East, as objects both of fear and worship. The question of the origin of the serpent's wickedness is not raised here. The phenomenon of the speaking snake (cf. Balaam's ass, Num 22:28–30) is a folkloric one.

In its conversation with the woman (3:1b–5) the serpent asserts that God's threat of immediate death for eating the fruit of the tree of knowledge (2:17) is a false one. The acquisition of the knowledge of good and evil (that is, of wisdom) will lead rather to the human pair becoming 'like God'. There is truth in what the serpent says: eating the fruit does not result in immediate death, and although the man and woman do not become wholly like God since they still lack immortality, God fears that if they also eat the fruit of the tree of life they will obtain full divine status (3:22). But the serpent fails to say what will be their actual fate.

The various punishments imposed by God on the guilty (3:14–19) all have aetiological bases: serpents have no legs and are thought to 'eat dust', and bite human beings but are killed by them; women are attached to their husbands, suffer pain in childbirth, and also suffer from their husbands' domination (contrast 'helper' and 'partner' in 2:18). The final clause of 3:19, probably a common saying, adds point to the first half of that verse, which refers back to 2:7. The derivation of the name Eve (ḥawwâ, 3:20) which occurs in the OT only here and in 4:1, is unknown. There is a play on words here: ḥawwâ echoes ḥay, 'living (person)'. This verse seems to have no connection with the previous verses, though it is separated from the notice of Eve's becoming a mother (4:1) by only a few verses.

The somewhat ludicrous picture in 3:21 of God's acting as seamstress for the man and his wife is an indication of his continuing concern for mankind now that he has abandoned his original intention to impose the death sentence (2:17) on them. 3:22–4 is not to be regarded as the imposition of an additional punishment: God has already made it clear that mankind's way of life must now change radically and for the worse.

The reason for the expulsion from the garden is specifically stated in 3:22: it is to prevent mankind from eating the fruit of the tree of life and so obtaining eternal life. The theme echoes Mesopotamian myths about mankind's failure to attain immortality (see ANET 89–96, 101–3). There is no implication here or anywhere else in chs. 2–3 that mankind was originally intended to be immortal.

In 3:24 God takes elaborate precautions to ensure that the man and woman do not re-enter the garden. The cherubim (cf. Ezek 10; Ps 18:10) are supernatural beings closely associated with God who carry out his commands, here as guardians; the flaming and turning sword reflects a Mesopotamian tradition.

(4:1–16) In its present context this story is a continuation of the previous chapter, as is shown by the mention of the name Eve. However, the use of a different source is indicated by the fact that God is now called not by the appellation 'the LORD God' (YHWH ʾĕlōhîm) but by the single name YHWH. In v. 1 there is a play on words: Eve called her firstborn Cain (qayin) because she had 'acquired' (qānâ) him from YHWH.

This is a story about Cain: his brother Abel's role is entirely passive. The account of Cain's murder of his brother Abel follows the pattern of ch. 3. This motif of fratricide is found in other ancient myths, for example in the Egyptian story of the murder of Osiris by his brother Seth and, in Roman mythology, that of Romulus's murder of Remus. The similarity of motif, however, does not help to elucidate the point of Gen 4:1–16. Some scholars have seen this in the difference between the brothers' occupations (v. 2) and in YHWH's acceptance of Abel's meat offering while he rejected Cain's fruit offering (vv. 3–5), which was the cause of Cain's anger. But no explanation is given in the text of God's preference, and it is not probable that the story, at any rate in its present form, reflects an age-old rivalry between pastoralists and farmers.

The story is of course significant in that this is the earliest instance in Genesis of death and also of violence committed by one human being against another. Although there is no suggestion in the text that the sin of disobedience committed by the first human pair is here seen as the cause of the universal corruption of human nature, the fact that the first murder immediately follows it can hardly be without significance. There is in these chapters a progression in evil which culminates in the statements in 6:5, 11 that mankind has become wholly corrupt.

In his reply to God's questioning (v. 9) Cain intensifies his sin by a lie: he pretends that he does not know where Abel is. He also declines responsibility for his brother—a denial of family solidarity that would be anathema to Israelite readers. The blood of Abel is understood as crying out from the ground (v. 10), demanding vengeance. God's answer to this cry is a curse (vv. 11, 12). Cain is condemned to have no permanent place to dwell: he will henceforth be a wanderer or fugitive on the earth (v. 14), subject to the vengeance of anyone who may meet him (v. 13). (The implication that there are other human beings on the earth shows that the story is not in fact a continuation of ch. 2–3; cf. the statement in 4:17 that Cain later married a wife.) But in v. 15 God mitigates his punishment, cursing in turn Cain's potential murderers, and puts him under his protection. The nature of the mark (ʾôt) that God placed on him as a sign that he was not to be killed is not explained in the text, and the various explanations that have been offered by scholars are purely speculative. The 'land of Nod (nôd)' to which Cain took himself (v. 16) should not be understood as a geographical location: the word probably means 'aimless wandering'.

(4:17–26) The genealogy in vv. 17–22 is in two parts: vv. 17–18 list six generations (making seven in all if Adam, v. 1, is included), while vv. 19–22 are of a different, collateral, type, listing the children of Lamech by his two wives. The latter passage has something of the character of an aetiology of the origin of various aspects of civilized life; the origin of cities is interestingly placed very early (v. 17). This propensity to satisfy a demand for historical information about origins by naming the inventors of existing aspects of life is not peculiar to Israel: we may compare the Sumerian 'seven sages' who taught mankind the pursuits of civilization, and the Greek myth of Prometheus, who gave mankind the gift of fire.

The song of Lamech (vv. 23–4) is an elaboration of the preceding genealogy. It may originally have been a boasting song; but in its present context its prediction of dramatically increased violence marks a new stage in the progress of human wickedness. vv. 25–6 appear to be a fragment of a separate genealogy (of Seth) from that of Cain; it is given in a more complete form in ch. 5. v. 25 refers back to 4:1. The name Seth is connected by the author with the verb šît, 'to put, procure' (NRSV 'appointed'). The statement at the end of v. 26 that mankind (ʾĕnôs—the word is identical with the name Enosh) began 'at that time' to invoke the name of YHWH appears to contradict Ex 6:2–3, where it is stated that the worship of YHWH began with Moses (cf. also Ex 3:13–15). The attempt to reconcile v. 26 with the Exodus passages by arguing that the former only refers to divine worship in general is hardly convincing. That there is a discrepancy here should be admitted. The proponents of the Documentary Hypothesis regarded the discrepancy as providing strong evidence of their source theory.

(5:1–32) The genealogy of Seth of which this chapter consists, which traces the history of mankind from the beginning to the birth of Noah, is linked to ch. 1 by the résumé in vv. 1–2. This is a somewhat different tradition from that of the genealogy of Cain in ch. 4, though it has some of the names in common. In this chapter Lamech becomes the father of Noah (v. 29). Enoch appears in both lists, but in v. 22 there is an additional note about his character and fate. He 'walked with God', as is also said of Noah in 6:9; and, presumably on account of this exceptional piety, he was mysteriously taken away by God and disappeared from the earth. (Cf. the similar translation of Elijah, 2 Kings 2:10–11.) (The late Jewish books of Enoch used this information to develop elaborate speculations about Enoch's adventures after his translation.)

There is a partial parallel between this list and the Mesopotamian King Lists, especially the old Babylonian (Sumerian) King List (ANET 265–6) which ascribes even more fantastically long reigns to kings who lived both before and after the Flood. However, these lists differ in important respects from Gen 5, and there is no reason to suppose that the latter was modelled on the former. But they do share a common notion of a succession of distant forebears; and they also have in common the idea that these human beings of the unimaginably remote past were of a quite different order of vitality and durability from the puny men and women of the present age.

v. 29 refers back to 3:17. The name Noah (nōaḥ) is improbably associated in the Hebrew text with the root n-ḥ-m, 'to comfort' (NRSV 'bring us relief'); the Greek translation seems to presuppose a form of the root n-w-ḥ, which would be closer to 'Noah' and would mean 'give rest'. This verse is evidently intended to introduce the story of the Flood, though this summary of Noah's achievements, whichever version is accepted, is not particularly appropriate.

(6:1–4) It must be admitted that the meaning and purpose of this story remain uncertain after a long history of attempts to interpret it. Every verse presents difficulties. v. 1 speaks of a great increase of human population—a motif of Mesopotamian origin-stories, where this constituted a threat to the gods; but as far as one can see this is not central to the biblical story. Especially problematic is the interpretation of the phrase 'the sons of God' (bĕnê-hāʾ ĕlōhîm), which can also be rendered by 'the sons of the gods', in v. 2. These are mentioned again in Job 1:6; 2:1 and—with slightly different wording (bĕnê ʾēlîm)—in Ps 29:1; 89:6. In those passages they are heavenly beings subordinate to YHWH and members of his council. In the texts from Ras Shamra (Ugarit) the sons of the gods are themselves gods and members of the pantheon of which the high god El is the head. The traditional view of the sons of God here in v. 2 is that they are angels; but the implication of vv. 1–4 as a whole is that their activities do not meet with YHWH's approval. There are other ancient myths describing marriages between gods and human women, and also well-known myths about a rebellion in heaven. The story here may have been derived from an otherwise unknown Canaanite myth.

In v. 3 YHWH is represented as speaking to himself, expressing his determination to limit the span of human life to 120 years. Here we have once more the motif of a divine prohibition of human immortality, which might have resulted from the union of divine beings with human women. God's spirit (rûaḥ) here is probably equivalent to the 'breath of life' of 2:7. v. 4 appears to be a series of comments on the story, identifying the nature of the children born of the divine–human union. They were the Nephilim, interpreted in Num 13:33 as giants. In the second half of the verse they are identified with the famous 'heroes (gibbōrîm) of old'. The reason why the author chose to include this strange story with its polytheistic overtones may be that it served as a further mark of the corruption of human nature and thus as an appropriate prelude to the story of the Flood in chs. 6–9.

(6:5–8:22) The Story of the Flood Stories of a great flood sent in primeval times to destroy mankind are so common to many peoples in different parts of the world between whom no kind of historical contact seems possible that the theme seems almost to be a universal feature of the human imagination. The flood story of Genesis is a clear example of a type that was characteristic of the Mesopotamian world. The two extant literary accounts that most closely resemble it are Atrahasis (ET in Lambert and Millard 1969) and Tablet XI of the Epic of Gilgamesh (ANET 93–5). The Babylonian text translated in ANET was, according to Lambert and Millard, largely derived from Atrahasis, although the latter in its fragmentary state lacks some of the details preserved in the former such as the sending out of birds to discover whether the waters had receded. But unlike Gilgamesh, Atrahasis resembles Genesis in that it contains an account of the creation of mankind from clay before proceeding to the story of the Flood.

As was pointed out long ago, there are a number of details in the Genesis story such as the chronology and the numbers of animals taken into the ark that are mutually contradictory. Attempts to reconcile these, however ingenious, can hardly be convincing. It is clear that more than one version of the story have been combined. But the text as it stands can no longer be separated into two complete versions: there is, for example, only one account of God's detailed instructions to Noah about the construction and dimensions of the ark (6:14–16), without which there could be no story. The author, who may have known several versions from which he could choose, has spliced two of them together without concerning himself about total consistency—a method already noted above with regard to chs. 2–3.

The story of the Flood in Genesis is the climax of a sequence that begins with the creation of the world and ends, after almost total disaster for mankind, with the renewal of mankind through Noah and his descendants. Despite similarities in some of the details of the account of the Flood itself, no such sequence is to be found in either Gilgamesh or Atrahasis. In the former, the Flood is only an episode recounted by the 'Babylonian Noah', one Utnapishtim; no information is given about the future of the survivors. In Atrahasis as in Genesis the Flood is part of a connected story, but a quite different one which involves a quarrel among the gods, while the fate of the survivors is barely sketched in the fragmented manuscripts that have been preserved. The Genesis story on the other hand has in the hands of the author acquired a purposeful theological meaning in the context of the book's presentation of human nature and of the *one* God's treatment of it which combines mercy and grace with severity.

vv. 5–12 give the reason for the bringing of the Flood: human wickedness has now become total and universal (Noah being the sole exception, 6:9); and God, faced with this apparently complete failure of his hopes, now regrets his decision to create human beings (6:6) and determines on their destruction together with all other living creatures (6:7). This striking anthropomorphism (i.e. the representation of God as fallible and reacting to a situation as with human weakness) is reminiscent of 3:22. Such a view of God runs counter to the belief expressed elsewhere in the OT (e.g. Num 23:19; 1 Sam 15:29), but is not unparalleled (cf. e.g. Ex 32:14; Am 7:3, 6), though in those instances God's 'repentance' is favourable rather than unfavourable to those concerned. More analogous to the present passage is God's threat in Ex 32:10 to destroy his rebellious people and to start again with Moses.

The statement that humanity had become totally corrupt is repeated in 6:11–12. Since there is a change in the appellation of God here—from YHWH to *'ĕlōhîm*—this verse has been thought to come from a different source (P as opposed to J); but in the present context the repetition is appropriate since it immediately follows the statement about the uniquely righteous Noah in 6:8–9. In 6:12, 13 'all flesh' evidently includes the animals, though some of these were to be preserved by being taken into the ark together with Noah and his family. The word 'ark' (*tēbâ*, 6:14) occurs in the OT only here and in the story of the infant Moses (Ex 2:3, 5). It is probably derived from an Egyptian word meaning a chest or box. The usual word for 'ship' has been avoided. The use of the word *tēbâ* may point to an earlier version of the story. The identity of the word rendered by 'cypress' (*gōper*, older English versions 'gopher') is uncertain. The impression given of the ark is that of a flat-bottomed box-like construction about 450 ft. long, 75 ft. broad and 45 ft. deep (6:15) with three decks, a roof or window (the meaning of *ṣōhar* is uncertain), and a door (6:16; 'finish it to a cubit above' is incomprehensible).

At 6:18 is the first mention of a covenant (*běrît*) in the book. This promise to Noah is reaffirmed in 9:11–17. Since Noah and his family were to be the only human survivors, it is by implication a covenant made by God with the whole future human race; it points forward also, however, to the specific covenant to be made later with the people of Israel. It is an obligation that God imposes on himself; its contents are unspecified, but it clearly implies divine protection and blessing, conditional only on Noah's complete obedience to God's instructions in 6:18–21, which he carried out (6:22).

In its specification of the numbers of each species of animal to be taken into the ark 6:19–20 differs from that of 7:2–3, which is clearly from a different source. In 7:2–3 a distinction is made between clean and unclean animals. This refers to the lists of clean and unclean animals in Lev 11:3–31 and Deut 14:4–20: it is an example of a tendency to carry back the origin of fundamental institutions (in this case, Mosaic laws) to primeval times. The main reason for the command to take seven rather than two pairs of the clean species into the ark was that some of the clean animals were to be reserved to be used, for the first time, as animal sacrifices (8:20).

The discrepancies in the statements about the duration of the Flood in 7:4–8:14, which are due to the combination of different sources, are difficult to disentangle, although the main outline of the narrative is clear. The immediate cause of the Flood is a dual one: the bursting forth of the 'fountains (i.e. springs) of the great deep (*tĕhôm rabbâ*)' below the earth (cf. 1:2) and the opening of the 'windows of the heavens' (7:11; cf. Isa 24:18; Mal 3:10) to let the torrential rain fall unremittingly for forty days and nights (7:12). This signalled the undoing of his creation by God's command: chaos had come again.

Ararat (8:4) is mentioned again in 2 Kings 19:37; Isa 37:38; Jer 51:27. It was known to the Assyrians as Urartu, and was an independent kingdom in the early first millennium BCE until its destruction in the sixth century BCE. The area corresponds roughly to that of modern Armenia. The *Epic of Gilgamesh* also records the landing of the ark on a mountain. The sending out of a raven and a dove to test the subsidence of the waters (8:6–12) also corresponds to a similar incident in *Gilgamesh*. The first animal sacrifice on the first altar (8:20) is an act of thanksgiving, not an attempt to propitiate God, who had already (6:8, 18) shown his acceptance of Noah. But this sacrifice inaugurates a new era in which the slaughter of animals was permitted (9:3–4). The anthropomorphical statement that God 'smelled the pleasing odour', unique in the OT, is no doubt a reminiscence of an earlier version of the story: it is a way of saying that he approved of the sacrifice. In *Gilgamesh* at this point in the story the gods 'smelled the savour' and 'crowded like flies about the sacrificer'. In determining never again to destroy mankind God now appears to accept that the evil tendency of the human heart is innate and ineradicable. The negative decision of 8:21 is then matched by a positive one: the orderly alternations of day and night and of the seasons will now resume and will not again be interrupted. 'As long as the earth endures' makes it clear, however, that it will not continue for ever but will have an end.

(**9:1–17**) In vv. 1–7 God, addressing Noah and his sons, inaugurates the new era and the renewed humanity. There are strong indications here that this is regarded as a new creation. The passage begins and ends with a blessing (cf. 1:28) and there is a repetition of the command to be fruitful and multiply and fill the earth and to rule over the animal world; but there are significant differences from ch. 1. The animals are now to *fear* their rulers (v. 2), and may be killed for food: things are not after all as idyllic as at the beginning. v. 4 prescribes the manner of their slaughter, once more carrying back the institution of a Mosaic law to the primeval period (cf. 7:2–3); this is the kosher law prohibiting the consumption of an animal's blood (cf. Lev 7:26–7 and other passages). vv. 5–6 forbid homicide: mankind, in contrast to the animals, was created in the image of God. The story of the Flood concludes in vv. 8–17 on a hopeful note with God's reaffirmation of the covenant that he had made with Noah (6:18), which now includes all living creatures as well as Noah's descendants. He reveals his previous decision (cf. 8:21–2) never again to destroy the earth, and makes the rainbow—literally a 'bow in the clouds'—a 'sign' of the covenant, a reminder both to himself and to mankind—another example of aetiology.

(**9:18–29**) The story of Noah's drunkenness can hardly be seen as related to that of the Flood. It appears to be a resumption of the history of human generations in chs. 4 and 5 with its theme of human sin and corruption. vv. 18–19, however, have a connection with the Flood story in their reference to the departure of Noah's sons from the ark. The notice in v. 18 that Ham was the father of Canaan is a link with vv. 20–7; an attempt to account for the curse on Canaan in vv. 25–7.

The statement in v. 20 that Noah was the inventor of viticulture is an aetiology comparable

with 4:20–2, but with a story attached to   point of the story in vv. 20–7 is not that Noah committed a sin in becoming drunk, but that Ham sinned in seeing his father when he was naked, an act which called forth a curse on Canaan, Ham's son. There is nothing in the text to support the view advanced by some scholars that Ham's sin was in fact either an act of homosexuality or the incestuous rape of his mother (Lev 18:6–19, which speaks of 'uncovering' nakedness, is not speaking of the same thing). Nakedness was shameful (3:7–11), and Ham humiliated his father by not decently covering him. In vv. 25–7 it is already presupposed that Noah's sons are to become the ancestors of different nations. The incongruity that it is Canaan and not his father who is cursed (vv. 25, 27) is connected with Israel's traditional hatred of the Canaanites, who are seen as destined to become slaves; but attempts to identify the circumstances in which these verses were written have not been successful. The name Japheth is here aetiologically associated with a rare Hebrew verb meaning 'to enlarge'.

(**10:1–32**) This chapter, often known as the 'table of the nations', is an attempt, on the basis of the presupposition that all humanity is descended from Noah's three sons, to name all the nations of the world and to state from which genealogical branch they are derived. It appears to be quite unique: no comparable ancient texts exist. Certain stylistic variations and inconsistencies in the lists of names have led the source critics to postulate a combination of the sources J and P, despite the fact that there is only one reference to God, where he is referred to by his name YHWH (v. 9). Many but by no means all the names are readily identifiable. The descendants of Japhet, for example, include the Medes (Madai), the Ionian Greeks (Javan), possibly the Cypriots (Kittim), and Rhodians (if the emendation of Rodanim from the Dodanim of the Hebrew text is correct). The list of Ham's descendants, which begins with Nubia (Cush), Egypt, and possibly Lybia (Put), also contains Canaan, a country which would in modern terminology be ranked as Semite (i.e. Shemite). This is true also of Babylon (Babel) and Assyria. The descendants of Shem, who is called 'the father of all the sons of Eber', that is, Hebrews, are listed last as more immediately relevant to the readers. There is some inconsistency here: Assyria, listed under Ham in v. 11, is given as a descendant of Shem in v. 22. Other well-attested peoples listed as descendants of Shem include Elam and Aram (the Arameans); but most of the remaining names in these verses are unknown or not certainly identifiable, as also is the territory mentioned in v. 30. By thus peopling the world the author has prepared for Abraham's world, which was already divided into nations. The cause of these divisions is given in 11:1–9.

(**11:1–9**) This is a compact and self-contained narrative. It contains an aetiological element in that it purports to explain why the human population, which had originally shared the same language, came to be divided by the development of many languages which prevented their mutual comprehension and so hindered co-operation; and also how they came to be dispersed throughout the world (though this is already implied in the command to 'fill the earth', 9:1, and its fulfilment in 9:19). But aetiology is not the main point of the story, which is another account (cf. ch. 3) of human ambition to rise above the human condition, the threat that this posed to God's supremacy, and the action taken by God to frustrate this. The story is located in the land of Shinar, that is, Mesopotamia (cf. 10:10); the city which they began to build, perhaps including the tower (v. 4) is identified in v. 9 with Babylon. There is nothing specifically in the text to indicate that the story was inspired by one of the Mesopotamian ziggurats: it is true that the Esagil in Babylon was supposed to link heaven and earth; but it was a completed building, not one left unfinished as was the city in v. 8. There is no extant Mesopotamian story comparable with this, though some of its motifs are found in a Sumerian epic. The anonymous builders ('they') are represented as the whole human population ('the whole earth', v. 1). This means that 'make a name for ourselves' implies a universal ambition to attain to a greatness superior to their present status, which must mean an infringement of God's absolute supremacy. God's decision to come down from heaven to see what his puny creatures are trying to do ('Let us go down', v. 7) is expressed in the same plural terms as are 1:26 and 3:22. In v. 9 the word 'Babel' is seen as related to the verb *bālal*, 'to mix, confuse'.

(**11:10–32**) This genealogy spans the generations from Shem to Abram (Abraham). It concentrates on succession from father to son, and deals with individuals: thus it is intended to be seen as the family history of a single individual, Abraham. It forms a link between the primeval world and that of the patriarchs, Abraham,

Isaac, and Jacob, the 'fathers' of Israel. vv. 27–32, the genealogy of Terah, Abraham's father, in fact function as the beginning of the story of Abraham, and introduce principal characters in that story: Abraham, his wife Sarai (Sarah), and his brother Lot. It briefly refers to Sarai's barrenness and a migration of the family from Ur of the Chaldeans, probably in southern Mesopotamia (but 'Chaldeans' is an anachronism), with the intention of settling in Canaan but instead getting no further than Haran, a city of northern Mesopotamia.

Abraham and his Family (chs. 12–36)

The world of Israel's ancestors, Abraham, Isaac, and Jacob, and their families, is different from that of chs. 1–11: here we are dealing with 'real' individuals and their life stories. Yet it is still not *our* world. Frequent attempts have been made to find historical situations into which these patriarchs can be fitted, but they have all failed to convince (see Thompson 1974). Gunkel, in his famous commentary on Genesis (1901), put forward a view which was long accepted: that most of these stories were independent short folk-tales (*Sagen*) which circulated by word of mouth for a very long time before they were combined into longer complexes and eventually set down in writing. That they have an oral origin and are not to be seen as accounts of the lives of historical personages remains a common opinion; but that they had a long history before their incorporation into the present work is regarded by some recent scholars as by no means certain (see Whybray 1987). The possibility that these stories may not be much older than the time of the final redactor of the Pentateuch is supported by the fact that the pre-exilic parts of the OT with one possible exception (Hos 12:3–4, 12) show no knowledge of Abraham, Isaac, and Jacob *as individuals* or of events connected with them.

The true purpose of this part of Genesis was theological rather than historical in the modern sense of the latter term. Like some other parts of the OT which must be regarded as historical fiction (e.g. Job, Ruth, Jonah, Esther, and Dan 1–6), its purpose is to teach a religious lesson. It is generally admitted that the three patriarchs were originally unrelated to one another and that their stories have been combined in order to create a family story whose main theme is set out at the very start (Gen 12:1–3), where Abraham is commanded by God to leave the country where he has been residing and to migrate to another country whose identity will later be revealed to him, where he will become the ancestor of a great nation, especially blessed and in turn conferring his blessing on other peoples. This theme of God's promise dominates these chapters: the promise is repeated on several more occasions to Abraham himself (15:4–7, 18–21; 17:4–8; 22:17–18) and then to Isaac (26:2–5, 24) and Jacob (35:11–12). The promise of future blessing implies material success; and it is made clear that God will guide the fortunes of the family. But the continuity of that family depends on the production of an heir in each succeeding generation; and the difficulties and dangers attending this provide the dramatic content of many incidents in the story.

The promise of the possession of the land, which proved to be the land of Canaan, was not in fact fulfilled in the course of the book of Genesis; but by the end of the book there had been a positive development. The twelve sons of Jacob, who were to be the ancestors of the twelve tribes of Israel, had been born, and had received their blessings (ch. 49). So the nation of Israel now existed in embryo. Their migration to Egypt during a famine, in the final section of the book, may be considered on the one hand as one of the many causes of delay of the fulfilment of the promise; but it is also to be seen as the springboard for the miracle at the Sea in the book of Exodus and for the subsequent series of events related in the rest of the Pentateuch which led eventually to the possession of the land. The readers were thus presented in these chapters with a picture of a God who was totally in control of events and who had marvellously created their nation and preserved it from the beginning, one whose promises they knew to have been ultimately fulfilled; but they were also made aware, through the account of the wanderings and vicissitudes of their ancestors, of the precariousness of the life of faith.

Basically these chapters fall into three sections, each concerned with the life of one of the three patriarchs, Abraham, Isaac, and Jacob. However, since in their present form they are a combination of separate parts to form the history of a single family, the three stories have been made to interlock so as to produce a continuous family saga. Thus Abraham's death is recorded in 25:8, but the birth of his heir Isaac had taken place long before (21:2); similarly the birth of Isaac's son Jacob is noted in 25:25–6, but Isaac's death only in 35:29. Jacob's own death (noted in 49:33) did not occur until the completion of his son Joseph's extraordinary success story (Joseph's birth is recorded in 30:23). (On

the story of the life of Joseph, chs. 37–50, which belongs to a different literary genre from the previous stories, see below.) Meanwhile the births of all Jacob's twelve sons had taken place, recorded at intervals between 29:32 and 35:18. Recently attempts have been made to reconstruct the stages of the process by which the patriarchal stories have been composed (especially Blum 1984), but these remain hypothetical.

The Story of Abraham (chs. 12–25)

(12:1–3) The story begins with a divine command and a dual promise. First, God promises to make Abraham into a great nation; this of course implies that Abraham himself will have a male heir and that the succeeding generations will all have numerous progeny, and also that the future nation will enjoy great political power (the word *gôy*, 'nation', suggests a fully organized group, and the 'great name' in this context implies international pre-eminence or superiority). The second promise is really implied by the first: it is a promise of divine blessing, which will ultimately be extended to all peoples. There is no specific promise of possession of the land here; this appears for the first time in 12:7 as a promise not to Abraham personally but to his descendants. A number of recent scholars, regarding 12:1–3 as representing the earliest stage of the Abraham story, have maintained that the promise of the land belongs to a later stage of redaction. This may be so; but the initial command to Abraham in v. 1 to travel to a land later to be identified cannot be without significance, especially to the original readers, who would naturally identify that land with the land of Canaan, which they knew had in fact come into the possession of Abraham's descendants. The fact that God had arbitrarily uprooted Abraham and exiled him from his original country would, however, remind them of the precariousness of their own residential status. In Gen 23:4 Abraham himself spoke of his being 'a stranger and an alien' in the land. In 12:1–3, then, the basic promises to the patriarchs are all already presented.

(12:4–9) takes Abraham on his journey south from Haran to Canaan, which God now identifies (v. 7) as the land to which he was to go (v. 1). His unquestioning obedience to God's command is seen by NT writers (Heb 11:8–10; cf. Rom 4; Gal 3) as an outstanding act of faith to be imitated. The reference in v. 4 to Lot (cf. 11:27,

31) as Abraham's travelling companion sets the stage for the story in 13:5–13. The oak of Moreh near Shechem (v. 6) is represented as an already sacred tree at which oracles were given (*mōreh* means 'one who teaches'); but it was God's appearance to Abraham that led him to build an altar there and—presumably—to offer sacrifice (cf. Noah's sacrifice, 8:20). On the invocation of the name of YHWH at the second altar that he built near Bethel (v. 8) see at 4:26 above. In travelling to the Negeb (the semi-desert area to the south of Judah) he reached the southern border of Canaan, having traversed the land completely from north to south. It is significant that it is not stated that he entered any of the ancient cities of Canaan; instead, he lived in tents as a travelling stranger.

(**12:10–20**) is one of a group of three stories in Genesis with the same theme. In 20:1–18, as here, Abraham passes Sarah off as his sister during a temporary residence in Gerar, with similar consequences, and again in 26:6–11 Isaac, driven by famine (26:1), as was Abraham in ch. 12, seeks refuge, again, in Gerar. It is generally recognized that these are three variants of one and the same story, which was defined by Gunkel as a folk-tale; but there is no agreement today about their relationship to one another or the reasons why despite their basic similarities they differ substantially in details. Attempts to discover which of the variants is the oldest have resulted in different conclusions.

Migrations of groups of people at various times across the eastern frontier of Egypt to seek more favourable conditions of life are well attested historically (see e.g. *ANET* 251). In the OT the migration of Jacob and his sons to Egypt (Gen 47) is another example of this. 12:10–20 is the first instance of many in which the fulfilment of the promise to Abraham is endangered. Not only is the departure from Canaan a move away from the promised land; even more serious is the threat to the marriage of Abraham and Sarah which is still childless, and so to the promise of progeny. Faced with a choice between death from starvation and the potential danger entailed in migrating to an alien and unknown country, Abraham chooses the latter course; but, fearful for his own safety, he sacrifices his wife to a life in Pharaoh's harem, which would also make the promise null and void. In contrast to his shabby conduct, which also involves telling a lie, the behaviour of Pharaoh, whose unsuspecting action is rewarded by God

with 'great plagues' (presumably soon cured; a lacuna in the story has been suspected between vv. 17 and 18) is exemplary and even generous (v. 20). Abraham is left speechless before Pharaoh's justified reproach. The story is told without the making of an overt moral judgement; but the contrast between the obedient Abraham of 12:1–9 and the Abraham of this story is unmistakable. The story considered by itself is clearly not favourable to Abraham; but in its present context it has become an illustration of the theme of the promise constantly endangered but never annulled. Paradoxically, Abraham emerges from this incident not only unscathed but rewarded with great wealth (vv. 16, 20). It is important to note that it is not said of Abraham as it is of Noah (6:9) that he was morally perfect. The point of the story in its present context is not his moral character but that he is the bearer of God's promise to him and his descendants. The threefold repetition of what is basically the same story cannot be adequately accounted for in terms of a dovetailing of written continuous strands that were originally independent of one another. The reason for it is of a literary nature. Repetition to create particular effects is a common literary device in narrative; and this is eminently the case in Genesis (see Alter (1981), especially on type-scenes, 47–62). Here each version of the story marks a crucial point in the total narrative. 12:10–20 stands at its head, immediately following the initial promise to Abraham of numerous descendants (12:2–3), and shows how God safeguards that promise, keeping both the prospective parents from harm in a dangerous situation. 20:1–18 occurs immediately before the crucial account of the birth of Isaac (21:1–2) which marks the first stage in the fulfilment of that promise. 26:6–11 is similarly closely connected with the birth of Isaac's son Jacob, the next heir (25:21–4) and is immediately preceded in 26:3–5 by a further reiteration of that promise. These repeated stories thus help to provide a structure for the patriarchal stories.

(**13:1–18**) This chapter and ch. 14, which are mainly concerned with relations between Lot and Abraham, are a kind of interlude or digression: Lot is not a leading character in the main patriarchal story; after the events of ch. 19 he disappears from it, though at the end of that chapter it is noted that he became the ancestor of the Moabites and Ammonites whose later dealings with Israel have a part to play in other OT books (19:37–8). Continuity with the main plot is, however, maintained in the incident which determines Abraham's future area of residence well away from the corruption and temptations of Sodom and Gomorrah, whose evil inhabitants (v. 13) were later to suffer destruction at the hands of YHWH (v. 10). The final verses of ch. 13 revert to the principal theme of the promise.

In v. 2 Abraham's wealth is again stressed, though he continued to live an itinerant life. The quarrel between Abraham's and Lot's herdsmen (vv. 5–7) is to be understood as due to inadequate living space for the herds in a land which was occupied by other, settled, peoples. (The identity of the Perizzites, v. 7, who are mentioned fairly frequently in Genesis, is uncertain.) Abraham's offer to settle the dispute, which was not of his making or of Lot's, by giving Lot the choice of territory is explained as due to a desire to preserve amicable relations with his kinsman (lit. brother), while Lot's disastrous choice is determined by the attraction of the fertility of the Jordan plain, which is compared to that of Egypt and of the garden of Eden. The passage ends with a more detailed reaffirmation of the promise to Abraham of numerous descendants and of the *whole* land, with the additional assurance that it will remain in their possession for ever (v. 15).

(14:1–24) This chapter is an unusual one in several respects. It is self-contained and appears to be unrelated to the surrounding chapters except for the names of Abraham and Lot and of Sodom and Gomorrah. The documentary critics with some exceptions were unable to connect it with any of their main sources (J, E, and P), and concluded that it is a quite independent episode. It is the only passage in which the otherwise entirely peaceable Abraham is represented as taking part in military activity. It begins in the style of a historical narrative; yet none of the nine kings mentioned (vv. 1–2) has been identified, nor is any war such as is described here known to have occurred. It puts Abraham in a very good light both as an outstanding warrior who comes to the aid of members of his family, and as forgoing the spoils of war. Its purpose thus seems to have been to glorify Abraham as a great and powerful hero of international stature. It has been argued that it is not a single unitary composition; the Melchizedek episode (vv. 18–20) has been thought by some scholars to be a later addition to the original story. There is no agreement about its date: while some believe that it is a reworking

of old traditions, its heroic character and also perhaps its style may point to a post-exilic origin.

The peoples named in vv. 5–6 are legendary groups who inhabited the Transjordan; the Valley of Siddim is unknown. The reference in v. 13 to Abraham as 'the Hebrew' conveys the impression that he has not been previously introduced to the reader. The word 'Hebrew' is used in the OT only by foreigners speaking about the Israelites and not by Israelites about themselves (see Jon 1:9). In Genesis it occurs elsewhere only in the story of Joseph when he is spoken of by Egyptians or addresses Egyptians. The tiny size of Abraham's military force, which consists entirely of members of his own household (v. 14) enhances his heroic stature.

Melchizedek, in v. 18, provides a royal banquet to welcome Abraham on his return after his victory. It is strange that he should suddenly appear in the story, having taken no part in the preceding events. He is a mysterious and enigmatic figure. His name probably means '(The god) Melek is righteousness' and closely resembles that of a pre-Israelite king of Jerusalem, Adoni-zedek ('The Lord is righteousness'), who was defeated and killed by Joshua (Josh 10). It is not clear whether Salem is intended to be identified with Jerusalem, as Jerusalem is never so-called in any of the non-biblical texts that refer to (pre-Israelite) Jerusalem. In the OT, only in Ps 76:2 is Salem equated with Zion, God's dwelling-place. In Gen 14:18 Melchizedek is described as a priest-king serving El Elyon (*'ēl elyôn*, 'God Most High') who is stated to be the creator of heaven and earth. In Ps 110:4, the only other OT passage where his name occurs, Melchizedek is taken to be a precursor of the later priest-kings of Israel. The author of Gen 14 clearly intended the reader to identify El Elyon with YHWH as is the case with the titles El Olam (*'ēl ʿôlām*, 'the Everlasting God', 21:33), El Shaddai ('God Almighty', (*'ēl šadday*, 17:1), etc. But in fact El was the high god of the Canaanite pantheon, who is not infrequently identified with YHWH in the OT, and Elyon sometimes occurs in the texts from Ugarit as an epithet of El. The phrase 'maker of heaven and earth' is virtually identical with what is said of El in those texts. In v. 22 El Elyon is specifically identified with YHWH in the solemn oath that Abraham swears to forgo his share of the spoils of victory.

(15:1–21) There has been much scholarly discussion about the composition of this chapter. It has proved resistant to a division into sources along the lines of the Documentary Hypothesis, and attempts to demonstrate that a relatively short piece has been massively supplemented by a late hand have also failed to be entirely convincing. Some recent scholars have reverted to something like the pre-critical position that it is mainly or wholly the work of a single author. But all agree that it is in two parts: vv. 1–6 and 7–21. Both contain further divine revelations to Abraham reiterating the earlier promises, but they differ considerably in the mode of revelation.

vv. 1–6 are introduced in the same way as a prophetical oracle, but take the form of a vision—the word 'vision' (*maḥāzeh*) is very rare and probably indicates a late date. The call not to be afraid is characteristic of Deutero-Isaiah (Isa 40–55). This is what is often called an 'oracle of salvation', and it sounds the note of encouragement. But it becomes clear that Abraham has begun to doubt whether God will carry out his promise to give him an heir of his body: he has been obliged to appoint his own servant Eleazar as his heir. YHWH reiterates his original promise and shows him the stars as a demonstration of how numerous his descendants will be. This direct vision of God convinces him: he believes, that is, trusts, God's word. The author's statement that YHWH 'reckoned it to him as righteousness', which forms the climax of the episode, has rightly been seen as one of the most significant in the whole of Scripture (see Gal 3:7–9; Jas 2:23; cf. Heb 11:8–10) and has been taken, together with other instances of Abraham's faith, particularly his readiness to leave Haran and his willingness to sacrifice his son Isaac (ch. 22) as the foundation of the doctrine of justification by faith, even though its precise meaning has been disputed. That it is an expression of Abraham's readiness to trust God's promise cannot be doubted.

vv. 7–21, like 1–6, are probably a creation of the author with no older tradition behind it. They are also concerned with the promise, but now specifically with the promise of the land rather than with the question of progeny. Like vv. 1–6, they present Abraham as hesitant to believe the promise and demanding to know how it is to be fulfilled. YHWH satisfies him by means of a solemn but curious ritual which Abraham is commanded to carry out. This ritual does not conform precisely with anything known from elsewhere, although the cutting of the animals into two is reminiscent of some covenant rituals. The animals specified are those used in sacrifice in the laws of the OT; but the purpose of the ritual is indicated by the solemn oath-like statement to Abraham by YHWH in vv. 13–16 and his making of a covenant with him (vv. 18–21). Its awesome accompaniments—the 'deep sleep' (*tardēmâ*, a rare word also used of Adam when Eve was created) and the terrifying darkness—add to the solemnity of the event. The smoking fire pot and the flaming torch (v. 17) represent YHWH's passing between the rows of animals to symbolize his binding himself to keep the covenant. vv. 13–16 are a 'prophecy after the event' foretelling the captivity in Egypt and the Exodus; its purpose is to account for the long gap between promise and fulfilment. The 400 years of v. 13 and the 'fourth generation' of v. 16 can hardly be reconciled; it has been suggested that v. 16, which foreshadows the Israelites' conquest of the Amorites (Canaanites), is a later revision of the prophecy. The Amorites are said not to be sufficiently wicked as yet to deserve this fate. The promise of vv. 18–21, which contains a comprehensive list of the peoples believed to have preceded Israel in the land, describes the boundaries of the land in very grand terms—from the borders of Egypt to the Euphrates. In fact the borders of the state of Israel were probably never as extensive (1 Kings 4:21 is hardly a sober historical statement). The covenant with Abraham (v. 18), who here represents the future nation of Israel, is a free, unconditional promise, unlike the covenant of Sinai.

(**16:1–16**) Like the stories in chs. 12, 20, and 26 (see above on 12:10–20), the story of Hagar in this chapter has a counterpart (21:9–21). These are clearly variants of an older folk-tale; and once again their placement in the ongoing story of Abraham is significant. Both are further examples of the threat to the fulfilment of the promise that Abraham will have a legitimate heir by his wife Sarah and of the setting aside of that threat (cf. 15:2–4). Ch. 16 immediately precedes the repetition of the promise guaranteeing Abraham's progeny and their destiny (17:1–8); 21:9–21 immediately follows the birth of Isaac (21:1–8) and confirms that it is he who is to be the heir. But the motif of God's protection of the rejected Ishmael which is common to both versions of the story is an indication that before the story was inserted into the Abraham narrative and placed in its two respective positions it was the figure of Hagar who was the centre of interest and the principal character. There is a somewhat similar story of acrimonious relations between a barren wife and her rival in 1 Sam 1:2–8.

The practice alluded to in vv. 2–3 was a common and accepted one in the ancient Near East; it is consequently not possible to fix the date of the story by reference to any particular extant Near-Eastern law or legal contract as has been proposed by some scholars. The words of the 'angel' (*mal'āk*) of YHWH who speaks to Hagar in 16:7 are identified with the words of YHWH himself in 16:13. Westermann's comment (1985: 244) is apt: 'God is present not in the messenger, but in the message.' The promise that YHWH makes to Hagar in v. 10, which is curiously like that made elsewhere about Isaac, identifies Ishmael as the ancestor of the Ishmaelites, whose supposed characteristics are described in v. 12. There are two aetiologies in the later part of the narrative, but they are subordinate to the main theme of the story. First, the name Ishmael, who is to be preserved by YHWH's intervention (v. 11), means 'God hears'. In the second aetiology the name El-rei (*'ēl rō'î*) (v. 13, probably 'God who sees me'), is stated in v. 14 to be the origin of the name of the—now unidentifiable—well where the angel spoke to Hagar. The aetiology, like others in Genesis, is not exact, as it is Hagar who 'sees' God, and not vice versa.

(**17:1–27**) This chapter is primarily concerned with the covenant (*běrît*) which God undertakes to make with Abraham—the word *běrît* occurs 13 times in the chapter. It reiterates the promises of progeny, of future greatness for Abraham's descendants, and of the gift of the land; but it contains several new and significant features. In v. 1 YHWH introduces himself as El Shaddai ('God Almighty'): the author supposes that at this time Abraham did not know YHWH by name. The name Shaddai, the meaning of which is uncertain (it may mean 'the one of the mountain' or 'the one of the field') was probably used as a divine epithet from an early period. This incident is regarded as opening a new stage in the life of Abraham: this is why he now receives a new name (v. 5). (So also with Sarah, v. 15.) Abraham is to be the father of not one but many nations, including that of the Ishmaelites; but the covenant is clearly for Israel alone, and will be for ever. It is to Israel that the land of Canaan is to be given 'for a perpetual holding' (v. 8) and YHWH will be their God. But the covenant is now to be two-sided: Abraham and his descendants must *keep* it by obeying God's command to practise circumcision, a rite not practised by the peoples of Mesopotamia from which Abraham has come. There is now for the first time in the Abraham story a

warning against the breach of the covenant, which will entail exclusion from its privileges and from the new special relationship with God; this could be a warning to Jews of the immediate post-exilic community who were tempted to abandon their Jewish identity. The concept of the crucial importance of circumcision was a particular characteristic of the post-exilic period.

Two further additional features of the chapter are the personal promise to Sarah (vv. 15–19) with the precise announcement of the time when her son will be born (v. 21) and the blessing of Ishmael (v. 20). Abraham's sceptical laughter at the announcement that Sarah will give birth combined with his deep obeisance (cf. Sarah's laughter on a parallel occasion, 18:12) is strange; but there is here a play on the name Isaac (*yiṣḥāq*, that is, 'he laughs', possibly an abbreviated form of *yiṣḥāq-'ēl*, 'God laughs'). Abraham's wish that Ishmael should be preserved under God's protection (v. 18) shows that he still places his hopes in Ishmael. God grants his wish, conferring a special blessing on Ishmael, but excludes him from the covenant that is for Isaac and his descendants. The chapter concludes with a notice that Abraham duly carried out God's commands about circumcision, which was performed on all Abraham's household (including Ishmael) as prescribed in later legislation (Ex 12:48).

(**18:1–16**) The motif of the appearance to human beings of gods in human disguise is a common mythological theme of the ancient world. A Greek myth, preserved by the Roman poet Ovid, tells of such a visit in which a miraculous birth is announced; there is a similar story in Judg 6:11–24. Gen 18:1, 13 make it clear that, although Abraham and Sarah are unaware of this, the three mysterious visitors (or one of them?) are in fact YHWH himself. This passage is thus another version of ch. 17, but expressed in a quite different, more circumstantial style, with a precise note of time and place. Abraham's treatment of the strangers is an example of the traditional customs of hospitality observed by tent-dwellers. The laughter of Sarah, like that of Abraham in 17:17, involves a play on words and is an expression of unbelief about the news that the visitors have brought. Sarah is firmly reminded that God has unlimited power and can bring about the impossible. Her denial that she laughed (v. 15) is caused by fear: she now dimly recognizes the identity of the speaker. The reference to Sodom in v. 16

introduces the theme that follows in the second half of the chapter and ch. 19. The passage is an admirable example of the high quality of Hebrew narrative art at its best.

(18:17–33) This passage is not based on an older folk-tale but is a discussion of a theological question of the utmost importance, that the author has himself composed in the form of a dialogue. The question, which is about God's justice (v. 25), was not, for the readers, a purely theoretical one, but one of immense *practical* importance, especially for those who had suffered, and were still suffering, the effects of the devastation of the Babylonian conquest of Judah in 587 BCE. It is raised in various forms in other OT books of a relatively late period, e.g. in Job, and Ezek 14:12–23. The fate of Sodom is here a paradigm of this much wider question.

The passage is remarkable in more than one respect. It begins (vv. 17–21) with the author's notion of YHWH's private thoughts: YHWH comes to a decision to inform Abraham of his intention—if the inhabitants of Sodom and Gomorrah prove to be as wicked as they have been reported to be—to destroy them, so that Abraham, whom he has chosen, may not imitate their wickedness and so prove unworthy of the promise (cf. 17:1–2, where Abraham's righteousness appears to have been made a condition of the making of the covenant with him). A second outstanding feature of the passage is Abraham's boldness in rebuking YHWH: although he frquently shows awareness of his temerity (vv. 27, 30, 31, 32), he dares to remind YHWH of his duty, as universal judge, to deal justly (v. 25)! His rebuke is reminiscent of the passionate speeches of Job. Equally remarkable is YHWH's readiness to listen to the rebuke and even to modify his intention. The precise accusation which Abraham makes is that in proposing to destroy the whole population of Sodom and Gomorrah YHWH intends to treat the righteous in the same way as the wicked (v. 25). He extracts from YHWH a promise that he will not do so (v. 26). The point appears to be not that YHWH fell short of his true nature but rather that he is shown to be a just God after all! There is no particular significance in the diminishing numbers of righteous persons for whose sake he will not destroy Sodom (vv. 28–32). The principle of justice towards individuals as against indiscriminate collective punishment has been established.

(19:1–29) This story is an episode in the life of Lot, who had chosen to live in the plain of Jordan, whose principal cities (unknown to archaeology) were Sodom and Gomorrah in the vicinity of the Dead Sea (13:10–13). But it is now also connected with ch. 18: the 'men' who visited Abraham (18:2) departed towards Sodom with the exception of YHWH himself, who remained to talk to Abraham (18:22). In v. 1 the other two, now called 'angels' or 'messengers' (mal᾽ākîm), who are clearly supernatural beings (v. 11), arrive in Sodom, presumably to investigate the reported wickedness of the inhabitants (it appears to be assumed that there are *no* righteous persons among them), where they find Lot sitting in the city gate. It is to be noted that there is no mention at all of Abraham in the main story: he appears only after the event (v. 27) and looks down on the catastrophe in the valley below. His absence may suggest that this was originally a story about an unnamed man (now identified with Abraham's nephew Lot) and the destruction of a city, which the author has incorporated into the story of Abraham. The reason for its inclusion is not obvious; however, it illustrates the consequences of grave sin against which Abraham has been warned. It should further be noted that the main story recounts only the fate of Sodom: Gomorrah is not mentioned until v. 24. But the two cities are regularly mentioned together in a number of passages elsewhere in the OT as examples of exemplary sin and consequent annihilation (e.g. Deut 29:22–4; 32:32; Isa 1:9–10; Jer 23:14).

It is strongly stressed in 19:4 that every male individual was involved in the homosexual attack intended against the two angels. This is no doubt to be seen as a justification of the subsequent annihilation of the whole populace; but the omission of any reference to the women of the city (or to the children) reflects at least a residuary notion of communal rather than of individual guilt. Lot's offer of his daughters (v. 8) also reflects a moral code, repulsive to the modern reader, which put the duty of hospitality above other ethical concerns. vv. 24, 28 attempt to describe the nature of the catastrophe that overwhelmed Sodom. That it was an earthquake that caused the release of combustible gases is a plausible guess; but—apart from the fact that no historical basis can be found for the story—it is not possible to be sure what the author had in mind. The city of Zoar (ṣōʿār) to which Lot was allowed to flee (vv. 18–23) actually existed in OT times (Isa 15:5; Jer 48:34). Like Sodom and Gomorrah, it lay in the valley, but was counted as belonging to Moab. Its name is here stated to be derived from a verb *ṣāʾar* meaning to be small or insignificant; Lot calls it 'a little one' (*miṣʿār*). The point of this conclusion to the story is to emphasize that it is Lot who is the central character and to present God's merciful nature towards those of whom he approves (19:29) as well as his punitive side. The incident of the fate of Lot's disobedient wife (v. 26) may be an aetiology based on a rock formation that existed in later times.

(19:30–8) These verses mark the conclusion of the story of Lot, who now disappears from Genesis. This is a story of double incest involving father and daughters; but no moral judgement is made or implied. The information that the children born of the incestuous union became the ancestors of the Moabite and Ammonite peoples is probably a secondary feature of the story rather than its main point. It is presupposed (v. 31) that the male population of the region has entirely perished in the catastrophe which befell Sodom; the observation that Lot is old cannot, in the context, mean that he is too old to father children; it probably means that he will not marry again and so have legitimate children. This is a situation in which the need to perpetuate the race is paramount, and sanctions desperate remedies. Like Noah (9:21), Lot is unaware, in his drunkenness, of what is happening.

(20:1–18) This story is a variant of 12:10–20 and 26:1–11 (see at 12:10–20 above). Its position immediately before the notice of the conception and birth of Isaac, which at last fulfilled YHWH's promise, is an example of dramatic irony: the reader is made to feel the danger of the situation. The relationship between the three variants is disputed. This version is fuller than 12:10–20, and there are a number of differences of detail. The scene is set not in Egypt but in Gerar, near Gaza (already mentioned in 10:19), and the king is Abimelech—a Canaanite name. Abraham's residence in Gerar is not due to a famine. The main variant detail is Abimelech's dream in which God speaks to him. God exonerates Abimelech as he has acted in ignorance of Sarah's status as Abraham's wife. An additional detail is Abraham's excuse, made on the specious grounds that Sarah is his half-sister as well as his wife (not previously mentioned!), together with his claim to know that the most basic moral standards are not observed in Gerar (vv. 11–12). Also, instead of the plagues inflicted on Pharaoh (12:17) we are told that YHWH had

made Abimelech's wives unable to bear children during Sarah's residence in his harem; and we are explicitly told that Abimelech did not have sexual relations with her. Like Pharaoh in 12:16, Abimelech behaves with great generosity to Abraham, while Abraham, though he is said by God to be a 'prophet' (v. 7) and bidden to pray for Abimelech, is portrayed as a guilty man. Nevertheless (21:1) God does not abrogate his promise.

(21:1–21) This story, although it begins with the birth of Isaac, is really about Abraham's two sons, Isaac and Ishmael. vv. 8–21 are a variant of the earlier story of the banishment of Hagar and Ishmael because of Sarah's jealousy (ch. 16). While it is emphasized that it is Isaac who is Abraham's promised heir, the author stresses God's concern for Ishmael, contrasting it with the harsh attitude and action of Sarah. According to the chronology given in 16:16 and v. 5, Ishmael would have been about 14 years old when Isaac was born, yet the story used here by the narrator assumes that he was a small child whom his mother put on her shoulder and carried away (v. 14). In v. 6 there is yet another explanation of the name Isaac (see on 17:17 and 18:12). The circumcision of Isaac (v. 4) is in accordance with the command in 17:12. Abraham's reactions to Sarah's demand (vv. 10–11) are more forthright than in 16:5–6, but he gives way when God intervenes. Hagar's distress in vv. 15–16 is depicted with psychological sensitivity. God's reaction to her distress illustrates his compassion (vv. 17–20). Finally when he grows up under God's protection Ishmael goes to live in the wilderness of Paran near the border of Egypt where he becomes the ancestor of the Ishmaelites.

(21:22–34) These verses presuppose ch. 20, but are not closely related to it. They are concerned to enhance Abraham's status: although he remains an alien (v. 34) he is recognized by Abimelech as especially protected and favoured by God; he is thus treated by a king, who commands an army, as an equal. In vv. 22–4 Abimelech thinks it important to safeguard himself by obtaining from him an oath that he will remain his ally (the phrase is *ʿāśâ ḥesed*) and that this alliance will continue in future generations. The second incident is quite different: Abraham becomes involved in a dispute with Abimelech over the possession of a well (vv. 25–32). The dispute is settled in Abraham's favour with the offering of seven lambs and the making of a treaty of friendship (*bĕrît*, v. 32). There are two different aetiologies of the name Beersheba here: it is the place of the well (*bĕˀēr*) of the oath (*šĕbūˀâ*) but also of seven (*šebaˁ*). The tree planted by Abraham marked the spot where the covenant was made. The 'Everlasting God' (*ˀēl ˁôlām*) worshipped by Abraham here, and implicitly identified with YHWH, was probably originally a local deity associated with Beersheba. The 'land of the Philistines' is an anachronism: the Philistines in fact arrived in Canaan and established their cities there near the Mediterranean coast during the twelfth century BCE and cannot have been known to Abraham. Abimelech has a Semitic name, and so was evidently a local Canaanite ruler, not a Philistine.

(22:1–19) This story is one of the most brilliantly told narratives in the book. It has generated an immense quantity of interpretative comment beginning in early times with Heb 11:17 and Jas 2:21 and continuing up to the present, and many works of art. It is widely agreed that no one interpretation is entirely adequate (see von Rad 1972: 243–5). Its psychological sensitivity and stylistic skill in portraying the distress of Abraham when commanded by God to kill his beloved son and heir are unequalled. It may be that somewhere in its background lies a story about human sacrifice, specifically the sacrifice of the firstborn; but there is no indication at all that that practice, which was not only forbidden but regarded with horror in Israel, was in the mind of the author of the present story. The statement in the opening verse that God's purpose in demanding Isaac's death was to test Abraham's obedience—to see whether he 'feared God' (v. 12)—is an accurate summary of the plot. Abraham was forced to choose between obedience to an incomprehensible and abhorrent command and his love for his child (v. 2). There is a terrible dramatic irony here: God did not intend that his command should be carried out; but Abraham had no means of knowing that. He passed the test. On a different level, this is yet another example of the theme of the endangerment of God's promise: with Isaac's birth the promise of an heir has apparently been miraculously fulfilled; but now the very life of that heir is—as far as the reader knows—to be prematurely brought to an end. The location of the 'land of Moriah' is unknown. A later tradition identified Moriah with the mountain on which Solomon later built the Jerusalem temple (2 Chr 3:1); but there is no indication in the text of Gen 22 that this is what the author had in mind. Every particular of the journey and of the preparations for the sacrifice (vv. 3–9) is meticulously recorded in order to retard the pace of the action and so increase the tension to an almost unbearable degree; it reaches its greatest intensity with 22:10 and is then suddenly released in v. 11. Abraham's reply to Isaac's question (vv. 7, 8) is understandably evasive, but he speaks more than he knows. The angel of YHWH is here clearly identified with YHWH himself. The name given to the place by Abraham (*YHWH yirˀeh*, 'Yahweh provides'—lit. sees, or looks out) echoes his reply to Isaac in 22:8; it expresses his joy that YHWH has now done so in a miraculous way. The note in v. 14*b* is a later addition to the story, perhaps linking the place with Jerusalem. vv. 15–18 are also probably an addition to the story: by its repetition of the promise of blessing this makes explicit its place in the wider context of Abraham's life—by his obedience Abraham has confirmed that he is worthy of the blessing.

(22:20–4) This genealogy defines Abraham's kinship with the Arameans (Aram) and points forward to Isaac's marriage with Rebekah (ch. 24).

(23:1–20) Full possession of the land of Canaan was a crucial matter for a people that had lost it with the Babylonian conquest in the sixth century BCE and were, even under the milder policy of the Persian empire, like Abraham, only 'strangers and aliens' (v. 4) in it, subject to foreign rule. Abraham's legal purchase from the 'Hittite'—that is, Canaanite—owner of a single field containing the cave where he could bury Sarah (vv. 17, 20) was a hopeful sign to these readers, even though it was no more than symbolic—the first fruits, as it were, of the promise that Abraham's descendants would possess the whole land.

The name Kiriath-arba, here identified with Hebron (v. 2), means 'city of four'—probably referring to its consisting of four districts or 'quarters' or to its position at the intersection of four roads. The name 'Hittite' here and elsewhere in the Pentateuch does not designate the great Hittite empire of Asia Minor, long extinct when this chapter was written, but is used as a general designation of the Canaanites. Abraham, having no settled home, is obliged to seek a place of burial for Sarah from the local inhabitants. The cave in question belongs to one Ephron (v. 8); but the decision to convey it to Abraham's use evidently rests with the people of Hebron as a whole—the 'people of the land' (vv. 10–13). The negotiation is carried on with great courtesy; it is a legal transaction, and the terminology resembles that used in extant neo-Babylonian legal contracts. Abraham, who is regarded by the Hebronites as a 'mighty prince' (v. 6), is first offered a choice of burial places, but not legal ownership. He insists that the latter is what he seeks; and he finally succeeds in buying the entire field, though at what is known to have been a very high price (v. 15).

(24:1–67) This is by far the longest story in this part of the book, and has with some justification been called a novella, or short story (in the modern sense of that term). It is divided into distinct scenes, and is told with great sensitivity and with acute psychological insight. An unusual feature is the extent to which dialogue is used to portray character and to move the action along: more than half the verses consist of or contain reported speech. Apart from its intrinsic interest as literature, the story marks a new and positive stage in the theme of the promise: Abraham's heir has not only survived; he is now provided with an eminently suitable wife, who is destined in turn to produce an heir, the inheritor of the promise in the third generation. The narrative speaks of the continued guidance of God at every stage.

Abraham, who is evidently too old to undertake a long journey (but note his second marriage in 25:1!), sends his trusted and confidential servant or steward, whom he has entrusted with all his possessions, to seek a wife for Isaac from among those of his kindred who have remained in Mesopotamia (Aram-naharaim, lit. Aram of the two rivers): marriage with an alien Canaanite is ruled out as unthinkable, and it is equally out of the question that Isaac should return to fetch his bride from the country from which his father had departed at God's command. If the girl chosen should refuse the match, the messenger is to return alone to Abraham.

The rite of touching the genitals of the other party while swearing an oath, mentioned in the OT only here (vv. 2, 9) and Gen 47:29, is attested in a Babylonian document and is also known from Arabic usage (TWAT 7, 984). Its significance is not clear; but it may be related to the more common practice of swearing by a person's life. The messenger sets out with an impressive retinue and carries valuable gifts appropriate to his master's great wealth and high status (v. 10). On arrival at his destination

he takes no action but kneels down at a well that he knows will be frequented by the young girls of the town when they come to draw water, and prays that YHWH will signify his choice of a bride for Isaac in a particular way (vv. 13–14); he is miraculously rewarded when the first girl who comes to draw water proves to be not only beautiful, a virgin, and of a kindly disposition but also Abraham's own niece, so confirming that YHWH has made his mission unexpectedly and completely successful (vv. 15–27; cf. 11:29; 22:22, 23). The reason why it is Rebekah's brother Laban rather than her father who plays the principal role in the remainder of the story (from v. 29) is not clear, though he is to be a principal character in later chapters (29–31). The reference to Rebekah's mother's house rather than that of her father (v. 28) might lead the reader to suppose that her father Bethuel was dead; but he appears in a minor role in v. 50.

Although it is not specifically stated that Rebekah's consent to the marriage was sought, this seems to be implied in her acceptance of the valuable jewellery and the ring (v. 22) and by her running home to tell the news (v. 28). It is also strongly implied by the fact that, when consulted, she agreed to leave her family immediately and accompany the servant home to meet her designated husband (v. 58). There is some difficulty about the Hebrew text of v. 62 and about Isaac's place of residence. According to 25:20 Isaac was 40 years old when he married, and had a separate establishment. The absence of any reference to Abraham in the last part of the story is strange: one would have expected that the servant would have first conducted Rebekah to Abraham and have made his report to him. The story concludes with the rare statement that Isaac loved his wife, paralleled in Genesis only by the love of Jacob for Rachel (29:18) and of Shechem the Hivite for Dinah (34:3).

(25:1–18) With these verses the story of Abraham comes to an end. They are a somewhat miscellaneous collection consisting mainly of genealogies but including a brief statement of Abraham's death and burial (vv. 7–10). They contain no real continuous narrative. The point of the genealogies is to continue the theme of Abraham as the 'father of many nations' (cf. 17:5, 20; 21:13). These lists contain the names of several nations and tribes known from elsewhere, notably Midian (v. 1) and the Ishmaelites (vv. 12–16). The note about

Abraham's life in v. 8 reflects the Israelite attitude towards both life and death. Death was not regarded as tragic if it closed a long and fulfilled, honourable life. The statement that Abraham was 'gathered to his people' (v. 8) obviously does not mean that his body was placed in an ancestral tomb, since only Sarah had yet been buried in the cave of Machpelah (v. 10): it was a conventional expression testifying a strong sense of family solidarity.

The Story of Jacob (25:19–37:2)

Of the three 'patriarchs' Abraham, Isaac, and Jacob only Isaac lacks a really independent story. Although as Abraham's heir and Jacob's father he obviously holds an essential place in the family history and is in his turn the recipient of the promise of blessing and of numerous descendants 'for Abraham's sake' (26:3–5, 23–5), he is the principal character in only one chapter (26). It must be presumed that the author or editor of the book did not possess a wealth of narrative material about Isaac as he did about Abraham and Jacob. A large part of the story of Jacob is concerned with the relations between Jacob and his elder brother Esau. God's choice of Jacob rather than Esau as the heir and recipient of the promise recounted in these chapters introduces a new major theme: God in his sovereignty is not bound by the 'natural' or legal principle of inheritance by primogeniture but inscrutably singles out younger sons to carry out his purpose (cf. the choice of David as king of Israel, 1 Sam 16:1–13). So not Ishmael but Isaac is chosen, and not Esau but Jacob; and, of Jacob's twelve sons, it is his eleventh son Joseph who is chosen to rule over his brothers (Gen 37:5–11) and to preserve the lives of the embryo people of Israel (Gen 45:5; 50:20). Similarly Ephraim is given precedence over his elder brother Manasseh (Gen 48:8–20).

(**25:19–34**) In vv. 19–20, which introduce the stories about Isaac's children, the author has inserted a short notice which repeats what the reader already knows, adding the information that Isaac was 40 years old when he married. But the chronology in this chapter is somewhat confused. If Isaac was 60 when Rebekah bore his first children (v. 26), Abraham, who was 175 when he died (25:7), would still have fifteen years to live, since he was 100 when Isaac was born (21:5)! The two stories about the birth of Esau and Jacob (vv. 21–6) and the birthright (25:27–34) both point forward to the later antagonism between the two and to

the precedence of Jacob over his brother. The former story, which begins with YHWH's decree that the elder is to serve the younger, contains a pun on the name Jacob (*ya'ăqōb*) who grasped the heel (*'āqēb*) in the womb (v. 26) and another on Esau, the ancestor of the Edomites (v. 30; 36:1) who 'came out red' (*'admônî*) from the womb. There is yet another pun on the name Edom in the second story, where Esau calls the dish that Jacob has prepared 'that red stuff' (*'ādōm*, v. 30). The two brothers are also caricatured as two contrasting types: the ruddy, hairy hunter (vv. 25, 27) who is an easy prey to the cunning 'quiet man' who stays at home (v. 27; Jacob is later to become a shepherd, ch. 29). vv. 27–34 especially have been seen as based on an earlier civilization story which reflected problems that arose when the sedentary way of life began to supersede the hunting stage (see Westermann 1985: 414–15). The motif is of crucial importance later in ch. 27; but the point of the present story is to show that Esau already forfeited the privileges of the elder son.

(**26:1–35**) This chapter is given a unity by the theme of Isaac's relations with Abimelech the 'Philistine' (i.e. Canaanite) king of Gerar. vv. 6–11 are a variant of 12:10–20 and 20:1–18 (on which see the commentary above), the main difference from both the other stories being that it concerns Isaac and Rebekah, not Abraham and Sarah. It contains motifs from both the other versions; and it is commonly held that its author was familiar with, and intended to make certain changes with regard to, both. In particular, the lie told by Isaac (v. 7) is the same as that told by Abraham in the other two versions, but the consequences are less critical, since Rebekah is not taken into the royal harem. vv. 1–5 introduce the story by accounting for Isaac's move to Gerar. It includes an appearance to Isaac by YHWH in which he repeats the promise of the land and of numerous progeny but couples it with an injunction not to depart from Canaan as Abraham had done in similar circumstances (12:10).

In vv. 12–33 the motif of the dispute with the Canaanites of Gerar over the ownership of the wells that were essential to life and livelihood (21:25–34) recurs. But Isaac, who was the first of the patriarchal family to grow crops (v. 12) as well as owning flocks and herds (v. 14) and who had become wealthy even beyond the wealth accumulated by his father, had aroused the envy of the 'Philistines' (vv. 12–14) who were making life difficult for him. However, this series of incidents ends with the making of a treaty of peace between Isaac and Abimelech, in which Isaac is credited with taking the initiative (vv. 26–31). The aetiologies of the names of the wells (v. Ezek 20, 'contention'; Sitnah, v. 21, 'quarrel, accusation'; Rehoboth, v. 22, 'broad space') probably come from ancient local traditions. The naming of Shibah (v. 33) is attributed, as is Beersheba in 21:31, to an oath, this time between Isaac and Abimelech (v. 31).

The Adventures of Jacob (chs. 27–33)

At one level this is a story of withdrawal and return, a familiar folk-tale motif. It is also a story of hatred between brothers followed by eventual reconciliation; but in the context of the book as a whole it is a continuation of the history of the promise made to the patriarchs. Although Esau has his reward in the end in terms of material wealth (33:9–11), it is made clear that he was deprived not only of his birthright but also of the blessing (27:36). He is to be the ancestor of the Edomites and not of Israel, and accordingly establishes his residence in the region of Seir, later to be part of Edom (32:3; 33:14, 16; cf. 36:9). Later events are clearly reflected here. Isaac's blessing of Jacob (27:27–9) and his lesser 'blessing' of Esau (27:39–40) reflect the history of the later relations between the state of Israel and Edom: Israel will rule over Edom, but eventually Edom will 'break his yoke' and achieve its independence (cf. 2 Sam 8:14; 1 Kings 11:14; 2 Chr 21:8–10). This account of Jacob's adventures is not made of whole cloth: it has incorporated many elements which the final author/editor has combined. In particular, one major section, ch. 29–31, which describes Jacob's extended residence in the house of his uncle Laban, originally belonged to a quite distinct tradition about the relations between two peoples: Israel and the Arameans.

(27:1–46) This chapter is another example of narrative skill. It is structured in a number of distinct scenes, in each of which, as in folk-tales, only two characters appear: Isaac and Esau in vv. 1–4, Jacob and Rebekah in vv. 5–17, Jacob and Isaac in vv. 18–29, Esau and Isaac in vv. 30–40, Esau alone in v. 41, Rebekah and Jacob in vv. 42–5, Rebekah and Isaac, v. 46. The theme is Jacob's trickery by which he obtains the paternal blessing that would normally be given to the elder son and the consequent implacable hatred of Esau for his brother which makes it necessary for Jacob to leave home and set out on his travels. One of the most remarkable features of the story is the portrayal of Rebekah, who plays a crucial role in the story and whose personality is thus displayed in marked contrast to the passivity of Sarah in the previous chapters (but we may compare the enterprising action of Rachel in 31:34–5). Despite Jacob's disgraceful behaviour in deceiving his aged and blind father, the story is presented in a way that arouses the reader's sympathy for such a rogue, though the depiction of Esau's distress (vv. 34–8) is intended to elicit some sympathy for him as well. There is also a humorous quality in the tale that should not be missed. The predominance of dialogue helps to give the narrative a particularly lively character. The fact that the action takes place entirely on the human plane, with no mention of God (except for his invocation in Isaac's blessing, v. 28, and Jacob's lying assertion in v. 20) sets the chapter, together with 25:27–34, apart from the surrounding chapters in which the hand of God is prominent.

It is noteworthy that it is Rebekah, who evidently loves her 'smooth' son Jacob more than the uncouth, hairy Esau (v. 11) and is even prepared to risk her husband's curse, who proposes the deception; but Jacob, in agreeing to her proposal, is equally guilty. The story turns on the belief that blessings and curses possess objective power and cannot be taken back (v. 33). In v. 36 Jacob's name is once more (cf. 25:26) associated with the root '-q-b, here in a verbal form and interpreted as 'supplant'. It is again Rebekah who takes the initiative, overhearing Esau's intention to kill Jacob and warning him to flee to Haran to his uncle Laban (vv. 43–5). The chapter ends with her fear that Jacob may marry a 'Hittite' (cf. 26:34–5)—an echo of the theme of 24:3–4.

(28:1–9) A different account of the circumstances of Jacob's departure to Laban is given in vv. 1–5 from that given in ch. 27. Here his father sends him off so that he may marry a girl from his own family as Isaac himself had done, and Isaac prays that he will inherit the promise once given to Abraham. Laban's home is now given as Paddan-aram, which may mean 'country of Aram' (so also in 25:20). This region of north Mesopotamia is called Aram-naharaim in 24:10. vv. 6–9 relate how Esau also conformed to Isaac's wish in that he now married a relation in addition to his previous Canaanite wives.

(28:10–22) On his way to Laban, whose home is now specified (as in 27:43) as the city of Haran, Jacob rests for the night at an unnamed place

(v. 11) and takes a large stone there as a pillow. He has a dream in which he sees a ladder (probably rather a ramp) stretching from earth to heaven on which God's angels—that is, heavenly messengers—are passing up and down to perform tasks assigned to them by God. He recognizes the ladder as 'the gate of heaven' (v. 17), that is, as the means of communication between God in his dwelling in heaven and his manifestations to human beings on earth; and so concludes with awe that the place where he is resting must therefore be 'the house of God', that is, a place where God manifests himself on earth. The imagery of the dream corresponds to Babylonian religious beliefs as expressed in their structures known as ziggurats. In the dream Jacob becomes aware that God is indeed communicating with him: God repeats to him the promise of the land of Canaan, in which he is now resting, and of numerous progeny, and adds a further promise that he will guide and protect him on his journey and wherever he may go (vv. 13–15).

It is generally agreed that this passage has undergone several accretions, but there is no consensus about the details. Jacob names the place Bethel (lit., 'house of God'), thus naming a place which was later to be one of Israel's most important sanctuaries. The story is thus to be seen as the origin story of the sanctuary of Bethel and will have been used from ancient times by the worshippers at that sanctuary. Its importance to later generations accounts for the fact that it later came to be embellished in various ways (for a recent study of its redactional history which understands it without ascribing it to an interweaving of two major written sources see Rendtorff 1982: 511–23). The stone used by Jacob as a pillow (v. 11), which he erected as a pillar and consecrated with oil (v. 18), marked the site as a holy place where God had revealed himself and so might be expected to do so again—that is, as a sanctuary. Such a pillar (*maṣṣēbâ*) might be no more than a memorial stone or marker, e.g. of a frontier (31:51); but it was often a feature of sanctuaries both Canaanite and Israelite, though later condemned in Israel (e.g. Lev 26:1). In his concluding vow (vv. 20–2) Jacob acutely translates God's promise of guidance into concrete, down-to-earth terms, and in turn promises to worship YHWH as his God. He also undertakes to pay a tithe of future produce, in anticipation of the cult that will be established at Bethel. He is clearly speaking as a representative of a future Israel and as the founder of the Bethel sanctuary.

(**29:1–30**) This chapter begins the story of Jacob and Laban which continues to the end of ch. 31. It is set in foreign territory, outside Canaan. As yet another story about an encounter at a well that ends with marriage of the heir to the promise to a member (here two members!) of his Aramean kindred, it has many affinities with ch. 24; but there are significant differences. There is again the apparently fortuitous meeting with the Aramean kindred; but, unlike Isaac, who was forbidden to leave Canaan to seek his wife, Jacob makes precisely that journey. He travels to 'the land of the people of the east' (a rather vague term denoting the land to the east of Canaan, but here including the more northern territory in the vicinity of Haran); but he does not go specifically to seek a wife, and does not at first realize where he is. Further, in contrast to the religious atmosphere of 28:10–22 and with the pious mission of Abraham's servant in ch. 24, this is a purely secular story in which God does not appear, although no doubt he is invisibly present in the background in the mind of the final editor.

vv. 1–14 are an idyllic tale that gives no hint of troubles to come. Jacob is presented as the mighty hero who is able alone to move the stone, which normally required several men to move it, from the mouth of the well to enable the flocks to be watered (cf. 28:18, where also he moves a massive stone); and he does this on perceiving the arrival of Rachel. The kiss which he gives her is no doubt a cousinly kiss (v. 11; cf. v. 13); but his weeping (for joy) surely speaks of love at first sight. The continuation of the story in vv. 15–30, however, already introduces the reader to the calculating character of Laban, who succeeds in employing Jacob for fourteen years without wages and in tricking him into marrying the unwanted Leah. There are two further motifs in this story: Jacob's marriages are a further example of the younger being preferred to the elder; and, in view of Jacob's earlier behaviour (25:27–34; 27), vv. 21–30 may be seen as an example of the motif of the deceiver deceived. Jacob's love for Rachel is again emphasized in vv. 20 and 30. In vv. 24 and 29 Laban's assignment of the two maids Zilpah and Bilhah respectively to serve Leah and Rachel prepares the reader for the accounts of the birth of Jacob's twelve sons, who are to be the ancestors of the twelve tribes of Israel.

(**29:31–30:24**) This section consists mainly of a miscellaneous collection of notices of the births of Jacob's first eleven sons (and one daughter,

Dinah), whose names are those of later Israelite tribes. The reasons given for their names, which all refer to the circumstances of the mothers (unlike the tribal blessings in ch. 49) are quite fanciful and hardly genuine popular etymologies. The words attributed to the mothers in naming their sons have been made to fit the names; but they do not fit very well. In some cases they involve the use of very rare words. The name Reuben (*rĕ'ûbēn*) would naturally be taken to mean 'Behold a son' (29:32), but has been connected with *'ônî*, 'affliction'. Simeon (29:33) is more reasonably connected with *šāma'*, 'to hear'. Levi (29:34) is supposedly derived from *lāwâ*, 'to join'. Judah (29:35) has been associated with the mother's exclamation *'ôdeh*, 'I will praise'; Dan (30:6) with the verb *dîn*, 'to give judgement'; Naphtali (30:8) with a rare verb *pātal*, possibly meaning 'to twist', here interpreted as 'wrestle'. Gad (30:11) is the name of a god of good fortune; Asher (30:13) is explained as related to *'iššēr*, 'to pronounce happy'; Issachar (30:18) as connected with *śākār*, 'hire, wages'. In two cases (and possibly a third, Reuben) two alternative explanations are given: the name Zebulon (30:20) is associated with a verb that occurs nowhere else in the OT but which may refer to exaltation, hence honour, but also with *zēbed*, 'gift', while Joseph (30:24) is related both to *'āsap*, 'gather, remove, take away', and to *yāsap*, 'add, increase'. It was not deemed necessary to offer an explanation of the name of the daughter, Dinah.

Only scraps of narrative and dialogue are attached to these birth notices. The motif of the two wives, one of whom is unable to bear children (29:31–2), is found also in the story of the birth of Samuel (1 Sam 1), but with significant differences. In both cases the childless wife is enabled to bear a son through divine intervention; but here this happens to the 'hated' wife (i.e. the one who is unwanted by her husband) whereas in 1 Sam 1 it happens to the one who is especially beloved; here too God takes the initiative rather than acting in response to prayer as in the case of Hannah. There are other OT parallels to God's initiative in such cases: not only in the case of Sarah but also in the story of the birth of Samson (Judg 13). All these stories differ considerably in detail; but behind them lies the conviction that God alone bestows or withholds life. 30:1–7 is another example of the custom of surrogate birth earlier practised by Sarah (so also 30:9–11). The 'birth on the knees' of Rachel (30:3) is a rite which ensures that the child born is to be regarded as Rachel's own. 30:14–18 reflects an ancient belief that the fruit of the mandrake plant has aphrodisiac properties, although the birth of Issachar is attributed to divine operation.

(30:25–43) The details of this story are not clear, and have puzzled the commentators. There are strange contradictions, no doubt due to glossators who themselves did not fully grasp what was happening but attempted to set matters right. The thrust of the story, however, is sufficiently plain. This is a battle of wits between Jacob and Laban from which Jacob emerges victorious. Jacob, who has suffered before from Laban's trickery, repays it in kind. The story begins with an abrupt request by Jacob to Laban for his release from his servitude which puts Laban in an embarrassing situation. Jacob points out that Laban has greatly benefited from his service, but now requests to be allowed to return to his homeland accompanied by his wives and children, who are of course Laban's own daughters and grandchildren (v. 26). This request may not have been within Jacob's rights: Ex 21:2–4 does not permit a freed slave to take his family with him; but Jacob's status is not clear (cf. Laban's action in ch. 31). Laban recognizes the value of Jacob's service to him, and adopts a conciliatory tone. He admits that his prosperity is due to Jacob, perhaps claiming that he has learned by divination (the meaning of this word is uncertain) that this is due to YHWH's having blessed Jacob (v. 27), but complains that the loss of Jacob may damage his own economic status. He makes an offer to reward Jacob, who replies that he is not asking for a reward, but then inconsistently requests to be allowed to keep some of Laban's flocks. He proposes (v. 32) that he should be given those animals that are particoloured (a rarity among sheep and goats) and promises to carry out this operation honestly. Laban pretends to agree, but then himself deceitfully separates the particoloured animals from the rest, and sends them away with his sons to be kept at a distance (vv. 35–6).

The account of Jacob's retaliatory action (vv. 37–42) is again somewhat muddled and repetitive, but here again its general import is clear. To gain an advantage over Laban Jacob had recourse to a trick based on a superstitious, farmers' belief (taken seriously by the author) that newborn animals (and also human babies) can derive certain characteristics from the visual impressions experienced by their mothers at the moment of conception. Taking advantage of

Laban's absence, Jacob arranged that the ewes, which mated while they were drinking, should do so while standing facing some rods which he had taken from appropriate trees that he had partly peeled and set before the drinking troughs, so producing particoloured young. (v. 40 is unfortunately obscure.) In addition (vv. 41–2) he selected for this purpose only the more robust animals. As a result he became the owner, following his previous arrangement with Laban, of the choice animals because they were particoloured, while Laban was left only with the feebler ones. By this device he increased his wealth, though the final verse of the chapter (v. 43) about the extraordinary wealth which he acquired in this way seems entirely disproportionate to the preceding account and is probably a later addition made to enhance the impression that the patriarchs, although landless, were nevertheless persons of substance in the world. This is another secular story in which (apart from Laban's remark in v. 27) God does not appear.

(31:1–55) This chapter concludes the Jacob–Laban stories. It is a continuation of ch. 30, but it also marks a return to the theme of the promise. The question of Jacob's departure broached in ch. 30 has remained unresolved. Now he has determined to leave, with his family, without Laban's permission, partly because relations with Laban and his sons have deteriorated, but above all because YHWH has commanded him to do so and has promised to continue to guide and protect him (vv. 2–3). Jacob meets his wives secretly and speaks to them of his reasons for departure: Laban's animosity towards him, restrained only by God's protection, and God's command, here represented as mediated by an angel in a dream (vv. 11–13). There are inconsistencies again here, e.g. Jacob's claim that Laban has changed his wages ten times does not accord with what has been said in the previous two chapters. In his account of his dream (v. 13) he cites God's command, but with an additional reference to ch. 28. Jacob's proposal to his wives, which involved for them the abandonment of their family and their community, is accepted without demur: they too have a grudge against their father, who has used for himself their bridal price and has thus 'sold' them and in fact treated them as foreigners (vv. 14–16). These verses involve legal questions of marriage and inheritance customs which are not completely clear to the modern reader; but what the wives are say-

ing is that owing to their father's actions they no longer belong to their community, and are prepared to put their trust in what Jacob has told them of God's call to him. So the heir of the promise effects his escape from the alien territory of Paddan-aram and returns to the land of promise.

The second scene (vv. 19–42) opens with Laban, accompanied by his kinsmen, pursuing Jacob, and overtaking him when he has reached the hill country of Gilead, east of the Jordan. Once more Laban receives a divine message warning him not to interfere with Jacob (v. 24); and in fact when they meet Laban exercises restraint. His final complaint against him is that he has stolen his 'household gods' (tĕrāphîm), though in fact it was Rachel who had stolen them without Jacob's knowledge (vv. 19, 32). The incident of the search for the teraphim (vv. 33–5) is recounted with crude humour. Teraphim, which are mentioned in several other OT texts, appear to have been fairly small hominiform images of gods whose use was not confined to Israel. There is a reference to their manufacture in Judg 17:5, and Hos 3:4 implies that they were in common use in Israel during the period of the monarchy. Later, however, they were condemned as idolatrous (Zech 10:2) together with the practice of divination with which they appear to have been associated (Ezek 21:21). They were obviously very important to Laban, who may have used them for divination. In recent times it was widely supposed, on the basis of purportedly similar practices known from second-millennium BCE texts discovered at the Mesopotamian city of Nuzi, that possession of such objects could be used to substantiate legal claims to the inheritance of property; but it has now been shown that this view is not tenable, at least as far as this passage in Genesis is concerned (see Thompson 1974: 272–80). There is nothing in the Genesis text that indicates why Laban's teraphim were so important to him.

Jacob in his defence of his conduct (vv. 36–42) attributes his present material success to the ancestral God, whom he here refers as 'The Fear of Isaac' (or possibly 'Kinsman of Isaac', probably an ancient name of a god who was later identified with YHWH). Laban (vv. 43–4) still maintains his legal right to all Jacob's possessions, but is forced to admit defeat. The treaty or covenant now made between the two is a non-aggression pact (vv. 48–50); but in a different version of the event (v. 52) it also defines a territorial boundary which each partner swears to observe. This is really an agreement not simply between two individuals but between representatives of two nations, as is indicated by the double naming of the boundary cairn that they have set up in two distinct languages: both Jegarsahadutha (Aramaic) and Galeed (Hebrew *galʿēd*) mean 'cairn of witness'. Behind this incident there undoubtedly lies an ancient tradition of an agreement once made between Israel and the Arameans, who were, however, later to be involved in territorial wars (cf. especially 2 Sam 8; 10; 1 Kings 11; 20; 22; 2 Kings 7–16).

(**32:1–21**) After reporting the peaceful solution of Jacob's dispute with Laban (31:54–5) the story resumes the account of his relations with his brother Esau, from whose hostile intentions he had fled (ch. 27). First, however, there is a short notice of a (presumably) favourable appearance of a group of divine messengers or angels (cf. 28:12) during his journey, which he perceives as 'God's camp' (*maḥănēh ʾĕlōhîm*) and so names the place Mahanaim. This incident is no doubt based on a local foundation legend about the city of Mahanaim in Gilead east of the Jordan, later to become an important Israelite city. Now, aware that he is close to the land of Edom, Esau's home, and fearful for his life and the lives of his family, he sends an embassy to Esau. Learning that Esau is advancing towards him with a strong military force (v. 6), he prays to God that he will protect him, and then makes preparations for the encounter, sending a further conciliatory message to Esau together with valuable presents which he sends by instalments, himself remaining behind with his family in the hope of protecting them in case of attack. Here again the reader finds the heir to the promise and his family in danger of their lives; and once again the narrative is slowed down to increase the dramatic tension.

(**32:22–32**) This incident, which interrupts the account of Jacob's concluding encounter with Esau, is of central importance in the story of Jacob, even more significant than Jacob's experience at Bethel (28:10–22). Here once more the heir to the promise is placed in danger of his life. But the incident remains essentially mysterious, and several of its features are difficult to interpret. This is at least partly due to the fact that it is evidently a pre-Israelite story that has been reworked, probably more than once. The original version strongly resembles pagan, even animistic, tales of spirits or demons guarding particular places such as streams, who at-

tack travellers who are endeavouring to pass on their way, but who are powerful only at night; here we are told that the sun rose only when the incident was over (v. 31). The place in question here is a ford over the stream Jabbok, which rises in the mountains east of the Jordan and descends precipitately to flow into the Jordan— a place where it is difficult to cross on foot. The supposed connection between its name and the rare Hebrew verb *ʾābaq*, 'wrestle' (v. 24) may have given rise to the story in its original version. The man (*ʾîš*) who attacked Jacob and struggled with him all night remains unidentified until v. 30, but is clearly possessed of supernatural power as well as of great physical strength (30:25), and is recognized by Jacob as one who is able to confer a blessing on him. He subsequently reveals himself as divine (*ʾĕlōhîm*, v. 28); but the statements that Jacob overmatched him and forced him to bless him (vv. 26, 29) remain mysterious in the face of Jacob's final realization that he has been locked in a struggle with God, and has seen him face to face (*pĕnîʾēl* means 'face of God'). At this point of the story, as in others, features of the original tale are still present. The central and crucial point of the story in its present form is that Jacob not only received the divine blessing (despite the refusal of the 'man' to declare his own name), but that his name is changed to 'Israel' (this name is here associated with the rare verb *śārâ*, 'struggle', used in v. 28). The passage thus declares Jacob to be not only a towering, heroic figure who has close dealings with God himself, but also the founder of the nation of Israel. Despite its evidently somewhat composite nature, attempts to analyse its sources have been controversial; but the final verse is certainly a separate comment on the incident as being the origin of an otherwise unknown food taboo.

(**33:1–20**) The reconciliation between Jacob and his wronged brother resolves the tension built up in 32:1–21. The chapter is a riot of deferential bowings and honorific expressions ('my lord', 'your servant') in oriental fashion on the part of Jacob and his household and magnanimity and solicitous concern on the part of Esau. Esau's emotional welcome of Jacob signifies his complete forgiveness, after so many years, of a grievous offence which is never mentioned, but of which Jacob still remains painfully aware. Until the moment of greeting he appears still to be apprehensive of Esau's intention; and even subsequently he is still reluctant to travel in his company, pretending that they will meet again in Seir, Esau's home territory (vv. 12–15), whereas in fact he makes for Succoth ('booths'), where he builds a house for himself and settles down. Another version (vv. 18–20), however, takes him across the Jordan, still living in tents, to the 'city of Shechem'. This phrase must, on grounds of Hebrew syntax, refer to a person of that name (cf. v. 19) who was the owner or founder of the city (see Westermann 1985: 528). The further reference to the man Shechem and to the sons of Hamor in v. 19 links this chapter to the events of ch. 34. Jacob's naming of the altar that he erects on the plot of land that he has bought ('God, the God of Israel') might be a reference to Jacob's new personal name Israel, but the reader would understand it as a proclamation that Jacob's God was to be the God of the *people* Israel.

(34:1–31) This brutal and—to the modern reader—repulsive story, which may be based on a reminiscence of some actual event in the early history of the Israelite tribes, is widely supposed to have existed in two versions, which have been combined and used by a later writer to make the point that Israelites should abstain from intermarriage with the Canaanites. The massacre which it describes is in conformity with the teaching of the Deuteronomists, who represent Moses as having demanded their extermination (Deut 7:1–3). The protagonists are Simeon and Levi, who first ensure by a trick that the victims will be in a weakened condition (vv. 25–6). Their brothers, however, all participate in the subsequent plundering of the city. That Jacob may not have figured in the original story is suggested by the fact that he plays only a marginal and passive role. Jacob's fear that the neighbouring Canaanites will take their revenge on his family and destroy it in turn (v. 30) qualifies the story as yet another example of the endangerment of the lives of the heirs to the promise, a situation that leads to Jacob's removal with his family to Bethel and is only relieved by the mysterious 'terror' that falls on the surrounding cities (35:5, which appears to be intended as the sequel to this story). The Shechemites are here (v. 2) specified as Hivites, one of the tribes supposed to have constituted the Canaanite people (cf. e.g. Gen 10:15–18; Deut 7:1). After forcing Dinah into illicit intercourse with him, Shechem falls in love with her and wishes to marry her at all costs. The inhabitants of the city, with Hamor as spokesman, attempt to negotiate the marriage in all innocence, but are rebuffed

(vv. 8–14). The imposing of circumcision on all the Shechemite men as a condition of the marriage is a trick with sinister and ironical overtones, a mere excuse for the real cause of the massacre, the desire for revenge for the initial rape (v. 31). In the Blessing of Jacob (49:2–27) in which Jacob foretells what will be the future destiny of each of his sons (now openly called the twelve tribes of Israel, 49:28), Simeon and Levi are not blessed but cursed (49:5–7) for their violent behaviour, with an apparent reference to the incident of ch. 34.

(35:1–15) Jacob's departure from Shechem to Bethel is here attributed to a positive command by God. The preparations for the journey (vv. 2–4) and the use of the technical term 'to go up' (ʿālâ) suggest that this was no ordinary journey but a pilgrimage. Alt (1959: 79–88), followed by others including von Rad (1972: 336), maintained that these verses reflect an actual annual pilgrimage made by the Israelites at later times. Bethel was the place where Jacob had already encountered God and set up a sacred pillar (28:10–22) during his flight to Laban, and which he had vowed to visit again on his return home 'in peace' (28:21). The connection between the two episodes is specifically made in vv. 1, 3, 7. The change of clothes (v. 2) was an act of purification necessary before an encounter with God (cf. Ex 19:10–14). More important is the putting away and burial of 'foreign gods' (vv. 2, 4). The fact that a similar rite, also performed at Shechem, is recorded in Josh 24:23 suggested to Alt (1959) that something of the kind constituted an essential feature of a regular pilgrimage from Shechem to Bethel, marking an annual demonstration of exclusive loyalty to YHWH. (On v. 5 see above on ch. 34.) The name given to the place where Jacob set up an altar (v. 7) is the same as in 33:20. In vv. 9–15 there occurs a further repetition of the promise of numerous descendants and of the land, followed by a further account of the setting up of a pillar and its consecration with oil.

(35:16–22) is concerned with events in Jacob's family. The birth of his twelfth and last son Benjamin is recorded. Jacob does not accept the name given to him by his dying mother, which means 'son of my sorrow', but gives him a name which may mean either 'son of the right hand' or 'son of the south' but perhaps, more appropriately and hopefully, 'son of good fortune' (Soggin 1961: 432–40). The incest committed by Reuben is condemned when Jacob blesses his sons (49:4). vv. 23–9 conclude the story of Jacob's adventures with his return home at last in time to be with his father Isaac before he dies. Jacob lived many more years after this (his death is recorded in 49:33, at the end of the story of his son Joseph's brilliant career), but he no longer plays an active role in the book.

(36:1–43) After the lengthy story of Jacob the author turns his attention to Esau, the ancestor of the Edomites, and his descendants—an indication that although Israel and Edom were often hostile to one another Israel still considered them to be 'brothers'. These genealogical lists are derived from different sources and contain not a few repetitions and inconsistencies. The extent to which they contain genuine information about a people about whom little is otherwise known is disputed. In vv. 20–30 the clan of the Horites appears to be reckoned as related to Esau, but in Deut 2:12, 22 the Horites are said to have been one of the former peoples whom the Edomites dispossessed. The lists distinguish between three types of socio-political organization, referring to heads of families (vv. 1–8, 20–8), tribal leaders (vv. 15–19, 29–30, 40–3), and kings (vv. 31–9). The kings of Edom are said to have reigned 'before any king reigned over the Israelites' (v. 31). This list, which obviously cannot be very early, may contain some genuine historical information (so Westermann 1985). The Edomites are known from the evidence of archaeology to have settled in their territory before the arrival of Israel in Canaan, and that they had acquired the status of a monarchy before Israel had done so is plausible (Num 20:14 mentions a 'king of Edom' in the time of Moses). That their monarchy was at first non-hereditary as stated in Gen vv. 31–9 is of interest in the light of recent studies of the early history of Israel.

The Story of Joseph (chs. 37–50)

These chapters are of a different kind from the rest of Genesis. Instead of a catena of brief incidents and notices about family and tribal affairs we have here—interrupted only by some obviously interpolated material, notably chs. 38 and parts of 48–50—a single, well-constructed, continuous narrative comprising some 300 verses in our Bibles and skilfully arranged in a series of distinct consecutive scenes, about the career of one man, Jacob's eleventh son, who rose to an undreamed-of eminence in Egypt as ruler of that whole land second only

to Pharaoh himself (41:40–4) and so became, under God's guidance, the saviour of his father Jacob and all his family (45:7–8; 50:19–21). This story raises for the reader a number of questions which have been the subject of much discussion, e.g.: What is its relationship to the rest of the patriarchal stories? What is its literary genre? Is it the work of a single author? Does it contain reliable information about ancient Egypt, and if so, of what period? What is its purpose?

The function of the story in the context of the foregoing patriarchal stories and of the following book of Exodus is that it bridges a gap in the chronological scheme of the Pentateuch. The material available to the compiler of Genesis about Abraham, Isaac, and Jacob appears to have come to an end. The story of Joseph, whose connection with that material is tenuous though real (his birth and his genealogy are recorded in Gen 30:22–4; 35:22–6) serves the purpose of accounting for the migration of Jacob and his family to Egypt, from which country the Exodus tradition recounts the subsequent departure of the Israelites (the sons of Jacob), so ensuring the continuity of the larger narrative tradition. At the same time, it constitutes yet another example of the theme of danger to the heirs of the promise—again as a result of famine—and their miraculous deliverance. But neither of these functions required or could account for such an elaborate narrative as this. Von Rad (1966b), who found parallels between the story and Egyptian short stories, saw it as narrative wisdom literature depicting Joseph as an ideal wise man. But others have questioned this assessment of the character of Joseph as here portrayed.

It is this quality that has led to a questioning of the conventional view that the story is the result of a combination of two separate versions, attributed respectively to J and E. Von Rad's attempt to combine the latter view with an appreciation of its literary quality was shown to be inconsistent by Whybray (1968), followed independently by Donner (1976). The possibility that it is the work of a single author, first proposed by Volz and Rudolph in 1933, who threw doubt on the existence of an E strand, is now seriously, though not universally, accepted. Whether the story betrays accurate knowledge of Egyptian life and customs of any period has been disputed by Egyptologists. Some (e.g. Vergote 1959) took a positive view of this, arguing that it fits well into the Ramesside period which was believed by some to be a plausible time for the career of a historical Joseph, but others (e.g. Redford 1970) were sceptical about the authenticity of the Egyptian allusions. Redford maintained that if the author did in fact have genuine knowledge of Egypt the work cannot be dated earlier than the seventh century BCE.

(37:1–34) The minor inconsistencies and duplications in this chapter (e.g. the apparent confusion between Ishmaelites and Midianites in v. 28; the duplication of Joseph's dreams in vv. 6–7 and 9; the similarity of the compassionate actions of Reuben and Judah in vv. 21–2 and 26–7) are not sufficient to show that two complete versions of the story have been interwoven; at most they may suggest that the author made use at some points of earlier oral material. The story itself is quite straightforward: it recounts the first of a series of incidents which once again put in danger of his life the person who is destined to hold in his hands the survival of the heirs of the promise. This destiny is foreshadowed here by Joseph's dreams; but the dramatic suspense is to continue concerning his fate for several more chapters. Another motif, that of hatred between brothers, is reminiscent of the hostility between Jacob and Esau; once again the issue is solved by the end of the story with the indication that it is not the elder brother who has been chosen by God to assure the continuation of the chosen race. vv. 1–2 are an introduction to the whole Joseph story, providing the necessary link between the earlier patriarchal stories and the present one. In v. 3 the precise nature of the 'long coat with sleeves' (*kĕtōnet passîm*) is not certain. Outside this chapter this garment is referred to in the OT only in 2 Sam 13:18, 19, where it is the apparel of a princess. Here it is a token of Jacob's especial affection for Joseph and a mark of esteem which incites the brothers' hatred. The description of Jacob's grief at the supposed death of his son (vv. 33–5) closes this first part of the story of Joseph, after which (in ch. 39) the scene changes to Egypt.

(38:1–30) This chapter, in which Joseph does not appear at all, is an interpolation that interrupts the Joseph story, which resumes in 39:1 at the point at which it is broken off at the end of ch. 37. Attempts to interpret it as in some way relevant to the events narrated in the surrounding chapters have hardly been convincing, although on the other hand no convincing explanation has been found for its interpolation. Probably, as a story about a member of

Jacob's family it was thought to deserve a place in the total narrative, but no satisfactory placement for it could be found. It is wholly concerned with events in the life of Judah, Jacob's fourth son. But he can hardly be called the hero of the story: it is his daughter-in-law Tamar who fills that role. The story is a complicated one and involves a number of customs that call for elucidation. These can only be briefly sketched here. vv. 1–11 are introductory to the main story. Judah's decision to settle apart from his brothers probably reflects the fact that the tribe of Judah was located in historical times in the south, away from the other tribes, and had a separate existence until politically united with them by David (Adullam and Timnah were both Judaean cities in later times). The story also reflects fraternization and intermarriage between Israelites and Canaanites. Tamar's second marriage, to Onan, conforms to the custom of levirate marriage (see Deut 25:5–6). With the death of her first two husbands Tamar evidently expected to be married to the third brother, Shelah; but, afraid that he too might die prematurely, Jacob made an excuse to avoid this; and Tamar, according to custom, returned to the unenviable state of living with her parents. In desperation she then tried to force Judah's hand. She arranged to have sexual relations with her father-in-law in the guise of a prostitute without his being aware of her identity, and retained proof of the relationship by keeping his cylinder seal with its cord and his staff as pledge for her fee (v. 18). It is not clear on what grounds she was condemned to death by Judah in his capacity as undisputed head of the family with powers of life and death (v. 24); it is perhaps assumed that she was betrothed to Shelah, though not actually married to him (cf. Deut 22:23–4). After Judah's recognition that her action was justified (!) the story ends with her giving birth to twin boys, Judah's children, whose names (Perez and Zerah) are interpreted as meaning 'breaking out' and (perhaps) 'bright, shining' respectively.

(39:1–41:57) This account of Joseph's humiliation and subsequent exaltation has some of the characteristics of the folktale, but is an integral part of the story of Joseph as a whole. It is full of dramatic tension: Joseph is again placed in great danger; but the tension is finally resolved in an equally dramatic fashion. It is several times (39:3, 5, 21, 23; 41:51–2) specifically emphasized that both his preservation in danger and his later success are due not to his own abilities but to the unseen operation of God. Although there is no evidence in extant Egyptian texts of any comparable elevation of a person of humble status to a position of great power, the theme of the elevation of exiled Jews by foreign potentates was evidently a favourite one in post-exilic times, and is found also in Dan 1–6 and Esther. 39:1, which repeats information given at the end of ch. 37, is deliberately resumptive following the interpolation of ch. 38. It specifies that it was Ishmaelites rather than Midianites who sold Joseph into slavery in Egypt (as in 37:28*b*). The Egyptian name Potiphar means 'the one whom Re gives'. The initial success of the good-looking Joseph (39:6) as Potiphar's trusted servant (39:2–6) is brought to a sudden end and his life once more endangered by the lie told by Potiphar's wife when he twice virtuously refuses her sexual advances (39:14–18). (On the use of the term 'Hebrew', 39:14, which occurs several times in the story of Joseph, see above on 14:13.) But the punishment which Potiphar imposes on Joseph is surprisingly mild for the crime of adultery, and suggests that Potiphar was not entirely convinced of his guilt. The chapter ends on a more positive note: Joseph's attractive personality (as well as God's protection) once more leads to success, when he obtains the favour of the jailer.

The chief cupbearer and chief baker, whom Joseph waited upon in prison (40:1–4) were high officials imprisoned for some undisclosed offences by the dictatorial king of Egypt. Unlike Joseph's own dreams in ch. 37, whose meaning needed no explanation, their dreams, as also those of Pharaoh in ch. 41, were dreams whose meaning was not obvious and which required an interpreter with special powers. The interpretation of such dreams was, both in Egypt and in Mesopotamia, the speciality and occult art of the professional diviner. Like Daniel, who was required not only to interpret Nebuchadnezzar's dream but also to remind the king of its contents (Dan 2:31–45), Joseph possessed the power to interpret dreams, but attributed this power to special divine revelation rather than to his own ability (40:8—although in 44:15 he speaks of his ability to practise divination (*niḥēš*). The difference between the cupbearer's and the baker's dreams—the fact that in the latter's dream the birds were eating from the basket of food which he was carrying to Pharaoh, whereas the cupbearer dreamed that he had resumed his former function—determined Joseph's interpretations, in which Joseph played—gruesomely—on two

meanings of the phrase 'to lift up the head', whose normal meaning was to restore to favour, but in the case of the baker referred to decapitation or hanging. Both interpretations proved to be correct. The last verse of the chapter reintroduces the tension into the story: although the cupbearer had promised to intercede for Joseph when he was restored to favour with Pharaoh, he forgot him, leaving him in prison with no apparent hope, and possibly again in danger of his life should judgement be given against him.

Pharaoh's dreams (41:1–7) are of the same symbolic kind as those of the cupbearer and baker, and required expert decipherment. Like Nebuchadnezzar in similar circumstances (Dan 2:4) Pharaoh sent for his experts (*ḥarṭummîm*, 'magicians', is a form of an Egyptian word meaning 'soothsayer-priest'), who proved to be incapable of the task. On the suggestion of the cupbearer, who at last remembered Joseph's talents, Joseph was sent for from his prison cell and, having shaved and put on clean clothes—matters of great importance to the Egyptians—appeared before Pharaoh. His preparations are symbolic of a great change in his life; from this moment he never looked back. But it was his successful interpretation of the dreams that—under God, 41:39—was the cause of his sudden elevation to greatness, together with his eminently practical advice about the measures to be taken in the face of an otherwise certain disaster. In a manner typical of the folktale, Pharaoh put his entire faith in this one demonstration of Joseph's ability (41:39–40) and lost no time in appointing him Grand Vizier of Egypt, endowing him with all the symbols and the reality of that office, which are attested in Egyptian art and tomb furniture. The meaning of the word '*abrēk* ('Bow the knee!', 41:43) may be related to the Semitic root *b-r-k*, 'kneel', or may be related to an Egyptian word meaning 'Watch out!' In receiving a new and Egyptian name (Zaphenath-paneah means 'God speaks and lives'), Joseph was received into the ranks of the Egyptian nobility; and this was confirmed by his being given the daughter of the high priest of Heliopolis ('On') as his bride. He is presented (41:34–6, 47–57) as a foresighted administrator. The establishment of large granaries against times of low grain production was a well-known Egyptian economic measure. The final verse of the chapter (57) prepares for the events of the following chapters by emphasizing the world-wide nature of the food shortage against which Joseph successfully prepared Egypt.

(42:1–45:28) With ch. 42 the scene switches back to Canaan and to Jacob and his other sons. Egypt was the granary of the ancient world; and journeys from such countries as Canaan to try to buy food in times of famine are recorded in extant Egyptian texts (see *ANET* 250–1) and depicted in Egyptian graphic art. The main problem of the interpretation of these chapters is to understand the reason for Joseph's harsh treatment of his brothers before he reveals his identity in ch. 45. One of his motives was certainly to force them to bring his youngest brother Benjamin to see him. But there can be little doubt that a main motive was connected with his brothers' treatment of him many years before (ch. 37). In his present position of unlimited power he was in a position to punish them, and he did so; but in the end brotherly love and family feelings proved stronger than his desire for revenge (ch. 45). The story is replete with dramatic tension and also with dramatic irony (the brothers do not know who he is, but the readers do) and is told with psychological subtlety. By pretending to believe that the brothers are spies (42:9), Joseph extracts the information that they have left their youngest brother behind with his father, and demands that he should be brought to him. Imprisoned for three days, they suppose that they are being punished for their earlier crime, even though they do not recognize Joseph (42:21). In releasing them all except Simeon, however, Joseph is deeply affected, and supplies them with corn and provisions; but the return of their money increases their fears (42:28, 35), and their misery is increased when on their return home Jacob, in a mood of self-pity, refuses to let Benjamin return with them to Egypt.

When a further supply of corn became an absolute necessity to Jacob and his family a second visit to Egypt was mooted, and Jacob was persuaded against his will to let Benjamin go with his brothers, with Judah as a guarantor of his safety (43:1–11). This time, fearful of their reception, they take with them tribute in the form of choice products of Canaan and double the previous sum of money, to prove their honesty (43:11–12). Joseph, however, was to continue to play his tricks on them (ch. 44). The scene with Joseph's steward (43:16–25) is intended to allay the brothers' fears: they are at first suspicious and naïvely afraid of a trap (in such a setting!), but are reassured. They have been naturally astonished and awed by the luxury of Joseph's house and by the invitation to dinner; but when Joseph arrives he shows his concern

for his aged father, and is overjoyed, and again deeply affected, on seeing Benjamin (43:30). There is again astonishment at Benjamin's treatment as guest of honour, and probably at Joseph's dining at a separate table in accordance with Egyptian rules of purity; but in the relaxed atmosphere they forget their fears and even drink to excess ('were merry') in Joseph's company, unaware of further trouble to come.

(44:1–34) By the repetition of the earlier incident of 42:35 with the planting in the brother's luggage of Joseph's cup (the reference to the money here is probably a later addition), the pursuit and apprehension of the brothers and the accusation of theft (vv. 1–13) the tension is still further increased. It seems to them that Joseph has now trapped them as they had feared all along, and that it is all up with them. The cup is particularly important to Joseph because he uses it to practise lecanomancy (v. 5), a form of divination in which oil was poured into a cup or bowl to give psychic insight (see Cryer 1994: 145–7, 285)—a practice somewhat resembling modern foretelling of the future by tea-leaves. Joseph's purpose in so tricking the brothers was to test them to see whether they had changed their nature, and whether they genuinely cared for their father and for Benjamin. They protest their innocence, but recognize that if found guilty they merit condign punishment (v. 9), though both the steward and Joseph himself are inclined to mercy except towards the thief, who must be enslaved (vv. 10, 17). Joseph adds to their dismay by claiming that he has the gift of divination even without the use of the cup, and knows what has occurred (v. 15). But Judah's lengthy speech in which he heartrendingly depicts the inevitable fate of Jacob if he is bereft of yet another son and offers himself as a scapegoat in Benjamin's place is a masterpiece of rhetoric which Joseph finds too hard to endure (45:1).

(45:1–28) This chapter probably marks the end of the Joseph story proper. With it all the tension is released and the problems solved; there is a reconciliation and a happy ending. From the literary point of view the story is complete, and the chapters that complete the book have rather the character of an appendix or series of appendices designed to provide an answer to the question, 'And how did it all end?' (46:1–5 already reverts to the style and concerns of the earlier patriarchal stories, with an appearance of God in the night to Jacob, reiterating the promise of making a great nation of him, but this time in Egypt rather than Canaan. The remaining chapters lack the high literary quality of the Joseph story proper, and are rather piecemeal in contents.) vv. 1–15 describe a touching scene in which, apart from the emotions that are expressed between Joseph and his brothers, the author is concerned to emphasize Joseph's forgiveness of his brothers and the hidden hand of God in preserving the lives of Jacob's family through Joseph's agency. In vv. 10–15, however, a new theme is announced: Jacob and his family are to migrate to Egypt to share in Joseph's good fortune. (His question in v. 3 is strange: the brothers have already told him that his father is still alive.) The rest of the chapter is concerned with the arrangements for the move. Joseph proposes it on his own initiative (vv. 9–11), and Pharaoh himself confirms this, offering the family the best land in Egypt for their residence. In vv. 21–8 Joseph's lavish provisions for the journey and Jacob/Israel's astonishment, incredulity, and final acceptance of the news of Joseph and of his offer are described.

(46:1–34) Jacob was last heard of as living in Hebron (37:14). Now he passes through Beersheba on his way to Egypt, and it is there that he has his reassuring message from God. The list of names of those who went with him (vv. 8–27) is supposedly a roll-call of the persons mentioned in vv. 6–7; but it clearly comes from a different source and interrupts the narrative. Among the total of sixty-six persons alleged to have made the journey (v. 26), expanded to seventy by (presumably) including Jacob himself and also Joseph and his two sons Ephraim and Manasseh, who are counted twice, though not named the second time (v. 27) there are some who are expressly stated not to have been among them: Er and Onan (v. 12) were already dead (38:7, 10), and Manasseh and Ephraim had been born in Egypt. Joseph, of course, was still in Egypt. Moreover, the statement that Benjamin had ten sons who accompanied him on the journey (v. 21) does not accord with what had previously been said about his youth. Probably this list was originally intended as a list of all Jacob's descendants through three generations and had no original connection with this narrative. vv. 28–34 are concerned with Jacob's projected meeting with Pharaoh and with the place of residence designated for the immigrants. Goshen (vv. 28, 34, already mentioned in 45:10) was an area on the eastern edge of the Nile delta, where the Egyptians, who were

suspicious of foreign immigrants, commonly settled them. There is a strong hint to the reader in v. 34 about the future in the statement that shepherds are abhorrent to the Egyptians, and in Joseph's advice to his father to be open in his interview with Pharaoh about his profession. However, Pharaoh is represented in 47:5–6 as being prepared to welcome Jacob for Joseph's sake on condition that he lived in Goshen, as he had already promised (45:17–20).

(47:1–26) The narrative of vv. 1–12 follows immediately on ch. 46, and is continued in v. 27. vv. 13–26 are an account of Joseph's economic policy as Grand Vizier, and has no connection, except for the motif of the famine, with the story of Jacob and his family in Egypt. The audience with Pharaoh (vv. 1–12) is in two parts: first Joseph presents five of his brothers to Pharaoh (vv. 2–6) and then, separately, his father (vv. 7–12). It is probable that two distinct versions have been used here; this is suggested by the fact that in v. 11 the land assigned to the immigrants is called (only here) the land of Rameses (cf. Ex 1:11) rather than of Goshen. The location, however, is probably the same. The point of the audience with the brothers seems to be that the brothers do not, as they might have done, try to use their kinship with Joseph to enhance their social status: they do not ask for permanent residence in Egypt, which would have been tantamount to Egyptian citizenship, and they wish to continue their hereditary profession, although Pharaoh suggests that some of them may be capable of positions of some responsibility (v. 6). The point of the second audience is to present Jacob as a dignified old man who is not overawed by Pharaoh but dares to bless him (vv. 7, 10). vv. 13–26 are designed to demonstrate Joseph's superior wisdom in using his control over the corn supply to make slaves of the whole Egyptian nation—a triumph which, whatever the modern reader may think of its morality, perhaps—although this is a secular story—foreshadows the later triumph of the Israelites over Pharaoh himself (Ex 6–15).

(47:27–48:22) The story of Jacob and his family is now resumed; but the narrative is not all of one piece. It contains a number of inconsistencies and incongruities, and is the result of the combination of several different kinds of material. 47:27–8 notes the family's successful life in the land of Goshen and the period of their residence there together with a note of the length of Jacob's life—though his death is not recorded until 49:33. 47:29–31, however, begins the account of his last years and death. His request to be taken back to Canaan for burial reintroduces—though indirectly—the theme of the promise of the land: life in Egypt is not to be the permanent destiny of the nation of Israel. In his deathbed speech in 48:1–4 Jacob first repeats the story of his blessing and the promise made to him at Bethel (35:6–12; Luz = Bethel; 28:19; 35:6) and then informs Joseph that he is adopting his (Joseph's) sons Ephraim and Manasseh as his own sons. This action, which points beyond the brothers as individuals to their future character as Israelite tribes, would mean that the traditional number of twelve tribes (implied, for example, in 35:23–6) is augmented to thirteen (if Ephraim and Manasseh are to be counted instead of their father). In fact the traditional number of twelve is a fiction; they are listed in several different ways in various places in the OT, and their numbers vary between ten and thirteen.

The scene of Jacob's blessing of Ephraim and Manasseh (48:8–20), in which Jacob is called by his other name Israel, appears not to presuppose the previous passage but to be from a different source. Since it is implied here that Joseph's sons are not yet adult and Jacob appears to be encountering them for the first time, the scene is evidently supposed to have taken place soon after Jacob's arrival in Egypt rather than just before his death (cf. 47:28). This is another example of the younger son being given precedence over the elder (cf. ch. 27). The right hand is assumed to confer the greater blessing. Jacob deliberately crosses his hands despite Joseph's protest, in order to give Ephraim, the younger, the greater blessing. 48:15–16 is somewhat confused, and interrupts the main narrative. It is stated here that it is Joseph who is blessed (48:15a), but in fact it is his sons who are blessed (48:16), and no difference is made between them. 48:20 also is a somewhat confusing addition to the story: it purports to be an alternative blessing of Ephraim and Manasseh ('them'), but in fact it is a wish rather than a blessing, and it is addressed to one person ('you' is singular). It is noteworthy that 'Israel' here (and perhaps also in 47:27) refers to the *nation* of Israel, not to the individual Jacob/Israel. The last sentence in the verse reverts to the main story, summing it up: Ephraim was preferred before Manasseh. There is a clear allusion in this story to the later predominance of the tribe of Ephraim (cf. e.g. Deut 33:17).

The significance of 48:22 is not clear. 'Joseph' here does not refer simply to the individual but to the 'house of Joseph', which comprised the tribes of Ephraim and Manasseh, and was to be the most powerful of the northern group of Israelite tribes. Jacob confers on 'Joseph' one 'portion' (*šĕkem*), here unidentified, more than he gives to the others. The word *šĕkem* is also the name of the city of Shechem, but as a common noun means 'shoulder'. Here it plainly means a shoulder of land or a mountain ridge. The military exploit of Jacob referred to here is unknown; certainly he did not capture the city of Shechem from the Amorites (= Canaanites; cf. ch. 34).

(49:1–33) The sayings about the twelve tribes of Israel preserved here in the guise of a deathbed address by Jacob to his twelve sons (vv. 3–27) are generally known as the Blessing of Jacob, partly on the basis of the statement in v. 28. v. 1, however, describes their character somewhat more accurately: in their present form the sayings are, to a large extent, *predictions* of 'what will happen' to the various tribes in the future. They vary considerably in their contents, and their assessments are by no means all favourable. They cannot be said to constitute a single poem, but differ greatly in form and length as well as in contents. They are in fact a collection of originally quite separate sayings or slogans each characterizing an individual tribe (in the case of Simeon and Levi, vv. 5–7, two are treated together), some of them alluding to particular incidents in which they were involved that are now wholly or partly obscure. Some have been greatly augmented; in those cases it is often possible to identify the original, usually pointed, saying. The intention of the author/ collector was to provide a complete survey of all the twelve tribes of Israel (Joseph, vv. 22–6 being treated as a single tribe—see above); however, the persistent tradition that Israel was composed of exactly twelve tribes is not derived from this chapter. This is not the only passage of this kind in the OT: Deut 33, known as the Blessing of Moses, is a parallel instance, and Judg 5, the Song of Deborah, also assesses the characters of almost all the tribes (Judg 5:14–18). The latter, however, is a unitary poem which comments on a single incident, and praises or blames the various tribes according to their co-operation or otherwise. Here in Gen 49 it is significant that Judah (vv. 8–12) and Joseph (vv. 22–6)—that is, the tribes which were later to become the most powerful and important tribes—are treated much more fully than the others.

The Blessing of Jacob is here presented as a scene that took place at Jacob's bedside just before his death in the presence of all his sons, and thus as a farewell discourse (a frequent feature in the accounts of the deaths of great men in the OT—cf. e.g. the Blessing of Moses, Deut 33; Josh 24; David's farewell speech, 1 Kings 2:1–9). However, it is clearly an independent piece that has been inserted at an appropriate point into the story of Jacob's death. In its present expanded form it cannot be earlier than the time of David, as it speaks of Judah as the ruler of the other tribes and of other peoples (v. 10). The full and favourable assessment of Joseph—that is, of the central tribes—as numerous and powerful (vv. 22–6) expresses a different picture of leadership; but it also clearly reflects a later period and has a different orientation from that of Judah. The chapter appears to have been subject to more than one process of redaction. The function of the individual sayings in their original brief state is not obvious and has been frequently debated. They were presumably comments by tribes about other tribes made at an early period; but the circumstances in which they were made remain obscure.

v. 2 is a formal poetical introduction to the collection of sayings, which are also in poetical form. Reuben (vv. 3–4) is addressed directly and accused of incest—probably referring to 35:22. Little is known of Reuben either as an individual or as a tribe. It played no prominent part in subsequent history; Deut 33:6 suggests that it died out as a distinct tribe at a fairly early period despite its initial prominence reflected in Reuben's being the eldest son of Jacob. Simeon and Levi (vv. 5–7) are not blessed but cursed. The crime of which they are accused in v. 6 is almost certainly their treacherous murder of the Shechemites in ch. 34, though no mention is made there of their hamstringing oxen. In historical times Levi was a priestly tribe which, unlike the others, had no inheritance in the land: it thus ceased to be counted among the ordinary tribes, though the connection between the Levi of this saying and the later priestly tribe is uncertain. According to Judg 1:3, 17 Simeon was associated with Judah in its invasion of Canaanite territory, and was probably absorbed into the more powerful tribe of Judah, so being 'scattered in Israel'. The use in v. 6 of the first person singular can hardly be supposed to be that of Jacob, and this is also true of 'are brothers' in v. 5. The

statement at the end of v. 7 reads like a divine pronouncement of judgement similar to those found in the prophetical books.

Judah (vv. 8–12) was David's tribe, pre-eminent in the time of the united kingdom; it was the name of the southern kingdom after the dissolution of the union until its destruction in the sixth century BCE. This passage has incorporated more than one shorter saying. The reference to Judah as a lion (v. 8) is the first of several examples in the chapter of the association of a tribe with a particular animal. The lion later became the traditional symbol of the tribe of Judah (cf. Rev 5:5). 'shall praise you' (yôdûkā) is a play on the word 'Judah'. 'Until tribute comes to him' (v. 10) is only one among many alternative renderings of the Hebrew phrase 'ad kî-yābō' šîlōh, the meaning of which is one of the unsolved problems of OT interpretation. Its literal translation could be either 'Until Shiloh comes' or 'Until he comes to Shiloh'; but no plausible connection between Judah (or David) and the Ephraimite city and sanctuary of Shiloh can be found. The Hebrew text may be corrupt, or the word 'Shiloh' may have some hitherto undiscovered meaning; but attempts to correct it or to find some other explanation based on comparative philology have achieved no consensus. 'Until' suggests that some event will put an end to Judah's domination; but the traditional notion that this is a prophecy of the coming of the Messiah to bring to an end temporal earthly rule lacks support in the text. That it should be a prophecy of the accession to rule of David is also improbable, as he can hardly be said to have put an end to the rule of Judah! Westermann (1986: 231) comments: 'It is no praiseworthy page in the history of O.T. exegesis that so many studies have been preoccupied with this one word [Shiloh]'. vv. 11–12 appear to be a somewhat fanciful prediction of great fertility and prosperity which will follow the accession of the future ruler, when wine will flow in abundance, and of the ruler's outstanding beauty. There is an analogous prediction of a future king in Num 24:5–9; the last two lines of v. 9 are repeated almost word for word in Num 24:9a.

The saying about Zebulon (v. 13) makes no comment on the character of this tribe, but only—somewhat vaguely—on its territorial location. These statements do not correspond very closely with the description of its location in Josh 19:10–16, which places it in Galilee to the east of the Sea of Tiberias, but at least ten miles from the Mediterranean at its nearest point. It is not known at what period it expanded its territory so far west. Ancient Israel was not, of course, a maritime people. The saying may have been intended to emphasize Zebulon's isolation from the other tribes, though in Judg 5:14 it is commended for its participation with other tribes in the battle against Jabin and Sisera in the nearby valley of Jezreel. Issachar's name and character (vv. 14–15) are probably associated here, as in 30:18, with śākār, 'hire, wages'. Although the tribe, like Zebulon, is praised in Judg 5:15, it is here portrayed as submitting itself to the harshest form of slavery—that is, under the neighbouring Canaanite cities. Dan's name (v. 16) is understood here, as in 30:6, to be derived from the verb dîn, 'to judge'; but whereas in 30:6 it is God who is the subject of the verb, here it is Dan who is the subject: he will be the judge of his people. In v. 17, however, Dan is described as a snake that attacks horsemen by biting the horses' heels. The analogy may be a reference to the small size of the tribe, that cannot attack enemies openly. This verse is probably intended as praise rather than condemnation, referring to attacks against the enemy Canaanites. v. 18 is probably a pious exclamation of a general kind, not specifically connected with the tribe of Dan.

The name of Gad (v. 19) is here derived from the Hebrew root g-d-d, 'to band together', which occurs in various forms four times in the verse. It is an appropriate name in that this tribe, which was located east of the Jordan bordering on the desert, would be subject to attacks by marauding raiders. The saying comments that it is known for its ability to give a good account of itself in such encounters. Asher (v. 20), whose name means 'happiness, good fortune' (cf. 30:13), settled in the fertile coastal strip between Carmel and the Phoenician border (Josh 19:24–31). But according to Judg 1:31–2 it was unable to drive out the local Canaanites and so lived among them. The 'royal delicacies' referred to here may refer to a period when Asher was renowned for its provision of delicacies for royal courts—either for those of Jerusalem or Samaria or for Canaanite or Phoenician royal courts. The saying about Naphtali (49:21) is obscure: the text may be corrupt. A different spelling of 'doe' ('ayyālâ) would yield 'terebinth' ('ēlâ); 'fawns' could also mean 'words'. But if the text is correct and 'fawns' is a correct interpretation, this is another animal analogy: Naphtali is called a female deer 'let loose', that is, free to roam at will in the mountains of Galilee.

The section on Joseph (vv. 22–6) is, like that on Judah, made up of a number of originally separate elements, not all of which are tribal sayings. It is divided into two main parts, a characterization of the 'tribe' of Joseph with an allusion to Joseph's behaviour when attacked (vv. 22–5a) and a series of blessings (vv. 25b–6). Unfortunately much in these verses is difficult to understand: there are rare and obscure words, and the syntax is sometimes unusual and difficult. There are probably textual corruptions and the rendering of NRSV—and of all other translations—is based to some extent on conjectural interpretation, v. 22 is a metaphorical reference to Joseph as a strong and flourishing plant well supplied with water; 'fruitful' (pōrāt) plays on the word 'Ephraim', the predominant member of the 'house of Joseph'. vv. 23–4 describe an incident, now unidentifiable, in which 'Joseph' was attacked by enemies but overcame them with God's help. v. 24b introduces a series of divine blessings, and prayers for blessings to be conferred on Joseph. In vv. 24–5 God is invoked with an amazing, and unique, concatenation of divine names, all found elsewhere in the OT together betraying a fairly late date of composition. 'Mighty One of Jacob' occurs in Isa 49:26; 60:16; Ps 132:2, 5. God is referred to as a shepherd a number of times, e.g. Ps 23:1 and 80:1. 'Rock' ('eben) of Israel' occurs only here, but there are fairly frequent references in the Psalms to him as 'Rock' (ṣûr), and in that form 'Rock of Israel' occurs in Isa 30:29. 'God of your father' most obviously refers to Abraham or Jacob, and similar epithets are found throughout Genesis. 'Almighty' (šadday) elsewhere in Genesis occurs in the phrase 'El Shaddai', but is found frequently by itself in Job and elsewhere. v. 26 is probably a very ancient form of blessing. In vv. 25 and 26a Joseph is addressed in the second person, but not in the previous verses or in v. 26b. v. 26b refers primarily to Joseph's separation from his brothers while in Egypt, but is also intended to emphasize his pre-eminence over the other tribes. The description of Benjamin (v. 27) refers to the tribe rather than to the individual: it has nothing in common with the Benjamin of the preceding narratives. This is a fierce tribal saying of great antiquity, unaugmented by later comment. Benjamin is here presented, and apparently commended, as a ruthless brigand-like fighter. Jacob's charge, now to all his sons, to bury him with his ancestors in the cave of Machpelah (vv. 29–32) essentially repeats his charge to Joseph alone in 47:29–31. The repetition was intended by the final redactor of the book to form a framework for the whole section about Jacob's arrangements in anticipation of his death that stretches from 47:29 to 49:32.

(50:1–26) This chapter forms an appropriate conclusion to the patriarchal stories that began in ch. 12. Like the deaths of Moses at the end of Deut (34:5–12) and of Joshua at the end of Josh (24:29–31), that of Joseph marks the end of an epoch. The chapter satisfactorily ties up several of the themes of the book, at the same time hinting that it marks no more than a temporary stopping-place in the history of the nation: the final words of the book, 'in Egypt', make this clear. The reconciliation of the brothers with Joseph is completed and their crime forgiven; God's promise of protection and guidance is once more affirmed and demonstrated; the promise of the land is renewed; and the future of the heirs of the promise is assured. Joseph's love for his father, already noted in his enquiry about him in Gen 45:3, is poignantly brought out in v. 1. The elaborate treatment of Jacob's corpse (vv. 2–3) and of his burial (vv. 4–14) reflects the almost royal position of Joseph in Egypt. Joseph's application for permission to bury Jacob in Canaan through the court officials rather than personally to Pharaoh (vv. 4–6), the granting of which was presumably a foregone conclusion, though his promise to return to Egypt afterwards (v. 5) may have some significance, is strange; it may mean that as a recent mourner he refrained from appearing at court. The great detail with which the ceremonies of the burial are described (vv. 7–13) certainly reflects his immense prestige among the Egyptians and so was a matter of great pride to the Israelite reader. The curious route taken by the funeral procession with a first stopping-place east of the Jordan before the actual burial in Machpelah (i.e. Hebron) on the western side (vv. 10–13) is also strange; it has been suggested that an alternative tradition about Jacob's burial place has been incorporated into the narrative (see von Rad 1972: 431). The place-name Abel-mizraim (v. 11) is interpreted here as meaning 'the mourning of Egypt'; its true meaning, however, may be 'brook of Egypt'.

(50:15–21) Joseph had given the brothers no cause to believe that he was only waiting for their father's death to take his revenge on them; but their consciousness of their guilt still remained, and they were afraid. Whether the author means the readers to understand that they invented the story—otherwise unattested—that Jacob had asked that Joseph should forgive them (v. 17) cannot be determined; to tell such a lie would be an indication of their panic. On the other hand, there is nothing in the text to suggest that they acted in bad faith. Joseph's weeping when they spoke in this way was a sign of deep emotion, but gives no hint of his thoughts. In their fear the brothers fell at his feet in supplication and acknowledged that their fate was in his hands, so unconsciously—though this was certainly in the mind of the author—fulfilling Joseph's former dreams that he would eventually rule over them (37:6–10). But his reply (vv. 19–21) reassures them completely. He first points out that it is not for human beings, however exalted, to take revenge, which is a prerogative of God, and then, as he had already done on a previous occasion (45:5–8), he attributes all that had happened to the hidden hand of God, whose purpose had been to preserve their lives so that they would become a 'numerous people' (the word *'am*, 'people', can denote a group or family, but here has also overtones of 'nation'). This speech, which expresses a high theology and also sums up a major theme of the book, is the climax of the whole.

(50:22–6) constitutes the epilogue to the book. v. 23 hints at the fulfilment of the promise of numerous progeny, reported in Ex 1:7 as having already been realized in Egypt. In v. 24 Joseph on his deathbed at the end of a long life affirmed the promise of the land—not a feature of the Joseph story proper; and in v. 25 he charged 'the Israelites' (lit., 'the sons of Israel'), to rebury him after they left Egypt and returned to Canaan. That they did so is recorded in Josh 24:32, after the land had been conquered and its territory distributed among the tribes. Meanwhile Joseph died in Egypt and was duly buried according to Egyptian custom, as befitted the man who had been the effective ruler of Egypt. Ex 1:6–7 takes up the story. So, the author tells us, Israel became a nation.

REFERENCES

Alt, A. (1959), 'Die Wallfahrt von Sichem nach Bethel', *Kleine Schriften zur Geschichte des Volkes Israel* I (Munich: Beck), 79–88.

Alter, R. (1981), *The Art of Biblical Narrative* (London: Allen & Unwin).

Blenkinsopp, J. (1992), *The Pentateuch. An Introduction to the First Five Books of the Bible* (London: SCM).

Blum, E. (1984), *Die Komposition der Vätergeschichte* (WMANT 57; Neukirchen-Vluyn: Neukirchener Verlag).

Cryer, F. H. (1994), *Divination in Ancient Israel and its Near Eastern Environment. A Socio-Historical Investigation*, JSOTSup 142 (Sheffield: JSOT).

Donner, H. (1976), *Die literarische Gestalt der alttestamentlichen Josephs-geschichte* (SHAW; Heidelberg: Carl Winter).

Driver, S. R. (1909), *An Introduction to the Literature of the Old Testament* (8th ed.; Edinburgh: T. & T. Clark).

Gunkel, H. (1964), *Genesis übersetzt und erklärt* (HK 1/1; Göttingen: Vandenhoeck & Ruprecht, 1901; 6th ed.).

—— (1901), *The Legends of Genesis* (New York: Schocken, 1964; German original).

Lambert, W. G., and Millard, A. R. (1969), *Atra-ḥasīs. The Babylonian Story of the Flood* (Oxford: Clarendon Press).

von Rad, G. (1966), 'The Form-Critical Problem of the Hexateuch', *The Problem of the Hexateuch and Other Essays* (Edinburgh and London: Oliver & Boyd) 1–78 (German original, Munich: Kaiser, 1958) 9–86.

—— (1966), 'The Joseph Narrative and Ancient Wisdom', *The Problem of the Hexateuch and Other Essays* (Edinburgh and London: Oliver & Boyd) 292–300 (German original, VT supplement, Leiden: Brill, 1953) 120–7.

—— (1972), *Genesis* (OTL; 2nd ed.; London: SCM) (German original, Göttingen: Vandenhoeck & Ruprecht).

Redford, D. B., (1970), *A Study of the Biblical Story of Joseph (Genesis 37–50)* (VT Supplement 20; Leiden: Brill).

Rendtorff, R. (1982), 'Jakob in Bethel. Beobachtungen zum Aufbau und zur Quellenfrage in Gen 28, 10–22', *ZAW* 94, 511–23.

Soggin, J. A. (1961), 'Die Geburt Benjamins, Genesis xxxv 16–20 (21)', *VT* 11, 432–40.

Van Seters, J. (1983), *In Search of History* (New Haven and London: Yale University Press).

—— (1992), *Prologue to History. The Yahwist as Historian in Genesis* (Louisville, Kentucky: Westminster/John Knox).

de Vaux, R. (1978), *The Early History of Israel* I, (London: Darton, Longman & Todd; French original, Paris: Gabalda, 1971).

Vergote, J. (1959), *Joseph en Egypte. Genèse chap. 37–50 à la lumière des études égyptologiques récentes* (OBL 3; Louvain: Publications Universitaires).

Volz, P., and Rudolph, W. (1933), *Der Elohist als Erzähler ein Irrweg der Pentateuchkritik?* (BZAW 63; Giessen: Töpelmann).

Westermann, C. (1985), *Genesis 12–36* (London: SPCK; German original, Neukirchen-Vluyn: Neukirchener Verlag, 1981).

Whybray, R. N. (1968), 'The Joseph Story and Pentateuchal Criticism', *VT* 18, 522–8.

—— (1987), *The Making of the Pentateuch. A Methodological Study*, JSOTSup 53 (Sheffield: JSOT).

5. Exodus

WALTER J. HOUSTON

INTRODUCTION

A. What Kind of Book is Exodus? 1. The second book of the Pentateuch is in many ways its centrepiece. Genesis is about Israel's ancestors, Exodus tells how they became a nation through the action of their God. It is Israel's foundation story, their identity document, telling them where they have come from and showing them their place in the world under God's sovereignty.

2. Is Exodus a work of history? That is, could it be appropriately put on the history shelves in a library? If we define a historical work as one whose 'chief purpose is to trace the network of causation between events at a mundane level' (Johnstone 1990: 31), then Exodus is not one. It portrays the entire sweep of events as the direct result of the purpose and intervention of God. Although people have sometimes tried

to understand parts of the story as heightened accounts of natural sequences of events (see EX 7:6–11:10, EX 16, or EX 19), this flies in the face of the basic intention of the text, which is to relate the glorious works of God. Not only does God intervene directly in an astonishing series of powerful acts, but he himself appears on the scene several times in more or less plainly visible forms (see EX 3:1–6). The writers draw freely on imagination or legend to create the scenes which we read. The historical setting is only very hazily sketched in. In brief, Exodus is not the kind of history recognized by the Greeks or by modern historians.

3. Yet several points show that its intention is to relate, however imaginatively, a story of the actual past, not a simple fiction. The story focuses on a people of history and is part of a continuous narrative (Genesis to 2 Kings) which takes their story down to the fall of

Jerusalem to the Babylonians in 587 BCE; and there are links with earlier and later parts of this narrative. Often the story serves to explain known facts, such as the name of Israel's God (see 3:13–15). Occasionally, chronological information is given, as in 12:40. If the writing of history can be defined as imaginatively re-creating a people's past so that they may understand themselves in the present, then Exodus is a work of history. As such, it has literary, historical, and theological aspects, which we shall briefly look at in turn in this introduction.

B. Exodus as Literature. 1. Exodus falls into the category of narrative, literature which tells a story. Even the large parts of the text which present law or instructions are cast into the form of speeches by God at appropriate points in the story. The story has two main themes. The first theme is the deliverance of the Israelites from oppression in Egypt by their God, usually referred to by his name YHWH (see EX 3:7–12). This theme is completed in the first fifteen chapters, which are set mainly in Egypt or on its borders. The second theme is how YHWH establishes his presence among the Israelites and brings them into obedience to himself. This is told mainly in the second half of the book, from 15:22 onwards, which is set in the wilderness to the east of Egypt, but it is foreshadowed in the earlier part of the book. The two themes are united in that both events are ways in which YHWH makes himself known and fulfils his promises to Israel's ancestors.

2. YHWH is the dominant character. The text underlines his sovereignty even at the expense of the interest of the story in places. Although the Israelites are essential to the story, they rarely act independently. Between the two stands Moses. He can be described as the hero of the story. He is hardly ever off-stage from the moment of his birth; the story alternates constantly between scenes between Moses and YHWH and scenes between Moses and the Israelites or Pharaoh. Yet even he, throughout the greater part of the story, acts simply as YHWH's agent, and it is only in places that he asserts his independence (Ex 32 is a notable example). The main foil to YHWH in the first part of the book is the Pharaoh of the plagues. Yet, as I will show in EX 7:6–11:10, YHWH increasingly constrains him to act in the way he does, and ultimately he seems to be little more than a puppet whom YHWH manipulates to demonstrate his own power (Gunn 1982).

3. The development of the plot has, then, decided limitations. Through much of the story the characters do not have sufficient independence to oppose YHWH's purposes. Nevertheless there is a plot. There is a struggle between YHWH and Pharaoh; its end is inevitable and clearly foreseen, but it is a struggle. Israel's acceptance that YHWH must be obeyed is not as automatic as it seems to be at first sight (in 19:8); they do rebel in Ex 32. Their rebellion is of course doomed from the start; the interest of this part of the story lies in whether Moses will persuade YHWH to restore the people to his favour, and here the end is by no means a foregone conclusion. The rebellion sets up a tension in YHWH himself, which Moses exploits. To destroy them and to restore them to favour are in different ways humiliating for YHWH. He resolves the tension by declaring himself a God of mercy, whose glory it is to forgive as much as to punish affronts to his honour.

4. But in general the story proceeds on lines that are not only expected but explicitly forecast (3:12, 16–20: 4:21–3), and its sympathies are unambiguous. In Ex 1–15 we are constrained to be against the oppressors, and on the side of the innocent sufferers and their deliverers. As D. Robertson (1977: 16–32) points out, there is no irony in the moral structure of the story. It is all black and white, there are no shades of grey. Of course, moral simplicity is to be expected in a nation's foundation story. The reader, however, may not find it so simple; could a righteous god destroy so many innocent lives for his own glory?

C. Exodus and History. 1. On the assumption that the book is intended as history, it is natural to ask how it has come by what it knows or claims to know about the early history of Israel. The first step is to ask about the history of the book itself; but as it is only a part of the Pentateuch we can refer to PENT for discussion of the various proposals. The view taken in this commentary (broadly that of Van Seters 1994) can only be stated here, that the work consists of two main strands with different styles and interests, which I refer to as J and P. J was created from a variety of source material by an author writing probably in the seventh or sixth century BCE. Some J material is earlier than Deuteronomy, some of it later and clearly dependent on that book; see e.g. EX 23:10–19 contrasted with 13:3–10. P was written by a priestly author in the later sixth or fifth century. It seems to me likely that P was not an independent work later combined with J, but was written from the beginning as an expansion of J.

2. Exodus, then, was developing during a time when the nation's continuing existence as a distinct community was in prolonged doubt. It was written to strengthen national feeling and support national identity. The two main traditions or ideas which J uses to achieve this are those of Israel's origin from a group of exploited aliens in Egypt, and of YHWH's covenant with them at Mt. Sinai. They were, according to this writer, a nation specially claimed by the God of all the earth as his own (19:5). His claim, his care and protection, and in return their exclusive attachment to him and faithful obedience to his moral direction would preserve them as a nation. The main ideas added by P were that of YHWH's covenant of promise to Israel's ancestors and that of his presence among his people in a sanctuary specially built at his direction, and this has obvious relevance to the time of restoration. Note that 'covenant' has various shades of meaning in the OT (see Mendenhall 1992a, Nicholson 1986).

3. Despite the great attention given by scholars in this century to what they have called 'tradition history' (I again refer to PENT for a brief survey), I do not believe it is possible to write a history of the way in which these traditions developed. The evidence is simply insufficient. Nor is there much to go on to distinguish traditional material from the authors' own contributions. However, the central narrative assertion, that YHWH delivered Israel's ancestors from slavery in Egypt, is certainly traditional: it is central to the prophecy of Hosea in the eighth century BCE, as well as to the book of Deuteronomy in the late seventh. It is much more doubtful that the claim that YHWH made a covenant with Israel at Sinai can be described as traditional (Nicholson 1986). It is important in Deuteronomy and writings influenced by it; but it plays no significant role in any prophetic book before Jeremiah, itself influenced by Deuteronomy. Still less securely rooted in tradition is the concept of the mobile sanctuary; although it depends on the ancient tradition of temple-building in the Near East (see EX 25–31), it appears practically only in the P strand in Exodus, Leviticus, and Numbers.

4. With the exception of the Exodus from Egypt itself, the major ideas of the book are not popular traditions but ideas of an intellectual élite striving to preserve or excite national feeling in a time of crisis, and to reshape the national spirit through an exclusive monotheistic ideal which they saw as the only way to preserve the nation at all.

5. What then is the likelihood that the traditions of Exodus reach right back, as the book claims, to the origin of Israel? (See, among others, S. Herrmann 1973; de Vaux 1978: i. 321–472; Ramsey 1981: 45–63: Houtman 1993: 171–90; Hoffmeier 1997.) If one abstracts the many miraculous elements, the story in itself is not implausible, and indeed similar events appear in Egyptian records (S. Herrmann 1973: 23–9, de Vaux 1978: i.374). The names Moses and Aaron are best explained as of Egyptian origin (Houtman 1993: 75. 83). It is generally assumed that before the traditions were committed to writing they were carried by oral tradition, maybe in connection with the feast of Passover which celebrates the Exodus, and possibly in poetry (Cross 1973: 124 n. 38), which is less subject to loss and distortion than a prose tale. The date of the event is most often put at the end of the Bronze Age, in the thirteenth century BCE. But some (e.g. Bimson 1978) maintain the fifteenth-century date suggested by the Bible's own chronology.

6. However, recent research into traditions about historical events in modern non-literate societies shows that it would be difficult for reliable historical knowledge to survive the hundreds of years separating any possible date for the events related and any likely date for the writing, even if that was much earlier than I have suggested (Kirkpatrick 1988). Moreover, the hard archaeological evidence that would show that the nation of Israel came from outside Canaan is lacking. The material culture of early Iron Age Israel is like that of Late Bronze Age Canaan, only poorer (Finkelstein 1988, Dever 1992). At most there could have been a small group which escaped from Egypt and passed on its traditions to related groups in Canaan (so Gottwald 1980: 36, etc.). And the Passover did not become a national festival until the end of the seventh century (2 Kings 23:22); could the rustic family celebration from which it arose have been the bearer of a national tradition?

7. It therefore remains unclear to what extent Exodus presents authentic historical events. It should in any case be clear from the *way* in which it speaks of history (see c. 2) that we cannot use the book as a historical source. Its aim is not to present an objective record, but to celebrate the glory of YHWH.

D. Exodus as Theology. 1. Exodus is based on a thoroughly monotheistic world-view. Even though YHWH is known by a name distinguishing him from other gods, he is the only God who counts as such: the others are mere idols. He is the creator (4:11), and to him the whole earth belongs (9:29; 19:5). Yet he has committed himself to one people, the people of Israel, long in advance (6:3), and in return asks for their exclusive commitment to him (20:3). Although his presence and power is made known to the Egyptians (7:5) and to the whole earth (9:16), it is permanently promised to Israel (29:45–6) in a specially beneficent form: he will 'dwell among them'.

2. This is not simply the theology *found* in Exodus: the story which it tells is intended as the foundation and legitimation of this theology. YHWH demonstrates that he is the God of all the earth in his victory over Pharaoh. No other god even enters the contest. He demonstrates his commitment to Israel in his calling of Moses, his revelation of his name, his deliverance of Israel from slavery in Egypt, and his appearance to them at Sinai. The covenant which he offers the Israelites embodies the basic demand that they should be committed to him alone, and governs the entire story of the nation from this point onwards. The instructions he gives to Moses in 25–31 are intended to govern the way in which his presence with his people is to be safeguarded for all time.

3. Obviously in the above two paragraphs I have combined points from the two or more main writers of the book. P's particular contributions are the recollection of the promise to the ancestors, the definition of the name YHWH as a new revelation, and the instructions for the building of the sanctuary for his presence.

4. Exodus raises questions about the character and motives of YHWH, which can be followed through the commentary. Miranda (1973:89) asserts that (in J) YHWH acts to deliver the Israelites from slavery simply because he is the God of justice who delivers the oppressed, and not because they are his people or because of any prior commitment. In the text as it stands the prior commitment is clearly stated (2:24 (P)). Even in J the prior connection between YHWH and the ancestors is emphasized. That is not to say that YHWH does not act because of his justice; 'justice' in the HB is a term of relationship, and denotes, among other things, acting in accordance with the commitments one has to other particular people. YHWH's self-proclamation in 34:6–7 lays great stress on the virtues of relationship, and his compassion, also emphasized there, has to be seen in that context.

5. There is, however, an increasing emphasis as one moves into the plagues narrative and beyond on YHWH's action for his own sake: 'that the Egyptians shall know that I am the LORD [YHWH]' (7:5). YHWH's need to achieve a resounding victory over Pharaoh leads him to manipulate him into fruitless opposition (see EX 7:6–11:10). His motive appears to be not so much compassion for or commitment to Israel as the need to have his own Godhead recognized (Durham 1987:99: Gunn 1982:84). This is a particular emphasis of the P material, though it is not absent from J. However, the ancient reader would have seen it differently. Human patrons' generous treatment of their clients redounded to their honour; likewise there was no contradiction between the divine patron's commitment to his people and to his own glory. Moreover, the good order of the world demanded that its ruler should be recognized.

E. Exodus and the Reader. 1. As with any great work of literature, what Exodus means is in the end up to the reader. Creative readings of the book depend not merely on the readers' needs and perspectives, but upon their propensity to read themselves into the book. Thus, although Miranda's reading of YHWH's motives in Ex 3 (see above, D.4) may seem distorted, we understand it when we realize that he speaks for the Latin-American base communities, conscious of their own oppression, who identify themselves with oppressed Israel and claim God's just deliverance for themselves. Thus Exodus, despite its emphasis on God's self-regarding motives and destructive activity, has taken a central place in liberation perspectives on the Bible (cf. also Gutiérrez 1988; Croatto 1981).

2. The book's original purpose was to create or strengthen the identity of the community of Israel, and that is certainly the way in which it has been read by Jews ever since. The book forms the warrant for the festival of Passover. In traditional Christian exegesis, on the other hand, Christians have seen themselves as the Israelites brought through the Red Sea by the hand of God, and the experience of the Sea has been identified with the Resurrection, as in John of Damascus's Easter hymns (e.g. 'Come ye faithful, raise the strain') or with baptism (1 Cor 10:1–5; Origen, *Homily on Exodus*, 5.5). For interpretations through the ages see Langston 2006.

3. More recently, some readers have read Exodus 'against the grain' of the text, identifying themselves with groups who are marginal to it, such as women (Exum 1993, 1994; Fewell and Gunn 1993), or simply reading as moderns sceptical of the values maintained by the book (Clines 1995a and b), and pointing to their socially relative character. This procedure, of course, makes it more difficult to embrace the witness of the book; but that does not make these any less legitimate readings. On the contrary, they should be welcomed as powerful tests of the validity of the far-reaching claims that the book makes.

COMMENTARY

(1:1–2:22) The first two chapters of the book set out the problem to which God responds and introduce the person through whom he will act; they are the exposition of the plot. God is hardly mentioned; it is implied that he is active behind the scenes, but he does not appear on stage until he hears the cry of his people (2:24). At first sight Pharaoh's command to kill the baby boys (1:16, 22) does not fit in with the main story in which the Israelites are subjected to forced labour, especially as it is not mentioned again after ch. 2. It was clearly intended as context for the traditional story in 2:1–10. However, there is no contradiction. In Pharaoh's speech Israel is presented not as a convenient source of labour but as a danger. The two measures have the same object: to crush and weaken the Israelites (Houtman 1993: 245). To destroy only boys is not a very efficient way of wiping out a nation: the object could rather be to deprive it of its leadership.

Most of 1:1–2:22 belongs to J, but P is responsible for 1:1–5, 7, 13–14.

(1:1–7) These verses form a link between Genesis and Exodus. They refer back to Gen 46:5–27 and 50:26, and set the scene for the story of the oppression and deliverance of Israel in Ex 1–15. We are reminded in v. 7 of the promise to the patriarchs that they would have a multitude of descendants (e.g. Gen 15:5), but at the same time it begins the exposition of the plot of Exodus. We are reminded of it twice in the following verses (12, 20); whatever the Egyptians may do, the Israelites continue to increase, so God is perhaps secretly at work. v. 1, the Jewish name for Exodus, šĕmôt, 'Names', comes from the first words. v. 5, seventy names are listed in Gen 46.

(1:8–14) This section relates the beginning of the oppression of Israel. The new king 'did not know Joseph'. 'Know' in Hebrew often has an

overtone of relationship. The relation of friendship and service set up between Joseph and the earlier king is forgotten. In the king's speech (vv. 9–10) the writer uses irony to undermine the king's credibility. He grossly exaggerates the numbers of the Israelites, but in doing so confirms the divine promise to the patriarchs. He says 'let us deal shrewdly with them', but the story shows that his plan is anything but shrewd; and he ends by posing the danger that the Israelites may escape—which was exactly what happened! The Israelites have to perform conscript labour for the state. Often the OT writers describe them as slaves. Strictly speaking this is not the same thing: a conscript labourer is not the property of his master. But understandably the writers tend to ignore the distinction. Forced labour was a practice of Israelite kings also, but the biblical tradition has a moral repugnance to it (1 Kings 12:18; Jer 22:13). v. 11, the names of the supply cities (see ABD for each, and Redford 1963; they are in the east of the Nile Delta) have often been taken as a clue to the historical setting of the Exodus. Rameses is probably the capital of Rameses II, abandoned after his death in 1212 BCE. On the other hand, the form of the name Rameses in Hebrew suggests that it was borrowed no earlier than 700 BCE (Redford 1963: 411–13). A writer at a later time could have used the names to give his story colour without having an old tradition.

(1:15–22) Pharaoh's attempt to deprive the Israelites of male leadership is first of all frustrated by the courage of two women, and three more frustrate the second stage of his plan. For feminist reflections on this irony, see Exum (1993, 1994). v. 15, 'the Hebrew midwives'. This is the first appearance of the word 'Hebrew' in the book. It is used to refer to the Israelites from the point of view of the Egyptians (or, later, of other foreigners). For the origin of the word see 'Hebrew', and 'Habiru, Hapiru' in ABD iii. v. 19. The midwives' lie is not disapproved of—the OT reflects the moral sense of ordinary people, not moral philosophers!

(2:1–10) The birth story of Moses appears to be based on a very old folk-tale, which we first find as the birth story of King Sargon of Akkad (about 2300 BCE; ANET 119). Moses is destined to die; the human compassion of Pharaoh's daughter impels her to disobey her father and rescue him. v. 1, 'a Levite woman': the Hebrew text actually says 'the daughter of Levi', but may be influenced by 6:20 (Schmidt 1988: 50). v. 9,

Moses is brought up as a Hebrew, even though adopted as an Egyptian. This ironic twist serves to explain his later role. v. 10, the name 'Moses' is probably derived from an Egyptian word often found in personal names such as that of the Pharaoh Thutmosis. But here, as so often in the OT, it is given a fanciful Hebrew derivation: 'Moses' is *Moshe* (*mōšeh*), which means 'one who draws out'.

(**2:11–15a**) Can it be right for the oppressed to take justice into their own hands? The story neither approves nor disapproves. It shows us that Moses is a man who is passionate for justice (so is God's choice of him so odd?), but also imprudent. For without the divine authorization which he later receives, there is no possibility that his action could succeed. As far as the plot is concerned, the episode gets Moses from Egypt to Midian, where he is to meet God.

(**2:15b–22**) Moses in Midian. The resemblance of this story to that of Jacob in Gen 29, and more distantly to Gen 24, has often been noted. It may be a literary convention, in stories of the hero's finding a wife in distant parts (Alter 1981: 47–62), or a deliberate imitation (Van Seters 1994: 32).

'Midian' was an Arab people occupying an area to the east of the Gulf of Aqaba; but it is possible that their shepherds came as far west as the Sinai peninsula (Mendenhall 1992b), where Mt. Sinai/Horeb (3:1, 12) has traditionally been located. In v. 17 the word translated 'came to their defence' is the word which the OT regularly uses of God's 'saving' people. Here is another sign marking Moses out as one who is ready to save people who are suffering injustice. v. 18, Moses' future father-in-law is called Reuel here and probably in Num 10:29, Jethro in 3:1 and 18:1–12, Jether in 4:18, and Hobab in Judg 4:11 and perhaps Num 10:29. He is a Midianite in Exodus and Numbers and a Kenite in Judges. Probably he originally had no name in the tradition (Schmidt 1988: 85–7), and the writers, or the traditions they draw on, have filled in the blank in various ways. In Exodus this may point to different source material. v. 22, there may be a hidden meaning in Moses' words. Which is the 'foreign land', Midian or Egypt?

(**2:23–5:21**) God's intervention: Act I In this section the Israelites call for help, and the God of Israel responds by appointing Moses as his agent, and promises him he will deliver the Israelites; but Moses' first attempts to ask

Pharaoh to let them go meet with failure. This creates a crisis which can only be overcome by a further and more powerful divine intervention.

The God of Israel is usually given his name YHWH, but in places he is referred to by the more general *'ĕlōhîm*, 'God'. 2:23–5 (and probably not much else here) belongs to P, who avoids using 'YHWH' before YHWH himself reveals the name. 3:9–15 is often ascribed to a distinct source, E; but the writer (J) may simply find it appropriate to use *'ĕlōhîm* in describing the dialogue with Moses, who does not yet know the name. See Moberly (1992: 5–35). 2:23, the statement about the death of the king expresses the passage of time, and prepares for 4:19. But this makes no difference to the oppression. 2:23–5 adds a theologically important link between the Israelites' oppression and God's action. God's action is a response not only to what he sees, but also to what he hears, the cry of a suffering people. His action is then determined by his prior commitment to Israel's ancestors (see Gen 17; 35:11–13; 6:2–8). 'Covenant' here refers to a solemn promise made by God to the patriarchs. In Israelite society it was the responsibility of the nearest relative to redeem a person from the grip of the creditor and the slaveholder (Lev 25:25, 47–9). P expresses YHWH's responsibility to Israel, which was not based on physical kinship, in the concept of this 'covenant' with the ancestors. See further EX 6:2–8.

(**3:1–4:17**) The Call of Moses This passage follows basically the same pattern as some other accounts of God's call of individuals to special tasks, e.g. Gideon in Judg 6:11–24, Jeremiah in Jer 1:4–10. In all of them, five things happen. There is a *meeting* between God and the chosen one; God gives him a *commission*; he *objects* that he is unfit; God *reassures* him; God gives him a *sign* (Habel 1965). Here, however, the pattern is expanded. It is complete by 3:12; but Moses keeps finding new objections, which God responds to seriously; the elements of commission and assurance are thus taken up again in various ways, and a whole section (4:1–9) is devoted to signs. It is often suggested that Moses is here cast in the role of a prophet. It is true that much of the material is typical of prophecy (e.g. Moses is to speak to a king in the name of God); but some is more typical of a military leader, for example the assurance 'I will be with you' (3:12; see Gowan 1994: 56–61). Moses is both. This simple storytelling device of repeated objections enables the passage to be

1 richer than a simple call to service. It is in the first place God's promise that he himself will act to deliver Israel. Moses' work takes its place within the divine plan, and is impossible without God's action. God's words dominate the passage, and they refer backwards and forwards; the whole of the Pentateuchal story is set out here. The story of Exodus is a plot with few surprises, because the chief character promises beforehand everything that is to happen. It is essential to this that God should here reveal his name YHWH (3:13–15), backing his promise with it, as we might sign our name to a contract.

The passage pictures the interplay of divine sovereignty and human freedom. It ends, of course, with total victory for YHWH. Moses, for all his show of independence, is forced to submit, and for many chapters will play the role of a mere agent. Yet he has not been deprived of his humanity, and will later (14:13–14 and esp. 32–3) show that he can take the initiative (Gunn 1982: 84–7).

(3:1–6) Moses' meeting with God is the experience of a mysterious and awe-inspiring, but attractive presence, an example of the experience of the holy, as defined by Rudolf Otto (Gowan 1994: 25–53). It cannot be described literally, but only pictured, as in e.g. Judg 5:4–5; Ps 18:7–15; 50:1–6; Hab 3. When God is described in such passages as coming in visible ways to judge and save, scholars call it a 'theophany'. Fire is the most regular accompaniment of theophanies. Therefore, although people have tried to explain what the burning bush was in natural terms, this misses the point. But who is it who appears to Moses? The narrator calls him first 'the angel' (lit. messenger) of YHWH ('the LORD') (v. 2), and then in one verse (4) both YHWH ('the LORD') and *ʾĕlōhîm* ('God'). It is common in theophanies for the one who appears to be called 'the angel of YHWH/ *ʾĕlōhîm*' (as in Judg 6:11–24); but it normally becomes clear (as in Judg 6:14) that it is YHWH himself who is speaking. In this way the narrator makes it clear that the event is a real visitation of God, but avoids saying that YHWH himself became visible. v. 6 finally makes it clear that the mysterious apparition is none other than the God who is spoken of in Genesis, and was known to Israel's ancestors and Moses' own father. v. 1, for Jethro see EX 2:18. Horeb and 'the mountain of God' are alternative names, particularly in Deuteronomy, for the mountain called Sinai in Ex 19 where God reveals himself to Israel. v. 5, similarly Josh 5:15. The practice of removing footwear in holy places is regular in Judaism, Islam, and Buddhism, but its meaning is disputed: see Houtman (1993: 351–2).

(3:7–12) The divine promise and commission, Moses' initial objection and God's fundamental reassurance. Because v. 9 seems to repeat the substance of v. 7, it has often been thought that vv. 9–12 come from a different source (E) from vv. 7–8. But it is important that God's promise to 'bring up' the Israelites out of Egypt stands alongside his commission to Moses to 'bring them out'. Neither the divine initiative nor the human agency can be dispensed with. The phrases in v. 8 are conventional. The list of former inhabitants occurs in many places with slight variations; it is impossible to give a precise meaning to the names, except for the Jebusites, who were the people of Jerusalem before David captured the city (2 Sam 5). Moses' objection in v. 11 is a standard expression to avoid commitment. See Judg 6:15, Jer 1:6, which get the same answer; 1 Sam 18:23. The 'sign' in v. 12 has caused problems, since it is not something that Moses can see and be convinced by now (contrast 4:1–9). Gowan (1994: 55–6) rightly says that 'I will be with you' is sufficient in itself as an assurance; if Moses hangs on to that, he will *eventually* see the confirmation of his mission in the meeting of all the people (the last 'you' is plural) with their God.

(3:13–15) Here the god in the bush, so far nameless to Moses, reveals his name. Why does Moses ask this question (v. 13)? The call is to be a messenger, and a messenger needs a name to authenticate his credentials. Moses, however, does not know the name of his 'father's god'; but he cannot be sure that the Israelites do not know it either. The story at this point does not commit itself on whether the Israelites know YHWH's name already; it focuses on *Moses'* ignorance, not Israel's. But while this is Moses' reason for raising the question, the author has a deeper motive for highlighting it. A strong tradition held that the bond between Israel and YHWH went back to the time of the Exodus from Egypt (see Hos 2:15; 11:1; 13:4; Jer 2:2–8). Therefore it is appropriate that it is at this point, when he announces his intention to save, that YHWH becomes known to Israel. But here the episode is part of a larger story in which Israel's ancestors have already encountered this God, so the story must be told in a way which allows for this. 6:2–8 (P) clears up the ambiguity of this passage.

God answers Moses' question in v. 15. But first he tantalizes him with a play on words. The Hebrew for 'I am' or 'I will be' is *ehyeh*. Changed into the third person this would be *yihyeh* or in an older form *yahweh*, which was probably the pronunciation of YHWH. Many meanings have been seen in 'I AM WHO I AM' or 'I WILL BE WHO I WILL BE'; probably the simplest is 'I will be whoever I will be', that is, while I will graciously reveal my name to you, I will not be bound or defined by it (Gowan 1994: 84). But as a word-play the meaning is not as important as the sound! The actual origin of the name YHWH is quite uncertain (see de Vaux 1978: i. 338–57).

(3:16–22) YHWH follows up his revelation of his name by telling Moses how he is to use it, and so goes into his *commission* in detail, along with the *assurance* that he will unleash his own power to compel the king to let the Israelites go. Thus the whole story up to Ex 12 is given here in outline.

'The elders of Israel' do not in fact accompany Moses to the king (v. 18, cf. 5:1). Is this an inconsistency in the story, or a mistake on Moses' part? The request they are to make of the king (v. 18) is of course a ruse, which ought not to worry anyone's conscience when dealing with tyrants (see EX 1:19). But it also picks up 3:12.

(3:21–2) The puzzling instruction is carried out in Ex 12:35–6. Daube (1947: 49–50) offers a plausible explanation. There was a custom (Deut 15:14) that a released slave should get a generous endowment. The Israelites are to deceive the Egyptians—if it is deception—into giving them their rightful due!

(4:1–9) Moses may well mean that *he* does not know whether to believe YHWH. YHWH's answer is to demonstrate his power by means of 'signs' that he enables Moses to perform. These signs achieve what that in 3:12 could not, in immediately convincing a wavering Moses. Such signs, however external and artificial they may appear to us, are common in OT narrative (compare Judg 6:17–22, 36–40). In the story that follows they are used not only to convince the Israelites (4:30), but, with variations, to impress the Egyptians (7:8–24; foreshadowed in 4:21).

(4:10–17) Moses offers his final excuse (v. 10). YHWH's answer (vv. 11–12) shows that the author takes for granted that YHWH is the Creator. Moses has now run out of excuses and simply turns the job down (v. 13). And

YHWH runs out of patience, but his answer harks back to Moses' pretext in v. 10. Moses *must* go, but his brother may do the speaking for him. However, in the event, this does not happen in any consistent way (explicitly only in 4:30); and Aaron sometimes performs the signs (as in 4:30; 7:10, etc.) rather than, or as well as, speaking. It is probable that Moses' pretext is simply, for the author, a device to bring Aaron into the story, for the sake of a group in Jewish society that was attached to him, presumably the priests who claimed descent from him. It is not clear why Aaron is called 'the Levite' (v. 14) when Moses was one himself according to 2:1. 'Probably "your brother the Levite" originally meant "your fellow Levite" (Propp 1998: 214).' 'You shall serve as God for him', Moses is told in v.16. That is, the relation between Moses and Aaron is like that between God and his prophet.

(4:18–26) Moses' return to Egypt is told in a rather disjointed narrative which probably shows the effect of the piecing together of different sources or traditions. v. 19 refers back to 2:23, but seems to ignore all that has happened in between, since Moses already has his marching orders and has even said goodbye. vv. 21–3 develop Moses' instructions in a new direction as compared with 3:20. Pharaoh will refuse to let Israel go *because YHWH so wills*. This important theme is taken up again at 7:3. The mention of the 'firstborn son' anticipates another major theme of the story (Ex 11–13).

In the obscure vv. 24–6 the biggest puzzle is: why should YHWH try to kill the messenger whom he has only just commissioned? There are other questions. Why does Zipporah do what she does and how does it work? What is the meaning of her words? Many scholars have regarded the piece as an old legend in which the attacker was a demon, possibly intended to explain the origin of the practice of the circumcision of infants. Maybe, but this does not really explain what it means in this context. The first question is not really answerable, but at least two other episodes are in some way similar: the command to Abraham to sacrifice Isaac (Gen 22) and Jacob's wrestling with God at the Jabbok (Gen 32). The God of the Bible has a dark side. Zipporah circumcises her son and touches Moses' own penis ('feet' is a euphemism) with the severed foreskin. Along with her words, this suggests a symbol legitimizing this marriage between the leader of Israel and a foreign woman, which may have been a scandal to some of the first readers of Exodus in the

Second Temple period (Römer 1994—only one of many proposals). For circumcision, see GEN 17 and 'Circumcision' in *ABD* i.

(4:27–5:21) describes Moses and Aaron's first attempt to carry out YHWH's commission. It fails, and Pharaoh's oppression of Israel is simply intensified; a common experience for many who have challenged tyranny. Significant for the future development of the story is Pharaoh's dismissal of their request in 5:2: 'I do not know the LORD'. The long series of 'plagues' in chs. 7–12, according to YHWH's own statement in 7:3, has just one aim: that the Egyptians *should* know YHWH. See EX 7:8–11:10. For 5:1 see EX 3:18. For 'the Hebrews' in 5:3 see EX 1:16. In 5:16 "'You are unjust to your own people'" is odd, since the Israelites are not Pharaoh's people. The text is uncertain, and a better reading may be 'The fault is with you.'

(5:21–13:16) The Intervention of God: Act II
This is the key act of the story, in which YHWH's powerful action enables the Israelites to leave Egypt, though not yet to escape finally from Pharaoh's reach. It has much the same structure as the previous act: the appeal to God, his response of promise and commission. Moses and Aaron's request to Pharaoh. The vital differences are God's supporting action (the plagues) on the one hand and his delaying action (hardening Pharaoh's heart) on the other.

(5:21–7:7) In response to Moses' despairing complaint, God again reveals his name, confirms his promise to deliver the Israelites from slavery, and repeats his commission to go to Pharaoh. 6:1 advances the story and points forward to the plagues. Eventually, in 7:3–5, we return to this point. But from 6:2 to 7:2 (except for 6:14–25) the episode appears to go over the same ground as 3:1–4:17, but with new language. In the context this is quite appropriate, since Moses has been brought to the point where only fresh encouragement and a fresh mandate from God can restore his confidence. But it is also the sign of a fresh hand at work. The whole passage from 6:2 is the work of P, probably working on the basis of the existing story. (6:14–25 may be a still later expansion.)

The formal speech of God in 6:2–8 has an elegant structure (see Auffret 1983 for details). The pronouncement 'I am the LORD [YHWH]' occurs in key places and is clearly the key to the entire speech (see also Zimmerli 1982). It is more than a bare statement of authority: it is

the self-giving of a person, whose personality and character are summed up in his name, but who can be fully known for who he is only in his gracious act of salvation (6:7). The ambiguity in 3:13–15 is cleared up in 6:3. How could Israel's ancestors have known the God whose name is now newly revealed? Answer: they knew him under another name. Therefore Moses can be sure that the promise to them is still valid. 'God Almighty' (NRSV, etc.) is a conventional translation of *'ēl šadday*. *'ēl* means 'God': the meaning of *šadday* is unknown. See Gen 17:1; 35:11; 28:3. For 'covenant' in 6:4 see EX 2:23–5. 6:5 takes up the wording of Ex 2:24.

Something new is introduced at 6:7*a* YHWH's rescue of Israel from Egypt is the beginning of a permanent relationship between them. This promise will be fulfilled at Sinai in Ex 19–40, with the establishment of institutions by which God and people are related. In 6:8 the speech returns to its beginning, by promising the imminent fulfilment of what God swore to Israel's ancestors.

For 6:12 see 4:10. The genealogical material in 6:14–25 is to our mind quite out of place in the middle of a story. But the author had different ideas of literary appropriateness. His object is expressed in 6:26–7: to locate the heroes of the tale within the Israelite social structure and so validate them as historical according to his ideas of history (Childs 1974: 116), and probably to claim them as members of his own social group. Social and political status depended mainly on kinship, and genealogies, real or fictitious, were essential to validate it (Wilson 1977). As in many genealogies in the Bible, many of the names are those of kinship groups who trace their descent from a supposed ancestor with the same name. Moses and Aaron, then, belong to the Kohathite Levites, and Aaron is the ancestor of the Jerusalem priests. Aaron's wife (6:23) is a Judahite (see Num 1:7), which signifies the close connection between the priests of Jerusalem and the people of Judah. Korah (6:21), the sons of Aaron (6:23), and his grandson Phinehas (6:25) will all play parts in the story which follows (Num 16; Ex 24 and Lev 8–10; Num 25). 6:28–30 takes up the story again by summarizing 6:2–13.

(7:1–5) This completes Moses' recommissioning, and like 3:20 and 4:21–3 points forwards very clearly, and in more detail, to the plague story, which follows straight away. 7:1–2 takes up the theme of 4:14–16. In 7:3–5 several points are made which define the meaning of the following episodes. I will discuss most of them at greater length in the next section, EX 7:8–11:10. YHWH will 'harden Pharaoh's heart'. The 'heart' in Hebrew refers to the understanding and the will. What YHWH will do is to make Pharaoh uncomprehending and obstinate. The effect is that he will 'not listen to you' (7:4), and it will trigger YHWH's move to 'multiply my signs and wonders', 'lay my hand on Egypt', and bring the Israelites out 'by great acts of judgement'. A sign is anything that shows God's power, a wonder is a remarkable event of any kind; 'hand' usually means power at work; and a judgement is not necessarily a punishment, but an act of force undertaken to effect the decision of a judge or ruler. So in several different ways YHWH makes it clear that by making Pharaoh obstinate he will be enabled to display his power as ruler of the world on the Egyptians. And the result is that they 'shall know that I am YHWH'. Israel will know YHWH in his gracious act of deliverance (6:7), Egypt in a very different way. 7:7, the apparently excessive ages of Moses and Aaron fit the widespread belief that age brings wisdom.

(7:8–11:10) The Narrative of the Plagues (a traditional rendering of the Hebrew word in 9:14, which would be better translated 'blows', with which YHWH *strikes* Egypt). Here general remarks will be made on the passage as a whole, not on the separate plagues, followed only by notes on individual verses.

There are ten plagues, starting with the turning of water to blood in 7:14–24 and finishing with the death of the firstborn in 11–12. But as the book has been edited, the section is introduced by 7:8–13, though it does not describe a 'plague' but only a sign, and closed by an obvious summary in 11:9–10; the last plague has been announced, but its execution is tied up with the Passover narrative. In this part of the story the narrative, usually so concise, spreads itself at length. Attempts to explain the series of plagues historically as the effect of natural causes (Hort 1957–8) surely miss the point of the story, that they are the direct work of God for his purposes. From a literary point of view, they can be seen as intended to create tension. Since we already know the final result (3:20; 6:6; 7:4–5), we know *that* YHWH will achieve his purpose but we can still be intrigued as to *how* he will. To some extent the number of the plagues and the length of the narrative may be accounted for by the likelihood that different

authors have had a hand in it. But the division of sources is very much disputed. The simplest theory (Van Seters 1994:80) is that the original narrative (J) had seven plagues, and the Priestly editor added three more, as well as extra material in the others.

Table 1. Patterns in Plague Narratives

Pattern 1: 'Go to Pharaoh in the morning'	Pattern 1: 'Go to Pharaoh'	Pattern 2: not to go to Pharaoh, but simply to bring the plague
1. blood, 7:14–24	2. frogs, 7:25–8:15	3. gnats, 8:16–19
4. flies, 8:20–32	5. cattle plague, 9:1–7	6. boils, 9:8–12
7. hail, 9:13–35	8. locusts, 10:1–20	9. darkness, 10:21–9

Patterns in the plague narratives. The story is composed by taking a couple of basic patterns and repeating them with variations (see Table 1). In the first pattern YHWH tells Moses to go to Pharaoh and require him to let YHWH's people go, and to threaten him with a plague if he does not. Moses' delivery of this message is not described, but taken for granted. (This is varied in plagues 8 and 10.) Pharaoh's response is not given either; YHWH's first speech is immediately followed (except in plagues 4 and 5) by another telling Moses (and often Aaron) to bring the plague. Except in plagues 1 and 5 Pharaoh then summons Moses and Aaron and attempts to negotiate, and asks Moses to pray to YHWH for the plague to be removed, which he does, and it is.

In the second pattern, there is no message to Pharaoh, but YHWH simply tells Moses to bring the plague. There are negotiations in plague 9. but in this pattern Pharaoh does not ask for the removal of the plague. In both patterns, and all the episodes except the last, the conclusion is the same, though expressed in different ways: Pharaoh's 'heart was hardened' (see above, EX 7:1–7, for the meaning of this), and he refuses to let them go. This enables another round to begin. It is P who has added the three plagues in the second pattern, each after two plagues in the first pattern. This helps to create a larger recurring pattern: three groups of three, according to the start of YHWH's speech to Moses, followed by the final plague.

We would expect the plagues to get steadily worse, and this is broadly true. Other climactic effects include the contest with the magicians. They can duplicate the staff-into-snake sign, and the first two plagues, but they stick on the third, and the boils, finally, make it impossible for them even to appear in Moses' presence (9:11). Then there is the series of negotiations between Moses and Pharaoh. Much of the interest of the section lies in them, for these are the only parts of the whole story where Pharaoh is allowed some human personality. Broadly speaking, Pharaoh's concessions (always withdrawn once the plague has gone) are progressively more generous (8:8; 8:25, 28: 9:28; 10:8–10; 10:24). True, if he realizes that the Israelites do not intend to come back, they are nicely calculated to be always unacceptable to Moses. So even before the removal of each plague Pharaoh seems not to understand the real situation, that he cannot win.

Other variations include the gradual downgrading of Aaron, who in spite of 4:14–16 and 7:1–2 never actually speaks, but uses his staff in the initial sign and the first three plagues, but never after that; and whether the protection of the Israelites is mentioned (8:22–3; 9:4, 6–7: 9:26; 10:23; 11:7—five out of nine).

'That they may know that I am YHWH'. More serious issues arise when we ask why YHWH brings the plagues. YHWH himself says that it is so that Pharaoh and his people (and Israel, 10:2) may know him: 7:5, 17:9:14; 10:2; cf. also 8:10, 22; 9:29; 11:7. Pharaoh had said in 5:2 that he did not know YHWH. He will now—to his cost. From each new round of the struggle he will find that YHWH, not he, emerges with the real power in his own land, and indeed throughout the world. 9:14–16 is especially clear. If it had just been a question of liberating Israel, one stroke would have been enough. This long-drawn torture has a different goal: 'that you may know that there is none like me in all the world'.

The hardening of Pharaoh's heart. We may well wonder why YHWH's demonstrations of his power must be so violent and destructive. And why do they have to be repeated so often, with increasing destructiveness? The answer is there at the end of every single episode. Pharaoh fails to draw the right conclusion from his experience, so it needs to be repeated. Other people get the point (9:20; 10:7), but not Pharaoh.

Now if we had not already had the clues in 4:21 and 7:3, we might at first think that Pharaoh was responsible for his own incomprehension and obstinacy, especially as in three places we are told that 'Pharaoh hardened' his own heart (8:15, 32; 9:34). It is after all quite natural in the first three episodes (7:13; 7:22; 8:15), when his own magicians can produce the same effects, so that there is no clear demonstration of YHWH's superiority; though even here we are reminded that YHWH had foretold it, and that only he can remove the effects (8:10). Pharaoh's obstinacy in 8:15 seems to be a response to the respite from the frogs, but as plague succeeds plague this gradually ceases to be a convincing explanation. The magicians themselves point out the truth after the third plague (8:19), and his continuing blindness at 8:32 and 9:7 becomes increasingly puzzling. From 9:12, after the sixth plague, it becomes increasingly plain that it is YHWH who is hardening Pharaoh's heart, for his own purposes; so in 10:1, 20, 27, and in the summary at 11:10. This is something which Pharaoh himself and his officials do not know, hence the officials' despairing protest at 10:7. Even if Pharaoh appears to act independently, he is in fact a puppet in the hands of YHWH. Taken as a whole the narrative gives little support to the common preacher's idea that Pharaoh falls victim to a paralysis of the will set up originally by his own free decision. (This paragraph summarizes the fine analysis of Gunn 1982.)

It is possible (Childs 1974: 172) that an older version of the story was much simpler: YHWH's sole purpose was to force Pharaoh to release the Israelites, and the successive plagues were simply a response to Pharaoh's own refusal to act sensibly. But that is not the case in the story as we have it. Here YHWH *prevents* Pharaoh from acting sensibly in order to have an excuse for bringing the plagues on him. Gowan's comment (1994: 138) is to the point: 'If freeing the Hebrews from slavery had been God's main intention…then for God to harden Pharaoh's heart so as to extend the agonies of the process would be indefensible on any grounds.' But if his purpose is as stated in 7:5, 17, etc., to make Pharaoh know that he is God, it is strange that he acts every time to frustrate his own purpose. For that is the effect of the 'hardening', to prevent Pharaoh from understanding the truth. However often and destructively YHWH displays his power, it will have no effect on Pharaoh until YHWH wants it to. As Gowan sees (1994: 138), the truth must be that the object is not to enlighten Pharaoh but to triumph over him, to 'gain glory over him' (14:4). He will truly 'know that I am YHWH' only at the very end of the process (14:18), when it will do him no good at all: this must be ironical. Durham (1987: 96) and Gunn (1982: 84) may well be right in suggesting that the true audience for the demonstration is Israel, certainly from the point of view of the authors. The account is shaped by a theology interested above all in maintaining the absolute sovereignty of the God they serve.

Believing readers will need to reflect on the question whether a God so anxious to display his power and triumph over his enemies is the God that they believe in. See Gunn 1982: 84; Croatto 1981: 29; Houston 2007. But Brueggemann (1995: 47) suggests that the struggle between YHWH and Pharaoh is not a matter of personalities; they are embodiments of opposed social policies; so that the victory of YHWH is the victory of a no-slavery policy.

Notes on individual verses. 7:8–13 develops 4:2–5. The motif of the contest between courtiers is a popular one (see Gen 41; Dan 2; 4; 5; 1 Esd 3–4), and it serves here as a comic counterpoint to the tragic struggle between YHWH and Pharaoh. Not that the magicians are clowns. They have real power, but it is soon shown not to compare with YHWH's (Durham 1987: 92). The turning of water into blood takes up 4:9, but is much more extensive and drastic. There is a seasonal reddening of the Nile waters at the time of the inundation (Hort 1957–8: 87–95), but it cannot be taken seriously as the origin of an account of water being actually turned into blood (Durham 1987: 97). For 'Hebrews' in 7:16 see EX 1:15, and for the request to Pharaoh, obviously a blind, see EX 3:18. In 8:10, the lesson about YHWH's power is derived by Moses from the exact fulfilment of *Pharaoh's* definition of the time. 8:16, 'gnats' (NRSV), or lice: biting insects at all events. 8:21, 'swarms of flies': the Hebrew simply says 'mixed swarms', without specifying the insects. 8:22: the land of Goshen, see Gen 45:10, has never been satisfactorily identified. There is no particular reason known why any animal the Israelites sacrificed would be 'offensive' (8:26; same word as in Deut 14:3) to the Egyptians; presumably it is meant to be the invention of the wily negotiator. It is odd that after all the Egyptians' livestock have died in the cattle pestilence (9:1–7), there are still some alive to be affected by the boils (9:10) and the hail (9:19–25). OT authors or editors are not concerned for narrative coherence in the way we might be.

In 9:13–35, the seventh and longest of all the plague episodes, except the last, things are moving towards a climax, and this is signalled by YHWH's especially detailed explanation of why he is acting as he is (9:14–16). 9:31–2 is a note added, not in the right place, perhaps to explain how the locusts had anything to destroy in the next plague. Pharaoh's remark in 10:10 is ironical, actually a curse. Of course he understands very well what Moses really wants: he imposes a similar unacceptable condition in 10:24.

Ch. 11 is awkward: Moses appears to be leaving in 10:29, but at 11:8 it turns out he has been speaking to Pharaoh since 11:4. No doubt there has been some rearrangement of the text, in order to accommodate the detailed ritual instructions which are given in 12:1–28 before the final blow is actually struck. But the chapter does impressively introduce this final act. 11:2–3 repeats the instructions of 3:21–2 (see EX 3:21–2). 11:9–10 sums up the section, so that it is tied up before launching into the Passover instructions, which will be followed by the final blow and then immediately by the leaving of Egypt.

(12:1–13:16) The Passover and the Exodus from Egypt Once more the style of the narrative changes abruptly. The climax of the account of YHWH's blows against Egypt does not come until 12:29–39, and this brief narrative is surrounded with detailed ritual instructions. Some of them concern not what the people are to do immediately, but how they are to repeat the rite in time to come, which to us seems inappropriate in the context. Once again we need to understand the motivation of the writers. They are not simply writing about the past; they are offering to their people an account of events which made them a people, events which are to be celebrated and relived. The little dialogues between child and parent in 12:25–7 and 13:14–15 show how by celebration a people can keep memory alive and recreate the saving and founding act of their God. As this passage is the climax of the story of deliverance, it is natural that the theme of observance should be concentrated here.

Three ritual observances are presented in this text as memorials of the Exodus, but the first two are held at the same time and virtually merged: Passover (*pesaḥ*), the Festival of Unleavened Bread (*maṣṣôt*), and the consecration of the firstborn. The first two celebrate the Exodus in other texts: Unleavened Bread in Ex 23:15, and Passover (and Unleavened Bread) in Deut 16:1–8; but the consecration of the firstborn is related to the Exodus only here (compare Deut 15:19–20). All three are widely believed to be very old rites of various origins which at some stage have been given an interpretation related to the Exodus. (For details see de Vaux 1961: 484–93; ABD vi. 755–65; Propp 1998: 427–61; Van Seters: 1994: 113–27 dissents.)

A widespread opinion (following Rost 1943) is that Passover was originally a rite carried out by shepherds when moving to new pastures in the spring, while Unleavened Bread was an agricultural rite, marking the beginning of the barley harvest (which takes place in spring in the Near East) by getting rid of all the remains of bread from the last year's harvest and starting afresh. However, if that is so the distinctive features of the rites are given quite different interpretations, relating them to the last night in Egypt. Propp (1998: 427–61) sees them as ancient rites of purification, but not linked to the agricultural year.

The very name *pesaḥ* is interpreted in this way. The verb in 12:13, 27 translated 'pass over' is *pāsaḥ*—a wordplay characteristic of Hebrew narrative. The verb is rather uncertain in meaning: it might be 'leap over' or 'protect'. This is connected with the use of the blood to protect each family. Though this may be an ancient rite, and may have been thought of as a kind of magic, forcing evil spirits to swerve away, the text avoids this idea: the blood is a 'sign' (v. 13), YHWH sees it and of his own goodwill 'passes'—or leaps—'over'. Then there is the continuing importance of Passover as a mark of identity. All Israelites must celebrate it, and no one who does not belong to the community may share in it (12:43, 47–8). But it is not only a question of national identity. The eating of the passover lamb is a family activity, must take place within the house, and cannot be shared with those who are not members of the household: 12:44–6. So the Passover serves to strengthen and celebrate ritually both the identity of the nation *and* its social structure of patriarchal extended families. Unleavened Bread is not explained in 12:14–20, simply commanded; but in 12:34, 39 it is explained in story terms. Probably the story was invented to explain it, and Moses' subsequent commands in 13:3–10 do not refer to it, simply emphasizing the feast's commemorative function.

The relation between the consecration of the firstborn, also probably a very ancient practice, and the events described in the story is obvious, and is explained in 13:15. It is not just that the firstborn males of cattle are consecrated to YHWH in sacrifice, but that human firstborn are redeemed (by payment or substitution), just as they were in Egypt. There may have been a time in Israel when firstborn sons were sacrificed—see Ezek 20:26; Jer 7:31. Therefore it is appropriate that the 'horrifying' edict, as Ezekiel calls it, should be presented as revoked as a symbol of the deliverance of the whole people from slavery.

Instructions for Passover and Unleavened Bread are also given at Deut 16:1–8; there are striking differences. Jewish interpreters have traditionally distinguished between 'the Passover of Egypt' and 'the Passover of the [subsequent] generations'. Critical scholars have tended instead to see the history of the rite in the differences: the usual view is that Passover began as a family observance, and was transferred to the temple in the time of Josiah as part of the centralization required by Deuteronomy, and that during the Exile P kept the festival alive by reviving its family character. 'But it is more likely that P was simply depicting "the Passover of Egypt" (Propp 1998: 445–51).'

YHWH gives instructions for each rite to Moses before Moses passes them on to the people; but the speeches are interwoven in a curious way which points to the editorial history of the text (see Table 2).

Table 2. Speeches of Moses and YHWH

	YHWH	Moses
Passover	12:1–13 (14) + 43–9	12:21–7
Unleavened Bread	12:14–20	13:3–10
Firstborn	13:1–2	13:11–16

In each case YHWH's speech is the work of the P writer, but scholars have disagreed about the attribution of Moses' speeches. The simplest solution is that in J Moses gave instructions for the Passover before the Exodus and for the other two observances after it; and that P added the speeches of YHWH, taking Passover and Unleavened Bread together because they belonged together in the liturgical calendar. However, many scholars take 12:21–7 as P work (see Van Seters 1994: 114–19).

The first speech falls into two parts. 12:1–13 gives immediate instructions, while 14–20 looks forward to the future. This part is generally thought of as referring exclusively to Unleavened Bread; but the natural order of the speech shows that it is closely bound up with Passover. 12:2, 3, 6, 18: the month of Passover is called Abib in Ex 23:15; Deut 16:1. This is the old name for the first month of spring. P, writing after the Exile, always uses numbers instead of names, and begins the year in the spring as the Babylonian calendar did. It is likely that under the monarchy the new year began in the autumn, as it does for Jews today, and possible that 12:1 is to be interpreted as a call for a new calendar. See 'Calendar' in *ABD* i. The Hebrew word translated 'lamb' in 12:3, etc. by NRSV is wider than our word 'lamb', as you can see from 12:5. The requirement for a yearling male is quite practical—these were the most expendable members of the flock. The 'bitter herbs' in 12:8 are today taken as a symbol of the bitterness of oppression: the interpretation of the rite is an ongoing process. The requirement for the animal to be roasted whole (12:9, 46) differentiates it from a public sacrifice, which was boiled (as in Deut 16:7), and also perhaps symbolizes the integrity of the family and the nation. The identification of the lamb as the passover is held back to the climax of YHWH's speech in 12:11.

Moses passes on the instructions in 12:21–7. 'The passover lamb' may be intended to refer back to 12:11. In 12:23, 'the destroyer' has been taken as a relic of an ancient belief in demons as the object of the blood-smearing; but it can just as well be interpreted as YHWH's own angel. 12:29 resumes the thread of the story broken off at 11:8. At 12:32 is a reference back to Pharaoh's last negotiations with Moses in 10:24–6, and at 12:35–6 to 11:2. 'Succoth' in 12:37 may be identified with Tell el-Maskutah on the east border of Egypt, close to the present Suez Canal (*ABD* s.v. Succoth).

The 600,000 in 12:37 is obviously historically impossible, but it is the standard biblical figure, repeated in the censuses in Num 1 and 26. The origin of the figure is disputed. But it was habitual for ancient scribes to exaggerate numbers. The writer produced a number which seemed fitting to him as a representation of the might of YHWH's people marching out in freedom.

The P editor, or a later one, adds his own reflections in 12:40–2. The figure of 430 years is fitted to his scheme of chronology. The Exodus happens 2,666 years after creation—two-thirds of 4,000 years (Blenkinsopp 1992: 48; but see Hughes 1990: 5–54). 12:41, 51 again liken the Exodus to the marching out of a military force.

In 12:43–9 some further provisions for Passover are added. They underline the close connection of the feast with the integrity of the nation, symbolized by circumcision, and of the family. The translation 'bound servant' in 12:45 NRSV is very dubious, and the word is more usually thought to refer to a lodger or temporary visitor. A very brief speech by YHWH in 13:1–2 ensures that the theme of the consecration of the firstborn is given divine authority; but Moses has first to introduce the Israelites to the festival of Unleavened Bread in 13:3–10. This speech has strong Deuteronomic overtones (see EX C.1); many of the phrases can be found in Deuteronomy (e.g. the sign on the hand and the emblem on the forehead is in Deut 6:8), and the device of the dialogue with the child is used in Deut 6:20–5. But there is also a reference back to Ex 3:8 in 13:5. Moses goes on to instruct the people about the consecration of the firstborn. The first offspring of every female, if it is male, whether human or of domestic animals, belongs in principle to YHWH. However, only cattle, sheep, and goats can be sacrificed. The donkey is an 'unclean' animal which cannot (Lev 11:3—it has undivided hoofs), so a sheep must be sacrificed instead, or the donkey simply killed (13:13). A substitute sacrifice must be offered in place of human firstborn.

(13:17–15:21) The Intervention of God: Final Act The Israelites have left Egypt, but they are not yet out of the reach of Pharaoh. His attempt to recapture them is rewarded with the total destruction of himself and his army. With the end of Israel's oppressors the story of their deliverance reaches a conclusion. It has been argued that the story of the deliverance at the sea is the original basic story of the Exodus (Noth 1962: 114–15). But we have already seen that the commemoration of the Exodus is concentrated on the last night in Egypt. It is better to see this as the last twist in the tale, the final example of the pattern where a crisis evokes a desperate cry from the people, to which YHWH graciously responds, as in 2:23–5 and 5:22–6:1. From another point of view this is the beginning of the Israelites' 'wanderings in the wilderness'. We are introduced to the way in which YHWH will lead them in the wilderness, and the story is the first of several in which the people complain to Moses and YHWH graciously provides for them.

(13:17–22) The Israelites are, in fact, not 'wandering' in the wilderness, even if it looks like it. Their movements are determined by the purposes of God. 13:17 tells us *why* God does not lead them by the obvious route; vv. 18, 20 trace the route on the map, first in general terms, then by mentioning the staging posts; and vv. 21–2 tell us *how* God leads them.

The quickest route to Canaan was along the Mediterranean coast. The author appears to suggest they would meet the Philistines there—an anachronism if the Exodus took place in the late thirteenth century BCE. But this is imaginative history which cannot be fixed in time (EX C.3).

Instead, they went inland 'by way of the wilderness toward the Red Sea'. In other places (23:31; Num 21:4; 1 Kings 9:26) 'the Red Sea' (Heb. 'sea of reeds, weeds') refers to the Gulf of Aqaba. It is often thought that the Gulf of Suez is meant here, or one of the lakes north of it, because 15:4, 22 and other texts (but not 14) fix it as the place where the great deliverance took place, and the Gulf of Aqaba is too far away (see 14:2). For Succoth (v. 20) see EX 12:1–13:16; Etham is unknown. For all topographical details from this point on, see Davies (1979). v. 19 refers back to Gen 50:25, and forward to Josh 24:32. In vv. 21–2 God's leadership is represented in a literal, visible manner. Cloud and fire are two of the commonest accompaniments of God's presence in theophanies (see EX 3:1–6). In the pillar of cloud and fire God's presence becomes permanent and mobile. This visible presence continues with them presumably to the borders of the promised land.

(14:1–31) It is clear that the action of this chapter is presented from two different points of view; but these do not clash, because they are focused on different characters. vv. 1–4, 15–18 are words of YHWH showing us the events from his point of view as the climax of his struggle with Pharaoh in the plagues narrative. (For a full discussion of this, see EX 7:8–11:10.) YHWH deliberately entices him out to recapture the Israelites, so that he may 'gain glory' for himself (vv. 4, 17). One last time, with deepest irony, he announces 'the Egyptians shall know that I am the LORD' (v. 18): as they sink to their deaths, they will know that YHWH is the true ruler of the world.

But in vv. 10–14, 30–1 we see things from the Israelites' point of view. They are in panic, but Moses tells them to trust in YHWH's deliverance: 'Do not be afraid ... you have only to keep still' (vv. 13, 14). Moses uses a form of assurance that recurs again and again in the accounts of Israel's wars, where prophets urge the king or commander not to be afraid, but to trust in YHWH. Cf. particularly Isa 7:4; 28:16; 30:15. However, in the end faith comes *as a result* of seeing YHWH's act of salvation (v. 31). This pattern of events is repeated several times in the story of Israel in the wilderness: three times in the next three chapters, so that the lesson is rubbed in.

Although these points of view do not clash on the theological level, there are obvious unevennesses in the story. v. 4 seems at first to be fulfilled in v. 5, but actually looks forward to v. 8. YHWH's order in v. 16 is carried out only in

v. 21 and has effect only next morning! According to a widely accepted source division, in J (vv. 5–7, 10–14, 19–20, 21b, 24–5, 27b, 30–1) Pharaoh changes his own mind, and the sea is driven back by the wind and then returns to overwhelm the Egyptians. This is the account which concentrates on the Israelites and Moses' call for faith. In P (vv. 1–4, 8–9, 15–18, 21a, 21c, 22–3, 26–7a (to 'over the sea'), 28–9) YHWH 'hardens Pharaoh's heart', and the sea is split into two walls when Moses stretches out his hand, which fall in when he stretches out his hand again.

On one central point the text is at one. The Israelites are delivered and the Egyptians destroyed by God's power. Whether he uses the natural elements or the hand of Moses, he triumphs in person over the enemies of Israel, who are his own enemies.

YHWH's opening instructions to Moses (v. 2) are to *turn back*. This is intended as deliberate deception: it is to make Pharaoh think the Israelites are lost, and tempt him to follow them (v. 3). The place-names in v. 2 cannot be located exactly, but they are on the borders of Egypt, and by 'the sea' (see EX 13:17–22). In v. 5 Pharaoh's motive is different. He receives an intelligence report that the Israelites have 'fled'. Since he knew they were going, this must mean that they have not returned as implied in the negotiations (7:16, etc.). In vv. 9. 18, 23, 26, 28 the NRSV has 'chariot drivers' where other versions have 'horsemen' or 'cavalry'. The Hebrew word normally means 'horseman'. NRSV is probably based on the fact that armies are known not to have had mounted cavalry before the first millennium BCE. But the author of Exodus would not have known that, and almost certainly meant 'horsemen'. A different word is translated 'rider' in 15:1, 21.

What the Israelites claim to have told Moses in Egypt (v. 12) they have not said anywhere in the text of Exodus; but this kind of allusion is very common in Hebrew narrative. In v. 15 YHWH asks Moses why he is crying out to him ('you' is singular), but the narrator has not told us he has. Moses may be assumed to have relayed the *Israelites*' cry in v. 10 to YHWH. In v. 19 as elsewhere (see EX 3:1–6) 'the angel of God' may be a substitute for YHWH himself (cf. 13:21). But the statement is repeated with reference to the pillar of cloud; so it is often held that in v. 19 there are two parallel sources. v. 29 is not a simple repetition of v. 22. It tells us that the Israelites had passed through in safety while the Egyptians were destroyed behind them.

(15:1–21) Pieces of poetry occasionally break the flow of prose in the Pentateuch, often at significant points. This one is particularly suitable here: it is fitting that Israel should praise YHWH when they are finally delivered from their oppressors. This is a victory song, but the victor is God, so it is also a hymn of praise and thanksgiving. It has parallels in the Psalms, which are pointed out in the notes, but it does not rigidly follow any one model of psalm. Psalms of praise often begin with a call to the people to praise, such as Ps 118:1–4. The song sung by Miriam in v. 21 is such a call and could be intended as the opening to which the men's song in 1–18 is the response (Janzen 1992). The song does not describe the previous state of distress or the cry to God for help, unlike many thanksgiving psalms (Ps 18: 30; 118). Everything is concentrated on YHWH and his victory. The song achieves its effect by repeating the account of the victory in several different vivid and allusive ways, punctuated with words of praise.

There is a dispute about the age of the song. One school (see Cross 1973), argues that the grammar and poetic style mark it out as very old, perhaps from the eleventh or twelfth century BCE, so a very ancient and important witness to the event of the Exodus. Others (e.g. Brenner 1991) say that the song relies on Ex 14 as it now stands, so that it must be quite late (fifth century?), and composed to occupy its present place; the author has deliberately created a song which looks old enough to be sung by Moses. But it is possible (Houston 1997) that v. 8 was the source from which the P author in Ex 14 took his account by interpreting its imaginative picture literally. This would make the song older than P, but not necessarily older than J. Of course, now that the song is part of the Ex text we inevitably read it in line with the account in ch. 14. The song looks forward to the completion of YHWH's work in the settling of Israel in his own land. All the promises in 3:7–12 and 6:2–8 are seen as fulfilled, really or virtually, in the miracle at the sea.

The song can be divided into: an introduction, vv. 1–3; a main section praising. YHWH for the victory, 4–12; and a coda looking forward to the entry into the promised land, 13–18. For 'rider' in vv. 1, 21 see the note on 14:9, etc. in EX 14:13–31. But the word here *could* mean 'charioteer', v. 2 is closely similar to Ps 118:14, 28. The word for 'heap' in v. 8 is used in the account of the Jordan crossing in Josh 3:13, 16. As the text stands, this verse has to be taken as describing the 'walls' of water in 14:22, 29; but if the poem is older, it could have been a poetic description of a wave rearing up and about to break; the breaking is described in 10 (Houston 1997).

For the question 'who is like YHWH' (v. 11) cf. Ps 89:6–8. 'Your holy abode' in v. 13 could be Sinai or the temple at Jerusalem, but v. 17 makes the latter more likely. The song praises YHWH not just for the settlement in Canaan but for the establishment of his dwelling among them at Zion. The final verse is another psalm-type motif: see Ps 93:1; 95:3; 96:10; etc. v. 19 recalls the essence of the story after the look into the future in vv. 13–18.

There was a custom, when men came back victorious from a battle, for women to come out from the towns to meet them (hence 'went out' in v. 20) with victory songs and dances (see 1 Sam 18:6–7). Since this victory has been won by YHWH, not by the men, the men have celebrated it, but the women's role is not forgotten, and may well be intended to be prior to the men's (see above, and Janzen 1992; against Trible 1994: 169–73). Miriam is called a prophet probably because of this song, which is seen as inspired.

(15:22–18:27) **Israel in the Wilderness** The two main accounts in Exodus are of YHWH's deliverance of Israel from Egypt and of his gracious provision for their future life with him at Sinai. But Israel have first to reach Sinai through the wilderness. What is meant by 'wilderness' in the Bible is not totally barren sand-desert, but steppe with low rainfall and sparse vegetation, suitable as pasture for sheep and goats but not much else. So there is a linking section describing this journey, but it is more than a simple link. The episodes are based on the well-known conditions of life in the wilderness, but these are used as an opportunity to develop the characterization of the Israelites and the relationship between them, Moses, and YHWH. The first three episodes in particular go very closely together. Two short stories about water frame the much longer one about the manna. In each the people raise a complaint against Moses, to which YHWH responds with gracious provision for their needs. In each Moses acts as the intermediary between YHWH and the people, both ruling them and interceding for them. The word used for 'complain' implies bad-tempered grumbling; in 16:3 and 17:3 they even suggest they would have been better off back in Egypt—thus rejecting YHWH's act of salvation. In spite of this YHWH is patient and gracious.

Yet there is a harder note to the relationship, for another word which occurs in each story is 'test'. YHWH tests Israel (15:25; 16:4) to see whether they will be faithful and obedient; Israel tests or provokes YHWH (17:2, 7) by their grumbling. The theological point is very clear: life for Israel depends on trust in God's provision and obedience to his requirements. This is a lesson that reaches far beyond their temporary life in the wilderness; the best commentary is Deut 8. The main outlines of the relationship that will be literally cast in stone at Sinai begin to emerge; hence we should not be surprised that most of these stories anticipate points that are eventually grounded formally in the law given there: the 'statute and ordinance' at Marah (15:25); the sabbath provision in the manna story (16:5; 22–30); the legal system established on Jethro's advice (18:13–27). There is a similar group of stories in Num 11; 12; 14; 16; 20:2–13, but in most of these the people's grumbling arouses YHWH's anger and his punishment. This arrangement is surely deliberate. Once the people have received the law and accepted the covenant, there is no excuse for them.

It is impossible to say to what extent these stories are based on a tradition in Israel (see EX C.2). The references to the wilderness time in Old Testament literature are very varied: in some it is a time of happiness and obedience in contrast to the apostasy of the time in Canaan (e.g. Hos 2:14; Jer 2:2–3), in some a time of disobedience (e.g. Deut 9:7; Ps 95). Deut 8 comes closest to Exodus in seeing it as a time of testing.

By putting in place-names, the authors must have intended to give a precise idea of the Israelites' route, but this no longer works for us because we do not know where the places are. The people are now on their way to Sinai. If Sinai was, as traditionally supposed, in the south of the Sinai peninsula (see Davies 1979: 63–9), the places mentioned in 15:22, 27; 16:1; 17:1 are likely to be strung out along the west side of the peninsula. But there are other theories about the location of Sinai, and they would change the location of these places.

(15:22–7) For general comments and comments on the location of the place-names, see the previous section. Nothing is said about how or why the 'tree' or 'piece of wood' (15:25) made the water sweet. It seems like magic, but to the author it is simply the way in which YHWH chooses to act. And it is YHWH who 'tests' them. They have known YHWH as a 'healer' in

his 'healing' of the water; they should beware lest he act in the opposite way (as he does in Numbers).

(16:1–36) For general comments and comments on the location of the place-names, see EX 15:22–18:27. This story seems to have originally been based on the fact that the tamarisk tree of the Sinai peninsula in May and June exudes drops of a sweet substance which is gathered and eaten by the local people, who still call it *man*. But the amounts are small, and obviously the story goes far beyond that natural fact. It speaks of a miracle which provides enough food every day, all the year round, to sustain a whole people on the march. And to that miracle of provision are added two further miracles which test the obedience and faith of the people. There is the miracle of precise quantity (vv. 17–18). God's providing is always enough for the day, it cannot be stored (v. 20). And there is the miracle of the sabbath exception to this miracle (vv. 22–30). The meaning of these miracles is found first in the saying in v. 5 which has echoed in one form or another through the narrative since 6:7. Here it is a rebuke to the Israelites who have spoken of *Moses and Aaron* as having brought them out of Egypt (v. 3). They need to understand that it is YHWH alone who can and will provide for them. The second lesson is that the generosity of YHWH is only of value to them if they on their part obey his commands. The full meaning of the sabbath will not be revealed until 20:11; but for the moment they need to understand simply that it is possible to rest for a day and still live, by YHWH's grace.

This chapter has been through a process of editing. It is mainly P, but there is probably an older narrative behind it. It is a somewhat awkward effect of the editing that when YHWH appears he simply repeats what Moses and Aaron have said already; and another awkward feature is the half-hearted way in which the quails are introduced into the narrative from Num 11, where they play a greater part. It is only the manna that the people eat for their whole time in the wilderness. v. 1, 'the second month'. The reckoning is inclusive: it is exactly a month since they left Egypt. In v. 7 'the glory of the LORD' is probably another way of referring to the way YHWH makes himself known in his miraculous provision; but in 10 it is the usual way in P of describing the appearance of YHWH in brightness wrapped in a cloud. In v. 15 the word translated 'what?' is *man*, which is not the normal word for 'what?' (*mah*), but near enough for a Hebrew pun: it is the word for 'manna' (v. 31). Aaron kept the preserved manna 'before the covenant' or 'testimony' (v. 34), that is before or in the ark, which is made in ch. 37. Since they 'ate manna forty years' (v. 35), Moses' order could have been given at any time: there is no anachronism.

(**17:1–7**) For general comments and comments on the location of the place-names, see EX 15:22– 18:27. The episode closely follows the general pattern of the two previous episodes; its distinctive feature is the people's 'testing' or 'provoking' of YHWH, which gives its name to the place (vv. 2, 7). Once again Moses directs their attention away from himself, whom the Israelites blame, to YHWH who is able to provide. 'Horeb' in v. 6 is the name in Deuteronomy, but not in Exodus (except 3:1), of the mountain of revelation. It may be identified with Sinai here, which cannot be far away. It is confusing that the place is given two names, not only Massah, 'testing', but Meribah, 'quarrelling', and that the latter is given to another place where a similar thing happens in Num 20:13. The poetic references at Deut 33:8 and Ps 95:8 use the two names. Possibly the author has taken both names from one of the poems and assumed they referred to the same place.

(**17:8–16**) Amalek was a nomadic people dwelling in the wilderness to the south of Canaan. All references to them in the HB are fiercely hostile: see especially Deut 25:17–19 and 1 Sam 15. There seems to be a long-standing feud: Deut 25 offers a reason for this, but it is not reflected in this story. The strangest feature of the story is the connection between the position of Moses' arms and the fortunes of the battle. Older commentators presume that his arms were raised in prayer; but if so why does the narrative not say he was praying? As Van Seters (1994: 203) points out, Josh 8:18–26 is similar. In both cases the automatic connection suggests magic; it is only implicit that God was in action. It is only the end of the story (17:14–16) that makes it clear that Israel's battle is, as always, YHWH's—to the death in this case. The Hebrew text in v. 16 is unclear. The NRSV's 'A hand upon the banner of the LORD' is the best suggestion, since it explains the name Moses has just given to his altar.

(**18:1–12**) This episode links up with the early part of the story (chs. 2–4). Cf. in particular v. 5

with 3:12. There are difficulties in the placement of the story. The Israelites have not at this point actually reached the mountain of God. Moses' father-in-law appears to be still with them in Num 10:29; and the measures of 18:13–27 are placed after leaving Horeb in Deut 1:9–18. For all these reasons it is often believed that the story originally belonged *after* the Sinai narrative; but the reason why it was moved is unclear (see Childs 1974: 322; Durham 1987: 242; Van Seters 1994: 209 n. 3. Propp 1998: 627–8 does not agree). Zipporah and her family also create a problem. In 2:22 we are only told of one son of Moses (but see 4:20); and we last heard of Zipporah and her son on the way to Egypt, not left behind with her father (4:24–6). The best explanation may be that 4:24–6 is a late addition to the narrative. 'After Moses had sent her away' would then be an addition in v. 2 to harmonize the narrative with 4:20–6. 'Took her back' in v. 2 (NRSV) is not a correct translation of the Hebrew, which refers to what Jethro did *after* hearing about Moses: he 'took her and her two sons … and came' (v. 5).

The author has a tolerant acceptance of foreign peoples, and sees no sharp distinction between their religion and Israel's. Jethro, a foreign priest, gladly acknowledges the supremacy of YHWH (v. 11): but he makes this acknowledgement from within his own religious tradition, not as an act of conversion. Probably for this reason (unless one accepts the existence of a special E source (see PENT)) the chapter tends to use *ʾĕlōhîm* rather than YHWH except in vv. 8–11. For the multiple names of Moses' father-in-law, see EX 2:15*b*–22.

(**18:13–27**) The theme of this section is also addressed in Num 11:11–17; Deut 1:9–18. It is not clear why the advice to Moses to share the burden is given by his father-in-law. Moses here is a judge deciding civil disputes, and a lawgiver mediating God's 'statutes and instructions'; and people come to him 'to inquire of God' (v. 15), that is, to seek directions in particular situations. There is no sharp line drawn between these functions in the Bible: so in Deut 17:8–13 the priest is associated with the judges in the decision of difficult cases, because the direction of God must be sought. The legal system which is established is actually based on a military organization (v. 21). Practice in the ancient Near East tended to give military and judicial functions to the same officers. The organization is artificial, it does not arise out of the existing social structure. Moses here acts like ancient kings, who tended to impose their systems on society. Possibly the story is intended to account for the later judicial system of the Israelite/Judean monarchy.

The interesting theological point is seen by Childs: that hard-headed, practical advice is seen as the 'command of God' (v. 23). There is no distinction between divine revelation and practical wisdom: the latter is as much the will of God as the former.

(19:1–40:38) The Establishment of Israel's Relationship with YHWH The people of Israel are no longer slaves. They have been saved from the land of oppression. But they are not yet a nation. The authors of Exodus believed that their being as a nation depended on the presence of their God with them, and that in turn depended on certain conditions. The second half of the book of Exodus is mainly concerned to set these out. The chapters contain two main kinds of answer to the question: on what conditions can Israel be YHWH's people and YHWH their God? The first answer is: on condition of obeying his commandments, which can be summed up as to worship him alone, and to behave with justice towards one another. These are set out in chs. 20–3, and the people's formal acceptance of them is narrated in ch. 24. This solemn imposition of requirements and undertaking of obedience is what this part of the book means by 'covenant' (19:5;24:7, 8; 31:18; for covenant see EX C.1; and for law and commandments, Patrick 1986). The book then goes on, in chs. 32–4, to deal with the question: what happens if the people break the covenant? They then depend essentially on the mercy of God (33:19). But interleaved with this account is another way of dealing with the question. It is not contradictory to the first, but its presuppositions are different. YHWH safeguards his presence among his people by locating it in a physical site which moves as they move, and is hedged about with restrictions so that they receive blessing rather than harm from the presence of the holy God among them (29:43–6). YHWH gives Moses directions for the establishment of this 'tent of meeting' or 'tabernacle' in 25–31, and it is set up in accordance with his directions in 35–40.

The first answer sees the relationship as above all a moral one—not a matter of morals in a narrow sense, but based on how God and people behave towards one another. It is deeply marked by the influence of the prophets and the Deuteronomic writers, and is the work of the author

I call J (see EX C.1). The second answer sees the main issue as being that of holiness. From God radiates a power that is the source of life and blessing, but is destructive to anyone who approaches too close or does not take precautions. This answer is the contribution of P.

(19:1–20:21) Before any of this can happen, the coming of YHWH to his people must be described. Mount Sinai becomes the symbol, not of the permanent presence of YHWH, which goes with them, but of his coming in unimaginable power and glory. This is the work of an imaginative writer, not a record from history. But it describes, symbolically, the experience of the presence of the holy and righteous God. The account proves difficult to follow, at least with our ideas of narrative logic. 19:3–8 appears to anticipate the whole process which culminates in ch. 24, and vv. 20–5 seem inconsequential. YHWH's speech to the people in ch. 20 begins abruptly: 19:25 breaks off with; 'and Moses said to them' which ought to be followed by what he said (NRSV 'and told them' smooths over the difficulty). After YHWH's speech, in 20:18–21, the people react in a way that suggests they have not heard what he has said. Two main types of solution are on offer. The first is that the difficulty arises from a complex literary history (see, for different analyses. Childs 1974: 344–51; Van Seters 1994: 248–52; Albertz 1994: 55; Propp 2006: 141–54). It is possible, for example, that the Ten Commandments are a late addition to this context, from Deut 5, although they are fundamental to the covenant in the text as it stands. The alternative is that a literary technique is being used which we tend not to understand. For example, Sprinkle (1994: 18–27) suggests that ch. 19 gives us an overview of events to come, which are described in greater detail later: possibly 20:1 picks up 19:19 and 20:21 picks up 19:20; YHWH's command to Moses in 19:24 is taken up again in 24:1–2. Patrick (1994) suggests that 19:3–8 makes clear at the outset the nature of the transaction. YHWH does not give commandments until the Israelites have formally declared themselves ready to accept them.

The description of YHWH's coming is created from traditional materials. So far as the site of the theophany (see EX 3:1–6) is concerned, there was a very ancient literary tradition describing the coming of YHWH in power from the deep southern wilderness, and one of the geographical names used was Sinai (Judg 5:5; Ps 68:8). The idea that the gods live on a high mountain was a very widespread one. But here the idea is more refined: YHWH does not actually live on the mountain, but comes down on it (19:11, 18; cf. 3:8). The theophany (19:16–20) is described in terms drawn from thunderstorms, earthquakes, and volcanic eruptions, the greatest displays of natural power that can be observed; and such descriptions are found in Hebrew literature of all periods—see e.g. Ps 18:7–15. They are ways of describing the indescribable, and certainly should not be taken to mean that what the Israelites actually saw was a thunderstorm or earthquake, or that Mt. Sinai was a volcano. The one unusual feature in the theophany is the sound of the trumpet (19:13, 16, 19; more precisely the ram's horn). This was used in temple services. YHWH comes so that the Israelites may come to him in worship. They have to make preparations to meet a holy God (19:10–15), preparations which are similar to those undertaken before entering a temple for sacrifice, and the mountain is fenced off in the same way as the most holy parts of a shrine are fenced off. 'On the third new moon', 19:1; more likely 'in the third month', reckoning inclusively. This would bring them in the Priestly calendar to the feast of Pentecost, when the Jews to this day celebrate the giving of the Law. 'A priestly kingdom and a holy nation' (19:6): each of the two phrases expresses both sides of Israel's future existence. They will be a nation, with a social and political structure; they will at the same time and *through* their nationhood and state structures be dedicated to YHWH as priests are dedicated to the God they serve. The covenant to be announced will explain how this will be possible. A further purpose of YHWH's coming is explained in v. 9: it is to confirm the position of Moses as the confidant of YHWH in the eyes of the people, so that they trust him (cf. 14:31). The severe rules for anyone touching the mountain in 19:12–13 arise from the idea that holiness is a physical infection which can be 'caught' and is dangerous for people in an ordinary state. The command 'do not go near a woman' (v. 15)—a euphemism for sex; the 'people' who receive the command are the men—again arises because of the conception that certain bodily states create a danger in the face of holiness (see Lev 15, esp. 31; 1 Sam 21:4). The mention of priests in 19:22, 24 is difficult, since at this point Israel has no priests. Presumably it means those who will become priests later (Lev 8–9).

(20:1–17) The Ten Commandments The central place which this passage has had in the

religious and moral teaching of Judaism and Christianity is a fair reflection of the centrality which it is given here in Exodus and in Deut 5. The Ten Commandments are, in this story, the prime expression of the covenant demands. They stand first in the account of the covenant-making. It is unclear whether they are spoken directly to the people; they certainly are in Deuteronomy. But the centrality also emerges from the very form and content of the text. In the first place it begins with YHWH's self-introduction (cf. 6:2 and see Zimmerli 1982), and asserts his right to authority, by recalling to the Israelites his goodness to them. And the first and much the greater part of the text is concerned with the requirements of his honour. Secondly, it is obviously designed to include all the most basic religious and moral requirements over a wide sphere of life. Thirdly, every command is expressed in the broadest possible way, sometimes by detailed elaboration (vv. 8–11), sometimes by avoiding any details which might narrow down the application (vv. 13–15). In a word, it is the most basic statement possible of the conditions on which Israel may be in relationship with YHWH. It combines in one text the specific demand for Israel to worship YHWH alone with those few moral requirements which are essential in one form or another for any human society.

But it is not a legal text. What laws in ancient Israel looked like we see in chs. 21–2. It is instruction addressed personally to Israel, or to the individual Israelite (the 'you' is singular and masculine, but that does not necessarily mean that women are not addressed; see below on vv. 8–11). It does not suggest how it is to be implemented or say what is to happen if the commands are ignored, but simply asks for obedience. (But Phillips 1970 regards it as Israel's fundamental law, and many scholars connect it with the form of ancient treaties: see Mendenhall 1992a.) If the setting in life of this type of text is not legal, what is it? Material of this kind, with its brief memorable clauses, could be designed as an aid to religious instruction in the home (Albertz 1994: 214–16). But this text goes beyond that function. With YHWH's self-announcement and personal demand for exclusive loyalty, vv. 2–6 belong nowhere else but in this present setting of covenant-making. Afterwards, in vv. 7–12, he is referred to in the third person, which is more suitable for a catechism. Perhaps catechetical material has been adapted to its place in the narrative.

This is the fundamental text of the covenant, but that does not mean that it is necessarily historically the earliest of the OT 'legal' texts, although many scholars firmly believe that it is, at least in an older form (see Durham 1987: 282). Reflection on all God's commands and requirements may have led to a more profound grasp of their basic meaning, which has then been expressed in this text. In fact vv. 2–12 are written very much in the style of Deuteronomy, except for v. 11, which is Priestly, so they are unlikely to be earlier than the late seventh century. Although this passage has always been called (literally) the Ten Words (Ex 34:28; Deut 4:13; 10:4), it is not obvious how the roughly twenty sentences of the text are to be grouped into ten. Different religious traditions have come to different conclusions. Jews call v. 2 the first Word and vv. 3–6 the second. Roman Catholics and Lutherans group vv. 2–6 as the first commandment and divide v. 17 into two to make up the tally of ten; other Christians separate v. 3 as the first commandment and treat vv. 4–6 as the second. (See further EX 20:2–6.) This commentary will simply use verse numbers. (For detailed discussion of the Commandments see Childs 1974: 385–439; Weinfeld 1991: 242–319.)

(20:2–6) The first section of the Commandments is quite different from the rest, being spoken in the first person and expressing what is most distinctive of the religion of the OT: the requirement to worship YHWH alone, and the prohibition of using images in worship. Two basic demands: can the Catholic tradition be right in treating it as one 'commandment'? Many scholars (e.g. Durham 1987: 286; B. B. Schmidt 1995) would see v. 4 as prohibiting images of YHWH in particular, after v. 3 has dealt with worshipping other gods. However, there is no sharp break anywhere in these verses: they treat throughout of YHWH's exclusive claim. The 'them' in v. 5 must refer to the 'other gods' in v. 3, because all the nouns in v. 4 are singular (Zimmerli 1968). This means that the command not to make an idol is part of a context forbidding the worship of any god but YHWH. That YHWH might be worshipped by means of an idol is simply inconceivable for this text. If you are using an idol, you must be worshipping another god. In those OT passages where people appear to be worshipping YHWH with idols (Ex 32:4; Judg 17; 1 Kings 12:28), the context implies that they are not genuinely worshipping YHWH. In the Syria–Canaan area generally, the central worship symbol in official

sanctuaries tended not to be an image, but images of subordinate gods and especially goddesses were freely used (Mettinger 1995). But in the pure monotheism demanded here YHWH brooked no such rivals.

Modern preachers interpret this command in a moralistic way: anything which absorbs a person's devotion is his/her god (cf. Luther). But this is not what it means in the OT context. It was not self-evident to people in OT times that there was only one God; the demand to worship only one God had to struggle against a polytheism which to many people seemed more natural, reflecting the complexity and unpredictability of the world. Even the Bible has to recognize the existence of other powers; the uniqueness of its demand is that even so only one of them is worthy of Israel's worship, the one 'who brought you…out of the house of slavery'; who is 'a jealous God'—better, perhaps, 'passionate', 'watchful of my rights'. The issue is one of YHWH's honour as the protector and saviour of his people. The harshness of the threat in 5b–6 (see also 34:7) has to be evaluated in the light of a far stronger community feeling than is normal with us. The worship of a god could not be an individual matter: the whole extended family shared in the sin—and therefore in the punishment. But contrast Ezek 18.

(20:7) It is uncertain what this command was intended to refer to: suggestions include deceitful oaths (as in Lev 19:12), unwarranted use of formal curses (Brichto 1963: 59–68), the use of God's name in magic spells, or all of these and other things (Childs 1974: 410–12). But it is quite clear that the improper use of the name YHWH is prohibited. The command is closely related to 20:2–6. It is YHWH's honour that is at stake. To wrest his name to one's own private and deceitful purposes is to dishonour the one who bears it.

(20:8–11) The sabbath likewise is an institution for the honour of YHWH; it is a sabbath 'to YHWH your God', and must be 'kept holy'. The day is dedicated to YHWH by abstaining from work, that is, from anything that is intended for one's own benefit, or human purposes generally. In order to ensure that the entire community keeps it, the householder is required to ensure that everyone in the house, which is also the work unit in peasant society, abstains from work on the seventh day. The list of persons does not include 'your wife'. The best explanation is that the lady of the house is not mentioned because she is addressed along with her husband (as in e.g. Deut 16:11; Smith 1918: 169; Weinfeld 1991: 307–8; contrast Clines 1995a). v. 11 gives a motivation for observing the commandment. The primary emphasis is on the special character of the day, determined by YHWH in the beginning, rather than on the need for people to rest (contrast Deut 5:15). The verse is obviously P, referring back to Gen 2:1–3 (so also Ex 31:14). The sabbath commandment is the only positive ritual requirement among the Ten Commandments. The main reason is likely to be that it had to be observed by every individual in the community without exception (the dietary laws, for example, did not have to be observed by aliens).

(**20:12**) Ancient Israel was a hierarchical society in which respect for superiors, parents in the first place, was fundamental. Care for their honour therefore comes next in the series after the honour of God (similarly Lev 19:3–4). This commandment is formulated positively, so its effect is broader than the law against insulting parents in Ex 21:17, etc. It will include care and comfort in old age (Mk 7:9–13). The commandments are addressed to adults, not children, and the need for this commandment may arise from tension between older men at the head of extended families and their sons with their own families.

The remaining commandments define serious transgressions against the rights of members of the community (generally of male householders).

(**20:13**) 'Murder' is the correct translation, i.e. the unlawful killing of a member of the community. The commandment does not cover capital punishment, killing in war, or the killing of animals for food; which is not to say that the OT is unconcerned with the ethical problems posed by these things.

(**20:14**) Adultery in the Bible is definable as intercourse between a married (or betrothed) woman and a man not her husband. The commandment is concerned with a man's rights over his wife. As in all traditional patriarchal cultures, the men of the family need to be assured of the faithfulness of their wives to be sure that their children are theirs. No similar restrictions apply to a husband in OT morality. It is the only sexual offence in the Ten Commandments, since others do not infringe the rights of a third party in a serious way.

(**20:15**) This commandment would include kidnapping as well as the theft of movable property. The word translated 'steal' does not cover

the violent or dishonest alienation of land and houses: that is probably covered by 20:17.

(**20:16**) This is concerned with testimony in the courts. In Israelite courts the witness was in effect a prosecutor, as there was no state prosecution system. False accusation could put one's life, not merely one's reputation, in danger (see 1 Kings 21; Deut 19:15–21).

(**20:17**) The dominant interpretation of this commandment is that it is concerned simply with the *desire* to possess what is not one's own as a sin in itself (Rom 7:7–8; Calvin 1953: i. 354–6). However, there is also an interpretation which sees it as concerned with overt action to dispossess one's neighbour (Mk 10:19; Luther, J. Hermann 1927). Even if the Hebrew word refers primarily to desire (Moran 1967), the concern is for the danger to one's neighbour posed by one's covetousness; and in particular the kind of covetousness described in Mic 2:1–2. As Luther saw, the machinations of the powerful to dispossess the weak are not covered elsewhere in the Ten Commandments.

(**20:18–21**) Moses' point is that they should not be terrified at the divine appearance because it is for their good: 'fear' in v. 20 is not the panic terror that is now seizing them, but reverence and awe which should lead to the right conduct that God asks of them. Once again (cf. 15:25) they are being 'tested' or 'challenged' to make the right response.

(**20:22–23:33**) The 'Book of the Covenant' The very long speech that YHWH now delivers to Moses to pass on to the Israelites includes a much wider range of religious, moral, and legal instruction than the Ten Commandments. The Ten Commandments make absolute demands; this speech shows how the demands of God for fairness and justice and for the proper honouring of himself work out in practice in a particular society. That is why much of it is at first sight of little interest to people who live in a different society under different conditions. It has been given the name Book of the Covenant by modern scholars, from 24:7. The name suggests that the speech existed as a single document simply slotted into the text. (There continues to be discussion among scholars about its date (see Albertz 1994: 182–3).) But it is unlikely ever to have been a single document. Most of the material has been taken from earlier sources, but it has been shaped to fit its narrative context (see 20:22; 22:21; 23:15

(13:6–7); 23:20–33), and as it stands is likely to have been put together by J.

The main areas covered are religious observance; civil law, specifically the law of bondage for debt, personal injury, and property torts; social justice; and judicial integrity. The arrangement of material sometimes seems capricious to us, but there is logic behind it, as Sprinkle (1994) shows. 23:20–33 is concerned with the immediate situation rather than with permanent rules, so it might be described as an epilogue. The remaining material is arranged as follows:

20:23–6	Rules for worship
21:1	Heading for 21:2–22:17
21:2–11	Release of slaves
21:12–32	Personal injury
21:33–22:17	Property damage (these two bridged by the case of the goring ox)
22:18–20	Offences against covenant holiness
22:21–7	Treatment of dependants
22:28–30	Treatment of superiors
22:31	Covenant holiness (bracketing with 22:18–20)
23:1–9	Judicial integrity
23:10–19	Sabbaths and festivals

The speech contains material of very different types. Most of the material between 21:2 and 22:17 is in an impersonal legal style which contrasts sharply with the personal address of most of the rest, in which YHWH speaks of himself in the first person and addresses Israel as 'you' (usually in the singular, sometimes the plural). For detail on these different types of law see Patrick (1986: 13–33). The impersonal style sets out a legal case, giving the situation 'when such-and-such happens', and laying down what should then be done. This is the style used in the Mesopotamian legal codes such as the Code of Hammurabi (see ANET 159–98), and it is technically referred to as 'casuistic' law. There is also a good deal of overlap in content between this section and the Mesopotamian codes (summarized by Childs 1974: 462–3). This does not mean that the laws have been borrowed from a foreign source, simply that legal style and stock examples were similar all over the ancient Near East. Laws of this type were probably not used as the basis of judicial decisions (see Jackson 1989: 186). Jackson considers them 'self-executing' laws, which would enable lay people to settle their disputes without recourse to a court. But even judges in the ancient Near East did not normally interpret written laws, but used their wisdom to apply traditional ideas of

justice. Laws like these embody such traditional ideas, not in the form of legal principles, but by evoking typical situations and giving appropriate solutions (Jackson 2006: 23–39). That is why they do not have the detail and precision one would expect in a modern body of law. They are probably borrowed from an old legal text to illustrate the kind of justice required by YHWH in the resolution of disputes.

The other main style is that of personal admonition. This is the kind of style in which a tribal elder might give moral instruction (cf. Jer 35:6–7; Gerstenberger 1965: 110–17), but in this text it is clear that God is the speaker. It is therefore unlikely to have been borrowed from a specific social setting; the suggestion of a ritual of covenant renewal (see Childs 1974: 455–6) is pure speculation. So although the content of the instruction would have been derived from Israel's moral and religious tradition, its form has been designed to fit its present literary setting.

In each case the style is appropriate to the subject-matter: casuistic for the settlement of disputes, personal address for religious instruction and for teaching about justice as a personal responsibility.

(20:22–6) Prologue: YHWH's Presence YHWH begins his address to Moses by speaking of his own person and presence in worship. The first point, as in the Ten Commandments, is his intolerance of idols, that is, other gods, alongside him: see EX 20:2–6, and Sprinkle (1994: 37–8) for a different view. He goes on to speak positively of how he should be worshipped. The altar must be of natural materials (E. Robertson 1948; for the different kinds of sacrifices, see LEV 1–7). The key religious point, however, is in v. 25. YHWH's presence and blessing depends not on the humanly organized cult, but on his own decision: 'where I proclaim my name'. This has generally been understood as permitting many altars for sacrifice, while Deut 12 permits only one, so that it would belong to an earlier stage in religious history than Deuteronomy. But it could be saying that while one altar is allowed, YHWH's blessing may be received quite apart from altars and sacrifice (Van Seters 1994: 281).

(21:2–11) The 'ordinances' begin with the demands of justice in relation to the use of people as slaves, no doubt because the people addressed have just been released from slavery themselves. For detail on the laws of slavery, see Chirichigno (1993); also 'Slavery' in ABD vi. The law is concerned with 'Hebrews' who are in bonded service for debt., not with foreign slaves who might be owned outright (ibid. 200–18: another view of the meaning of 'Hebrew' in e. g. Childs 1974: 468). Someone taking out a loan might hand over a child of the family to work off the debt, or might sell a child into service in order to pay off debts (Neh 5.1–5); and a creditor was entitled to seize a defaulting debtor or his/her child (2 Kings 4:1) and either sell or use him/her as a slave. A creditor could seize a defaulting debtor or a member of his family (2 Kings 4:1) and either sell or use him/her as a slave; or a man could sell a member of his family into bondage to pay off his debts (Neh 5:1–5). The law limits the period of such bondage to six years. Permanent bondage could only be at the bondsman's own choice; but often he may have had no genuine choice. 21:7–11 is concerned with a girl who is sold as a concubine or slave-wife. A woman who had been sexually used and might be the mother of her master's children could not normally be released after six years; but the law lists situations in which justice would demand that she should be. In effect she is given the privileges of a legal wife.

(21:12–17) Four capital cases are listed in descending order of severity. All are worthy of death; this indicates how seriously the requirement to honour parents (20:12) was taken. In v. 17 'dishonour' or 'reject' might be a better translation than 'curse'. It was customary for the relatives of the victim to take vengeance. v. 13 limits this by protecting someone who is accidentally responsible for a person's death (Deut 19:1–13 elaborates): traditionally the altar provided sanctuary (1 Kings 2:28). Frequently the victim or relatives would accept monetary compensation (see 21:30), though in the case of murder Num 35:31 forbids this.

(21:18–27) The general principle of justice exemplified here is that of fair compensation for injury. The principle is stated in general terms in the famous vv. 23–5. Later this was interpreted as requiring reasonable monetary compensation (Daube 1947: 106–9; Childs. 1974: 472), but at some earlier stage its literal application prevented excessive vengeance and would have ensured the rich were not at an advantage. In the case of slaves, the compensation for serious injury or unintended killing (v. 21) is that the owner loses his property. If he murders his slave he must face punishment (v. 20). It is important that as against Mesopotamian codes the slave is treated as a legal person.

(21:28–36) The case of the goring ox is a topic also in Mesopotamian codes. It serves as a standard example of the way to treat cases of negligence, and of how to distinguish between accident (vv. 28, 35) and culpable negligence. The one feature that would not be found in contemporary or modern laws is that the ox itself, if it has killed a person, is treated as a criminal and stoned rather than slaughtered in the normal way (vv. 28, 29, 32). Here religious factors enter in. The ox has transgressed boundaries between human and animal and between wild and tame animals (see Houston 1993: 182–200), so is treated as ritually detestable and not simply dangerous; see Gen 9:5.

(22:1–15) The principle adopted in the property section of the laws is that equal compensation is acceptable for negligence (vv. 5, 6, 12, 14), but is enhanced as a deterrent to deliberate theft or fraud (vv. 1,4, 7, 9); while no compensation is payable in the case of accident or *force majeure* (vv. 11, 13).

Theft and sale of livestock (v. 1) is treated more severely than theft of money or articles (v. 7), perhaps because they represented the farmer's livelihood; oxen are compensated on a higher scale than sheep perhaps because of their working capacity (Daube 1947: 133). vv. 2–3a draw a line between justified killing in self-defence and unnecessary killing, which is murder. The time of day is simply an example of the factors that could be taken into account. The other issue raised in this section is that of evidence. Where the matter could not be settled by witnesses, the only recourse was religious. 'Before God' (8, 9) probably means at a sanctuary; but how was the decision made? In 11 it is clearly by oath; this may be true in 8 and 9 as well (Sprinkle 1993: 146–7); other suggestions include ordeal and divination by the priest.

(22:16–17) Seduction is treated on the one hand as a matter of responsibility on the part of the seducer: he does not have the right to decide not to marry the girl. On the other, it is a matter of the father's rights. Normally a father had the right to dispose of his daughter, and to receive 'bride-price' for her. If he chooses to exercise his right, he is compensated for the difficulty he will have in giving her away. The girl has no say in the matter.

(22:18–20) gives a series of three practices which the advocates of exclusive loyalty to YHWH saw as fundamentally threatening to it, and therefore deserving of death. We do not know precisely what is meant by sorcery, but it probably involved treating with spiritual powers other than YHWH. Bestiality transgressed fundamental ritual boundaries (cf. 21:28 and see Lev 18:23). Here it is the community which must inflict punishment on YHWH's behalf.

(**22:21–7**) Earlier sections have treated disputes in the community as resolvable by applying norms of justice. But there were great disparities in wealth and power in Israelite society, as in ours. Some people were in a dependent situation either temporarily or permanently. It was easy to take advantage of them and prevent them from obtaining legal redress. So those who hold power over them must be both reminded of what is just and warned of the possible consequences when they have to deal with a just God (See Houston 2008: 105–14.). The 'resident alien' meant an incomer from another area without a property stake in the local community. Widows and orphans were vulnerable because they had no adult male protector in the immediate family. A 'poor' person means primarily a family head who has insufficient resources to maintain his family (Houston 2008: 61–4) and so needs a charitable loan.

(**22:28–30**) As the independent Israelite has duties to his dependants, he also has duties to those above him, especially God (see also 13:11–16).

(**22:31**) In an economy of scarcity, people would be inclined to make use of any source of food, however suspect. But being dedicated to YHWH means using a diet fitted to his dignity. Mangled meat is fit only for the universal scavenger. This theme is developed in much more detail in Lev 11; Deut 14; see Houston (1993: 241–4, 248–53).

(**23:1–9**) It is all very well to have norms of justice. But unless they can be enforced fairly and impartially, they are of no use v. 3: 'the poor' is probably a textual error for 'the great' (Van Seters 2003: 137; Houston 2008: 114–15; against, Houtman 2000: 240–41), vv. 4, 5, which do not seem to fit this theme, underline the requirement of total impartiality. You may have a long-standing dispute with another family: but you should be fair to them in daily life, and, just the same, you should show no partiality against them in court. v. 9 ties up the section on social justice by repeating the warning not to oppress the alien which begins it in 22:21.

(**23:10–19**) A people dedicated to YHWH, who are called by him to act with justice, honour him particularly in ways which serve the cause of justice. Two institutions particularly characteristic of Israel's religious culture are the sabbath year (vv. 10–11) and the sabbath day (v. 12). Neither of them is called that here, possibly because the name was attached to a different holy day in the pre-exilic period when these verses may have originated (Robinson 1988). The original function of the sabbath year (cf. Lev 25:1–7) is unclear, but here it is given a charitable purpose; likewise the sabbath day is commended for its beneficial effects on dependants, as in Deut 5:15, not as in 20:11 (P!) for its sacral character in itself. v. 13 looks like a concluding verse, so what follows may be an addendum. vv. 14, 17 bracket the brief instruction about the major pilgrimage festivals of the agricultural year. Passover is not mentioned, possibly because it was not yet a pilgrimage festival at the time of writing. The Israelites are reminded that they have already been told (13:3–10) of Unleavened Bread. The other two festivals are described in exclusively agricultural terms, and are given different names from those customary later. 'Harvest' is Weeks or Pentecost, Deut 16:9–12; Lev 23:15–21; 'Ingathering', when all produce is taken in before the autumn rains begin, is Booths or Tabernacles, Deut 16:13–15; Lev 23:33–6.

The instructions in vv. 18–19 are connected with festival worship. The taboos in v. 18 possibly arise because the ideas of fermentation and corruption are opposed to the purity of the sacrifice. The 'kid in mother's milk' prohibition is an old conundrum. See the full discussion in Milgrom (1991: 737–41); also Houston in *DOTP*: 333–4.

(**23:20–33**) **Epilogue: Entering the Land** As the whole of the speech has looked forward to Israel's settled life in the land, it is appropriate that it should be concluded with a word of promise, along with some admonition, about their journey to and entering of it. The promise of an 'angel' or messenger does not really revoke YHWH's personal presence with them (13:21–2)—see EX 3:1–6; especially in view of YHWH's statement that 'my name is in him'. vv. 23–33 look back to the promises in 3:7–10 and expand them. Here, as in Deuteronomy (see Deut 7 especially), the native nations stand for the constant threat of the worship of the gods of the land (seen as idols, as in the opening of the speech at v. 24): 'you shall . . . demolish *them*') to the exclusive loyalty demanded by YHWH. He will do all the fighting for them (as in ch. 14!); their sole responsibility is to be faithful to him. v. 31 very much exaggerates the territory that Israel ever held at any time in her history; but as in vv. 25–6 the implication may well be that they never received the fullness of the promise because they were *not* faithful.

(24:1–8) The Conclusion of the Covenant Ch. 24 is the climax of the Sinai narrative, but it contains a number of themes rather roughly pieced together. There has never been any consensus among critics about the sources or editing of the chapter. vv. 1–2 take us back to the end of ch. 19. v. 1*a* is most accurately translated in the Jerusalem Bible: 'To Moses he *had* said', i.e. in 19:24. YHWH's invitation here includes more people, but variation is common when speeches are repeated. Though we are reminded of the invitation here, it is only taken up at v. 9. vv. 3–8 are the account of the ceremonial sealing of the covenant on the basis of the words which YHWH has given to Moses, that is the Ten Commandments and the Book of the Covenant. The meaning of the covenant has already been explained in 19:4–6. There (19:8) we heard of the people's response in advance, and it is repeated twice here (vv. 3, 7): first Moses secures their acceptance of YHWH's terms, then he formally seals their covenant with YHWH by writing the terms down, reading them to them, and hearing their acceptance again; then he consecrates them as YHWH's holy people (19:6) in a sacrificial ritual. Nicholson (1986: 171–2) has shown that although there is no ritual precisely like this in the OT we can understand its meaning by comparing rituals which have some similarity, such as the ordination of priests in 29:20. The blood of the holy offering makes them holy to YHWH. This is an imaginative way of expressing in narrative form the bond of will and obedience between YHWH and Israel.

(24:9–18) Vision of God on the Mountain The invitation of 24:1 (19:24) is now taken up. Representatives of the people, and of the future priests (Aaron and his sons), ascend the mountain and receive a vision of God himself. As with other similar visions (Isa 6; Ezek 1), the Bible avoids describing the appearance of God, but simply gives one vivid glimpse of the glory that surrounded him. 'Sapphire' (NRSV) should probably be 'lapis lazali', a common material in the decoration of

temples. The eating and drinking of the people's representatives in the presence of YHWH himself is an appropriate conclusion to the story of how they became his holy people. The promise of 19:13*b* is at last fulfilled. (See Nicholson 1986: 121–33, 173–4.) vv. 12–14 prepare for YHWH's giving of the tablets of stone to Moses, and it also makes a bridge to ch. 32. What exactly is written on the tablets is not made clear here: it is only at 34:28 (and Deut 5:22) that it emerges it is the Ten Commandments. It is also unclear how the tablets relate to the document that Moses has written. The tablets are to be placed in the Ark when it is made (25:16; 40:20; Deut 10:2–5); as Cassuto (1967: 331) notes, this is similar to the provisions in ancient treaties for copies to be placed in the sanctuaries of the contracting parties. Perhaps, then, the tablets are meant to be the official original of the covenant, while copies on papyrus may be made for practical purposes. vv. 15–18 are a P paragraph preparing for the giving of the instructions about the tabernacle which now follow.

(25:1–31:17) The Prescriptions for the Sanctuary This third long speech by YHWH from Sinai is an entirely Priestly passage. He gives instructions here for the building of a portable structure which has two functions. It enables the living presence of YHWH, which the Israelites have met at Sinai, to go with them on their journey and continue to bless them (40:34–8); and it enables Moses to continue to receive instructions from YHWH after the people have left Sinai (see 25:22; 29:42; Lev 1:1).

This double function is reflected in the names 'tabernacle' and 'tent of meeting'. In part, these names refer to different parts of the structure (see ch. 26, especially v. 7): the tabernacle is the arrangement of frames or boards over which curtains of fine material are stretched, and the tent is the curtains of goat's hair which cover the tabernacle. But theologically the name 'tent of *meeting*' implies (as in 33:7–11) the place where God meets with Moses as the prophetic representative of Israel: while 'tabernacle' (*miškān*, lit. 'dwelling') implies the place where God dwells among his people. Both these understandings are expressed in the conclusion to the main body of instructions in 29:43–6.

But though the name 'tent of meeting' is rather the commoner of the two, the physical image is that of a temple, differing from other temples only in being portable; and a temple was primarily thought of as a god's permanent dwelling-place on earth. (For thorough discussion of the priestly picture of the tabernacle and its service see Haran 1985: 149–259.)

The main body of instructions, chs. 25–9, moves outwards from the centre which represents the divine presence. First (25:10–40) the sacred furniture is prescribed, beginning with the ark and its cover which stand in the innermost sanctum; then (ch. 26) the tabernacle-tent structure which screens these sacred objects from public view, then (ch. 27) the altar outside and the hangings which surround the court where it stands. A consecrated priesthood is required to serve in this holy place, so the instructions proceed by prescribing their vestments (ch. 28) and the rite of their ordination (ch. 29) which qualifies them to serve. Chs. 28–9 on the priesthood are framed by two passages which prescribe the permanent daily service which is to be carried on, and so explain why a priesthood is necessary: 27:20–1 on the tending of the lamp in the tabernacle; and 29:38–42 on the daily burnt offerings.

The instructions are rounded off (29:43–6) with a statement by YHWH of how he will use the sanctuary, as the place of meeting and of presence. However, some additional prescriptions follow in ch. 30; the first (vv. 1–10) is part of the main speech, the others, like those in ch. 31, are added as separate short speeches. As a conclusion has already been given to the instructions, and the incense altar and basin have not been mentioned in their logical places, these prescriptions are generally taken as later additions.

The whole passage is framed by the call for contributions in 25:2–9 and the provisions for design and manufacture in 31:1–11. Why this is followed by the repetition of the sabbath commandment in 31:12–17 is discussed below.

The general outline of the sanctuary is similar to that of Solomon's temple described in 1 Kings 6, and to that of many of the shrines in Palestine and its surrounding area found in archaeological excavations. It clearly reflects very ancient ideas of the deity's dwelling in the temple and having his needs attended to there by his priestly servants. A covered rectangular structure stands in an open court, and is divided by a crosswise partition into two rooms (for a slightly different picture see Friedman 1992). The inner, smaller room contains the principal symbol of the presence of the deity. The two cherubim originally represented a throne for the invisible YHWH (see 1 Sam 4:4). In the outer room stands furniture required for the

personal service of the deity: the lampstand for light, the table for the 'bread of the Presence', and the incense altar for pleasant scent. Outside in the court stands the 'altar of burnt offering', where offerings are burnt, wholly or partially, as a 'pleasing odour' to YHWH (29:18, etc.).

Taken literally, this mode of service would imply a very crude conception of God. But the ritual goes back to time immemorial, and the text does not imply such a literal conception. It avoids implying that YHWH was enthroned over the ark (Mettinger 1982: 88), and gives no indication beyond the use of traditional clichés that YHWH was literally benefited by his service. In fact no one had ever believed that gods literally lived in their temples, in the sense that they were bounded by them. God's true temple is in heaven, where he sits enthroned in glory (see Isa 6): the temple on earth is a copy of this (Ex 25:9; Cassuto 1967: 322), and there he makes himself present to his people in a particular way.

The presence of God in the centre is believed to generate an intense holiness which is like a physical influence, radiating outwards in declining degree. This is marked by the materials used and by the persons allowed to enter. The materials decrease in value as one moves outwards (Haran 1985: 158–65). No one may enter the inner sanctum except the high priest once a year (Lev 16:2, 29); no one but priests may enter the outer hall or ascend the altar. The high priest (Aaron) and the priests (the sons of Aaron) are specially consecrated (29) and must preserve a special degree of ritual purity (Lev 21) so that they can venture into these holy areas. Any Israelite who is ritually clean for the time being (see Lev 11–16) may enter the court, but the hangings mark out the area beyond which the unclean may not proceed. (For further details see Haran 1985: 158–88.)

Clearly this whole arrangement is symbolic. At the centre of the people's life stands the Presence of God, and order, life, and blessing flow out from there. But there are also powers of disorder and death that have to be kept at bay. Contact between these would be deadly: hence the carefully ordered gradation of boundaries, material, and personnel. (See also Jenson 1992: 56–88.) At the same time the system would have served to guarantee the power of the priests who controlled it.

The system is more obviously appropriate for a settled people, despite the great care with which it is adapted to life on the move. No doubt it represents what the priests believed about the temple. The question arises whether the picture of the mobile tabernacle is imaginary or derived from a real sanctuary. Portable shrines existed, but the one described is far too elaborate to have been produced in the wilderness. Critical scholars have tended to argue that it is an imaginary projection of the Jerusalem temple into the period of the wilderness. Some (e.g. Friedman 1992), however, have suggested that there was a real portable shrine, not as elaborate as is here described, referred to in Ex 33:7–11 and in Num 11 and 12, which was preserved at Shiloh and perhaps later at Jerusalem, and that this is what the writer is describing.

But if P is dependent on the earlier sources, it is likely that it has taken the idea of a tent-shrine and the name 'tent of meeting' from 33:7, and with it the function of the shrine as a place of meeting between God and his prophet, and has combined that with the temple image (similarly Childs 1974). But there are details that do not accord with the Jerusalem temple either before or after the Exile.

(25:1–9) The Israelites are to make a 'holy place' (v. 8; NRSV 'sanctuary'), a place marked out for and by YHWH's presence. The verse is echoed by 29:43 at the end of the main body of instructions. In v. 9, YHWH does not merely tell Moses what to make: he shows him a 'pattern' (very necessary in view of the obscurity and ambiguity of some of the prescriptions!). Perhaps the writer believed that the tabernacle was a copy of a heavenly temple (as Heb 8:5 deduces). Other ancient Near-Eastern priestly writers claimed this for their temples.

(25:10–22) The word translated 'covenant' (vv. 16, 25) in the NRSV and 'testimony' in many other versions is not the same as the word for 'covenant' earlier; it is P's term for the document on the stone tablets which YHWH gives to Moses in 31.18. In the Pentateuch as it now stands this must be the ten commandments (see Deut 10:2–5), but possibly not in P originally (Propp 2006: 383–5). vv. 17–22. The 'mercy-seat' or 'cover' (NRSV margin; Heb. *kapporet*) is the central site where atonement or purification is made for Israel on the Day of Atonement (Lev 16:13–15) v. 18, 'cherubim' were probably imaginary winged four-footed creatures such as are found constantly in ancient Near-Eastern art. YHWH is depicted as 'riding' or 'seated' on cherubim in e.g. Ps 18:10; 80:1.

(25:23–40) The table is used both for the bread of the Presence (v. 24; see Lev 24:5–9) and for

vessels for drink-offerings; however, these were not offered inside the tabernacle. The prescriptions for the lampstand are hard to follow, but the well-known relief of the lampstand from Herod's temple on the Arch of Titus in Rome probably gives a fair idea of what the writer had in mind; see also Meyers (*ABD*iv.142; cf. Meyers 1976). Solomon's temple had ten lampstands (1 Kings 7:49), but it is not said that these were branched. The branched lampstand appears to be a later innovation, thrown back into the time of the wilderness.

(26:1–37) The description is ambiguous, and various reconstructions have been made. The main structure is the 'frames', or boards, described in vv. 15–25. These are set up on end, so that the height of the tabernacle is 10 cubits (a cubit was about 50 cm. or 1ft. 8 in.); but disagreement arises over whether they are set side by side, giving the tabernacle a length of 30 cubits, or overlapping (Friedman 1992), giving a length of (perhaps) 20 cubits. The breadth is very uncertain, because of the difficulty of vv. 23–4. The tabernacle curtains are meant to be stretched over the top of the structure, forming its roof and hanging down the sides; they are joined together lengthwise to make an area 28 × 40 cubits, with the long side running the length of the tabernacle and hanging down the back; similarly with the tend curtains which are stretched over the top of the tabernacle curtains and cover the parts these cannot reach.

The key ritual element here is the 'curtain' (not the same word as in v. 1, etc.) in vv. 31–5, which marks off the 'most holy place' (Heb. 'holy of holies'). Within the curtain is the ark, outside it the other furniture. Most scholars envisage the curtain as dividing the tabernacle crosswise in the same way as the solid wall dividing the main hall from the inner sanctum of permanent temples, with the pillars side by side; Friedman however sees it as a canopy hanging down from four pillars set in a square.

(27:1–8) This description is once again very ambiguous. The altar is a hollow box of wooden boards overlaid with bronze: so much is clear. But as it is doubtful whether such a structure could stand a fire, it is argued by Cassuto (1967:362) that it has no top and in use would be filled with stones or earth (cf. 20:24–6), so that the fire would be laid on the stones. Even more unclear is the placing and function of the 'grating'. The horns (v. 2) at least are a regular feature of altars in that cultural area. Their origin is uncertain, but their use in Israelite ritual appears in 29:12.

(27:9–19) The dimensions and function of the enclosure which surrounds the altar and tabernacle are clear, even though details of the spacing of the pillars on which the hangings are hung are not, and the placing of the altar and tabernacle within the court is not specified.

(27:20–1) It is not immediately clear why this passage is placed here (it is repeated almost word for word in Lev 24:2–4): for my suggestion see above. EX 25:1–31:17. Why it speaks of only one light is also unclear; it is likely that it is a fragment of a different tradition from that which calls for seven, which has become dominant in the text.

(28:1–43) This chapter now introduces the priesthood to serve in the holy place, and details the vestments they are to wear for that purpose. Aaron is to be the high priest, his sons the priests. Obviously what is said of Aaron will apply to each high priest after him. Most of the chapter (vv. 2–39) is concerned with Aaron's vestments, which are designed for officiating within the tabernacle (Haran 1985: 210–13). v. 40 lists the garments of Aaron's sons, for service at the altar, and v. 41 points forward to their vesting and ordination prescribed in detail in the next chapter. The undergarments or drawers prescribed in vv. 42–3 may be a later development, but as their function is a negative one (cf. 20:26) they might in any case not be mentioned along with the garments which are designed for 'glorious adornment' (vv. 2, 40). These are made of the same costly materials (v. 5) as the tabernacle itself. The ephod (vv. 6–14) appears to be a sort of apron with shoulder-straps; it is the most visible and impressive of the vestments. The 'breastpiece of judgement' (vv. 15–30) is so called because it holds the Urim and Thummim (v. 30), which are objects used for divination (Num 27:21). The robe (vv. 31–5) is worn under the ephod, and is of simpler workmanship, except for the hem. The bells protect Aaron (v. 35) perhaps by preventing him making an unannounced approach before the throne (Cassuto 1967: 383). Like the other elements of ritual in the tabernacle, they go back to a more primitive conception of deity. The tunic goes under the robe, but it may have sleeves, unlike the other vestments.

The balance and structure of the account emphasize those elements in Aaron's attire which express his representative function: the stones on which he bears the names of the sons of Israel 'before the LORD'—that is, in the tabernacle; Urim and Thummim in which he would 'bear the judgement of the Israelites'; the rosette with its inscription, which reminds YHWH that the whole people (not just Aaron) is 'holy to YHWH', so that any unintentional failures may be overlooked. During the monarchy, it was the king who was the representative of the people before God; it is likely that it was in the post-exilic period that the high priests took over this function, and perhaps much of the array ascribed here to Aaron was originally the king's.

(29:1–37) This chapter prescribes a ritual which is carried out in Lev 8, where it is again described in detail; Lev 9 goes on to describe the ritual of the eighth day, when Aaron enters fully on his priesthood. Fuller comment will therefore be found at LEV 8–9; for the details of the different sacrifices LEV 1–4; and for the 'elevation offering' (vv. 24, 26) Lev 7:28–38. Briefly, the elements of the ordination ritual are as follows: investiture in the sacred vestments (vv. 5–6, 8–9); anointing, a symbol of appointment (v. 7; only for Aaron, though 28:41 mentions anointing for them all); and ordination proper (vv. 10–35), which is a seven-day rite of passage (v. 35) consisting of particular sacrifices. The defining moment is the ritual in vv. 19–21, in which some of the blood of the 'ram of ordination' is smeared on representative extremities of the ordinands and the rest dashed on the sides of the altar. Cf. 24:6–8: the smearing or sprinkling of a token portion of the blood of a sacrifice which is at the same time made holy by its offering to God makes the person holy to God. The altar (vv. 36–7) also requires purification from any uncleanness it may have contracted, and consecration. 'Sin offering' and 'atonement' (NRSV) are clearly unsatisfactory translations in reference to an inanimate object: 'purification offering' and 'purification' (Milgrom 1991: 253–4) are better. Its consecration is not simply dedication: it becomes actively holy so as to engulf in its holiness anything that touches it: this is a warning, for it is certain death for anyone who is not already consecrated.

(29:38–42) Mention of the altar leads into instruction for its one regular daily use; but as I have suggested it also serves, with 27:20–1, to frame the instructions for the priesthood with a representative reminder of the daily need for a priesthood: Aaron to enter the tabernacle to dress the lamps, and his sons to serve at the altar. The prime reason for the existence of a public sanctuary is to offer public offerings paid for out of public resources (see 30:11–16) as a formal expression of the community's homage to its God. The Jerusalem temple under the monarchy would have had such a regular offering paid for by the king: P needs to emphasize the importance of continuing it by placing its beginning in the wilderness.

(29:43–6) The speech comes to a fitting climax in which YHWH defines the purpose of all the elaborate provisions which he has been reciting, and makes it clear that they are the fulfilment of the promise he had made while the people were slaves in Egypt, that 'I will take you as my people, and I will be your God' (6:7). What he had not said there was that he would *meet* with them and *dwell* among them. It is the tent of meeting that makes this possible. And even though he has been giving directions for *Moses* to consecrate the tent, the altar, and the priests, he makes it clear that it is he himself, YHWH, who will really consecrate them, and he will do this by his presence, which is summed up in the symbol of his 'glory', which for P is a literal dazzling radiance. 'And they shall know...' (v. 46): of all the acts by which Israel comes to know their God, this, for P, is the supreme one, that he dwells among them and speaks with them.

(30:1–10) This may reflect an addition to the furniture of the Second Temple. Incense was at all times in the ancient Near East a common element of ritual; its sweet smell was held to attract the favour of the deity and appease the deity's wrath. But we more commonly hear of its being offered in censers carried in the hand. Although it is an addition to the ritual, it is fully integrated into the complex of acts of 'service' which Aaron performs in the tabernacle (vv. 7–8) (Haran 1985: 230–45). For v. 10, see Lev 16.

(30:11–16) During the monarchy the regular offering would have been the king's responsibility; in Neh 10:32–3 we find the community as a whole taking the responsibility on themselves through a poll-tax; the census ransom is P's version of this. It was an ancient belief that carrying out a census was a dangerous act which might arouse the envy of the deity: see 2 Sam 24. The token offering averts this, as well as providing for the offering.

(30:17–21) The concern here is not for ordinary dirt, but for ritual uncleanness (Lev 11–15), which to the priests, who are constantly in the holy place and handling holy things, is a constant threat. Washing the body is the normal way of removing low-grade uncleanness.

(30:22–38) These two sections each provide for the compounding of distinctive substances which are to be used exclusively in the service of the tabernacle. They are 'holy' (vv. 25, 36) both in this sense and as far as the oil is concerned in the sense that it is a sign which conveys holiness to the objects and persons which are anointed with it.

(31:1–11) Bezalel's qualifications come to him by a twofold action of YHWH, who both calls him and fills him with divine spirit. Although these graces are most frequently referred to as bestowing gifts of leadership and of prophecy, they are clearly not confined to those connections. P has laid stress throughout on the importance of the materials and design of the tabernacle and its furniture; they help to give them their holy character. It is therefore natural that the skill which is needed to create them should be seen as a divine gift.

(31:12–17) It is appropriate that the sabbath command should be repeated here, with its grounding in the creation account in Gen 1:1–2:3. The tabernacle represents God's heavenly dwelling-place, where he rested after his exertions in creation, and the sabbath represents his heavenly rest (cf. Levenson 1988: 79–99). The passage bears a number of marks of the style and concerns of the editor of the Holiness Code (Lev 17–26), who may have been the final editor of the Priestly material (Knohl 1994). The sabbath is not only holy itself, but is a way God has given of expressing the holiness of the people (v. 13). For the first time a penalty is given for breaking it (vv. 14–15): as with other offences against Israel's holiness to YHWH, it is death (cf. Lev 20).

(Chs. 32–4) Covenant Breaking and Renewal (For a thorough treatment of 32–4, see Moberly 1983; also Van Seters 1994: 290–360.) The story here takes a turn which is of great importance for the theological message of the book. After the people have solemnly accepted YHWH's covenant on the basis of his commandments, the first thing they do is to break the most fundamental of them; they desert the worship of YHWH for an idol. This is a 'test' (see 17:2) of the covenant, and of YHWH's commitment to his people, of the most radical sort. He would have every justification in destroying them and starting afresh, and says so in 32:10. But this does not happen; why not?

The story makes Moses responsible for reconciling YHWH to the people. Moses struggles with YHWH from 32:11 to 34:9, first to avert the threatened destruction, and then to ensure the full restoration of his presence with them and graciousness to them. And this he achieves. The people do nothing towards this, and make no renewed promises. They express no repentance for their apostasy; Moberly (1983; 60–1) shows that their mourning in 33:4 is not repentance. Moses here comes into his own as a heroic figure (see EX A). For months he has simply obeyed orders; now he not only acts on his own initiative, but, with deference but determination, sets himself against YHWH's expressed intention and fights on behalf of the people whom YHWH himself has made his responsibility, ignoring inducements (32:10), and putting his own life on the line for their sake (32:32). Aaron makes a pitiful contrast: 'Aaron was too weak to restrain the people; Moses was strong enough to restrain even God' (Childs 1974: 570). But if Moses acquires new stature in this episode, so too does YHWH. What Moses appeals to is YHWH's own promise and character. He cannot persuade him to do something that he does not want to do. And when YHWH at the climax of the story proclaims his own characteristics, what comes first is his mercy, steadfast love, and forgiveness (34:6–7). He proves himself a God able in the end to bear with a people who not only have sinned but are likely to go on sinning, as Moses confesses (34:9). The legalistic interpretation of the covenant, that breaking the commandment means death, suggested in 20:5, 23:21, and 32:10, is set aside without being formally repudiated (34:7b). It is on this basis that YHWH's presence is able to go with the people, as he has already promised in 33:17; and so the elaborate provisions that he has made for this are able to go forward.

We may treat this passage as a literary unity, though many would see 32:9–14 and 25–9 as later expansions (see Moberly 1983: 157–86 and Van Seters 1994: 290–5). Interesting questions arise when we compare the story, particularly 32:1–6, with the story of Jeroboam and his calves in 1 Kings 12. In both cases the cultic object is described as a golden calf, and the cry

in 32:4 is identical to Jeroboam's announcement in 1 Kings 12:28. There can be no doubt that one or other of the writers has deliberately described the event in terms drawn from the other account. It is likely that Kings is the source. The bull was a common symbol of deity in Canaanite culture; it fits with this that the kingdom of Israel should have had bulls as its official cult symbols, and the story in 1 Kings 12 is a slanted and polemical account of how they were introduced. Calling the bulls 'calves' is deliberate disparagement, probably begun by Hosea (Hos 8:5, 6; 10:5). I follows his usual practice of tracing back key themes in Israel's later history into the wilderness period. (For another view, see Moberly 1983: 161–71.)

(32:1–6) The calf which Aaron makes is in the first place a subsitute for Moses, who represented God's guidance in a concrete way. Without him, the people feel the need for a visible expression of divine guidance. The course they urge on Aaron is described in terms which suggest that they are behaving exactly like pagans. Gods are something that can be made. Why 'gods', when there is only one image? Because to speak of 'gods' in the plural is typical of pagans (see 1 Sam 4:7–8; 1 Kings 20:23); the sentence is probably taken from 1 Kings 12:28, but not unthinkingly—the fact that there are two calves does not make it more appropriate there (see Moberly 1983: 163). Is the calf intended as an image of YHWH? It is hailed as having 'brought you up out of the land of Egypt', and the feast which Aaron announces is a festival for YHWH. But the author leaves no doubt that they are not really worshipping YHWH. See EX 20:2–6. Therefore the people have indeed broken the first commandment.

(32:7–14) This passage has caused difficulty. Why should Moses react so violently in v. 19 if YHWH had already told him on the mountain? How can the long process of intercession in 32:30–34:9 be understood if Moses has already secured YHWH's forgiveness in v. 14? It is a matter of literary technique. The key issues are set out here, right after the account of Israel's sin, and they govern the whole story. There is, in any case, no real difficulty in understanding Moses' reaction on actually seeing the worship of the golden calf; and it is often overlooked that Moses is not himself told of YHWH's change of heart. v. 14 is a narrative comment which gives the reader the advantage over Moses; as far as he knows, there is everything still to play for; and YHWH, as befits the seriousness of the sin, will not immediately reveal his forgiveness. 'Stiff-necked' (v. 9) is one of the motifs of the story, repeated in 33:3, 5:34:9. In YHWH's demand 'Now let me alone', 'he pays such deference to [Moses'] prayers as to say they are a hindrance to him' (Calvin 1854: iii. 341); and he then indirectly reminds Moses of the right basis for such prayers. 'Of you I will make a great nation' recalls his promise to Abraham, Gen 12:2. Moses in his reply picks this up, as well as reminding YHWH of the danger to his reputation, which had been one of the main themes of the struggle with Pharaoh.

(32:15–24) The tablets are the focus in vv. 15–19. Moses' breaking of them appears to signify that the covenant is at an end, and this is confirmed in ch. 34, where a new covenant is made on conditions inscribed on new tablets. Could a calf made of gold be burnt and ground to powder? It is possible that the description has simply been taken over from Deut 9:21 (Van Seters 1994: 303–7); Deuteronomy does not say what the calf was made of. vv. 21–4 recall Gen 3. Aaron contrives to throw all the blame on the people and minimizes his own part, in contrast with Moses, who identifies himself with the people in his struggles with God.

(32:25–9) is another passage that has caused difficulty, partly because Moses inflicts a fearful punishment on the people, whereas elsewhere he pleads for forgiveness, partly because the punishment seems quite random. It should be noted that what Moses pleads against is the total destruction of the people, and then YHWH's withdrawal of his presence from Israel's midst; this does not rule out an exemplary punishment. v. 35 expresses the same idea, though it has been interpreted as the much later fulfilment of the threat in v. 34. The passage serves to account for the special position of the Levites in Israelite society.

(32:30–33:6) In this episode of intercession, Moses clearly does not achieve his object, though it is not easy to follow the conversations between Moses and YHWH because of their polite and allusive language. 32:33 rejects Moses' offer, and v. 34 warns that a time of punishment is yet to come. YHWH is not yet reconciled. For v. 35, see above on vv. 25–9. In 33:1–3 YHWH sends the people off to Canaan, but without his presence

among them. The 'angel', as in 23:20, may represent YHWH and even be a form of his presence. But what he refuses to give them is his presence *among* them. Moberly (1983: 62–3) suggests that this presence would be experienced through the medium of a sanctuary; and the following section supports this.

(33:7–11) This section is a digression from the main thread of the narrative, but not an irrelevant digression. It describes not what Moses did next, but what he regularly did; the period over which he did it is not specified, but see Num 11 and Deut 31:14–15. It is mentioned to make clear how Moses was still able to communicate with YHWH although he had refused his presence in their midst. He does it through the medium of a tent shrine; but unlike the one provided for in chs. 25–6 it is pitched way outside the camp, a clear enough sign of the danger of YHWH's coming any closer. v. 11 underlines the special privilege of Moses in speaking with YHWH 'face to face', and this leads in appropriately to the next passage of intercession.

Although P takes over the name 'tent of meeting', there are many differences between this tent and his, besides its location. It is a place not of priestly service and sacrifice but of prophetic revelation, and YHWH appears not in its innermost recesses but at its entrance. It has been conjectured that this tent of meeting was an ancient prophetic institution in Israel. But Van Seters (1994: 341–4) suggests that it is J's imaginative reconstruction.

(33:12–23) The story of Moses' intercession with YHWH is taken up again at the point where it was left in 33:4. Moses' object is to gain YHWH's personal presence among the people. In v. 14 the translation 'I will go with you' (NRSV and others) makes nonsense of the conversation. Only in v. 17 does YHWH finally grant Moses what he has been asking for, his presence *with* the people. At v. 14 all he says is 'My presence will go', without the vital word 'with'. Moses' success is remarkable: a holy God has agreed to be present with a people who are still sinful and show no serious sign of repentance. Moses' further request in v. 18 seems at first sight to be purely selfish. But it becomes clear when YHWH grants it (in his own way) in 34:5–7 that the vision of his 'goodness' which he has promised Moses has everything to do with the people's need of mercy and forgiveness. Moses has achieved much, but he has still not gained the main point, absolute forgiveness.

The answer he got to the direct request in 32:32 was not encouraging, so he tries an indirect one, and this time receives definite, though still indirect, encouragement (v. 20). YHWH is merciful, though he reserves to himself absolute discretion in deciding whom to be merciful to.

(34:1–9) The episode moves to its climax. YHWH's order to Moses in v. 1 leaves no doubt now that he intends to restore the covenant shattered with the tablets in 32:19. Moses alone goes up the mountain. The people's rebellion leaves them no role but humbly to accept their Lord's good pleasure. YHWH's proclamation of his own name and qualities in vv. 6–7 is another version of the descriptions in 20:5–6 and Deut 7:9–10, and is itself repeatedly quoted elsewhere (e.g. Ps 103:8). It lays stress on his forgiveness, and avoids saying that he is gracious 'to those that love me and keep my commandments'. The centre is his 'steadfast love' (Heb. ḥesed; other translations 'faithfulness', 'mercy'). This is the gracious favour which a patron shows to those who have come under his protection (or the loyalty which they show to him); it is gracious and yet at the same time required of him by the relationship, an idea difficult for us to grasp in a society which has separated institutional obligation and personal motivation (cf. Kippenberg 1982: 32). There remains a paradox in the proclamation: YHWH forgives iniquity, and yet he also punishes it, even to the fourth generation. As we have already seen, punishment is not excluded even where he has resolved to forgive. The essential thing is that the relationship is restored and maintained in perpetuity, however much Israel's sinfulness may test it.

(34:10–28) And this is what YHWH promises in his proclamation 'I hereby make a covenant'. A covenant, because what he now does is new. The precise reference of the rest of v. 10 is unclear; even whether 'you' is Moses or Israel; but it is clear that the covenant is primarily YHWH's promise to Moses to forgive Israel. There are conditions; they are not new, but almost entirely a selection of the commandments from the Book of the Covenant (see EX 20:22–23:33) with particular emphasis on the exclusive worship of YHWH. vv. 11–16 are a rewriting of 23:23–4, 32–3; v. 17 is a version of 20:23; and vv. 18–26 are 23:15–19 with some expansion, mostly from 13:12–13 (cf. 22:29–30). The implication is that, as YHWH has already said in 34:1, the covenant terms are still in force,

but it is not necessary for the author to repeat the entire code, as only certain things need to be emphasized. Moses is commanded to write the words, as he had done in 24:4. The text in 28 seems to say that Moses wrote on the tablets. But YHWH has already said (34:1) that he himself would write the words on them. So probably the subject of the last sentence in v. 28 is YHWH, and Moses is thought of as writing a separate copy. But what did YHWH write? Up to this point the implication has been that it would be the words in vv. 11–26, yet the text adds that it was 'the ten commandments'. This can only mean 20:2–17. The likely explanation is that someone has added the words 'the ten commandments', remembering that in Deut 5 it is these which are written on the tablets and trying to make Exodus and Deuteronomy agree.

(34:29–35) The shining of Moses' face as a sign of intense spiritual experience is not unparalleled: one might think of Jesus' transfiguration (Mk 9:2–8) or the experience reported of St Seraphim of Sarov. It is not clear why Moses puts a veil over his face when he has finished reporting YHWH's commands, unless perhaps simply to avoid standing out unnecessarily when not performing his religious and leadership functions.

(Chs. 35–40) The Building of the Sanctuary With the covenant relationship restored, the instructions given by YHWH to create a sanctuary for him can now be carried out. This account obviously depends very closely on chs. 25–31; in the parts which describe the actual construction the instructions are reproduced word for word with the appropriate changes. As the incense altar and laver are described in their proper places, the account was obviously written from the start in dependence on the whole passage chs. 25–31 including its afterthoughts. Every paragraph concludes 'as YHWH had commanded Moses' to underline the authority behind the construction. As the instructions had concluded with the repetition of the sabbath command, Moses' commands to the Israelites begin with it. A detailed account of the offering follows in 35:4–36:7, together with the calling of Bezalel and Oholiab. The construction of the various items occupies 36:8–39:43. The account begins with the tabernacle itself before moving on to the furniture which is placed in it. It is broken only by the account of the contributed metals in 38:24–31. This does not reproduce any single passage in 25–31, but is deduced from its data; as far as the silver is concerned the figure in 38:25 is derived from the census figure in Num 1:46 on the assumption that the ransom commanded in 30:11–16 was intended for the construction.

(38:8) No one can really explain this odd note. 1 Sam 2:22 is no help.

When all is complete, YHWH gives the order to set the tabernacle up and consecrate it and ordain its priesthood (40:1–15). For the fulfilment of much of this we must wait till Lev 8; but here we are told of the setting up of the tabernacle (40:16–33), and this is followed immediately by the climax of the whole account, the entry of the glory of YHWH into his dwelling-place. The glory is described as cloud and fire, as it appeared on Sinai in 24:16–17. The object of all the work has been achieved: the presence of YHWH, as it had been on Sinai, is with his people for ever, and guides them on their journeys.

REFERENCES

Albertz, R. (1994), *A History of Israelite Religion in the Old Testament Period* (2 vols.: London: SCM).

Alter, R. (1981), *The Art of Biblical Narrative* (London: Allen & Unwin).

Auffret, P. (1983), 'The Literary Structure of Ex. 6.2–8', *JSOT* 27: 46–54.

Bimson, J. J. (1978), *Redating the Exodus and Conquest*, JSOTSup 5 (Sheffield: JSOT).

Blenkinsopp, J. (1992), *The Pentateuch: An Introduction to the First Five Books of the Bible* (London: SCM).

Brenner, M. L. (1991), *The Song of the Sea: Ex. 15, 1–21*, BZAW 195 (Berlin: de Gruyter).

Brichto, H. C. (1963), *The Problem of 'Curse' in the Hebrew Bible*, JBL Monograph Ser. 13 (Philadelphia: Society for Biblical Literature and Exegesis).

Brueggemann, W. (1995), 'Pharaoh as Vassal: A Study of a Political Metaphor', *CBQ* 57: 27–51.

Calvin, J. (1854), *Commentary on the Four Last Books of Moses, arranged in the Form of a Harmony*, tr. C. W. Bingham (4 vols.; Edinburgh: Calvin Translation Society).

—— (1953), *Institutes of the Christian Religion*, tr. H. Beveridge (2 vols.; London: James Clarke).

Cassuto, U. (1967), *A Commentary on Exodus* (Jerusalem: Magnes).

Childs, B. S. (1974), *Exodus: A Commentary* (London: SCM).

Chirichigno, G. C. (1993), *Debt-Slavery in Israel and the Ancient Near East*, JSOTSup 141 (Sheffield: JSOT).

Clines, D. (1995a), 'The Ten Commandments, Reading from Left to Right', in *Interested Parties: The Ideology of Writers and Readers of the Hebrew Bible* (Sheffield: Sheffield Academic Press), 26–45.

—— (1995b), 'God in the Pentateuch; Reading against the Grain', ibid. 187–211.

Croatto, J. S. (1981), *Exodus: A Hermeneutics of Freedom* (Maryknoll, NY: Orbis Books).

Cross, F. M. (1973), 'The Song of the Sea and Canaanite Myth', in *Canaanite Myth and Hebrew Epic* (Cambridge, Mass.: Harvard University Press), 112–44.

Daube, D. (1947), *Studies in Biblical Law* (Cambridge: Cambridge University Press).

Davies, G. I. (1979), *The Way of the Wilderness: A Geographical Study of the Wilderness Itineraries in the Old Testament*, SOTSMS 5 (Cambridge: Cambridge University Press).

Dever, W. G. (1992), 'Israel, History of (Archaeology and the "Conquest")', *ABD* iii. 545–58.

DOTP = *Dictionary of the Old Testament: Pentateuch*, eds. T. D. Alexander & D. W. Baker (Downers Grove, IL: InterVarsity Press, 2003).

Durham, J. J. (1987), *Exodus*, WBC (Waco, Tex.: Word Books).

Exum, J. C. (1993), '"You Shall Let Every Daughter Live": A Study of Exodus 1.8–2.10', *Semeia*, 28: 53–82, repr. in Athalya Brenner (ed.), *A Feminist Companion to Exodus to Deuteronomy* (Sheffield: Sheffield Academic Press, 1994), 37–61.

—— (1994), 'Second Thoughts about Secondary Characters: Women in Exodus 1.8–2.10', ibid. 75–87.

Fewell, D. N. and Gunn, D. M. (1993), *Gender, Power and Promise: The Subject of the Bible's First Story* (Nashville: Abingdon).

Finkelstein, I. (1988), *The Archaeology of the Israelite Settlement* (Jerusalem: Israel Exploration Society).

Friedman, R. E. (1992), 'Tabernacle' in *ABD* vi. 292–300.

Gerstenberger, E. (1965), *Wesen und Herkunft des 'apodiktischen Rechts'*, WMANT 20 (Neukirchen Vluyn: Neukirchener Verlag).

Gottwald, N. K. (1980), *The Tribes of Yahweh: A Sociology of Liberated Israel, 1250–1050 B.C.E.* (London, SCM).

Gowan, D. E. (1994), *Theology in Exodus: Biblical Theology in the Form of a Commentary* (Louisville, Ky.: Westminster/John Knox).

Gunn, D. M. (1982), 'The Hardening of Pharaoh's Heart', in David J. A. Clines, David M. Gunn, and Alan J. Hauser (eds.), *Art and Meaning: Rhetoric in Biblical Literature*, JSOTSup 19 (Sheffield: JSOT), 72–96.

Gutiérrez, G. (1988), *A Theology of Liberation*, rev. edn. (London: SCM).

Habel, N. (1965), 'The Form and Significance of the Call Narratives', *ZAW* 77: 297–323.

Haran, M. (1985), *Temples and Temple Service in Ancient Israel*, 2nd edn. (Winona Lake, Ind.: Eisenbrauns).

Herrmann, J. (1927), 'Das zehnte Gebot', in A. Jirku (ed.), *Sellin-Festschrift* (Leipzig: A. Deichert), 69–82.

Herrmann, S. (1973), *Israel in Egypt*, CSBT 2nd ser. 27 (London: SCM).

Hoffmeier, J. K. (1997), *Israel in Egypt: the evidence for the authenticity of the Exodus tradition* (New York: Oxford University).

Hort, G. (1957–8), 'The Plagues of Egypt', ZAW 69: 84–103; 70: 48–59.

Houston, W. J. (1993), *Purity and Monotheism: Clean and Unclean Animals in Biblical Law*, JSOTSup 140 (Sheffield: JSOT).

—— (1997), 'Misunderstanding or Midrash?', *ZAW* 109: 342–55.

—— (2007), 'The Character of YHWH and the Ethics of the Hebrew Bible: Is *Imitatio Dei* a Safe Principle?', *JTS* 58, 1–25.

—— (2008), *Contending for Justice: Ideologies and Theologies of Social Justice in the Old Testament* (2nd ed., London: T & T Clark).

Houtman, C. (1993), *Exodus*, Historical Commentary on the Old Testament, vol. i (Kampen: Kok).

—— (1996), *Exodus*, vol. ii (Kampen: Kok).

—— (2000), *Exodus*, vol. iii (Leuven: Peeters).

Hughes, J. (1990), *Secrets of the Times: Myth and History in Biblical Chronology*, JSOTSup 66 (Sheffield: JSOT).

Jackson, B. S. (1989), 'Ideas of Law and Legal Administration', in R. E. Clements (ed.), *The World of Ancient Israel* (Cambridge: Cambridge University Press), 185–202.

—— (2006), *Wisdom-Laws: A Study of the Mishpatim of Exodus 21:1–22:16* (Oxford: Oxford University).

Janzen, J. G. (1992), 'Song of Moses, Song of Miriam: Who is Seconding Whom?', *CBQ* 54: 211–20, repr. in Athalya Brenner (ed.), *A Feminist Companion to Exodus to Deuteronomy* (Sheffield: Sheffield Academic Press, 1994), 187–99.

Jenson, P. P. (1992), *Graded Holiness*, JSOTS 106 (Sheffield: Sheffield Academic Press).

Johnstone, W. (1990), *Exodus*, Old Testament Guides (Sheffield: JSOT).

Kippenberg, H. G. (1982), *Religion und Klassenbildung im antiken Judäa: Eine religionssoziologische Studie zum Verhältnis von Tradition und gesellschaftlicher Entwicklung* (SUNT 14), 2nd edn. (Göttingen: Vandenhoeck & Ruprecht).

Kirkpatrick, P. (1988), *The Old Testament and Folklore Study*, JSOTSup 62 (Sheffield: Sheffield Academic Press).

Knohl, I. (1994), *The Sanctuary of Silence: The Priestly Torah and the Holiness School* (Minneapolis: Fortress).

Langston, S. M. (2006), *Exodus Through the Centuries*, Blackwell Bible Commentaries (Oxford: Blackwell).

Levenson, J. D. (1988), *Creation and the Persistence of Evil* (San Francisco: Harper & Row).

Luther, M. (1896), 'The Larger Catechism', in Wace and Buchheim (eds.), *Luther's Primary Works*, ii.

Mendenhall, G. E. (1992a), 'Covenant' in ABD, i. 1179–1202.

—— (1992b), 'Midian' in ABD, iv. 815–18.

Mettinger, T. N. D. (1982), *The Dethronement of Sabaoth: Studies in the Shem and Kabod Theologies*, ConBOT 18 (Lund: Gleerup).

—— (1995), *No Graven' Image? Israelite Aniconism in its Ancient Near Eastern Context*, ConBoT (Stockholm: Almqvist & Wiksell Int.).

Meyers, C. (1976), *The Tabernacle Menorah* (Missoula, Mont.: Scholars Press).

Milgrom, J. (1991), *Leviticus 1–16*, AB 3 (New York: Doubleday).

Miranda, J. P. (1973), *Marx and the Bible* (London, SCM).

Moberly, R. W. L. (1983), *At the Mountain of God: Story and Theology in Exodus 32–34*, JSOTSup 22 (Sheffield: JSOT).

—— (1992), *The Old Testament of the Old Testament: Patriarchal Narratives and Mosaic Yahwism* (Minneapolis: Fortress).

Moran, W. L. (1967), 'The Conclusion of the Decalogue (Ex. 20, 17 = Dt. 5. 21)', *CBQ* 29, 543–4.

Nicholson, E. W. (1986), *God and his People: Covenant and Theology in the Old Testament* (Oxford: Clarendon).

Noth, M. (1962), *Exodus: A Commentary* (London: SCM).

Patrick, D. (1986), *Old Testament Law* (London: SCM).

—— (1994), 'Is the Truth of the First Commandment Known by Reason?', *CBQ* 56: 423–41.

Phillips, A. C. J. (1970), *Ancient Israel's Criminal Law: A New Approach to the Decalogue* (Oxford: Blackwell).

Propp, W. H. C. (1998), *Exodus 1–18*, AB 2 (New York: Doubleday).

—— (2006), *Exodus 19–40*, AB 2A (New York: Doubleday).

Ramsey, G. W. (1981), *The Quest for the Historical Israel* (London: SCM).

Redford, D. B. (1963), 'Exodus I, II', *VT* 13: 401–18.

Robertson, D. (1977), *The Old Testament and the Literary Critic* (Philadelphia: Fortress).

Robertson, E. (1948), 'The Altar of Earth (Exodus xx, 24–26)', *JJS* 1:12–21.

Robinson, G. (1988), *The Origin and Development of the Old Testament Sabbath*, BBET 21 (Bern: Peter Lang).

Römer, T. (1994), 'De l'archaïque au subversif: le cas d'Exode 4/24–26', *ETR* 69: 1–12.

Rost, L. (1943), 'Weidewechsel und altisraelischer Festkalendar', *ZDPV* 66: 205–16.

Schmidt, B. B. (1995), 'The Aniconic Tradition: On Reading Images and Viewing Texts', in Diana

V. Edelman (ed.), *The Triumph of Elohim* (Kampen: Kok Pharos), 75–105.

Schmidt, W. H. (1988), *Exodus 1. Teilband: Exodus 1–6*, BKAT (Neukirchen-Vluyn: Neukirchener Verlag).

Smith, G. A. (1918), *The Book of Deuteronomy*, Cambridge Bible for Schools and Colleges (Cambridge: Cambridge University Press).

Sprinkle, J. M. (1994), *'The Book of the Covenant', a Literary Approach*, JSOTSup 174 (Sheffield: JSOT).

Trible, P. (1994), 'Bringing Miriam out of the Shadows', in Athalya Brenner (ed.), *A Feminist Companion to Exodus to Deuteronomy* (Sheffield: Sheffield Academic Press), 166–86: repr. from *Bible Review* 5/1 (1989), 170–90.

Van Seters, J. (1994), *The Life of Moses: The Yahwist as Historian in Exodus–Numbers* (Kampen: Kok Pharos).

—— (2003), *A Law Book for the Diaspora: Revision in the Study of the Covenant Code* (New York: Oxford University).

Vaux, R. de (1978), *The Early History of Israel* (2 vols.; London: Darton, Longman & Todd).

—— (1961), *Ancient Israel, its Life and Institutions* (London: Darton, Longman & Todd).

Weinfeld, M. (1991), *Deuteronomy 1–11* AB 5 (New York: Doubleday).

Wilson, R. R. (1977), *Genealogy and History in the Biblical World*, YNER 7 (New Haven: Yale University Press).

Zimmerli, W. (1968), 'Das zweite Gebot', in *Gottes Offenbarung* (Munich: Kaiser), 234–48.

—— (1982), 'I am Yahweh', in *I am Yahweh* (Atlanta: John Knox), 1–28.

6. Leviticus

LESTER L. GRABBE

INTRODUCTION

A. Structure and Contents. 1. The structure and content of Leviticus as a whole can be briefly outlined as follows:

Sacrificial system (chs. 1–7)
 Introduction (1:1–2)
 Whole burnt offering (1:3–17)
 Cereal offering (ch. 2)
 Well-being offering (ch. 3)
 Sin offering (chs. 4–5)
  Normal sin offering (ch. 4)
  Graduated sin offering (5:1–13)
  Guilt offering (5:14–6:7 (HB 5:14–26))
  Laws (*tôrôt*) of the offerings (chs. 6–7)
   Law of burnt offering (6:8–13 (HB 6:1–6))
   Law of cereal offering (6:14–18 (HB 6:7–11))
   Offering at Aaron's anointment (6:19–23 (HB 6:12–16))
   Law of sin offering (6:24–30 (HB 6:17–23))
   Law of guilt offering (7:1–10)
   Law of well-being offering (7:11–18)
   Miscellaneous instructions (7:19–38)
Initiation of Aaron and sons to the priesthood (chs. 8–10)
 Consecration of priests (chs. 8–9)
 Death of Nadab and Abihu (10:1–11)
 Question of consuming the offerings (10:12–20)
Purity and pollution (chs. 11–15)
 Clean and unclean animals (ch. 11)
 Childbirth (ch. 12)
 Skin diseases ('leprosy') (chs. 13–14)
 Genital discharges (ch. 15)

Atonement for sanctuary and people (scapegoat ritual) (ch. 16)
Holiness code (chs. 17–26)
 Question of blood (ch. 17)
 Forbidden sexual relations (ch. 18)
 Miscellaneous laws on being holy (chs. 19–20)
 Laws for priests (ch. 21)
 Laws on holy things and sacrifice (ch. 22)
  Who may eat of holy things (22:1–16)
  No blemished animals (22:17–25)
  Miscellaneous laws (22:26–30)
  Concluding admonition (22:31–33)
 Festivals (ch. 23)
 Lamps and bread of presence (24:1–9)
 Question of blasphemy (24:10–23)
 Sabbatical and jubilee years (ch. 25)
 Blessings and curses (ch. 26)
Appendix: vows and tithe of livestock (ch. 27)

2. At various points in this commentary, the form critical structure of passages will be discussed. For further detailed information on the structure and contents of Leviticus, one should consult the Leviticus volume of the Abingdon series, the Forms of Old Testament Literature, when it appears. In the meantime, the commentary by Hartley (1992) is very valuable for its extensive discussion of the form criticism of each section of the book.

B. History of the Tradition. 1. We can say with some confidence that the book of Leviticus has had a long period of growth, with numerous additions and editings. Scholarship is practically unanimous on this point. We can also state that much of the material within it seems to derive from priestly circles. Thus, Leviticus is a 'Priestly' document as it now stands, whether or not there was a P source as envisaged by the Documentary Hypothesis. More controversial are the precise stages of this growth. In recent years many monographs, as well as commentaries, have attempted to tease out the different layers (in addition to the writers cited below, see Reventlow 1961; Kilian 1963; Rendtorff 1963; Koch 1959).

2. The Documentary Hypothesis has dominated study of the Pentateuch for the past century (see INTROD. PENT B). According to that theory, most of Leviticus belongs to the Priestly source (P), though the P writers may have used a diversity of material in composing it. For example, many would see chs. 17–26 (usually referred to as H, for the Holiness Code) as originally a separate block of material which was taken over by P. Since Wellhausen's time, this dating to the sixth century—whether the exilic or the early post-exilic period—has remained fairly constant among critics. An exception was Vink who put it in the fourth century, though few have followed him. All agree that this is only the date of the final form of the work, though, since the editor/author drew on various priestly traditions, some of them of substantial antiquity.

3. In recent years, however, there have been two challenges to this consensus: (1) some ask whether P may not date from before the Exile (see below), and (2) others have questioned whether the traditional alleged sources exist at all (Whybray 1987). Although biblical fundamentalists have continually rejected the Documentary Hypothesis for dogmatic reasons, it should not be assumed that recent challenges fall into the same category. While some of the arguments may have been around a long time, those who oppose the old consensus do so for critical reasons which have nothing to do with a desire to 'defend' the biblical text.

4. The question of P is discussed at length above (INTROD. PENT B.5) and need not be repeated here. I shall only point out that the composition and dating of the book of Leviticus is very much tied up with the question of when P is to be dated—assuming that it exists. One school of thought, currently a minority but with a growing number of adherents and a strong voice in the debate, now favours a pre-exilic dating (Haran 1978; Milgrom 1991; Hurvitz 1982, 1988;

Zevit 1982). Indeed, Milgrom even suggests that P was originally composed for the pre-monarchic territory centring on the temple at Shiloh. On the other hand, Gerstenberger (1993) continually discusses how the book fits into the situation in the post-exilic community, and Blenkinsopp (1996) has recently challenged the linguistic arguments of Hurvitz and others for a pre-exilic dating. A further factor to consider is the current debate on the history of Israel in which a number of scholars are arguing that the present text of the HB is no earlier than the Persian period and perhaps even later (see e.g. Lemche 1993). This debate has taken on a new impetus with the launch of the European Seminar on Historical Methodology (see Grabbe 1997).

5. The question is rightly being vigorously debated on several fronts, and I believe it is premature to anticipate the outcome. Yet we should not forget that there is some agreement on several issues. One is that the present form of the book was not reached until the Persian period; another is that the text as it now stands incorporates some material of considerable antiquity. Finally, the book probably says a good deal about the temple cult in the Second Temple period, but one should be cautious in assuming it is an actual description of what went on at that time. For this last point, see further below ('Leviticus and the Actual Temple Cult').

6. Throughout the rest of this commentary on Leviticus, I shall often refer to P, by which the material normally identified as part of the P document is being referred to. However, in each case one should always understand the qualifying phrase, 'if it exists' or 'as normally identified'. I have no intention of begging the question of whether P exists or, if so, what it consisted of.

7. The Holiness Code. Lev 17–26 is commonly divided off from the rest as the so-called Holiness Code (H), with ch. 27 as an appendix to the book. Not all would accept this delineation, but most would agree that within 17–26 is another document which has been incorporated into the present book but is not necessarily fully integrated with 1–16. That is, both 1–16 and 17–26 are collections with their own stages of growth, but each has a relative unity which marks it off from the other. There are tensions between the two parts, with some major differences of outlook on certain issues. There is also the difficult problem of trying to give the relative dates of the two collections. In the past it was customary to consider H earlier than most of the material in 1–16. Nevertheless, a number of prominent scholars had not accepted the existence of H as such. For example, Elliger had proposed several independent legal corpora which had been brought together, with several redactional hands. A. Cholewski took a similar view. I. Knohl (1995; cf. 1987), although accepting the existence of H, has come to the conclusion that it was later than Lev 1–16. He argues the question mainly on the basis of Lev 23 which he thinks is constructed on Num 28–9. Knohl concludes that there were two priestly schools, one that produced the earlier P document and the other that not only wrote H (the later document) but also did the final editing of the Pentateuch. Similarly, Milgrom (1991) has taken the position that most of H is later than most of 1–16, and in his opinion H was one of the editors of the book.

8. Methods and Approaches to Interpretation. Having now seen a general consensus that the book grew up over a long period of time, the reader might ask, 'What level of the book do we interpret?' There is more than one legitimate answer to the question. In recent years, many interpreters have argued for the final form of the text as the primary object of study, whatever the stages of growth of the book or its dating. This has led to a number of new disciplines under the general rubric of the 'literary approach' to the biblical text, including 'close reading', structuralism, deconstruction, and rhetorical criticism. So far, few seem to have applied these to Leviticus specifically (but see Damrosch (1987) and Schwarz (1991) for examples). From a different perspective, those interested in the 'canonical' form of the text for theological purposes are also concerned mainly with the final form of the text (see esp. Childs 1979). Douglas (1993: 8–12) has recently argued that the book can be properly understood only if one recognizes a basic ring structure of the text in its present form.

9. This does not mean that the final form of the text has been ignored even by some of the traditional disciplines. For decades, many form critics have practised a structural analysis of the text as we have it before asking questions of growth or even questions of genre and the like. The results of this approach can be seen in the series Forms of Old Testament Literature edited by R. P. Knierim and G. Tucker. Knierim's recent book (1992) on exegesis combines traditional form criticism with broader concerns, including theological and sociological ones. Some exegetes, while not abandoning traditional source criticism, have severely demoted it in their concerns. For example, although Rendtorff (1982–95: 4) does not reject 'reconstruction' of earlier phases of the tradition, he thinks these should be seen primarily as an aid to understanding the present text.

10. This by no means suggests that older methods of source criticism and the like can be forgotten. On the contrary, they are often presupposed in the new methods. This means that traditio-historical analysis is very important for two further legitimate stages to be interpreted. The second level of interpretation is that of the book as a part of the P document (see below). A third object of interpretation would be the various levels in the growth of the book as determined by form and redaction criticism. This is the most hypothetical and is less favoured today for that very reason (cf. Rendtorff 1982–95: 4), yet most commentators give some attention to the internal growth of the book, and many see it as their primary concern.

C. Importance of the Cult to Ancient Israel. 1.
It is easy for modern Christians to dismiss the Levitical and other passages dealing with the sacrificial cult as outdated or irrelevant. For that reason, the cult is often slighted or even ignored when Israel's religion is discussed. But it must not be forgotten that many Jews still observe the regulations concerning ritual purity, in some form or other, even though the sacrificial regulations can no longer be applied in the absence of a functioning temple. Any description of Israelite religion has to take stock of its complexities, but one cannot get away from the fact that the sacrificial cult, especially blood sacrifice, lay at the heart of worship in Israel. On the other hand, the Israelite cult, like all religious ritual—and all religions have their ritual—was extremely meaningful to the participants even if we do not always understand it from our time and culture millennia later. A number of recent studies have focused on the symbolism of the cult and attempted to decipher the priestly world-view that lay behind it. For example, Gorman (1990) argues that a complex creation theology is presupposed and represented by the cult, and Jenson (1992) has made similar points. The priestly view had a cosmological and sociological dimension, as well as a cultic. In order to express this, it made distinctions between holy and profane, clean and unclean, life and death, order and chaos.

2. The idea of sacrifice seems to be ubiquitous among human societies the world over.

Even those which have abandoned it in their contemporary form, especially in the developed countries, have sacrifice as a part of their past. Since the concept goes so far back in human history that its origins are no longer traceable, we are left only with hypothesis and speculation as to how sacrifice came to be a part of the religious culture of most peoples. (For further information, see the account of the debate in Grabbe 1993: 43–7.) But the inescapable conclusion seems to be that central to most sacrifices are the notions of expiation, cleansing, and re-establishment of cosmic— or at least microcosmic—harmony. If evil cannot be removed, sin wiped away, pollution purified, and harmony restored, there would be little point in sacrifice. Therefore, regardless of the precise terms in which sacrifices are conceived (substitution, ritual detergent, etc.), the desired outcome is clear. The scapegoat sort of ceremony is perhaps not strictly a sacrifice, in that the animal is not killed (though according to later Jewish tradition, the scapegoat was pushed over a cliff: m. Yoma 6:6; cf. Grabbe 1987), but the concept seems to be very much the same as that of sacrifice. In this case, the sins are heaped onto the head of the victim which is then separated from the community. In other cases, the victim is in some way identified with the offerer even if precise identification is not required. The laying of the hands on the victim by the offerer in Israelite sacrifice may have a function along these lines. But regardless of the rite, the desire is to cause the sins, pollutions, illness, or troubles to vanish.

3. Perhaps one of the most misunderstood concepts is that of ritual purity. It has little or nothing to do with hygiene or with the clean/dirty distinction in a physical sense. For example, in the Israelite system, excrement was not usually included in the category of unclean; even though ancient Israelites had much the same view towards it that we do today. One of the important discoveries of anthropology in the past half-century is that purity and pollution systems are not arcane, primitive superstition. The precise form of the rituals may well be arbitrary, at least to some extent, but recent study suggests that broader concerns are at the heart of the purity system. The insights offered by social and cultural anthropology have gone a long way towards explaining the deeper meaning and foundation of these laws which may seem primitive to many today. Purity and pollution form an important mirror of the society itself, especially its social relations and attitudes.

They map the ideological cosmos of the people who hold these views. These regulations can be seen as a language, in the broad sense of the term, communicating to those within the society the 'correct' attitudes towards relations between the sexes, marriage, kinship, and intercourse with outsiders. Ritual cleanliness tells the people how to classify the entities— human and animal—which inhabit the world around them and communicates to the society how to fit in new forms which enter its world. The animal world and how it is treated is also a map of human society, and the human community is represented by the body of the individual.

4. One of the major attempts to work out the meaning of the biblical system in detail was by Mary Douglas in her seminal book *Purity and Danger* (1966; for an account of this book and criticisms of it, see Grabbe 1993: 56–9). Despite some criticisms against Douglas, some of her points about the meaning of the system in Israelite society have not been affected and still seem valid, especially the notion that the system of permitted and forbidden animals was a microcosm of the world according to the Israelite view. The many forbidden animals represented the surrounding nations; the few clean animals, the Israelites; and the sacrificial animals, the priests. Just as Israelites were not to eat certain animals, they were not to mix with other nations. The dietary regulations had both a practical and a symbolic function; symbolically they stood for the fact that Israel was to keep itself free from intercourse with non-Israelites; practically, inability to eat certain animals meant that Jews could not socialize with those who ate these animals. The rules of pollution and purity also drew strict boundaries around the altar and sanctuary. No pollution and no polluted persons were allowed to penetrate into the sacred area. This clear and rigid boundary drawing suggests a concern with political boundaries as well as social ones. Just as the Israelites were concerned about mixing with the surrounding peoples, so their political boundaries may have been threatened by others who claimed the territory for themselves. If so, the message of the rules which, on the surface, might seem arcane ritual turn out to be a rich symbolic system with significant meaning for understanding the concerns of ancient Israel.

D. Women and the Cult. 1. The place of women in society and literature has become a much-discussed subject in the past couple of decades (see e.g. Newsom and Ringe 1992; Schüssler Fiorenza 1994a and b). Some have seen the treatment of women as very negative. It is not my purpose to enter into this debate, but Wegner (1992) gives a mainly positive assessment of Leviticus on women, recognizing its general context in the ancient world. Women are mentioned specifically in only two sections of Leviticus: one concerns childbirth, which made a woman impure for ritual purposes (Lev 12). In order to be allowed to re-enter the temple, she had to undergo a period of cleansing which culminated in sacrifices in the temple. The implication is that the woman herself is envisaged as participating in the sacrificial cult. Although the directions relating to sacrifice are addressed in the masculine form of the verb (whether singular or plural), this could be thought to include women under normal circumstances. Women are not specifically excluded in the P legislation. If women were not allowed to enter the altar area, as was the case in the time of the Second Temple, this is nowhere stated.

2. The other occasion of impurity with women was menstruation (15:19–24). The regulations about bodily issues in Lev 12–15 do not make a particular point about menstruation; on the contrary, it is only one of a number of issues of blood or fluid which are polluting. Nevertheless, most of the other regulations concern unusual occurrences, whereas the rules about menstruation would regularly affect all women between puberty and menopause, as well as their families more indirectly. It is clear that these purity regulations were extremely important to all Israelites of both sexes. However, it should be noted that menstruation, like the impurity contracted from normal sexual intercourse, did not require a sacrifice for cleansing. These were in a different category from 'abnormal' discharges.

3. Anthropological studies have suggested that regulations about menstruation often mirror the relationship between the sexes and the place of either sex within the society. Societies in which women have considerable freedom of choice and independence from men will usually have this reflected in various customs about ritual purity, including menstruation. Those societies in which women are restricted to a particular place and function and are discouraged from entering the province of men will usually have constrictive regulations about menstruation.

4. It seems clear that in Israelite society, women had a particular sphere and place in which they were confined. They were not generally allowed to participate in activities which were associated with the male Israelite. These customs were not necessarily absolute since the OT tradition has stories of exceptional women who broke through the traditional boundaries. But any woman who carefully observed the rules about menstrual pollution would have found her activities severely restricted in certain ways. A similar purpose seems to be associated with the rules surrounding childbirth. The longer purification time after bearing a daughter could be a symbol that women had an appropriate place in society which was different from that of men. On the other hand, any evaluation of these regulations would do well to take account of the fact that many Jews still observe these or similar regulations today and give them a positive value (cf. Wegner 1992).

E. Leviticus and the Actual Temple Cult. 1. Does Leviticus (or it and the rest of P) describe the rites in the temple, or is it merely a theoretical document, a programme, or even a mere fantasy? We can say with some confidence that Leviticus does not describe the cult in a tabernacle built by the Israelites under Moses during 40 years in the wilderness. The whole story as described in the biblical text (from Exodus to the end of Deuteronomy) is now generally rejected by biblical scholars. A generation ago, many would have given greater credence to the story, or at least certain parts of it. New archaeological information and further study has convinced most that Israel did not enter the land as a unified group out of the wilderness after escaping from Egypt. Rather, even if some had been in Egypt, they would have been a small group. The bulk of those who came to make up Israel were probably indigenous people in some sense, though there may also have been immigrants from outside the area. Those who coalesced to produce Israel no doubt had their shrines, permanent or portable, but the description of building the tabernacle in Exodus is fiction as it stands. For example, the altar described in Exodus is made of wood and bronze. This sort of construction would hardly stand the heat of the fire necessary to consume the sacrificial portions, and any actual altar was probably made of stone and earth (Gerstenberger 1993: 29). Nevertheless, some reality may have lain behind it. What might that have been?

2. It is possible that the description in P is purely hypothetical or utopian. Priests who had a vision of an idealized cult could write it up and present it as if that was what happened long ago under Moses. There is no doubt that we find a certain amount of idealization in the description of the tabernacle and the setting up of its cult. However, most scholars would see some relationship to what went on in an actual temple or shrine. Those who date P to the post-exilic period consider the Priestly material to reflect generally the situation in the Second Temple which was built in the early Persian period. If P is dated to the exilic period, one would expect that it is presenting a programme for a renewed cult in Jerusalem (which was expected imminently), with the hope of influencing the structure of the new cult.

3. Cross (1947) advanced the thesis that the tent of David, which housed the ark before and after its removal to Jerusalem but before the temple was built, was the basis of the tabernacle tradition. The proposal of Haran (1962), followed by Milgrom (1991), makes the core of Leviticus relate to the temple at Shiloh in the early period of the monarchy. Part of Milgrom's argument concerns later editings which attempted to bring the material up to date, with some of these even as late as the post-exilic period. Therefore, despite possible earlier origins the cult and regulations in the present text of Leviticus in most cases can be related to the practice in the First Temple.

4. What most would accept is that Leviticus represents to a large extent actual cultic practice, despite some tensions and contradictions. No doubt there have been editings, perhaps in part because of changes and developments in actual practice. But it is also likely that many cultic procedures remained essentially unchanged over long periods of time (Rendtorff 1985–92: 5; Grabbe 1995: 207). The many differences in detail between Leviticus and other passages in the OT do not suggest major differences in the overall shape of the cult. Those who see Leviticus as by and large a description of cultic observance in the Second Temple period are probably correct since, even if much of it goes back to the First Temple, the same practices were probably continued when the temple was rebuilt.

COMMENTARY

Chs. 1–7 describe the sacrificial system. Contrary to popular opinion, there is more to the book of Leviticus than just a description of various sacrifices. Nevertheless, the cult was central to Israelite worship, and it is important to understand the sacrifices if one wishes to understand Israelite religion (see C.1–2 above). It was through the sacrificial cult that sins were forgiven and evil was removed from the land. And an important question is what was thought to happen when an animal was slain at the altar. Milgrom (1976) has dismissed the idea of the sacrificial victim being a substitute for the sinner. He does acknowledge, though, that on the 'day of *kippûrîm*' (Day of Atonement) the sins were placed metaphorically on the head of the goat for Azazel. In this case, there is no sense of 'wiping off' but of the transfer of sins from the people to the animal (see further at LEV 1:4 and 16). That this is really a type of substitute or surrogate for the sinner, however, is a point well made by Kiuchi (1987). Kiuchi argues that the sin offering is envisaged as a substitute for the sinner, in other words, it purges the sin of the individual and not just, as Milgrom asserts, the effects of these sins on the sanctuary. (The transfer of sins in the Day of Atonement ceremony may be somewhat different from this, since the victim is sent away and not slain. Nevertheless, he argues that the scapegoat ceremony is a form of sin offering.) This transfer of sins might be indicated when the offerer lays hands on the animal's head. Kiuchi (1987: 112–19) notes that there are a number of interpretations of this act. Although he favours the interpretation that it represents substitution, he recognizes that the evidence is scanty. Knierim (1992: 34–40) opposes the idea of substitution and considers the gesture (which he translates as 'firm pressing down of the hand') a means of denoting transfer of ownership, i.e. from the offerer to God. If so, this aspect of the discussion does not help resolve the main problem of the elimination of sin.

Perhaps part of the problem is being too literal in interpretation. The sacrificial system was a symbolic system, filled with metaphor, allegory, and analogy. It would be a mistake to assume that only one symbol or metaphor was used for removing sin (e.g. ritual detergent). In the same way, the cultic terminology may have a more general meaning and should not be defined in terms of the specific metaphor used. The individual's sins were removed, whatever the precise symbolic conceptualization used.

Chs. 1–5 tend to address the whole people, lay as well as priest, in contrast to 6–7 which seem aimed primarily at the priests. The main term for offering is *qorbān*, a generic term which refers to a variety of different types (cf. the reference to the term in its Greek transliteration *korban* 'gift' in Mk 7:11). The instructions about how to prepare the sacrifice are often stereo-typed, so that similar instructions are given about those which are parallel; however, it is interesting to notice that small differences in wording are often found, even when the same instructions seem to be in mind. The sacrificial pattern for animals generally goes according to the following schema:

1. The sacrificer laid hands on the head of the animal.
2. It was killed at the entrance to the tabernacle, north of the altar, and cut up. The most natural interpretation of the Hebrew word-ing is that the slaughtering was done by the one making the offering rather than by the priest. If so, it contradicts Ezek 44:11, where it is done by the Levites, and 2 Chr 29:22, 24 where it is done by the priests.
3. Blood was sprinkled or dashed or poured, usually on the sides and/or base of the altar.
4. The parts burned for cattle included the en-trails with their fat, the kidneys and suet, and the caul of the liver; the same was true with sheep or goats, except that the fat tail was also added.
5. Except for the whole burnt offering, the breast of the animal went to the priests as a body, while the right thigh went to the pre-siding priest specifically.

(1:1–2) is an introduction to the entire section of chs. 1–7 and forms an *inclusio* with 7:37–8, to mark off chs. 1–7 as a unit.

(1:3–17) describes the whole burnt offering ('*ôlâ*). Sometimes referred to as the 'holocaust', this whole burnt offering was the complete sacrifice, for none of it went to the sacrificing priest (except for the hide, 7:8) or to the one bringing the offering. The entire animal was 'turned into smoke', to use the Hebrew expres-sion (*hiqtîr*). The offering could be from the herd or flock, a male animal in either case, or from the birds (turtle-doves or pigeons). Although the animal was cut up, all the pieces (not just the fat, kidneys, etc.) were placed on the altar. The legs and entrails were washed but placed on the altar as well. The burnt offering had expiatory function, as indicated by 1:4, 9:7, 14:20, and 16:24 (cf. also Ezek 45:15, 17). But it also seems to have been used for a wide range of functions, according to other passages, includ-ing entreaty (1 Sam 13:12) and appeasement of God's wrath (1 Sam 7:9; 2 Sam 24:21–5). It could

also be used as an occasion for rejoicing (Lev 22:17–19; Num 15:3). It has been proposed that because of its ubiquity in early texts, it and the well-being offering (Lev 3) were the only sacri-fices in the earliest period, with the sin and guilt offerings being added later when the temple was established. Gerstenberger (1993: 31) also suggests that the sin offering was a later replace-ment for the whole burnt offering.

(1:4) says that the purpose of the sacrifice is for 'atonement' for the one making the offering. The Hebrew word is *kipper* and is used in a number of contexts to describe the removal of sin or ritual impurity. Although often translated as 'atone' or 'cover up', the precise connotation has been much debated. The denominative verb can mean 'serve as a ransom, expiation gift'. Levine (1974: 56–77) has argued that it means 'remove, wipe off' impurity, not 'cover up'. In the cult, the word was used primarily in functional terms to mean 'perform rites of expiation' rather than 'to clean'. Milgrom (1991: 1079–84) sees a develop-ment in the word from a basic meaning 'purge'. It also carried the idea of 'rub, wipe', so that the meanings 'cover' ('wipe on') and 'wipe off' are complementary rather than contradictory. In rit-ual texts, the idea of 'wipe off' predominated in that the blood was thought of as wiping off impurity, acting as a sort of cultic detergent. With certain rituals, such as those on the Day of Atonement or involving the red cow (Num 19:1–10), the idea of 'ransom' or 'substitute' was the main connotation. This finally led to the meaning 'atone, expiate' in some passages, espe-cially with regard to all sacrifices where blood was not daubed on the horns of the altar.

Central to the cult was the shedding of blood. There is a major disagreement about the func-tion of the blood between Milgrom and Levine, however. Levine argues that it has two func-tions: (1) an apotropaic function for the deity; that is, the blood was placed on the altar to protect God from the malignancy of impurity which was regarded as an external force; (2) purificatory or expiatory, in which the blood served as a ransom substituting for the life owed by the offerer. According to Milgrom, the idea of demonic or malignant forces which might harm the deity had no place in the thought of the P tradition. Impurities did com-promise the holiness of the sanctuary and altar, so the purpose of the offering was to remove these. As noted above, Milgrom's opinion is that the blood acted as a ritual detergent, washing off the impurities which had attached themselves to the sacred things. For further comments on the blood, see at LEV 17:10–14.

(1:14–17) gives instructions for a whole burnt offering of birds. There are differences from those of other animals. For birds the neck was wrung off but, rather than being cut up, the body was torn open by the wings without severing it. The crop and excrement were placed on the ash pile. The whole of the offering was done by the priests, perhaps because only the poorest, such as slaves, used birds and were perhaps not as observant of the cult (Gerstenberger 1993: 27–8). On fowls for the sin offering, see at LEV 5:14–6:7.

(2:1–16) describes the cereal or meal offering (minḥāh). The word minḥāh means 'gift' and is used with such a general meaning in some texts (e.g. in reference to animals in Gen 4:3–4 and 1 Sam 2:17). It could even have the meaning of 'tribute' (Judg 3:15; 2 Sam 8:2). In Leviticus and priestly tradition in general, it refers exclusively to the offering of grain or meal. The cereal offering was the only non-blood sacrifice. It had two functions: (1) it was often an accompanying offering to one of the others, in particular the burnt and thanksgiving offerings; (2) it could be offered in its own right as an independent sacrifice. The meal offering follows this basic pattern:

1. Choice flour was to be used, with oil mixed in before cooking or added afterwards; anything cooked was always unleavened; frankincense accompanied the offering.
2. The frankincense and a token portion of the flour or cake were burnt on the altar.
3. The rest of the offering went to the priest.

It could be raw flour (mixed with oil) or it could be baked in an oven, cooked on a griddle, or fried in a pan. It was always unleavened since no leaven was to be burnt on the altar (v. 11), and was to be salted (v. 13) as a sign of the covenant. Other vegetable offerings could be brought: first fruits (v. 12: rē'šît, no details given) and a cereal offering of first fruits (bikkûrîm) which was to consist of roasted grain with the usual oil and frankincense (vv. 14–16).

In his recent study Marx (1994) argues that the vegetable offering plays a central role in the system of P (including Ezek 40–8 and Chr), and is an accompaniment not only of the whole burnt offering but also of the well-being offering, the sin offering, and the guilt offering. (P represents a utopian ideal which views vegetarianism as the original state of man-kind.) As

noted above, the cereal offering can also stand alone and be offered independently of other offerings. By contrast, the J source (followed by Deut, Hos, and Ezek 1–39) limits its horizon to the blood offering, according to Marx.

(3:1–17) describes the šĕlāmîm offering. There is no agreed translation for this term. It was long connected with šālôm 'peace' and called the 'peace offering', a translation still found in the RSV. More recent translations have often derived the name from šālēm 'well-being', the translation used in the New Jewish Publication Society translation and the NRSV (the NEB and REB have 'shared-offering'). Levine himself suggests the meaning 'gift', based on the Akkadian šulmānu which means 'gift of greeting'. These are all only educated guesses, and exactly how one renders the term is to some extent arbitrary. The actual terminology used for the well-being offering is zebaḥ šĕlāmîm 'sacrifice of well-being'. The term zebaḥ is often translated by the general term 'sacrifice'; however, it seems to be limited to those sacrifices which were eaten by the offerer and would not be applied to the burnt offering or the sin offering since these were burnt whole or eaten only by the priests. The question is why the double terminology is used. Rendtorff has suggested that two originally separate offerings must have been combined, since such double terminology is unparalleled in cultic language. Also, zebaḥ šĕlāmîm is limited to Leviticus and Numbers; zebaḥ often occurs by itself outside these two books, but šĕlāmîm is never alone and often in the context of the burnt offering. Milgrom (1991), on the other hand, argues that zebaḥ šĕlāmîm is merely a synonym for šĕlāmîm. This passage does not discuss the various sorts of well-being offerings, and one must see the later treatment at 7:11–18 for a breakdown of the types of usage for this offering.

v. 11: A number of offerings are said to be 'iššeh, which is often translated as 'offerings by fire'. This depends on the presumed origin of the word from 'ēš 'fire', which is also reflected in later translations. This presents two difficulties: some offerings are referred to as 'iššeh even when they are not burned (e.g. the wine offering: Num 15:10), whereas some offerings burned on the altar (e.g. the sin offering) are not called 'iššeh. Milgrom has related the zword to Ugaritic iṯṯ 'gift' and perhaps Arabic 'aâu 'possession of every kind'. He suggests the translation 'food gift', perhaps a shortened term from leḥem 'iššeh 'food gift' (Lev 3:11, 16). In his opinion, the word may have become obsolete by exilic times since it is absent from later OT collections.

(4:1–6:7) (HB 4:1–5:26) treats the sin and guilt offerings. There is considerable difficulty in separating these. The guilt offering especially has been a notorious problem since antiquity. Early Jewish commentators already had difficulties in interpreting it (cf. Philo, *Spec. leg.* 1.226–38; Josephus, *Ant.* 3.9.3 §§ 230–2). The same quandary has afflicted modern commentators, with various solutions proposed. For example Kellermann (1977) suggested that the guilt offering developed from the sin offering, to provide a form of sacrifice between the sin and burnt offerings, as the atonement sacrifice for all cases of gross negligence. In Lev 5:15, however, it is probably equivalent to the sin offering. Levine (1974) believes that it was not originally an altar sacrifice but a cultic offering presented to the deity in the form of silver or an object of value in expiation for certain offences. A necessary precondition is that the sin be done inadvertently, although Lev 5:20–6 may seem to go against this, because a false oath cannot be given inadvertently, Levine explains this as a separate category of crime. Milgrom (1976) opposes Levine with the view that the guilt offering must be a blood sacrifice. Any mention of silver has reference to buying an animal to sacrifice. Milgrom thinks he has found a solution in the meaning of the name, which he takes to mean 'feel guilt' when there is no verbal object. The notion common to all offences which call for it is that they are all cases of sacrilege against God, i.e. either an actual infringement of holy things or a trespass against the name of God.

(4:1–35) The term *ḥaṭṭāʾt* is traditionally translated 'sin offering' because the word also means 'sin'. The difficulty with this translation is that the sacrifice is required in certain cases where no sin is involved (e.g. Lev 12:6). Therefore, Milgrom argues for the translation 'purificatory offering'. His point is well taken; however, it seems a cumbersome title and one which may not be readily apparent to those more used to 'sin offering'. For this reason, 'sin offering' is still used here despite being somewhat problematic. The sin offering is to be offered when one has committed a sin unwittingly. The instructions vary according to the rank of the person offering it, and the pattern differs in certain details from that given at the head of this section on LEV 1–5. It is clear that two sorts of sin offering are in mind here. There is the one which is offered because of the sin of the priests or the congregation as a whole and is burnt entirely. The other, offered on behalf of the ordinary Israelite (including the tribal chieftain), was eaten by the priests after the normal parts were burned on the altar. vv. 3–12, if the anointed priest (high priest?) is atoning for his own sin, he is to offer a bull. The blood is sprinkled inside the tabernacle itself, before the curtain covering the Holy of Holies, and some of it put on the horns of the incense altar. The normal portions are burnt on the altar, but the rest of the animal is taken outside the camp and burned where the ashes from the altar are dumped. vv. 13–21, if the whole community has sinned, the ceremony is the same as for the priest, except that the elders take the part of the offerer. vv. 22–6, if a tribal chieftain (*nāśîʾ*) has sinned, a male goat is offered, with blood put on the horns of the altar of burnt offerings. In this case only the normal portions are burned, while the rest goes to the priest to be eaten. vv. 27–31, if an ordinary person (*ʿam hāʾāreṣ*) has sinned, a female goat or sheep is offered, with the other details being the same as for the chieftain.

(5:1–13) is generally interpreted as describing the graduated sin offering. That is, there are two sorts of sin offering: the normal sin offering (4:1–35) and the graduated sin offering. Confusion is caused by the fact that the term *ʾāšām* is used here (vv. 6–7) as in 5:14–6:7 (HB 5:14–26), suggesting that the offerings of ch. 5 are separate from ch. 4. However, it is usually argued that *ʾāšām* means 'atonement for guilt' in vv. 6–7 rather than 'guilt offering', especially since reference is specifically made to the 'sin offering' in vv. 6, 7, 11. The breaches for which this is offered do not form a clear pattern: not acting as a witness, uttering a rash oath, or touching the corpse of an unclean animal or some other unclean thing without realizing it. The person must first confess the sin, then bring an offering of a female goat or sheep. If he does not have enough wealth for sheep or goat, he can bring two turtle-doves or two pigeons, one for a burnt offering and one for a sin offering. Since there are no instructions about fowls for a sin offering, some details are given: the neck is wrung but the head not severed from the body, and part of the blood is sprinkled on the side of the altar while the rest is poured out at the base. What happens then is not stated. The flesh of the guilt offering normally went to the priest, after the fat etc. were burned on the altar, but we do not have precise instructions about birds. The other bird is treated as a burnt offering. If the person does not have enough for birds, a tenth of an ephah of fine flour (without oil or frankincense) is offered. A token portion is burnt, and the rest goes to the priest, as is normal in cereal offerings. This is the only case where a cereal offering can serve for a transgression (though cf. Num 5:15).

(**5:14–6:7**) (HB 5:14–26) describes the guilt offering. The precise meaning of ʾāšām is not clear. The verb can mean 'commit an offence' and 'become guilty' (by committing an offence); hence, the traditional translation 'guilt offering'. Milgrom (1976) opposes this, arguing that when confined to cultic usage it has four meanings: (1) reparation, (2) reparation offering, (3) incur liability to someone, (4) feel guilt. It is especially this last which he emphasizes. The translation 'realize guilt' or 'become conscious of guilt', as found in a number of translations, he thinks is wrong. Rather, the clue to the sacrifice lies in the fact that the person becomes conscience-stricken, afraid that he has committed an offence. For the offering itself, he uses the translation 'reparation offering'.

5:14–16: the first transgression relating to the guilt offering involves unwitting violation of the 'holy things' of God (qodšê yhwh). The type of violation is not described, but the later ceremony suggests that the person has used something belonging to God for his own purposes, for restitution has to be made with another 20 per cent (fifth part) added to it (v. 16). A ram is also brought (v. 15; cf. 6:6 (HB 5:25)). A debate has arisen concerning the expression 'convertible into silver' (v. 15). Does this mean that only the value of the ram in money was brought rather than the animal itself (Noth 1977: 47)? Hartley (1992: 81–2) disagrees. However, Levine (1974: 98–100) thinks this was the earlier practice which later developed into the use of a ram of a minimal value, while Milgrom (1991: 326–7) argues that the value of the ram could be assessed and the equivalent value paid. vv. 17–19 follow the instructions about the transgression with regard to holy things by a general statement that a ram is to be brought for any transgressions of YHWH's commands which at first escape the person's notice. 6:1–7 (HB 5:20–6) expands the the concept of 5:17–19 further to include defrauding one's neighbour by illicitly appropriating a pledge or not returning a lost object. Again, restitution has to be made, with 20 per cent added, and a ram or its equivalent value is brought for a guilt offering.

(**6:8–7:38**) (HB 6:1–7:38) gives the laws (tôrôt) of the offerings. The term tôrâ in these texts often refers to a priestly ruling. The sacrifices enumerated in chs. 1–5 are covered once more, but this time the instructions relate to the responsibilities of the priests rather than focusing on the offerings from the point of view of the lay person. It also emphasizes the priestly dues to be given over from each sacrifice. 6:8–13 (HB 6:1–6) gives the law of the burnt offering; cf. 1:3–17. 6:14–18 (HB 6:7–11) gives the law of the cereal offering; cf. Lev 2. 6:19–23 (HB 6:12–16) discusses the offering at Aaron's anointing. This section seems out of place because of its subject, though it was probably put here because a cereal offering is being described. It seems to be referring to a type of tāmîd or daily meal offering. It consisted of a tenth of an ephah of fine flour (about 2 litres), mixed with oil, and cooked on a griddle. Half is offered in the morning and half in the evening. This is burned entirely on the altar, with no portion eaten by the priests. We know that there was a daily or tāmîd offering made on the altar, and it seems to have included a cereal offering as well as a burnt offering in the morning. The daily offering was extremely important in antiquity because it was the chief sign that the temple was functioning and God accessible to the people. The times when the daily sacrifice was stopped were times of dire consequences, as when the temple was destroyed by Nebuchadnezzer or the Romans, or when the sacrifice was stopped by force in the time of the Maccabees. Surprisingly, though, what constituted the daily offering is not clear. Leviticus mentions only the cereal offering of the high priest, made in the morning and in the evening. Other priestly passages mention a daily burnt offering of two lambs, one in the morning and one in the evening (Ex 29:38–42; Num 28:3–8). Was this separate from the cereal offering or was the cereal offering thought of only as a companion offering? If the cereal offering accompanied it, why is this not mentioned in Leviticus, and why is the required drink offering also ignored? Other passages are different yet again. Dating from the time of the Maccabees, the practice of sacrificing the tāmîd twice a day is attested in Dan 8:11–14, while 9:21 mentions an evening cereal offering. 2 Kings 16:15 refers to a morning whole burnt offering and an evening cereal offering. Ezek 46:13–15 differs from Exodus, Leviticus, and Numbers by describing a daily sacrifice of one lamb (not two), accompanied by one-sixth of an ephah of flour (instead of one-tenth).

The question is, What is the offering of 6:19–23? Is it identical with the cereal offering of the *tāmîd*? Most likely, it is a separate offering but one offered daily by the high priest (Milgrom 1991).

6:24–30 (HB 6:17–23) gives the law of the sin offering; cf. 4:1–5:13. 7:1–10 gives the law of the guilt offering; cf. 5:14–6:7. 7:11–21 gives the law of the well-being offering. 3:1–16 gives the details of the ritual, but it is only here that the basic rationale is given, i.e. the various sorts of well-being offering. Three types seem to be included under the well-being offering:

1. The freewill offering (*nědābâ*), given voluntarily on the part of the offerer, without any special motivation.
2. The votive offering (*nēder*). Whenever a vow was made, it was completed by an offering.
3. The thanksgiving offering (*tôdâ*), given as an expression of thanks for deliverance in time of trouble. There are several problems with understanding this offering.

Is it the same as the freewill offering? Some scholars have thought so. Others (e.g. Milgrom 1976) think the two are always clearly distinguished in the OT and should be kept separate. There are certain anomalies about the *tôdâ* offering when compared with the other well-being offering, suggesting that it was once considered separate. The main distinction from the other similar offerings is that it is accompanied by a cereal offering and must be eaten the same day it is offered. The freewill and votive offerings do not have the accompanying cereal offering and can be eaten both on the day of the offering and the next day. Indeed, in other passages the thanksgiving does seem to be an independent offering along-side the well-being (Lev 22:21, 29; Jer 17:26; 2 Chr 29:31–3; 33:16) and only in the supposed P source is it made a subdivision of the well-being offering.

7:22–38 has a set of miscellaneous instructions. Formally, it consists of two speeches of YHWH to Moses, and it seems to form a sort of appendix or supplement to instructions on the various sacrifices: vv. 22–7 prohibit the eating of any fat or blood, under pain of the penalty of being 'cut off' (*nikrat*; also in 7:21). This expression of being 'cut off' has been much debated but without a clear resolution (e.g. Levine 1989: 241–2; Milgrom 1991: 457–60). In some passages it refers to an early death, perhaps because of judicial punishment (Lev 20:2–3). Others have argued that passages with the expression generally imply divine punishment, not human.

Some passages envisage that one's line of descendants would be cut off, not necessarily involving human action (1 Sam 2:30–4; Ps 109:13; Mal 2:12; Ruth 4:10). vv. 28–36 talk specifically of the well-being offering, but the main theme concerns those portions of the animal which are due to the priests: the breast and the right thigh. In Leviticus the maintenance of the priest-hood is alluded to only in chs. 6–7, plus a brief discussion of tithing of animals (see at LEV 27:26–7). But the priesthood could not have been supported on portions of sacrifices alone, and other P passages speak of tithes and other support; see the discussion in Grabbe (1993: 70–2). vv. 37–8 are a concluding summary for the entire section on sacrifices, i.e. chs. 1–7; cf. 1:1–2.

(**Chs. 8–10**) describe the initiation of Aaron and sons into the priesthood and an unfortunate episode relating to priestly service in the sanctuary. Chs. 8–9 concern the ceremony in which Aaron and his sons were anointed and consecrated to their offices. There is general agreement that this is a priestly fiction; that is, these chapters do not describe an actual event involving a literal Aaron and Moses in the wilderness of Sinai. On the other hand, these chapters may tell us something about priestly belief or practice. Leviticus seems to envisage the anointing of Aaron and his sons as a once-only event, setting apart their descendants to the priesthood forever, as apparently does Exodus (29:9; 40:15). But each new high priest was customarily designated by anointing (Lev 6:22 (HB 6:15)). The lengthy ritual described in Lev 8–9 has many characteristics of what is often referred to as a 'rite of passage' (Gennep 1960). This is an anthropological term for rites which take place as a person passes from one stage to another, such as from boyhood to manhood or girlhood to womanhood. There is first a rite of separation, next a transitional rite during which the person is in a 'liminal' state (on the doorstep between one phase and another). There may be dangers while in this liminal state, and various rituals have to be carefully performed to protect the one undergoing the transition. In the case of Aaron and sons, they were under-going the passage from 'common' to 'sacred'. Various purification and burnt offerings and washings were performed, a special ordination offering carried out (8:22–9), and the anointing done. Those involved were then required to remain a week segregated in the Tent of Meeting (transitional rite). The final act was a ritual of incorporation, in this case sacrifices and ceremonies on the eighth day (Lev 9). Thus, the ceremony of consecration in Lev 8–9 is very much parallel to rites of passage known both from preliterate modern societies and from many examples in modern Western culture. Ch. 10 seems to be an inset chapter relating the incident of Nadab and Abihu (sons of Aaron) and its consequences, though the chapter follows naturally on the anointing ritual of Aaron and his sons.

(**10:1–20**) vv. 1–7 describe the death of Nadab and Abihu as a result of offering 'alien fire' (*'ēš zārâ*) on the altar. The episode is very puzzling since the 'sin' of the two sons is never clearly indicated, with the result that the passage generated many explanations in later Judaism (Hecht 1979–80; Kirschner 1982–3). Thus, as with the Golden Calf episode, one must ask what lies behind the story. Those who date this part of Leviticus late usually look for some event in the exilic or post-exilic period. For example, Noth (1977) thought he saw internal disputes between different priestly groups. However, others are willing to ascribe the background to one or other event during the time of the monarchy. Milgrom (1976) suggests that it is a polemic against private offerings of incense. There are textual and archaeological indications that it was common for Israelites to offer incense to God in their homes and elsewhere outside the Jerusalem temple. Those who believed in cult centralization would have disapproved of this practice. Thus, a graphic story like that in Lev 10 would serve as a salutary reminder that private incense offerings were fraught with danger. vv. 6–7 command Aaron and his other sons not to mourn for Nadab and Abihu. This is parallel to the passage in 21:10–12 which forbids the high priest to mourn for his near kin. vv. 8–11 give a general instruction about not drinking alcohol when on duty in the sanctuary, another possible occasion for divine punishment for a serving priest. vv. 12–20 use the the death of Aaron's sons related in the previous verses to discuss a particular situation—the question of consuming the offerings in a time of mourning.

(**Chs. 11–15**) form an important section on ritual purity and pollution. An explanation now almost universally rejected is that the various laws in this section have hygiene as their basis. Although some of the laws of ritual purity roughly correspond to modern ideas of physical cleanliness, many of them have little to do with hygiene. For example, there is no evidence that

the 'unclean' animals are intrinsically bad to eat or to be avoided in a Mediterranean climate, as is sometimes asserted. For a further discussion, see LEV C.3–4.

(**11:1–47**) describes the clean and unclean animals. Eating was very much involved with purity. Certain things were not to be eaten. The Israelite was especially to be concerned about the types of animal considered fit for consumption and how they were to be prepared. Lev 11 (paralleled by Deut 14) lists the various animals available for food and those to be avoided. There are some difficulties here because it is not always clear which animals were being referred to. The standard treatment of this chapter is now the study by Houston (1993). He argues that the animals allowed or forbidden under Israelite law were generally those similarly permitted or prohibited in the surrounding cultures. The laws of the Pentateuch thus reflect and systematize the general habits not only of the Israelites but also of their north-west Semitic neighbours. Thus, the animals permitted or forbidden seem to have come first, and the criteria for distinguishing them were worked out only subsequently. The presentation in this chapter is an intellectual exercise, a learned attempt to systematize and provide formal criteria and probably had little practical significance (Houston 1993: 231).

In vv. 2–12 the mammals and sea life are fairly easy to identify. For mammals (vv. 2–8) two questions are asked: 'Does it chew the cud?' 'Does it have cloven hooves?' If 'yes' is the response to both these, the animal can be eaten; if 'no' to either or both, it is off limits. A few borderline cases are mentioned to clarify the situation: the pig has cloven hooves but does not chew the cud; the camel chews the cud but does not have cloven hooves; the hare might be thought to chew the cud, because of the movements of its jaws, but it has no hooves. In scientific terminology, mammal food is limited to the ruminating bi-hooved ungulates. The practical implications were that edible mammals were limited to those offered on the altar and to their wild counterparts. Although pigs are attested in many areas of Palestine (Hübner 1989), the number seems to have declined fairly rapidly during the Iron Age. There is almost no evidence for their being used for sacrifice (even where they were eaten), with the possible exception of some special rites to underworld gods. However, it should be noted that pigs were included in these particular sacrifices *because* they were unclean, rather than that they were declared unclean because of being used in cults, as so often asserted (Houston 1993: 253). So the Israelite avoidance of pork fits with the general practice in the west Semitic area.

Consumption of sea creatures is restricted to those that have fins and scales (vv. 9–12). No animals are named, but it is clear that some fish (those without scales), all crustaceans, and most other fresh and saltwater animals are forbidden. The birds are hard to categorize because not all can be positively identified (vv. 13–19). Nevertheless, the majority of those which can be recognized are carnivorous or scavengers. Other flying things are also discussed here, including the bat (unclean) and some insects. A few insects could be eaten, mainly of the locust, cricket, or grasshopper type (vv. 20–3). This concession of some insects seems to be because of common dietary habits among the people, since insects seem to have been forbidden in the parallel passage in Deut 14:29 (Houston 1993: 236). vv. 24–40 seem to repeat earlier instructions, with quadrupeds again (vv. 24–8), followed by a long section on 'swarming things' (vv. 29–45). However, some sort of structure does emerge with a closer look, since vv. 24–40 are primarily about the carcasses of unclean animals, not the animals themselves. Then, vv. 41–5 are about the swarming things which had not really been discussed in vv. 1–23. Despite a somewhat coherent structure, though, most critics have seen evidence of growth and supplementation here. Further evidence of this is found in vv. 43–5 which use language reminiscent of H: 'be holy as I am holy'. vv. 41–5 discuss the 'swarming things', which seem to be a miscellaneous collection of small animals regarded as abhorrent by the Israelites. vv. 46–7 are a summary of the chapter.

(**Ch. 12**) gives directions about the purity procedure which follows childbirth. The first form of impurity for women listed in Leviticus is that of childbirth. If a woman bore a boy, she was unclean for 7 days, until the circumcision of the boy on the eighth day. For another 33 days she was not unclean as such (i.e. passing on uncleanness to others who had contact with her) but was not allowed to come into the sanctuary or touch any holy thing.

These periods were doubled for the birth of a girl: 14 days and 66 days. The allotted period was completed and purity restored with a lamb for a burnt offering and a pigeon or dove for a sin offering. A poor person could substitute two pigeons or doves, one for the burnt offering and one for the sin offering.

(**Chs. 13–14**) discuss a variety of skin diseases under the general Hebrew term of *ṣāraʿat*. Although this is often presented in older English translations as 'leprosy', the modern condition of leprosy is limited to Hanson's disease; by contrast, it is not clear that modern leprosy is even covered by the ancient disease; in fact, there is some question as to whether Hanson's disease was known in the Mediterranean world before the Hellenistic period. Also, some objects can be infected with 'leprosy'.

(**13:1–59**) Various skin afflictions are listed in vv. 1–46, along with the priestly response to them. The main function of the priest was to examine any affliction or inflammation brought to him, isolate the individual if it looked like the real disease, check again after seven days, and finally pronounce the afflicted person whole or leprous. Despite the length of the regulations, they are fairly repetitive, with slightly different criteria for scaly patches, burns, boils, and so on. As with Lev 11, the text is not dealing with medical treatment or hygiene but rather with ritual. What is being discussed is not how to treat the various diseases under the rubric *ṣāraʿat* but only how to recognize them and how to view them from the point of view of cultic purity. The medical question was no doubt of concern in Israel but it is not within the scope of the discussion here. The job of the priest was to pronounce on ritual purity and impurity, and the text gives some guidance on how to decide whether the person is clean or not, but he was not treating the disease as such. Even the isolation was not a quarantine for purposes of preventing the spread of the disease but only a way of allowing it time to develop or recede so an authoritative pronouncement could be made about it. In vv. 47–59 the infected object is a piece of cloth or leather. This is an additional complication to the identification of the disease(s) falling under the generic term *ṣāraʿat*. This section appears to deal with mould or fungus infections. From a medical point of view, there is no connection between these and the skin diseases otherwise dealt with. This reinforces the view that something other than pathological conditions is in the mind of the writer.

(**14:1–53**) In vv. 1–32 a good deal of space is devoted to the question of re-entry into the cultic community once the disease is cured.

A major feature was a ritual in which two birds were taken, one killed but the other released into the open country. As is obvious, this ritual has certain features in common with the scapegoat ritual, especially the use of two creatures, one of which is slain and the other released (see further at LEV 16). The cured person then had to wash himself and his clothes, shave off his hair, and remain outside his tent (though within the camp) for a further 7 days. He then presented three lambs (one for a guilt offering, one for a sin offering, and one for a burnt offering), a cereal offering, and a quantity of oil. Some of the blood of the guilt offering and some of the oil was put on different parts of the former sufferer's anatomy. A poor person need bring only one lamb (for the guilt offering), two turtle-doves or pigeons (for the sin and burnt offering), the cereal offering, and the oil. The range of offerings required in this case is paralleled only by those required for the nazirites to finish their vow (Num 6:13–20). vv. 33–53 envisage that a house could get ṣāraʿat, in the same way as a piece of cloth or leather. Again, it seems to be some sort of fungus which the writer has in mind. As with a person, the cleansing would be completed with the ceremony of the two birds.

(15:1–30) deals with a variety of genital discharges, normal and abnormal, for both men and women. vv. 2–24: a number of discharges were regarded as more or less normal, because they were a part of everyday life, and the person becoming polluted by them would be purified by washing and the passage of time. There was no requirement to offer a sacrifice. First to be treated, in vv. 1–16, are men. If there is an abnormal emission of semen or other penile discharge, the man (*zab*) becomes impure. The pollution is passed on to anyone touching him or anything on which he sits, as it is also if he spits on anyone or touches anyone without first washing his hands. The person so polluted was required to bathe in spring water, wash his clothes, and would become clean with the going down of the sun. A normal discharge of semen in marital intercourse (vv. 16–18) was also polluting, though less contagious than an abnormal discharge. The man and woman both were to wash themselves and remain unclean until evening. Any cloth or leather object on which semen fell was also to be washed and remain unclean until evening.

With regard to women (vv. 19–24), the flow of blood caused by childbirth was already dealt

with in 12:1–8. The most basic and regular genital discharge was the monthly menstrual period. The time of impurity lasted 7 days even if the actual flow of blood finished sooner. During this time the woman transmitted impurity by direct contact or indirectly via anything on which she sat or lay. The person who touched her or that on which she lay or sat would need to wash himself or herself and his or her clothes and be unclean until evening. A man who had sexual relations with her would be unclean for 7 days. Any other prolonged discharge of blood for a woman also brought on uncleanness on the same order as menstruation (vv. 25–30). If the flow stopped, the woman would become clean after 7 days. In this case, though, there was a significant difference, for she had to make a sacrifice. On the eighth day she was to bring two pigeons or doves, one for a burnt offering and one for a sin offering.

(16:1–34) describes the atonement for sanctuary and people popularly known as the 'scapegoat ritual'. The central core of the ritual was the ceremony with the two goats. One goat was for God and one was for 'Azazel' (on this word, see at v. 8), the choice being determined by lot. This ceremony differs from most of the cultic rituals in having the sins of the people placed on a live animal rather than sacrificing one and putting its blood on the altar. Part of the peculiarities of this chapter may arise from its origins. A variety of possibilities have been suggested, the most recent seeing parallels— and perhaps even the origin—of the rite in southern Anatolia and northern Syria (Janowski and Wilhelm 1993). Expiation rituals in the Hittite and Hurrian texts have some striking points in common with the scapegoat ritual (ibid. 134–57; Wright 1987: 31–60).

v. 1 connects the chapter back to the regulations about the priests in chs. 8–10, linking it with the one proper occasion when a priest (limited to the high priest) could appear before God in the Holy of Holies. That is, whereas Adab and Abihu had acted improperly (though their sin is never specified) and had been punished by death, the right ceremony at the right time could allow the right priest to come into God's actual presence. vv. 2–14, before the high priest could come into God's presence, he first had to offer a bull as a sin offering for himself and his household. Then he went inside the veil and placed incense on the coals of his censer to make a cloud of smoke and hide the ark, thus protecting himself from God who was seated on top of the ark, and sprinkled the blood of the bull on the ark. This was all to atone for his own sins. Before this was done, however, two goats were chosen to perform separate roles by lot (vv. 7–10). One goat was for YHWH, the other for 'Azazel' (v. 8). What was this Azazel? Unfortunately, it remains an enigma. No explanation is found in the text of Lev 16, and the word does not occur elsewhere in the OT or early inscriptions. Various etymologies have been proposed, but none is clearly compelling. Later Jewish tradition identified Azazel with the leader of the fallen angels (Grabbe 1987). Although this identification may itself be the result of exegesis, scholars have often proposed that Azazel represents some sort of demonic figure. This is suggested by the context as well as later Jewish interpretation. While accepting this interpretation as the one which developed in Judaism, Janowski and Wilhelm (1993: 161–2) argue that the original meaning of the word was 'for (the elimination of) God's wrath'. vv. 15–19, after the priest had sacrificed for himself and his family, he next sacrificed the goat on whom the lot for God had fallen. This goat became a sin offering and was sacrificed and the blood sprinkled on the ark, which atoned for the holy place (polluted because of the sins of the people). The altar was atoned for by sprinkling on it the blood from both the bull and goat. vv. 20–8, in the rituals earlier in the chapter the various sacrifices had been used to atone for the sins of the high priest himself and then to cleanse the sanctuary of impurities because of the sins of the people. Now a unique ceremony takes place in which the sins of the people are removed by the treatment of the goat 'for Azazel'. It was not slain. Rather, the high priest laid hands on it and confessed the sins of the congregation, thus transferring them to its head. The goat was then taken away and sent into the wilderness, bearing away all the sins of Israel on its head. As noted above, the different conceptualization of removing sins in this ritual may be due to its origins.

vv. 29–34 summarize the ceremony and associate it with the tenth day of the seventh month. The detailed ceremony of ch. 16 is only at this point connected with the Day of Atonement listed as one of the festivals of Israel (Lev 23). It also specifies that the day should be one of fasting by the people. This suggests that the ritual of ch. 16 may have been only secondarily connected with the Day of Atonement in the list of festivals (Noth 1977). Before this it was likely to have been a ceremony evoked by the high priest whenever it was needed (Milgrom 1991: 1061–5).

Chs. 17–26 form the Holiness Code according to a long-term consensus in scholarship; nevertheless, there have been significant voices raised against this identification. See LEV B. 7 above.

(17:1–16) Ch. 17 does not provide a formal introduction to the Holiness Code (assuming one accepts the idea of H). Indeed, Gerstenberger sees chs. 16–26 as a unit separate from chs. 1–15, and puts ch. 17 in with ch. 16 as a thematic unit on 'the prime festival and the prime rule of the offerings' (1993: 17). The subject of ch. 17 is proper sacrifice; under this heading come matters of handling blood and of eating meat. The reason for these is that eating of meat is intimately associated with cultic sacrifice in the mind of the writer.

vv. 3–7 cover the law regarding slaughter, requiring that domestic animals be killed at the altar. The reason is that the blood can be disposed of at the altar, and people will not sacrifice to goat demons (vv. 6–7). It is generally assumed that this chapter envisages all slaughter as being done at the altar so that the blood can be dashed against the altar and the fat burned on it. The exception to this rule was the case of clean wild animals or birds which could be hunted, killed, and eaten apart from the shrine as long as the blood was drained out onto the earth. If so, all slaughter of domestic animals for food would have to take place in a sacrificial context. How could this be carried out from a practical point of view, if no butchering or eating of meat could be done apart from the shrine? The difficulty is highlighted by Deut 12:20–5 which seems to be changing just such a regulation when it states that profane slaughter is now allowed, as long as the blood is drained out of the animal. This means that Lev 17 must either be an idealized system divorced from reality or have in mind a society small enough in numbers and territory to allow a trip to the altar and back within a day or so. The post-exilic community had just such a size, and the majority of scholars apply this to the post-exilic community (cf. Gerstenberger 1993: 216–17). Milgrom, however, argues that the original setting was the pre-monarchic community, which was also quite small and allowed such laws to operate. Another interpretation argues that only the sacrifice of well-being offerings is in mind and that profane slaughter for food was permitted outside the temple (cf. Hartley 1992), though this seems to go against the most obvious meaning of the passage.

vv. 8–9 are a separate law and seem to repeat vv. 3–7. They may have had a separate existence at one time and thus came to be included in the collection despite some duplication. The penalty of being 'cut off' is characteristic of Leviticus (see at LEV 7:22–7). vv. 10–14 focus on the question of blood which is a central element in this chapter. The life of both humans and animals is in the blood (vv. 11, 14). For that reason, blood should not be eaten but dashed on the altar or poured on the ground and covered with dust. Blood functions as a potent symbol within the sacrificial cult and must be given due weight in any theological discussion of the meaning of the cult (see at LEV 1:4). Schwartz (1991: 55–61) argues that *kipper* in 17:11 has the meaning of 'ransom' and is the only biblical passage where sacrificial blood is said to be a ranson for human life. Elsewhere blood has the quality of purifying or cleansing, so v. 11 is a unique verse. Because of the characteristic of blood to serve as a ransom for life, its consumption is prohibited.

(17:15–16) deals with eating that which dies of itself or is killed by animals. One of the reasons is no doubt that the blood is still in the animal and has not been drained away as required (vv. 6, 11, 13–14). Surprisingly, though, such eating is not prohibited but only requires the eater to bathe, wash clothes, and be unclean until sunset. No sacrifice is necessary. Priests were specifically prohibited from eating meat not properly slaughtered in Lev 22:8, while Ex 22:31 (HB 22:30) and Deut 14:21 are even more stringent, and prohibit Israelites from eating such meat at all.

(18:1–30) discusses primarily forbidden sexual relations, in two sets of laws (vv. 7–18 and 19–23). Much of this chapter covers what is usually referred to as incest, that is, sexual relations forbidden because of the closeness of kinship of the person involved; however, some other sorts of sexual acts are also mentioned. Sexual relations sit at the heart of social practice within any community. Each society has strict views about which sort are allowed and which are not; these views may change over time and—human nature and passions being what they are—such rules are often breached, but they are still there even in what might seem the most promiscuous of societies. Indeed, promiscuity in one area of a society may be matched by great rigidity in another. Social anthropologists have found that laws about permitted and forbidden sexual

relationships are an important clue to attitudes towards relatives and outsiders (cf. LEV c.3–4). In many preliterate societies elaborate codes govern marriage. Often these force exogamy, even if the only source of wives or husbands might be an enemy tribe. Israel's rules here are very lenient (despite the claim that 'the Canaanites' allowed sex with close of kin), allowing even first cousins to marry. Israel was thus an endogamous society. This fits their emphasis on rigid barriers to non-Israelites. Easy marriage between groups internally would, of course, help to prevent any feeling of need for marriage to outsiders.

vv. 1–5: the prohibited relations are framed in two sets of admonitions or paranaetic material (vv. 1–5, 24–30). The sections justify the laws by an appeal to the 'abominations' of the Egyptians and Canaanites (vv. 3, 24–8). In fact, there is no evidence that these peoples were less moral than the Israelites, nor that their sexual practices were necessarily that different. There may have been some differences in definition of what constituted incest among these peoples compared with Israel, as is to be expected, but they had their own strict society codes. (The 'abominations of the Egyptians and Canaanites' is a fiction which still dominates some discussions, especially with regard to Canaanite religion.) On the theological construction of the Canaanites in the biblical text, see Lemche (1991).

The following sexual relations are considered off limits for the Israelite male (vv. 7–23): first are those 'with his own flesh' (i.e. near of kin): mother or step-mother (vv. 6–7); sister, half-sister, stepsister, or sister-in-law (vv. 9, 11, 16); daughter-in-law (v. 10, 15); aunt (vv. 12–14); a woman and her daughter or granddaughter (v. 17). Other regulations seem to have to do more with what is deemed appropriate: not to take a wife's sister as rival wife (v. 18); not to have sex during the menstrual period (v. 19) or with the neighbour's wife (v. 20), with another male (v. 22), or with animals (v. 23). One should not offer one's children to Molech (v. 21—on this, see further at LEV 20:1–6). Omitted is prohibition of relations with a daughter or a sister. The reason may be that the laws are phrased to forbid violation of one's father and one's mother (Rattray 1987). Also omitted is any prohibition against homosexual acts between women, though the framers of the laws may not have envisaged that such even existed.

vv. 24–30 put blame for exile from the land on the sins of the inhabitants. The Israelite is the object of the command but, as noted above in the general comments on ch. 18, the attribution of such abominable sins to the original inhabitants of the land is not based on any objective criteria. Sexual mores were fairly uniform throughout the ancient Near East. For example, adultery was universally condemned (cf. Codex Hammurabi 129–32). Sex with animals seems otherwise unattested in the Near East at this time (Gerstenberger 1993: 232).

(Chs. 19–20) list a set of miscellaneous laws on being holy. The term 'miscellaneous' is used from a modern perspective; no doubt the ancient authors/compilers had their own view and may have arranged the material according to a perfectly logical pattern from their standpoint. The contents of this section have a number of parallels with the Covenant Code (Ex 21:1–23:33) and Deut 12–24, as well as with laws known elsewhere in the ancient Near East (on Israelite law in the context of ancient Near-Eastern law, see Grabbe (1993: 23–8) and the bibliography cited there).

(Ch. 19) has a series of laws preceded by an introduction (vv. 1–2) and with a concluding verse (v. 37): revere parents (v. 3); unusually, the mother is mentioned first; keep the sabbaths (v. 3); avoid idols (v. 4); law of well-being sacrifice (vv. 5–8); leave some of harvest for the poor (vv. 9–10); do not steal (v. 11); do not lie or deceive (v. 11); do not swear falsely (v. 12); do not exploit others: friend, hired person, deaf, blind (vv. 13–14); judge justly (v. 15); do not be a slanderer (v. 16); do not hate your fellows but love them (vv. 17–18); avoid mixtures (v. 19); if a man has sex with a betrothed slave woman (vv. 20–2); the first fruits of a fruit tree (vv. 23–5); do not eat blood (v. 26); do not practice divination (v. 26); do not disfigure yourself for the dead (vv. 27–8); do not make your daughter a prostitute (v. 29); keep the sabbaths and honour the sanctuary (v. 30); do not seek to contact spirits of the dead (v. 31); show respect for the elderly (v. 32); love the resident alien (vv. 33–4); have honest scales and measures (vv. 35–6).

Many of these are what we might call civil law, but here they are given a religious sanction and thus brought under cultic law. The motive clause, '(for) I am YHWH', occurs frequently. The laws proper (vv. 3–36) are not of a piece because there is some overlap between the various ones. For example, the sabbath is mentioned twice (vv. 3, 30). It has been noted that vv. 11–18 have a common vocabulary in 'friend'

($r\bar{e}a^c$), 'associate' ($^c\bar{a}m\hat{i}t$), and 'people' (^cam) (Wenham 1979: 267). Scholars have noted connections between the Decalogue (Ex 20; Deut 5) and this chapter (Morgenstern 1955). Some have thought they could even find two decalogues (Kilian 1963: 58–9) or a dodecalogue and a decalogue (Elliger 1966: 254), though a good deal of textual rearrangement is required and the precise construction is not agreed on. It is true that the contents of much of the Ten Commandments are echoed here: graven images (19:4 || Ex 20:3); using God's name in vain (19:12 || Ex 20:7); the sabbath (19:3, 30 || Ex 20:8–12); honouring parents (19:3 || Ex 20:12); murder (19:16 || Ex 20:13); adultery (19:29 || Ex 20:14); stealing (19:11, 13 || Ex 20:15). Lev 19 also has a command against lying (v. 11) which might be taken as somewhat parallel to bearing false witness (Ex 20:16). Nevertheless, the wording and even the precise concept is often different, and the order of presentation has nothing in common, and there is much here not in the Ten Commandments. Thus, there is no obvious relationship between this chapter and the Decalogue. Comparison of the OT and the legal material elsewhere in the ancient Near East suggests a large amount of traditional exhortative material widespread in the area. The coincidences between the traditional Decalogue and this chapter are most likely due to this fact.

(20:1–8) is a section prohibiting seeking after false sources of supernatural aid. It primarily concerns dedicating children to Molech (vv. 2–5) but also forbids necromancy (v. 6). The prohibitions about Molech raise two questions: what does it refer to, and why should it be in this collection? There has been much discussion about the first question (cf. Day 1989; Heider 1985). Who or what is Molech? Some have argued that the term refers to a type of sacrifice; others assert that Molech is a deity of some sort. Although recent writings have favoured the latter hypothesis, it cannot be said that the matter is settled. Similarly, the expression 'pass (a child) over to Molech' has been taken to mean only 'to dedicate to' Molech or, more drastically, 'to sacrifice (the child) to' Molech. Again, recent writings have tended to support the latter viewpoint. The same prohibition occurs in a similar series in 18:19–23, but there the writer/editor must have seen a connection between the sexual acts and offering children to Molech. Its presence is more easily explained here in ch. 20. But why is the law included in a series having to do with sexual relations? Perhaps both were seen as threatening to family solidarity (Hartley 1992: 289–90). As its position here indicates, worship of Molech may be a form of seeking the deities of the underworld. Necromancy was another means of gaining help from the dead and the forces associated with death and the netherworld. The precise development of the cult of the dead and its significance is debated (cf. the summary in Grabbe 1995: 141–5), some thinking it was early in Israel's history (Bloch-Smith 1992) while others think it developed only fairly late (Schmidt 1994). What is clear is that in Leviticus, as in other passages (e.g. Deut 18:9–14), the practice of necromancy was known and forbidden, suggesting that it was practised at the time of writing, whenever that was.

(**20:9–27**) has parallels to Lev 19 and, especially, Lev 18. vv. 10–21 primarily concern the question of sexual relations between relatives and others, though it is introduced by a prohibition against cursing one's parents (v. 9). These are similar to Lev 18:6–23. vv. 22–6 give the rationale for these laws (the previous inhabitants did these things and the land vomited them out) in a manner parallel to 18:24–30. The section finally ends in a prohibition against necromancy (v. 27). This probably forms an *inclusio* with 20:1–6 (i.e. the chapter begins and ends with the same subject), suggesting that ch. 20 was composed as an independent unit. This implies that the repetition between chs. 18 and 20 is probably due to their being originally separate collections. If so, the final editor included both, despite the parallel material, rather than choosing between them or attempting the difficult task of editing them together. Gerstenberger (1993: 262–6), however, argues that one of the chapters must be dependent on the other, most likely the editor of ch. 20 was dependent on ch. 18; the intention of this revision is to give new perspectives relating to the community.

(**21:1–23**) The concentration in chs. 17–20 has been the community and people; now the text turns to laws relating primarily to the priests. Formally, the passage is divided into two parts by two speeches by YHWH to Moses. The first speech (vv. 1–15) is addressed to all the priests, whereas the second (vv. 16–23) is specifically to Aaron. The reason the second speech is addressed to Aaron may be because he (and subsequent high priests) were the ones to decide whom to allow near the holy food (Hartley 1992: 346). Otherwise, all the regulations relate to all the priests, since they were all thought of as descendants of Aaron.

vv. 1–9: the presumption is that all Israel is to be holy, but the priests had to be even more rigorous. They were not allowed to defile themselves by contact with a corpse by participating in funerals other than of close blood relatives: only for a mother, father, son, daughter, brother, or an unmarried sister (vv. 1–4). They were not to carry out mourning rites by disfiguring their hair, beards, or flesh by cutting it (vv. 5–6). They were not allowed to marry a harlot or divorcee, and the priest's daughter who became a harlot was to be burned (vv. 7–9). However, v. 8 makes the holiness of the priests a responsibility of the whole community. vv. 10–15, the OT as a whole does not say much about a high priest, though we know that the high priest became very important in Second Temple times (Grabbe 1992: 73–83). Leviticus does envisage a high priest, however, as this and other passages (e.g. Lev 16) show. The special nature of his office is shown by special restrictions which were even more stringent than in 21:1–9: he was not to participate in a funeral, even for a close relative, or engage in mourning rites of any kind; he was to marry only a virgin of his own people. vv. 16–23, the regulations about the physical condition of those who could preside at the altar were also rigorous. Just as animals to be sacrificed were to be without physical defect, so the officiating priests were to be without physical blemish. A number of these defects are described, though they may be only representative. Nevertheless, even priests whose physical deformity or disease prevented them from carrying out their priestly duties were still allowed to eat of the priestly gifts.

(**22:1–33**) carries on the theme at the end of ch. 21 by giving laws on holy offerings and who may eat of them. Certain portions of the sacrificial animal and other offerings were to go to the priests, as noted in chs. 5–7. These were sacred and to be eaten only by those qualified and only under certain conditions, vv. 3–16, priests and their families who were in a state of purity, and they alone, were to partake of these offerings. The various sorts of uncleanness are specified, but these do not differ from those already known. The basic rule was that only members of the priest's household could eat, including slaves but not hired servants, and unmarried daughters but not married ones. Any unqualified person who ate of holy things had to restore it plus 20 per cent; cf. at 5:14–16.

vv. 17–25 link again the bodily perfection of both sacrificial animals and the presiding priests. The first part of ch. 22 covers the priest; this section now specifies that all offerings were to be whole, normal animals without major physical defects. Anything which was blind, injured, maimed, or had certain sorts of disease was rejected. Neither was a castrated animal to be accepted. (The implication is that Israelites did not castrate their animals, contrary to the normal practice of those around them.) An animal with a limb extraordinarily short or long could be accepted for a free-will offering but not for a vow. This was the only explicit concession made about blemishes, though how the rules might be interpreted in practice we do not know. v. 21 mentions only the votive (*nēder*) and the free-will (*nēdābâ*) offerings as falling under the well-being offering; this seems to differ from the description given at 7:11–18 which also seems to include the thanksgiving offering (*tôdâ*), though even this is a moot point. See the discussion at LEV 7:11–18. vv. 26–30 list another set of miscellaneous laws. A newborn animal was not to be sacrificed until it had been with its mother 7 days (v. 26), nor were it and its mother to be sacrificed on the same day (v. 27). Any thanksgiving offering had to be eaten on the day it was offered, and anything left over after that time had to be burnt (vv. 29–30). This agrees with 7:15. vv. 31–3 provide a concluding admonition to the chapter.

(Ch. 23) is one of several lists itemizing the major religious festivals (cf. Ex 23:14–17; 34:18–26; Deut 16:1–17), but it tends to be the most detailed and, in the opinion of many, one of the latest. There is also a late list of festivals in Ezek 45:18–25; however, this one is a bit difficult to correlate with the others because it focuses on the duties of the 'prince' and perhaps was not meant to be comprehensive in other respects. The list to be most closely compared to Lev 23 is Num 28–9, however. The conventional view of scholarship has been that Num 28–9 (a part of the P document) is secondary to Lev 23 (a mixture of P and H). This view has now been stood on its head by Knohl (1995; cf. 1987) who argues that H is secondary to P. Specifically, he thinks Lev 23 is an adaptation of Num 28–9 and thus represents the later list. Form-critically, ch. 23 is divided into five commands to Moses for him to speak to Israel: 23:1–8, 9–22, 23–5, 26–32, 33–44. This serves to give each festival an independent treatment, but it also highlights the fact that the weekly sabbath does not fit easily in the list and draws attention to what seem to be additions made to the original list, especially vv. 39–43 (Feast of Booths). For further information on a number of the festivals, see Grabbe (1993: ch. 6).

(23:3) the word 'sabbath' is from the Hebrew root *š-b-t* which means 'rest, cessation'. The basic characteristic of the sabbath was that no work (*mēlā'kâ*) of any kind was to be done. What exactly made up that prohibited work is not stated in this passage and is nowhere else spelled out as such. Outside Leviticus one passage notes that work is also prohibited on the holy days except 'that which each person must eat' (Ex 12:16), suggesting that the preparation of food was allowed on these annual sabbaths but not on the weekly sabbath. The sabbath seems to have a long history in Israel and was hardly invented by the Priestly writers, but it is difficult to say how far back the development of sabbath observance can be pushed. It was once common to regard the sabbath as primarily a post-exilic innovation. Sabbath observance is emphasized mainly in exilic and post-exilic texts (e.g. Isa 56; Neh 13:15–22). There is also the question of the sabbath passage here, since from a form-critical point of view, v. 3 appears to be a later insertion and not part of the original list. Yet some texts generally acknowledged to be pre-exilic seem to presuppose sabbath observance (Hos 2:11; Am 8:5; Isa 1:13), indicating that it was known and followed in some circles as early as the eighth century BCE. Some have even argued for an earlier observance based on such passages as Ex 23:12 and 34:21 (cf. 2 Kings 4:23). Although it does not seem to be clearly attested as early as some of the annual festivals, certain scholars have argued that the weekly sabbath goes far back in Israel's history and is not a late development (see Andreasen 1972; Shafer 1976).

(23:5) briefly mentions the Passover, but Leviticus is otherwise silent about this important celebration. This may not be significant if there is a P document since other passages normally labelled P include a lengthy description of the observance, especially Ex 12:1–20. The important point about Leviticus is that Passover is presupposed but intimately tied up with the Festival of Unleavened Bread (23:6–8). This was the 7-day period when only unleavened bread (*maṣṣôt*) was eaten and no leavening or leavened products were allowed in the land. The festival was inaugurated by the Passover meal, at which unleavened bread was eaten, on the evening between 14 and 15 Nisan. The first full day

(15th) was a holy day, as was the last day (1st). A major question is when the Passover became associated with the Feast of Unleavened Bread. It is now generally admitted that some early traditions do mention the Passover (e.g. Ex 23:18; 34:25). Haran (1962: 317–48) has argued that the Passover was associated with Unleavened Bread from an early time and is already so linked in all the biblical sources. However, his argument that the Passover goes back to a 'nomadic' way of life, with Unleavened Bread arising in settled conditions, is problematic in the light of recent discussion about nomadism and the Israelite settlement (cf. Lemche 1985: esp. 84–163). Haran also makes the point that the Passover in Ex 12 and elsewhere is actually envisaged as a temple sacrifice.

(23:9–14) An important day within the festival of unleavened bread was the Wave Sheaf (ʿōmer) Day. On this day a symbolic sheaf of grain was cut as the first fruits of the harvest and presented before God. In addition, certain specific offerings are enjoined: a male lamb as a burnt offering, a cereal offering of two ephahs of flour mixed with oil, and a quarter hin of wine as a drink offering. This ceremony marked the start of the grain harvest. No bread or grain from the new crop was to be eaten until the first sheaf had been brought. The ceremony took place on the Sunday ('the day after the sabbath') during the days of unleavened bread. In later centuries, the various sects disagreed over whether the 'day after the sabbath' meant the day after the first annual sabbath (the holy day on 15 Nisan) or after the weekly sabbath, but the most natural reading of the Hebrew text was that which interpreted it as the weekly sabbath (cf. Grabbe 2000:141). This date also affected the date of Pentecost.

(23:15–21) The spring grain harvest began on the Wave Sheaf Day and continued for 7 weeks until the Feast of Weeks. For some reason, though, no specific term ('Feast of Weeks' or otherwise) occurs for this festival in Leviticus. The Feast of Weeks did not fall on a specific day of the month but was counted from the Wave Sheaf Day, reckoning 7 sabbaths. The Feast of Weeks (ḥag šabuʿôt: Ex 34:22) was on the day after the seventh sabbath, called the fiftieth day when counting inclusively (i.e. including both the starting and finishing day in the total). Hence, in later times the day was given the Greek name of Pentēkostē 'fiftieth (day)', from which the English Pentecost comes. From later Jewish sources, we know that there

was disagreement among the various sects about the day of this festival. The dispute concerned whether one counted 7 weeks from a floating annual sabbath on 15 Nisan or 7 sabbaths from the first day of the week, to arrive at another first day of the week. (As noted above, the debate mainly concerned the exact time of the Wave Sheaf Day.) Some translations and lexicons render the Hebrew phrase šebaʿ šabbātôt as 'seven weeks', but this would be the only place where šabbāt means week in the OT; more likely is that the word means 'sabbath' here as elsewhere. It was only in Second Temple times that the meaning 'week' developed and allowed some sects to try to count from a fixed day of the month. Hebrew usage and later priestly practice indicate that Shavuot was always celebrated on a Sunday as long as the temple stood and only later became fixed on 6 Sivan as it is among most Jews today (Grabbe 1992: 486). Shavuot also had its own specific offerings. Two loaves of bread were baked from flour made from the new grain and presented before God. Unusually, they were to be baked with leaven; this seems the only exception to the requirement that cereal offerings were to be unleavened, though nothing is said about their being burnt on the altar.

(23:23–5) the first day of the seventh month (Tishri) was a holy day celebrated by the blowing of trumpets. The type of trumpet used is not specified. Another passage usually associated with P mentions a set of silver trumpets to be used for ceremonial occasions and war (Num 10:1–10). One might therefore think of these, but the symbolic blowing may not have been confined to them. The ram's horn (šôpār) associated with the festival in modern times may have been a later development or interpretation, but we have no way of knowing. Other than the blowing of trumpets and the command to do no work, nothing further is stated about this day here. Num 29:1–5 lists sacrifices to be offered, though why they should be omitted here is a problem.

(23:26–32) The tenth day of the seventh month was the Day of Atonement (yôm hakkippûrîm). This passage states that the day is a time of no work, fasting ('you shall afflict your souls'), a holy convocation, with an 'offering of fire' (see at 3:11) to be carried out. No further data are given. Yet we know that the ceremony of the two goats was also associated with this day, as Lev 16 describes in detail. Was the ceremony of Lev 16 once an independent observance which only later became associated with 10 Tishri? Most of the chapter gives no indication of when the ceremony was to take place. It is only towards the end of the chapter (16:29–34) that the ritual is connected with the Day of Atonement known from Lev 23.

(23:33–6, 39–43) The Feast of Booths or Tabernacles (*sukkôt*) was the final festival of the year, celebrated after the autumn harvest (23:33–6, 39–43) on 15–22 Tishri. It probably arose from the practice of farmers who would build a temporary shelter (booth) in the field to sleep in to protect the harvest and maximize the daylight until it was gathered. The people were to take fruit, palm leaves, tree branches, and willows and make booths as a part of the celebration. The first day was a holy day on which no work was to be done, as was the eighth day. As with the Day of Trumpets, no sacrifices are listed for Sukkot in Leviticus. At Num 29:12–39, however, we find that an elaborate series of sacrifices was to take place, with each of the eight days having its own particular ceremony. They followed a diminishing series, beginning with 13 bulls on the first day, 12 bulls on the second, and so on down to 7 bulls on the seventh day. The eighth day had its own separate ceremony.

(24:1–9) describes the lamps and the bread of the presence in the foyer of the temple. Why this section and the next (24:10–23) go here is not immediately apparent, but both 24:2–4 and 24:5–9 relate to the area inside the Holy Place, in front of the curtain separating it from the Holy of Holies. A very pure olive oil was to be provided to keep the lampstand burning on a regular basis (vv. 2–4). (The concept of a perpetual lamp occurs in 1 Sam 3:3.) There was also to be a table on which 12 loaves (along with frankincense) were to be placed each sabbath. The frankincense was burned at the end of the week, and the priests were allowed to eat the loaves. This was known as the 'bread of presence' or 'show bread'. It is these loaves or something similar which David and his men ate in 1 Sam 21:1–6. This bread is referred to in passing at Ex 39:36, but it is a puzzle why an actual description is delayed until this point in Leviticus.

(24:10–23) discusses the question of blasphemy. Here and there within Leviticus narrative replaces direct commands. In such cases, the episode seems meant to explain what should be done by example rather than just instruction. It is similar to Lev 8–10 which is

also a narrative section and, especially, to Num 15:32–6 where a sinner is likewise imprisoned until God decides the punishment for the crime (in this case, the sin is sabbath-breaking). The passage is made of up two sections: a narrative about the blasphemer and his ultimate fate (vv. 10–12, 23), and the command of YHWH not only about blasphemy but also other sins (vv. 13–22). The narrative tells how a man with an Israelite mother but an Egyptian father used God's name in a blasphemous way. He was put in custody until God could be consulted. God's judgement was that he be stoned to death by the entire community. Anyone in the future blaspheming with God's name was likewise to be executed by stoning. The commands of YHWH (vv. 13–22) concern not only blasphemy but also causing death to a man (which brings the death penalty) or a beast (compensation has to be paid), and they apply not only to Israelites but also to the resident alien. Within this section is an inset paragraph about life and reciprocation of punishment, otherwise known as the *lex talionis*.

(24:17–22) makes the point of the importance of life, especially human life. The one who kills a person is to be executed. Anyone who kills an animal must make restitution. There is also the principle that injuries were to be compensated by having a reciprocal injury done to the perpetrator, the famous 'eye for an eye and a tooth for a tooth'. This law has often been misunderstood as if it were a primitive barbaric practice which embarrassed legislators later did their best to soften. In fact, the earlier principle was that a person injuring another was to pay compensation. For example, the earliest Mesopotamian law codes (Eshnuna 42–7; Ur-Nammu 15–19 = A324–325? || B§§13–24) have monetary compensation. In the case of an extended family or community, that was the simplest way of handling it. The injured party received some benefit, or at least his family did. On the other hand, the later law codes (Hammurabi 195–223) evoke the *lex talionis* for those of equal status (though monetary compensation applies to injury of someone of lower status). The *lex talionis* was an important advance in jurisprudence for two reasons: first, it made all equal before the law. The rich man could not get away with his crime of injuring another by monetary payment. The 'eye for an eye' principle was a great leveller. Secondly, it marks the stage at which the tribe or state takes over the function of justice from the local community.

(Chs. 25–6) seem to be envisaged as a unit by the author or editor, because they consist of one speech by YHWH to Moses and because they are marked off by an *inclusio* (the phrase 'on Mount Sinai') in the first verse (25:1) and the last verse (26:46). Each of the two chapters has different subject-matter and can be treated separately, but they are also connected in that the punishments of ch. 26 are in part the result of not observing the sabbatical year commanded in ch. 25.

(Ch. 25) describes two year-long observances: the seventh or sabbatical year (year of release: *šĕmiṭṭâ*) in vv. 2–7, and the jubilee (*yôbēl*) year in vv. 8–55. Comparison has been made with the Mesopotamian *mîšarum* and the *andurāru* (Lewy 1958) which go back to the Old Babylonian and Old Assyrian periods (early second millennium BCE). Among the points to note are the following: Babylonian *andurāru* is cognate with the Hebrew *dĕrôr* release. A king would declare a *mîšarum* which was a general declaration of justice. He might also declare an *andurāru* 'release', which could include a remission of certain taxes, a release of debts, reversion of property to its original owners, or manumission of slaves. It was common for a king to declare such in his first year of reign. The Israelite innovation was to declare a jubilee at regular intervals rather than in the first year of a king as in Mesopotamia. The Akkadian evidence for the *mîšarum* and *andurāru* is generally accepted (cf. Finkelstein 1961), but its interpretation in relation to the Israelite institution is not necessarily simple. In solidly argued studies of both the biblical and the Mesopotamian evidence, N. P. Lemche (1976; 1979) found a lot of sloppy comparison in earlier studies. For example, OT material was used to interpret the Old Babylonian which was then used to interpret the Israelite, with clear dangers of circular reasoning. The existence of the practice of a king's granting a release in his first year in the Old Babylonian period proves nothing about the antiquity of the jubilee in Israel which is, after all, somewhat different. Lemche admits some evidence for the antiquity of a seventh fallow year in agriculture, but the development of a sabbatical year with all its social accoutrements seems late.

(25:2–7) envisages a basic cycle of 7-year periods or sabbatical years. The last year of this cycle was a year when the land had to be left fallow. No crops were to be sown. That which grew up by itself (volunteer growth)

was allowed, and the people could eat it for food on a day-to-day basis, but no harvesting as such was permitted. Of course, by a divine miracle there would be no hardship since the land would produce enough in the sixth year to tide the inhabitants over to the harvest of the crops sown in the new cycle (vv. 19–22). In Leviticus the seventh year seems to be primarily an agricultural observance (cf. also Ex 23:10–11). According to some passages, however, loans and the enslavement of Israelites were also cancelled in the seventh year (Deut 15:1–3, 12–15; Jer 34:8–16). If so, the seventh year would have been an integral part of the nation's life, with widespread implications for the economy. On the other hand, there seems to be a contradiction between Leviticus, which sees the year of release as the jubilee, and those other passages which ascribe release to the sabbatical year (see below). This suggests that we find two separate systems, one in which the year of release is the seventh year, and the other in which the year of release is the fiftieth. Those texts which view the seventh year as the year of release do not seem to envisage a jubilee year at all.

The existence of a sabbatical year is attested in historical sources of the Second Temple period (Grabbe 1991: 60–3). This included a rest from growing crops, at least from the time of the Maccabees (1 Macc 6:49, 53; Josephus, *Ant.* 13.7.4–8.1 §§ 228–35; 14.16.2 § 475). We also know from actual documents found in the Judean Desert that the cancellation of debts and return of property in the seventh year was a known institution (*Murabba'at* 18; 24). There is no mention of the jubilee year, however, except in literature such as the *Book of Jubilees*. The indication is, therefore, that the sabbatical year but not the jubilee was observed in Second Temple times. It is also reasonable to conclude that the seventh year was in some way observed in early post-exilic times, though how much further back it can be projected is a question. Whether the jubilee was ever observed is a matter of speculation.

The tithing cycle is not mentioned in Leviticus (or other P passages) but, if a sabbatical year existed, the tithes of Deut 14–15 would work only if operated on a 7-year cycle. That is, the tithe of the third year (Deut 14:28–9) would have to be coordinated with the seventh year, or it would sometimes fall on the sabbatical year when there was no produce on which to pay tithes. Thus, the tithe of the third year would have been paid on the third and sixth year out of the cycle rather than forming an independent

3-year cycle. On the matter of tithing in general, see Grabbe (1993: 66–72).

(25:8–55) describes the jubilee which took place after seven sabbatical-year cycles. The text is somewhat ambiguous. On the one hand, the jubilee might be thought to coincide with the last year of the seventh cycle (Lev 25:8); on the other hand, it is explicitly said to be the fiftieth year (Lev 25:10–11). If it was indeed the fiftieth year, it would mean two fallow years in a row, yet nothing is said about the effects of such a situation or how to cope with it. The later Jewish *Book of Jubilees* definitely counts a jubilee cycle of 49 years, showing that the 'fiftieth year' might be counted inclusively (i.e. including both the starting and finishing years in the calculation). It may be that this is what the author of Lev 25 has in mind, but the point is never clarified.

vv. 13–28, the jubilee was also a fallow year but, according to Leviticus, it was more than this; it was a year of release (also Lev 27:16–24; Num 36:4). Land was to return to its original family. Agrarian land was considered an inalienable heritage granted by God and to be kept in the family in perpetuity. Therefore, the land could not be sold permanently. Any sale was viewed really as a long-term lease which reverted back to the family in the jubilee year. The sale price was determined according to the length of time to the next jubilee, so that the purchaser was really paying for the number of crops obtained before it reverted to the original owners; the less time until the jubilee, the less was paid for the property. vv. 29–34 note that town property was treated differently and could be transferred without right of repossession, after a probation year in which the seller could change his mind and redeem it. On the other hand, Levitical property was treated like agrarian land in that it would revert to the original owner at the jubilee. vv. 35–55 deal with the question of helping the poor and needy among the Israelites by necessary loans, without charging interest. It moves on to the question of debt slavery. Slavery was accepted as an institution (as, indeed, it was in the NT). Foreign slaves could be bought and sold as chattels (vv. 44–6), though there were laws which regulated how they were treated (e.g. Deut 21:15–17). But Israelites were not to be treated as slaves. If someone sold himself or his family because of debts or poverty, the person was to be treated as a hired servant. He may also redeem himself or be redeemed by a relative, the redemption

price being calculated according to the number of years until the jubilee. If he is not redeemed, he and his family were allowed to go free in the jubilee year. On the question of the release of slaves and cancellation of loans, there is some contradiction between Leviticus and other passages, as already noted above. Lev 25 and Lev 27 are the only descriptions of the jubilee year.

(26:1–46) is mainly composed of a list of blessings for obedience and curses for disobedience, and makes a fitting end to the book. An appropriate literary closure of a book such as this is a section which demonstrates the consequences of heeding or not heeding the commands contained in it. A similar conclusion is found in Deut 28. Such blessings and curses are well known from other ancient Near-Eastern literature. International treaties usually ended with a list of blessings and, especially, curses for disobedience (cf. McCarthy 1978: 172–87). The so-called 'law codes' often include a similar section. For example, the epilogue to the Code of Hammurabi spells out how the gods will punish the king in various ways for not heeding the marvellous laws which had just been listed (*ANET* 163–5). Probably the clearest example of an international treaty is that of Esarhaddon (Wiseman 1958; *ANET* 534–41). As with the list in Lev 26, the curses tend to dominate, with the blessings listed only briefly.

vv. 1–2 at first sight seem out of place in the context of chs. 25–6. However, they may form a connecting section between the two chapters. vv. 3–13 list the blessings for obedience which come first. There seem to be four of these, based on the formal structure (Hartley 1992): rain in due season (vv. 4–5), peace (vv. 6–8), fertility (vv. 9–10), and God's presence (vv. 11–13), though victory over enemies could be said to be a fifth (vv. 7–8), judging from the content (Porter 1976). vv. 14–38 give a much longer and more clearly structured section on the curses for disobedience. Five sections are marked off with the phrase, 'If you (still) disobey, I will punish you sevenfold' or similar words. The desire seems to be to create a crescendo effect, so that the longer the Israelites refuse to obey, the stronger becomes the punishment, multiplying sevenfold each time. This does not seem to be carried through consistently, though there is a sort of climax in the exile from the land. In fact, the individual curses seem to be listed by subject rather than according to any sense of increasing malignancy: defeat in battle (vv. 14–17), drought (vv. 18–20), wild animals (vv. 21–2), war, pestilence, famine (vv. 23–6), dire conditions and exile (vv. 27–39). Finally, hope is expressed for repentence and a return from captivity (vv. 39–45).

vv. 31–45 end the chapter with reference to an exile and return, which led many scholars to claim that this shows knowledge of the Exile of the Jews in 587/586 BCE and their return in 538. This may be a correct interpretation, but it is interesting to note that one of the traditional punishments is to have the people of the land taken captive (e.g. Codex Hammurabi, xxvi. 73–80; xxviii. 19–23). If the actual Exile is presupposed, the writer is surprisingly vague about the details; alternatively, the account of the Exile known to him was rather different from that described elsewhere in the OT. This suggests that the punishment of exile was a traditional one in such curses and not necessarily to be related to the historical situation. v. 46 forms a concluding piece. Is it the conclusion of ch. 26 only or is it a conclusion to a larger section? Its reference to 'statutes' (ḥuqqîm), 'judgements' (mišpāṭîm), and 'laws/teachings' (tôrôt) suggest that something larger than a chapter or even a couple of chapters is intended. Thus, this seems to be a concluding formula for the entire book (Hartley 1992: 414).

(Ch. 27) describes vows and tithe of livestock. It is also an important chapter about support for the priesthood. The chapter is usually seen as an appendix to the book and not part of the Holiness Code proper. The reason is that ch. 26 makes an appropriate ending with its general blessings and curses and, as noted above, 26:46 fits well as a concluding statement for the entire book. On the other hand, in the present structure of the book ch. 27 is parallel with chs. 1–7 in giving specific halakic instructions. Also, just as Deuteronomy does not end with the blessings and curses of ch. 28, so the final editors of Leviticus may have been reluctant to end with ch. 26. Therefore, Lev 27 may indeed be a later addition but one which the final editors regarded as appropriate and even essential.

(27:1–29) Much of this chapter is devoted to the question of vows and consecration of objects and property to God. It was possible to dedicate human beings, animals, houses, and land to God. vv. 2–8: if the dedicated object was a person, then he or she had to be redeemed by money. The valuation of the redemption money was according to age and sex and seems to be primarily economic; that is, it is

according to how much the person is likely to earn by physical labour. This means that males were worth more than females of a similar age, and adults in their prime were worth more than children, youths, or the elderly. vv. 9–13, if an animal suitable for offering had been vowed, it had to be sacrificed, with no substitution being allowed. Any attempt at substitution meant that both the original vow and the substitute became dedicated to God. However, in the case of an unclean animal no sacrifice was possible. Therefore, it had to be redeemed by its valuation plus 20 per cent. vv. 14–15, if a house was dedicated, it could also be redeemed by paying its value plus 20 per cent. vv. 16–24: land was valued in relation to the jubilee year. In other words, the number of harvests remaining until the jubilee was calculated and the value set according to that number. Inherited land could then be redeemed for its valuation plus 20 per cent. If the owner did not redeem the land and it was sold, however, it was no longer in his power to redeem. Instead it became priestly property. According to Deut 18:1–21, Levites (including priests) were not to own land as individuals. Apparently, though, the temple and priesthood could own land jointly. (We know that such was the case in the Second Temple period.) Land which had been purchased (as opposed to inherited) did not belong perpetually to the purchaser but reverted to the original owner in the jubilee. Thus, if such land was consecrated, it would still go back to the owner in the jubilee, so its valuation without any addition was given to the priests.

vv. 26–7, firstling animals belonged automatically to God. This brief mention is all that Leviticus has on the subject. Other passages of priestly instruction fill this out (Ex 13:11–15; 34:19–20; Num 18:15–18): all clean animals were to be offered at the altar, with the appropriate portions burned, but the rest of the meat went entirely to the priests. Unclean animals were more complicated since there seems to be more than one set of instructions. It is clear that they were normally to be redeemed, though Ex 34:20 says this was to be with a lamb, whereas Lev 27:27 states that it is by their monetary value plus 20 per cent. Similarly, if not redeemed, 27:27 says they were to be sold for their assessed value, with the money going to the temple personnel, but Ex 34:20 says the animal's neck was to be broken.

vv. 28–9 devoted things (ḥērem) belonged solely to God and were not to be made use of by man. They could not be sold or redeemed.

A devoted human being was to be put to death. This last statement is puzzling because normally the human beings which belonged to God were to be redeemed. For example, the first-born were to be redeemed for money because their place was taken by the Levites (Num 3:5–13; 18:15). It seems unlikely that an Israelite would be allowed to devote another Israelite to God in this way. Therefore, it is unclear who the devoted person might be who would be put to death; however, there are several examples of prisoners-of-war being slain at God's orders, suggesting that this might be what was in mind (cf. Josh 10:24–7; 1 Sam 15).

(27:30–3) speaks of the tithe of livestock. The tithe of animals is nowhere else referred to in the Pentateuch. They were to be tithed apparently by running them past and cutting out every tenth animal, regardless of whether it was good or bad. If the owner tried to substitute an animal, not only was the original tithe animal still considered as belonging to YHWH but also the substitute. The point was that no substitution was to be made. Nothing is said about how the tithe was to be used. By inference from other passages (2 Chr 31:6), it was to go to the priests as a part of their income. A number of questions arise. Why is not the tithe of animals referred to elsewhere in the OT (apart from 2 Chr 31:6)? How was the tithing to be carried out? If the entire herd or flock was run by each year, the breeding stock would gradually become decimated (literally). Would it just have been the new crop of calves, kids, and lambs each time? This makes sense, but no discussion is given. Why? Is it because this was only a theoretical law which was never put into practice? Giving the first-born of each breeding animal would equal roughly 10 per cent, so how did the tithe relate to the command about the first-born? The question of how these instructions of Leviticus related to the actual situation in Israel is brought forcefully to our attention in these verses. For a further comment on the situation, see LEV E.4 above.

REFERENCES

Andreasen, N.-E. A. (1972), *The Old Testament Sabbath*, SBL Dissertation 7 (Missoula, Mont: Scholars Press).

Blenkinsopp, J. (1996), 'An Assessment of the Alleged Pre-Exilic Date of the Priestly Material in the Pentateuch', *ZAW* 108: 495–518.

Bloch-Smith, E. (1992), *Judahite Burial Practices and Beliefs about the Dead*, JSOTSup 123; JSOT/ASOR MS, 7 (Sheffield: JSOT).

Childs, B. S. (1979), *Introduction to the Old Testament as Scripture* (Philadelphia: Fortress).

Cross, F. M. (1947), 'The Priestly Tabernacle', *BA* 10: 45–68 (= *BAR* 1: 201–28).

Damrosch, D. (1987), 'Leviticus', in R. Alter and F. Kermode (eds.), *The Literary Guide to the Bible* (London: Collins), 66–77.

Day, J. (1989), *Molech: A God of Human Sacrifice in the Old Testament*, University of Cambridge Oriental Publications, 41 (Cambridge University Press).

Douglas, M. (1966), *Purity and Danger: An Analysis of the Concepts of Pollution and Taboo* (London: Routledge & Kegan Paul).

—— (1993), 'The Forbidden Animals in Leviticus', *JSOT* 59: 3–23.

Elliger, K. (1966), *Leviticus*, HAT 4 (Tübingen: Mohr [Siebeck]).

Finkelstein, J. J. (1961), 'Amisaduqa's Edict and the Babylonian "Law Codes" ', *JCS* 15: 91–104.

Gennep, A. van (1960), *The Rites of Passage* (London: Routledge & Kegan Paul).

Gerstenberger, E. S. (1993), *Das dritte Buch Mose: Leviticus*, ATD 6 (Göttingen: Vandenhoeck & Ruprecht); ET *Leviticus: A Commentary*, OTL, tr. Douglas W. Stott (London: SCM; Louisville, Ky.: Westminster/John Knox, 1996).

Gorman, F. H., Jr. (1990), *The Ideology of Ritual: Space, Time and Status in the Priestly Theology*, JSOTSup 91 (Sheffield: Sheffield Academic Press).

Grabbe, L. L. (1987), 'The Scapegoat Ritual: A Study in Early Jewish Interpretation', *JSJ* 18: 152–67.

—— (1991), 'Maccabean Chronology: 167–164 or 168–165 BCE?' *JBL* 110: 59–74.

—— (1992), *Judaism from Cyrus to Hadrian*, i. *Persian and Greek Periods*; ii. *Roman Period* (Minneapolis: Fortress); British edn. in one vol. (London: SCM, 1994).

—— (1993), *Leviticus*, SOTS, Old Testament Guides (Sheffield: JSOT).

—— (1995), *Priests, Prophets, Diviners, Sages: A Socio-Historical Study of Religious Specialists in Ancient Israel* (Valley Forge, Pa.: Trinity Int.).

—— (ed.) (1997), *Can a History of Israel Be Written?* JSOTSup 245 = European Seminar in Historical Methodology, 1 (Sheffield: Sheffield Academic Press).

—— (2000), *Judaic Religion in the Second Temple Period: Belief and Practice from the Exile to Yavneh* (London: Routledge).

Haran, M. (1962), 'Shilo and Jerusalem: The Origin of the Priestly Tradition in the Pentateuch', *JBL* 81: 14–24.

—— (1978), *Temples and Temple-Service in Ancient Israel* (Oxford: Clarendon).

Hartley, J. E. (1992), *Leviticus*, WBC 4 (Dallas: Word Books).

Hecht, R. (1979–80), 'Patterns of Exegesis in Philo's Interpretation of Leviticus', *Studia Philonica*, 6: 77–155.

Heider, G. C. (1985), *The Cult of Molek: A Reassessment*, JSOTSup 43 (Sheffield: JSOT).

Houston, W. (1993), *Purity and Monotheism: Clean and Unclean Animals in Biblical Law*, JSOTSup 140 (Sheffield: Sheffield Academic Press).

Hübner, U. (1989), 'Schweine, Schweineknochen und ein Speiseverbot im Alten Israel', *VT* 39: 225–36.

Hurvitz, A. (1982), *A Linguistic Study of the Relationship between the Priestly Source and the Book of Ezekiel: A New Approach to an Old Problem*, Cahiers de la Revue Biblique, 20 (Paris: Gabalda).

—— (1988), 'Dating the Priestly Source in Light of the Historical Study of Biblical Hebrew: A Century after Wellhausen', *ZAW* 100 Suppl., 88–100.

Janowski, B. and Wilhelm, G. (1993), 'Der Bock, der die Sünden hinausträgt: Zur Religionsgeschichte des Azazel-Ritus Lev 16,10.21 f', in Bernd Janowski, Klaus Koch, and Gernot Wilhelm (eds.), *Religionsgeschichtliche Beziehungen zwischen Kleinasien, Nordsyrien und dem Alten Testament: Internationales Symposion Hamburg 17.–21. März 1990*, OBO 129 (Fribourg: Universitätsverlag; Göttingen: Vandenhoeck 69.

Jenson, P. P. (1992), *Graded Holiness: A Key to the Priestly Conception of the World*, JSOTSup 106 (Sheffield: Sheffield Academic Press).

Kellermann, D. (1977), *"āshām"*, *TDOT* (Grand Rapids, Mich.: Eerdmans), i. 429–37.

Kilian, R. (1963), *Literarkritische und formgeschichtliche Untersuchung des Heiligkeitsgesetzes*, BBB 19 (Bonn: Peter Hanstein).

Kirschner, R. (1982–3), 'Rabbinic and Philonic Exegesis of the Nadab and Abihu Incident (Lev. 10:1–6)', *JQR* 73: 375–93.

Kiuchi, N. (1987), *The Purification Offering in the Priestly Literature: Its Meaning and Function*, JSOTSup 56 (Sheffield: JSOT).

Knierim, R. P. (1992), *Text and Concept in Leviticus 1:1–9: A Case in Exegetical Method*, FAT 2 (Tübingen: Mohr [Siebeck]).

Knohl, I. (1987), 'The Priestly Torah Versus the Holiness School: Sabbath and the Festivals', *HUCA* 58: 65–117.

—— (1995), *The Sanctuary of Silence: The Priestly Torah and the Holiness School* (Minneapolis: Fortress).

Koch, K. (1959), *Die Priesterschrift von Exodus 25 bis Leviticus 16: Eine überlieferungsgeschichtliche und literarische Untersuchung*, FRLANT 71 (Göttingen: Vandenhoeck & Ruprecht).

Lemche, N. P. (1976), 'The Manumission of Slaves—the Fallow Year—the Sabbatical Year—the Jobel Year', *VT* 26: 38–59.

Lemche, N. P. (1979), 'Andurārum and Mīšarum: Comments on the Problem of Social Edicts and Their Application in the Ancient Near East', *JNES* 38: 11–22.

—— (1985), *Early Israel: Anthropological and Historical Studies on the Israelite Society before the Monarchy*, VTSup 37 (Leiden: Brill).

—— (1991), *The Canaanites and Their Land: The Tradition of the Canaanites*, JSOTSup 110 (Sheffield: Sheffield Academic Press).

—— (1993), 'The Old Testament—a Hellenistic Book', *SJOT* 7:163–93.

Levine, B. A. (1974), *In the Presence of the Lord: A Study of Cult and Some Cultic Terms in Ancient Israel*, SJLA 5 (Leiden: Brill).

Lewy, H. (1958), 'The Biblical Institution of D^erôr in the Light of Akkadian Documents', *EI* 5: 21*–31*.

McCarthy, D. J. (1978), *Treaty and Covenant*, 2nd edn., AnBib 21A (Rome: Biblical Institute).

Marx, A. (1989), 'Sacrifice pour les péchés ou rites de passage? Quelques réflexions sur la fonction du, *ḥaṭṭā't*, *RB* 96: 27–48.

—— (1994), *Les Offrandes végétales dans l'Ancien Testament: Du tribut d'hommage au repas eschatologique*, VTSup 57 (Leiden: Brill).

Milgrom, J. (1976), *Cult and Conscience: The ASHAM and the Priestly Doctrine of Repentance* (Leiden: Brill).

—— (1991), *Leviticus 1–16*, AB 3 (Garden City, NY: Doubleday).

—— (1992), 'Priestly ("P") Source', *ABD* v. 454–61.

Morgenstern, J. (1955), 'The Decalogue of the Holiness Code', *HUCA* 26: 1–27.

Newsom, C. A., and Ringe, S. H. (eds.) (1992), *The Women's Bible Commentary* (Louisville, Ky.: Westminster/John Knox; London: SPCK).

Noth, M. (1977), *Leviticus: A Commentary*, OTL, rev. trans. (London: SCM).

Porter, J. R. (1976), *Leviticus*, Cambridge Bible Commentary on the New English Bible (Cambridge: Cambridge University Press).

Rattray, S. (1987), 'Marriage Rules, Kinship Terms and Family Structure in the Bible', *Society of Biblical Literature Abstracts and Seminar Papers*, 26, ed. K. Richards (Atlanta: Scholars Press), 537–44.

Rendtorff, R. (1963), *Die Gesetze in der Priesterschrift: Eine gattungs-geschichtliche Untersuchung*, 2nd edn. (Göttingen: Vandenhoeck & Ruprecht).

—— (1982–95), *Leviticus*, BKAT 3 (Neukirchen-Vluyn: Neukirchener Verlag).

Reventlow, H. G. (1961), *Das Heiligkeitsgesetz formgeschichtlich untersucht*, WMANT (Neukirchen-Vluyn: Neukirchener Verlag).

Schüssler Fiorenza, E. (ed.) (1994a), with the assistance of S. Matthews, *Searching the Scriptures*, i. *A Feminist Introduction* (London: SCM).

—— (1994b), with the assistance of A. Brock and S. Matthews, *Searching the Scriptures* ii. *A Feminist Commentary* (London: SCM).

Schmidt, B. B. (1994), *Israel's Beneficent Dead: Ancestor Cult and Necromancy in Ancient Israelite Religion and Tradition*, FAT 11 (Tübingen: Mohr[Siebeck]).

Schwartz, B. J. (1991), 'The Prohibitions Concerning the "Eating" of Blood in Leviticus 17', in G. A. Anderson and S. M. Olyan (eds.), *Priesthood and Cult in Ancient Israel*, JSOTSup 125 (Sheffield: Sheffield Academic Press), 34–66.

Shafer, B. E. (1976), 'Sabbath', *IDBSup* 760–2.

Wegner, J. R. (1992), 'Leviticus', in C. A. Newsom and S. H. Ringe (eds.), *The Women's Bible Commentary* (Louisville, Ky.: Westminster/John Knox; London: SPCK), 36–44.

Wenham, G. J. (1979), *The Book of Leviticus*, NICOT (Grand Rapids, Mich.: Eerdmans).

Whybray, R. N. (1987), *The Making of the Pentateuch: A Methodological Study*, JSOTSup 53 (Sheffield: JSOT).

Wiseman, D. J. (1958), 'The Vassal-Treaties of Esarhaddon', *Iraq* 20, Part 1.

Wright, D. P. (1987), *The Disposal of Impurity: Elimination Rites in the Bible and in Hittite and Mesopotamian Literature*, SBL Dissertation, 101 (Atlanta: Scholars Press).

Zevit, Z. (1982), 'Converging Lines of Evidence Bearing on the Date of P', *ZAW* 94: 481–511.

7. Numbers

TERENCE E. FRETHEIM

INTRODUCTION

A. Character. 1. The book of Numbers, named for its census lists, is the most complex of the books of the Pentateuch. This can be seen in the variety of types of literature represented, e.g. lists, itineraries, various statutes, ritual and priestly prescriptions, poetic oracles, songs, wilderness stories, and even a well-known benediction (6:22–7). The interweaving of law and narrative characteristic of Exodus and Deuteronomy is most evident in Numbers; specific statutes again and again emerge from specific life situations, revealing a dynamic relationship of law and life.

2. Moreover, some of these texts border on the bizarre, with talking donkeys, curses from a non-Israelite diviner turned into blessings that have messianic implications, the earth swallowing up people, copper snakes that have healing powers, an almond-producing rod, an execution for picking up sticks on the sabbath, Miriam turning leprous, and repulsive instructions for discerning a wife's faithfulness. One is tempted to claim that these strange goings-on were constructed to match the incredible character of Israel's response to its God. To complicate these matters, God is often depicted in ways that challenge traditional understandings; at times it seems that God's identity is in the process of being shaped too.

B. Source and Tradition. 1. The origin of Numbers is also complex. Most scholars consider the book to be a composite of sources (both oral and written) from various historical periods. The book itself speaks of sources, the Book of the Wars of the Lord (21:14) and popular songs (21:17–18, 27–30). The tradition most identifiable is the Priestly writing (in several redactions), with its interest in matters of worship and priesthood; it is most attested in chs. 1–10; 26–36, and provides continuity with Ex 25–40 and Leviticus. Other sources, such as J and E (esp. in chs. 11–25), are more difficult to distinguish; it is common to speak simply of an older epic tradition. The association of blocks of texts with three primary locales (Sinai, 1:1–10:10; Kadesh, chs. 13–20; Moab, chs. 22–36) could reflect a way in which traditions were gathered over time. Beyond this, editorial activity seems unusually common (for detail, see Milgrom 1990: pp. xvii–xxi).

2. Also of scholarly import has been the study of individual traditions and their development, e.g. the Balaam cycle, the murmuring stories, the censuses, the wilderness encampment, the Transjordan conquest, the cities of refuge, land apportionment, and the priesthood. It is clear from such work that various Israelite interests from different times and places inform the present redaction. These traditions have in time (perhaps during and after the Exile) been brought together to form a unified composition, but the character of that unity has been difficult to discern.

C. Structure. 1. The structure of Numbers, often thought to be non-existent, is best seen from two angles, those of the census lists and the geography of a journey.

2. The Census Lists (for detail, see Olson 1985). The overarching structure of the book is laid out in terms of its two census lists (chs. 1; 26). The first registers the generation that experienced the Exodus and the giving of the law at Sinai, which is prepared to move towards the land of promise. When faced with dangers, however, the people do not trust the promise; they experience God's judgement (14:32–3) and finally, in the wake of apostasy, die off in a plague (25:9). Even Moses and Aaron mistrust God and are prohibited from entering the land (20:12); only the faithful scouts, Caleb and Joshua, and the young (14:29) are allowed to do so. The oracles of Balaam (chs. 22–4) provide a hopeful sign of things to come, as God blesses the insiders through this outsider.

3. The second census (ch. 26) lists the members of the new generation (though no births are reported in Numbers). They are a sign of God's continuing faithfulness to ancestral promises and will enter the land. The following texts (chs. 27–36) raise issues focused on the future in the land. No deaths, no murmurings, and no rebellions against the leadership are in view, while various hopeful signs are presented. This new generation is the audience for Deuteronomy.

4. Generally speaking, the censuses include representatives from each of the twelve tribes. This inclusiveness may have functioned in the wake of various devastating events in Israel's history as an assurance that all tribes were included among the chosen (see Douglas 1993).

5. The Geography of a Journey. The movement through Numbers can also be tracked in terms of three stages of a journey toward the fulfilment of the land promise, with all the problems encountered along the way in spite of careful preparations. The itinerary of 33:2–49 emphasizes the importance of the journey as such, apart from specific occasions. Laws are integrated into the story, providing for an ongoing ordering of the community as it encounters new situations. The positive opening and closing sections enclose a sharply negative picture.

(*a*) Numbers begins with the people still situated at Sinai, preparing to leave (1:1–10:10). That includes the organization of the camp and various statutes, especially regarding the sanctuary and its leadership. A somewhat idealistic picture emerges: a community ordered in all ways appropriate to God's dwelling in the centre of the camp, and the precise obedience to every divine command (e.g. 1:17–19, 54). The reader may wonder how anything could go wrong.

(*b*) In episodic fashion, Israel moves through the wilderness from Sinai to Transjordan (10:11–

25:18). The disjunction with the opening (and closing) chapters is remarkable: obedience to God's command turns to rebellion; trust becomes mistrust; the holy is profaned; order becomes disorder; the future of the people of God is threatened. Continuities with the wilderness journey story in Ex 15:22–19:1 are seen in the gifts of quail and manna, the ongoing complaints, and military victory; but discontinuities are also sharply presented, evident especially in the conflict among leaders, sin, and divine judgement. Integrated with these journey reports are miscellaneous statutes (chs. 15; 18; 19), focused on purification and leadership support, the need for which grows out of these experiences.

(*c*) The journey concludes in the plains of Moab (26:1–36:13). This is an entirely positive stage. Conflicts are resolved through negotiation and compromise and land begins to be settled. Various statutes anticipate the future in the land; the community is to so order its life that this new dwelling-place of both God and people will not be polluted.

6. These three stages may also be characterized in terms of Israel's changing relationship with God, moving from fidelity to unfaithfulness and back to fidelity. But, through all these developments, God remains faithful and does not turn back from the ancestral promises to Israel (articulated most clearly by Balaam). Though Israel's journey involves judgement, that judgement is finally in the service of God's objectives of blessing and salvation.

7. Such a portrayal mirrors the situation of the implied (exilic) readers of the Pentateuch (for details, see the proposal in Fretheim 1996: 40–65). Israel's apostasy and experience of divine judgement lie in their recent past; signs of a hopeful future are articulated in both law and promise. The paradigm of old generation and new generation would be especially pertinent during the years of exile in a situation which could be seen to have parallels with that of the Israelites in the wilderness.

D. Leading Themes. 1. Certain themes provide compass points for negotiating the journey through Numbers: the wilderness book, the ancestral promises, the divine presence and guidance, divine revelation and human leadership, and holy people and holy priests.

2. A Wilderness Book. The entire book is set in the wilderness. Appropriately, 'In the Wilderness' is the Hebrew title for Numbers. This setting presents problems and possibilities for shaping a community identity for the newly redeemed people of God. As a long-oppressed community, Israel has a deeply ingrained identity as 'slave'. It does not have the resources to move quickly to a 'slaves no more' (Lev 26:13) mentality; God must be at work to enable them to 'walk erect' once again. The period of wandering is a necessary buffer between liberation and landedness for the sake of forming such an identity. Such a process does not unfold easily for Israel or for God; even the most meticulous preparations for the journey are not able to make things go right. It is possible to take the people out of Egypt, but it proves difficult to take Egypt out of the people. The familiar orderliness of Egypt seems preferable to the insecurities of life lived from one oasis to the next. In other words, the problem is not so much the law as an inability to rely on the God who has brought freedom and keeps promises.

3. Israel's time in the wilderness is finally shaped by God's extraordinary patience and mercy, and the divine will to stay with Israel in this time of adolescence. No divine flick of the wrist is capable of straightening them out without compromising their freedom. If God wants a mature child, the possibility of defiance must be risked. But it soon becomes clear that the process of maturation will take longer than a single generation. God will not compromise in holding Israel to high standards.

4. Ancestral Promises. God is committed to the ancestral promises, especially of land. As Israel moves out from Sinai, the goal is the land God is 'giving' (10:29 and often). Conditions regarding the land promise are expressed (14:8), which affect the future of individuals—even an entire generation—but not finally Israel as such. Beyond that, the promises are spoken almost exclusively by Balaam. His oracles ironically gather the clearest references to the promises in Numbers; no Israelite, including Moses, has standing enough left to bring them to expression.

5. The middle section (chs. 11–25) problematizes the movement toward fulfilment; the wilderness is a time of endangered promises. Again and again the people trust the deceptive securities of the past more than God's promised future (11:5; 21:5). Hence, they experience disasters of various kinds that threaten progress towards the goal, including plagues (11:33; 16:49), an abortive conquest (chs. 13–14), and snake infestation (21:6).

6. The final section (chs. 26–36), with the new generation in place, bespeaks confidence in the promises with the apportionment of lands (26:53–6) and the specification of boundaries (34:1–15). Initial settlements in Transjordan function as a 'down-payment' on the fulfilment of the promise (chs. 31–2). Moreover, various laws dealing with emerging issues constitute a hopeful sign in the midst of much failure and grief; a community will exist to obey them. In some sense, the ongoing promulgation of *law* is a witness that the *promise* of land will indeed be fulfilled.

7. Divine Presence and Guidance. God, not Moses, has given birth to this people (11:12) and has chosen to stay with the family and to dwell in the heart of their camp (5:3). From this womb-like centre blessings flow out into the encircled community. This intense kind of presence is promised for Israel's future in the land as well (35:34). Even Balaam testifies to the presence of such a God among this people (23:21–2).

8. Because of the intense presence of God in Israel's midst, and the recognition of God's holiness, the tabernacle was to be protected from casual contact. This concern is sharpened in view of the golden calf apostasy and the near annihilation of Israel (Ex 32:9–10). Precautions must be taken to prevent a recurrence for the sake of the integrity of the divine–human relationship. The tribe of Levi was consecrated for service at the tabernacle and made responsible for guarding this holy place (1:50–3). Sharp warnings about intrusion are issued (1:51–3; 3:10, 38); even Levites could die if furnishings were mishandled (4:17–20). Strikingly, encroachment is not a serious problem in the subsequent narratives, except as related to conflict over leadership (ch. 16). The more problematic issue is mistrust and rebellion with respect to God and God's chosen leaders. These forms of sinfulness in particular pervade chs. 11–25 and deeply affect the character of the journey and the shape of Israel's future. On God's wrath and judgement, see especially at NUM 1:53 and ch. 14.

9. Israel's God not only dwells in the midst of Israel, but also goes before them. The accompanying presence of God is associated with the pillar of cloud/fire; 9:15–23 speaks of it in such a way that the itinerary is not predictable or routinized. This symbol is linked to the ark of the covenant, which represents the presence of God (10:35–6). God's ongoing presence is the decisive factor in Israel's journey, but various texts witness also to the importance of human leadership; for example, the passage regarding Hobab's skills (10:29–32) is placed immediately before the ark text (10:33–6). God works in and through what is available, even characters such as Balaam, to move towards the divine objectives.

10. Divine Revelation and Human Leadership. Revelation is not confined to Sinai; it occurs throughout Israel's journey. Statutes and other divine words newly enjoin Israel all along the way. This was the case with Israel's wanderings *before* Sinai as well (15:26; 18:23). God's word is not delivered in a once-and-for-all fashion; it is a dynamic reality, intersecting with life and all its contingencies. This is demonstrated in the very form of this material in the interweaving of law and narrative (for detail, see Fretheim 1991: 201–7).

11. God's word is usually mediated through Moses, but not uniquely so. This becomes an issue during the journey. Challenges to Moses' (and Aaron's) leadership that began in the pre-Sinai wanderings are intensified in Numbers, and other leaders take up the argument. Related issues and disputes are pursued in various chapters (11; 12; 16; 17).

12. The issue is voiced most sharply by Miriam and Aaron: has God spoken only through Moses (12:2)? The response is negative. God is not confined to only one way to speak to this community; indeed, if need be, God will go around the chosen ones to get a word through. God's spirit even rests upon the outsider Balaam who mediates remarkably clear words of God (24:2–4, 15–16). Nevertheless, Moses does have a special relationship with God and challenges to his role are not countenanced.

13. God communicates to and through Moses often in Numbers; indeed, 7:89 speaks of Moses' contact with God in an almost routinized way. In 12:8 God himself claims for Moses a unique face-to-face encounter. Moses actually 'beholds the form of the LORD' and lives to tell about it. One facet of this relationship is especially remarkable: the genuine interaction between them as they engage issues confronting the wandering community. Characteristic of their relationship in Exodus (chs. 3–6; 32–4, cf. GEN 18:22–33), it intensifies in Numbers (chs. 11; 12; 14; 16; 21; cf. Ps 106:23).

14. This says something about both Moses and God. Moses' leadership credentials are considerable, including a capacity to tolerate threats to his authority (11:29) and to persevere with God (chs. 11; 14; 16), calling forth the strong statement regarding his unique devotion (12:3). God also is remarkably open to such discourse, treats the relationship with integrity, and

honours the insights that Moses offers. Indeed, God may shape a different future in view of the encounter (14:13–20; 16:20–2). But such divine openness to change will always be in the service of God's unchanging goals for Israel and the creation (Balaam's point in 23:19).

15. Some of the disputes are focused on Aaron (and his sons) and their priestly leadership (chs. 16; 17). Actual tests are carried out which substantiate their unique role with respect to the sanctuary in the eyes of God. Members of this family also take actions that have an intercessory function; they stand 'between the dead and the living' and a plague is averted (16:47–50; cf. 25:7–13). This correlates with their mediating role in various rituals (chs. 5; 15).

16. Interest in the proper succession of leaders (Eleazar, 20:22–9; Joshua 27:12–23) demonstrates the crucial importance of good leaders for the stability of the community. Rebellion against God-chosen leaders is deeply subversive of God's intentions for the community and risks death short of the goal. But the leaders themselves are not exempt from strict standards (20:10–12). They may be held to a higher standard, because the impact of their mistakes has such a deep and pervasive effect on the community.

17. Holy People and Holy Priests. The call in Leviticus for the people to be holy (i.e. to live a life that exemplifies the holy people they are) is continued here (15:40). What constitutes a holy life, or that which is inimical to it, is continuous with the provisions of Leviticus in some ways. Various uncleannesses—whether moral or ritual in nature—are incompatible with holiness (chs. 5; 6). Yet, for Numbers, Israel's sins are focused on matters relating to leadership, mistrust of God and failure to believe in promises, and finally idolatry (ch. 25).

18. A case for more democratic forms of priestly leadership is pursued by Korah on the basis of the holiness of all the people (16:3). Moses' reply assumes gradations of holiness; even if all are holy, God chooses from among them certain persons to exercise priestly leadership, and this chosen status constitutes a holiness that sets them apart from other holy ones. The disaster experienced by Korah and his company (16:23–35) demonstrates their special status (16:40), as does the test with staffs (ch. 17).

19. Gradations of holiness are also evident within the members of the tribe of Levi. The Levites are set aside to care for the tabernacle, symbolized by their encampment between the tabernacle and the people. Among the Levites the family of Aaron is especially set aside for priestly duties (16:40; 17; 18:7–11, 19). Indeed, a 'covenant of perpetual priesthood' is made with this family because of the mediatorial actions of Phinehas (25:10–13).

20. The NT works with several themes from Numbers. It cites God's providing for Israel in the wilderness and lifts up Israel's infidelity as a warning for the people of God. These themes are carefully interwoven in 1 Cor 10:1–13, where many texts from Num 11–25 are referenced; it is carefully noted that these passages were 'written down to instruct us' (cf. Jn 3:14; Heb 3:7–4:11; 2 Pet 2:15–16; Jude 5–11; Rev 2:14–17).

E. Outline

COMMENTARY

Israel Prepares to Leave Sinai (1:1–10:10)

This entire section comes from the Priestly tradition. The chronological report (1:1) situates the census one month after the completion of the tabernacle (Ex 40:17) and nineteen days before the departure from Sinai (10:11), where Israel had been for almost a year (Ex 19:1). The tabernacle stands in the centre of the camp. Encamped around it are members of the tribe of Levi. Encircling them are the various tribes of Israel, three in each direction. The tabernacle situated in the centre of the camp expresses a divine centring for the community generally. At the same time, while God dwells among the people and guides them through the wilderness (9:17), the nature of that guidance is divinely limited. Hence, while God leads them from one oasis to the next, the divine guidance is not all-controlling and human leadership is crucial (10:29–32). The divine presence does not issue in a situation where the people have no option but to obey; disobedience is a lively possibility. Indeed, warning signs punctuate the narrative (e.g. 1:53); they alert Israel to the care needed by the community with respect to the near presence of God in their midst and the importance this has for the shape of the journey.

(1:1–54) The First Census The early mention of the 'tent of meeting' (v. 1) signals its importance for what precedes as well as what follows; it is synonymous with the tabernacle. How it is to be related to the tent of the epic tradition (Ex 33:7–11) is uncertain; the tabernacle may have assumed the role of the tent (see 7:89). The rare phrase, 'tabernacle of the covenant' (1:50, 53; 10:11; Ex 38:21) extends the designation for its major sacred object, the 'ark of the covenant'; the language focuses on the God–Israel relationship and the divine speaking associated with that.

This census list plays an important structural role in Numbers (see NUM c.2). God commands the census and also names one male from each tribe to assist (except Levi; two Joseph tribes keep the number at twelve, see Gen 48), 'the leaders of their ancestral tribes' (v. 16; cf. 2:3–31; 7:12–83; 10:14–28). To appear on this list was a continuing sign assuring each tribal group of their present identity and future place among God's chosen.

The census is to include the males of the old generation, 20 years and older. The purpose is conscription, to determine 'everyone able to go to war' (cf. 2 Sam 24:9); battles are expected (though there will be few to fight, see 21:1–3). Israel has good reason to be confident with these numbers (but they are not, 14:1–4). The results of the census (perhaps the same census as in Ex 38:26; cf. 12:37): 603,550 males; the second census yields 601,730 (26:51), though the tribal distribution changes somewhat. When women, children, and Levites are added, the total must have been about 2 million. The unrealistic number has not been resolved (for a survey, see Ashley 1993: 60–6); probably it was thought, if mistakenly, to be actually this large. Whether literal or symbolic, the number testifies to God's blessing and preserving this people, and keeping the divine promises. This generation will be unfaithful and, by divine decree (14:22–30), will die off in the wilderness. At the time of the new census, 'not one of them was left', except Joshua and Caleb (26:65).

The Levites, who do not bear arms and are not registered here (see 3:14), are given duties with respect to the tabernacle and its furnishings (detailed in NUM 4). They are charged to encamp around it, protect it from casual contact, maintain it, carry it during the journey, and pitch it at each stop. The 'outsider' (v. 51) refers to all who are not Levites, whether Israelite or alien (16:40). The sense of 'come near' is 'encroach (see Milgrom 1990: 342–3). Violation of the tabernacle precincts means death, not as a court verdict, but as a penalty delivered on the spot by the levitical guards (see 18:7).

This drastic action is in the interests of the community as a whole, so that it will not experience the wrath of God (v. 53). God's wrath in Numbers is impersonal in its basic sense; it 'goes forth' or 'comes upon' (16:46; 18:5). Wrath is not a legal penalty, or a divine decision, but inevitably issues from the deed as a matter of the moral order; it is an effect intrinsically related to, growing out of, the violation of the place of God's presence or the divine–human relationship (see NUM 14). God is not conceived in deistic ways, however, and sees to the movement from deed to consequence, in sometimes sharp language (11:33). The effect

may be death, often in Numbers because of plague (16:46–50; 31:16). It can be overcome by various means, from sacrificial ritual (8:19) to priestly intercession (16:47–50; 25:11).

Looming large over the exacting concern for the tabernacle are Israel's past infidelities, especially the golden calf *débâcle*, where Israel violated its relationship with God and jeopardized its future (Ex 32:9–10). God graciously chose to dwell among them; but, given the people's propensity to apostasy, safeguards had to be instituted. These strict measures are not to protect God from the people or the people from God (though violation could mean violence, v. 53), but to preserve a proper *relationship* between God and people. Israel has been honoured by this incredible divine condescension, but God remains God and this divine move is not to be presumed upon without the endangerment of life.

In v. 54 and throughout chs. 1–9, the Israelites are reported to have done exactly as God commanded. One wonders how anything could go wrong. Later failures cannot be blamed on faulty preparations.

(2:1–34) The Encampment With the tabernacle centred in the camp, and the Levites camped immediately around it (see NUM 3), God commands that the tribes be precisely ordered around the perimeter. They are to be ordered as companies ('hosts' or 'armies'), specifying military readiness. Three tribes are to be positioned at each side of the tabernacle, under their distinctive banners; each triad is named for the dominant tribe of the three (seen from the perspective of Israel's later history; cf. Gen 49), which is flanked by the other two tribes in each case—the camp of Judah (the most dominant) to the east, the side where the tabernacle opening was located, and Moses and the Aaronides were camped; Reuben to the south; Ephraim to the west; Dan to the north (the leaders of the tribes as in 1:5–15). This order of the tribes is the order for the march, beginning with Judah. The tabernacle, set in the midst of the Levites (v. 17), is to move between the camps of Reuben and Ephraim. God's commands are again followed. This camp may have been modelled after an Egyptian pattern (see Milgrom 1990: 340).

(3:1–4:49) The Levites This section describes two censuses of the tribe of Levi, its organization, and its responsibilities for transporting and guarding the tabernacle and its furnishings. The genealogical formula (3:1) links the generation of Moses and Aaron with those in Genesis (the last is 37:2; cf. Ex 6:14–25).

(3:1–13) occurs 'at the time when God spoke with Moses on Mount Sinai' (v. 1). Since that time Aaron's sons, Nadab and Abihu, have died childless (Lev 10:1–2); this reference alerts the reader to dangers associated with handling holy things, and the tasks of the Kohathites in particular (4:15–20). Aaron's other sons, Eleazar and Ithamar, were ordained as priests by Moses (the 'he' of v. 3; cf. Lev 8:30) and served with their father throughout his lifetime.

A distinction is made within the tribe of Levi between the descendants of Aaron, who attend to priestly duties, and other Levites, who assist the priests, with responsibilities for 'service at the tabernacle' (cf. 1:50–3 for an earlier summary). vv. 11–13 (restated in 8:16–18) recall the killing of the Egyptian firstborn and the sparing of the Israelite firstborn (see Ex 13:1–2, 11–15), in remembrance of (or repayment for) which God had consecrated the latter to a life of religious service; the Levites serve as substitutes for them (and their livestock for Israel's firstborn livestock). While the Levites are responsible to the sons of Aaron, it is as representatives of all Israel. It may be that God himself takes the census of the Levites and reports the results to Moses (3:12, 15–16).

(3:14–39) continues in narrative time and space from 2:34 and describes God's command of a census of the non-Aaronide Levites (total: 22,000), their encampment positions, and their specific responsibilities. The census of Levites was prohibited in 1:47–9 because they were non-military, served the tabernacle, included all from one month and older, and represented all Israel's firstborn (cf. 3:40–1). The levitical camp is ordered in terms of Levi's sons (Gershon, Kohath, and Merari); their clans encamp on three sides of the tabernacle and have varying duties with respect to its transit. The Kohathites (from whom Moses and Aaron are descended) are responsible for the most sacred objects (4:4; e.g. the ark), the Gershonites for the fabrics, and the Merarites for the supporting structures (responsibilities are detailed in 4:1–33). Aaron and his sons encamp on the pre-eminent, entrance (eastern) side of the tabernacle (v. 38). Aaron's son, Eleazar, is in charge of the leaders of the three clans (v. 32) and has general oversight of the tabernacle and certain special details (4:16); his brother Ithamar has oversight over the work of the Gershonites and the Merarites (4:28, 33).

Again, God's commands are followed (3:16, 39, 42, 51).

(3:40–51) The firstborn system is detailed more fully here, where the firstborn of all Israel are numbered (22,273); each of the 273 persons over and above the 22,000 Levites is redeemed by five shekels apiece (paid apparently by the firstborn, v. 50, and given to the priests; cf. Lev 27:6). The figure of 22,273 seems too low in view of the census numbers in 2:32 (even assuming an equal number of female to male firstborn, this would entail an average of fourteen male children per family); no satisfactory explanation has been given. The redemption of the firstborn keeps the exodus action of God explicitly before the people as a reminder of their redeemed status. The recurring phrase 'I am the Lord' (common in Leviticus) is shorthand for the divine origin of the commands.

(4:1–33) delineates God's commands regarding the second levitical census, taken to determine the number of those (ages 30–50) who are to perform the actual duties; these ages differ somewhat from 8:24–6 and from other OT texts (e.g. Ezra 3:8), perhaps reflecting expanding community needs. Aaron and his sons are responsible for packing and unpacking the most holy things, with differently coloured cloths marking gradations of holiness (vv. 5–15); only they are allowed to see and touch them. The responsibilities of the three levitical groups for certain sanctuary items, as noted above, are also divinely commanded in detail, so that each item is exactly accounted for (Kohathites, vv. 1–20; Gershonites, vv. 21–8; Merarites, vv. 29–33). A special emphasis is given regarding the work of the Kohathites (4:17–20), not because their status is higher, but because they handle the 'most holy things'. God graciously takes their greater risk into account and specifies precautionary procedures for their handling of these objects. To die for improper contact with the most holy objects (vv. 15, 19–20) seems to have reference to direct, though mediated action by God (see NUM 1:53; Lev 10:1–2). This concern may be rooted in the golden calf apostasy, where the holiness of God was compromised.

(4:34–49) describes the implementation of God's commands; once again, they are obeyed to the letter (vv. 46–8 summarizes the results). The encampment is now fully prepared for the journey through the wilderness.

(5:1–6:21) **Purification of the Camp** This section, probably added late in the redactional process, deals with matters needing attention for the journey. Why these particular issues are collected at this point and ordered in this way is uncertain; some links are evident (e.g. 'be unfaithful' in 5:6, 12; guilt offerings) and they deal both with matters of ritual purity and moral living among the laity (male and female), and the priests have responsibilities relating to both spheres. More generally, matters of purity are important in recognition of God's dwelling in the camp (5:3), but so also are matters of moral wrongdoing, which 'break faith with the Lord' (5:6). Several cases extend or modify statutes in Leviticus.

(5:1–4) Persons who are ritually (and communicably) unclean for various reasons are to be put outside the camp to live in tents or caves, without access to worship, so as not to contaminate the community or defile the tabernacle. This statute reinforces or extends those in Leviticus (see Lev 13:45–6; 15:31–3; 21:1–3, 11).

(5:5–10) extends Lev 6:1–7; the new focus is on wrongdoing (including a false oath) where the injured party dies without next of kin, in which case priests receive the appropriate restitution. The public confession of this deliberate sin against the neighbour (see Lev 5:5) is also newly integral to the ritual; note that the sin against the neighbour 'breaks faith with God'. vv. 9–10 note that priests are to receive their rightful dues.

(5:11–31) has a complex history given the literary difficulties; yet at least some features (e.g. repetition) serve a purpose in the present redaction (for detail, Milgrom 1990: 350–4). Though often called a trial by ordeal, the coalescence of verdict and sanction, effected by God not the community, suggests rather an oath that is dramatized. The focus of this case-law is a wife, possibly pregnant, whose husband suspects ('is jealous of') her of adultery but has no evidence, whether she has actually committed adultery (vv. 12–14a) or is only suspected of doing so (14b). In the former case, this text softens the penalty prescribed for an adulteress in Lev 20:10, probably because there was no evidence. In the latter case, a woman unjustly accused could be vindicated; so the jealous husband (or the community) could not arbitrarily decide her fate.

In either case, the man brings his wife (who is 'under [his] authority', vv. 19, 29) to the priest with a grain offering, though without the usual oil and frankincense (Lev 2:1–10), as was the case with sin offerings (Lev 5:11). Such offerings bring 'the [potential] iniquity to remembrance' before God. The procedure: the priest prepares a mixture of holy water (see Ex 30:17–21) and dust from the tabernacle floor, probably thought to have potency because of its contact with holy things, in an earthen vessel (which could be broken after use, Lev 11:33). The priest is then to bring the woman 'before the LORD' (the altar), loosen her hair—a sign of (potential) uncleanness, Lev 13:45—and put the grain offering in her hands. The priest has her take an oath regarding the suspicions registered (vv. 19–22): if she has been faithful, she will be immune from the water; if unfaithful, the water will cause her sexual organs to be affected adversely in some way (the effect is correlated with the crime) and she will be ostracized among the people (see Job 30:9) and precluded from having children (v. 28). If the woman is pregnant, the effect may be a miscarriage. The nature of the effect of the water upon the woman is considered a sign as to whether the woman has told the truth. The repeated 'Amen. Amen' ('so be it'), expresses her willingness to accept either result of the ritual (see Deut 27:15–26). Unlike her husband, she is given no other voice in the ritual.

In 5:23–8 (v. 24 anticipates 26b, as v. 16a does 18a), the priest writes the curses on a surface from which the ink could be washed off into the water the woman is to drink; the imbibed water is thought to contain the power of the curses (cf. Ex 32:20; Ezek 3:1–3). The priest takes the grain offering from her and burns a portion of it on the altar, after which she drinks the water (vv. 25–6). If the woman has been unfaithful, she will experience distress (no time frame is specified), hence the phrase, 'waters of bitterness'. The potion actually has no bitter taste nor brings pain in itself, but this would be the effect if God adjudged the woman guilty (v. 21; cf. Zech 5:1–4; Jer 8:14; 9:15).

(5:29–31) summarizes the essence of the two types of case for which this ordeal would be applied. The husband is freed from any responsibility for a false accusation (the need to express this is striking, and it opens the way to frivolous expressions of jealousy). If the woman is guilty, she bears the consequences (by divine agency).

One might claim that the ritual could not accurately determine the truth; but, as in the sacrificial system, it is God, before whom the woman is brought, who knows the truth of the situation and is believed to act in the ritual and to effect the proper result. Yet, one wonders if this procedure ever verified suspicions; perhaps the threat was sufficient to elicit confessions. It was only women who lived under such threat, and the ritual is degrading; that no comparable law existed for the male, or no concern is expressed that undisclosed male infidelity might contaminate the camp, is revealing of the patriarchy involved. The language of jealousy is also used in the marriage analogy for Israel's relationship with God, her husband (who is jealous, e.g. Ex 20:5; 34:14), and may have informed prophetic rhetoric (e.g. Isa 3:16–17; Ezek 23:31–4). Jesus' attitude towards women (Lk 7:36–50; Jn 4:1–30; 8:1–11) breaks open the one-sidedness of the Numbers ritual (see Olson 1996: 38–9).

(6:1–21) provides for a temporary, voluntary nazirite vow (from *nāzîr*, meaning 'set apart'; the unpruned vine was also called a *nāzîr*, perhaps a symbol of Israel as consecrated to the Lord; the word for uncut hair is *nezer*). As with the other statutes in this section, the laity are the focus of concern; yet these statutes highlight priestly obligations relating thereto (and may suggest priestly control over their activity). The text does not institute the nazirite vocation, but regulates a consecrated life in certain ways. Vows, always individual acts, were common in ancient Israel (see 30:1–16) and this vow was 'special' (v. 2).

Yet, the precise purpose for becoming a nazirite remains elusive. Generally, nazirites were male or female individuals who took a vow of consecration for a special vocation. Am 2:11–12 states that God raised up nazirites; the parallel with the prophets means they had a high calling (as does their parallel with the priests). That they generated opposition among the people, who made them drink wine and thereby prevented them from fulfilling their calling, suggests their importance. The stories of Samson and probably Samuel, lifelong nazirites (dedicated by their parents from the womb, cf. Jer 1:5), suggest that God called such persons to specific tasks (cf. Judg 5:2; Gen 49:26). Wenham (1981: 85) calls them 'the monks and nuns of ancient Israel', but we do not know if this was considered an 'office', whether many took the vow, or how long a term was.

The nazirite vow entailed separation from products of the vineyard (and other intoxicants), haircuts, and corpses; their return to secular life was signified by cutting the hair. As such, these persons were highly visible members of the community, signs to all of total dedication to God. They bore similarities to the Rechabites (2 Kings 10:15; Jer 35), conservative proponents of ancient Israelite traditions who rejected Canaanite culture, including viticulture and building houses.

Like the high priests, nazirites were not to come into contact with (even within sight of) a corpse, but unlike them, accidental contact required rites of purification (vv. 6–12; cf. 5:2–3; 19:11–12, 19). Upon being purified, they were to 'sanctify the head [hair]', i.e. be reconsecrated (vv. 11c–12). vv. 13–20 describe the ritual at the completion of their consecration; the range of offerings (cf. Lev 8) suggests the high status of the nazirite; returning to secular life was a major step. The ritual includes the shaving of the head and the burning of the hair (because it is considered holy). v. 21 summarizes the force of the previous verses. On possible links to Jesus, John the Baptist, and the early church, see Mt 2:23; Lk 1:15; Acts 18:18; 21:23–4; on nazirites in Second-Temple Judaism, see Milgrom (1990: 355–8).

(6:22–7) The Aaronic Benediction The placement of this benediction seems unusual; it may be another item that prepares the people for the journey through the wilderness. This is the blessing for the time of departure, and daily throughout their journey. Each line, with God as subject, is progressively longer (three, five, seven Hebrew words); besides the name YHWH, twelve Hebrew words signify the twelve tribes.

This benediction in some form was widely used in ancient Israel, especially at the conclusion of worship (see Lev 9:22; Deut 21:5; 2 Chr 30:27; Ps 67:1; 121:7–8; see its ironic use in Mal 1:8–10). Putting the name of God on the people may have been understood literally, given the inscription on two cigarette-sized silver plaques found near Jerusalem, dating from the seventh–sixth centuries BCE (for such parallels, see Milgrom 1990: 360–2). The blessing has been commonly used in post-biblical Jewish and Christian communities.

One probably should not see a climactic arrangement in the clauses; so, for example, blessing would include peace. Perhaps the second verb in each case defines the first more specifically, but together the six verbs cover God's benevolent activity from various angles and state God's gracious will for the people.

Blessing has a wide-ranging meaning, touching every sphere of life. It testifies most basically to the work of God the Creator, both within the community of faith and without. No conditions are attached. It signifies any divine gift that serves the life, health, and well-being of individuals and communities. Keeping is a specific blessing to those with concerns for safety, focusing on God's protection from all forms of evil (Ps 121:7–8), pertinent for wilderness wandering.

God's face/countenance (the same Hebrew word) is a common anthropomorphism (esp. in Psalms; see Balentine 1983). The shining face of God (contrast the hiding face) signifies God's benevolent disposition towards the other, here in gracious action, for which Israel can make no claims (Ps 67:1). The lifting up of the Lord's countenance signifies a favourable movement towards the other in the granting of peace, that is, wholeness and fullness of life. Putting God's name on the people (supremely by means of the word) emphasizes the divine source of all blessings.

(7:1–8:26) Final Preparations for Tabernacle Worship The chronological note at 7:1 indicates that what follows is a flashback (it continues through 10:10); it is one month earlier than the time of 1:1 and coincides with Ex 40 and the day Moses set up the tabernacle; yet it assumes Num 3–4 and the provisions made for carrying the tabernacle. This literary technique suspends the forward movement of the narrative and returns the reader to the occasion of the divine descent to dwell among the people and their grateful response.

(7:1–88) describes the consecration of the tabernacle in connection with which offerings were made by the leaders of the twelve tribes. vv. 1–9 describe one gift: six wagons and twelve oxen to carry the tabernacle and its furnishings. The Merarites received two-thirds of the wagons and oxen because they carry the supporting structure; the Kohathites carry the most holy things by hand. 7:10 refers to the offerings presented in both vv. 1–9 and 12–88. vv. 11–83 specify other gifts: necessities for the public altar sacrifices and the priesthood—silver and gold vessels, animals, and flour mixed with oil and incense—to be offered at the altar whenever needed (not at one dedication occasion). The tribal leaders, in the order given in 2:3–31, each give the same offerings on the successive days of the celebration; they are listed out twelve times, and vv. 84–8 provide a total.

This striking repetition underlines the unity and equality of the tribal groups and the generosity of their support for the tabernacle.

(7:89) seems out of place, but it emphasizes that God's ongoing commitment to Israel (not only to dwell among them, but to speak to Moses) matches the people's obedient response regarding God's dwelling-place. The mercy seat is the cover of the ark of the covenant, upon which were fixed two cherubim, sphinx-like creatures, shaped to form a throne for the invisible God (1 Sam 4:4; 2 Sam 6:2); in effect, the ark was God's footstool (2 Kings 19:15; 1 Chr 28:2; for description, see Ex 25:17–21). From this place, God will speak to Moses on a regular basis when he enters the tabernacle; this fulfils God's promise in Ex 25:22 and is reported in the narrative that follows (Num 11:16–30).

(8:1–4) specifies lighting directions for the seven tabernacle lamps (commanded by God in Ex 25:37, but not reported in Ex 37:17–24), with a reminder of how the lamps were constructed. Their seven branches and flowery design may have symbolized the tree of life (see 1 Kings 7:49 for the temple lampstands; cf. also Zech 4:1–14; Rev 11:4); the branched lampstand or menorah remains an important symbol of light in Judaism.

(8:5–26) (the setting is still as Ex 40; cf. Num 3:11–13); the Levites are consecrated 'to do service at the tent of meeting' (v. 15; cf. Lev 8; the priests are sanctified, while the Levites are purified). vv. 5–19 state the divine command and rationale for the ceremony and vv. 20–2 stress that it was obeyed. This entails participation in a purification rite (vv. 5–7; cf. 6:9; 19:1–22; Lev 14:8–9) so they can perform this service without endangering themselves or the community. The Levites are then presented 'before the LORD' (v. 10) and before 'Aaron and his sons' (v. 13) in the presence of the people. The people lay their hands on them, symbolizing that the Levites have become their sacrifice, a 'living sacrifice' dedicated to the service of God in their stead (vv. 10–11; cf. 3:40–51). The Levites in turn lay their hands on the head of the bulls, which are sacrificed to cleanse the sanctuary (the whole burnt offering, v. 8a) and to atone for sins they had committed (v. 12b). God claims that the choice of the Levites is rooted in the Exodus events (3:5–13), and that they are 'mine...unreservedly given to me from among the Israelites' (vv. 14–16); God in turn gives them to the

Aaronides for service at the tabernacle (see 3:9). This constitutes an act of atonement for the Israelites (for whom the Levites undertake the work) to prevent any plague resulting from too close a contact with the holy things. The section concludes with the typical reference to obedience and a summary of the Levites' cleansing (vv. 20–2), followed by a reference to age requirements (vv. 23–6; cf. 4:47) and a clarification that they are not priests, but assist the Aaronides in their responsibilities.

(9:1–14) The Passover at Sinai This section continues the flashback begun at 7:1. vv. 1–5 report a second celebration of the Passover in fulfilment of the 'perpetual ordinance' of Ex 12:24. This celebration also precedes the wilderness journey, and enhances this moment of departure in Israel's life.

A question is presented to Moses (and Aaron) as to whether those who had become unclean through touching a corpse (see 5:1–4; 19:11–20) could celebrate Passover. Upon consulting the Lord (see 7:89), Moses is told that such unclean persons (and possible descendants) should not be denied Passover and are to keep it one month later, i.e. the fourteenth day of the *second* month. In view of v. 6 ('could not keep') this represents an adjustment in the law (see NUM D.10). The (later?) addition of another case of persons away from the camp (v. 9) assumes the land settlement and is a still further adjustment of passover law. For stipulations regarding celebration, see Ex 12:10, 46. For reference to not breaking the bones of the passover lamb (9:12), see Jn 19:36.

Supplemental instructions also adapt older regulations for those who are clean and at home (v. 13). Such a strict ordinance at this point reflects a concern that others might delay celebration until the second month. A permissive rubric in v. 14 is given for the aliens, non-Israelites who are residing permanently in the land (cf. Ex 12:19, 48–9). Being 'cut off from the people' is explained as bearing (the effects of) one's own sin, which is either banishment or execution, either judicially or at God's own hand. As in 5:31, the last seems likely (see Milgrom 1990: 405–8).

(9:15–23) Divine Guidance in the Wilderness This section begins (v. 15) with a flashback to Ex 40:34 and supplements Ex 40:36–8 regarding the relation between the cloud/fire and the stages of Israel's journey. It describes in advance an ongoing feature of that journey; the actual departure is not reported until 10:11. vv. 17–23

anticipate the march, stressing Israel's obedience to the divine leading at every stage.

In Israel's pre-tabernacle journeying, God 'in' (not 'as') the pillar of cloud and fire led them through the wilderness (Ex 13:21–2). Divine leading follows this Passover as it did the first. This was a single pillar, with the fire within the cloud (Ex 14:24; 40:38); references to the 'glory' of the Lord in the cloud (Ex 16:10) refer to the fire (Ex 24:17). Here this 'glory-cloud' is linked to the tabernacle (and the ark, 10:33–6); its rising and setting schedule the stages of Israel's journey. It is likely that the cloud would rest on the tabernacle and, while the tabernacle remained in the middle of the marching people, the cloud would proceed to the front of the procession (see v. 17; 14:14). The various timings of this cloud activity (v. 22) emphasize obedience and the need to follow a schedule ('charge') set by God, however irregular. At the same time, divine activity does not function apart from human agency (see 10:1–10, 29–32).

(10:1–10) The Two Silver Trumpets God commands Moses to make two trumpets of hammered silver (about 1 ft. long with a wide bell). They are to be blown by priests on various occasions: summoning the congregation or its leaders (vv. 3–4), breaking camp (vv. 5–6, presumably all four sides according to the order in Num 2, so the LXX), engaging in battle (v. 9; see 31:6), and on days of rejoicing (see 2 Kings 11:14; Ezra 3:10), appointed festivals (see chs. 28–9), and monthly offerings (v. 10; see 28:11–15). In vv. 9–10, the language anticipates the land settlement. A distinction is made (v. 7) between an 'alarm', perhaps a series of short blasts, and a 'blow', one long blast.

A rationale for the blowing of trumpets is given in vv. 9–10: to bring Israel's situation before God, who is thereby called to act on their behalf, either in battle (salvation from enemies) or in and through the offerings (forgiveness and well-being). The call of the trumpet is picked up in eschatological contexts (Zech 9:14; 1 Cor 15:51–2), exemplifying continuity across all generations of God's people. The blowing of the trumpets by the sons of Aaron complements the rising and the setting of the cloud. With the role of Hobab in 10:29–32, it becomes apparent that clear-sighted human leadership is integral to effective divine guidance.

The Wilderness Journey (10:11–25:18)

This middle section of Numbers describes Israel's journey from Sinai to the plains of Moab. The emphasis upon Israel's obedience to this point stands in sharp contrast to what follows. The beginnings of the march (10:11–36) signal no problems, but with 11:1 the carefully woven fabric comes apart at the seams. In spite of precise preparations, disloyalty now fills the scene and severely complicates the move towards the land. Warnings of divine judgement have been given (1:53; 3:4, 10; 4:15, 18–20; 8:19), but they go unheeded, with disastrous results.

Many of these narratives (a mixture of the traditional sources) are ordered in a comparable way (see at 11:1–3) and mirror the wilderness stories of Ex 15:22–18:27. Once again we hear of manna, rocks producing water, battles with desert tribes, and non-stop complaints. But Numbers is different. The complaints in Exodus are tolerated, as if a long-oppressed people is entitled to some grumbling. In Numbers, however, in view of the giving of the law and the golden calf débâcle, the themes of sin, repentance, and judgement are introduced. The people are sharply identified as rebellious, against both God and Moses/Aaron, and the judgement of God is invited into the picture again and again.

(10:11–28) Departure from Sinai The date in v. 11 is nineteen days after the census (1:1), which was eleven months after arrival at Sinai (Ex 19:1). The time of departure is set by divine command, signalled by the cloud (see 9:15–23). In vv. 14–28 the marching order of the tribal units according to a three-tribe standard (or regiment) follows the arrangement in Num 2. The positioning of the Levites, those who carry the tabernacle items (vv. 17, 21), is not precisely symmetrical (see chs. 3–4). For the leaders see 1:5–15; 2:3–31; 7:12–83. The end of the first stage of the journey is anticipated in the reference to the settling of the cloud in the wilderness of Paran (v. 12; see 12:16), the setting up of the tabernacle framework (v. 21), and the reference to three days' journey (10:33).

(10:29–36) Human and Divine Guidance These verses formed part of the older epic tradition. Both v. 29 and the tradition are ambiguous as to whether Hobab or Reuel is Moses' father-in-law; in Ex 2:18 Reuel is, but in Judg 4:11 Hobab is so identified (and Jethro in Ex 3:1; 18:1). Perhaps 'father-in-law' refers to any relative by marriage. The Midia-nites are often mentioned positively (contrast chs. 25; 31); being a desert tribe, they would know the wilderness. Moses' invitation shows that the guidance of the cloud is not deemed sufficient. The marching community is in need of the 'eyes' of a human guide, even from outsiders such as Hobab (cf. also Balaam; Jethro in Ex 18). Both divine and human activity are necessary for the people to find their way (so also the spies in ch. 13). Moses promises that Hobab's people will obtain the goodness the Israelites receive from God (see Judg 4:11).

The ark in association with the cloud (see 9:15–23) precedes the community here (v. 33). The second 'three days' journey' is probably a dittograph. Moses' directives to the Lord (vv. 35–6), at the departure and arrival of the ark, are old poetic pieces. They portray the march as a liturgical procession. God was believed to be intensely present wherever the ark was (7:89; see Ps 68:1; 132:7–8). God, the Lord of Hosts ('the ten thousand thousands of Israel'), leads Israel in battle against its enemies (14:44; 1 Sam 4:1–7:2). That Moses would invite the Lord to become active on behalf of Israel demonstrates again the integration of human activity and divine.

(11:1–3) A Paradigm of Rebellion These verses provide a pattern in both form and content for several episodes that follow: murmuring; judgement; cry (of repentance); intercession; deliverance (on Exodus parallels, see above; for content see NUM 13:1–14:45). Place-names are at times etymologized for convenient recall of the story.

The peoples' complaints of unidentified misfortunes are not specifically directed to God, but God hears them. The divine anger is provoked and 'the fire of the LORD', perhaps lightning (see Ex 9:23–4; 2 Kings 1:9), consumes outlying areas of the camp (a threat to its integrity). The people direct their response to Moses, who intercedes on their behalf, and the storm stops. The place was called Taberah ('Burning'), referring to both divine anger and its effects.

(11:4–35) Rebellion and Leadership The coherence of this passage is difficult, perhaps reflecting different traditions; yet good sense can be made of the awkwardness. On the 'miraculous' provision of food in the wilderness see NUM 20:1–13.

This murmuring immediately follows the first; complaining has become a pattern of life. The complaints of the rabble (non-Israelites, Ex 12:38), intensified by Israelites, despise God's gifts of food (vv. 6, 18) and deliverance (v. 20). Nostalgically recalling the (mostly vegetable!) diet typical for Egyptians, they cry out for fish (cf. v. 5). God's gift of manna (see EX 16), which the narrator notes was tasty and choice, was not thought to provide the strength they needed.

This amounts to a rejection of God and a request for the Exodus to be reversed (v. 20)!

God's anger is revealed to Moses, who joins the people in complaint about a related matter (vv. 10–15). In language typical of lament psalms, Moses complains that, given what the people have become, God has mistreated him, placed too heavy a leadership burden on him (see Ex 18:18), and provided insufficient resources. Feeling caught in the middle, he asks for either relief or death. The maternal imagery Moses uses is striking; God has conceived and birthed this people (see Deut 32:18), and hence God should assume the responsibilities of a wet-nurse and see to their nourishment. Moses should not have to carry this burden 'alone', implying that God is somehow negligent.

A lively exchange between God and Moses follows (vv. 16–23). God replies to Moses in two respects: he will share the spirit given to Moses with others, who will help bear the burden (see vv. 24–30); God will provide the meat for which the people have asked (see vv. 31–2). Regarding the latter, however, God's anger at the people remains. Repeating their complaints, God declares that they are to prepare for an encounter with him; they will indeed get meat, a month's worth, but so much that it will become loathsome. Moses responds by wondering how meat can be found for so many people (only soldiers are counted, 1:46). God responds with a rhetorical question: in effect, God's hand is not too short (NRSV fn.; no general statement is made about divine power; cf. Isa 50:2; 59:1) to provide this amount of food. God will show that his word is good.

As for burden-sharing (vv. 16–17, 24–30), Moses obeys God and gathers seventy elders around the tent (probably in the centre of the camp in spite of vv. 26, 30, which may speak of movement within the camp). God shares Moses' spirit (rûaḥ, not quantitatively understood), which had its source in God, with the elders, who prophesy. Such a charisma was given to various leaders (see 24:2, 27:18, 1 Sam 10:5–10) and was transferable (see 2 Kings 2:9; on prophecy and ecstasy, see Milgrom 1990: 380–4). While they prophesy only once (unlike Moses), 16:25 suggests they assume some ongoing burdens. Even two elders who remained in the camp (Eldad and Medad) receive a share of God's spirit. In the face of efforts by Joshua to stop them, Moses refuses any protection of his authority or restriction of the divine word to established channels (see 12:1–16; Balaam); indeed, he wishes that all God's people could receive this charisma.

The gift of meat (vv. 18–20, 31–5) comes in the form of quails (see Ex 16:13; Ps 78:26–31), carried into the camp on a wind (rûaḥ) provided by God. They cover the ground for miles to a depth of two cubits (about 3 ft.); the least that anyone gathered was ten homers (probably 60 bushels). But before they had finished eating (the entire amount; cf. vv. 19–20), God's anger was provoked and a plague (related to the food?) swept the camp.

The place was called Kibroth-hattaavah ('Graves of craving'), recalling the people's complaint (v. 4) and the effects of the plague.

(12:1–16) Familial Challenge to Moses' Leadership This text concerns the authority of the Mosaic tradition in view of rival claims regarding divine revelation; it may reflect later power struggles among priestly groups (cf. NUM 16).

Challenges to Moses as a unique spokesman for God are brought by his sister and brother (though God alone hears them, v. 2?). The stated basis for the challenge is that Moses had married a Cushite woman. Cush usually refers to Ethiopia (if so, this would be Moses' second wife; so the LXX), but here it probably refers to a Cush in northern Arabia (see Hab 3:7). If so, she would be Zipporah, a Midianite (10:29; Ex 2:15–22).

Why this issue is raised remains uncertain. If v. 1 is integral to the reason given in v. 2, the issue centres on intrafamilial conflict regarding authority in view of Zipporah's (growing?) leadership role and/or influence with Moses (see Ex 4:24–6; 18:2). Miriam and Aaron assume that God has spoken through them (cf. Mic 6:4), confirmed by God in v. 5, for Miriam is a prophet (Ex 15:20) and Aaron speaks for God (Ex 4:15). 11:4–35 has shown that God does not speak only through Moses; moreover, God's spirit will rest upon Joshua (27:18) and even on Balaam (24:2–4, 15–16). God is not restricted to a single way into this community.

Yet, challenges to Moses' status with God are not countenanced. The narrator bases this point on Moses' unique relationship with God, stated generally (v. 3, devout, humble before God) and, in an act of conflict resolution, God's own words to Aaron and Miriam in Moses' presence. God customarily speaks to prophets in visions and dreams, but Moses is different for two reasons: he is uniquely entrusted with the house of Israel (see Ex 40:38) and God speaks to him directly (lit. mouth to mouth) and he sees the form of YHWH, a human form that God assumes (cf. 14:14; Ex 24:9–11; Deut 34:10; in

Deut 4:15, the *people* see no form). The issue pertains both to what is heard (that is, clarity) and what is seen (God). Unlike with dreams or visions, Moses' entire person, with all senses functioning, is engaged in the experience (for detail, see Fretheim 1984: 79–106). God assumes (v. 8c) that Miriam and Aaron were aware of this uniqueness, and his response is anger (see 11:33).

When Miriam becomes leprous (an unidentified skin disease), Aaron interprets it as a consequence of *their* foolish sin and pleads ironically to 'my lord' Moses that he (not God!) spare both Miriam and himself. The Hebrew 'do not lay sin upon us' (NRSV fn.) should not be translated 'punish'; rather, the effect is intrinsic to the deed. The whiteness of Miriam's skin (a reversal of the dark skin of Moses' wife?) occasions the stillborn analogy, in effect: do not let her waste away to death. Aaron may not suffer the same effects because of his confession and plea or perhaps because he is high priest (see Lev 22:4), revealing a clerical (and male) bias.

Moses prays to God on Miriam's behalf, but God responds that she is to be barred from the camp for seven days. The levitical regulations speak of a fourteen day process for leprosy (Lev 13:4; 14:8), so the banishment is probably an external sign of shame (like a parent spitting in a child's face, Deut 25:9). Miriam bears her shame, and the people honour her by not resuming the march until she returns (apparently healed). v. 16 probably means they remain in the wilderness of Paran (see 10:12).

(13:1–14:45) The Spy Mission The setting for chs. 13–20 is Kadesh-barnea (13:26), about 50 miles south of Beersheba in the wilderness of Paran (or Zin, 20:1). On historiographic considerations, see Levine (1993: 372–5). This passage interweaves at least two traditions; the epic story has Caleb as hero and the Priestly tradition adds Joshua. This rebellion proves to be the decisive one for the future of Israel.

Twelve scouts, one from each tribe, are sent to spy out the land of Canaan at God's command (cf. 32:6–13; Deut 1:22–45). Moses gives instructions regarding destination (the Negeb and the hill country) and observations to be made regarding military readiness and the character of the land (13:17–20). According to 13:21 they scout the entire length of the country, from the wilderness of Zin in the south to Rehob in the north; 13:22–4 (from the epic tradition) reports only on the Negeb and Judah, from which they bring back fruit; especially noted is a cluster of grapes (hence the name Eshcol), the season for which is July/August. After some forty

days the scouts bring back a mixed report. The initial report (13:28–9) is realistic; the land is bountiful but filled with strong people and fortified cities. The identity and placement of indigenous peoples is not always clear (cf. 13:29 with 14:25, 45), reflecting different traditions. The Amalekites are a perennial enemy of Israel (see EX 17:8–16). The Anakites (13:22, 29, 33) are a people remembered as giant in stature and associated with the Nephilim (see GEN 6:1–4); they are later defeated (Josh 15:14). For the other peoples, see GEN 15:19–21.

Unrest among the people at the report (13:30) occasions a division among the spies. Caleb responds by expressing confidence in Israel's ability to overcome all obstacles. The other scouts (Joshua is not separated out until 14:6–9, 30) give 'an unfavourable report of the land' (13:32), voicing alarm at the size and strength of its inhabitants and their cities and expressing a belief that Israel would be defeated (so 'devours' in 13:32). This report is exaggerated for effect; it succeeds. The people are seduced by the negative report (14:36), despise God's promise of land (14:31), and complain against Moses and Aaron out of fear for their lives and the fate of their dependants (cf. 31:13–18). They plot to choose a new leader and reverse the Exodus (14:4)! They persist in spite of the leaders' urgent pleas ('fell on their faces'; 16:4, 22), expressions of distress ('tore their clothes'; Gen 37:34), and assurances that the indigenous peoples are 'bread' (that is, we will 'devour' them, not they us, contrary to 13:32; cf. Ps 14:4) and their gods will provide no protection (lit. 'shadow'; cf. Ps 91:1), for 'the LORD is with us'. Rather than rejoice in the report of 'an exceedingly good land' and trust that God will see to the promise, the people 'rebel against the LORD' and threaten to stone Joshua and Caleb to death.

To these developments God responds (on 'glory' see 9:15–23). This response has several dimensions. If this kind of detail were present in the other sin and judgement stories, a comparable understanding would no doubt be evident.

1. God voices a lament (14:11), echoing those of the people and Moses (11:11–14), using language familiar to the psalms (cf. Ps 13:1–2). God does not remain coolly unaffected in the face of these developments. But the judgement that follows is spoken, not with the icy indifference of a judge, but with the mixed sorrow and anger of a suitor who has been rejected. That God's lament is repeated in 14:26, interrupting the announcement of judgement, reinforces this

understanding (see Fretheim 1984: 107–26). The phrase 'you shall know my displeasure' (14:34) may refer to this divine frustration.

2. God announces a disastrous judgement (14:12), comparable to that visited upon Egypt (Ex. 9:15). God will disown Israel and start over with Moses. Given what follows, this is a preliminary announcement, a point for debate with Moses (cf. 16:20–1; Ex 32:9–14). Yet, such a judgement would be deserved.

3. God engages Moses in conversation (14:13–35). Moses argues (cf. EX 32:11–14; Deut 32:26–7) that God's reputation among the nations (the Egyptians and, remarkably, the Canaanites) is at stake; they will conclude that God failed in his promise to give them the land. Their opinion should count with God; God agrees that it does, for God's goal is that his glory fill the earth (14:21). Moses also appeals to God's promise from that previous interaction (see EX 34:6–7), pleading for God to act according to his steadfast love: to forgive the people as he had done 'ten times' (frequently, Gen 31:7). Such intercession is reported elsewhere as prayer (11:2; 21:7) or action that 'turned back my wrath' (25:11) and diminished the effects of a plague (16:46–50).

4. God responds favourably to Moses and forgives Israel (14:20); but forgiveness, while it ameliorates the effects of sin (Israel is not annihilated), does not cut off all consequences. This is true for all acts of forgiveness; the consequences of sin, which can catch up the innocent (as here), need ongoing salvific attention (e.g. abuse in its various forms). In this case, the build-up of the effects of sin means that the old generation will die in the wilderness and their children suffer the fall-out of the adults' infidelity (14:33; 26:64–5; 32:10–12). Those who brought the bad report die off early (14:37). Yet, the consequences are not total: the children, ages 1–19 (14:29, 31; cf. 1:3), and the *clans* (see Josh 14:6–14) of Caleb (14:14) and Joshua (14:30) will enter the land. So, finally, God does not disinherit this people, and a new generation will possess the land. But the entire community is now to turn away and continue their wandering for a generation (14:25, 34).

5. God announces the judgement (14:21–35), this time as a solemn oath, made as certain as God's own life (14:21, 28), and details that judgement in moral order terms, i.e. what goes around comes around (14:28–35). They have sinned, they will bear (the effects of) their sin (14:34). A key verse is 14:28, 'I will do to you the very things I heard you say'. In effect: your will be done, not mine. Their desire for death in the

wilderness (14:2) is granted (14:32–3); their rejection of the land (14:3) is agreed to (14:30); their desire for a return to Egypt (14:3–4) is brought close to hand (14:25); their claim that the children would become booty (14:3) causes the children to suffer that fate at their own hands (14:33) rather than in the land (14:31); they want different leaders (14:4), they will get them (14:30). They do not believe that God is with them (14:8–9); they discover he is not (14:43–4). The forty days of scouting become forty years of wandering (14:34). Judgement is intrinsic to the deed ('you shall bear your iniquity', 14:34; cf. 32:23); God does not introduce it into the situation. God is not arbitrary, but facilitates a consequence that correlates with the deed. One might speak of a wearing down of the divine patience in view of 14:22; the other side of the coin is that persistent negative human conduct will in time take its toll, and God will see to the proper functioning of the moral order.

Having heard these words of judgement, the people mourn at what has been lost, confess their sin, and seek to make things right by taking the land on their own (14:39–45; cf. Deut 1:41–5). Moses sees that it is too late. God has now issued a new command (14:25) and they will be defeated, for God will not be with them (cf. 14:9). The die has been cast, and God's word about their future is certain. Moses' word proves to be correct; God (the ark) does not go with them and they are defeated. God's presence, not human strength, is what finally will count in Israel's life.

(15:1–41) Statutes for Life in the Land The wilderness narrative is interrupted by a series of statutes—probably late Priestly additions— pertaining to the time 'when you come into the land' (vv. 2, 18) 'throughout your generations' (vv. 15, 21, 23, 37). For the coherence of this chapter in its context, see Olson (1996: 90–101). Such laws, following upon rebellion and judgement, function to assure the community in a concrete way that God still intends a future for them; hence, law essentially functions as promise, at least for the new generation. For the old generation, however, the laws would function only as threat, for they would not live to obey them. Such an interweaving of law and narrative is common in the Pentateuch, and is revealing of the dynamic relationship of law and changing life circumstances.

One such matter pertains to the non-Israelites in the camp. The statutes in vv. 1–31 apply equally to outsiders (vv. 14–16, 26, 29, 30;

cf. 9:14). They are given equal status before God: 'you and the alien shall be alike before the LORD' (v. 15; cf. Lev 19:33–4, 'you shall love the alien as yourself'). Other changes are evident.

(15:1–16) prescribes that a grain offering (flour mixed with oil) and a drink offering (wine)—agricultural products—are to accompany each animal (vv. 11–12) presented for the 'offerings by fire' listed in v. 3 (for detail, see LEV 1–7). What was previously required only for the offering of first fruits and the festival of Weeks (Lev 23:12–18) and for the nazirite consecration (6:14–17) now applies to all offerings. The amount of these offerings increases with the size of the animal (lamb, vv. 4–5; ram, vv. 6–7; bull, vv. 8–10). The repeated reference to 'a pleasing odour to the LORD' (vv. 3, 7, 10, 13, 14, 24) is a vivid way of speaking of that which brings pleasure to God (see GEN 8:21–2) because it signifies a healthy relationship.

(15:17–21) prescribes, on the occasion of baking bread (in the land), a donation of one loaf from the first batch of dough. A donation is any gift for the service of the sanctuary, given to acknowledge that all such gifts come from God. In this case the bread would be food for the priests. This statute broadens earlier statutes regarding first fruits to include that produced by humans (see Ex 23:19; Lev 23:9–14; cf. 18:13–18).

(15:22–36) Various sacrifices for atonement for unintentional sins (cf. LEV 4:13–21; for detail see Milgrom 1990: 402–5), for the 'whole people' (vv. 22–6) and for the individual (vv. 27–9), and penalties for individuals who commit 'high-handed' sins, i.e. who are defiant and unrepentant (vv. 30–1; see Milgrom 1990: 122–5). In 5:5–8 (cf. LEV 6:7) even intentional sins can be atoned for, apparently because the persons are repentant (though see 16:46). The priests are those who make atonement for both congregation and individual (vv. 25, 28). This is the means God has established in and through which to effect both corporate and individual forgiveness.

Those who sin defiantly (the old generation of chs. 11–14 is in view) will be 'cut off' from the people (see 9:13). The following incident of intentional sabbath-breaking (vv. 32–6) illustrates such defiance. The sabbath-breaker's labour did carry the death penalty (see EX 31:14–15; 35:2–3); yet it was not clear what to do with him (15:34). Though much disputed (see Milgrom 1990: 408–10), this may mean (cf. LEV 24:12) that,

though the death penalty was clear, the community awaited a word from God either regarding the means of execution or before proceeding to such a severe punishment (gang stoning).

(15:37–41) (cf. Deut 22:12) pertains to clothing. Tassels are to be attached to each corner of the garments of all Israelites, with a blue(-purple) cord on each (still worn on prayer shawls by Orthodox Jewish men). This cord was a public sign of Israel's status as a holy people and a reminder of what that entailed. The call to be holy (v. 40; see EX 19:6; LEV 19:2) is a call to exemplify that holiness in daily life, to be true to the relationship in which they already stand. The fundamental way in which the people do justice to this relationship is by obedience to the commandments. Israel's holiness is not simply an internal disposition; it is to be expressed in every sphere of life. The fundamental grounding for this is the fact that God is YHWH, the Lord who brought them out of Egypt.

(16:1–50) The Rebellions of Korah and Others Num 16–18 focuses on issues relating to the value and legitimacy of leadership within Israel, especially priestly leadership as it relates to service at the tabernacle.

This passage in its present form portrays two major rebellions, one by Korah, Dathan, Abiram, and 250 lay leaders (vv. 1–40) and, in response to their deaths, a second rebellion by 'the whole congregation' (vv. 41–50). The role of Korah, one of the Levites (about whom the narratives have been silent heretofore), draws the entire community into a rebellious stance. The conflict between the Levites and the Aaronides may reflect later controversies between rival priestly groups (cf. 12:1–16; 17:1–13).

Issues of coherence make it likely that at least two major traditions have been interwoven. The epic tradition centred on a revolt led by the Reubenites (Dathan and Abiram, vv. 12–15); it has been overlaid by a Priestly tradition, wherein Korah leads the rebellion (vv. 3–11, 16–24, 35). Other expansions may be evident, e.g. the role of the 250 lay leaders, but it is possible to read the whole as an (awkwardly ordered) unity.

Korah, a son of Kohath, belonged to the Levite clan responsible for the tabernacle's 'most holy things' (4:4), but they were not to touch or see them (4:15, 20). Korah is the eponymous ancestor of a later group of temple singers (1 Chr 6:31–48; his name occurs in eleven

Psalm superscriptions, e.g., 44–9). Dathan and Abiram (and On, not mentioned again) were members of the tribe of Reuben, the firstborn son of Jacob (the demotion of the tribe may be due to this rebellion, 26:9–11). These persons (probably with different agendas) make common cause against Moses and Aaron. They are joined by 250 lay leaders and confront Moses and Aaron with the charge that they 'have gone too far' in 'exalting' themselves above other members of the community (vv. 3, 13). While this charge may have been sparked by their prominence in 15:1–41, it may also be related to their harsh words about the old generation (14:26–35), among whom the rebels would be numbered.

The claim (v. 3) that 'everyone' in the camp is holy is not incorrect (as just noted in 15:40, and perhaps prompted by it); the problem is the implication drawn, namely, that Aaron and Moses have no special prerogatives for leadership. The claim for the holiness of everyone is not simply related to a move to gain priestly prerogatives for all Levites (as Moses interprets it, v. 10), though this is primary. The presence of Reubenites and 250 laymen reveals another interest, namely, extending 'secular' leadership prerogatives beyond Moses to representatives from all twelve tribes, especially firstborn Reuben (so vv. 12–15).

Moses responds in deed and word to this confrontation (vv. 4–17). After 'falling on his face' (see 14:5), Moses proposes a test. The antagonists are to bring censers (metal trays that hold hot coals on which incense is burned, cf. LEV 10:1–2) to the tabernacle and prepare them for offering incense. If God accepts their offerings, their priestly status would be recognized. The phrase 'and who is holy' (v. 5) assumes gradations of holiness; even if all are holy, God chooses the priest and this status entails a holiness that sets him apart from other holy ones (cf. 6:8). So *God*, not Moses, will decide the identity of 'the holy one' who is to approach the altar. But Moses makes his opinions clear. *They* (and here Levites, whom Korah represents, become the focus), not *we* (v. 3), have gone too far (v. 7)!

The reply in vv. 8–11 addresses the Levites' challenge to Aaron's leadership (v. 11). Their displeasure with the duties they have been assigned by God (1:48–54), and their desire for higher status, is a move 'against the LORD' (v. 11). They have elevated privilege above service. Next Moses speaks to challenges to his own leadership (vv. 12–15), sending for Dathan and Abiram. They twice refuse to come, believing themselves

to be deceived (to 'put out the eyes'). In their complaint about Moses' authoritarianism (after all, Reuben was the firstborn son), they give Moses' own words in v. 9 an ironic twist (v. 13), and even call *Egypt* the land of milk and honey! Moses tells God (spitefully?) to ignore their offerings, i.e. not act through them on their behalf, for he has taken nothing (cf. 1 Sam 12:3) from them or harmed them. Finally, Moses repeats his instructions to Korah, adding that Aaron is also to appear (vv. 16–17).

The time for the divine decision arrives (vv. 18–35). Each of the men stands before the Lord at the tent with his censer prepared. In addition, Korah assembles the entire congregation, apparently in sympathy with him, to watch the proceedings. The glory of the Lord appears (see 9:15–16) and God tells Moses and Aaron to move away for God is going to destroy the assembled congregation (in essence, the old generation; cf. v. 45) immediately. But Moses and Aaron intercede on behalf of the congregation (v. 22), for not all should bear the consequences for the 'one person' (an exaggeration for Korah is representative of the rebellious group; cf. GEN 18:22–33). The 'God of the spirits of all flesh' (cf. 27:16) is an appeal to God as Creator, who gives breath (i.e. spirit) to all.

God responds positively to the intercession and separates the congregation from the 'dwelling' (sing. here and v. 27; since sing. is used only for God's dwelling, does it refer to their 'tents', v. 26, ironically?) of the rebels and their families. Dathan and Abiram had refused to leave their homes (16:14) and Korah had apparently joined them. The 250 men remain at the tent to offer incense, and are later consumed by fire (v. 35; cf. 3:4; 11:1; LEV 10:1–2). The inclusion of the families and the command not even to touch (v. 26) suggests their sins have polluted all that is theirs (on corporate guilt, see JOSH 7:24–6).

When the separation occurs, Moses sets up a test to demonstrate that this is God's decision not his own. If these people die a natural death, then he is wrong; if God 'creates something new' (a creation for this moment) and the ground opens up and swallows them, and they descend prematurely to Sheol (the abode of all the dead; cf. the image in Isa 5:14), then they have despised the Lord (note: not Moses). The latter happens immediately to 'everyone who belonged to Korah and all their goods' (v. 32). Korah, Dathan, and Abiram are not specifically mentioned (they are in 26:9–10; cf. Deut 11:6; Ps 106:17). The people panic, perhaps because of complicity; it quickly turns to accusation, v. 41.

In the wake of the killing of the 250 men because of their presumption, special attention is given to their censers (vv. 36–40), which became holy because of the use to which they were put, even by unqualified persons ('at the cost of their lives'). They are gathered from the fire by Eleazar and not Aaron (see Lev 21:11) and, at God's command, hammered into an altar covering (perhaps a supplement; cf. Ex 38:2) to serve as a reminder that only Aaron's sons can approach the Lord to offer incense.

The congregation, however, remembers only the killings, blames Moses and Aaron, and threatens them (16:41). Again the glory of the Lord appears, this time to Moses and Aaron, and God again threatens to annihilate this people (cf. vv. 19–21). Once again Moses and Aaron intercede by falling on their faces, presumably pleading with God (cf. v. 22). In the absence of God's response, they take the initiative and act to make atonement for the (intentional! cf. 15:22–31) sins of the people through the use of incense (unprecedented, but appropriate for this story). They do so with haste, and at some risk (he 'stood between the dead and the living'—a job description for a priest!), because a plague had already broken out (on divine judgement, see NUM 13–14; note that wrath is impersonally described, see NUM 1:53). The act of atonement had the effect of stopping the plague, but not before many died (14,700).

The disaster experienced by Korah and his company proves the special status of both Moses (vv. 28–9) and Aaron (v. 40). It is not that such leaders never fail (12:1–16; 20:12) or that other persons are never channels God might use to reveal his will (11:24–30; Balaam), but these persons are chosen and are deserving of respect. Implicit is that the way to adjudicate differences with leaders in the community is not through envy or personal attack (common in Numbers), but through a careful discernment of God's will for the flourishing of the community. God goes to enormous lengths to protect the place of good leaders (on the divine wrath, see NUM 1:53).

(17:1–13) Aaron's Blossoming Rod Whereas 16:1–40 was concerned about the status of both Aaron and Moses, and Aaron among other Levites, this passage focuses on Aaron 'the man' (v. 5) among other tribal leaders. In view of the renewed rebellions of the people *and* Aaron's risking his life on their behalf (16:41–50), God makes another effort to demonstrate Aaron's priestly status. Whereas 16:40 showed

that through an ordeal that led to death, this passage makes the same point through an ordeal that symbolizes life (the budding staff), emblematic of Aaron's life-saving actions in 16:46–50. Both the bronze covering for the altar (16:38) and Aaron's staff serve as ongoing visual signs for the community of God's choice of Aaron's priestly leadership. This story, best designated a legend (with parallels in many cultures), may reflect later struggles between rival priestly groups. Yet, unlike 16:3–11, rivalry with the Levites is not evident.

God's effort on behalf of Aaron's priestly status is settled by means of a unique ordeal. At God's command, Moses places twelve staffs (a symbol of authority; 'staff' and 'tribe' translate the same Hebrew word) from the leaders (cf. 16:2) of the tribes, each inscribed with a leader's name, before the Lord, i.e. the ark (see 10:35–6), in which the 'covenant', the Decalogue, was placed (Ex 25:16, 21). Aaron's staff, the powers of which had already been demonstrated (EX 7:8–12, 19; 8:16–17), was added to them (the Levites are the thirteenth tribe in Numbers). God set the terms: the staff that sprouts would indicate which leader God had chosen for priestly prerogatives. Upon Moses' inspection the following morning, only the staff of Aaron had sprouted; moreover, it flowered and bore *ripe* almonds (symbolic of the life-enchancing, fruit-bearing capacity of priests for the community). Moses shows the evidence to all the people. At God's command Moses put Aaron's staff before the ark, to be kept as a warning (Hebrew 'sign') to the rebels. For usage of this image in messianic texts, see ISA 11:1–2.

God had performed such a sign 'to put a stop to the complaints' against 'you' (pl.; Moses and Aaron) and 'me' (vv. 5, 10); it soon becomes clear that God did not succeed in his objective (see 21:5).

The concluding verses (12–13) lead into the next chapter. The people, apparently convinced, express their dismay and worry about dying. Yet the focus is not on what they have done, but on the possibility of encroaching upon the tabernacle precincts. The next chapter provides protections against such a possibility.

(18:1–32) Rights and Responsibilities of Priests and Levites The Priestly material of chs. 18–19 constitutes a second break in the narrative flow (cf. 15:1–14). On law and narrative, see NUM 15.

Given the establishment of Aaron's status with the people and other Levites (chs. 16–17),

and the concern of the people about encroachment on the tabernacle (17:12–13), a redefinition
of the responsibilities of the tribe of Levi is now
given along with their means of support
(though the people are not said to hear this).
vv. 1, 8, 20 contain the only cases (except Lev
10:8), of God's speaking to Aaron alone, indicating its importance for Aaronides.

vv. 1–7 gather previous material (see 1:50–3;
3:5–10, 14–39; 4:1–33; 8:14–19) and delineate the
relationship among the various groups regarding their duties at the tent of meeting ('covenant', 17:7). The protection of the community as a
whole ('outsider') from 'wrath' (v. 5, see NUM 1:53)
is a prime concern (vv. 1a, 4–5, 7, 22; 'outsider' in
v. 7 would also include Levites). Aaronides and
Levites alone (not laity) 'bear responsibility for
offences', that is, suffer the consequences for
violations (their own and that of the laity) relative to the sanctuary (vv. 1a, 23). In addition,
priests are responsible for other priests (v. 1b)
and priests and Levites for Levites (v. 3, 'they and
you'). God stresses to the Aaronides that priesthood is a gift from God as is the service of their
'brother Levites' (vv. 6–7; cf. v. 19); they cannot
presume upon their office in relationship to
their brothers or all Israel.

vv. 8–32, a gathering of materials from Lev
6–7; v. 27 primarily reviews the God-com-
manded portion due to the Aaronides from
the people (vv. 8–20) and the Levites (vv. 25–
32, a new provision) and that due to the Levites
(vv. 21–4), in perpetuity (vv. 8, 11, 19, 23), in spite
of their failures.

In vv. 8–20 the 'portion' consists of those
'holy gifts' the people give to the Lord, which
in turn God 'gives' to the priests and Levites and
their 'sons and daughters' for the sake of their
support and for that of the sanctuary. vv. 9–10
specify the 'most holy' gifts, reserved for the
priests: 'every offering of theirs' (those parts
not burned, 'reserved from the fire'). vv. 11–18
specify the 'holy' gifts (v. 19), 'elevation offerings' (*tĕnûpâ*) or gifts dedicated to God, to be
eaten by any clean member of the priests' families. They include first fruits ('choice produce');
anything 'devoted' to the Lord's service, pro-
scribed under the provisions of the ban (see
LEV 27:21, 28); and firstborn human and unclean
animals, for which the priests receive the redemption price (v. 15 is detailed in 16–18). On
the redemption of the firstborn, see NUM 3:11–13,
40–51.

These holy gifts of God to the priests are
called 'a covenant of salt forever before the
LORD' (v. 19). Salt is presented with all offerings

(Lev 2:13); as a preservative it becomes a symbol
for an everlasting covenant (see 2 Chr 13:5). This
provision is God's commitment to the priests in
perpetuity, for the Aaronides have no property.
God alone is their share and possession, that is,
they are dependent for life and health upon
the gifts of God, albeit gifts mediated through
human beings, rather than on land.

The Levites' portion for their work is
the Israelites' tithe of agricultural produce (vv.
21–4). The tithe belongs to YHWH (v. 24) and is
given to the Levites (on the title see Milgrom
1990: 432–6). They also have no tribal territory,
but are given forty-eight cities with pasture land
(see 35:1–8). On vv. 22–3, see vv. 1–7.

Finally, in a speech to Moses, God commands
the Levites to give a tithe of the tithe they have
received (the 'best of it') to the Aaronides (vv.
25–32). The other nine-tenths of the offering
shall be no longer holy and become in effect
their own produce, 'as payment for your service'. But if they do not give their tithe, that will
'profane' the holy gifts, and they shall die.

(19:1–22) Ritual of the Red Heifer 5:1–4 stipu-
lated a measure to be taken in cases of 'contact
with a corpse'. Such unclean persons were to be
placed 'outside the camp' so as not to defile the
community. This passage expands upon that
statute, providing for rituals of purification for
such persons in perpetuity (mostly laypersons,
Israelite and alien), especially in view of all who
had died (e.g. 16:32–5, 49) and would die
(14:32–5). Caring for the dead is a necessary
(and dangerous) task, so this impurity is not
linked to sin. On purity issues, see Nelson
(1993: 17–38). The origin of this ritual is unknown, but it probably can be traced to ancient
Near Eastern rites developed to deal with the
same issue. These statutes are to be conveyed to
the Israelites (v. 2; contrast 18).

The choice of a (brownish-)red heifer (actually, cow) perhaps symbolized blood/life (red
animals were so used in the ancient Near East);
it was to be unblemished (see Lev 21:16–24;
22:20) and never used for work (Deut 21:3–4).
The burning of the entire animal (including its
blood/life, v. 5, uniquely here) may have been
thought to concentrate life in the ashes which,
when mixed with water and applied to the
unclean person or thing, would counteract (literally thought to absorb?) the contagious impurity of death and the diminishment of life in
the community. This happened, not in some
magical way, but because God had decreed it
so. The placement of cedar wood and hyssop

(cleansing agents), and crimson material (symbolizing blood?), during the burning intensified the purifying quality (literal and symbolic) of the resultant ashes. The sprinkling of the blood/life seven times *towards* the entrance of the tabernacle (that is, towards God; cf. Lev 4:6) shows the importance of the ritual for maintaining the integrity of the community in relationship to God (19:4, 13, 20).

vv. 1–10 specify the procedure by which the life-giving and cleansing agent was prepared under the supervision of the priest (the absence of reference to death may mean an earlier, more general application). Eleazar is charged with this duty (Aaron dies in 20:28); he and those who assist him must be clean, but they become unclean in the process (because of contact with the holy) and short-term 'decontamination' rituals are prescribed for each.

vv. 11–13, detailed in 14–22, specify the use to which the ashes and fresh ('running') water are put for persons and things (vv. 14–16) that have had contact with death. As in other cases (see Lev 12:2) they are unclean for seven days; during this time, if they are to become clean, they must twice be sprinkled with this mixture by a clean person (vv. 17–19; outside the camp? cf. v. 9 and 5:3–4). Otherwise they 'defile the tabernacle' where God dwells (5:3) and shall be 'cut off from Israel' (19:13, 20; see NUM 9:13) for the sake of the community's wholeness.

(20:1–29) The Disobedience of Moses and Aaron The text returns to a narrative mode, explaining why Israel's key leaders did not enter Canaan. It is enclosed by the deaths of Miriam and Aaron and marked especially by the 'rebellion' of Moses and Aaron. It may be a reworking of the story in EX 17:1–7, which also took place at a place called Meribah ('Quarrelled'). Priestly materials surround a report from the epic tradition in 20:14–21.

v. 1 is difficult given the reference to Kadesh in 13:26. Perhaps God's command in 14:25 to wander back towards Egypt was in fact carried out (contrast 33:36–7), and so they arrive again in Kadesh (they set out again in v. 22). Probably the forty years in the wilderness has been completed, as v. 12 and the time of Aaron's death (v. 28 with 33:38) suggests. The 'first month' in v. 1 would thus be in the fortieth year. On the problems of redaction in chs. 20–1 see Milgrom (1990: 463–7).

The people again complain to Moses and Aaron about wilderness conditions, but this time the narrator agrees that 'there was no

water' (vv. 2, 5). They return to the basic questions they had in 14:2–4; events have apparently not changed this people. They even express the wish that they had died with Korah, Dathan, and Abiram (16:32–5, 49)! Again, Moses and Aaron fall on their faces and turn towards God (14:5; 16:4); again the glory of the Lord appears (see 9:15–16).

The reader expects to hear about God's judgement; but God has a different response this time, recognizing that the people's need for water is real. God commands Moses to take 'the staff' (from v. 9 this is Aaron's staff that had been placed in the tent, 17:10–11; 'his' staff refers to the one he was using, v. 11) and '*command* [speak to] the rock before their eyes to yield its water' (my itals.). The reference to 'the rock' (v. 8) suggests a prominent rock in the area. This was the way in which Moses was 'to bring water out of the rock for them'.

Moses takes the staff as God had commanded him. The reference to Moses' obedience usually concludes his actions; here it breaks into the sequence, suggesting that his following actions are less than what God commanded. Having gathered the people, Moses calls them rebels (as does God, 17:10), and asks them:'shall *we* bring water for you out of the rock?' (my itals.). He proceeds to *strike* the rock twice with Aaron's staff, and water flows. God's response is negative: Moses and Aaron did not trust God to 'show my holiness' before the people, and hence they will not lead the people into the land. The place name Meribah is linked to the *people's* quarrelling with God (as in EX 17:7, without judgement) and to God's showing his holiness, perhaps because of the gift of water (but apparently less so than if Moses and Aaron had trusted, v. 12).

A much debated question: what did Moses and Aaron (Aaron stays in the background) do to deserve this divine response (for the history of interpretation, see Milgrom 1990: 448–56)? The charge in v. 12—they did not 'trust' in God (used of the people in 14:11, with the same result) 'to show my holiness' before Israel; in v. 24— they 'rebelled against my command'; in 27:14— they 'rebelled against my word…and did not show my holiness' before Israel; in Deut 32:51— they 'broke faith…by failing to maintain my holiness among the Israelites'; in Deuteronomy elsewhere (1:37; 3:26; 4:21)—God was angry towards Moses because of the *people*, as if Moses suffered vicariously; in Ps 106:32–3—the people make Moses' spirit bitter and his words rash (v. 10?), qualifying Moses' fault.

It is difficult to bring coherence to this variety; it may be purposely ambiguous. The 'we' of v. 10 could suggest that this was their work not God's, hence reducing the witness to God. But the focus in v. 24 and 27:14 is 'rebelling against' God's command (a major issue in Numbers), ironically using Moses' own word regarding the people (v. 10). This could entail a lack of trust or breaking faith. Neither the questioning of the people nor the striking of the rock (rather than speaking to it) followed God's command. The former, with its negative address, does not recognize the real needs of the people (as God did *twice* in v. 8), and the latter would be less a witness to God's power. Thus God's compassion and power, both analytic of God's holiness, are compromised 'in the eyes of' the people.

The point is sharply made that the end result (here, water to drink) is not only what counts as a witness to God, but also the means by which that result is achieved. The most trusted of God's leaders fall into the trap of thinking that the end justifies any means. The reader should beware of both 'rationalization' and supernaturalism in interpreting stories such as this (as with the manna and quail, 11:7–9, 31). The provision of food and water is not to be divorced from a recognition of nature's God-given potential. Even in the wilderness God's world is not without resources. In ways not unlike the gifts of manna and quail, water courses through rock formations. God is not creating out of nothing here; water does not materialize out of thin air. God works in and through the natural to provide for his people. The rock itself plays a significant role in this.

(**20:14–21**) Before reporting the death of Aaron, an interlude recounts developments in Israel's journeying. They are 'on the edge' of Edom (v. 16) and request permission from the Edomites to use the King's Highway (the major north–south route through Transjordan) to pass through and, presumably, enter Canaan from the east (cf. the failure from the south in 14:39–45). Edom's refusal to allow Israel to pass creates an external difficulty that matches the internal difficulties in the chapter. Together they raise questions about endangered promises. The text gives no reason for the reader to think this request of Edom was unfaithful because God was not consulted.

The Edomites are the first people Israel encounters since Sinai (cf. GEN 25:19–36:43 on Jacob/Esau). Moses initiates the contact by sending messengers to the 'king of Edom' (no evidence exists that Edom was a kingdom at this time; cf. the chieftains of GEN 36). Moses' letter, typical in that world, uses the word 'brother' for Edom, a dual reference assuming a relationship of both ally and actual brother (see Gen 33:9).

Moses briefly recounts Israel's history from the descent into Egypt through the Exodus to the present time. Notable is the confessional character of this account: they cried to YHWH, who heard and sent an angel, God in human form (see NUM 9:15–23; EX 14:19; 23:20–3), to bring them out. It is assumed that the king of Edom knows who YHWH is (cf. Ex 15:11)! Given the last reference to an Edom–Israel encounter, which ends on an ambivalent note (33:4–17), it is not surprising that Edom refuses (Judg 11:17). Edom refuses even though Israel promises not to trouble them and, after negotiation, even promises to pay for water (vv. 19–20). Edom's show of military force convinces Israel to go 'around' Edom (so 21:4; Judg 11:18; Deut 2:4–8 has access to a memory that the Israelites passed through Edom without incident).

(**20:22–9**) returns to internal issues, with the installation of Eleazar as successor to his father as high priest and the death of Aaron. The people continue their journey along the border of Edom and come to Mount Hor (site unknown). In view of Aaron's imminent death, and at God's command and as a reminder of their rebellion ('you' is pl.), Moses, Aaron, and Eleazar climb to the top of the mountain (cf. Moses' death in DEUT 32:50; 34). Aaron's vestments are transferred to Eleazar before 'the whole congregation', an assuring sight signifying continuity into the future. Aaron dies (is 'gathered to his people', cf. Gen 25:8) and is mourned by Israel for thirty days (as with Moses, Deut 34:8), rather than the usual seven.

The next five chapters are transitional. The new generation seems to be essentially, if not entirely in place (20:12). And so the texts portray a mix of the old and the new.

(**21:1–35**) Victory, Complaint, and Healing The narrative from 11:1 to this point has been predominantly negative. The promulgation of laws for life in the land (chs. 15; 18; 19) and the installation of Eleazar have given signs of hope. As the narrative moves towards the census of the new generation (ch. 26), these signs become more frequent. Indeed, from this time on Israel will be successful in all its battles. Yet negative realities still abound. In this passage military victories enclose a negative report about further complaint and judgement.

Victory over Arad (vv. 1–3): this text functions paradigmatically for other holy war texts in a way that 11:1–3 did for the complaint passages; it summarizes the essence of what is at stake. For the geographical and chronological problems associated with Canaanite contact at Arad and Hormah (a region in the Negeb), given the references to Edom in 20:21 and 21:4, see Milgrom (1990: 456–8).

The Canaanites of Arad fought with some success against Israel; this prompts 'Israel' to make a vow to wage holy war against them if God would give them victory (cf. Jephthah's vow, Judg 11:30–1). Israel's victory reverses the earlier failure at Hormah (14:45).

Israel then fulfils the vow, utterly destroying the people and their towns. Such texts (see also ch. 31) are virtually genocidal in their ferocity towards others. These understandings are grounded in a concern about infidelity and extreme danger to Israel's future (Deut 20:16–18) and unfaithful Israel experiences similar destruction (see Deut 28:15–68). Such practices are followed only in this era of land settlement (and hence are not paradigmatic, even for Israel). Yet they rightly remain incomprehensible to modern sensibilities. That Israel understands their God to want such destruction makes this practice even more difficult to fathom. The canon as a whole subverts such understandings (see Isa 2:1–4).

(21:4–9) returns for a final time to the complaining mode (for form, NUM 11; for content, NUM 14), qualifying the victories that enclose it. The seriousness of the complaint is evident in that it is directed for the first time against both God and Moses (though see 14:2–3), yet for the first time the people sincerely (cf. 14:40) confess their sin, and the segment ends on a healing note. This occurs as the people turn towards the Red Sea, that is, the Gulf of Aqaba, and begin their journey around Edom. The complaint focuses on the lack of (palatable) food and water, and God is charged with intending death in the Exodus. The God-facilitated effect of their complaining is an infestation of poisonous (lit. fiery, because of the burning) snakes that results in many deaths (not unheard of in this area). The people confess their sin to Moses and request his intercession to have the snakes taken away. Though the people repent (and presumably are forgiven), the snakes are not removed nor kept from biting. In other words, as is typical, the effects of sin continue beyond forgiveness. But God works on those effects by

commanding a means (a homeopathic Egyptian technique to ward off snakes and heal snake-bite), with which the promise of God is associated, through which to heal those who are bitten (cf. Wis 16:7; the combination of prayer and medicine in 2 Kings 20:1–7). Moses makes a copper image of a snake and sets it upon a pole for all to see; God is true to promises made, healing those who look to it and trust the means God has provided. The copper snake ends up in the temple, but its meaning is distorted and Hezekiah has it destroyed (2 Kings 18:4). On snakes as symbols of both death and life in the ancient Near East and the discovery of copper snakes in that area, including a copper snake 5 in. long near Timnah in a copper-smelting region, see Joines (1974); Milgrom (1990: 459–60) (for NT usage, see JN 3:14–15).

(21:10–20) Travel in Transjordan: the tempo of the journey picks up as Israel moves through various places on its way to Canaan. The character of the journey changes as well; water is provided at the *divine* initiative at Beer (v. 16, meaning 'well', the first positive etymology in Numbers) and the people sing songs of appreciation (vv. 17–18, 27–30, from unknown sources).

Though several sites cannot be identified (and do not fully correspond to the itinerary in 33:41–9), the route takes Israel around Edom and Moab. The Wadi Zered is the boundary between Moab and Edom and the Wadi Arnon the northern boundary of Moab. The Arnon prompts the narrator to insert a portion from the otherwise unknown Book of the Wars of the Lord (apparently an early collection of poems about Israel's conquests). This poetic piece (though not spoken by Israel) and the songs in vv. 17–18 and 27–30 contribute to the increasingly anticipatory character of the march. Finally, they arrive at Mount Pisgah 'across the Jordan from Jericho' (22:1).

(21:21–35) Victories over the Amorites: these reports probably precede 21:10–20 chronologically. For greater detail, cf. Deut 2:24–3:7. With Israel situated on the 'boundary of the Amorites' (21:13), Moses sends a message (similar to 20:17) to King Sihon requesting safe passage. Moses receives the same reply as he got from Edom, but Sihon also pursues Israel in battle. In response, Israel defeats his armies, kills him, and takes possession of his lands, to the border of the Ammonites in the east (at the Wadi Jabbok), including the capital Heshbon, perhaps a short distance east of Jericho. These lands include former Moabite lands, and the

song in 21:27–30 (cf. Jer 48:45–6) praises the
victory of the *Amorites* over the Moabites and
their god Chemosh (21:29) and the capture of
their lands, now belonging to Israel. Notable is
Israel's integration of a non-Israelite story into
their own story of these events. Because Sihon
defeated Moab and Israel defeated Sihon this
enhances Israel's strength. Israel's 'settling' in
the land of the Amorites sets up a later controversy (see NUM 32).

The victory over the aggressor Og, another
Amorite king (vv. 33–5), mirrors that of the
victory over Arad in 21:1–3 (cf. Josh 10:8), with
its stress upon holy war, and this in express
response to a word from God. The total destruction is like what was done to Sihon (v. 34).

Israel is now situated at the boundary of the
promised land and is given a foretaste of victories and settlements to come. Those promises are
now raised in the story of Balaam.

(22:1–24:25) The Story of Balaam This text has
been deemed intrusive in its context, and its
central figure Balaam thought less than worthy
of God's purposes for Israel. He is a travelling
professional seer, and a non-Israelite at that,
who seems all too ready to pronounce curses
if the price is right. But the story with its oracles
has in fact been cleverly woven into the larger
fabric of Numbers and God uses Balaam in
remarkable ways to bring blessing to Israel.

Source-critical attempts to divide this story
into J and E (only 22:1 is P) have not been
successful. Coherence difficulties and the various divine names may reflect a long history of
transmission and editing of both narrative and
poetry, the earliest forms of which may date
from before the monarchy. An Aramaic inscription from the eighth century BCE has
been found at Tell Deir 'Alla in Jordan, the
contents of which are ascribed to a 'seer of
the gods' named 'Balaam, son of Beor'. He
reports a vision of a meeting of the gods who
are planning disaster for the earth (for text and
details, see Milgrom 1990: 473–6). Scholars
agree that this text and Num 22–4 both have
roots in Transjordan traditions about this legendary figure. A few biblical traditions have a
negative assessment of Balaam, perhaps having
access to still other traditions (cf. Num 31:8, 18;
Josh 13:22; Rev 2:14).

The text combines a narrative and four poetic
oracles, the basic content of which is blessing.
Literary studies have noted the repetition of key
words such as '(not)seeing' and the number
three, including a probable tripartite structure:

(*a*) Balaam's three encounters with God (22:1–
40); (*b*) Balak's three attempts to curse Israel
thwarted by Balaam's three blessings (22:41–
24:13); (*c*) A climactic fourth blessing (24:14–25).

The function of this material at this juncture
in Numbers has been delineated by Olson (1985:
156–64) especially. With its focus on the blessing of Israel and its remarkable reiteration of
divine promises, the story envisages a marvellous future for Israel at a key transition between
old generation and new. The material also functions ironically; a non-Israelite with less than
sterling credentials voices God's promises in a
way that no Israelite in Numbers does, not even
Moses. God finds a way to get the word through
in spite of the rebellions of Israel and its leaders
(and Balaam's own failings, 22:22–35; 31:8, 16).
The disastrous activities in 25:1–18 make the
words of Balaam stand out all the more
brightly. That the people do not actually hear
these words is testimony that, contrary to appearances, God continues to be at work in fulfilling these promises. Indeed, God turns even
the worst of situations (the potential curses of
Balaam) into blessing.

(22:1–40) Balak, king of Moab, is fearful that
Israel, given their numbers and victories over
the Amorites, will next turn on what is left of
his kingdom (which includes Midianites, 22:4, 7;
31:7–9) and overcome his armies with ease. And
so, as kings were wont to do in that world (cf. 1
Kings 22), he turns to a mercenary diviner from
Syria (the exact location is uncertain), famous for
his effective blessings and cursings (v. 6, an ironic
statement, given later developments!). Messengers, prepared to pay for his services, inform
Balaam of Balak's request to have him curse Israel
so that he can defeat them (in v. 11 the compli-
ment of v. 6 is omitted). Note that the curses were
not thought to be finally effective apart from
Balak's subsequent actions. Divination (usually
condemned in Israel, Deut 18:9–14) was a widely
practised 'art' whereby the meaning and course of
events was sought through various natural phenomena.

Asking for a delay in order to consult
YHWH(!), Balaam has the first of three encounters with God. That YHWH's name is placed in
the mouth of Balaam, that he is called 'my God',
converses with him, and is accepted as a matter
of course by the visitors, is remarkable. Such a
usage expresses, not a historical judgement, but
the narrator's conviction that the god with
whom Balaam had to do is none other than
YHWH (cf. Ex 15:15; Gen 26:28). The divine

enquiry into the visitors' identity (v. 9) is designed to elicit the response Balaam gives; how he responds—absolute divine foreknowledge is not assumed—will shape the nature of God's response. God prohibits Balaam from going to Moab to curse Israel, for they are blessed (see 6:22–7). Balaam obeys God and recounts the divine refusal to the visitors (both acts relate to Balaam's faithfulness to God), who report back to Balak but without any reference to God (v. 14).

Readers would expect such a reply from God and think this is the end of the matter, but not Balak: he sends a larger and more distinguished delegation, who make a more attractive offer—promising honour and writing a blank cheque (v. 17). Even with such a tempting offer, Balaam again demonstrates his faithfulness by consulting with 'YHWH my God' and telling the visitors that he is subject *exactly* (not 'less or more', v. 18) to the divine command. In view of Balaam's demonstrated and promised faithfulness, God changes the strategy and *commands* him to go and do 'only what I tell you to do' (v. 20), a word which the reader is led to think God can now speak with more confidence. Balaam goes, but the reader is left to wonder what God might tell him to do.

What follows is surprising (v. 22), probably to both ancient and modern readers (in view of various disjunctions most regard vv. 22–35 as a later interpolation). The reader (but not Balaam) is told of God's anger because he departed (for the translation, 'as he was going', see Ashley 1993: 454–5); indeed, God has become Balaam's 'adversary'. To create curiosity about the reason, the narrator delays informing the reader until v. 32, where it is clear that God still has questions about Balaam's faithfulness, remarkable in view of his responses in vv. 13–21. This strange encounter thus amounts to a 'blind' test. The reader will remember Jacob in GEN 32:22–32 and Moses in EX 4:24–6, both of whom encounter a God who creates trials as they embark upon a new venture relative to God's call. The language is also similar to Joshua's experience (JOSH 5:13–15). At the end of this test (v. 35), God's command to Balaam remains the same as it was in v. 20—to speak only what God tells him.

But to get to that goal, the narrator makes use of fable motifs with a talking donkey (cf. GEN 3:1–6; JUDG 9:7–15) to portray the test. God here uses irony and humour to get through to Balaam. The donkey becomes his teacher (!), one who sees the things of God (including potential disaster) more clearly than Balaam sees and subverts Balaam's supposed powers.

Balaam's treatment of the donkey during the journey is a sign of his unfaithfulness; he does not see the God who stands before him in increasingly inescapable ways and respond appropriately (cf. Joshua in JOSH 5:13–15). The donkey is a vehicle through which God works to show Balaam's dependence upon God for his insight and words and to sharpen his faithfulness.

With sword drawn, the angel of YHWH (God in human form, see 9:15–23) confronts Balaam and donkey three times in increasingly restrictive circumstances. The donkey alone sees the figure in the road; twice it is able to avoid a confrontation, but the third time it proves impossible and so it lies down under Balaam. Each time Balaam strikes the donkey, becoming angry (like God in v. 22) the third time. God opens the donkey's mouth and it questions Balaam about its mistreatment. Balaam thinks that he has been made to look the fool; if he had had a sword, he would have killed the animal. When the donkey queries him about their long history together, Balaam admits that the donkey has not acted this way before.

At this point God opens Balaam's eyes so that he can see as the donkey sees. When he sees the angel with drawn sword he falls on his face, presumably pleading for his life. It was not the donkey who was against him but God. The angel gives the reason for the confrontation, noting that if it had not been for the donkey's manœuverings, he would have killed Balaam. Balaam responds that, though he did not know that God opposed him, he has sinned; he offers to return home if God remains displeased. But God renews the commission (v. 35) and Balaam proceeds.

The three episodes of Balaam with his donkey are mirrored in the first three oracles of 22:41–24:13. These oracles show that the experiences of Balaam with his donkey parallel the experiences of Balak with Balaam. The donkey's experience becomes Balaam's experience. Just as the donkey is caught between God's threatening presence and Balaam's increasing anger so Balaam is caught between God's insistence on blessing and Balak's increasing anger about the curse. From another angle, Balaam's difficulties with the donkey are like God's experience with Balaam. It is a conflict of wills. Balaam has to be brought more certainly to the point where he will allow God to use him as God sees fit (see v. 38). God will open Balaam's mouth just as God opened the donkey's mouth (v. 28). From still another angle, the donkey becomes a God figure(!), speaking for God and reflecting *God's* relationship to Balaam (vv. 28–30). God has been mistreated by Balaam along the journey because Balaam thinks this trip is making him look the fool. The donkey reminds Balaam of their long life together and his faithfulness to him.

Having arrived at the boundary of Moab (v. 36), Balaam is greeted by Balak, who chides him for his initial refusal. Balaam responds by saying, rhetorically, that he does not have the power 'to say just anything' (v. 38). What God puts in his mouth, as with the prophets (see Jer 1:9; 15:16; Ezek 2:8–3:3), this is what he must say (cf. Jer 20:7–9).

(22:41–24:13) Balaam's first three oracles. The first two oracles are integral to the surrounding narrative; the third (as with the fourth) is less so but still has close links. Each situation contains seven similar elements; the third time around breaks the pattern in key ways (cf. Olson 1996: 145–7):

1. Balak brings Balaam to a high point overlooking the Israelite camp (22:41; 23:13–14, 27–8), a people so vast he cannot see them all (23:13). The place changes each time and Balak hopes that the venue (and the sight of a smaller portion of the people) might change the word spoken; in the third instance Balak uses (will of) God language (23:27). But the place makes no difference, and he finally sees all the people (24:2).

2. Balak builds seven altars and sacrifices a bull and a ram on each (23:1–2, 14, 29–30), the first and the last at Balaam's request. Sacrifices were a typical part of the diviner's art, perhaps to appease the deity and to look for omens in the entrails. Balaam's purpose may be to show Balak that he is proceeding in a proper manner. But, in fact, divination is seen to be bankrupt as a means of revelation (23:23; 24:1).

3. Balaam twice turns aside from the offerings to consult with YHWH, but the third time he does not 'look for omens' (24:1; diviner's language is used for consulting with YHWH). In the first case, he is uncertain that YHWH will meet him and informs God about the offerings (23:3–4); the second time he is certain and says nothing about offerings (23:15).

4. God twice meets Balaam and puts a word in his mouth and commands him to return and speak that word (23:5, 16). God's insistence on what he must say recognizes that Balaam does have options. It becomes increasingly clear, even to Balak (23:17), that God reveals through the word, not divination. In the third instance,

the spirit of God comes upon him (see 11:17, 25–6) without consultation after he 'sets his face' and 'sees' Israel's situation (24:2).

5. Balaam speaks God's blessings on Israel rather than curses. The blessings become less descriptive, more future oriented, and more properly blessings as one moves through the four oracles. Even more, those who curse Israel will themselves be cursed, while those who bless will be blessed (24:9). Prominent throughout is the language of seeing; the one who did not see the purposes of God (22:22–30) now does see them (23:9, 21, 23–4; 24:3–4, 15–17). Indeed, the clarity of his seeing increases over the course of the oracles; the most expansive claims are the 'knowledge' of 24:16 and the seeing into the future of 24:17. Falling down but alert (24:4, 16) may refer to a qualified ecstatic reception of God's word.

Balaam 'sees' Israel's history and God's promises, moving from the past through the present to a more and more specific future: election from among the nations (23:9); promise (and fulfilment) of many descendants, like the dust of the earth (23:10; see Gen 13:16, 28:14), and blessing (24:9, cf. GEN 12:3); exodus (23:22; 24:8); God's presence among them and his care in the wilderness (23:21; cf. 24:5–6). He anticipates a successful conquest, as both Israel and God are imaged as lions (22:23–4; 24:7–9), the rise of the monarchy and specific conquests relating thereto (24:7, 17–19). The overall scene for Balaam is a blessed people: numerous, confident, flourishing, powerful, and its king is God. In Balaam's words (23:10):'let my end be like his!'

Balaam 'sees' some of Israel's basic convictions about God. God is not a human being, is not deceptive, blesses Israel, reveals his word to people such as Balaam, and makes promises and keeps them (23:19–20). The claim that God has spoken and will not change his mind (23:19) refers to these promises for Israel and is not a general statement about divine immutability (see Gen 6:5–6; Ex 32:14) or a general claim about prophecy (see Jer 18:7–10). This God chooses to dwell among this people and is acclaimed as their king (23:21), is a strong deliverer, imaged as strong animals (23:22; 24:8–9), and will defeat Israel's enemies (24:8–9).

6. Balak's reactions to Balaam's oracles are increasingly negative, issuing finally in anger and dismissal (23:11, 25–6; 24:10–11). But Balak comes to recognize that Balaam's God is the one with whom he has to do (23:17, 27) and finally blames YHWH for the fact that Balaam will not be paid for his services (24:11).

7. Balaam's response to Balak in each case is a testimony to the word of God (23:12, 26; 24:12–13). That he must 'take care' to say what God has put in his mouth again indicates that he does have other options. But he knows he must speak in view of the source of the words.

(**24:14–25**) Balaam's fourth oracle stands outside the form delineated above and comes directly from Balaam, with no reference to the spirit of the Lord (as in 24:2), but with a claim that he himself 'knows the knowledge of the Most High' (24:16). This oracle is suddenly introduced as Balaam's word to Balak upon his departure, a word that ironically makes clear that Balak and Moab are expressly in Israel's future. Israel will bring Moab (24:17, and perhaps Ir in 24:19; cf. 22:36), Edom, and the other peoples in the region (the Shethites) under the aegis of Israel and its God and will be exalted among the nations.

The means by which this will be accomplished is anticipated in the kingdom language of 24:7; God will raise up a star and sceptre (the future 'him') of 24:17a; from the tribe of Judah, for whom lion imagery is also used (see Gen 49:9–10), and Israel will be established among the nations (24:17–20). These royal images are usually associated with the Davidic dynasty and its victories over Moab and Edom (2 Sam 8:2, 12–14) and have been messianically interpreted.

The obscure (and possibly added) brief oracles against the nations (24:20–4) name the Amalekites (cf. its king Agag, 24:7, and 1 SAM 15; 30); the Kenites (Kain), a subgroup of the Midianites; Assyria (or an obscure tribal group, Gen 25:3); Eber (perhaps another tribal group in the area); and the Philistines or other sea people (Kittim). The oracles announce their ultimate demise. In all of these events Israel's God will be the chief actor (24:23).

But the Moabites come back to haunt Israel almost immediately. The Israelites remain at the boundary of Moab across from Jericho.

(**25:1–18**) **The Final Rebellion** Scholars agree that this chapter combines two separate stories about Israelite men and foreign women (often assigned to JE and P), with a conclusion that assumes both stories. The second story may have been added to illustrate the first and to raise up the stature of the Aaronic line (at the expense of Moses?). The chapter is highly condensed and the reader must fill in many gaps. The focus is violation of the first commandment, the first notice of idolatry since Ex 32

(for parallels, see Olson 1996: 153–4), anomalous given God's blessings in chs. 22–4. In these events the old generation seems finally to die off (14:26–35; 26:64–5). The decks are cleared for the new generation (whose census follows in ch. 26).

The first story (vv. 1–5; cf. Deut 4:3–4) involves Moabite women who, through acts of prostitution, invite Israelite males into idolatrous practices associated with the god (sing.) Baal, the Canaanite god of Peor (on Balaam's advice, 31:16). God tells Moses to impale the chiefs of Israel so that the anger of God is turned away from Israel; no notice is given of obedience (unusual in Numbers; a failure of Moses?). Moses issues a different command, namely to kill only the idolaters (also not executed). vv. 8–9 speak of a severe plague, which v. 18 and 31:16 associate with the idolatry of Peor, and must have begun in 25:3 (cf. weeping in 25:7). Because the wrath of God was not turned away by following God's command to execute a few, a more devastating plague occurred, a working out of the consequences of the deed (see NUM 1:53; 14).

The second story (vv. 6–15) involves a relationship between a Midianite woman and a Simeonite; the detail given in vv. 14–15 testifies to their status (and may link the man with v. 4). The phrase 'into his family' (v. 6) suggests marriage, but the Hebrew is 'to his brothers'; the tabernacle setting suggests something more sinister, as does the word 'trickery' in v. 18 (see 31:16). He did this 'in the sight of Moses' and *all* Israelites as they voiced their lament to God at the tabernacle. The wrong committed is uncertain, but the combination of marriage to a Midianite (paired with idolatrous Moabites, v. 18) and the defiance exhibited in parading themselves before the lamenting people suggests idolatrous practice.

Perhaps Moses had difficulty acting because he himself had married a Midianite. In any case, the blatant act exhibited in his sight was serious enough to call for a decisive response. Moses' failure entails two instances of disobedience in quick succession. But Phinehas, grandson of Aaron, does not hesitate. He enters their tent (perhaps a nearby shrine?—the Hebrew word occurs only here) and pierces them through. The single act suggests they were having intercourse and the tabernacle vicinity suggests an act of cultic prostitution, which would link back to v. 1. The effect of his action (in effect a 'sacrifice') was to 'make atonement for the Israelites' (v. 13; cf. 16:46–8) and stop the plague, which God's command to Moses in v. 4 had called for, and Phinehas now fulfils at least in part. God interprets this action as a zeal exercised on behalf of the divine jealousy (the related Hebrew words show that God's zeal became Phinehas's), which links the action to idolatry (see Ex 34:14–16; Hos 9:10). So, this is a zeal for the first commandment (and the first reference to Baal, which may account for the god's later infamy, e.g. Ps 106:28).

This action of Phinehas becomes the basis for God's establishing with the Aaronides an everlasting covenant of peace, which is interpreted to mean a covenant of perpetual priesthood ('my' means that its fulfilment is solely dependent on God). What is new, given earlier divine commitments to Aaron (Ex 29:9; 40:15; cf. Mal 2:4–5)? Covenant (of peace) language is new (see Isa 54:10; Ezek 34:25), suggesting a formalization of a prior commitment.

This text may reflect later priestly rivalries. The status of Phinehas is raised up over Aaron's other son Ithamar (whose descendants were banished by Solomon, 1 Kings 2:26–7) and God's commitment to Phinehas, whose descendants were Zadokites (1 Chr 6:4–10; Ezek 44:15), is eternal.

The conclusion (vv. 16–18) combines elements from both stories (known to Num 31:8–16 and Ps 106:28–31). The divine word to 'harass [be an enemy to] the Midianites' is directly correspondent to their harassment of Israel; see NUM 31, where Israel goes to war against the Midianites and Balaam is killed for his participation in Israel's apostasy. The condemnation of a Simeonite, when combined with the actions of Levites and Reubenites in ch. 16, means that the curse on these three tribes in Jacob's last testament (Gen 49:1–7) is brought to completion (see Douglas 1993: 194–5).

The New Generation on the Plains of Moab (26:1–36:13)

The balance of Numbers (all Priestly material) contains little narrative in the usual sense, though enough to keep the law and narrative rhythm alive (see chs. 31; 32). Various statutes and lists are presented that prepare Israel for its life in the land.

This census marks the beginning of the new generation without the presence of the old (see NUM C.2). Given the obedient preparations for the journey in chs. 1–10, the reader may wonder whether anything external can be developed to prevent the rebellions of a new generation. The oracles of Balaam, however, have made it clear

that God will be true to promises made, and those promises have been focused on this new generation by God himself (14:24, 31). From the assumptions of land ownership and allocation in chs. 27–36, this new generation will inherit the land, regardless of what it does. Hence, these chapters have a promissory force (see NUM 15).

Yet this does not lessen the call to be faithful (Caleb and Joshua stand as examples) and so chs. 27–36 (and Deuteronomy, also addressed to the new generation) seek to assist Israel in its faithfulness through new orderings of a community confronted with many of the same issues. Many signs of hope will surface, not least the complete absence of death notices. But this picture dare not contribute to undue optimism. Deut 28–31 will make it clear that this new generation will be no more faithful than the old and will experience many of the same failures and consequences (see Deut 29:22–8; 31:20–9). On parallels between Num 1–25 and 26–36, see Olson (1996: 158–9).

Characteristic of chs. 27–36 is the recognition that older law may need to change in view of new life situations. The heart of the matter is community justice and stability; for that reason God becomes engaged in social and economic change. Such ongoing divine involvement witnesses to a dynamic understanding of law, in which the tradition is reinterpreted for the sake of life in a new situation. Instead of an immutable, timeless law, Israel insists on a developing process in which experience in every sphere of life is drawn into the orbit of law, but always in the service of life and the flourishing of community.

(26:1–65) The Census of the New Generation

The second census begins as did the first (cf. v. 2 with 1:2–3), with military service in mind, Eleazar replacing his father Aaron, and land allotment issues paramount. The reference to all these persons having come out of Egypt seems strange; perhaps this is how they identify themselves as a *community*. See GEN 46:8–24, whose list of seventy individuals have here— basically—become seventy clans (cf. also 1 Chr 2–8). Even with the failures of certain tribal groups and the diminishment of numbers, the twelve-tribe reality remains intact here (only Manasseh and Ephraim are inverted). The listing focuses on clans rather than individuals (for land allotment); the totals are given for each *tribe* and the total for all: 601,730 compared to 603,550 in 1:46. Even with all the deaths in chs. 11–25, the numbers remain essentially the same.

God's blessings have been at work behind the scenes.

Several events of previous chapters are recalled, the rebellion of Korah and the Reubenites (vv. 9–11; cf. also v. 19), the deaths of Er and Onan (v. 19; cf. Gen 38:3–10), the deaths of Nadab and Abihu (v. 61; cf. Lev 10:1–2), and a reference to Jochebed, the mother of Moses (v. 59). Another reference to women anticipates events yet to occur (v. 33), and is the reason for the lengthier generation list of Manasseh. A new reason for the census is given in vv. 52–6, i.e. land apportionment is to be based on tribal size after the conquest is complete (though the location of land will be based on lot, a means of eliminating human bias). Such a method sought to ensure a fair distribution of the land to the various families.

The Levites are also newly enrolled (cf. 3:14–39, with an increase of 1,000), separately as before (1:48–9), with reference to the absence of tribal allotment (18:23–4). As God had said (14:20–35), no member of the old generation is still alive except Caleb and Joshua and, for a time, Moses.

(27:1–11) The Daughters of Zelophehad Because ancestral lands are to be kept within the tribe (see Lev 25; 1 Kings 21:1–4), a way to pass on the inheritance must be found if a man has no sons. In such cases daughters may inherit; that possibility is here given Moses' blessing (it occurs in Josh 17:3–6). A restriction is added in 36:1–2, providing an *inclusio* for Num 27–36 (for less restrictive practices in that world, see Milgrom 1990: 482–4).

The daughters of Zelophehad take the initiative with Moses in pursuing inheritance rights inasmuch as their father had no sons (see the census, 26:33). The allusion to their father not being with Korah may refer to the 250 laymen of 16:2; 'his own sins' may refer to the old generation (26:64–5). They note that their father's name would still be associated with this land (27:4); apparently their sons would pass on the name (see 36:1–12; Ezra 2:61). Moses consults with God, who agrees with the daughters. In addition, God decrees other ways in which the inheritance is to be passed on in the absence of sons, with preference given to direct lineage (see Sakenfeld 1995). Levirate marriage (Deut 25:5–10) was probably not applicable here, either because the mother was dead or no longer of child-bearing age.

Israel's patrilineal system sought to ensure the endurance of the family name (see 27:4;

Deut 25:5–6), a questionable issue from a modern perspective; yet, such a concern sought to safeguard a just distribution of land among the tribes (see 36:1–12). These women challenge the practice that only males inherit land; yet their appeal remains fundamentally oriented in terms of their father's name (vv. 3–4), perhaps practising politics as the art of the possible. So they commendably challenge current practice, and take an important step toward greater gender equality, but they do not finally (seek to) overturn the patrilineal system. (See Fishbane 1985: 98–105.)

(27:12–23) From Moses to Joshua This segment describes the transfer of authority from Moses to Joshua. A good case can be made, especially given the reference to the death of Moses (v. 13), that the report of Moses' death (now in Deut 34; note also the similarity between Num 27:12–14 and Deut 32:48–52) originally stood here (or after 36:13) and concluded an earlier version of the 'Pentateuch'.

The need for a successor to Moses on the eve of the entry into the land is made clear by his (and Aaron's) earlier rebellion (v. 14; see 20:12). It is striking that Moses is the one who initiates the issue of succession (v. 15), appealing to God as Creator, the one who gives breath (spirit) to all people (see 16:22), in an apparent reference to God as the one who has given Joshua the spirit, a specific charisma for leadership (27:18; cf. 11:17, 26; Deut 34:9). Joshua has been an 'assistant' to Moses since the Exodus (11:28; Ex 24:13; 33:11). Here his responsibilities are especially associated with leading the Israelites in battle (see Ex 17:8–14), the basic meaning of 'go out before them and come in before them' (27:17, 21; Josh 14:11). Yet the image of sheep and shepherd suggests a more comprehensive leadership role, even royal in its basic sense (see 2 Sam 5:2).

In response to Moses, God commands him to take Joshua and commission him by laying his hand upon him, a symbolic act signifying the transfer of authority through which God was active (so v. 20; cf. 8:10–11; Deut 34:9). The investiture is public, before 'all the congregation', so that it is clear that he is the one whom the people are to obey (v. 20). The act is also to take place before Eleazar the high priest (see 20:22–9), to whom Joshua is responsible with respect to the discernment of the will of God (esp. regarding battle) through the use of Urim and Thummim (see EX 28:29–30). The latter explains why only 'some' of Moses' authority was given to Joshua (v. 20; cf. Moses' role in 12:6–8; Deut 34:10; Josh 1:7–8). Moses did as God had commanded him.

(28:1–29:40) Offerings for Life in the Land In chs. 28–9 offerings are instituted for various regular and festival occasions (the number seven is prominent throughout) for Israel's life in the land. They assume all previous texts in the Pentateuch regarding these matters (e.g. LEV 23; cf. NUM 7; 15; DEUT 16:1–17) and may be a late addition. Whereas the opening chapters of Numbers centre on the spatial ordering of the community, these ordinances focus on its temporal ordering, in anticipation of a more settled life in the land. By marking out these times Israel placed itself in tune with God's temporal ordering in creation, a rhythm and regularity essential for the life God intends for all (for links to Gen 1, see Olson 1996: 170–3). At these times through the year Israel is to be attentive to offerings given by God in and through which God acted for the sake of the life and well-being of the community (indeed, the cosmos). For a convenient summary of the significance of offerings, see Nelson (1993).

(28:1–2) introduces all the offerings (brought by the people) that belong wholly to YHWH (whole burnt offerings; purification or 'sin' offerings; each with meal and drink offerings, cf. NUM 15) for the various times. This totals thirty days of the year (252 total male animals—lambs (140), rams (20), bulls (79), and goats (13) for the purification offerings), besides the daily and sabbath offerings (two lambs in each case). 29:39–40 concludes the list, with a list of private offerings not covered here. On 'pleasing odour' (28:2, 24) see NUM 15:3.

The first three offerings (28:3–15) mark the basic temporal frame of days, weeks, and months. The remainder mark out the festival year, set primarily in terms of the beginning of the two halves of the year, the first month (Passover and Unleavened Bread) and the seventh month (Rosh Hashanah, Day of Atonement, and Booths), with Weeks between these major seasons. These three festival periods are closely timed to Israel's three harvest times, and in time become associated with three events of Israel's early history (Exodus; giving of the law; wilderness wanderings).

(28:3–8) Daily (continual) Offerings (*tāmîd*), offered every day (even on special days) at dawn and dusk, the points of transition between night and day. See EX 29:38–42.

(28:9–10) Sabbath Offerings, which help focus on that hallowed seventh day of creation, separated from all other days. No purification offering is presented on the sabbath because of the theme of joyfulness.

(28:11–15) Monthly (New Moon) Offerings. Cf. NUM 10:10.

(28:16–25) Passover and Unleavened Bread, celebrated in the first month. v. 16 assumes the provisions for Passover (see 9:1–14; Ex 12:1–27; Deut 16:1–8). Unleavened bread (vv. 17–25; see Ex 13:3–10) was celebrated on the seven days following Passover; it was begun and concluded with a 'holy convocation', on which days there was to be no occupational work.

(28:26–31) Festival of First Fruits (Weeks; Harvest; Pentecost), one day with no occupational work. Celebrated fifty days (a sabbath plus seven times seven days) after Unleavened Bread at the start of the wheat harvest (June). See LEV 23:15–21; DEUT 16:9–12.

(29:1–6) The first day of the seventh month is the traditional New Year's Day (this time in the autumn is thought to be the first month in an older agricultural year calendar, cf. Ex 23:16; 34:22). This is an occasion for a holy convocation, with no occupational work. The shofar is blown (v. 1); on blowing the trumpets at the appointed festivals, see NUM 10:10.

(29:7–11) Day of Atonement (Yom Kippur), celebrated on the tenth day of the seventh month, with a holy convocation, fasting, and no work at all (as on sabbath). See LEV 16:29–34; 23:26–32.

(29:12–38) Tabernacles (Booths; Sukkot; Ingathering) is the autumn harvest festival. Celebrated from the fifteenth day (when there was no occupational work) of the month for seven days, offerings are specified for each day, with many more animals than at other festivals. Fewer offerings are ordered for an eighth day, a day of 'solemn assembly' (the seventh one for the year) with no occupational work, which ends the celebration. See LEV 23:33–6, DEUT 16:13–15.

The large number of animals and amounts of produce anticipate settlement in a land of abundance. These statutes will help the wilderness community face into the future.

(30:1–16) Vows and their Limits The mention of votive offerings in 29:39 perhaps provides the link to this material (see LEV 7:16–18; 22:17–25; 27; NUM 15:1–10). These statutes in casuistic style (cf. DEUT 23:21–3) concern vows or pledges (*nēder*) made by men (v. 2), who are bound by their word, and by women who are as well (vv. 3–15). But women are usually (v. 9) bound to their vows within limits placed by the actions of a father or husband. These are (sworn) promises to God ('oath' is used with human beings) related to service (nazirite, 6:2) or in exchange for the (potential) fulfilment of a request, often in crisis (see 21:2; Jacob in GEN 28:20–2; Jephthah in JUDG 11:30–1; Hannah in 1 SAM 1:11).

Three categories of women whose vows are conditional are presented: those who are still in their father's house and under his authority (vv. 3–5); women who are under vows (even rash ones, see Lev 5:4) at the time they are married, vows not annulled by the father (vv. 6–8); women who are married and under their husband's authority (vv. 10–15). Widows and divorcees are excluded because they are under no man's authority (v. 9).

In the cases presented essentially the same principles are operative. If a father or husband disapproves of a vow, he must speak up at the time he hears (of) the vow (not least a vow to fast, v. 13) or the vow stands. If the father or husband disapproves, the vow is annulled, the woman is forgiven by God and is to suffer no consequences. The fourth case is expanded (3:14–15): if a husband annuls his wife's vow after some time has passed, then he (not she) will be guilty of breaking the vow and will have to suffer the (unspecified) consequences (see Deut 23:21).

These statutes assume dependence of the woman upon the man rather than a culture of reciprocity. They protect both men (from having the responsibility to fulfil a vow a woman has made) and, to a lesser extent, women (whose vows remain intact unless there is immediate male response). Lines of responsibility are thus clearly drawn. The overarching concern is that voiced in v. 2—individuals are to keep their word. Failed promises adversely affect one's relationship to God and disrupt the stability of a community.

(31:1–54) War Against the Midianites This narrative (with 32:1–42) focuses on traditions associated with Israel's conquests and settlement in the Transjordan. It is often called a Midrash, with its frequent reference to prior

texts in Numbers and its exaggerations (e.g. the amount of spoil and that no Israelite warrior was lost in battle, v. 49). Certainly the entire narrative is idealized, probably in the interests of the portrayal of the new generation, though a nucleus seems rooted in some event.

vv. 1–2 pick up the story line from 25:17–18. God had commanded Israel to attack the Midianites in response to their corresponding attacks on Israel. v. 16 interprets this harassment in terms of Moabite/Midianite—merged here—women, at the instigation of Balaam, seducing Israelite men into idolatrous practices. Israel's obedient response to God's command is military in character and is interpreted as 'avenging' (n-q-m) Israel and God (vv. 2–3). But the language of 'vengeance' for n-q-m is problematic; preferred is the sense of vindication, to seek redress for past wrongs. Israel is God's instrument of judgement against the Midianites, which would vindicate the honour of both God and the Israelites.

This narrative is also linked to two earlier successful battles against Canaanites and Amorites (21:1–3, 21–35), each waged according to holy war principles in which their entire populations were destroyed (cf. Josh 6:20–1; 10:28–42). This battle takes a somewhat different turn. It has the earmarks of a Holy War, with the presence of the priest as 'chaplain' (see Deut 20:2–4; Phinehas rather than Eleazar because of Lev 21:11) and the sanctuary vessels (v. 6, presumably including the ark, 14:44) and the sounding of alarm (10:9). Only 1,000 men from each tribe are engaged, a small percentage of those available (26:51; cf. Judg 7:2–8; 21:10–12). The battle itself is only briefly described (vv. 7–8) and every male (including Balaam) is killed and their towns destroyed (v. 10; cf. Josh 13:21–2). The presence of Midianites in Judg 6–8 would seem to question this, but there were other Midianite clans (see Hobab in 10:29–32). Then (unlike Num 21) the women and children (and animals) are not killed but taken captive and (with other booty) brought before Moses, Eleazar, and the congregation (v. 12). This action represents a variation in the practice of Holy War as outlined in Deut 20:13–18 (and 21:10–14), where a distinction is made between the peoples of Canaan (including Amorite areas where some tribes settled, 32:33) and others more distant. Apparently the Midianites are considered among the latter, though qualified in view of Israel's prior history with them (ch. 25).

Moses expresses anger that captives have been taken, or at least that 'all the women' have (vv. 14–15). He isolates 'these women here', because they were involved in the Peor apostasy. But he commands not only that they be killed, but all women who are not virgins (because all are suspect?) and all male children (certainly a genocidal move), while female virgins can be preserved alive 'for yourselves', as wives or slaves (vv. 16–18). No word from the Lord is given regarding this matter (common in Numbers), and there is no arbitration, so the reader might ask how legitimate it is. One cannot help but wonder if the unmarried women were checked one by one! The text informs the reader only indirectly that these commands of Moses were carried out (see v. 35).

The commands regarding purification for persons (soldiers and captives) and organic materials which have come into contact with the dead are begun by Moses (vv. 19–20; in terms of NUM 19, as is v. 24) and extended by Eleazar (vv. 21–3, in terms of a word of God to Moses not previously reported) with respect to distinctions between flammable and nonflammable (metallic) items.

vv. 25–47 focus on the distribution of the spoil. God speaks for the first time since v. 2 (vv. 25–30) with commands regarding the disposition of captives and booty. They are to be divided evenly between the warriors and the rest of the congregation (cf. 1 Sam 30:24). One in 500 of the warriors' items are to be given to the priests as an offering to the Lord; one in fifty of the congregation's items (more because of less risk) are to be given to the Levites (see NUM 18:8–32 for other such portions; cf. also NUM 7). This command is carried out (v. 31) and vv. 32–47 detail the disposition and quantity of the spoil; the total—just of the officers!—is immense: 808,000 animals, 32,000 young women, and (from v. 52) 16,750 shekels of gold. vv. 48–54 deal with non-living booty. The officers approach Moses with information that no Israelite was killed and announce their gift to YHWH of the precious metals each soldier (v. 53 includes everyone) had taken. These valuables are brought to Moses to make atonement for themselves and as a memorial before God—through tabernacle furnishings made from the metals—regarding this event (vv. 50, 54). The need for atonement is usually linked to EX 30:11–16 and the taking of a military census, but this seems strained; it might have to do with the taking of human life, not fully commanded by God in this case (see above).

On the offensiveness of these holy war practices, see NUM 21:1–3. This victory is the first of the new generation and bodes well for the future.

(32:1–42) Early Land Settlement Issues This chapter reports a crisis among members of the new generation regarding land settlement to the east of the Jordan (outside the usual definition of Canaan, but present in some texts, GEN 15:16–21, Exod 23:31). Its resolution by means of compromise stands in sharp contrast to earlier experiences (see 32:6–13) and witnesses to a change in this Israelite generation.

The focus is on tribes who settled in the highlands of Gilead east of the Jordan river—Reuben, Gad, and the half-tribe of Manasseh (see also Deut 3:12–20; Josh 13:8–32; 22:1–34). These tribes receive a somewhat mixed evaluation here and elsewhere in the tradition (see 16:1; Gen 49:3–4; Josh 22:10–34; Judg 5:15–17; 11:29–40; 1 Chr 5:23–6).

In 21:21–35 the Israelites had defeated the Amorite kings Sihon and Og and obliterated their communities; this happened at God's command (21:34). This theological point is correctly made by Reuben and Gad (32:4) in their request for this territory as their possession (32:1–5). These areas with their fertile pasture lands were now 'vacant', and their availability attracted the attention of these cattle-rich tribes (later joined by the half-tribe of Manasseh, 32:33–42).

Their final words, 'do not make us cross the Jordan', trigger Moses' memories of past disasters associated with reluctance to enter the land (32:8–15; see NUM 13–14; 'land' here understood to mean Canaan. Moses questions whether they are trying to avoid upcoming battles; indeed, he considers them 'a brood of sinners' (v. 14) who repeat the unfaithfulness exhibited by the spies, the effects of which he rehearses, and which could now recur with even more disastrous consequences—the destruction of Israel.

But, unlike Israel in chs. 13–14, these tribes propose a compromise (vv. 16–19). They will settle in the Transjordan and leave their families and animals behind. And they will fight, indeed serve in the vanguard of the Israelites as they move across the Jordan. They will not return to their homes until 'all the Israelites' are secure and they will not inherit any of those lands (vv. 16–19).

Moses responds positively, if cautiously, and mention of God is especially prominent. Picking up on the 'vanguard' of v. 16, they are to go 'before the LORD' (vv. 20–2), that is, before the ark (see JOSH 4:12–13; 6:7–13). If they follow through on their agreement they have fulfilled their obligation. If they do not, they can be sure that their sin will find them out (vv. 20–4). The effects of sin are here understood to have an intrinsic relationship to the deed and such effects will in time reveal what they have done (see NUM 14).

Gad and Reuben, using deferential language ('your servants', 'my lord'), agree with those terms (vv. 25–7). And so Moses commands Eleazar, Joshua, and tribal heads to witness and honour (he will soon be dead) this agreement and these tribes formally and publicly agree (vv. 28–32). If these tribes fail, they will have to take lands west of the Jordan (v. 30). The words, 'As the LORD has spoken' (v. 31) are striking because the text does not report God having so spoken; Moses' word seems to be as good as God's. When the agreement has been made, Moses gives the lands to these tribes, who rebuild Amorite cities and rename them (vv. 33–8; see JOSH 13:8–32 for land allotments).

The integration of the half-tribe of Manasseh (vv. 33, 39–42) into the tribes settling in Transjordan comes as something of a surprise; it may be an old tradition added later (see 26:29–34; Josh 13:29–32). They oust more Amorites for their lands, and hence their situation is different from that of Gad and Reuben who possess already conquered lands. The land for two and one-half tribes is thus already in place before the Jordan is crossed.

(33:1–49) The Wilderness Journey Remembered This passage is a recollection of the forty-two stages of Israel's journey through the wilderness, from Egypt (vv. 3–5) to their present situation across the Jordan (v. 49). Its placement may recognize the end of the journey narrative and the beginning of the land settlement. The itinerary is represented as something Moses wrote at God's command (v. 2); it probably has its origin in one or more ancient itineraries that circulated in Israel through the generations (see Milgrom 1990: 497–9). Many sites are not mentioned elsewhere (vv. 13, 18–29); most are not geographically identifiable. The itinerary is a surprisingly 'secular' document; divine activity is mentioned only at the beginning (v. 4) and at the death of Aaron (v. 38). This omission emphasizes the importance of human activity on this journey.

The reader can recognize two uneven segments, up to and following the death of Aaron (vv. 38–9), perhaps betraying priestly interests, and the reference to the king of Arad (v. 40), perhaps because this is the first contact with Canaanites. Only v. 8 speaks of the travel time involved.

The first segment is vv. 3–37 (see Ex 12:37–19:1; Num 10:11–20:29). Noteworthy is the detail regarding the Passover, and the note about it as a battle among the gods (see v. 52; cf. Ex 12:12; 15:11). Strikingly, Sinai is simply another stop along the way (vv. 15–16), with no mention of the giving of the law, and the sea crossing is mentioned only in passing. The presence and absence of water is raised (vv. 9, 14), perhaps because of its import for the journey. This levelling of the journey to its bare bones highlights the journey itself rather than the events along the way.

The second segment (vv. 41–9; see Num 21:1–22:1) moves quickly to the present situation (with a passing reference to Mt. Nebo, the site of Moses' death and burial).

(33:50–6) Directions for Conquest of Canaan This segment constitutes hortatory instructions from God to Moses regarding the nature of the attack on Canaan, which God has given for Israel to possess (v. 53). In possessing the land, they are to drive out (not exterminate; cf. Ex 23:23; Deut 7:1–6) all the present inhabitants, destroy their images and sanctuaries, and apportion the land by lot according to the size of the clans (v. 54, essentially a repetition of 26:54–5, perhaps because of the events of NUM 32). If they do not drive out the inhabitants (which is what actually happens; cf. JUDG 1:1–2:5; 1 Kings 9:21), those left shall 'be as barbs in your eyes and thorns in your sides' (v. 55), which is what they prove to be over the years (see Judg 2:11–3:6). The reader will recognize these themes from EX 23:23–33 and 34:11–16; they anticipate such texts as Deut 12:2–4. The final verse (v. 56) anticipates the destructions of Samaria and Jerusalem and the exiling of Israel, a warning that will be more fully developed in Deuteronomy (see esp. chs. 28–31).

(34:1–29) The Apportionment of the Land This chapter delineates the boundaries of the promised land (vv. 1–15) and the leaders who are to apportion that land among the tribes (vv. 16–29). Both are chosen by God. The content suggests that the land will soon be in Israel's hands.

The boundaries of the land of Canaan are idealized; they do not correspond to the boundaries known from any time during Israel's history. On the other hand, the boundaries correspond well to the Canaan known from Egyptian sources prior to the Israelite settlement and a few other texts (see Josh 13–19; Ezek 47:13–20). Several sites are not known and so the boundaries cannot be determined with precision (see Milgrom 1990: 501–2).

The southern border (vv. 2–5) moves from the southern end of the Dead Sea south and west across the wilderness of Zin to south of Kadesh to the Wadi of Egypt to the Mediterranean (the western boundary, v. 6). The northern border (vv. 7–9) is less clear, extending from the Mediterranean to Mount Hor (not the southern mountain, 20:22–9) into southern Syria (Lebo-hamath). The boundary to the east moves from a line north of the eastern slope of the Sea of Chinnereth (Galilee) down the Jordan river to the Dead Sea (vv. 10–12). Hence, the boundaries given here do not include Transjordan where two and one-half tribes had settled (v. 32), confirmed by Moses' statement (vv. 13–15). From the perspective of v. 2 (cf. 32:17; 33:51), Israel has not yet entered the land of its inheritance. Yet God had commanded the destruction of the Amorites (21:34) and cities of refuge are assigned in the Transjordan (35:14). Deut 2:24–5 includes the area west of the Jordan.

Ten tribal leaders (not from Reuben and Gad) are appointed to apportion the land, generally listed from south to north (vv. 16–29). Eleazar and Joshua (v. 17) are to supervise the work.

(35:1–34) Special Cities and Refinements in the Law These stipulations are given by God to Moses for the enhancement of life for various persons in the new land. The taking of human life puts the land in special danger. vv. 1–8 allocate cities for the Levites (for lists see Josh 21:1–42; 1 Chr 6:54–81). Stipulations for land distribution in Num 34 are here continued, with provision for the Levites, who have no territorial rights (see 18:21–4; 26:62). Inasmuch as they will be active throughout the land (with unspecified functions more extensive than care for the tabernacle, such as teaching), they are to be allotted forty-eight cities (six of which are cities of refuge, vv. 9–15). These cities provide for their housing and for grazing lands for their livestock, though not as

permanent possessions (and others would live in them). 1,000 cubits (450 m.) in each direction from the town wall issues in a square of 2,000 cubits per side (see Milgrom 1990: 502–4). The various tribes will contribute cities according to their size.

(35:9–15) institutes cities of refuge (cf. Ex 21:12–14; Deut 4:41–3; 19:1–3, 9; for a list see Josh 20:1–9). When established in the land, the people were to choose three cities of refuge on each side of the Jordan (well distributed north to south). These cities were set aside as a place of asylum for persons (Israelite or alien) who killed someone without intent, until their case could be properly tried. Their purpose was to ensure that justice was done and to prevent blood feuds. As long as such persons remained within one of these cities they were secure from the avenger. The avenger of blood (or redeemer, gōʾēl; cf. Lev 25:25, 47–9) was the relative of the deceased charged to ensure proper retribution for the sake of the land (see 35:33). These cities were probably functioning during the monarchial period.

(35:16–34) Distinctions are made in the homicide laws between murder (including death through negligence) and unpremeditated killing (on the intentional/unintentional distinction, see 15:22–31; Ex 21:13–14). The burden of proof is on the slayer. Those who murder another with intent, regardless of the means or motivation (six examples are given, vv. 16–21), are to be put to death by the avenger (vv. 19, 21), though not without trial (v. 24 covers both cases, see below) and, according to the supplement (vv. 30–4), evidence of more than one witness (v. 30; cf. Deut 19:15–21), and no monetary ransom ('loophole') is possible (v. 31). Murder pollutes the land and its wholeness, not least because God dwells there (v. 34); only the blood of the killer can expiate the land, that is, remove the impurity that the murder has let loose (vv. 33–4). The avenger's action is necessary for the sake of the future of the land and its inhabitants.

On the other hand, killing without intent and hostility issues in a different response (vv. 22–3). A trial is to be held (v. 24, outside the city of refuge, with national judges representing the congregation, cf. Deut 19:12; Josh 20:4–6) to decide whether the killing was truly unintentional. If so decided, the slayer was returned to the city where he originally took refuge (cf. Josh

20:6), where he remained until the high priest died.

The cities of refuge were a kind of exile, a home away from home for those who killed unintentionally, so this was a penalty. Because the city of refuge only masked the polluting effects of the murder, expiation was still necessary. This was accomplished through the death of the high priest, which had expiatory significance, issuing in a kind of general amnesty. Only then was release possible. If the slayer left the city before this happened (and no ransom was possible, v. 32), he was not protected from the avenger, whose actions would not incur guilt.

(36:1–13) Once Again: The Daughters of Zelophehad This chapter picks up the issues raised by the daughters of Zelophehad; they provide an *inclusio* for Num 26–36. In 27:1–11 they had requested Moses that they inherit their father's property inasmuch as he had no sons. They based their case on the continuance of their father's name and his property in their clan (27:4). Now members of their tribe (Manasseh) come to Moses, recall the previous arrangement (v. 2), and ask for an interpretation in view of the fact that upon marriage any property held by the wife became that of her husband. Hence, if a daughter were to marry outside her tribe, the property would transfer to that tribe and Manasseh (in this case) would lose its full original allotment. Even the jubilee year property transfer would not return it to the family, because the property would have been inherited rather than sold (v. 4; see LEV 25:13–33). Moses agrees with this reasoning and apparently receives a word form the Lord on the matter (it may be his interpretation of the 'word of the LORD' more generally, cf. Ex 18:23). The daughters may marry whom they wish, but it must be from within their own tribe (common in patrilineal systems) so that the tribal allotment of every tribe remains as originally determined. The daughters of Zelophehad—Mahlah, Tirzah, Hoglah, Milcah, and Noah—actually marry within their *clan*, sons of their father's brothers.

The final verse in Numbers speaks of God's commandments given through Moses since 22:1, when Israel arrived by the Jordan at Jericho. These commandments have been essentially forward-looking, anticipating Israel's future life in the land. Inasmuch as Deuteronomy takes place over the course of a single day, at the end of Numbers Israel's entrance into the promised land is just hours away.

REFERENCES

Ashley, T. R. (1993), *The Book of Numbers*, NICOT (Grand Rapids: Eerdmans).

Balentine, S. E. (1983), *The Hiding of the Face of God* (Oxford: Oxford University Press).

Douglas, M. (1993), *In the Wilderness: The Doctrine of Defilement in the Book of Numbers* (Sheffield: Sheffield Academic Press).

Fishbane, M. (1985), *Biblical Interpretation in Ancient Israel* (Oxford: Oxford University Press).

Fretheim, T. E. (1984), *The Suffering of God: An Old Testament Perspective*, Overtures to Biblical Theology, (Philadelphia: Fortress).

—— (1991), *Exodus*, Interpretation: A Bible Commentary for Teaching and Preaching (Louisville, Ky.: John Knox).

—— (1996), *The Pentateuch*, Interpreting Biblical Texts (Nashville: Abingdon).

Joines, K. R. (1974), *Serpent Symbolism in the Old Testament: A Linguistic, Archaeological, and Literary Study* (Haddonfield, NJ: Haddonfield House).

Levine, B. (1993), *Numbers 1–20: A New Translation with Introduction and Commentary*, Anchor Bible (New York: Doubleday).

Milgrom, J. (1990), *Numbers*, JPS Torah Commentary (Philadelphia: Jewish Publication Society of America).

Nelson, R. D. (1993), *Raising Up a Faithful Priest: Community and Priesthood in Biblical Theology* (Louisville, Ky.: Westminster/John Knox).

Olson, D. (1985), *The Death of the Old and the Birth of the New: The Framework of the Book of Numbers and the Pentateuch*, Brown Judaic Studies, 71 (Chico, Calif.: Scholars Press).

—— *Numbers*, Interpretation: A Bible Commentary for Teaching and Preaching (Louisville, Ky.: John Knox).

Sakenfeld, K. D. (1995), *Journeying with God: A Commentary on the Book of Numbers*, International Theological Commentary on the Old Testament (Grand Rapids: Eerdmans).

Wenham, G. J. (1981), *Numbers: An Introduction and Commentary*, Tyndale Old Testament Commentary (Downer's Grove, Ill.: Inter-Varsity).

8. Deuteronomy

CHRISTOPH BULTMANN

INTRODUCTION

A. Character. Deuteronomy represents a major strand of Judean theology of the seventh to fifth centuries BCE. Its anonymous authors develop pivotal ideas such as the uniqueness of YHWH, the human 'love' and 'fear' of God (6:4–5, 24), and the excellence and accessibility of Israel's law (4:5–8; 30:11–14). The book contains a version of the Decalogue and relates all other laws to these basic commandments (ch. 5). It gives expression to the ideas of a 'covenant' between YHWH and Israel and of Israel's 'election' through YHWH (5:2; 7:6; 26:16–19). Deuteronomy focuses narrowly on Israel's land, while at the same time viewing it from a perspective of expectation (6:10–12, 17–18; 30:20). Its concern for the exclusiveness and purity of the worship of YHWH results in drastic admonitions about the conquest of the land (7:1–2; 12:1–4, 29–31) and harsh regulations concerning apostasy (13:1–18; 17:2–7). Originally the document of a religious movement, the oldest parts of the book functioned as a law to enforce the centralization of the sacrificial cult at the temple in Jerusalem (ch. 12) and as a law to promote social solidarity in Judah (ch. 15). The spirit of Deuteronomy in regard to cultic matters may be grasped from the law on religious vows in 23:21–3 (MT 22–4), and in regard to ethical matters from the law on just measures in 25:13–16. Deuteronomy reflects a tendency towards rationalization within the Israelite religious tradition. However, as the book developed over a long period, there are many tensions within it.

B. Name. The name 'Deuteronomy' is derived from the LXX where it is called *deuteronomion*, the 'second law'. This goes back to a misinterpretation of 17:18 by the LXX translators, where the expression *mišneh hattôrâ* means a 'copy of (this) law'. In the Jewish tradition, the name of the book is *dĕbārîm* (words), which is a name taken from the opening verse of the book.

C. Place within the Canon. I. Deuteronomy is the fifth book of the Pentateuch. Its last chapter reports the death of Moses and thus, on the plane of narrative, concludes the story of the Exodus which began with the oppression of the Israelites and the call of Moses in Exodus. With its numerous references to the patriarchs it also relates to the patriarchal stories in Genesis. Above all, Deuteronomy indicates the end of the era of divine legislation for Israel. All of the laws which Moses delivers to the people were revealed to him at Mount Horeb (which is called Mount Sinai in Exodus and Numbers). According to Deuteronomy, however, they were only promulgated by Moses towards the end of his life in the 'land of Moab' (except for the Decalogue). This concept allowed later redactors of the Pentateuch to co-ordinate competing laws which claimed Mosaic authority by making Deuteronomy a sequel to the so-called Priestly Document.

2. Deuteronomy is the first book of a historical work which consists of Deuteronomy plus the Former Prophets (Joshua, Judges, Samuel, Kings). Thus, it is the opening of what is known as the Deuteronomistic History and leads directly on to the book of Joshua (Noth 1991; McKenzie 1994). In many instances, Deuteronomic laws function as criteria for the representation of Israel's history in the land during the period from the crossing of the river Jordan to the fall of Jerusalem. The process of the formation of the Pentateuch loosened the literary link between Deuteronomy and its continuation.

D. Literary Genre and Structure. I. A clue to the problem of genre lies in 1:5 which says that Moses set out 'to expound this law' (*bĕ'ēr 'et hattôrâ hazzō't*). From 1:6 to 30:20, Deuteronomy is a great oration with a didactic purpose. However, the speaker is presented to the readers of Deuteronomy by a narrator, who framed the oration with short narrative sections in 1:1–5 and 34:1–12, thus making the oration the valedictory address of Moses before his death in the land east of the Jordan. This concept is also reflected in a few more instances where the voice of a narrator is heard in Deuteronomy (e.g. 4:41–3, 44–9; 5:1; 27:1; 29:1, 2 (MT 28:69; 29:1); 31:1, 2, 7, 9–10, and see Polzin 1993).

2. Deuteronomy is a multifaceted oration. 'To expound *tôrâ*' means more than just the transmission of a law code. The speaker relates the laws to the land as the area of their future application as well as to the Decalogue as the essential compilation of commandments for Israel. He instructs his audience about the theological significance of the Torah and calls for faithful obedience. This gives Deuteronomy its unrivalled paraenetic tone. The speaker also predicts the consequences of violating the law and even hints at the prospects beyond. The resulting structure of the oration is very complex indeed. Historical reviews in 1:6–3:29; 5:1–33; 9:7–10:11 and paraenetic sections in 4:1–40; 6:4–9:6; 10:12–11:25 form a prologue to the laws in 12:1–26:15, a large collection of blessings and curses in 28:1–68 and a further paraenetic section in 29:2–30:20 forms an epilogue to them. In addition, the speaker gives instructions for a future ritual commitment to the law after the crossing of the Jordan in 11:26–32 and 27:1–26. At the climax in 26:16–19, the speaker himself enacts a declaration of covenantal relationship between Israel (his audience) and YHWH. The overall form of an oration thus combines a number of distinct materials.

3. Many attempts have been made to describe the literary unity of Deuteronomy in more precise terms than that of an oration. A basic structural pattern of four elements consisting of a historical and paraenetic prologue—laws—covenant (26:16–19)—blessings and curses, was regarded as reflecting the pattern of a cultic ceremony (von Rad 1966). A similar basic pattern of four main elements, namely a historical prologue—a fundamental statement of allegiance (6:4–7)—detailed stipulations—blessings and curses, was regarded as reflecting a pattern of ancient Near-Eastern political treaties (McCarthy 1978; Weinfeld 1992: 65–9). However, a simple basic pattern of laws, introduced by a prologue and concluded by an epilogue with curses, may already be found in the Code of Hammurabi of the eighteenth century BCE (where the curses threaten any future king who might abolish or alter the laws: ANET 163–80). Deuteronomy cannot be reduced to a literary structure which directly corresponds to any typical pattern because its erudite authors freely employ several elements from a common Near-Eastern cultural background.

E. History of Research. From patristic times onwards there was always a tradition that Deuteronomy was somehow related to the 'book of the law' (sēper hattôrâ) which, according to 2 Kings 22:1–23:25, was found in the Jerusalem temple during the reign of Josiah in the late seventh century BCE (e.g. Jerome, CChr.SL 75. 5). T. Hobbes, in his Leviathan (1651, chs. 33, 42), explicitly identified that law code with Deut 12–26 and emphasized that, in his opinion, it had been written by Moses. One hundred and

fifty years later (1805–6), W. M. L. de Wette at the University of Jena came to the conclusion that Deuteronomy was not only the book which was found in the temple but had also been written not long before Josiah's times (see Rogerson 1992: 19–63). Whereas for de Wette this hypothesis meant that Deuteronomy was a late part of the Pentateuch, later research into the history of the Israelite religion, conducted by A. Kuenen and J. Wellhausen around 1870, established the view that most parts of the Pentateuch were even later than the Josianic Deuteronomy (for a convenient presentation of this view see W. Robertson Smith 1892: 309–430). The valuable commentary by S. R. Driver (1895) rests on this seminal model of the history of Israel's religious traditions. Subsequent scholarship tried to identify several editions of Deuteronomy which had been conflated into the extant book or to discover distinct redactional layers within it (see Mayes 1979; for a retrospective discussion see Nielsen 1995; for the current state of debate see Veijola (forthcoming)). Meanwhile it has become clear that the age of Josiah only stands for the beginnings of the literary development of Deuteronomy which reaches well into the Second Temple period.

F. Historical Background. 1. The age of Josiah, king of Judah 639–609 BCE (2 Kings 22–3), was characterized by the decline of the Neo-Assyrian empire. As very little is known about the impact of Assyrian politics and religion upon Judah, which since the second half of the eighth century had to some extent been a vassal state of Assyria, it is hard to decide what liberation from Assyrian domination would have meant to the Judeans (see McKay 1973; Spieckermann 1982; Halpern 1991). However, even in a very critical reading of Kings, scholars accept the historicity of the information given in 2 Kings 23:11–12, according to which Josiah removed Assyrian religious symbols from the temple in his capital Jerusalem (Würthwein 1984: 459; cf. Uehlinger 1995). It is less certain whether he also carried out the centralization of sacrificial worship which is attributed to him in 2 Kings 23:8–9, and whether this was instigated by the Deuteronomic law or conversely inspired the composition of a corresponding law code (see Lohfink 1985; Clements 1996). Even more disputed is the historical reliability of the information about Josiah's encroachment on the territory of the former Assyrian provinces north of Judah (2 Kings 23: 15–20). Any general conclusions concerning the spirit of the Josianic age are severely restricted by the nature of the historical sources informing us about his times (cf. also P. R. Davies 1992: 40–1). Nevertheless, even if most of 2 Kings 22–3 is only legendary, the historical background of the representation in these chapters of Josiah's religious reform in 622 BCE may be sought in the activity of a movement which promoted the exclusiveness and purity of the Judean religion and gave literary expression to these ideas in a law code which later became the core of Deuteronomy. It is therefore not amiss to attribute the origin of Deuteronomy to a 'YHWH alone movement' in the seventh century BCE (M. Smith 1987: 11–42) and even to a distinct class of scribes who were educated in a Judean wisdom tradition (Weinfeld 1992: 158–78, 244–319).

2. An important factor in the development of the Deuteronomic movement is the language of political treaties in the ancient Near East (McCarthy 1978; Weinfeld 1992). Although the dependence of Deuteronomy upon such documents has often been overstated (see the critique by Nicholson 1986: 56–82), there are clear parallels in terminology and in the compositional function of a curse section. The relevant texts for comparison may be found in Parpola and Watanabe (1988) and ANET 531–41, also 201–6. The succession treaty of the Assyrian king Esar-haddon in favour of his son Assurbanipal, which dates from 672 BCE, is of particular interest here. Copies of this treaty were discovered during an excavation in Nimrud on the upper Tigris in 1955. They represent versions of the treaty as it was concluded with vassal states in the eastern periphery of Assyria and one can assume that the same treaty was also concluded with vassal states in the west, including Judah. The treaty must have been known to the scribe who wrote Deut 28:20–44 (Steymans 1995) and may also be alluded to in Deut 13. However, the question of under what political circumstances a Judean scribe would have borrowed those motifs from ancient Near-Eastern traditions remains open to conjecture.

3. The literary history of Deuteronomy developed further after the Babylonian conquest of Jerusalem in 587 BCE. According to Noth's theory of a Deuteronomistic History (see DEUT c.2), the author who wrote the history of Israel in her land must be seen against the background of this exilic age (see, however, Cross 1973). That author opened his narrative with Deut 1–3; 4; 31; 34 (apart from some later additions) and placed the book of the law which had been passed on to him into this narrative framework. Further-

more, not only do such passages as 4:25–31 and 29:22–30:10 refer to Israel in exile; the entire concept which dominates the paraenetic sections, namely that Israel finds herself outside the promised land and has to regain it, looks like a response to the end of monarchic Judah.

4. More refined analyses of the distinct redactional layers within the Deuteronomistic History led many scholars to the conclusion that the work of the Deuteronomistic scribal school extended far beyond the middle of the sixth century BCE and right into the Persian period. Passages which secondarily add theological reflections on the relevance of the Torah to preceding narrative or paraenetic texts (such as Josh 1:7–8; Deut 6:17–18) are seen as an expression of a specific 'nomistic' or 'covenant-related' stage in the Deuteronomistic tradition (Smend 1971; 1983; Veijola 1996a). Modifications in anti-syncretistic paraenetic passages which seem to reflect later historical experience of the Second Temple period (e.g. Deut 7:22; 7:3–4; cf. Neh 13:23–7; Ezra 9:1–2) are another point in question. An important formal criterion for these analyses is the recurrent shift of address in Deuteronomy between second person singular and second person plural (cf. DEUT 12:1–32) for which, however, an explanation in purely stylistical terms has also been suggested.

G. Sources. 1. The legal core in chs. 12–26 incorporates many older materials. A direct comparison is possible between Deuteronomy and the so-called Book of the Covenant in Ex 20:22–23:33. This shows parallels between Ex 20:24–5 || Deut 12:13–14, Ex 21:2–11 || Deut 15:12–18, Ex 21:12–14 || Deut 19:1–13, Ex 22:25–7 (MT 24–6) || 23:19–20 (MT 20–1); 24:10–13, Ex 23:4–5 || Deut 22:1–4, Ex 23:10–11 || Deut 15:1–11, Ex 23:14–18 || Deut 16:1–17. These as well as some less obvious parallels make it clear that the Deuteronomic law represents a later stage in the history of Israelite law (Otto 1996a; Levinson 1997; contrast Van Seters 1996), although the Book of the Covenant may itself contain post-Deuteronomic as well as pre- and proto-Deuteronomic materials. At least two more collections of laws were taken up by the authors of the law code, namely a collection of family and sex laws (21:15–21; 22:13–29; 24:1–4; 25:5–12) and a collection of laws on warfare (20:10–14, 19–20; 21:10–14; 23:10–15) (Seitz 1971; Rofé 1987; 1985b). Further laws may have been taken up from oral tradition, possibly with some paraenetic elements attached to them urging and motivating obedience, such as, e.g. 22:6–7. The series of curses in 27:16–25 belongs to the apodictic law in Israelite tradition which commands an unconditional condemnation of or punishment for certain offences.

2. The large section of blessings and curses in ch. 28 contains a traditional series of blessings in vv. 3–6 (which are reversed in vv. 16–19). vv. 20–44 closely follow a sequence of curses in Esar-haddon's succession treaty (see DEUT F.2).

3. Ch. 5 contains the Decalogue (vv. 6–21) which found its place also in Exodus (20:2–17). However, instead of being a source of Deuteronomy, it is a composition which originated inside the Deuteronomic movement (Hossfeld 1982).

4. On the plane of the history of ideas, Deuteronomy is often seen as belonging to a Hoseanic prophetic tradition. The basic command of Deut 6:4–5 which centres on the notion of 'love' of God is regarded as a consequence of the theological concern and the metaphorical language of Hosea. As a second instance of Hoseanic influence the law concerning the king over YHWH's people (Deut 17:14–20) is appealed to. However, the available evidence does not sufficiently support the conclusion that Deuteronomy originated in the monarchy of northern Israel and was taken to Judah by refugees after the defeat of Israel in 722 BCE (Alt 1953).

5. The historical reviews in 1:6–3:29; 5:1–33; 9:7–10:11 show a relationship with narrative traditions in Exodus and Numbers and presuppose the Yahwistic work in the Pentateuch. Whether 11:26–32 and 27:1–14, together with Josh 8:30–5, reflect an ancient tradition (Nielsen 1995; Weinfeld 1991) remains doubtful.

6. Two independent documents have been added to Deuteronomy, in ch. 32 the Song of Moses, and in ch. 33 the Blessing of Moses. Whereas the collection of sayings about the tribes in ch. 33 mostly predates the seventh century, the poem of ch. 32 has its origin in the context of later reflections about the relationship between YHWH and Israel amongst the nations.

H. Literary History. 1. Deuteronomy developed from a law code to an oration of Moses within a narrative frame. The original law code aimed at a cultic reform in Judah and addressed its lay audience in the second person singular. It consisted of laws which were relevant to the centralization of sacrificial worship (12:13–19; 14:22–9; 15:19–23; 16:1–17; 18:1–8) and probably also of laws concerning social and judicial matters (15:1–18; 16:18–19; 17:8–13; 19:1–21; 21:1–9; cf.

Morrow 1995), family and sex laws (see DEUT G.1), laws promoting equity in response to poverty (mainly in 23:15–25:16), and some ritualistic materials (e.g. 21:22–3; 22:9–10; 23:17–18), cf. Crüsemann 1996. 6:4–9 may have been the prologue to this law code. However, any detailed reconstruction of the original law code remains highly hypothetical. Whether or not it was presented as a law of Moses depends on the evaluation of 4:44–5 as its superscription.

2. The incorporation of Deuteronomy into the Deuteronomistic History was a distinct stage in its literary history (see DEUT C.2 and F.3), which created an explicit interrelation between the law and the issue of Israel's land as well as the differentiation between the law code and the Decalogue in ch. 5. In this process, the historians added laws to the code which look towards the subsequent history of Israel, such as the law on the king (17:14–20) and the law on the conquest (20:10–18, and further laws on warfare, see DEUT G.1).

3. The literary development of the paraenetic sections in 4:1–40; 6:4–11:25; 29:2–30:20 as well as of the laws which are primarily concerned with the problem of syncretism or religious assimilation such as 12:1–7, 29–31; 13:1–18; 18:9–20 is a special problem (see DEUT F.4). Many suggestions have been made for attributing the respective texts to only a few successive editions or redactional layers. However, it seems more appropriate to think in terms of a prolonged literary process which led to what ideally may be called the canonical shape of Deuteronomy no earlier than the 4th century.

I. Outline

Review of the Conquest of the Land East of the Jordan ((1:1–5) 1:6–3:29)

Discourse on the Excellence of the Law (4:1–40 (41–3, 44–9))

Review of the Covenant at Horeb and the Decalogue (5:1–33 (6:1–3))

Discourse on Faithful Obedience to the Law (6:4–11:25 (26–32))

Promulgation of the Laws (12:1–25:19 (26:1–15))

Declaration of Mutual Commitments between YHWH and Israel (26:16–19)

Instructions for a Ceremony West of the Jordan (27:1–26)

The Consequences of Obedience and Disobedience through Blessings and Curses (28:1–68)

Discourse on the Significance of the Law ((29:1) 29:2–30:20)

Report of Moses' Parting from Israel, Including his Poem and his Blessings (31:1–34:12)

COMMENTARY

Review of the Conquest of the Land East of the Jordan ((1:1–5) 1:6–3:29)

(1:1–5) Moses as Orator The superscription to Deuteronomy introduces the book as the words of Moses to all Israel at a location east of the river Jordan. As Moses is never to cross the Jordan (3:23–8), the following oration will be his valedictory address. This, however, is only explicitly indicated in 31:1–2 (cf. 4:22). The basic form of the superscription, 'These are the words that Moses spoke to all Israel beyond the Jordan as follows', has been considerably expanded. v. 5, which may be part of a specific compositional scheme (cf. 4:44; 29:1 (MT 28:69)), emphasizes the qualification of Moses' oration as law (tôrâ). 'Of all the terms for God's instructions, none better characterizes Deuteronomy, since it connotes both law and an instruction that must be taught, studied, and pondered, and it is expected to shape the character, attitudes, and conduct of those who do so' (Tigay 1996: 3). For v. 4 see further on 2:24–3:11. v. 2 can best be explained as a misplaced gloss on 1:19, while v. 1b, which adds some topographical information, remains elusive. v. 3 reflects an interest in chronology that is typical of Priestly texts in the Pentateuch, cf. e.g. Ex 40:17; Num 10:11.

(1:6–3:29) The Conquest of Israel's Land Moses gives an account of the partly unsuccessful and partly paradigmatic beginning of Israel's taking possession of the promised land. The section gives expression to a deliberate concept of the land as YHWH's gift to Israel which Israel entered from outside at a certain moment in history. The Deuteronomistic History (see DEUT C.2) thus starts with an idealized image of the conquest of the land, and ends with a somewhat stylized image of the loss of the land, cf. 2 Kings 15:29; 17:6, 23; 25:21, 26. It thus shapes a coherent overall view of one extended period of Israel's history. Although the Deuteronomistic authors of the sixth and fifth centuries BCE include several historical traditions in their composition, their work cannot be called historiographical in a strict sense.

(1:6–8) YHWH's Command Moses' retrospective does not start from the Exodus but with a reference to Mount Horeb. Thus it alludes to all the events which this name implies (cf. 5:2; 9:8). The land which Israel is to conquer is called 'the hill country of the Amorites' (har hā' ĕmōrî) by a designation based on the name for the area in Neo-Assyrian inscriptions. An alternative general designation is 'the land of the Canaanites' ('ereṣ hakkĕna'ănî), and elsewhere in Deuteronomy a list of peoples is used for describing the population of the land (cf. 7:1; 20:17). Whereas chs. 2–3 carefully define Israel's territorial claims east of the Jordan (cf. 3:8), the vision of Israel's land as extending to the north as far as the river Euphrates (v. 7; cf. Josh 1:4) is alien to the concept of a conquest as well as to Israel's historical traditions. It may be either an echo of imperial rhetoric (Weinfeld 1991:133–4) or a reflection of political experience in the late seventh century when victory in a battle at Carchemish on the Euphrates in 605 BCE made the Neo-Babylonians the political overlords of Palestine (cf. Jer 46:2; 2 Kings 24:7). v. 8 emphasizes that Israel's hope for the land is founded on an oath which YHWH swore to her ancestors, cf. Gen 15:18. The verse forms an inclusio with 30:20.

(1:9–18) Officers in Israel This insertion, which separates vv. 6–8 from its continuation in v. 19, authorizes an organization of the people modelled on 16:18–19 and 17:8–11. The passage is remarkable in that it grounds the position of 'leaders' on the consent of the people (v. 14) and specifies their qualification as 'wise, discerning, and reputable' persons (v. 13)—a profile which one may read as a self-portrait of the Deuteronomistic school. The designation of these leaders (rā'šîm) in military terms (śārîm, šōṭĕrîm, v. 15) corresponds with the literary context of the conquest narrative. Their designation as 'judges' (šōpĕṭîm) may reflect their actual function in the society of the author's time. A similar concern with the institution of leaders is expressed in Ex 18:13–27; 2 Chr 19:5–10; Num 11:14–17, 24–5, whereas no details about the appointment of officials during the time of the Judean monarchy (cf. e.g. Jer 36:12; 2 Kings 24:15) are known vv. 16–17, integrity of the judges is essential to the idea of justice, and just claims of the poor merit protection (cf. 24:14–15; Am 5:10–12).

(1:19–2:1) The Failed Conquest In an artistic retrospective account, Moses indicates the reason why, after the Exodus, the Israelites did not conquer the promised land west of the Jordan from its southern border (cf. also the time-scale implied in 1:2). Disobedience (1:26; cf. 1:7–8) and lack of faith (1:32, RSV; contrast Ex 14:31) led to divine punishment of the Exodus generation (1:34–5; cf. 2:14–15). Kadesh-barnea has been identified with an oasis about 80 km. to the south-west of Beersheba, the town which normally marks the southern border of Judah (1 Kings 4:25 (Mt 5:5); 2 Kings 23:8; cf. however Josh 15:2–4). Instead of being the starting-point for the conquest, it becomes the starting-point for a journey of nearly forty years southeastwards to the Red Sea and back northwards on the eastern side of Mount Seir until the successful conquest begins with the crossing of the Wadi Arnon (2:24), a wadi which runs towards the Dead Sea from the east opposite En-gedi. The narrative has been constructed upon the basis of a tradition about the Calebites who had expelled 'the three sons of Anak' from the fertile Hebron area (cf. Josh 15:14 and some fragments in Num 13–14).

(2:2–23) The Neighbouring Nations The second episode in Moses' account opens with a phrase similar to 1:6–7. The approach to the Wadi Arnon offers an opportunity to define Israel's territorial claims against the Edomites, the Moabites, and the Ammonites (see *ABD*, ad loc.). The section has been expanded by several successive scribes. One basic feature is the idea that YHWH, and not the respective national deities, assigned these three peoples their territories (vv. 5, 9, 19; contrast Judg 11:12–28, esp. v. 24). A second basic feature is the analogy between Israel's conquest of her land and the way in which these and other peoples took possession of their respective territories 'just as Israel did in the land they were to possess, which the Lord had given to them' (v. 12, NJPS). According to this view, the history of the historical nations follows on a mythological age in which 'Rephaim' (giants) inhabited the land. They may be called 'Emim', or 'Zamzummim', or 'Anakim' (vv. 10–11, 20–1), and are comparable with 'Horim' and 'Avvim' in other regions (vv. 12, 22–3; cf. also Am 9:7). As far as the Rephaim are concerned, a mythological tradition has been identified through a Ugaritic text (c.14–12th cents. BCE) which also establishes a link between Rephaim and the place-names Ashtaroth and Edrei (cf. 1:4; 3:11; see Margulis 1970). All these glosses amount to a striking reinterpretation of the conquest imagery which finds expression also in 9:2. vv. 14–15, pointing back to 1:34–5, these verses mark a transition between two periods of Israel's history after the Exodus.

(2:24–3:11) The Model Conquest YHWH's command also stands at the beginning of the third episode in Moses' account. 2:32–6, the first

act of the conquest draws on an ancient tradition about a Transjordanian city ruler which has been preserved in the parallel narrative in Num 21:21–31. The account follows a highly stylized pattern: YHWH gives the enemy over, and the Israelites' army then 'strikes him down—captures his towns—utterly destroys all human beings in them—keeps the livestock and plunder as spoil' (2:33–5 and again in 3:3–7). This pattern agrees with the Deuteronomistic law on warfare in 20:10–18 and especially the injunction to 'utterly destroy' (ḥ-r-m hifil) all former inhabitants of the land (20:16–17; see DEUT 7:1–2). Moses is thus represented as conducting an exemplary war against the Amorites east of the Jordan, cf. 3:21; 31:4. 2:25–30, the basic structure of the account has been supplemented by several additions which focus on divine providence: YHWH puts 'the dread and fear' of Israel upon the peoples (2:25), YHWH 'hardens the spirit' of the Amorite king (2:30). Moses acts in accordance with the law of 20:10 although neither this law nor the analogy with Israel's passing through the land of the neighbouring nations applies to the case of the Amorite territory (2:26–9). 3:1–7, the second Amorite king is seen not as a city ruler but as king of a vast region; see, however, 1:4 and DEUT 2:10–11, 20–1. His name has been adopted from an etiological tradition which links this mythological figure to Rabbah of the Ammonites (3:11, however, the Ammonite territory itself is exempted from the land which the Israelites claim, 2:19, 37). The description of the conquered towns probably depends on 1 Kings 4:13. 3:8 states the result of Moses' ideal conquest which a scribe, probably in the sixth century BCE, created from very remote memories of some early history of Israelite tribes in the land east of the Jordan.

(3:12–20) Tribal Territories On the distribution of the land see Josh 13:8–32. vv. 18–20, the 'rest' (n-w-ḥ hifil I.) which YHWH has given to these tribes is an ideal for all Israel. Therefore, these tribes are summoned to support the conquest of the land west of the Jordan, cf. Josh 1:12–15; 22:1–4 (for the notion of 'rest' cf. also Deut 12:9; Josh 23:1; 2 Sam 7:1; 1 Kings 8:56). The notion of a rest in which the towns may be left without any defence (v. 19) conveys a peaceful vision in strong contrast with the military ideology of 2:34.

(3:21–9) The End of Moses' Leadership vv. 21–2, Moses' and Joshua's leadership in the conquest are seen in close parallel, cf. Josh 1:5. v. 28 is resumed in 31:7; Josh 1:6. The scene of Moses' rejected prayer is not continued by the narrator until 34:1–3. Moses wants to 'cross over' into the land and 'see' it (v. 25), but he may only 'see' it, whereas Joshua is to 'cross over' into it (v. 27–8). Moses thus becomes the symbol for an unfulfilled hope to live in the promised land. The reason for this is that YHWH makes him bear the consequences of the people's lack of faith—which Moses deplored in 1:32 (v. 26; the same thought has been added in 1:37–8). Not unlike 9:13–14, 25–9, the scene thus includes reflections on the relationship between Moses and the people. The opening of the prayer proclaims YHWH's uniqueness (as in 1 Kings 8:23); one might compare the hymnic praise of the sun god in an Akkadian hymn (Lambert 1960: 129 ll. 45–6; ANET 388): 'Among all the Igigi (gods) there is none who toils but you, | None who is supreme like you in the whole pantheon of gods.'

Discourse on the Excellence of the Law (4:1–40)

This great discourse has been inserted between the historical retrospective and the superscription to the law in 4:44. Although it combines several components and although the form of address changes between second person plural and second person singular (see DEUT F.4 and Begg 1980), it eventually forms a unit framed by vv. 1–2 and 40. The discourse gives an interpretation of the Exile after the destruction of Jerusalem in 587 BCE as a time of 'serving' gods who are nothing but 'wood and stone' (v. 28; cf. 28:64) and addresses the issue of Israel's 'return' to YHWH (v. 30; cf. 30:1–2). It presupposes the prohibition of idols in the Decalogue (vv. 12–13, 16; cf. 5:8) and contains an explicit monotheistic confession (vv. 35, 39). Both these fundamental theological doctrines are being derived from the visual scene of YHWH's revelation at Mount Horeb and presented as an epitome of the Torah.

(4:1–8) Israel's Wisdom Obedience to the 'statutes and ordinances' brings with it the promise of life (v. 1; cf. 30:15–16) and is also seen as a condition for the conquest of the promised land (v. 1; cf. 6:17–18). At the same time, the 'statutes and ordinances' are defined as rules for life in the land (v. 5; cf. 12:1). The substance and the extent of the law must be protected from any changes (v. 2). This principle lies on the way to the formation of a canon. In vv. 6–8, a scribe gives expression to the ideal of Israel as a 'wise and discerning people' (ʾam ḥākām wĕnābôn). Israel will be recognized as such a people from YHWH's protection (v. 7) as well as from her divine law (v. 8, cf. DEUT 1:5). Obedience to this

incomparable law would counteract the 'foolishness' of the people which is attacked in Jer 4:22. The designation of Israel as a 'great nation' echoes Gen 12:2, cf. Deut 1:10. In the final shape of Deuteronomy, the admiration of the nations in 4:6–8 corresponds with their puzzlement in 29:24–8 (MT 23–7). vv. 3–4, the warning against apostasy may be a gloss based on Num 25:1–5, cf. also Hos 9:10.

(4:9–14) YHWH's Voice at Mount Horeb The praise of the Torah is complemented by a graphic representation of the revelation of the Decalogue. The Israelites are to keep that day in their memory and their heart and pass the tradition on to all future generations (v. 9). YHWH revealed the Ten Commandments directly to the people so that they could hear 'the sound of words' (v. 12; cf. 4:33; 5:24), and he thus established his 'covenant' (bĕrît) with them. The poetic imagery underlines the priority of the Decalogue over the several statutes and ordinances (vv. 12–14). The account is based on 5:1–6:3 which, in turn, depends on fragments of older traditions in Ex 19–34. It makes the special point that Israel did not see any 'form' (tĕmûnâ; 'shape' NJPS, 'similitude' KJV) in the theophany (v. 12).

(4:15–20) Prohibition of Idols and Astral Cults Like 5:8, Moses' warning excludes all sculptured images in wood or stone (pesel) from Israel's cult. No image of the deity can signify religious truth, because the fundamental tradition of YHWH's theophany at Mount Horeb knows of no anthropomorphic or zoomorphic shape, cf. also the imagery of 1:33; Ex 13:21–2, contrast Ex 32:4. The strongly anthropomorphic language of the HB should be considered in the light of this critical thought. The section takes the law of 16:21–2 one step further and reflects a development which is also indicated by Isa 40:18–20, 25–6; Jer 10:14–16 (on religious iconography in Israel in antiquity see Keel and Uehlinger 1998). Astral cult, which is also an issue in the law code itself (17:2–7), seems to have been a major threat to Judean religious identity in the late monarchic period, cf. 2 Kings 23:11–12; Zeph 1:4–6; Jer 8:1–3, and see the quotations from an Assyrian treaty at DEUT 28:1–68. This type of religion is interpreted in vv. 19–20 on a line with 32:8–9, according to which YHWH as the God most high assigns celestial beings as deities to the nations, whereas Israel is his own people (ʿam naḥălâ, cf. 1 Kings 8:51–3 and the term ʿâm sĕgullâ in

26:18). However, the polemics in v. 28 and the confession in v. 35 seem to invalidate this interpretation of polytheism.

(4:21–31) Moses' Prophetic Warning A scribe here gives Moses a prophetic role on his parting from Israel (cf. 31:14–30). Moses foresees YHWH's wrath and YHWH's mercy in Israel's future history which centres on the Exile after the defeat of Jerusalem in 587 BCE. He confronts Israel's faith with two conflicting views of God: 'the LORD your God is a jealous God', and 'the LORD your God is a merciful God' (vv. 24, 31; cf. 5:9–10; Ex 34:6–7). The tension between these two statements should not be superficially resolved, as both perceptions of God claim their place in religious experience and stimulate as much as restrict theological reflection. In the present context, the experience of divine punishment is seen as a consequence of violating the prohibition of idols (v. 23), not of the service of 'other gods' as e.g. in 29:24–5 (MT 25–6); cf. also Rom 1:22–3. On the other hand, the expectation to 'find' YHWH 'if you search after him with all your heart and soul' (v. 29; cf. Jer 29:13–14; Am 5:4) is founded on YHWH's covenant with the ancestors (cf. 29:13 (MT 12)) which, unlike the covenant at Mount Horeb (4:13, 23) does not depend on obedience to the law (cf. Gen 15:6). v. 31, therefore, shows a greater kerygmatic depth than a passage like 28:58–68.

(4:32–40) A Confession of Monotheism vv. 32–5, this unique statement in Deuteronomy must be seen on one level with Isa 45:5–6, 12, 18, 21–2; 46:9–10, although it may reflect a later liturgical adaptation of these sayings from the sixth century BCE. In a perspective of a theology of creation, the unit leads to a climax in a monotheistic creed, cf. 32:39. In a universal horizon, YHWH's revelation at Mount Horeb in a voice 'out of the midst of the fire' (RSV, cf. vv. 12–13) and his prodigious actions in the Exodus (cf. 5:15; 34:11–12) are considered a proof of his exclusive divinity. The knowledge of God (v. 35) which Israel will arrive at through an understanding of her traditions is finally to become the knowledge of 'all the people of the earth': 1 Kings 8:60; cf. Isa 49:6. vv. 36 (cf. 8:5) and 37–9 read like homiletic amplifications of the preceding sections. In liturgical diction, v. 38 refers to the completed conquest of the land. vv. 39–40 echo v. 35 and vv. 1–2 respectively and form a finale to the discourse.

(4:41–3) Cities of Refuge Based on 19:1–13, a narrative insertion identifies three towns

in the allotted territory east of the Jordan (3:12–17) as places of refuge. This is repeated in Josh 20:1–9.

(4:44–9) A Superscription v. 44 marks the transition from Moses' historical review in 1:6–3:29 to the publication of the *tôrâ* in a more limited sense than that implied by 1:5. Still, the notion of *tôrâ* includes paraenesis as well as laws. Together with the subscription in 29:1 (MT 28:69), the superscription in v. 44 forms a frame around the extended law code as the document of a covenant, and 31:9 may refer to this unit. A parallel superscription in v. 45, which is taken up in 6:20–5, is terminologically interesting, cf. 5:31. The term 'decrees' (*ʿēdōt*) may designate the Decalogue, cf. 2 Kings 17:15 and the singular noun in such priestly texts as Ex 25:16; 31:18. As neither of these superscriptions can be shown to have been the original superscription to the law code which Hilkiah is said to have sent to Josiah (2 Kings 22:3–10), it remains an open question whether that document had already been attributed to Moses then. vv. 46–9, these later additions are based on chs. 1–3. Instead of 'the land of Moab' as in 1:5, they speak more correctly of 'the land of . . . Sihon'.

Review of the Covenant at Horeb and the Decalogue (5:1–33 (6:1–3))

(5:1–5) The Covenant at Mount Horeb The superscription which announces the Torah (4:44) is not directly followed by a code of laws, but instead by an explanation of the relation between the laws of Deuteronomy and the Decalogue (5:1–31) as well as by a series of discourses on faithful commitment to YHWH (chs. 6–11). Chs. 5–11 may altogether be attributed to Deuteronomistic scribes of the sixth and fifth centuries BCE; cf. DEUT F.3, H.3. The Decalogue is the foundation of YHWH's covenant with Israel (v. 2) which is linked to the place name 'Horeb' (as 'Sinai' in Exodus) and the imagery of God's speaking to the Israelites directly from 'out of the fire' (v. 4). Two further considerations have been added to this original concept: v. 3 emphasizes the continuous relevance of the covenant to all generations of Israel. The weight of this issue becomes clear in contrast to Jer 31:32 where the original covenant refers to the 'ancestors' and, after a history of unfaithfulness, needs eschatological renewal. v. 5 emphasizes the role of Moses as mediator between YHWH and Israel. A similar concern guides the narrators in Ex 19–24; 32–4. For a circumspect analysis of Deut 5 see Hossfeld (1982).

(5:6–21) The Decalogue A proper biblical perspective on the Decalogue can be gained through 5:24 (cf. 4:33): 'Today we have seen that God may speak to someone and the person may still live.' The Decalogue is fundamental not only to the covenant relationship between YHWH and Israel, but through Israel as God's revelation to humankind. Within the Christian tradition, it remains a valid exposition of the commandment to love God and one's neighbour (Mk 12:28–34; Rom 13:8–10). The Decalogue is a literary composition of the Deuteronomists and may be more original in its context in Deut 5 than in Ex 20. It could, however, always function as a self-contained sequence of basic commandments and probably originated independently of its literary setting. The Decalogue integrates several distinct elements; see also Schmidt (1993). Its three main sections are the self-presentation of YHWH and the prohibition of other gods (vv. 6–10), the sabbath commandment (vv. 12–15) and the series of six prohibitions in vv. 17–21.

vv. 6–10, in a first person singular address of YHWH, two basic features of Israel's faith are being expressed: the God who demands obedience to his commandments is the God who delivered his people from oppression in Egypt, and this God is a 'jealous God' ('ēl qannā') and therefore demands exclusive worship. God's punishment for 'iniquity' ('āwôn) extends to an entire family, i.e. to the four generations which may at most be living at any one time. Ezek 18 revises this doctrine of 5:9–10 and Ex 34:7 in an extensive theological discussion, cf. especially 18:19–20 and also Deut 7:10; 29:18–21 (MT 17–20). The first section of the Decalogue is framed by a witness to the gracious God who is known to those who love God through the Exodus and through a promise to show 'steadfast love' (ḥesed). The human being's response is to love God (v. 10; cf. 6:5), and this implies acknowledging God's uniqueness (v. 7) and keeping God's commandments (v. 10). v. 8, which separates v. 7 from its continuation in v. 9, is an addition which anchors the concern of 4:15–18 in the Decalogue. The prohibition effects a sharp distinction between visual representations of God and metaphorical representations of God in human language, v. 11, invoking the name of a deity is part of an oath (cf. 6:13; Jer 5:2; Ps 24:4). The prohibition reflects the strong concern with judicial matters typical of Deuteronomy (cf. 16:19; 19:15–19).

vv. 12–15, the Decalogue includes only one distinctive religious custom, namely keeping the sabbath as a weekly day of rest from work. The commandment continues an older tradition (cf. Ex 23:12; 34:21) and at the same time probably transforms the day called šabbāt from a celebration of full moon (cf. e.g. 2 Kings 4:23; Hos 2:11 (MT 13)) into a weekly day of rest. vv. 14–15 particularly emphasize the social significance of a periodical day of rest and call for generous treatment of all dependent persons, whether they be formally linked to a family as slaves or live as 'resident alien[s] in your towns'. Obeying this commandment is a way of remembering God's liberation of Israel from oppression in Egypt (cf. 15:15; 26:6–8). In Ex 20:11, this motivation has been substituted with the concept of a cosmic dimension of a seven-day week, cf. Gen 1:1–2:3. Notwithstanding this notion of its universal character, the sabbath must also be protected as a 'sign' of the unique relationship between YHWH and Israel, cf. Ex 31:12–17.

v. 16, except for v. 12, this commandment of the Decalogue is the only one which is expressed in a positive form. It has a traditional background in the legal sentences in Ex 21:15, 17; cf. also Deut 21:18–21. It aims at protecting solidarity within a family and securing support for parents in their old age by their sons and daughters. The first part of the motive clause (cf. 22:7) reflects the idea that honourable behaviour will repay the person who exercises it. The second part refers to life in Israel's land, and this shows that the Decalogue was given preeminence over the 'statutes and ordinances' for observance in the land (5:31; 12:1) only through the literary construction of 5:1–5, 22–31.

vv. 17–19, these three prohibitions are probably based on Hos 4:2 and are alluded to in Jer 7:9. Fundamental ethical criteria for accusations in prophetic speech are being reformulated as positive law here. The life of the community is to be guided by three essential principles: the protection of human life, of marriage, and of property. Natural indignation at any offences against these rules is a powerful demonstration of their universal validity. The death penalty within a society (cf. 19:11–13) and war between hostile societies (cf. 20:10–14) are not addressed by the commandment at v. 17, cf. also Gen 9:6. However, as the commandment expresses great respect for human life, it should strengthen a commitment to peace and protection of life in all fields. vv. 20–1, the three concluding prohibitions can be related to the three preceding ones. Bearing false witness may be used as a strategy for causing another person's death, cf. 19:15–21; 1 Kings 21:8–14. Coveting a married woman may lead to adultery, and desiring another person's property may end in its misappropriation. The authors of the Decalogue have thus reduplicated the three basic rules of vv. 17–19 in order to warn against the psychological origin of obvious violations of basic ethical norms, cf. Job 31:5–12. The same line of interpretation is pursued further in Jesus' teaching in Mt 5:21–2, 27–8. As much as the social world of ancient Judah can be recognized behind 5:12–21, and as strongly as the conflict between the God of the Exodus and 'other gods' in Israel's religious history characterizes 5:6–11, the Decalogue still remains the most comprehensive compilation of life-enhancing religious and ethical insights within the OT.

(5:22–31) Moses as Mediator The idea which was only secondarily added in 5:5, that Moses is the unique mediator of YHWH's revelation of the law (cf. 34:10), is fundamental to this section of Moses' review of the events at Mount Horeb. YHWH invites Moses, 'stand here by me' (v. 31), after approving of what the people demanded of Moses (vv. 28, 30). Following the people's pledge to listen and do whatever YHWH would tell Moses (v. 27, cf. Ex 19:7–8), YHWH begins to tell Moses the whole instruction (*kol-hammiṣwâ*), and 'the statutes and ordinances' which Moses in turn shall teach the people (v. 31). All the laws are thus referred back to a revelation at Mount Horeb although, prior to entering the land, the Decalogue is the only law known to the people. In correspondence with this differentiation between the Decalogue and all other laws, the idea that YHWH wrote the Ten Commandments on two stone tablets further underlines their significance (v. 22; cf. 9:8–10; 10:1–5; Ex 24:12; 31:18). Scribal comments (vv. 24b, 26) on the notion of the divine voice from 'out of the fire' reflect on the uniqueness of God's revelation (cf. 4:32–3) as well as the frailty of the human being beside God (cf. Isa 40:6–7; Jer 17:5–8). v. 29, which has a close parallel in Jer 32:39–40, is a further comment on Israel's pledge to obey the laws: the ideal of 'fear of God' as the true disposition for obedience to the law was realized in an exemplary situation during the foundational theophany. This 'fear' is 'not terror but inner religious feeling' (Weinfeld 1991: 325).

(5:32–6:3) Exhortations 5:32–3 may be a reflection of liturgical practice, cf. 6:17–18; 7:11. In general terms, a scribe here relates obedience to God's will to the rewards which an obedient person will gain from it. Within the OT, such a

liturgical and doctrinal tradition, which is characteristic of Deuteronomistic writing (cf. also 8:1; Josh 1:7; Jer 7:23), is questioned by the book of Job which gives expression to a different religious experience. 6:1 marks the beginning of Moses' teaching Israel the 'instruction' (*miṣwâ*) which YHWH commanded him (5:31). A further superscription in 12:1 introduces the 'statutes and ordinances', cf. already 4:44, 45. 6:2–3 may again reflect liturgical practice. A strong endeavour to keep the religious tradition alive throughout the generations also motivates 6:20–5.

Discourse on Faithful Obedience to the Law (6:4–11:25 (26–32))

(6:4–9) The Central Confession The opening vocative in v. 4 gives this section its name, Shema, and vv. 4–9 together with 11:13–21 and Num 15:37–41 form a liturgical text of highest importance in Jewish worship. The translation of the second half of v. 4 (*YHWH ʾĕlōhênû YHWH ʾeḥād*) is much debated and remains ambivalent. Stylistically, the words may form one prose sentence or, alternatively, two parallel hymnic exclamations. Thematically, the words may be a statement about YHWH or, alternatively, a statement about YHWH's relationship with Israel. The translation adopted by NRSV and NJPS, 'The LORD is our God, the LORD alone', is probably the best, cf. however LXX and Mk 12:29. The audience is being admonished and confesses that Israel stands in an exclusive relationship with YHWH. This excludes the worship of any other deities (cf. 5:7; 17:2–7) as well as a consort of YHWH (cf. DEUT 16:21). Josh 24 reflects a similar concern regarding Israel's exclusive allegiance to YHWH. At a later stage in the history of Israel's religious thought, this fundamental confession could be accommodated to a monotheistic creed like 4:35, 39; 32:39; and in this sense Zech 14:9 unfolds the universal dimension of v. 4; cf. also 1 Cor 8:4. v. 5, cf. Mk 12:30. What human sentiment can correspond to the confession of v. 4? A scribe here designates the true faith commitment as 'love of God'. This notion has been further developed in 30:16–20, and it equals the notion of 'fear of God' as in 5:29, see DEUT A.I. The fact that v. 5 is an injunction need not surprise. First, it may have been modelled after a demand of undivided loyalty in the political sphere (cf. Parpola and Watanabe 1988: 39 (ll. 266–8); *ANET* 537). Secondly, as faith is a human response to divine revelation (cf. 5:6, 24), it can be given guidance, and the notion of love here functions as the fundamental guiding idea; cf. also Mic 6:6–8. The scribe circumscribes the totality of the human being with three terms in order to emphasize the seriousness of a faith commitment, cf. the idealized characterization of Josiah in 2 Kings 23:25 and also 1 Kings 8:46–50; contrast Jer 12:2. vv. 6–9, all Israelites are asked to memorize, to teach, and to publicly confess the dogma of v. 4. As the intrusive relative clause 'that I am commanding you today' (cf. 7:11) shows, this later came to be understood of the entire law; see Veijola (1992a, b) and on the customs mentioned in vv. 8–9, Keel (1981).

(6:10–19) Against Forgetting YHWH The paraenetic discourses in chs. 6–11 are styled so as to correspond to the imagined situation of Moses' audience east of the Jordan (1:1–5; 3:29; 4:46). Taking possession of the promised land (cf. 1:8) is seen by the Deuteronomists as the one great threat to Israel's belief in the God of the Exodus (5:6). Looking back to the defeat of Jerusalem in 587 BCE, these scribes understand the catastrophe as caused by the 'anger' ('ap) of YHWH who, as a 'jealous God' (cf. 5:9), punishes apostasy (v. 15; cf. 29:25–8 (MT 24–7)). The extraordinary thought that YHWH might 'destroy' Israel (v. 15) is made the subject of reflection in 9:7–10:11, especially 9:13–14; cf. also Am 9:8 and Deut 28:63. 'Forgetting YHWH' while devoting oneself to the worship of local, autochthonous deities is a recurring reason for accusations in Hosea (2:13 (MT 15); 8:14; 13:6) and Jeremiah (2:32; 13:25; 18:15; 23:27), cf. 8:7–20. v. 14 reflects a situation of Israel as a community not yet consolidated after the destruction of the central royal sanctuary. Like ch. 13, the verse indicates the Deuteronomists' anti-assimilationist concerns. v. 16 points back to Ex 17:1–7: YHWH's presence in Israel must not be 'put to the test'. For vv. 17–18 cf. DEUT 5:32–3. v. 19 reflects the same situation as v. 14, cf. Josh 23:5 and see on 7:1–6.

(6:20–5) Basic Religious Instruction The section emphasizes that the Exodus creed is the foundation of the law, as the internal structure of the Decalogue also makes clear. The introduction shows the catechetical purpose of a unit such as vv. 21–4, cf. Ex 13:14–15. The graphic elaboration in v. 22 may be secondary, cf. García López (1978). v. 25 formulates a fundamental theology of the law: observing the law (kol-hammiṣwâ) will be 'righteousness (ṣĕdāqâ) for us'

(RSV), 'to our merit before the LORD our God' (NJPS), cf. 24:13. LXX offers a remarkable translation: 'mercy (eleēmosynē) will be for us, if . . . ' In the NT, Paul in Phil 3:9 expresses his acceptance and his rejection of this theological thought, cf. also Gal 2:16–17, 21.

(7:1–11) The Election of Israel v. 1 takes 6:10 as a model, and v. 4 depends on 6:15. However, the perspective in which the land is seen is totally different from the one adopted in 6:10–15 and 8:7–18 or such texts as Hos 2:2–13 (MT 4–15); Jer 2:5–7 where the wealth and fertility of the land are considered a threat to Israel's allegiance to YHWH. According to vv. 1–5, the land is a territory where the religious habits of many ancient 'nations' prevail and where, because of this, Israel's identity is in danger. This idea is being expressed through the imagery of a military conquest. v. 2 represents the same concept which underlies 2:32–5; here as in 20:16–17 it is shaped as a command to 'utterly destroy' (h-r-m hifil) the nations of the land. (On the antiquarian list of names see the entries for the respective names in ABD.) The concept of 'ritual destruction' of entire communities can be traced back to at least the ninth century BCE as it is also found on the Mesha stone, a Moabite royal inscription from about 830 BCE, which includes this episode:

And Chemosh said to me, 'Go, take Nebo [a town east of the Jordan] from Israel!' So I went by night and fought against it from the break of dawn until noon, taking it and slaying all, seven thousand [men and women], for I had devoted them to destruction [hrm] for (the god) Ashtar-Chemosh. And I took from there the [vessels] of Yahweh, dragging them before Chemosh. (ll.14–18 (abbreviated): cf. ANET 320)

However, v. 2 does not intend to document ancient military practice, but rather to construe an ideal of Israel's conquest of the land. This ideal does not tell anything about Israel's early history, but mainly has two functions: it serves as a basis for explaining the defeat of Jerusalem in 587 BCE in terms of Israel's apostasy which is seen to have been induced by her assimilation to the nations of the land in defiance of a Mosaic command (cf. 20:18; 29:25–8 (MT 24–7); Josh 23:1 to Judg 3:6), and it serves as a warning against assimilation for the community of those who are faithful to the law, probably at some time in the Second Temple period. v. 3 may be directly related to the policy of Nehemiah in the fifth century BCE, cf. Neh 13:23–7 and also Gen 24:3; 28:1. v. 5 proscribes all cultic sites besides the temple, cf. 12:3; Ex 34:13. In vv. 1–2, Israel's claim to the land and fear of apostasy resulted in an ideal which induces doubt about God's relation to humankind and frightens the human being away from God. Even within Deuteronomy itself, this voice finds a theologically more promising context, cf. 4:19–20, 32–5 (however, also 36–8); 9:1–6. v. 6 can justify a separation from people who worship 'other gods' (v. 4; 20:18), but not the ideal of vv. 1–2. On the exegetical problem of vv. 1–2 see Barr (1993: 207–20).

v. 6 (cf. 26:16–19) puts the exclusive relationship between YHWH and Israel (cf. 6:4) into a universal horizon in relating it to the entire created world (cf. Ex 19:5; Am 3:2), thus going far beyond an orientation towards Israel's land. The connection between mythological primeval history and YHWH's call of Abraham in Gen 9:18–12:3 gives a narrative representation of this creed. Its climax in Gen 12:3 (cf. Jer 4:1–2) must be considered an aspect of the canonical context of Deut 7:6. vv. 7–8, Israel's election is founded solely on YHWH's love, cf. Hos 11:1, which also manifests itself in YHWH's promise to the ancestors, cf. Gen 22:16–18. A scribe here confronts the triumphant conception of vv. 1–2 with a deliberate antithesis which sees Israel as 'the fewest of all peoples'. vv. 9–10 quote 5:9–10 but restrict YHWH's punishment to any individually responsible person.

(7:12–26) Hope and Israel's History This section presents further Deuteronomistic elaborations of some of the subjects addressed in 6:10–7:11. YHWH's oath to Israel's ancestors (7:8) will only motivate YHWH to keep the 'gracious covenant' if Israel observes the commandments; v. 12, together with 8:19–20, thus relate the theology of 7:7–8 to the doctrine of YHWH as a 'jealous God' (5:9–10; 6:15; 7:9–10). God's love unfolds in blessings in the spheres of daily life (vv. 13–15; cf. Ex 23:25–6; Deut 28:1–14). v. 16 forms a transition to scribal reflections on the impossible vision of 7:1–2 in the light of the historical experience of a small community living amongst different peoples (cf. 6:14). Although hope remains that taking possession of the land will eventually be as successful as the Exodus from Egypt (vv. 18–19; cf. 1:30; Ex 13:17–14:31), YHWH will 'clear away' (NRSV; dislodge: NJPS: *nāšal*, v. 22 as in 7:1) the peoples only 'little by little', cf. Ex 23:28–33; Josh 23:6–13. This concept prepares for the biblical picture of Israel's early history as much as for an understanding of the post-exilic period in the light of YHWH's exuberant promises. In the realm of history,

what is essential is not to allow the religions of these peoples to become a 'snare' (v. 16) for the people of YHWH. Cf. also the liturgical use of the warning example of the earlier generations in Ps 106:34–41.

(8:1–20) Knowledge of God and Praise Characterized by its poetic beauty and a rich diversity of paraenetic verbs, ch. 8 returns to the subject of 6:10–15: the wealth of the land as a possible threat to Israel's faithful adherence to the God of the Exodus. For a critical analysis see Veijola (1995 a). vv. 7–10 ('When the LORD your God brings you into a good land . . . then you shall bless the LORD your God . . .'; cf. Weinfeld 1991: 391) is an exhortation to praise God for all the good which the community enjoys. In v. 11, the notion of 'forgetting YHWH' is explained in terms of disobedience to the law. vv. 12–18 enlarge on the preceding texts, notably in hymnic praise of YHWH's mighty deeds. A scribe here warns against impious arrogance (cf. Hos 13:4–6), as Israel's wealth is owed to God's blessing (7:13; cf. Hos 2:8 (MT 10)). vv. 19–20 add a reinterpretation of vv. 7–18 on the lines of 7:1–5, turning the concept of annihilation into a conditional threat against Israel, cf. 6:15. vv. 1 and 6 (cf. 6:1) frame the first unit of ch. 8 which demonstrates how the imagery of Israel's forty years wandering in the wilderness (cf. 1:3; 2:14; Am 2:10; Ex 15:22–17:7; Num 10:33–12:16; 20:1–21:20) should lead towards a knowledge of God. To the several interpretations of this period (cf. 1:31; 32:10–11; Hos 2:14–15 (MT 16–17); Jer 2:2), v. 2 adds the aspect of God's 'testing' (*n-s-h* piel) Israel's faithfulness (cf. Judg 3:4). This thought may even prepare the ground for the discussion of the problem of theodicy in the book of Job. In v. 5, this interpretation is modified by the concept of God's 'disciplining' (*y-s-r* piel) Israel, cf. Zeph 3:2; Jer 2:30; 30:11, 14; 31:18. v. 3 is a keystone of theology within the OT. A scribe here develops an understanding of religious faith and, at the same time, claims that this faith must have its foundation in God's words of promise and command; cf. 5:24; 30:15–16; also Mt 4:4.

(9:1–6) Righteousness and the Conquest of the Land Rhetorically, this section has been carefully adapted to the fictitious situation indicated by 1:1–5; 3:28; cf. also 31:3–6. It is probably an insertion, and borrows a number of motifs from its literary context. Moses 'encourages and strengthens' Israel in such a way that his words even create a contradiction between v. 3 and

7:22. However, the specific subject of vv. 1–6 is the question of why YHWH would destroy the nations of the land, cf. 7:1–2; 8:19–20. Israel is being warned not to ascribe YHWH's great deeds to her own 'righteousness' (*ṣĕdāqâ*; contrast 6:25; 8:1). Instead, the nations of the land are being qualified by a 'wickedness' (*rišʿâ*) which provokes divine punishment, cf. Ezek 18:20 and also Gen 15:16; Lev 18:24–30. There is no way of determining what the 'wickedness' of these nations who could not have offended against the laws from Mount Horeb is seen to have been, although one might refer to the 'abhorrent things' (*tôʿēbôt*) according to 12:31; 18:9–12; 20:18. This problem may have motivated the scribe who, by adding v. 2, altogether transforms the imagery of conquest. Building on elements adopted from 1:28 and 7:24, this scribe imagines the entire land as populated not by ancient nations, but rather by 'the offspring of the Anakim' (see DEUT 1:28), i.e. mythological creatures, cf. Am 2:9; Josh 11:21–2; Bar 3:24–8. Mythological imagination thus counter-balances the rhetoric of annihilation.

(9:7–10:11) YHWH's Wrath at Mount Horeb
This section reads like a homily on the doctrine of YHWH as a 'jealous God' in 6:15. Looking back to Mount Horeb as the place of a 'covenant' ceremony (9:9, based on 5:2, 22), a scribe here reflects on the threat that YHWH might 'destroy' (*š-m-d* hifil, 6:15; 9:8, 13–14) Israel. In his representation of Israel's foundational period under Moses' leadership, he shows how, in a paradigmatic way, this threat had been averted through Moses' intercession for the people. Thus, Israel's future is grounded in the Mosaic age (as well as in the promise to the ancestors, 9:27; cf. 7:7–8), although the catastrophe of 587 BCE could not be averted, cf. Jer 5:18–19; 30:11, the interdiction of intercession theme in Jer 7:16; 11:14; also 15:1. The basic narrative, which may have included 9:7–18, 26–9; 10:10b–11, is based on an earlier version of the story of the Golden Calf in Ex 32–4; see Driver (1895 (1901)) and especially Aurelius (1988). Several additions have been joined to it, notably referring to Aaron (9:20; 10:6–7), the Levites (10:8–9), and the ark (10:1–5; cf. 1 Kings 8:9). The section starts from a striking reinterpretation of the period in the wilderness (9:7; cf. Jer 7:24–6, and see DEUT 8:2), and this has been enlarged by more instances of Israel's rebellious character as a 'stubborn people' (*ʿam qĕšê-ʾōrep*, 9:13) in 9:22–4 (for which cf. 1:19–46; Ex 17:1–7; Num 11:1–34; Ps 106:19–33).

(10:12–11:32) Nomistic Paraenesis The exhortation 'So now, O Israel' opens a sequence of loosely connected paraenetic addresses which borrow many elements from the preceding chapters. Although the section may include some vague reminiscences of a treaty form (cf. Mayes 1979: 30–4, 207–9), it has no overall coherence. Regarding the conquest of the land west of the Jordan, 11:22–32 returns as it were to the point where Moses' historical review had left the reader in 3:29.

The first unit, 10:12–11:1, builds upon 6:2, 5 and emphasizes that 'fear of God' and 'love of God' denote a belief in God which is the basis for all faithful obedience to the divine commandments. vv. 14–15 refer to Israel's election in a universal horizon (cf. 7:6–8; 4:32–5), and vv. 17–18 establish a connection between election and behaviour (cf. 4:5–8; Ps 146:6–9). v. 19 gives an example of how hymnic praise of a just and benevolent God must entail practical ethical consequences for the life within a community. For the command itself cf. Lev 19:18b, 33–4. The 'sojourner' (RSV; NRSV translates 'stranger' in 10:19, but 'resident alien' in 5:14; 24:17, etc.) is a typical needy person because he holds no property in land and does not belong to a landowner's household either. In dense metaphorical language, v. 16 gives a paraenetic response to 9:13 (cf. also Jer 4:4; 6:10); however, in 30:6 a scribe arrives at an even more radical understanding of human opposition to the divine word and of God's will to overcome this opposition, cf. Jer 31:33–4; Ezek 18:31; 36:26. For v. 22 cf. Gen 46:27. The second unit, 11:2–9, gives an enumeration of the mighty deeds of God (cf. esp. Ex 14; Num 16) that will contribute to an understanding of God's 'greatness', cf. 3:24. As v. 2 is an anacoluthon, it is not clear in what sense a scribe here addresses the problem of the succession of generations in Israel, cf. 29:14–15 (MT 13–14); Josh 24:31; Judg 2:7, 10. The liturgical fragment does not take the situation of Moses' oration into account, cf. 1:34–5, 39; 2:16. For vv. 8–9 cf. 8:1. vv. 10–12, cf. 8:7–10: the praise of the land also implies a rejection of idolatrous fertility cults, cf. Hos 2:2–13 (MT 4–15). vv. 13–15 cf. 7:12–15, a scribe here turns the praise into a conditional promise, cf. Jer 5:23–5. vv. 16–17 are based on 6:15 and echo the curse of 28:23. For vv. 18–21 see DEUT 6:6–9. vv. 22–5 (cf. 7:16–24; 9:1; Josh 1:1–9): this unit leads on to the conquest narratives of the book of Joshua. For the ideal delineation of Israel's territory cf. 1:7 and Josh 1:4. For the motif of the nations' dread of Israel cf. 2:25; Josh 2:9–11, 24.

11:26–32 (cf. 27:11–13; 30:15–20). Crossing the Jordan and entering into the land marks the situation for a decision between faithful adherence to YHWH, the God of the Exodus, and apostasy: obedience or disobedience, blessing or curse are being presented as straightforward alternatives. A similar ceremony at Shechem, i.e. between Mount Gerizim to the south and Mount Ebal to the north, is narrated in Josh 24, cf. especially vv. 14–15. A puzzling gloss in v. 30 transfers the ceremony of v. 29 to a location directly in the valley of the Jordan, cf. Josh 4:20; 5:10. Here as elsewhere in chs. 4–11, the great paraenetic alternative is as much a reflection of liturgical practice as it is part of the Deuteronomistic literary invention of Moses' oration.

Promulgation of the Laws (12:1–25:19 (26:1–15))

(12:1–32 (MT 12:1–13:1)) The Law of Centralization of Sacrificial Worship Ch. 12 contains the law which defines the place of Deuteronomy in the history of Israelite cult. It is based on an opposition between a multiplicity of cultic sites ('any place you happen to see') and 'the place that the LORD will choose' as the one legitimate place for performing acts of sacrificial cult (vv. 13–14). On the one hand, the law contradicts that of Ex 20:22–6 which gives permission to erect 'an altar of earth' or 'an altar of stone' in many places, for that law includes the divine promise that 'in every place where I [YHWH] cause my name to be remembered I will come to you and bless you'. On the other hand, the law is presupposed by the Priestly Document. In that code, the one single 'place' of sacrificial worship is imagined as a sanctuary the design of which was revealed to Moses on Mount Sinai, and this unique sanctuary was to allow YHWH 'to dwell among the Israelites' (wĕšākantî bĕtôkām, Ex 25:8–9 MT). The law of Deut 12 in its hypothetical original form is often regarded as the law which caused the Judean king Josiah 'to defile the high places… from Geba to Beersheba', i.e. throughout his kingdom, and to leave only 'the altar of the LORD in Jerusalem' (2 Kings 23:8–9; see DEUT F.1), and this historical connection remains a plausible assumption. The law does not name Jerusalem directly but, instead, speaks of 'the place that the LORD will choose'. This may be due to the fact that, according to Israel's historical tradition, it was David who first conquered Jerusalem and made it an Israelite city in the tenth century BCE (2 Sam 5:6–10). The temple at Jerusalem, therefore, was not a sanctuary of

YHWH from time immemorial (cf. also 2 Sam 6–7; 1 Kings 5–9). However, there is no reason to suppose that the formula 'the place that the LORD will choose' should be interpreted in a distributive sense as 'at all the respective places that YHWH will choose', even if, according to Jer 7:12–15, Shiloh had at some time been a sanctuary of the same legitimacy as Jerusalem. Deut 12 clearly has Jerusalem in view.

The law of Deut 12 is addressed to a laity which must be seen as living outside the capital in a rural milieu (v. 17). It has several repetitions and employs the second person singular as well as plural. There is a broad scholarly consensus which says that the sections in the plural (or mixed forms of address) are later than those in the singular, and that the singular sections may have been part of the original Deuteronomic law code. As far as cultic matters are concerned, 12:13–19; 14:22–9; 15:19–23; 16:1–17 represent the core of the Deuteronomic legislation. A correspondence has often been noted between these laws on cultic centralization and the concept of YHWH's unity and uniqueness as expressed in 6:4. For an extensive discussion of Deut 12 see Reuter (1993), Levinson (1997).

(12:1–7) Centralization and Anti-Syncretism v. 1 is a superscription to the law which closely follows 5:31; cf. 6:1. It introduces a second-person plural section (however, in the MT the formula relating to the land and its conquest is in the singular). vv. 2–3 echo 7:5 and introduce into the Deuteronomic law a criterion for the judgement of Israel's history of the monarchic period which is pronounced in Deuteronomistic historiography (cf. 1 Kings 14:23–4; 2 Kings 17:7–12). The stereotypical description of the high places may be based on Hos 4:13; Jer 2:20. Their interpretation as the remains of the cult of an earlier non-Israelite population represents a distinct development within Deuteronomistic thought, which results from the concept of the legitimacy of one single sanctuary of YHWH only. In 1 Sam 9:11–14, for example, the fact that a country town ('îr) has its shrine on a hilltop (bāmâ) does not worry the narrator. The list of cult-related objects in v. 3 also represents a late stage of religious polemics when compared to 16:21–2; 5:8.

(12:8–12) Centralization and the Periodization of Israel's History vv. 8–12 are another second-person plural section. Like Jer 7:21–2, the text builds upon the idea that Israel did not receive laws concerning cultic matters prior to entering the land. However, according to this Deuteronomistic scribe, the period of cultic tolerance lasted not only until the age of Joshua (cf. Josh 21:43–5; 23:1) but until that of Solomon, during which the temple in Jerusalem was built. Like 1 Kings 8:16, Deut 12:8–12 identifies the moment at which YHWH 'chose' the place of the only sanctuary with the inauguration of the temple in Jerusalem, cf. 1 Kings 5:3–5 (MT 5:17–19); 2 Sam 7:1 for the notion of 'rest'. It is clear from these links between the law and the narrative that vv. 8–12 are an addition to the Deuteronomic law after it had become part of the Deuteronomistic History.

(12:13–19) Centralization and Sacrifices vv. 13–19 are a second-person singular section and are the most original and the most radical part of the legislation of the Deuteronomic reform movement in the late-monarchic era (see DEUT F.1). The first and the last sentences of this section open with the imperative 'take care that you do not …' and it may be debated whether this is an appropriate beginning for a law (cf. 8:11; however, in 6:10–12; 12:29–31 the imperative follows a temporal clause). However, no alternative beginning suggests itself. In vv. 13–14, the lawgiver commands the restriction of sacrifices to the one single place 'that the LORD will choose' and thus puts an end to all other cultic sites which used to exist in Judah. A connection between the concept of a single sanctuary and the concept of tribal territories is made only here (and, depending on this verse, in 12:5), and the Deuteronomistic authors are not agreed on whether Jerusalem could be claimed by Judah (Josh 15:63) or by Benjamin (Judg 1:21).

The formula concerning the chosen place of sacrificial worship in v. 14 lacks a complement as in 14:23; 16:2, 6, 11; 26:2 which qualifies the chosen place as a place which YHWH chooses 'to make his name dwell there' (lĕšakkēn šĕmô šām; also in a second-person plural text in 12:11; a later variation reads 'to put his name there' as in 12:5 etc.). The concept of the sanctuary as dwelling-place not of the deity, but of the divine 'name' reflects a critique of a concept of holiness which is founded upon too anthropomorphic a notion of the deity (see Weinfeld 1992: 191–209; Mettinger 1982: 38–79). It counter-balances a theological understanding of the temple which may have been prevalent in the monarchic era and again in the Second Temple period (cf. Ps 46:5). According to 26:15, the 'heaven' is YHWH's 'holy habitation', and this idea also underlies Solomon's prayer in 1 Kings

8:22–53. The LXX translators may have had this prayer in mind when they translated the phrase 'to make his name dwell there' as 'for his name to be invoked there', cf. also Isa 56:7 and Mk 11:17.

vv. 13–14 speak of one type of sacrifice only, the 'burnt offering' ('ôlâ), when the entire animal is presented to the deity. It gives permission to slaughter (zābaḥ) animals for food 'within any of your towns' (v. 15) and thus makes slaughter a secular matter which does not have to be performed at an altar any more (see Maag 1956). In consequence, no ritual purity is demanded of those who eat the meat. v. 16 adds a detailed instruction concerning the blood which was formerly put on an altar. vv. 17–18 deal with cultic offerings which can no longer be brought to a local shrine but are not entirely divested of their ritual quality either. On the tithe see the additional law in 14:22–9, on the firstlings the law in 15:19–23, on pilgrimages to the sanctuary the laws in 16:1–17. The LXX has the second half of v. 17 in the second person plural which might suggest that the references to 'votive gifts' (nĕ-dārîm, cf. 23:21–3 (MT 22–4)), 'freewill offerings', and 'donations' are a later addition. The law envisages cultic celebrations of the entire family and makes 'rejoicing' the main characteristic of a religious festival. In the LXX, the list of participants does not include the Levite but rather the 'resident alien', as in 5:14. v. 19 commands permanent support of the Levite who used to be the priest at a local shrine and was to lose his cultic functions through the centralization of sacrificial worship (see, however, 18:6–8).

(12:20–8) Restrictions on Profane Slaughter The section gives a restrictive interpretation of v. 15. Permission is given to 'eat' meat 'whenever you have the desire', but an animal may be 'slaughtered' (zābaḥ) 'within your towns' only if, after the expansion of the territory, the sanctuary is 'too far from you' (v. 21; the structuring of the verse in the NRSV is not convincing). vv. 23–5 show the great concern this scribe has about the blood taboo (cf. Gen 9:4; Lev 17:10–12). v. 27 restores the zebaḥ type of sacrifice as a consequence of the restrictions on the law of v. 15, and this is presupposed in the enumeration of offerings in vv. 6, 11. At an even later stage, the law of Lev 17:1–7 abrogates Deut 12:15 (Cholewiński 1976: 149–78; see, however, Rofé, quoted in Fishbane 1985: 228, who suggests that vv. 20–8 should be understood as a late scribal harmonization of Deut 12:13–19 and Lev 17:1–7).

(12:29–32) Anti-Syncretistic Paraenesis In a second-person singular section, the same concept as in vv. 2–7 is being repeated, namely that even after the extinction of the nations in the land west of the Jordan, a temptation will remain for Israel to imitate religious rites which the divine ceremonial law does not permit. For paraenetic purposes, all 'abhorrent' rites are equated with a syncretistic corruption of Israel's religion (and vice versa). The end of v. 31 addresses a ritual practice which is severely criticized in such Deuteronomistic texts as e.g. Jer 7:30–4; 2 Kings 21:6. This type of child-sacrifice may betray Phoenician influence in Judah in the period after the fall of Jerusalem in 587 BCE (see Müller 1997). v. 32 (MT 13:1) concludes the law of centralization with a general exhortation and a formula which serves to protect the text from any changes and thus leads towards its canonical status (cf. 4:2). The law of Deut 12 was not only of enormous importance in the religious history of ancient Israel, but it retains its theological significance as a reflection on God's presence in worship in relation to God's supreme freedom.

(13:1–18 (MT 13:2–19)) Incitement to Apostasy The law deals with incitement to apostasy or idolatry in three paragraphs and in each case commands the death penalty (vv. 5, 10, 15) as in 17:2–7. The laws echo some motifs which are also found in Esar-haddon's succession treaty (see DEUT F.2), and thus apply instructions concerning disloyalty in the political sphere to apostasy in the religious sphere. Whether this betrays a revolutionary atmosphere in late seventh century Judah (Weinfeld 1992: 91–100; Dion 1991; Otto 1996*b*) or whether a later learned scribe employed the language of political treaties for paraenetic variations on the commandment of 5:7 (Veijola 1995*b*) remains open to debate. It may be useful to quote some lines from the Assyrian treaty for comparison here:

If you hear any evil, improper, ugly word which is not seemly nor good to Assurbanipal...either from the mouth of his ally, or from the mouth of his brothers...or from the mouth of your brothers, your sons, your daughters, or from the mouth of a prophet, an ecstatic, an inquirer of oracles, or from the mouth of any human being at all, you shall not conceal it but come and report it to Assurbanipal...If anyone should speak to you of rebellion and insurrection...or if you should hear it from the mouth of anyone, you shall seize the perpetrators of insurrection, and bring them before Assurbanipal...If you are able to

seize them and put them to death, then you shall destroy their name and their seed from the land... (ll. 108–46: Parpola and Watanabe 1988: 33–4; ANET 535–6; an Aramaic treaty of the 8th cent even includes the instruction to destroy a treasonous town: Sfire stela, 3. 12–13; ANET 661).

(13:1–5) Prophets The possibility of magic acts in the name of other gods than YHWH is also a motif in the Exodus narrative (cf. Ex 7:8–13). However, in the light of Jer 23:9–32, especially vv. 25–32, it is doubtful whether prophetic incitement to apostasy was ever an issue in late-monarchic Judah. The problem of untrue oracles in the name of YHWH is addressed in Deut 18:9–22. The author of vv. 1–2 interprets the criterion of fulfilment of an oracle as referring to thaumaturgic competence and decidedly subordinates it to the first commandment of the Decalogue (5:6–10). The law exhibits a concern for the exclusiveness of the worship of Israel's God, probably against a background of strong tendencies towards assimilation to foreign cults after the fall of Jerusalem (cf. 12:29–31). The second half of v. 3 which is based on 6:5 aims at a theological understanding of any conceivable enticement to a new religious allegiance.

(13:6–11) Family The second law concentrates on an instigator's confidentiality with the tempted believer and is therefore supported by an explicit order to suppress any feelings of sympathy. In comparison to the careful legal proceeding spelled out in 17:2–7 ('...and you make a thorough inquiry, and the charge is proved true'), the instructions for punishing the offender in vv. 8–9 look awkward. A double textual tradition for the beginning of v. 9 reads 'you shall surely kill him' (MT) or, alternatively, 'you shall surely report him' (LXX). However, it is clear that the formal legal verdict 'and he shall die' (*wāmēt*, cf. 19:12 contrast 19:4 'and he shall live', *wāḥāy*, and cf. 24:7 etc.) is only pronounced in v. 10 (MT 11; cf. also Tigay 1996: 132). The law represents a specific conception of 'Israel' in whose midst (MT vv. 2, 6, 12, 14) any attempt to incite apostasy must be punished. At a later literary stage within Deuteronomy, this is restricted to a threat of divine punishment (29:16–21 (MT 15–20)). v. 7 (28:64) may reflect an awareness of the religious world of antiquity in which Israel struggled to retain her faith.

(13:12–18) An Insurrectionary Town The model idea of ritual destruction of the nations in the promised land (7:1–2) is applied to an Israelite town in the case of its turning to the worship of foreign gods. The detailed instructions about the 'ban' (*ḥērem*) are reminiscent of Josh 6–7, cf. also Deut 7:25–6. vv. 17*b*–18 prove the author to have lived some time after the fall of Jerusalem, which was explained by the Deuteronomists as the consequence of YHWH's 'fierce anger' (*ḥărôn'ap*, cf. 2 Kings 23:26). The community lives in the expectation of YHWH's 'compassion' (*raḥămîm*), and faithful obedience to the law is understood as a condition for future restoration.

(14:1–2) Rites of Mourning This law, a late insertion into the law code, forbids two rites still considered to be habitual rites in Judah in Jer 16:6. The Israelites must neither gash their skin nor 'make baldness between the eyes', i.e. on the forehead. The kerygmatic introductory statement employs parent–child imagery in a way reminiscent of Isa 63:8–9, 16. Its metaphorical aspects are more evident in 8:5; Isa 1:2–3; Jer 3:19. In the monarchic period, the title of a 'son' of YHWH could be given to the king in royal ideology (cf. Ps 2:7; 2 Sam 7:14), and also the entire people could be called YHWH's 'son' (Hos 11:1). v. 2 is a repetition of 7:6.

(14:3–21) Dietary Laws The law opens with the general instruction not to eat 'any abhorrent thing' (*kol-tô'ēḇâ*) This is explained by detailed lists which have a more extended parallel in Lev 11. The section may be a secondary addition induced by the question of profane slaughter (12:15). A theological reason for these distinctions is given in Lev 20:22–6; for an interpretation of these rules see Douglas (1966: 41–57). v. 21, animals which have died of natural causes are a taboo for the people to which the law code is addressed but may be given as a charitable support to members of the non-landowning class, cf. 24:19–22, and may even be sold to foreigners. Later laws in Lev 11:39–40 and 17:15–16 only demand rites of purification after eating such meat. The prohibition at the end of v. 21 may reflect religious awe in regard to an animal and its mother as at 22:6–7, cf. Ex 23:18–19.

(14:22–9) Tithes A detailed law on tithes further clarifies 12:17–19. The tithe (or a less clearly defined offering: Ex 23:19) seems to have been a conventional contribution which peasants gave for ceremonies at local shrines, cf. Am 4:4–5. Any suggestion to link it to royal taxation re-

mains speculative (Crüsemann 1996: 215–19). The tithe is made the subject of a formal command in Deuteronomy in an attempt to abolish the traditional rites and to link the offering to the central sanctuary. A tendency towards desacralization of the tithe is reflected by the permission to turn it into money and to reserve the money for a pilgrimage. A later scribe restricted this permission by adding a conditional clause like that at 12:21 ('if/because the place . . . is too far from you', v. 24). In legislation of the Second Temple period, the tithe is formally declared a source of income for the Levites, cf. Num 18:20–32; Neh 13:10–14. vv. 28–9 (cf. 26:12–15), twice within a seven-year cycle (15:1), the tithe must be put to charitable support of the poor in the country towns. The attached promise makes it clear that divine blessing does not depend on any fertility rites.

(15:1–11) Remission of Debts and God's Blessing Within the sequence of cultic laws, the law indicates that the divine blessing on which economic success of farming depends (v. 10, cf. v. 18) may be won through humanitarian behaviour. vv. 1–3 revise the traditional institution of a fallow year (cf. Ex 23:10–11) and either complement or even replace it by a command to remit any debts which a fellow farmer might have incurred. It is clear from the context that the law concerns a loan which helped the 'neighbour' or 'brother' (RSV) to survive until the next harvest. The law does not include 'foreigners', because they did not belong to the community of those who had to observe the 'release' (*šĕmiṭṭâ*) that was proclaimed in YHWH's honour. A lucid philosophical understanding of this controversial differentiation (cf. again in 23:19–20 (MT 20–1)) has been suggested by H. Grotius who says that the Israelites owed the foreigners only whatever was demanded by 'natural law' because of the unity of humankind, but not what would have been motivated by an extraordinary benevolence ('Talibus incolis debebantur ob humani generis cognationem ea quae sunt iuris naturalis: non etiam ea quae maioris sunt bonitatis,' *Annotata ad Vetus Testamentum*, 1644).

The instruction of vv. 7–10 implies rich observations on the human heart and comes close to the commandment of Lev 19:18 to love one's neighbour (cf. Deut 10:17–19; Mk 12:31). In vv. 4–5, a later scribe expresses a vision of the fullness of God's blessing in response to the people's faithful obedience (cf. Isa 58:6–9) and v. 11 reconciles this expansion with the original intention of the law. v. 6 may be a late gloss on vv. 4–5 which is partly based on 28:12 and possibly reflects a political hope of the community in the Persian empire.

(15:12–18) Debt Servitude The law commands that any Hebrew slave is to be set free (*ḥopšî*) after six years of service. This seven-year period is not directly related to the year of release of vv. 1–11. The law is based on Ex 21:2–6. However, it does not take up the second law of Ex 21:7–11 (which is more a family law), but instead extends the force of the first law to apply equally to male and female slaves. The term 'Hebrew' (*ʿibrî*) is known from narratives which confront the Israelites with the Egyptians or the Philistines (e.g. Ex 1; 1 Sam 4). It remains doubtful whether it was originally related to the term *ḥab/piru* which, in Egyptian and Near-Eastern texts of the second millennium BCE, designates a certain stratum of society (see ABD iii. 6–10, 95). The subject of the law has a parallel in the Code of Hammurabi (18th cent. BCE) which decrees: 'If an obligation came due against a seignior and he sold (the services of) his wife, his son, or his daughter . . . they shall work (in) the house of their purchaser . . . for three years, with their freedom reestablished in the fourth year' (§117, ANET 170–1). The version in Deuteronomy puts special emphasis on the obligation to provide the slave generously with some goods on leaving, 'in proportion to YHWH's blessing' which the master had enjoyed (v. 14, following the LXX reading). However, it does not become clear on what economic basis former slaves would sustain themselves, and instead of becoming landless poor, it might be more advantageous for them to stay with their masters (vv. 16–17). In the circumspect social vision of Lev 25, the release of slaves is connected to the restitution of landed property in the jubilee year; cf. also Neh 5:1–13. v. 15 adduces the fundamental article of Israel's faith according to Deuteronomy in order to encourage unrestrained obedience. 'Remembering' (*zāḵar*) is a vital act of faith. Additionally, a rational argument in v. 18 says that a slave gives his master 'double the service of a hired man' (NJPS; NRSV's translation is based on a contentious interpretation of *mišneh* as 'equivalent').

(15:19–23) Firstlings Instructions for annual offerings in 14:22–7 and here form a framework for the humanitarian laws in 14:28–15:18 which refer to three-year and seven-year cycles or periods respectively. On firstlings see Ex 13:1–2; 34:19–20.

(16:1–8) Pesaḥ and the Feast of Unleavened Bread The law conflates *pesaḥ* and the *maṣṣôt* feast into one festival in the month of Abib (March/April; a later name is Nisan; see also Lev 23:5). The *pesaḥ* is thus integrated into the traditional cycle of three agricultural festivals (Ex 23:14–19). For a critical analysis of vv. 1–8 see Veijola (1996b); Gertz (1996). Read in conjunction with 12:13–19, it appears that the *pesaḥ* is the main *zebaḥ* type offering in the original law code. It may only be offered at the central sanctuary (vv. 2, 5–6). The ancient prohibition of eating leavened bread with a *zebaḥ* (Ex 23:18) forms a transition to the instructions concerning the Feast of Unleavened Bread. This is to last for seven days and radiates into the entire territory (vv. 3–4). At a later stage, v. 8 introduces a cultic assembly at the close of the festival week. In the history of the *pesaḥ*, this law is unique in that it does not allow the slaughtering of the passover lamb in the individual homes, cf. Ex 12. For the Deuteronomic movement, this festival in spring is of foremost religious significance because it causes the participants to remember the Exodus as the foundational intervention of God in Israel's history; cf. also 2 Kings 23:21–3.

(16:9–12) The Feast of Weeks In Ex 23:16a, the *šābuʿôt* festival is called 'the feast of harvest'. The date of this feast depends on the beginning of the grain harvest which would normally fall in April. Its main characteristic is the liberal consumption of portions of the new yield, and therefore it is supposed to include all the people within the rural community. The appeal to generosity is underlined by v. 12 in a way similar to 15:15. According to the Deuteronomic law, 'rejoicing' in YHWH's presence is the primary *raison d'être* of the harvest festivals (vv. 11, 14–15; cf. 12:18, see Braulik 1970), which, in pre-Deuteronomic times, may have had numerous and confusing mythological aspects, cf. Hos 2:2–15 (MT 4–17).

(16:13–15) The Feast of Booths In Ex 23:16b, the *sukkôt* festival is called 'the festival of ingathering'. It is the autumn festival which follows the grape harvest. Before the beginning of the calendar year in ancient Israel was moved to spring in the late seventh or early sixth century, the festival must have coincided with the New Year and many suggestions have been made concerning its ritual aspects, notably as a celebration of YHWH's enthronement as a 'king' and 'creator god' (Mowinckel 1962: i. 118–30; Mettinger 1982: 67–77).

(16:16–17) **The Rule of Pilgrimages** The law summarizes the festival calendar with a revised version of the rule of Ex 23:17. It is clear from vv. 11, 14; 12:18; 14:26 that 'all your males' includes entire 'households', if not entire villages. 31:10–13 gives a more extensive list of participants in a religious festival.

(16:18–20) **Judges** Possibly as one aspect of royal administration and judicature, the law institutes judges (*šōpĕṭîm*) in the Judean country towns. These are coupled with 'officials' (*šōṭĕrîm*), i.e. a certain type of scribe, to which the specification 'according to your tribes' (RSV) may relate, possibly a secondary addition (as in 1:15) which alludes to a tribal and military model, cf. 20:5–9. The city gate was the normal place for trials, cf. 21:19; Am 5:10. One layer of laws in Deuteronomy, esp. the collection of family laws (see DEUT G.1), is built upon the judicial authority of the 'elders' (*zĕqēnîm*) of a town who may have been a more traditional body. v. 19 is a concise expression of the juridical ethos which, in 10:17–18, is even related to God as example. Taking a bribe (cf. Ex 23:8) is condemned as a threat to justice in all currents of Israel's religious thought, cf. e.g. Am 5:12; Isa 5:23; Ps 15:5; Prov 17:23; cf. also Lambert (1960: 133). v. 20 is a later addition which makes taking possession of the land depend on obedience to the law as in 6:17–18. The subject of legal procedures is further pursued in 17:8–13; 19:1–21; 21:1–9.

(16:21–2) **Cultic Sites** This pair of instructions concerning the features of a sanctuary is puzzling in its literary context. The reference to 'the altar that you make for the LORD your God' is reminiscent of Ex 20:24–5 rather than Deut 12:13–14. The temple at Jerusalem does not seem to be an obvious place for an *'ăšērâ*, a sacred tree or a wooden object, nor a *maṣṣēbâ*, a standing stone (cf., however, 2 Kings 23:6). In Deuteronomistic literature, these objects are normally connected with cultic sites in the open country (1 Kings 14:23) and are ascribed to the pre-Israelite population (Deut 7:5; 12:2–3). Following recent archaeological discoveries, it is strongly debated whether an asherah might originally have been devoted to the goddess Asherah as a divine consort of YHWH, see Wiggins (1993); Frevel (1995).

(17:1) **A Sacrificial Rule** The mention of an altar entails a rule like that of 15:21 concerning sacrifices, cf. further Lev 22:17–25.

(17:2–7) **Apostasy as a Legal Case** This law may be more original in Deuteronomy than 13:1–18 from which laws it is distinguished by the prescription of a careful legal procedure. Apostasy is explicitly called a breach of the covenant (*bĕrît*) between YHWH and Israel. This points back to the interpretation of the Decalogue (esp. 5:6–10) as the main stipulation of a 'covenant' in 5:2, cf. also 4:12–13. Whether or not this idea of a covenant can be ascribed to the Josianic age depends on the critical understanding of Hos 8:1 and 2 Kings 23:1–3; see Nicholson (1986).

(17:8–13) **The Authority of a High Court** As the abolition of local sanctuaries eliminates the possibility of seeking an ordeal (cf. Ex 22:7–8), the law establishes the judicial authority of the priests at the central sanctuary (cf. 12:13–14). Later additions in vv. 9, 12 seem to anchor the office of a judge in this text which is presupposed in the book of Judges. The death penalty for 'presumptuously' (*bĕzādôn*) disregarding divine authority is commanded in a second case in 18:20–2.

(17:14–20) **The Israelite King** The law deals with the legitimacy of the Israelite, i.e. Judean monarchy, as does the Deuteronomistic discourse in 1 Sam 8. It is often regarded as the core of a supposed Deuteronomic constitutional law in 16:18–18:22. As such, it could be directed against revolutionary tendencies as known from the history of the northern kingdom (cf. 1 Kings 15:27–8; 16:9–10, 16; 2 Kings 9:14; 15:10, 14, 25, 30; Hos 8:4) or it could be a utopian model for the political role of a future Israelite king after the destruction of the Judean monarchy in 587 BCE (cf. Lohfink 1971a). However, a more plausible interpretation sees the law related to the diverse reflections within the Deuteronomistic representation of Israel's history (see DEUT C.2 and F.3) about the responsibility of the kings for the national disasters under the Assyrians and Babylonians (2 Kings 15:17–25:21). In any case it is worth noting that the law does not mention any royal officers (cf. 1 Kings 4:1–6).

According to vv. 14–15, instituting a monarchy was fundamentally legitimate although not without ambivalence, as it meant that Israel would become similar to 'all the nations that are around', thus verging on apostasy. The prohibition against appointing a foreigner (v. 15) as well as the reference to the king and his descendants (v. 20) intend to protect the Davidic dynasty, cf. 2 Sam 7. However, the restrictions imposed on the king in vv. 16–17, 20 are an indirect critique of Solomon, cf. 1 Kings 9:10–11:13. They correspond to the more general paraenesis of 8:11–14 and can even be traced back to prophetic criticism in Isa 31:1. The reference to a divine oracle in v. 16b (and again in 28:68) may reflect controversies which also lie behind Jer 41:16–43:7. At a later stage, the law was supplemented by vv. 18–19 which emphasize the pre-eminence of the Torah in Israel. The king shall have his own copy of the law which may lead him like any Israelite to fear God (6:24) and keep God's commandments (5:31–2). Deuteronomy ideally subjects the supreme representative of political power to the same religious and ethical obligations of the highest possible moral standard (4:8) which are valid for the entire community. It is this concern which invites comparison of this law with Paul's reflections on political power under the conditions of the Roman empire (Rom 13:1–7).

(18:1–8) Priests The law, which may originally have followed on 17:13, only addresses two issues which concern the typical audience of the law code in the Judean country towns. In a legislative form similar to 15:1–2, it defines claims of the priests at the central sanctuary (cf. Ex 23:19). The priests, who are not entitled to landed property, are regarded as levitical priests, and vv. 6–8 state that all Levites have a right to perform priestly duties, even if, due to the centralization of the cult, they lose their functions outside Jerusalem. The relation between this law and Josiah's actions as reported in 2 Kings 23:8–9 is a controversial issue (see DEUT F.1). In additions to the law in vv. 1, 2, 5, a scribe underlines YHWH's 'electing' the entire 'tribe of Levi'. However, in later legal developments the priesthood is restricted to the descendants of Aaron (Num 3:9–10).

(18:9–22) Prophets As sacrificial cult does not exhaust all religious energies, a section on divination and magic has been added to the law code. Like 17:14, vv. 9–12 reflect the Deuteronomistic narrative framework of Deuteronomy. As in 12:2–4, 29–31, what is 'abominable' to Israel's God is equated with the religious practices of the former inhabitants of the land, cf. also Lev 20:1–8, 22–7. Besides child sacrifice (see DEUT 12:31), seven forms of superstition make a contrast to the one exclusive form of communication between God and his people through a prophet (nābî'). vv. 16–18, the author establishes

the notion of a succession of prophets by the same interpretation of the events at Mount Horeb which is employed to define the relation between the Decalogue and the law code in ch. 5. The idea of a prophet in v. 18 and the law concerning a 'presumptuous' prophet in vv. 20–2 are closely related to the book of Jeremiah (Jer 1:7–9; 23:9–32). Israel's prophetic traditions are thus anchored in the Torah. However, 34:10 makes a distinction between Moses and all later prophets. On theories concerning the end of the prophetic age sometime during the Persian period see Barton (1986: 105–16).

(19:1–13) Cities of Refuge The law continues the section on judicial matters which began in 16:18. However, it does not mention any judges but only the 'elders' of a city (v. 12). The introductory v. 1 appears to be an addition made after 17:14–20 and 18:9–22 had been inserted into the law code. The institution of three cities of refuge in Judah compensates for the abolition of local sanctuaries where, prior to the reform, an asylum-seeker could have found protection (Ex 21:13–14; cf. 1 Kings 1:49–53). vv. 8–9 are an addition which provides for three cities of refuge east of the Jordan, cf. 4:41–3; Num 35; Josh 20. The central concern of the law finds expression in v. 10 and is the same as in 21:1–9.

(19:14) Boundaries Laws such as this (cf. 27:17); 23:24–5 (MT 25–6); 24:19–22, and also 15:7–11 address likely causes of conflict in a rural community and may be compared with the laws on agriculture in Plato's Laws, 842e–846c (Driver (1895) 1901: 234). The issue is also dealt with in wisdom literature: Prov 23:10–11; the Egyptian Instruction of Amen-em-ope (12th cent. BCE: ANET 422, 'Do not carry off the landmark at the boundaries of the arable land, | Nor disturb the position of the measuring-cord; | Be not greedy after a cubit of land, | Nor encroach upon the boundaries of a widow' (7.12–13)), Akkadian series of incantations, Shurpu (copies from the 7th cent. BCE: Reiner 1958: 14, 'He set up an untrue boundary, (but) did not set up the [tr]ue bound[ary], | He removed mark, frontier and boundary' [the sun god is asked to release this person] (2, 45)).

(19:15–21) Legal Witnesses v. 15 is of great consequence for setting up standards for legal proceedings, vv. 16–21 nevertheless discuss the problem of false testimony by a single witness and threaten him with a penalty based on the lex talionis. This rule, which applies to manslaughter and bodily harm, intends to keep punishment and revenge within strict limits (cf. Ex 21:23–5). Taken out of its original legal context, it is rejected in Mt 5:38–42, whereas within that context a line of interpretation within Judaism leads towards monetary fines (Tigay 1996: 185).

(20:1–21:14) Laws on Warfare Except for 21:1–9, these laws form a sequence of four laws on the army, on conquest, and on booty. Their background in antiquity is well illustrated by 2 Sam 8:2; 12:26–31, and 2 Kings 15:16; and especially in view of 20:10–14 it is worth comparing Thucydides, *Peloponnesian War*, 5: 84–116. The first two laws have been heavily supplemented. In 20:1–9, a priest has been given a role beside the officials (*šōṭĕrîm*) in vv. 2–4, and the officials' enquiry has been reinterpreted in v. 8, cf. Judg 7:1–7. In 20:10–18, the original law of vv. 10–14 has been given an opposite meaning in accordance with the idea of a military conquest of the promised land in vv. 15–18 (cf. Rofé 1985b). Whereas the original sequence of laws aimed at restricting destructive energies in case of war, the eventual result of its reworking provides another affirmation of the concept of annihilation of the peoples in the land, see DEUT 7:2. The anti-assimilationist motive for this fictitious historiographical concept is emphasized in v. 18, cf. 18:9–13. However, the authors of 1 Kings 14:24; 2 Kings 21:2 point towards the futility even of this concept.

(21:1–9) Expiation for Unresolved Murder Thematically contiguous to 19:1–13, the rite allows the elders of an Israelite town to make atonement for a murder in a case where the murderer cannot be identified and punished, v. 5 is a later attempt to see this unique ceremony directed by priests, cf. Lev 4:20.

(21:15–23) Family Laws vv. 15–17, the rule that the firstborn son shall inherit twice as much of his father's estate as any other heirs must not be violated (cf. E. W. Davies 1986). vv. 18–21, conversely, parents must be able to rely on that son for support in their old age, cf. 5:16; Ex 21:15, 17. The elders of a town play a remarkable role in traditional family law in Deuteronomy, cf. 22:15; 25:7. The law imposes a death penalty and stresses its function as a deterrent. By association, it is followed by a regulation which limits public exhibition of an executed offender.

(22:1–4) Fairness and Co-operation Like Ex 23:4–5, the law looks at disturbed social rela-

tions in a rural community and forbids 'ignoring' (*hitᶜ allēm*) obvious cases for mutual help. Although it also draws a distinction between lost property and theft, its main characteristic is the strong paraenetic tone which aims at overcoming indifference and irresponsibility.

(22:5–12) Ordinances Protecting Life and Manners This section, notably vv. 5, 9–12, must be seen against the background of the notion that certain practices would be 'abominable' to YHWH. Of special interest is the restriction on human greed and power over animal life in vv. 6–7. It concludes with a motive clause similar to the one in 5:16, and from this one may infer that respect for the parent-child relationship stands behind the law, cf. also 14:21b.

(22:13–30 (MT 23:1)) Family and Sex Laws Part of a more extended collection (see DEUT G.1 and Otto 1993), the laws address issues of dishonesty and violence in sexual relations. They are arranged according to the marital status of a woman. The death penalty is imposed in most cases, although vv. 23–7 reflect a development towards restricting this through careful considerations. In one case only (v. 19) a fine is imposed, even if this seems to contradict the principle expressed in 19:19. A complementary law to vv. 28–9 can be found in Ex 22:16–17 (MT 15–16). v. 30, if a man was married polygamously, his son must not marry any of his father's former wives; cf. 27:20; Lev 18:8.

(23:1–8 (MT 23:2–9)) The Assembly of the Lord The law probably concerned local assemblies in monarchic Judah (cf. Mic 2:5), however, it does not indicate what functions such an assembly (*qĕhal YHWH*) would have had. Edomites and Egyptians are to be admitted under certain conditions, whereas Ammonites and Moabites are not (see ABD). vv. 1–2 may allude to cultic perversions, however, this is not entirely conclusive, and the designation 'born of an illicit union' (NRSV) follows the LXX interpretation of the unknown Hebrew word *mamzēr*. The law originally seems to think of Jacob as Israel's ancestor (v. 7; cf. Gen 25:21–6) and, in v. 3, to express the same spirit of contempt as Gen 19:30–8. The list of peoples does not exhaustively reflect the political situation of Judah (cf. e.g. 2 Kings 23:13; Jer 27:3; Zeph 2:4–9) but concentrates on those three Transjordanian neighbours with whom 2:2–23 is also concerned. vv. 4–6 are obvious secondary additions based on reinterpretations of 2:8–25 and Num 22–4. 1 Kings 11:2; Ezra 9:12; Neh 13:1–3 refer to this law in combination with 7:3–4. It has been suggested that Isa 56:3–7 abrogates this law (Donner 1985).

(23:9–14) The Military Camp Possibly by association a transition is made from the assembly (*qāhāl*) to the camp (*maḥăneh*). YHWH is not seen to appear in an epiphany during a campaign (cf. Judg 5:4–5; 2 Sam 22:8–16), instead, the law is intended to protect the deity's continuous presence in the camp (cf. 20:2–4).

(23:15–16) A Fugitive Slave The law may originally have followed on v. 8 since it deals with slaves who presumably have fled from a foreign country: they are given permission to settle 'in any one of your towns'. If a political dimension should be implied here, the law overturns provisions such as are known from an Aramaic treaty of the eighth century BCE which specifies that a fugitive must be returned (Sfire stela, 3, 4–6; ANET 660). If, however, the law must be understood within a domestic horizon only, it is worth comparing contrary regulations in the Code of Hammurabi (§16, ANET 167).

(23:17–18) Laws against Prostitution As in 23:1–2, it is not clear what kind of cultic rites, if any, lie behind these laws (cf. ABD v. 505–13). Even Hos 4:13–14 and 2 Kings 23:7 hardly offer a firm basis for historical explanation.

(23:19–25:12) Religious, Economic, and Civil Laws 23:19–20, like 15:1–3, the law is intended to facilitate a fellow Israelite's economic survival. 23:21–3, the law is typical of the conflation of religious and sapiential thought in Deuteronomy (Weinfeld 1992: 270–2). On the one hand it fully recognizes and teaches the religious implications of a vow, on the other hand it asserts that this custom is dispensable, thus putting into effect the liberating power of reflection. A further development of this line of thought can be found in Mic 6:6–8. If someone made a vow, whatever had been dedicated to the deity would have to be taken to the central sanctuary (12:17–18). 23:24–5, a number of rules, such as this, in the final section of the law code (also 24:6, 10–13, 14–15, 17–18, 19–22) anticipate conflicts in a rural community. Most of them express the same spirit as 22:1–4 or 15:7–11. They refer to the relationship between economically independent 'neighbours' (*rēaʿ*) as well as between such peasants and the landless poor

who are employed as 'labourers' (*śākîr*) or are not attached to any household at all (*gēr*, also needy orphans and widows). The rules are based on an ethos of fairness and generosity, and this is an obvious moral consequence of a faith which centres on the Exodus creed (24:22; cf. 5:6–21, esp. 14–15). 24:1–4, a man had the right to divorce his wife (cases such as 22:13–19, 28–9 excepted), and he could get married to more than one woman (cf. 21:15). By implication, a woman had the right to get married more than once. However, a man did not have the right to call back his divorced wife once she had been married to and thus 'defiled' by (*ṭāmēʾ*) another man. As generally in Deuteronomy, the law does not take the perspective of the woman, whose fate may be deplorable. For discussions about this law in early Christianity cf. Mk 10:2–12; Mt 19:9; 5:31–2. 24:5, cf. 20:5–7. 24:7, the death penalty is imposed on anybody who kidnaps a person, cf. Ex 21:16. In the Code of Hammurabi a similar law reads: 'If a seignior has stolen the young son of another seignior, he shall be put to death' (§ 14, ANET 166). 24:8–9, a later addition to the collection, asserts the authority of the levitical priests in cases of an infectious disease which LXX identifies as leprosy. Lev 13–14 offers detailed instructions for dealing with such diseases. The concluding exhortation points to Num 12. 24:16, capital punishment (cf. e.g. 24:7) must be executed only on the person of the offender. Thematically, this belongs to a group of laws on the administration of justice (21:22–3; 25:1–3). Although in its immediate context the term for 'crime' (*ḥēṭ*) is also being used for 'guilt' in a religious sense (24:15), the principle of individual responsibility here does not engage with the teaching of 5:9 which states that YHWH will punish 'iniquity' (*ʿāwôn*) through four generations. 25:1–3, a further law on practical legal matters. The notion of 'degradation' within the community also underlies the two following laws. 25:4, proverbial from its reinterpretation in 1 Cor 9:9–11, may have been linked with 24:19–22. In four Hebrew words it says a lot about treatment of animals and its original sense merits pondering. Prov 12:10 may be a help. 25:5–10, if a man dies without leaving a son, his name is 'blotted out of Israel', and this is seen as a great misfortune (the same view may be implied in 24:5). Where circumstances allow, securing the continuity of a deceased man's family through levirate marriage has first priority. Fear of disgrace is to motivate a reluctant brother-in-law. 25:11–12, except for the *lex talionis*

(19:21), this is the only instance of mutilation as punishment in the law code.

(25:13–16) Fairness and Honesty The concluding paragraph of the law code is permeated by the sapiential spirit of humanism typical of many sections of Deuteronomy. The law on just weights and measures has parallels in Israelite as well as ancient Near-Eastern wisdom texts (Prov 11:1; 20:10, 23; *Shurpu*, 8. 64–7 (Reiner 1958: 42–3); cf. Code of Hammurabi, §94 (*ANET*169)). It appeals to a common sense of what is just in order to keep the human being from doing 'unrighteousness' (ʿāwel); cf. also Lev 19:35–4; Ezek 18:5–9. Moral behaviour guided by such self-evidently just principles is related to the blessing of a long life, whereas its opposite is considered an 'abomination' (tôʿēbâ) for God. However, in such laws as 15:1–11 and 23:19–20 (MT 20–1), Deuteronomy goes beyond the limits of this moral order: fairness is not enough in the service of Israel's God.

(25:17–19) War against Amalek A historical reminiscence of relations between Israelites and Amalekites may have been preserved in 1 Sam 30, whereas the traditio-historical background behind the three texts in Ex 17:8–16; Deut 25:17–19; 1 Sam 15:1–35 remains obscure; cf. Foresti (1984). The peculiar episode in Ex 17:8–16 is taken up here (in a secondary addition to the law code in the 2nd person pl., like 23:4*a* (MT 5*a*); 24:9) and reinterpreted in terms of a lack of 'fear of God' (cf. Gen 20), in order to account for the command to exterminate the Amalekites. Looking forward to a time when Israel will enjoy 'rest from all her enemies' (cf. 12:9–10) prepares the ground for the story of 1 Sam 15 (although this is not coherent with 2 Sam 7:1). Cf. also the motif of just retribution in Jer 2:3; 30:16.

(26:1–11) A Form for Liturgical Recitation On a redactional level similar to 17:14–20, a Deuteronomistic scribe makes the traditional custom of taking the first fruits to a YHWH sanctuary (Ex 23:19*a*; Deut 18:4) the occasion for a pilgrimage which seems not to coincide with one of the three main festivals (16:1–17). The core of the instruction is an artistic composition in vv. 5–10. In twentieth-century scholarship, it has often been considered an ancient confessional formula on which the oldest literary source of the Pentateuch was modelled (von Rad 1966). However, it is more likely that the confession did not originate in Israelite cult in pre-monar-

chic times, but instead within the Deuteronomistic School (cf. Richter 1967; Lohfink 1971*b*). The confession starts from a reminiscence of an ancestor who was 'a perishing Aramean' (NRSV reads 'a wandering'; see, however, Janzen 1994). As this must refer to Jacob, the scribe here integrates the Jacob tradition into the Exodus tradition and thereby to a certain degree invalidates the former which was closely linked to the sanctuary at Bethel (Gen 28; 35; cf. 2 Kings 23:15). The confession then unfolds four times in three sentences with a characteristic pause at the end of each section (cf. RSV). It is built on numerous allusions to the Exodus narrative, notably Ex 1:9–14; 3:7–10, 15 (in v. 8, 'signs and wonders' may be secondary as is 6:22). v. 10 leads up to the actual ceremony which is followed by a celebration. A scribe here designs a concise picture of Israel's salvation history and thus gives profound witness to God's mercy in a perspective of Judean theology. The basic structure of the composition reflects the conviction of biblical faith that God helps the oppressed who cry out to him (cf. Judg 3:9; Ex 22:20–3), even if his ways are inscrutable (cf. Ex 34:10; Isa 55:6–9). vv. 3–4, as v. 10 instructs the farmer himself to set down his basket 'before YHWH', the reference to a priest must have been introduced at a later stage, perhaps sometime during the Second Temple period (cf. Neh 10:35–7 (MT 36–8)).

(26:12–15) A Declaration of Obedience A declaration at the sanctuary corresponds to the law of 14:28–9 and also responds to an exhortation such as 6:17–18. It includes a list of three forbidden abuses of the third year's tithe, which presumably are related to some form of death-cult, possibly a problem in the Second Temple period. For the designation of heaven as YHWH's dwelling place cf. 1 Kings 8:27–30 and also Zech 2:17; Isa 63:15; 2 Chr 30:27.

Declaration of Mutual Commitments between YHWH and Israel (26:16–19)

In its present literary context, the passage represents the covenant ceremony which is presupposed in 29:1 (MT 28:69). It has been suggested that it originated in a cultic event and that this might even be identified with the covenant ceremony under King Josiah which is narrated in 2 Kings 23:1–3 (Smend 1963). After its introduction (v. 16*a*; cf. 6:1; 12:1), the declaration revolves around the solemn statements: 'You have affirmed this day that the LORD is your God', and 'And the LORD has affirmed this day that you are [...] His treasured people' (NJPS). In the unique form of a mutual declaration, this corresponds to 6:4. The covenant relationship between YHWH and Israel has an ethical dimension, and the Deuteronomists are strongly concerned with the ensuing idea of a divine law. This accounts for the first explication concerning Israel's obligation 'to walk in his ways, and to keep his statutes [...] and his ordinances, and to obey his voice'. Equally, the covenant relationship has a universal dimension. This is expressed in the second explication concerning YHWH's promise to Israel 'to set you high above all nations that he has made, in praise and in fame and in honour' (cf. RSV; there are some further additions to the text which partly may depend on 7:6). God the creator of all humankind sets his people 'high above' (ʿelyôn) all nations 'that he has made'. A similar thought is expressed in Ex 19:5–6, where the clause 'for all the earth is mine' also implies a theology of creation which in its hymnic form may have been a constituent motif in the cult of the Jerusalem temple even in the monarchic period (cf. Ps 24:1). Deut 7:6, too, refers to 'all the peoples that are on the face of the earth'. All these reflections (cf. also 32:8–9) should be understood in a dialectical relation to Gen 12:3 or Isa 49:6 which speak of the blessing that comes to all humankind through Israel.

Instructions for a Ceremony West of the Jordan (27:1–26)

In vv. 1, 9, 11, as well as in 29:1–2 (MT 28:69; 29:1), the narrator interrupts Moses' speech, which comes to an end only in 31:1. Concurring conceptions of cultic ceremonies on entering the land have been combined here just as in the book of Joshua. v. 2–3, the scribe who commands the erection of stelae with the law code written on them may be responding to the accusation that Israel spoiled her land as soon as she entered it (cf. Jer 2:7). Josh 4:20 mentions twelve memorial stones in Gilgal near the river Jordan (on the place-names see ABD). vv. 5–7, a second scribe thinks of sacrifices and consequently of the need for an altar, built in accordance with Ex 20:24–5, but not with Deut 12:13–14. The location of this altar, which Joshua is said to have built (Josh 8:30–1), is near Shechem, to where v. 4 also transfers the stelae. vv. 11–13, the valley between Mount Gerizim and Mount Ebal is defined as the place for a third ritual (cf. 11:29–30). vv. 14–26, this in turn has been expanded by a liturgy (cf. Neh 8:1–8). The series of curses, framed by vv. 15 and 26, has its focus

mainly on clandestine evil deeds which threaten human dignity and a peaceful society.

The Consequences of Obedience and Disobedience through Blessings and Curses (28:1–68)

As part of his address to Israel, Moses gives conditional promises of divine blessings (vv. 1–14) and curses (vv. 15–68) respectively. The parallel introductory clauses to these two sections (vv. 1–2, 15) presuppose the shaping of the law code as an oration of Moses (cf. Mayes 1979: 348–51). They refer back to the declaration in 26:16–19, and this connection to the idea of a covenant scene is further underlined by the subscription in 29:1 (MT 28:69). However, it is disputable whether 28:1–68 originated as part of a covenant pattern or as a homiletic elaboration based on a pattern of a good and a bad alternative, cf. the Deuteronomistic passages in 1 Kings 9:4–7 and Jer 22:3–5. The latter suggestion would account for the promise of blessings which cannot be traced back to treaty rhetoric.

There is strong evidence that the section of curses, notably vv. 20–35, incorporates material adopted from Esar-haddon's succession treaty of 672 BCE (see DEUT F.2 and on Deut 13; Weinfeld 1992: 116–29; Steymans 1995). In this treaty an extended series of curses invoking the gods of the Assyrian pantheon is pronounced against anyone who should breach the oath imposed by the Assyrian king:

37 May Aššur, king of the gods, who decrees [the fates], decree an evil and unpleasant fate for you. May he not gra[nt yo]u long-lasting old age and the attainment of extreme old age. 38 May Mullissu, his beloved wife, make the utterance of his mouth evil, may she not intercede for you. 38A May Anu, king of the gods, let disease, exhaustion, malaria, sleeplessness, worries and ill health rain upon all your houses (cf. 28:22). 39 May Sin, the brightness of heaven and earth, clothe you with leprosy and forbid your entering into the presence of the gods or king. Roam the desert like the wild ass and the gazelle (cf. 28:27). 40 May Šamaš, the light of heaven and earth, not judge you justly. May he remove your eyesight. Walk about in darkness! (cf. 28:28–9). 41 May Ninurta, the foremost among the gods, fell you with his fierce arrow; may he fill the plain with your blood and feed your flesh to the eagle and the vulture (cf. 28:25–6). 42 May Venus, the brightest of the stars, before your eyes make your wives lie in the lap of your enemy; may your sons not take possession of your house, but a strange enemy divide your goods (cf. 28:30).... 63 May all the gods that are [mentioned by name] in th[is] treaty tablet make the ground as narrow as a brick for you. May they make your ground like iron (so that)

nothing can sprout from it. 64 Just as rain does not fall from a brazen heaven so may rain and dew not come upon your fields and your meadows; instead of dew may burning coals rain on your land (cf. 28:23–4).... 69 Just as [thi]s ewe has been cut open and the flesh of [her] young has been placed in her mouth, may they make you eat in your hunger the flesh of your brothers, your sons and your daughters (cf. 28:53). (Parpola and Watanabe 1988: 45–52; ANET 538)

In addition to this Assyrian treaty, an Aramaic treaty of the eighth century BCE has been adduced as a possible source for motifs in 28:38–42 (Sfire stela, 1A. 27–8; ANET 659–60).

The curses of Deut 28, notably vv. 20–42, must be seen against this ancient Near-Eastern background, and it seems most likely that they were contrived once the disaster which Judah and Jerusalem suffered in 587 BCE had come to be interpreted as the experience of a divine curse (cf. 29:24–7 (MT 23–6); 1 Kings 9:8–9). In this process, YHWH became the subject of all those curses on an almost monotheistic level, cf. Isa 45:6–7. Referring back to the curses and 'afflictions' pronounced in vv. 20–35, a scribe in vv. 58–9 calls them a 'stupendous' doing of YHWH (p-l-ᵓ hifil).

(28:1–14) Moses promises God's blessing for obedience to the law. vv. 3–6 may be a traditional formula of blessing which originated in a cultic setting, cf. 1 Sam 2:20; Ps 24:5; 118:26; 121:8. vv. 7–14 can best be described as an attempt by later scribes to counterbalance the curses in vv. 20–44 (see Seitz 1971: 273–6). The blessing of Israel functions as a witness to YHWH's divinity (v. 10; cf. 1 Kings 8:43).

(28:15–68) vv. 15–19, the curse section opens in close correspondence with vv. 1–6. vv. 20–9, the second section adopts a rhetoric from the political sphere, see above. vv. 30–3, the third section, marked off by the repetition of expressions from v. 29 in v. 33, refers to a typical military defeat, cf. 20:5–7, 10–14. vv. 34–5, the fourth section, partly an inverted repetition of vv. 27–8, lays an elaborate curse upon the mental and bodily state of an individual. vv. 36–7, the fifth section goes beyond the motifs of vv. 30–3 and refers to the entire nation's exile, cf. v. 64 and 4:27–8. The scribe looks back to the Babylonian conquest of Jerusalem in 587 BCE, cf. 1 Kings 9:7; Jer 24:9. vv. 38–44, the sixth section to a certain degree runs parallel to vv. 30–3; it includes a series of so-called futility curses (vv. 38–42) which again reflect the rhetoric of political documents, see above. The elaborate curse in 43–4 envisages a total subversion

of the social order in which 'aliens' were the landless poor, cf. 14:28–9. vv. 45–8, the seventh section is a transitional passage which forms a conclusion to vv. 15–44 and an introduction to vv. 49–57. The curses in vv. 20–44 are called 'a sign and a wonder' (RSV), which expression may even allude to the Egyptian plagues (cf. 6:22) and thereby draw a parallel between these two sets of images of punitive disasters. The following reflections on the Exile and the fall of Jerusalem (as well as some additions in vv. 20, 25) betray connections to the book of Jeremiah. For vv. 47–8 cf. Jer 5:18–19 and 28:13–14. vv. 49–53, the eighth section gives a stylized representation of the Babylonian attack on Jerusalem. Cf. Jer 5:15–17; 6:11; 19:9; 48:40. v. 51 reverses the blessing of 7:13. Whether v. 53 refers to historical experience during the siege of Jerusalem or only alludes to a recurring motif in treaty curses (see above, and Weinfeld 1992: 126–8) is not conclusive (cf. also Lev 26:26, 29). vv. 54–7, the ninth section elaborates the scenes of horror during a siege, cf. also 2 Kings 6:24–9. vv. 58–68, the concluding section adds several scribal reflections on what is written in the 'book of this law (tôrâ)'. vv. 58–61 focus on the issue of diseases (vv. 21–2, 27, 35) and reverse the blessing of 7:15. The line of interpretation of the curses as 'a sign and a portent' in v. 46 seems to be continued here. v. 62 points back to 26:5 on the one hand, and 1:10 on the other. The verse implies a total reversal of Israel's salvation history, even if it might still hint at a vague possibility of a new beginning. This in turn is excluded by v. 68 which refers back to Ex 14:13 (Reimer 1990) and leaves no room even for the expectation of a miserable life in Egyptian slavery. vv. 64–7, the threat concerning life in the Diaspora cuts Israel off from any relationship with YHWH, the protection of which is the central concern of Deuteronomy, cf. 13:6–11 (MT 7–12). The frightful picture of the conditions of that life enlarges v. 34 in a different age. v. 68 sets a seal on the nullification of the relationship between YHWH and Israel (cf. 5:6) in case of disobedience to the Torah.

A most extraordinary interpretation of the curse section and, by implication, of the destruction of Jerusalem, is given in v. 63a. The verse is an artistic expression of the climax of negativity. While its structure may depend on such oracles as Zech 8:14–15; Jer 31:28; 32:42, the verb employed (śîś) may have been adopted from other promises of salvation (cf. Deut 30:9; Zeph 3:17; Jer 32:41 MT; Isa 65:18–19). This peculiar statement finds a wider context in reflections on YHWH's compassion (r-ḥ-m piel, n-ḥ-m nifal; cf. e.g. Jer 4:28; 13:13–14; 18:7–10; Deut 4:31; 30:3).

Discourse on the Significance of the Law ((29:1) 29:2–30:20)

(29:1 (MT and LXX 28:69)) The Covenant in the Land of Moab Whether this verse is a subscription to the preceding law or a superscription to the following speech of Moses is subject to debate. As it cannot be demonstrated that a traditional ancient Near-Eastern covenant pattern underlies 29:2b–30:20 (see, however, Weinfeld 1992: 100–16; Rofé 1985a), it is more likely that v. 1 is a concluding statement and that 4:44–28:68 are subsumed under the expression 'these are the words of the covenant'. Thus, the verse is part of an editorial framework around the law, and it also connects to 1:1–5 and to 5:1–5. Just as a 'covenant at Horeb' defines the theological dimension of the Decalogue, so a 'covenant in the land of Moab' defines that of the Deuteronomic law. However, the unique concept of two covenants which supplement each other does not blur the distinction between the Decalogue and the Deuteronomic law which is developed in ch. 5.

(29:2 (MT 29:1)) A Concluding Address The narrator introduces a speech which reaches as far as 30:20 and mainly consists of three thematically distinct units. 29:3–21 focuses on the religious obligation of every single Israelite and on the limitation of divine punishment for apostasy to an individual. 29:22–30:10 gives an interpretation of the fall of Jerusalem in 587 BCE and turns towards a prediction of future salvation. 30:11–20 is a general reflection concerning the law delivered by Moses and functions as a magnificent coda to it.

(29:2–9) Exhortations The notion of 'covenant' in 29:1 triggers off a paraenetic discourse which seems to be looking at the conquest of the land (cf. the verb 'to succeed', ś-k-l hifil, in v. 9 (MT 8) and in Josh 1:7–8). vv. 2–3 highlight the mighty deeds of YHWH in the Exodus, cf. 6:22. vv. 7–8 remind the reader of the paradigmatic conquest of the land under Moses' leadership as narrated in 2:24–3:17. v. 4, which may depend on Isa 6:9–10, is a gloss on vv. 2–3: unless God himself directs the human heart, even his mighty deeds which are represented through the kerygmatic narrative tradition will not lead to faith. vv. 5–6 quote from Deut 8 in direct

speech by YHWH (MT; LXX reads the 3rd person). The final clause of 8:3 is substituted by a formula which mostly occurs in Ezekiel and in the Priestly Document in the Pentateuch (e.g. Ezek 20:20; 28:26; Ex 6:7), and this demonstrates a combining of diverse theological traditions.

(29:10–15) Covenant and Oath This section sets forth a liturgical scene comparable to the one narrated in Neh 10. The term 'covenant' (bĕrît) is doubled by the term 'oath' or 'curse' (ʾālâ, v. 12; cf. Neh 10:29 (MT 30)). The idea of a covenant ceremony finds a less direct expression than in 26:16–19. The reference to the ancestors (cf. Gen 17:7) sees the patriarchal age as the foundation of Israel's existence as the people of God in an even more fundamental sense than that of the concept of a divine promise of the land (1:8; 30:20). According to vv. 14–15, the covenant also includes people who are not present at the assembly, although this is not coherent with the fictional setting of Moses' speech. The addition may be by a scribe having in mind the Jewish Diaspora in the Persian empire (cf. 30:3–4).

(29:16–21) A Warning against Apostasy The view of the 'nations' in this homiletic passage is informed by 1 Kings 11:1–8 and 2 Kings 23:13 rather than Deut 2:1–23. The polemics against foreign gods and their visual representations echo such passages as Ezek 20:1–44; Isa 44:9–20; Jer 10:1–16. Historically, it betrays a strong tendency towards a separation from rival groups within the land, cf. Neh 10:28 (MT 29). The metaphors of v. 18 (cf. also Am 6:12), as well as the term 'stubbornness of heart' (šĕrîrût lēb), link the passage with Jer 9:12–16 (MT 11–15). The threat of divine punishment is restricted to an individual and left entirely to YHWH. A scribe thus revises 5:9–10; 17:2–7, and also gives the curses of ch. 28 a new application.

(29:22–8) The Devastated Land The passage looks back to the destruction of Judah in 587 BCE. The rhetorical form of vv. 24–8 has close parallels in 1 Kings 9:8–9 and Jer 22:8–9 and is also known from an Assyrian source from the seventh century where a report of a punitive campaign reads: 'Whenever the inhabitants of Arabia asked each other: "On account of what have these calamities befallen Arabia?" (they answered themselves:) "Because we did not keep the solemn oaths (sworn by) Ashur, because we offended the friendliness of Ashurbanipal, the king, beloved by Enlil!"' (ANET

300). v. 25 is founded on the first commandment of the Decalogue as the central stipulation
of the covenant at Horeb (5:1–10, cf. also 4:20;
Judg 2:11–15). vv. 22 (cf. 1 Kings 8:41–3) and 23 (cf.
Jer 49:18; Gen 19) may be later additions.

(29:29) Secret and Revealed Things Taken
in its literary context, this verse may refer to
the human inability to fully understand the past
(29:25–8) or the future (30:1–10). It may also
refer to a concealed background of the Torah
which would be irrelevant to obedience (30:11–
14), or an interpretation in the light of Ps 19:12
(MT 19:13), which speaks of 'secret faults', might
also be a possibility. NJPS reads: 'Concealed acts
concern the LORD our God; but with overt acts,
it is for us and our children ever to apply all the
provisions of this Teaching.'

(30:1–10) Hope for Future Restoration From
the image of the land devastated by a curse, the
speech turns towards predictions of salvation.
These have close parallels in the book of Jeremiah (e.g. Jer 29:10–14; 32:36–41). As in Deut
4:25–31, Israel is envisaged as returning to
YHWH who will show his mercy to the people
(rāḥam: 4:31; 30:3). However, whereas according
to vv. 1–2 returning to YHWH is a precondition
for better fortunes, a scribe in v. 6 (contrast
10:16) makes Moses pronounce an unconditional promise, cf. Jer 31:33–4. Within this horizon of expectation, v. 7 gives a new
interpretation of the curses in ch. 28. vv. 8–10
are based on motifs adopted from 28:11, 63.

(30:11–14) The Accessibility of the Law Here
as in 6:1, 25, 'commandment' (miṣwâ) designates
the entire law which Moses delivers in his
speech. In terms of composition, the declaration may be seen as an equivalent to 4:5–8.
Whereas the expression 'in your mouth' refers
to the regular repetition of the received law (cf.
6:7; Josh 1:8), the expression 'in your heart' takes
the internalization of the law even further than
6:6 does, cf. also Jer 31:33–4. The scribe demonstrates the essential conformity of the divine
law to the human being with the help of impressive poetic imagery. In Rom 7, especially vv.
7–13, Paul opposes this anthropological concept
of Deuteronomistic theology in the light of his
understanding of sin, and therefore, in Rom
10:5–8, applies the figures of Deut 30:11–14 to
'the word of faith which we proclaim'.

(30:15–20) Choice between Good and Evil
This solemn finale to Moses' speech reflects an
aspect of the wisdom tradition, cf. Prov 11:19;
Am 5:14–15. The invitation to 'choose' (bāḥar) in
v. 19b recalls the scene in Josh 24, especially vv.
14–15. v. 20, the revealed law is the source of life
(cf. Lev 18:5 and Rom 10:5), and true obedience
to its commandments is based on the love of
God (cf. Mk 12:28–34). Faith is a possible decision in the face of death and 'evil' (RSV). The
beginning of the secondary vv. 16–19a has been
lost in the MT but can be restored following the
LXX, cf. 7:12–13; 8:19–20.

Report of Moses' Parting from Israel,
Including his Poem and his Blessings (31:1–34:12)

(31:1–8) The Appointment of Joshua NRSV
rightly restores the beginning of this section
following the LXX and the fragmentary MS 1Q
Deut[b] from Qumran (DJD 1. 59). The narrator
resumes 3:28–9 and prepares the transition to
the book of Joshua, cf. Josh 1:1–9. Additions in
vv. 3, 4–6 take up material from 7:17–23; 9:3;
29:7–8 (MT 6–7). What is presented in 2:33–4
and 3:3, 6 as actions of the Israelites, is interpreted directly as a divine action in v. 4, cf.
3:21–2.

**(31:9–30) Codification of the Law and
Announcement of Moses' Poem** Two themes
overlap in this section: a description of the
Torah as a book, and, in vv. 16–22, the designation of a Mosaic poem as a 'witness' against
Israel. vv. 9–11, the written Torah is handed
over to the levitical priests and significantly
also to representatives of the laity. Its public
reading gives the festival of the tabernacles
(ḥag hassukkôt) in every seventh year (following
15:1–3) a theological significance as great as that
of the Passover which is designed to remember
the Exodus (16:1–8). In a later addition in vv. 24–
7, the book of the Torah is brought into connection with the ark in which, according to
10:1–8, the tablets of the Decalogue are being
kept. The same scribe possibly also depicted the
levitical priests in v. 9 (cf. 17:18) as those 'who
carried the ark of the covenant'. vv. 14–15 make
the tent of meeting ('ōhel mô'ēd) the place where
YHWH speaks to Moses, cf. Ex 27:21; 33:7–11, etc.
vv. 16–22 are motivated by the problem of what
will happen to Israel once her incomparable
first leader has died and the foundational period
of her history has come to a close, cf. the analogous problem in Josh 3:11 to Judg 23:1. The
author introduces an independent poem in
32:1–43 which he wants to hand down as a
song of Moses. He makes YHWH address
Moses in a prophetic speech which characterizes

Israel by her breach of the covenant on entering the land, cf. 5:2, 7; Jer 31:32; Hos 13:4–6. The notion of YHWH concealing himself (v. 18) which is predicted in the poem (32:20; cf. Jer 18:17; 33:5; also Isa 8:17 and Ps 44:24 (MT 25); 80:3 (MT 4) et al.) is a remarkable interpretation of the motif of YHWH's anger which elsewhere dominates in the Deuteronomistic literature (e. g. 29:27 (MT 26); Judg 2:14–15; 2 Kings 23:26). The secondary vv. 20–1 borrow from 6:10–12, and, with the notion of 'inclination' (yēṣer), possibly even allude to the framing verses of the Flood story in Gen 6:5; 8:21. vv. 24–9 imitate the introduction to the Song of Moses and make the entire Torah a 'witness' against Israel. This thought is further underlined in 32:45–7 with material taken from 30:15–20.

(32:1–43) Moses' Poem The Song of Moses adds a new facet to the Mosaic oration and thus to the picture of the Mosaic age in Deuteronomy. Attributed to Moses as it is, the poem has a prophetic purpose (cf. 31:16–22), although its main characteristic is that of wisdom poetry. It has its climax in a monotheistic creed in v. 39, and this is prepared by a theodicy (vv. 4–5), a reference to mythological primeval history (vv. 8–9), a résumée of the earliest salvation history (vv. 11–12), an explication of YHWH's concealing of himself (v. 20), and a critique of a polytheistic misinterpretation of Israel's apparent abandonment by her God (vv. 30–1). S. R. Driver was right when he wrote: 'The Song shows great originality of form, being a presentation of prophetical thoughts in a poetical dress, on a scale which is without parallel in the OT' (1895 (1901): 345). A notable feature of the poem is its wealth of metaphors and images (e.g. in vv. 6, 10, 11, 13, 15, 18–19) as well as mythological motifs (vv. 8–9, 22, 23–4). Stylistically, it is characterized by the typical parallelism of two sentences or expressions which together form a poetic line; cf. Alter (1990, notably 24–5 on vv. 10, 13).

The poem's basic structure is built upon Deuteronomistic motifs. Israel first became guilty before YHWH when she prospered in her land and forgot her God (vv. 15–18; cf. 6:10–12; 8:7–18). In consequence, YHWH's anger was aroused (vv. 21–2; cf. 6:15; 29:24–8 (MT 23–7)). However, when the poet speaks of YHWH's mercy (v. 36), he does not see Israel's return to YHWH as a condition for it, in contrast to the Deuteronomistic vision of Israel's future restoration in 4:29–31; 30:1–3. The concept of YHWH taking revenge on his enemies and destroying them

(vv. 34–5, 40–1) leads beyond Deuteronomistic expectations. Instead, it has parallels in oracles in Nahum; Jer 46–51; Isa 63:1–6, etc.

The poem is anthological in character and obviously presupposes the development of monotheistic thought as reflected in Deutero-Isaiah (Isa 45:5–7). Despite the attempt by Sanders (1996), in his authoritative study of Deut 32, to demonstrate a pre-exilic origin of the poem, it is more plausibly considered a composition from, the Second Temple period.

(32:1–6) The poet and wisdom teacher stresses the perfection and justice of God in sharp contrast to the foolishness of the people. Upon the doctrinal foundation which is established by this antithesis, any historical experience of disaster will be reflected in a straight scheme of theodicy. It is worth noting how the poet places himself within a horizon of hymnic praise of YHWH (v. 3) and thus responds to the superior importance of the concept of 'fear of the LORD' in the wisdom tradition (Prov 9:10). There is a striking similarity between the opening of Moses' poem and the introduction to Isaiah (Isa 1:2–3).

(32:7–9) An insight into right behaviour as well as a knowledge of God's actions in a mythical primeval age are preserved in the wisdom of former generations (v. 7; cf. Job 8:8–10; Jer 6:16–17; Isa 45:20–1; 46:8–11). Therefore, the poet grounds the Deuteronomistic notion of Israel's election (7:6) on a mythological concept of the primeval age and adduces a polytheistic concept of the order of the nations corresponding with the number of celestial beings. It has been suggested that this may be traced back to Ugaritic mythology which, in the epic The Palace of Ba'al of the fourteenth century BCE, has the 'seventy sons of Athirat', cf. the seventy nations in Gen 10 (see Lipiński 1998: 300–1; Gibson 1978: 63; ANET 134). v. 8 thus is a poetic echo of polytheistic mythology as e.g. Ps 82:6–7; 89:5–14 (MT 6–15); Job 38:7. Whereas the LXX reads 'according to the number of the angels of God' (one MS reads 'of the sons of God'; cf. 4Q Deutʲ (DJD 14. 90), and see Sir 17:17), the Hebrew text testifies to a revision which reads 'according to the number of the sons of Israel' (for which cf. Gen 46:27; Deut 10:22). The designation of God as 'the Most High' (ʾelyôn) in v. 8 refers to Israel's God as much as does the divine name 'the LORD' (YHWH) in v. 9; cf. the use of ʿelyôn in Ps 18:13 (MT 14); 83:18 (MT 19); 97:9, etc. and see the discussion in Sanders (1996: 362–74).

(**32:10–14**) For the poetic images of the eerie desert and the prodigious land, cf. 8:1–18. The poet mentions neither the theme of the Exodus, nor that of the conquest of the land, cf. also Jer 2:2. The fascinating imagery of v. 10b is unique in the OT, that of v. 11 has a parallel in Ex 19:3–4. Against the background of the splendour of Israel's early salvation history, v. 12 prepares the ground for the monotheistic creed in v. 39. In contrast to the obvious uniqueness of YHWH in this early period, the foreign gods to which vv. 15–18 refer are called 'new ones recently arrived' (v. 17).

(**32:15–18**) The representation of Israel's sin stands in the tradition of prophetic accusations (Hos 11:1–3; 13:4–6). The poet compares Israel to a rebellious animal that 'kicks out' (LXX *apolaktizein*), cf. Hos 4:16. 'Jeshurun' as a name for Israel has only three other references in the OT, namely in the poems which frame the Blessing of Moses in 33:2–5, 26–9, and in Isa 44:1–5. The name is a nominal form of the root *y-š-r* 'to be straight/right', perhaps in a play on the name 'Jacob' which, in Hos 12:3 (MT 4), is derived from the root '*-q-b* possibly meaning 'to deceive'. LXX translates the name as 'the beloved' (*ho ēgapēmenos*).

(**32:19–25**) The poet attributes to the hiddenness and to the anger of YHWH all disastrous events which strike Israel. In vv. 21 and 25 he refers to military catastrophes, in v. 22 he represents YHWH's anger in a cosmological dimension (cf. Job 9:5–6). vv. 23–4 portray mythical powers of destruction as 'arrows' which YHWH will shoot at his people (cf. Ezek 5:16; Job 6:4).

(**32:26–7**) YHWH who is the God Most High, is also the originator of Israel's disaster (cf. Isa 45:6–7). However, the nations do not understand his work, because they attribute their triumph over Israel to their own strength (cf. Isa 10:5–15). Therefore, the relationship between YHWH and Israel which existed ever since the mythological origin of history (vv. 8–9) does not permit YHWH to destroy Israel totally, because then his name could not be known and honoured any more, cf. Isa 48:9–11.

(**32:28–33**) Israel's enemies are portrayed as being foolish (some commentators, however, suggest that vv. 28–30 refer rather to Israel). In v. 31, the poet points to the impotence of the enemies' gods who, following v. 8, can at most be subordinate divine beings.

(**32:34–5**) The future destiny of Israel's enemies has been decided by YHWH long ago, and the time of its arrival is conceived of as imminent. The nations will be hit by YHWH's 'vengeance'. This is a recurring motif in oracles of doom against the nations in the prophetic books (Jer 50:15; Isa 34:8; see Peels 1995). At the beginning of v. 35, the reading of the Samaritan Pentateuch and the LXX, 'for the day of vengeance and recompense' may be more original than the MT which, however, is clearly presupposed in Rom 12:19, where Paul combines Deut 32:35 and Lev 19:18 in a paraenetic call. In the *Targum Onqelos*, the phrase 'for the time when their foot shall slip' is rendered as 'for the time when they go into exile', because the entire passage, vv. 28–35, is seen as referring to Israel.

(**32:36–8**) The central idea is that of YHWH, the gracious God, who has 'compassion' on his people, cf. 4:31. Looking back to vv. 15–18, the poet derides Israel's aberration from her faith in YHWH, the only true God.

(**32:39**) The climax of Moses' poem. Even the most contradictory experiences which Israel may suffer must be referred to YHWH. The uniqueness of God has been given expression in 6:4 and it is now emphasized in a monotheistic creed. As a prayer of an individual, the Song of Hannah in 1 Sam 2:1–10 has close parallels to this verse, which may be considered the culmination of such passages as Hos 6:1–3 and Isa 45:5–7, cf. also Rom 4:17.

(**32:40–2**) The image of YHWH's hand raised for an oath (cf. Ezek 20) introduces an amplification of the expectation of vv. 34–5. The poet portrays YHWH as a warrior. Arrows and a sword as YHWH's weapons are mentioned in many oracles of doom, cf. e.g. Nah 3; Hab 3. The poet envisages the total extinction of the enemy. Within the OT as a whole, this image of vengeance finds its counterpart in the vision of universal peace as in Isa 2:2–4. That vision breaks up the dualism of 'compassion' and 'vengeance' which underlies any apocalyptic concept of 'salvation' and 'doom'.

(**32:43**) As in v. 8, MT has been revised in order to avoid all possible reminiscences of polytheism. Where MT reads 'praise, O nations, his people', a MS from Qumran reads 'praise, O heavens, his people, | worship him, all you gods' (4QDeut^q, see DJD 14. 141; this is followed by NRSV; cf. also Ps 97:9 and see Rofé (2000)), which partly corresponds to the double reading in LXX 'rejoice, O heavens, with him, | and let all the sons of God worship him; | rejoice, O nations, with his people, | and let all the angels of God confirm for him'. The last colon of v. 43 goes beyond the thrust of the poem and addresses the question of impurity and atonement (*kipper*), which according to the LXX and 4QDeut^q refers to Israel's land, but according to MT refers to the people as well as the land; on this theological issue cf. Ezek 36.

(**32:48–52**) **Moses on Mount Nebo** Harmonizing between different sources of the Pentateuch, a late redactor makes an instruction by YHWH precede the report of Moses' death in 34:1–8. He does not refer to 3:26–7, where no sin of Moses is thought of, but rather adopts motifs from Num 20:1–13, 22–4; 27:12–14. Deut 10:6 represents a different tradition about Aaron's death.

(**33:1–29**) **The Blessing of Moses** It has been suggested that the framing verses in vv. 2–5 and vv. 26–9 (together with v. 21b) originally formed an independent psalm from the earliest period of Israel's history (Seeligmann 1964; Jeremias 1987: 82–92). However, the text and its numerous mythological allusions pose many virtually unanswerable philological and traditio-historical questions. It opens with a hymnic description of a theophany of YHWH, surrounded by celestial beings (vv. 2–3, cf. Steiner 1996; Müller 1992: 30) and ends with praise of the incomparability of Israel's God (vv. 26–9). If v. 5a has YHWH as subject and is more original than v. 4, the poem may originally have celebrated the kingship of YHWH in 'Jeshurun' (see DEUT 32:15, and cf. e.g. Ps 93). Parallels to consider would have to include Judg 5:4–5 and Hab 3:3–6, also 1 Kings 8:23, 56 and Num 23:9.

(**33:6–25**) **The Blessings** On the individual tribes see ABD. Here, as in Gen 49, the tribes are mostly characterized by metaphors. In general, the sayings date from before the Assyrian expansion to the west in the eighth century BCE. The order of the tribes does not follow an established system like e.g. that of Jacob's sons according to Gen 29:31–30:24; 35:16–20. v. 6, Reuben, a tribe mostly paired with Gad in the land east of the Jordan, is seen as nearing extinction. v. 7, the saying about Judah is a blessing for success in a military campaign. The expression 'bring him to his people' has often been interpreted as commenting on the division

of Solomon's reign (1 Kings 12) from a northern Israelite perspective. However, it refers rather to a return from battle. vv. 8–11, Levi is a tribe which does not have its own territory (10:8–9; 18:1). It is characterized as a priestly tribe by the Urim and Thummim, technical means for giving oracles, cf. Ex 28:30. The reference to a trial of Levi at 'Massah' and 'Meribah' gives a surprising interpretation of the story of Ex 17:1–7 (cf. Deut 6:16); Num 20:1–13, which may allude to Ex 32:25–9. An addition in vv. 9b–10 makes the Levites the true teachers of the Torah, cf. 31:9. vv. 12–17, Benjamin, Ephraim, and Manasseh are tribes in the hill country north of Jerusalem. vv. 18–19, the saying about Zebulun and Issachar may refer to a former border sanctuary. vv. 20–1, Gad has its territory east of the Jordan. It is also mentioned there as a tribe in the Mesha stone of the ninth century BCE (see ANET 320–1). vv. 23–5, Dan, Naphtali, and Asher are tribes in the north of Israel's territory.

(**34:1–12**) **Moses' Death and Praise of Moses** The scene resumes the command in 3:27. The exact location of 'the top of Pisgah' (cf. Num 23:14) is unknown and its identification with Mount Nebo conflates two different traditions (cf. 32:48–52). v. 6 is based on 3:29; however, the important point is that no veneration for the site of Moses' burial may arise as it is said to be unknown. Moses' survey of the land from Gilead in the north-east to the Negeb in the south-west is reminiscent of Gen 13:14–15, and YHWH thus confirms his promise to Israel's ancestors (v. 4, cf. 1:8; 30:20). v. 5, like 29:1 (MT 28:69), refers back to the concept of 1:5: the era of Moses, who delivered the Torah to Israel, comes to a close in the land east of the Jordan. v. 7, Moses died at the highest age that, according to Gen 6:3, a human being could possibly reach; see, however, Num 33:39 and cf. Josh 24:29. v. 10, in a paradoxical way, stresses the primary importance which prophecy has for the Deuteronomistic school. On the one hand the verse classifies Moses as a prophet, on the other, it underlines his incomparable status (contrast 18:18) and thus subordinates all later prophets to the Torah; see Blenkinsopp 1977: 80–95. The expression 'face to face' may refer to the scene at Horeb as represented by 5:5, 31; the motif has been elaborated further in Ex 33:8–11, cf. also Num 12:1–8. v. 9 again addresses the problem of succession and continuity after Moses' death and portrays Joshua according to an ideal of wisdom. vv. 9–10 thus relate Torah, prophecy, and wisdom to each other.

vv. 1a, 7–9 are often considered fragments of the Priestly Document, see, however, Perlitt (1988). Finally, vv. 11–12 follow the same tendency of magnifying the miraculous which can be observed in 6:22. The verses stimulate the poetic imagination of the readers with a reference to the miracles that Moses wrought in Egypt and thus emphasize God's intervention when Israel's history started with the Exodus.

REFERENCES

Alt, A. (1953), 'Die Heimat des Deuteronomiums', in id., *Kleine Schriften zur Geschichte des Volkes Israel* (Munich: Beck), ii. 250–75.

Alter, R. (1990), *The Art of Biblical Poetry* (Edinburgh: T. & T. Clark); first pub. 1985.

Aurelius, E. (1988), *Der Fürbitter Israels: Eine Studie zum Mosebild des Alten Testaments*, ConBOT 27 (Stockholm: Almqvist & Wiksell).

Barr, J. (1993), *Biblical Faith and Natural Theology* (Oxford: Clarendon).

Barton, J. (1986), *Oracles of God: Perceptions of Ancient Prophecy in Israel after the Exile* (London: Darton, Longman & Todd).

Begg, C. T. (1980), '*The Literary Criticism of Deut 4, 1–40*', EThL 55: 10–55.

Blenkinsopp, J. (1977), *Prophecy and Canon* (Notre Dame, Ind.: University of Notre Dame Press).

Braulik, G. (1970), 'Die Freude des Festes: Das Kultverständnis des Deuteronomium—die älteste biblische Festtheorie', (1988) in id., *Studien zur Theologie des Deuteronomiums*, SBAB 2 (Stuttgart: Katholisches Bibelwerk; ET in id., *The Theology of Deuteronomy* (N. Richland Hills, Tx.: BIBAL Press, 1994), 27–65.

Cholewiński, A. (1976), *Heiligkeitsgesetz und Deuteronomium*, AnBib 66 (Rome: Biblical Institute).

Christensen, D. L. (1993) (ed.), *A Song of Power and the Power of Song*, Sources for Biblical and Theological Studies, 3 (Winona Lake, Ind.: Eisenbrauns).

Clements, R. E. (1996), 'The Deuteronomic Law of Centralization and the Catastrophe of 587 B.C.', in J. Barton and D. J. Reimer (eds.), *After the Exile* (Macon, Ga.: Mercer University Press), 5–25.

Cross, F. M. (1973), 'The Themes of the Book of Kings and the Structure of the Deuteronomistic History', in id., *Canaanite Myth and Hebrew Epic* (Cambridge, Mass.: Harvard University Press), 274–89.

Crüsemann, F. (1996), *The Torah: Theology and Social History of Old Testament Law* (Edinburgh: T. & T. Clark); first pub. in German 1992.

Davies, E. W. (1986), 'The Meaning of pî šěnayim in Deuteronomy XXI 17', VT 36: 341–7.

Davies, P. R. (1992), *In Search of 'Ancient Israel'*, JSOTSup 148 (Sheffield: JSOT).

Dion, P. E. (1991) 'Deuteronomy 13: The Suppression of Alien Religious Propaganda in Israel during the Late Monarchical Era', in B. Halpern and D. W. Hobson (eds.), *Law and Ideology in Monarchic Israel*, JSOTSup 124 (Sheffield: JSOT), 147–216.

Donner, H. (1985), 'Jesaja LVI 1–7: Ein Abrogationsfall inner-halb des Kanons—Implikationen und Konsequenzen', VTSup 36: 81–95.

Douglas, M. (1966), *Purity and Danger: An Analysis of Concepts of Pollution and Taboo* (London: Routledge & Kegan Paul).

Driver, S. R. (1895), *Deuteronomy*, ICC; 3rd edn. 1901; repr. (Edinburgh: T. & T. Clark).

Fishbane, M. (1985), *Biblical Interpretation in Ancient Israel* (Oxford: Clarendon).

Foresti, F. (1984), *The Rejection of Saul in the Perspective of the Deuteronomistic School* (Rome: Edizioni del Teresianum).

Frevel, C. (1995), *Aschera und der Ausschließlichkeitsanspruch YHWHs*, BBB 94 (2 vols.; Weinheim: Beltz Athenäum).

García López, F. (1978), 'Deut. VI et la tradition-rédaction du Deutéronome', RB 85: 161–200.

Gertz, J. (1996), 'Die Passa-Massot-Ordnung im deuteronomischen Festkalender', in T. Veijola (ed.), *Das Deuteronomium und seine Querbeziehungen* (Göttingen: Vandenhoeck & Ruprecht), 56–80.

Gibson, J. C. L. (1978), *Canaanite Myths and Legends* (Edinburgh: T. & T. Clark).

Halpern, B. (1991), 'Jerusalem and the Lineages in the Seventh Century BCE: Kinship and the Rise of Individual Moral Liability', in B. Halpern and D. W. Hobson (eds.), *Law and Ideology in Monarchic Israel*, JSOTSup 124 (Sheffield: JSOT), 11–107.

Hossfeld, F.-L. (1982), *Der Dekalog*, OBO 45 (Göttingen: Vandenhoeck & Ruprecht).

Janzen, J. G. (1994), 'The "Wandering Aramean" Reconsidered', VT 44: 359–75.

Jeremias, J. (1987), *Das Königtum Gottes in den Psalmen*, FRLANT 141 (Göttingen: Vandenhoeck & Ruprecht).

Keel, O. (1981), 'Zeichen der Verbundenheit: Zur Vorgeschichte und Bedeutung der Forderungen von Dt 6, 8f. und par.', in P. Casetti, O. Keel and A. Schenker (eds.), *Mélanges Dominique Barthélemy*, OBO 38 (Göttingen: Vandenhoeck & Ruprecht), 160–240.

Keel, O., and Uehlinger, C. (1998), *Gods, Goddesses, and Images of God in Ancient Israel* (Edinburgh: T. & T. Clark); first pub. in German 1992.

Lambert, W. G. (1960), *Babylonian Wisdom Literature* (Oxford: Clarendon).

Levinson, B. M. (1997), *Deuteronomy and the Hermeneutics of Legal Innovation* (Oxford: Oxford University Press).

Lipiński, E. (1998), 'naḥal', in TDOT 9 (Grand Rapids, Mich.: Eerdmans), 319–35.

Lohfink, N. (1993), *Das Hauptgebot: Eine Untersuchung literarischer Einleitungsfragen zu Dtn 5–11*, AnBib 20 (Rome: Pontificium Institutum Biblicum).

——(1971a), 'Die Sicherung der Wirksamkeit des Gotteswortes durch das Prinzip der Gewaltenteilung nach den Ämtergesetzen des Buches Deuteronomium (Dt 16,18–18,22)', in id., *Studien zum Deuteronomium und zur deuteronomistischen Literatur*, SBAB 8 (Stuttgart: Katholisches Bibelwerk, 1990), i. 305–23; ET in Christensen (1993), 336–52.

——(1971b), 'Zum "kleinen geschichtlichen Credo" Dtn 26,5–9', in id., *Studien zum Deuteronomium und zur deuteronomistischen Literatur* (as above), i. 263–90.

——(1985), 'Zur neueren Diskussion über 2Kön 22–23', in id. (ed.), *Das Deuteronomium: Entstehung, Gestalt und Botschaft*, BETL 68 (Leuven: Leuven University Press), 24–48; ET in Christensen (1993), 36–61.

Maag, V. (1956), 'Erwägungen zur deuteronomischen Kultzentralisation', in id., *Kultur, Kulturkontakt und Religion* (Göttingen: Vandenhoeck & Ruprecht, 1980), 90–8.

McCarthy, D. J. (1978), *Treaty and Covenant: A Study in Form in the Ancient Oriental Documents and in the Old Testament*, rev. edn., AnBib 21A (Rome: Biblical Institute Press); first pub. 1963.

McKay, J. W. (1973), *Religion in Judah under the Assyrians*, SBT 26 (London: SCM).

McKenzie, S. L. et al. (eds.) (1994), *The History of Israel's Traditions: The Heritage of Martin Noth*, JSOTSup 182 (Sheffield: Sheffield Academic Press).

Margulis, B. (1970), 'A Ugaritic Psalm (RS 24.252)', *JBL* 89: 292–304.

Mayes, A. D. H. (1979), *Deuteronomy*, NCB (Grand Rapids, Mich.: Eerdmans); repr. 1991.

Mettinger, T. N. D. (1982), *The Dethronement of Sabaoth*, ConBOT 18 (Lund: Gleerup).

Miller, P. D. (1990), *Deuteronomy*, Interpretation (Louisville, Ky.: John Knox).

Morrow, W. S. (1995), *Scribing the Center*, SBLMS 49 (Atlanta, Ga.: Scholars Press).

Mowinckel, S. (1962), *The Psalms in Israel's Worship* (2 vols.; Oxford: Blackwell).

Müller, H.-P. (1997), 'molæk', in *TDOT* 8 (Grand Rapids, Mich.: Eerdmans), 375–88.

——(1992), 'Kolloquialsprache und Volksreligion in den Inschriften von Kuntillet 'Ajrud und Hirbet el-Qōm', *Zeitschrift für Althebraistik*, 5: 15–51.

Nicholson, E. W. (1986), *God and His People: Covenant and Theology in the Old Testament* (Oxford: Clarendon).

Nielsen, E. (1995), *Deuteronomium*, HAT 1/6 (Tübingen: Mohr[Sie-beck]).

Noth, M. (1991), *The Deuteronomistic History*, JSOTSup 15, 2nd ed. (Sheffield: Sheffield Academic Press); first pub. in German 1943.

Otto, E. (1993), 'Das Eherecht im Mittelassyrischen Kodex und im Deuteronomium', in id., *Kontinuum und Proprium*, Orientalia Biblica et Christiana, 8 (Wiesbaden: Harrassowitz, 1996), 172–91.

——(1996a), 'The Pre-exilic Deuteronomy as a Revision of the Covenant Code', in id., *Kontinuum und Proprium* (as above), 112–22.

——(1996b), 'Treueid und Gesetz', *Zeitschrift für Altorientalische und Biblische Rechtsgeschichte*, 2: 1–52.

Parpola, S., and Watanabe, K. (1988), *Neo-Assyrian Treaties and Loyalty Oaths*, SAA 2 (Helsinki: Helsinki University Press).

Peels, H. G. L. (1995), *The Vengeance of God*, OTS 31 (Leiden: Brill).

Perlitt, L. (1988), 'Priesterschrift im Deuteronomium?', in id., *Deuteronomium-Studien* (Tübingen: Mohr[Siebeck], 1994), 123–43.

Polzin, R. (1993), *Moses and the Deuteronomist* (Bloomington, Ind.: Indiana University Press); first pub. 1980.

Rad, G. von (1966), 'The Problem of the Hexateuch', in id., *The Problem of the Hexateuch and other Essays* (Edinburgh and London: Oliver & Boyd), 1–78; first pub. in German 1938.

Reimer, D. (1990), 'Concerning Return to Egypt: Deuteronomy XVII 16 and XXVIII 68 Reconsidered', in J. A. Emerton (ed.), *Studies in the Pentateuch*, VTSup 41 (Leiden: Brill), 217–29.

Reiner, E. (1958), *Šurpu: A Collection of Sumerian and Akkadian Incantations*, AfO 11 (Graz: Selbstverlag des Herausgebers (Ernst Weidner)).

Reuter, E. (1993), *Kultzentralisation*, BBB 87 (Frankfurt am Main: Anton Hain).

Richter, W. (1967), 'Beobachtungen zur theologischen Systembildung in der alttestamentlichen Literatur anhand des "kleinen geschichtlichen Credo"', in L. Scheffczyk et al. (eds.), *Wahrheit und Verkündigung* (Paderborn: Ferdinand Schöningh), i. 176–212.

Rofé, A. (1985a), 'The Covenant in the Land of Moab (Deuteronomy 28:69–30:20)', in Lohfink (ed.), *Das Deuteronomium* (1985), 310–20; repr. in Christensen (1993), 269–80.

——(1985b), 'The Laws of Warfare in the Book of Deuteronomy', *JSOT* 32: 23–44.

——(1987), 'Family and Sex Laws in Deuteronomy and the Book of Covenant', *Henoch*, 9: 131–59.

——(2000), 'The End of the Song of Moses (Deuteronomy 32:43)', in R. G. Kratz et al. (eds.), *Liebe und Gebot*, FRLANT 190 (Göttingen: Vandenhoeck & Ruprecht), 164–72.

Rogerson, J. W. (1992), *W. M. L. de Wette: Founder of Modern Biblical Criticism*, JSOTSup 126 (Sheffield: JSOT).

Sanders, P. (1996), *The Provenance of Deuteronomy 32*, OTS 37 (Leiden: Brill).

Schmidt, W. H. (1993), *Die Zehn Gebote im Rahmen Alttestamentlicher Ethik*, ErFor 281 (Darmstadt: Wissenschaftliche Buchgesellschaft).

Seeligmann, I. L. (1964), 'A Psalm from Pre-Regal Times', *VT* 14: 75–92.

Seitz, G. (1971), *Redaktionsgeschichtliche Studien zum Deuteronomium*, BWANT 93 (Stuttgart: Kohlhammer).

Smend, R. (1963), 'Die Bundesformel', in id., *Die Mitte des Alten Testaments*, BEvT 99 (Munich: Kaiser, 1986), 11–39.

——(1971), 'Das Gesetz und die Völker', in id., *Die Mitte des Alten Testaments* (as above), 124–37.

——(1983), 'Das uneroberte Land', in id., *Zur ältesten Geschichte Israels*, BEvT 100 (Munich: Kaiser, 1987), 217–28.

Smith, M. (1987), *Palestinian Parties and Politics that Shaped the Old Testament* (London: SCM); first pub. 1971.

Smith, W. Robertson (1892), *The Old Testament in the Jewish Church*, 2nd edn. (London: A. & C. Black).

Spieckermann, H. (1982), *Juda unter Assur in der Sargonidenzeit*, FRLANT 129 (Göttingen: Vandenhoeck & Ruprecht).

Steiner, R. C. (1996), '"dat" and "ʿen"', *JBL* 115: 693–8.

Steymans, H. U. (1995), *Deuteronomium 28 und die 'adê' zur Thronfolgeregelung Asarhaddons*, OBO 145 (Göttingen: Vandenhoeck & Ruprecht).

Tigay, J. H. (1996), *Deuteronomy*, JPS Torah Commentary (Jerusalem: Jewish Publication Society).

Uehlinger, C. (1995), 'Gab es eine joschijanische Kultreform?', in W. Groß (ed.), *Jeremia und die 'deuteronomistische Bewegung'*, BBB 98 (Weinheim: Beltz Athenäum), 57–89.

Van Seters, J. (1996), 'Cultic Laws in the Covenant Code (Exodus 20:22–23:33) and their Relationship to Deuteronomy and the Holiness Code', in M. Vervenne (ed.), *Studies in the Book of Exodus*, BETL 126 (Leuven: Leuven University Press), 319–45.

Veijola, T. (1992a), 'Das Bekenntnis Israels: Beobachtungen zur Geschichte und Theologie von Dtn 6, 4–9', *TZ* 48: 369–81.

——(1992b), 'Höre Israel! Der Sinn und Hintergrund von Deuteronomium VI 4–9', *VT* 42: 528–41.

——(1995a), '"Der Mensch lebt nicht vom Brot allein": Zur literarischen Schichtung und theologischen Aussage von Deuteronomium 8', in G. Braulik (ed.), *Bundesdokument und Gesetz: Studien zum Deuteronomium*, Herders Biblische Studien, 4 (Freiburg: Herder), 143–58.

——(1995b), 'Wahrheit und Intoleranz nach Deuteronomium 13', *ZTK* 92: 287–314.

——(1996a), 'Bundestheologische Redaktion im Deuteronomium', in id. (ed.), *Das Deuteronomium und seine Querbeziehungen* (Göttingen: Vandenhoeck & Ruprecht), 242–76.

——(1996b), 'The History of the Passover in the Light of Dtn 16, 1–8', *ZAR* 2: 53–75.

——(forthcoming), *Deuteronomium*, ATD (Göttingen: Vandenhoeck & Ruprecht).

Weinfeld, M. (1991), *Deuteronomy 1–11*, AB 5 (New York: Doubleday).

——(1992), *Deuteronomy and the Deuteronomic School* (Winona Lake, Ind.: Eisenbrauns); first pub. 1972.

Wevers, J. W. (1995), *Notes on the Greek Text of Deuteronomy*, Septuagint and Cognate Studies Series, 39 (Atlanta, Ga.: Scholars Press).

Wiggins, S. A. (1993), *A Reassessment of 'Asherah'*, AOAT 235 (Kevelaer: Butzon & Bercker).

Würthwein, E. (1984), *Die Bücher der Könige*, ATD 11–2 (Göttingen: Vandenhoeck & Ruprecht).

Bibliographical Guide to Old Testament Studies: the Pentateuch

History and Theology, Old Testament

Barr, J. (1999), *The Concept of Biblical Theology: An Old Testament Perspective* (London: SCM).

Bright, J. (1981), *A History of Israel*, 3rd edn. (London: SCM).

Brueggemann, W. (1997), *Theology of the Old Testament: Testimony, Dispute, Advocacy* (Philadelphia: Fortress).

Clements, R. E. (1978), *Old Testament Theology: A Fresh Approach* (London: Marchall, Morgan, and Scott).

Eichrodt, W. (1961–7), *Theology of the Old Testament* (2 vols.: London: SCM).

Hayes, J. H., and Miller, J. M. (1990), *Israelite and Judaean History* (London: SCM).

Herrmann, S. (1981), *A History of Israel in Old Testament Times* (Philadelphia: Fortress).

Jagersma, H. (1982), *A History of Israel in the Old Testament Period* (London: SCM).

—— (1985), *A History of Israel from Alexander the Great to Bar Kochba* (London: SCM).

Noth, M. (1960), *The History of Israel*, 2nd edn. (London: A. & C. Black).

von Rad, G. (1975), *Old Testament Theology* (2 vols.; Edinburgh: T. & T. Clark).

2. Introduction to the Old Testament

Barton, J. (1991), *What is the Bible?* (London: SPCK).

—— (1997), *Making the Christian Bible* (London: Darton, Longman & Todd).

Blenkinsopp, J. (1984), *A History of Prophecy in Israel from the Settlement in the Land to the Hellenistic Period* (London: SPCK).

Childs, B. S. (1979), *Introduction to the Old Testament as Scripture* (London: SCM).

Crenshaw, J. L. (1981), *Old Testament Wisdom: An Introduction* (Atlanta: John Knox).

Davies, P. R. (1998), *Scribes and Schools: The Canonization of the Hebrew Scriptures* (Louisville: Westminster/John Knox).

Hayes, J. H. (1982), *An Introduction to Old Testament Study* (London: SCM).

Kaiser, O. (1975), *Introduction to the Old Testament: A Presentation of its Results and Problems* (Oxford: Blackwell).

Laffey, A. (1988), *An Introduction to the Old Testament: A Feminist Perspective* (Philadelphia: Fortress).

Noth, M. (1966), 'The Laws in the Pentateuch: Their Assumptions and Meaning', in his *The Laws in the Pentateuch and Other Essays* (Edinburgh and London), 1–107.

Soggin, J. A. (1989), *Introduction to the Old Testament: From its Origins to the Closing of the Alexandrian Canon* (London: SCM).

Theissen, G. (1984), *Biblical Faith: An Evolutionary Perspective* (London: SCM).

3. Introduction to the Pentateuch

Albertz, R. (1994), *A History of Israelite Religion in the OT Period*, ET (2 vols.: London: SCM).

Alt, A. (1966), 'The Origins of Israelite Law', in *Essays on Old Testament History and Religion*, ET (Oxford: Blackwell), 87–132. First published 1934.

Blenkinsopp, J. (1992), *The Pentateuch: An Introduction to the First Five Books of the Bible* (London: SCM).

Brueggemann, W., and Wolff, H. W. (1975), *The Vitality of OT Traditions* (Atlanta: John Knox).

Clements, R. E. (1976), *A Century of OT Study* (Guildford: Lutter-worth).

Clines, D. J. A. (1978), *The Theme of the Pentateuch* (Sheffield: JSOT).

Lohfink, N. (1994), *Theology of the Pentateuch: Themes of the Priestly Narrative and Deuteronomy* (Edinburgh: T. & T. Clark).

Nicholson, E. W. (1997), *The Pentateuch in the Twentieth Century* (Oxford: Oxford University Press).

Noth M. (1972), *A History of Pentateuchal Traditions*, ET (Englewood Cliffs: Prentice-Hall): from German original, *überlieferungsgeschichle des Pentateuch*, 1948.

Patrick, D. (1986), *Old Testament Law* (London: SCM).

Pritchard, J. B. (ed.) (1969), *Ancient Near Eastern Texts Relating to the Old Testament*, 3rd edn. (Princeton: Princeton University Press).

von Rad, G. (1962), *OT Theology*, ET (Edinburgh: Oliver & Boyd).

Wellhausen, J. (1885), *Prolegomena to the History of Israel*, ET (Edinburgh: A. & C. Black); from German original, *Geschichte Israels 1*, 1878.

Whybray, R. N. (1987), *The Making of the Pentateuch: A Methodological Study* (Sheffield: JSOT).

4. Genesis

Blenkinsopp, J. (1992), *The Pentateuch. An Introduction to the First Five Books of the Bible* (London: SCM).

Gunkel, H. (1964), *The Legends of Genesis* (New York: Schocken).

McKane, W. (1979), *Studies in the Pentateuchal Narratives* (Edinburgh: Handsel).

Noth, M. (1972), *A History of Pentateuchal Traditions* (Englewood Cliffs: Prentice-Hall).

Redford, D. B. (1970), *A Study of the Biblical Story of Joseph (Genesis 37–50)*, VTSup 20 (Leiden: Brill).

Rogerson, J. W. (1974), *Myth in Old Testament Interpretation*, BZAW 134 (Berlin: de Gruyter).

Thompson, T. L. (1974), *The Historicity of the Patriarchal Narratives*, BZAW 133 (Berlin: de Gruyter).

Van Seters, J. (1975), *Abraham in History and Tradition* (New Haven and London: Yale University Press).

von Rad, G. (1966), 'The Joseph Narrative and Ancient Wisdom', in *The Problem of the Hexateuch and Other Essays* (Edinburgh and London: Oliver & Boyd), 292–300.

—— (1972), *Genesis*, OTL, 2nd edn. (London: SCM).

Westermann, C. (1974), *Creation* (London: SPCK; Philadelphia: Fortress).

—— (1980), *The Promises to the Patriarchs. Studies on the Patriarchal Narratives* (Philadelphia: Fortress).

—— *Genesis* (3 vols.: London: SPCK, 1984, 1985, 1987).

—— *Genesis* (Grand Rapids: Eerdmans, 1987; London: SPCK, 1988).

Whybray, R. N. (1987), *The Making of the Pentateuch. A Methodological Study*, JSOTSup 53 (Sheffield: JSOT).

5. Exodus

Bruckner, J. K. (2008), *Exodus*, NICOT (Milton Keynes: Paternoster)

Brueggemann, W. (1994), 'Exodus', in *The New Interpreter's Bible* (vol. 1; Nashville: Abingdon).

Cassuto, U. (1967), *A Commentary on Exodus* (Jerusalem: Magnes).

Childs, B. S. (1974), *Exodus: a Commentary* (London: SCM).

Coggins, R. J. (2000), *The book of Exodus*, Epworth Commentaries (Peterborough: Epworth).

Croatto, J. S. (1981), *Exodus: a Hermeneutics of Freedom* (Maryknoll, NY: Orbis Books).

Durham, J. I. (1987), *Exodus*, WBC (Waco, Tex.: Word).

Fretheim, T. E. (1991), *Exodus* (Interpretation) (Louisville, Ky.: Westminster/John Knox).

Gowan, D. E. (1994), *Theology in Exodus: Biblical Theology in the Form of a Commentary* (Louisville, Ky.: Westminster/John Knox).

Gunn, D. M. (1982), 'The Hardening of Pharaoh's Heart', in D. J. A. Clines, D. M. Gunn, and A. J. Hauser (eds), *Art and Meaning: Rhetoric in Biblical Literature*, JSOTSup 19 (Sheffield: JSOT), 72–96.

Haran, M. (1985), *Temples and Temple Service in Ancient Israel*, 2nd edn. (Winona Lake, Ind.: Eisenbrauns).

Houtman, C. (1993–), *Exodus*, Historical Commentary on the Old Testament (3 vols.; Kampen: Kok).

Johnstone, W. (1990), *Exodus*, Old Testament Guides (Sheffield: JSOT).

Langston, S. M. (2006), *Exodus Through the Centuries*, Blackwell Bible Commentaries (Oxford: Blackwell).

Meyers, C. L. (2005), *Exodus*, NCBC (Cambridge: Cambridge University).

Moberly, R., and Walter, L. (1983), *At the Mountain of God: Story and Theology in Exodus 32–34*, JSOTSup 22 (Sheffield: JSOT).

Nicholson, E. W. (1986), *God and his People: Covenant and Theology in the Old Testament* (Oxford: Clarendon).

Patrick, D. (1986), *Old Testament Law* (London: SCM).

Propp, W. H. C. (1998), *Exodus 1–18*, AB 2 (New York: Doubleday).

—— (2006), *Exodus 19–40*, AB 2A (New York: Doubleday).

Van Seters, J. (1994), *The Life of Moses: the Yahwist as Historian in Exodus-Numbers* (Kampen: Kok Pharos).

6. Leviticus

Anderson, G. A. (1987), *Sacrifices and Offerings in Ancient Israel: Studies in their Social and Political Importance*, HSM 41 (Atlanta: Scholars Press).

—— and Olyan, S. M. (eds) (1991), *Priesthood and Cult in Ancient Israel*, JSOTSup 125 (Sheffield: Sheffield Academic Press).

Blenkinsopp, J. (1976), 'The Structure of P', *CBQ* 38: 275–92.

Cassuto, U. (1961), *The Documentary Hypothesis and the Composition of the Pentateuch* (Jerusalem: Magnes).

Cross, F. M. (1973), *Canaanite Myth and Hebrew Epic* (Cambridge, Mass.: Harvard University Press).

Grabbe, L. L. (1991), 'Maccabean Chronology: 167–164 or 168–165 BCE?', *JBL* 110: 59–74.

Kaufmann, Y. (1961), *The Religion of Israel From its Beginnings to the Babylonian Exile* (tr. and abr. M. Greenberg) (London: George Allen & Unwin).

Levine, B. A. (1989), *Leviticus*, JPS Torah Commentary (Philadelphia: Jewish Publication Society).

McKeating, H. (1979), 'Sanctions against Adultery in Ancient Israelite Society, with Some Reflections on Methodology in the Study of Old Testament Ethics', *JSOT* 11: 57–72.

Noth, M. (1972), *A History of Pentateuchal Traditions* (Englewood Cliffs, NJ: Prentice-Hall).

Polzin, R. (1976), *Late Biblical Hebrew: Toward an Historical Typology of Biblical Hebrew Prose*, HSM 12 (Missoula: Scholars Press).

Rentdorff, R. H. (1990), *The Problem of the Process of Transmission in the Pentateuch*, JSOTSup 89 (Sheffield: Sheffield Academic Press): German original, *Das überlieferungsgeschichtliche Problem des Pentateuch* (1977).

—— (1993), 'Two Kinds of P? Some Reflections on the Occasion of the Publishing of Jacob Milgrom's Commentary on Leviticus 1–16', *JSOT* 60: 75–81.

Van Seters, J. (1983), *In Search of History: Historiography in the Ancient World and the Origins of Biblical History* (New Haven/London: Yale University Press).

Vink, J. G. (1969), 'The Date and Origin of the Priestly Code in the Old Testament', *OTS* 15:1–144.

Weinfeld, M. (1972), *Deuteronomy and the Deuteronomic School* (Oxford: Clarendon).

—— (1992), *Deuteronomy 1–11*, AB5 (Garden City, NY: Doubleday).

Wellhausen, J. (1885), *Prolegomena to the History of Israel* (Edinburgh: A. & C. Black).

7. Numbers

Ashley, T. R. (1993), *The Book of Numbers*, The New International Commentary on the Old Testament (Grand Rapids: Eerdmans).

Budd, P. J. (1984), *Numbers*, Word Biblical Commentary, 5 (Waco, Tex.: Word).

Douglas, M. (1993), *In the Wilderness: The Doctrine of Defilement in the Book of Numbers* (Sheffield: Sheffield Academic Press).

Fretheim, T. E. (1996), *The Pentateuch*, Interpreting Biblical Texts (Nashville: Abingdon).

Gorman, F. H., Jr. (1990), *The Ideology of Ritual: Space, Time and Status in the Priestly Theology*, JSOTSup 91 (Sheffield: Sheffield Academic Press).

Gray, G. B. (1903), *A Critical and Exegetical Commentary on Numbers*, International Critical Commentary (Edinburgh: T. & T. Clark).

Levine, B. (1993), *Numbers 1–20: A New Translation with Introduction and Commentary*, Anchor Bible (New York: Doubleday).

Milgrom, J. (1990), *Numbers*, JPS Torah Commentary (Philadelphia: Jewish Publication Society of America).

Moore, M. (1990), *The Balaam Traditions: Their Character and Development*, SBLDS, 113 (Atlanta: Scholars Press).

Nelson, R. D. (1993), *Raising Up a Faithful Priest: Community and Priesthood in Biblical Theology* (Louisville: Westminster/John Knox).

Noth, M. (1968), *Numbers: A Commentary*, Old Testament Library (Philadelphia: Westminster); tr. J. D. Martin.

Olson, D. (1985), *The Death of the Old and the Birth of the New: The Framework of the Book of Numbers and the*

Pentateuch, Brown Judaic Studies, 71 (Chico, Calif.: Scholars Press).

—— (1996), *Numbers*, Interpretation: A Bible Commentary for Teaching and Preaching (Louisville: John Knox).

Sakenfeld, K. D. (1995), *Journeying with God: A Commentary on the Book of Numbers*, An International Theological Commentary on the Old Testament (Grand Rapids: Eerdmans).

Wenham, G. J. (1981), *Numbers: An Introduction and Commentary*, Tyndale Old Testament Commentary (Downer's Grove, Ill.: Inter-Varsity).

8. Deuteronomy

Christensen, D. L. (ed.) (1993), *A Song of Power and the Power of Song. Essays on the Book of Deuteronomy* (Winona Lake, Ind.: Eisenbrauns).

Crüsemann, F. (1996), *The Torah* (Edinburgh: T. & T. Clark)

Driver, S. R. (1986), *A Critical and Exegetical Commentary on Deuteronomy (ICC)*, 1895, 3rd edn. 1901 (Edinburgh: T. & T. Clark).

Levinson, B. M. (1997), *Deuteronomy and the Hermeneutics of Legal Innovation* (New York, Oxford: Oxford University Press) (includes bibliography).

Miller, P. D. (1990), *Deuteronomy (Interpretation)* (Louisville, Ky.: John Knox).

Rofé, A. (1988), *Introduction to Deuteronomy*. Part I and further chapters [Hebrew] (Jerusalem: Akademon Publishing House).

Tigay, J. H. (1996), *Deuteronomy (The JPS Torah Commentary)* (Philadelphia/Jerusalem: The Jewish Publication Society).

Weinfeld, M. (1972), *Deuteronomy and the Deuteronomic School*, reprinted (Winona Lake, Ind.: Eisenbrauns).

Joshua

Aharoni, Y. (1967), *The Land of the Bible* (London: Burns and Oates).

Auld, A. G. (1980), *Joshua, Moses and the Land: Tetrateuch, Pentateuch, Hexateuch in a Generation since 1938* (Edinburgh: T. and T. Clark).

Baltzer, K. (1971), *The Covenant Formulary in Old Testament, Jewish and early Christian Writings* (Oxford) (= *Das Bundesformular: sein Ursprung und seine Verwendung im alten Testament* [WMANT 4] (Neukirchen: Neukirchener Verlag, 1960)).

Index